Writing
Today

THIRD EDITION

New!
2016
MLA
Updates

RICHARD JOHNSON-SHEEHAN
Purdue University

CHARLES PAINE
University of New Mexico

Reader   Genre   Proposals   Reviews

Argument   Research   Plan   Draft

Design   Collaborate   Handbook

Boston Columbus Hoboken Indianapolis New York San Francisco Amsterdam
Cape Town Dubai London Madrid Milan Munich Paris Montréal Toronto Delhi Mexico City
São Paulo Sydney Hong Kong Seoul Singapore Taipei Tokyo

Vice President and Editor in Chief: Joseph Opiela
Lead Program Manager: Lauren A. Finn
Senior Development Editor: Anne Brunell
    Ehrenworth
Vice President, Marketing: Roxanne
    McCarley
Marketing Manager: Allison Arnold
Executive Digital Producer: Stefanie Snajder
Content Specialist: Erin Jenkins

Project Manager: Denise Phillip Grant
Project Coordination, Text Design, and Electronic
    Page Makeup: Cenveo® Publisher Services
Design Lead/Cover Designer: Heather Scott
Cover Image: Viktoria Kurpas/Shutterstock
Senior Manufacturing Buyer: Roy L. Pickering, Jr.
Printer/Binder: R.R. Donnelley/ Crawfordsville
Cover Printer: Phoenix Color/ Hagerstown

Acknowledgments of third-party content appear on pages 791–794, which constitute an extension of this copyright page.

PEARSON, ALWAYS LEARNING, and MYWRITINGLAB are exclusive trademarks, in the United States and/or other countries, of Pearson Education, Inc., or its affiliates.

Unless otherwise indicated herein, any third-party trademarks that may appear in this work are the property of their respective owners and any references to third-party trademarks, logos, or other trade dress are for demonstrative or descriptive purposes only. Such references are not intended to imply any sponsorship, endorsement, authorization, or promotion of Pearson's products by the owners of such marks, or any relationship between the owner and Pearson Education, Inc., or its affiliates, authors, licensees, or distributors.

Library of Congress Cataloging-in-Publication Data

Johnson-Sheehan, Richard.
 Writing today / Richard Johnson-Sheehan, Purdue University, Charles Paine
 University of New Mexico.—Third edition.
    pages cm
 Includes index.
 ISBN 978-0-321-98465-4
 1. English language–Rhetoric. 2. Report writing. 3. Study skills. I.
Paine, Charles. II. Paine, Charles. III. Title.
 PE1408.J753 2016
 808'.042—dc23   2014042173

1 2 3   18 17 16

Student Edition ISBN 10: 0-13-458641-7
Student Edition ISBN 13: 978-0-13-458641-0

A la Carte ISBN 10: 0-13-458255-1
A la Carte ISBN 13: 978-0-13-458255-9

www.pearsonhighered.com

Contents

PART 2
Using Genres to Express Ideas

PART 3

Developing a Writing Process

PART 4

Strategies for Shaping Ideas

PART 5

Doing Research

PART 6
Getting Your Ideas Out There

PART 7

Anthology of Readings

PART 8

Handbook

Preface

We began *Writing Today* with a few basic assumptions in mind. First, we believe college students want to learn the kinds of writing that will help them succeed in college and in their careers. Second, they want a guide to writing that presents information clearly, simply, and in a way that is easy to reference. Third, students' writing instructors prefer a teaching tool that is both practical and flexible, allowing them to adapt its content to their own pedagogical approaches and teaching styles.

In this third edition, we also added coverage that responds directly to three important trends in higher education: (1) critical reading and analytical thinking, (2) teaching for transfer, and (3) writing assessment. The new Chapter 4, "Reading Critically, Thinking Analytically," allows instructors to teach students advanced critical thinking and analytical reasoning skills. Meanwhile, teaching for transfer has been addressed throughout the book by highlighting how the writing skills learned in each chapter will transfer to advanced courses and careers. In addition, to meet increasing calls for assessment, we have also enhanced Chapter 31, "Succeeding on Written Exams and Assessments," to help students do their best on college exams and assessment tests.

That said, the core concepts of *Writing Today* are the same. *Writing Today* teaches *genres* of writing (memoirs, analyses, reports, proposals, etc.) and *strategies* for writing (narration, comparison, argumentation, etc.) as well as *processes* for writing (planning, drafting, revising, etc.). This approach shows students that genres are not rigid templates but are rather a set of versatile tools that guide every aspect of the writing process. *Writing Today* helps students to develop *genre awareness* and *genre know-how* so they can learn how communities get things done with words and images.

Writing Today is an easy-to-use book that fits the way today's students read and learn. Students respond best to an interactive writing style, so our instruction is brief and to the point. Key terms are immediately defined and reinforced. Sections and paragraphs are kept short to make them accessible. Important points are clearly labeled and supported by helpful visuals. We emphasize practical application and keep the academic explanations to a mininum, even though *Writing Today* is thoroughly grounded in contemporary theories of rhetoric and writing.

We also wanted to maximize flexibility for instructors. Our own experiences as writing teachers and writing program administrators tell us that instructors can be successful in a variety of different ways. The best books on college writing provide multiple pathways that work for a diverse group of instructors, allowing them to be creative and innovative. With *Writing Today*, instructors can choose the order in which they teach the chapters and combine them into units that fit their course designs.

Our approach is informed by our own classroom experience and by much of the research done in the field of writing studies over the last twenty years. The approach is also supported by findings emerging from our research with the Consortium for the Study of Writing in College (a collaboration between the National Survey of Student Engagement and the Council of Writing Program Administrators). Surveys conducted since 2008 by the CSWC of more than 200,000 students at over 200 different schools found that when faculty assigned challenging and diverse writing assignments, students reported deeper learning, increased practical competence, and greater personal and social gains.

New to This Edition

More Attention to Audience and Purpose. Each of the ten chapters in Part 2, "Using Genres to Express Ideas" now begins with an in-depth discussion of audience, purpose, and primary considerations students should think about before writing in a particular genre (Chapters 5–14).

New Chapter on Critical Reading. A new Chapter 4, "Reading Critically, Thinking Analytically," offers strategies for previewing, annotating, analyzing, and responding to any text. In addition, it guides students to strengthen their writing by both evaluating what others have written *and* using what others have written in students' own writing.

New Chapter on Collaboration Underscores the Importance of Peer Response. A new Chapter 23, "Collaborating and Peer Response," now covers strategies for working in groups and in teams, with an added focus on using peer response to improve writing. New content shows students how to effectively provide feedback to others and includes both strategies and guidelines, in tandem with helpful examples of rubrics and peer response worksheets, to assist students in this very important part of the writing process.

New Coverage of Citing Sources. In Chapter 26, citing sources is now given prominence as one of four methods of incorporating sources into writing. Explanation of when and how to cite, via parenthetical citations, shows students how to properly attribute the research of others in their own writing.

Focus on Assessment. A revised Chapter 31 now incorporates the important topic of assessment. Coverage includes how to study for exams in which your understanding of a course's key concepts and fundamental ideas will be measured and how to use rubrics to your advantage.

Streamlined Coverage of the Writing Process. Part 3, "Developing a Writing Process," provides students with the tools they need to begin their writing immediately. Instruction on drafting introductions and conclusions has been moved into Chapter 16, "Organizing and Drafting," for better ease of use.

New Microgenres Examples. Seven new full microgenre examples include the bio (Chapter 6), the rave (Chapter 7), the ad critique (Chapter 9), the letter to the editor (Chapter 10), the rebuttal (Chapter 11), the pitch (Chapter 12), and the explainer (Chapter 13) so that students can explore related genres.

New Engaging, Effective Readings. Over 15 new readings cover topics such as racial equality, video games, the Second Amendment, fast food, college sports, depression, and more to keep class discussion lively and suggest a range of topics students might consider for their own writing.

Features of This Book

Interactive Writing Style. Instruction is brief and to the point. Key concepts are immediately defined and reinforced. Paragraphs are short and introduced by heads that preview content. This interactive style helps students skim, ask questions, and access information when they are ready for it—putting them in control of their learning.

At-A-Glance. Each Part 2 chapter opens with a diagram that shows one or two common ways to organize a genre's key elements, giving an immediate and visual orientation to the genre. Students learn to adapt this organization to suit their rhetorical situation as they read the chapter.

End-of-Chapter Activities. Exercises conclude every chapter in the book to help students understand and practice concepts and strategies.

- **Talk About This** questions prompt classroom discussion.
- **Try This Out** exercises suggest informal writing activities students can complete in class or as homework.
- **Write This** prompts facilitate longer, formal writing assignments.

One Student's Work. A student-written example in each writing project chapter shows the kinds of issues students might explore in a specific genre of writing as well as the angles they might take. Annotations highlight the writer's key rhetorical decisions so the reading can be used either for discussion or as a model.

Quick Start Guide. This practical review includes action steps and appears in each chapter to get students writing quickly. Students spend less time reading about writing and more time working on their own compositions. They can also use the Quick Start Guide as a quick way to gain familiarity with a genre before reading the chapter.

Microgenre. A microgenre applies features of major genres to narrow rhetorical situations. For example, in Chapter 11, students apply features of a proposal to a pitch; in Chapter 5, those of a memoir to a literacy narrative. Each Microgenre in Part 2 includes a description, an example, and a writing activity, encouraging students to experiment and play by stretching genre conventions.

Readings and Prompts. Six readings—two in each project chapter and four in the anthology—offer models of each genre. Question sets after each reading encourage critical engagement.

- **A Closer Look** questions facilitate analytical reading.
- **Ideas for Writing** questions prompt responses, analyses, and different genres of writing.
- **A Few Ideas for Composing** activities (in the anthology) encourage writing that further explores each genre's possibilities.

A Multimodal Approach. Today's writers compose electronic texts, work with visual and audio tools, insert graphics, and collaborate with others online. Each chapter includes strategies for working in a multimodal environment. Multimodal assignments appear in "Write This" and in "A Few Ideas for Composing." Chapters in Part 6 offer guidance on creating and posting compositions in online environments.

How This Book Is Organized

Writing Today features brief chapters and plainly labeled sections, creating obvious access points that help students find what they need when they need it.

PART 1

Getting Started

Purposefully brief, the first four chapters are designed to get students up and running right away. They introduce the five elements of rhetorical situations (topic, angle, purpose, readers, and context) and explain why and how using genres will help students to write successfully. The fourth chapter teaches strategies for reading critically and thinking analytically.

PART 2

Using Genres to Express Ideas

These chapters help students master ten commonly assigned kinds of writing that form the foundation of an adaptable portfolio of skills. Students explore expressive, informative, analytical, persuasive, and argumentative genres that help them respond effectively to a majority of academic and workplace writing situations.

PART 3

Developing a Writing Process

Stand-alone chapters on planning, organization, style, design, and revision offer strategies students can apply to any writing situation. Instructors can assign them alongside the genre chapters.

PART 4

Strategies for Shaping Ideas

Straightforward chapters on drafting introductions and conclusions, developing paragraphs and sections, and incorporating rhetorical strategies (such as narration, classification, and comparison and contrast) provide resources for writing those sections of papers where students often find themselves stuck. A chapter on argument explores appeals and fallacies, and a chapter on collaboration helps students work effectively in groups.

PART 5

Doing Research

The ability to research effectively is critical to students' success in college and in their careers. Students learn to engage in inquiry-driven research, evaluate sources, and work with sources by paraphrasing, quoting, and synthesizing. Up-to-date coverage of MLA and APA styles includes citation examples and model papers.

PART 6

Getting Your Ideas Out There

Today's students have more opportunities to present their work publicly than ever before. Students learn how to use social networking and other Web applications for rhetorical purposes. Students learn best practices for creating a professional portfolio of their work. Basics such as succeeding on essay exams and giving presentations are covered in depth as well.

PART 7

Anthology of Readings

The anthology showcases the ten genres of writing explored in Part 2. These additional readings serve as models, suggest situations in which specific genres are particularly effective, offer material for response, and help students discover their own research topics.

PART 8

Handbook

Designed to be as accessible and usable as possible, the handbook gives students a quick resource for issues of grammar, usage, and punctuation.

Ways to Fit This Book to Your Teaching Approach

Flexibility is a chief strength of *Writing Today*. The first four chapters form a foundation, but remaining chapters can be taught in any order or combination to suit individual teaching approaches and objectives.

A Process Approach. Students want to learn a writing process that suits their own working habits and writing styles. The chapters in Part 2 tailor the writing process with strategies specific to different genres. Part 3, "Developing a Writing Process," provides additional chapters on prewriting, drafting, designing, revising, and editing that can be assigned with any project.

A Genre-Based Approach. Genres aren't templates into which writers pour words: they are tools writers can use to help them invent ideas and plan, research and draft, design and edit. *Writing Today* covers real-world writing—such as analyses, reviews, reports, proposals—that help students solve real problems and achieve specific goals.

A Purposes or Aims-Based Approach. Instructors who teach an aims approach to writing encourage students to be aware of their audience and purpose as they write to express, inform, analyze, or persuade. This approach works hand-in-hand with a genre-based approach: knowing the genre helps writers better understand a text's purpose, readers, and context.

A Strategies or Patterns-Based Approach. Instructors who teach rhetorical patterns (narrative, description, comparison and contrast, cause and effect, etc.), will find them embedded in this book. Part 4, "Strategies for Shaping Ideas," shows how strategies work with and within genres to help students organize and shape their ideas. *Writing Today* applies the strengths of a patterns-based approach to more complex kinds of documents.

An Academic Approach. Students learn the kinds of writing common in the General Education curriculum, such as narratives, rhetorical analyses, literary analyses, reviews, and argument essays. They also learn the foundations of the kinds of writing common in advanced academic classes, such as profiles, commentaries, reports, and proposals. Strategies for writing from sources—including paraphrasing, quoting, citing, and documenting sources—are covered in Part 5.

An Argument-Based Approach. *Writing Today* presents a rhetorical approach to writing. Several genres in Part 2, such as rhetorical analyses, commentaries, arguments, and proposals, are purposefully designed to be argument-based; this content is labeled with ARGUMENT in the table of contents. Chapter 22 helps students determine what is arguable and anticipate opposing points of view while also explaining the four stases, the classical appeals, and logical fallacies.

An Integrated, Multimodal Approach. Instructors teaching multimodal composition courses know there are few writing guides that teach critical twenty-first-century composing skills and even fewer that offer multimodal assignments. *Writing Today* assumes that students compose electronically and research online, and it offers strategies for writers to plan and collaborate online, include visuals in print texts, create visual texts, create media projects, and post compositions to the Web.

Distance Learning and Online Teaching. *Writing Today* was designed to be easily adaptable to online and hybrid learning environments. The book's comprehensiveness and flexibility provide strong scaffolding on which distance learning, online, and hybrid courses can be developed. Its highly accessible design allows students to quickly find the information they need while learning on their own and composing at their computers. The Pearson eText can be used alone or embedded in a suite of online writing, research, and grammar resources delivered in *MyWritingLab*.

Correlation to the Revised (2014) WPA Outcomes Statement

Writing Today helps teachers and students address learning outcomes for first-year composition courses identified by the Council of Writing Program Administrators: rhetorical knowledge; critical thinking, reading, and writing; processes; knowledge of conventions; and composing in electronic environments. Both of us have been leaders in this organization, and we believe strongly that these outcomes reflect the kinds of abilities that students should master in these courses. Specific connections between chapters and the WPA Outcomes appear in the Instructor's Manual.

Resources for Students and Instructors

MyWritingLab is an online homework, tutorial, and assessment program that provides engaging experiences for teaching and learning. Flexible and easily customizable, *MyWritingLab* helps improve students' writing through context-based learning. Whether through self-study or instructor-led learning, *MyWritingLab* supports and complements course work.

Writing at the Center. With the new composing space and Review Plan, *MyWritingLab* unites instructor comments and feedback on student writing with targeted remediation via rich multimedia activities, allowing students to learn from and through their own writing.

Writing Help for Varying Skill Levels. For students who enter the course under-prepared, *MyWritingLab* identifies those who lack prerequisite skills for composition-level topics, and provides personalized remediation.

Proven Results. No matter how *MyWritingLab* is used, instructors have access to powerful gradebook reports, which provide visual analytics that give insight to course performance at the student, section, or even program level.

A Deeper Connection between Print and Media: The *MyWritingLab* logo (MyWritingLab) is used throughout the book to indicate exercises and writing activities that can be completed and submitted through *MyWritingLab* (appropriate results flow directly to the Instructor Gradebook).

The Instructor's Manual. The Instructor's Manual opens by discussing how genre theory can be applied to the first-year writing curriculum. Subsequent chapters discuss classroom management, syllabus building, and teacher-student communication in traditional, hybrid, or online learning spaces. The second section is a collection of syllabi that includes rhetorical strategies/patterns approaches or purposes/aims-based approaches. The third section offers teaching strategies and support for *every* chapter in the book, as well as discussion of how each chapter aligns with WPA Outcomes. The last section provides additional support for teaching the readings and using the activities and prompts in the Anthology.

Acknowledgments

A book like this one is never the work of one or two people, even though our names appear on the cover. We would like to thank our editors, Joe Opiela and Anne Brunell Ehrenworth, for their great ideas and persistence. We would also like to thank our colleagues, Scott Sanders, Susan Romano, Wanda Martin, Michelle Kells, Karen Olson, David Blakesley, Irwin Weiser, and Shirley Rose, for their feedback on our ideas. We also want to thank our students, especially our graduate students, for trying out some of these materials in their classes and helping us refine the ideas and approaches in this book. We are appreciative of our thoughtful and enthusiastic reviewers, whose feedback helped us improve the effectiveness of *Writing Today* as a teaching and learning tool: Shawn Adamson, *Genesee Community College;* Ryan Allen, *University of Louisville;* Jennifer Aly, *University of Hawai'i Maui College;* Ellen Arnold, *Coastal Carolina University;* Katherine Baker, *College of Southern Nevada;* John Barrett, *Richland College;* Sharon Bartkovich, *College of Coastal Georgia;* Lisa Bickmore, *Salt Lake Community College;* Jacqueline A. Blackwell, *Thomas Nelson Community College;* Patricia Webb Boyd, *Arizona State University;* Jo Ann Buck, *Guilford Technical Community College;* Gary Cale, *Jackson College;* Genesea M. Carter, *The University of New Mexico;* Jacqueline Cason, *University of Alaska Anchorage;* John Castellarin, *Germanna Community College;* Marlys Cervantes, *Cowley College;* Ron Christiansen, *Salt Lake Community College;* Gail S. Corso, *Neumann University;* Paul Craven, *Alamance Community College;* T. Allen Culpepper, *Tulsa Community College, Southeast Campus;* Tamera Davis, *Northern Oklahoma College;* Louise Dekreon Watsjold, *University of Alaska Chugia— Eagle River Campus;* Dominic Delli Carpini, *York College of Pennsylvania;* Jason DePolo, *North Carolina A&T State University;* Paul Dombrowski, *University of Central Florida;* Carlton Downey, *Houston Community College;* Chitralekha Duttagupta, *Arizona State University;* Jeremiah Dyehouse, *The University of Rhode Island;* Charles Ellis, *Wiregrass Georgia Technical College;* William FitzGerald, *Rutgers University–Camden;* Mary Sue Fox, *Central New Mexico Community College;* Dayna V. Goldstein, *Georgia Southern University;* Deborah Goodwyn, *Virginia State University;* Pamela Hardman, *Cuyahoga Community College;* Susanmarie Harrington, *The University of Vermont;* Matthew Hartman, *Ball State University;* Karen Hattaway, *San Jacinto College North;* Dave Higginbotham, *University of Nevada, Reno;* Krista Jackman, *The University of New Hampshire;* Jay Jordan, *The University of Utah;* Chad Jorgensen, *Metropolitan Community College;* Margaret Konkol, *University at Buffalo, The State University of New York;* Andrew J. Kunka, *University of South Carolina Sumter;* Betty LaFace, *Bainbridge College;* Karen Laing, *College of Southern Nevada;* William B. Lalicker, *West Chester University of Pennsylvania;* Steve Lazenby, *University of North Carolina at Charlotte;* Robert Lively, *Truckee Meadows Community College;* MacGregor Frank, *Guilford Technical Community College;* Joleen Malcolm, *University of West Florida;* Terri Mann, *El Paso Community College;* Linda Martin, *Coastal Carolina University;* Rachel Maverick, *Richland College;* Sharon McCamy, *ITT Technical Institute;* Miles McCrimmon, *J. Sargeant Reynolds Community College;* James McWard, *Johnson County Community College;* Eileen Medeiros, *Johnson & Wales University;* Shellie Michael, *Volunteer State Community College;* Susan Miller, *The University of Utah;* Rhonda Morris, *Santa Fe College;* Mary Ellen Muesing, *University of North Carolina at Charlotte;* Lori Mumpower, *University of Alaska Anchorage;* Margie Nelson, *El Paso Community College;* Sarah Nielsen, *DeVry University;* Annie Nguyen, *Community College of Baltimore County;* Matthew Oliver, *Old Dominion University;* Michael Pennell, *The University of Rhode Island;* Jason Pickavance, *Salt Lake Community College;* Jennifer Pooler-Courtney, *The University of Texas at Tyler;* Sarah A. Quirk, *Waubonsee Community College;* Timothy D. Ray, *West Chester University of Pennsylvania;* Peggy L. Richards, *The University of Akron;* Shewanda Riley, *Tarrant County College–Northeast Campus;* Christy Rishoi, *Mott College;* Mauricio Rodriguez, *El Paso Community College;* Jane Rosecrans, *J. Sargeant Reynolds Community College;* Dan Royer,

Grand Valley State University; Stephen Ruffus, *Salt Lake Community College;* Andrew Scott, *Ball State University;* Brittany Stephenson, *Salt Lake Community College;* Mitchell Summerlin, *Calhoun Community College;* Stacey Tartar-Esch, *West Chester University of Pennsylvania;* Bradley A. Waltman, *College of Southern Nevada;* Elizabeth Wardle, *University of Central Florida;* Leah Williams, *The University of New Hampshire;* Margaret Wintersole, *Laredo Community College;* Kristy Wooten, *Catawba Valley Community College,* John Ziebell, *College of Southern Nevada.*

About the Authors

Richard Johnson-Sheehan is a Professor of Rhetoric and Composition at Purdue University, where he is currently the Director of the Purdue Writing Lab and the Purdue OWL. At Purdue, he has directed the Introductory Composition program, and he has mentored new teachers of composition for many years. He teaches a variety of courses in composition, professional writing, and writing program administration, as well as classical rhetoric and the rhetoric of science. He has published widely in these areas. His books on writing include *Argument Today*, co-authored with Charles Paine, *Technical Communication Today,* now in its fifth edition, and *Writing Proposals,* now in its second edition. Professor Johnson-Sheehan was awarded 2008 Fellow of the Association of Teachers of Technical Writing and has been an officer in the Council for Writing Program Administrators.

Charles Paine is a Professor of English at the University of New Mexico, where he directs the Core Writing and the Rhetoric and Writing programs. He teaches first-year composition and courses in writing pedagogy, the history of rhetoric and composition, and other areas. His published books span a variety of topics in rhetoric and composition, including *The Resistant Writer* (a history of composition studies), *Teaching with Student Texts* (a co-edited collection of essays on teaching writing), and *Argument Today* (an argument-based textbook). An active member of the Council of Writing Program Administrators, he has served on its Executive Board and served as co-leader of the WPA Summer Conference Workshop. He cofounded and coordinates the Consortium for the Study of Writing in College, a joint effort of the National Survey of Student Engagement and the Council of Writing Program Administrators. The Consortium conducts general research into the ways that undergraduate writing can lead to enhanced learning, engagement, and other gains related to student success.

Writing and
Genres

In this chapter, you will learn how to—

1.1 describe what genres are and how they help writers and readers communicate.

1.2 use genres to communicate with readers.

1.3 develop a writing process that will help you write efficiently and effectively.

1.4 use "genre know-how" to become a versatile writer in college and in the workplace.

Writing gives you the power to get things done with words and images. It allows you to respond successfully to the people and events around you, whether you are trying to strengthen your community, pitch a new idea at work, or just text with your friends.

The emergence of new writing situations—new places for writing, new readers, and new media—means writing today involves more than just getting words and images onto a page or screen. Writers need to handle a wide variety of situations with diverse groups of people and rapidly changing technologies. Learning to navigate among these complex situations is the real challenge of writing in today's world.

What Are Genres?

In this book, you will learn how to use *genres* to interpret complex situations and respond to them successfully. Defining the word *genre* is difficult. Sometimes, genres are defined by their structure alone (e.g., "A report has five parts: introduction, methods, results, discussion, and conclusion"). But this understanding of genre is too simplistic. Genres are not fixed or rigid patterns to be followed mechanically. They are not templates into which we insert sentences and paragraphs.

1.1 describe what genres are and how they help writers and readers communicate.

Genres are ways of writing and speaking that help people interact, communicate, and work together. In other words, genres reflect the things people do, and they are always evolving because human activities change over time to suit new social situations and fresh challenges. Genres *do* offer somewhat stable patterns for responding to typical situations. More importantly, though, they reflect how people act, react, and interact in these situations. Genres are meeting places—and *meaning* places. They are places where writers and readers make meaning together.

Using Genres to Write Successfully

1.2 use genres to communicate with readers.

For writers, genres offer flexible patterns that reflect how people in communities interact with each other. They provide strategies for analyzing and interpreting what is happening around you. Once you understand your current situation, you can then use genres to focus your creativity, generate new ideas, and present those ideas to others.

Readers use genres, too. For readers, genres are guideposts for orienting themselves to a text. Genres help readers to anticipate what they are likely to find in a document and how they can use the information in it. When you understand what your readers expect, you can make strategic choices about what information you will include and how you will present it (Figure 1.1).

Writing with Genres

Here are the most important things to remember about genres:

Genres Are Flexible. Genres are as flexible and changeable as the human activities they represent. It is important to know the common features of each genre, so you can use them to help you interpret new social situations and then respond to them appropriately and successfully.

Genres Are Adaptable to Various Situations. When the audience or context changes, a genre needs to be adjusted to suit the new situation. An argument that worked previously with some readers or in a particular context might not work with different readers or in another context.

Genres Evolve to Suit Various Fields. Each discipline adapts common genres to its own needs and purposes. A report written by a biologist, for example, will share many characteristics with a report written by a manager at a

FIGURE 1.1 College Writing Requires Genre Know-How

Writing matters because it is one way people get things done. College writing will teach you "genre know-how," the ability to size up writing situations and respond to them appropriately.

corporation, but there will also be notable differences in the content, organization, style, and design of the text.

Genres Shape Situations and Readers. When you choose a particular genre, you are deciding what kinds of issues will be highlighted and what role your readers will play. For instance, readers know that when they encounter a memoir (a literary genre), they should read thoroughly and follow the story line. Quite differently, when readers encounter a report (a workplace genre), they assume that they can "raid" the text for the specific information they need—that is, they can skip and skim.

Genres Can Be Played With. You can be creative and play with the conventions of genres. You can combine, blend, or even "mash up" genres into new ones. Genres are stretchy. But if you are going to go against your readers' expectations of the genre, you need to do so consciously and for a specific purpose.

Genres in Movies

You are already familiar with the concept of genres in media and entertainment (Figure 1.2). Movie genres include romantic comedies, action flicks, documentaries, murder mysteries, musicals, science fiction and fantasy, horror, thrillers, and others. These genres aren't formulas that the writers and directors must follow. Instead, they are familiar patterns that audiences will recognize and understand.

Once audience members recognize the genre of a movie, they form specific expectations about what kinds of things they will—and will not—experience. For example, a romantic comedy usually explores the amusing awkwardness and pratfalls of a new relationship. Two people meet and feel an attraction to each other. But then, events

FIGURE 1.2 Movie Genres

Usually, moviegoers recognize the genre of a movie even before they step into the theater. Movie studios use posters and previews to help audiences know what to expect and how to interpret the movie.

beyond their control keep them apart and cause humorous misunderstandings. Eventually, the two star-crossed lovers realize they truly do love each other and find a way at the end of the movie to be together.

Directors of successful romantic comedies use the boundaries and conventions of this genre to help them work creatively and produce a film that is familiar but also fresh. Genres aid the director's creativity by providing guidelines about how the movie should be structured, scripted, visually designed, musically scored, and even edited.

Movies that flop often fail to follow a recognizable genre or—even worse—they follow a common genre in a trite way. A movie that follows a genre formulaically feels painfully predictable and shallow.

Like successful movie directors, effective writers need to understand the genres they are using. Genres help writers figure out where to start and how to proceed. They allow writers to create something fresh and new, while also helping them to organize and control their message in a way that readers will recognize and comprehend. In this sense, good writers (like good movie directors) are always balancing the old, familiar, and stable with the new, creative, and dynamic.

Genre and the Writing Process

1.3 develop a writing process that will help you write efficiently and effectively.

So, how can genres help you write better? Think of something you already do well. To do something well, you first needed to learn the *process* for doing it. Someone else, perhaps a teacher, coach, parent, or friend, showed you the process and helped you get better at it (Figure 1.3). Writing is similar to the other things you enjoy doing. To write well, you first need to develop your own writing process. Strong writers aren't born with a special gift, and they aren't necessarily smarter than anyone else. Strong writers have simply mastered a reliable writing process that allows them to generate new ideas and shape those ideas into something readers will find interesting and useful.

Using a Writing Process

Over time, you will develop your own unique writing process, but the following six steps work well as a starting place:

Analyze the rhetorical situation. Define your topic, state your purpose, and analyze your readers and the contexts in which your text will be read or used.

Invent your ideas. Use inquiry and research to generate your own ideas and discover what others already know about your topic.

Organize and draft your paper. Arrange and compose your ideas into familiar patterns that your readers will recognize and find useful.

Choose an appropriate style. Use techniques of plain and persuasive style to clarify your writing and make it more compelling.

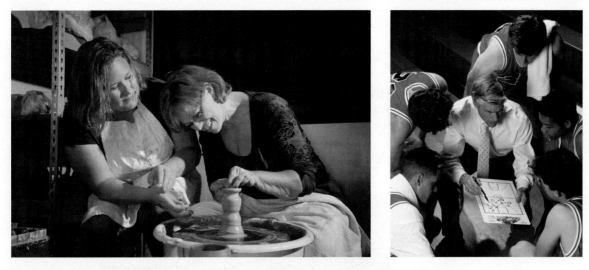

FIGURE 1.3 Learning to Do Something Involves Learning a Process

In order to do something you enjoy, you first had to learn a step-by-step process for doing it. Once you mastered the process and it became second nature, you could make it yours by refining and adapting it.

Design your document. Develop an appropriate page layout and use visual or audio features to make your ideas more accessible and attractive to readers.

Revise and edit your work. Improve your writing by rewriting, reorganizing, editing, and proofreading your work.

Experienced writers tend to handle each of these steps separately, but a writing process shouldn't be followed mechanically from one step to the next. Instead, experienced writers tend to move around among these steps as needed (Figure 1.4).

Why bother with a writing process at all? A reliable writing process helps you do things one step at a time. In the long run, following a writing process will save you time and will help you to write with more confidence and creativity.

Using Genre as a Guiding Concept

The genre you are using should influence each stage of your writing process, as shown in Figure 1.4. For example, if you are writing a movie review, the "review genre" (discussed in Chapter 7, "Reviews") will help you make decisions about what kinds of information your readers will expect. Should you tell them the plot of the movie? Should you describe the characters? Should you give away the ending? The genre will provide you with a model organization, so you can arrange your ideas in a pattern that your readers will expect. The genre also helps you to make informed decisions about what kind of style and design would work.

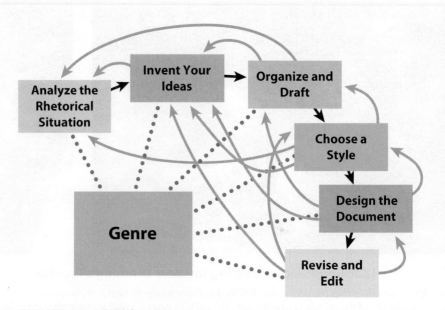

FIGURE 1.4 A Writing Process

Good writers tend to go through steps as they develop their work. They move among these steps in ways that fit their own work habits and personalities.

The purpose of a genre is to help you figure out how people tend to act, react, and interact in the situation in which you are writing. So if you tell your readers you are giving them a "movie review," they will have some predictable expectations about the content, organization, style, and design of your text.

Transfer: Using Genres in College and in Your Career

1.4 use "genre know-how" to become a versatile writer in college and in the workplace.

The genre-based approach to writing might be new to you, but it's really just the next step toward preparing you to succeed in college and in your career. By working with the genres in this book, you will develop *genre know-how*, the practical knowledge and skill to write effectively for a variety of purposes and situations. You will learn how to recognize and adapt genres for your own needs, and you will learn how to use genre know-how to adjust your writing for unique situations and specific readers.

In other words, the communication skills you learn in this book will "transfer" to your advanced classes and your career. Now is good time to begin mastering the genres you will need to be successful.

At the end of each chapter in this book, you will find something called the "Quick Start Guide." The purpose of the Quick Start Guides is to help you get up and running as soon as possible. You can use these guides for review or to preview the essential information in the chapter. Here is the essential information in this chapter.

KNOW What a Genre Is

Genres are ways of writing and speaking that help people communicate and work together in specific situations. Genres offer relatively stable patterns for writing, but more importantly they reflect how humans act, react, and interact in everyday situations. Genres are meeting places—and *meaning* places.

LEARN "Genre Know-How"

Genre know-how is the ability to use genres to analyze and interpret what is happening around you. When you have genre know-how, you can use genres to focus your creativity, generate new ideas, and present those ideas to others.

KEEP in Mind That Genres Are Flexible

Genres are as flexible and changeable as the human activities they represent. They need to be adjusted to suit evolving situations. They can be stretched, blended, and messed around with to fit unique situations.

DEVELOP Your Writing Process

A writing process leads you from your basic idea to a finished document, from inventing ideas to final editing. Developing and refining your writing process will save you time and effort in the long run.

USE Genres in College and in Your Career

A genre-based approach to writing helps you master a "genre set" that will transfer to your advanced college courses and to the workplace. The genre set taught in this book will cover most of the texts you will write in college and in your career.

1. With a group of people in your class, have each person talk briefly about his or her favorite movie genre; then, as a group, choose one of those genres to discuss. Describe the genre and its common features.

2. In your group, brainstorm and list all the television shows you can think of. Then divide these shows into genres. What characteristics did you use to sort these shows into categories? How do the producers of these shows follow and bend the genres to come up with something new?

3. With your group, brainstorm and list all the restaurant genres you can think of. Then choose one restaurant genre to explore further. How does the genre of the restaurant encourage specific kinds of behavior from its employees and its customers?

1. On the Internet, find a Web page or Web site that conforms to a familiar Web site genre. For your professor (who may not know about this genre), write a one-page document that describes the Web site and explains the genre and how it works.

2. When a movie uses the well-known features of a genre to make fun of that genre, it's called a *parody*. Write a one-page description of a movie that parodies a particular genre, the genre it makes fun of, and the features of the genre that are specifically targeted by the parody.

3. For five minutes, freewrite about your favorite movie or television show. Freewriting means just putting your pen on the paper (or your fingers on the keyboard) and writing anything that comes to mind. Then, in your group, discuss what you wrote in your freewrite.

4. Consider a kind of writing activity that you are good at (e.g., texting, e-mail, essays, short stories). What kind of content is typical; how is that content organized; what kind of language is used? In what ways does the genre determine who the participants can and cannot be?

5. Imagine that you have been asked to direct a movie that crosses two very different genres. For example, you might be asked to tell a horror story as a romantic comedy, or you might be asked to convert a historical documentary into an action flick. In a one-page paper written for your professor, explain how this merging of genres might offer some creative opportunities.

1. **Analyze a genre.** Find a longer nonfiction document that seems to be using a specific genre. Write a three-page analysis in which you describe the document's content, organization, style, and design.

2. **Review a movie for a Web site or blog.** Write a three-page review of a movie you saw recently to post on a blog or movie review Web site. In your review, identify the genre of the movie and the common characteristics of that genre. Then, show your readers how the movie exhibited those characteristics. Toward the end of your review, tell your readers whether you thought the movie was good by discussing how well it worked within its genre.

Go to **MyWritingLab** to complete this chapter's exercises and test your understanding of its objectives.

Topic, Angle,
Purpose

In this chapter, you will learn how to—

2.1 develop and narrow your topic to respond to any writing situation.

2.2 develop your angle, the unique perspective you'll bring to the topic.

2.3 identify your purpose, or what you want to accomplish.

2.4 use your identified purpose to develop a thesis sentence (or main point).

2.5 choose the appropriate genre for your purpose.

One of your professors has just given you a new writing assignment. What should you do first? Take a deep breath. Then, read the assignment closely and ask yourself a few specific questions about what you need to do:

What am I being asked to write about? (Topic)

What is new or has changed recently about this topic? (Angle)

What exactly is the assignment asking me to do or accomplish? (Purpose)

Who will read this document, and what do they expect? (Readers)

Where and when will they be reading this document? (Context)

Whether you are writing for your class or for the workplace, you can use these questions to help you identify the basic elements of your document's "rhetorical situation" (Figure 2.1).

The rhetorical situation has five elements: topic, angle, purpose, readers, and context. In this chapter, we will discuss the first three elements. Gaining a clear understanding of your topic, angle, and purpose will help you decide which genre is most appropriate for your writing project.

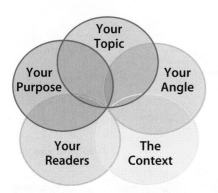

FIGURE 2.1 Five Elements of the Rhetorical Situation

Before you start writing, consider these five elements of the rhetorical situation, which will help you get started on your work.

Topic: What Am I Writing About?

In college, your professors will either provide the topics for your papers or ask you to come up with your own. When your professor supplies the topic, he or she will usually define the topic broadly, saying something like this:

2.1 develop and narrow your topic to respond to any writing situation.

> For this paper, I want you to write about the Civil Rights movement in the 1960s.

> Our next project will research "dating and mating in college," and we will be using our own campus for field research.

If your professor does not supply a topic, you should pick a topic that intrigues you and one about which you have something interesting to say.

In your career, you will write about topics that are different than the ones you wrote about in college. Nevertheless, you should still begin by clearly identifying your topic. For instance, your supervisor or a client may request a document from you in the following way:

> Our organization is interested in receiving a proposal that shows how we can lower our energy costs with wind and solar power.

> We want you to explore and report on the causes behind the sudden rise in violence in the Franklin South neighborhood.

Once you have clearly identified your topic, you should explore its boundaries or scope, trying to figure out what is "inside" and what is "outside" the topic. A good way to determine the boundaries of your topic is to create a concept map like the one shown in Figure 2.2.

To make a concept map, start out by writing your topic in the middle of a sheet of paper or your computer screen. Circle it, and then write down everything connected with it that comes to mind. Mapping on paper works well, but if you prefer mapping on screen you can use free or low-cost apps like *Coggle, XMind, Freemind,* or *Inspiration.*

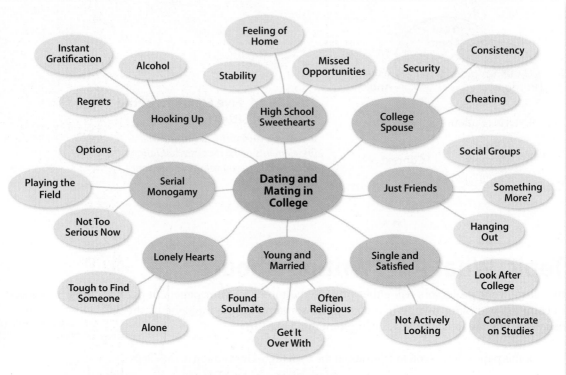

FIGURE 2.2 Creating a Concept Map About Your Topic

A concept map is a helpful way to get your ideas onto the screen or a piece of paper.

While mapping, write down all the things you already know about your topic. Then, as you begin to run out of ideas, go online and enter some of the words from your map into a search engine like *Google, Yahoo!,* or *Bing.* The search engine will bring up links to numerous other sources of information about your topic. Read through these sources and add more ideas to your concept map.

As your map fills out, you might ask yourself whether the topic is too large for the amount of time you have available. If so, pick the most interesting ideas from your map and create a second concept map around them alone. This second map will often help you narrow your topic to something you can handle.

Angle: What Is New About the Topic?

2.2 develop your angle, the unique perspective you'll bring to the topic.

You don't need to discover a new topic for your writing assignment. Instead, you need to come up with a new *angle* on an existing topic. Your angle is your unique perspective or view on the issue.

What Has Changed That Makes This Topic Interesting Right Now?

Let's say you are searching for information about college dating trends. At your library, you find a 2011 book by Laura Sessions Stepp titled *Unhooked: How Young Women Pursue Sex, Delay Love, and Lose at Both* (Figure 2.3). The book seems a little out of date, but you mostly agree with the author's main points, especially her arguments about women avoiding long-term relationships while in college so they can focus on their studies and careers. However, you also believe new forms of social networking like *Twitter* and *Tumblr* have somewhat cooled off the hooking up culture that once existed. Now, college students can use social networking to get that feeling of intimacy with others rather than seeking intimacy by pairing off for the night. That could be your angle on this topic.

What Unique Experiences, Expertise, or Knowledge Do I Have About This Topic?

Your experiences as a college student give you some additional insights or "angles" into college dating. For example, perhaps your own experiences tell you that the

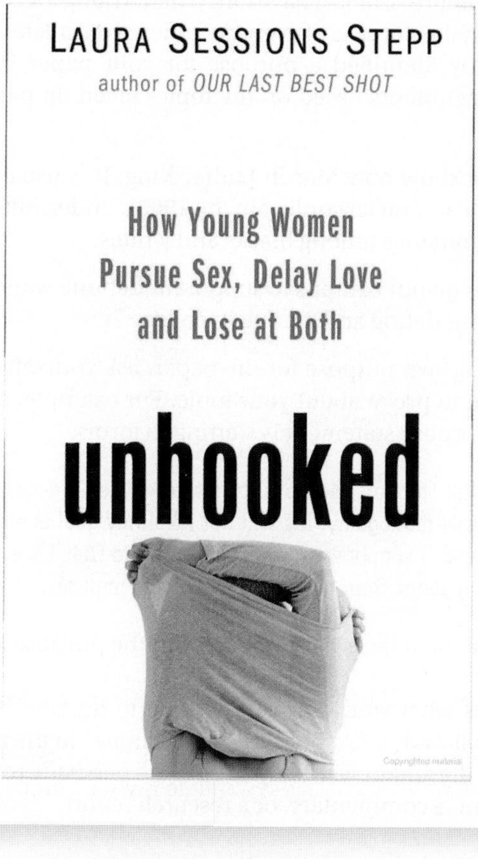

FIGURE 2.3　A Book on Your Topic

This book, published in 2011, looks like a great source for information on your topic, but it's a little dated. Your own experiences as a college student today may give you some new ways to see the topic.

hooking-up culture has been replaced by a culture of "serial monogamy" in which college students now go through a series of short-term emotional and physical relationships while they are in college. These so-called monogamous relationships may last a few months or perhaps a year, but most people don't expect them to lead to marriage. That's another possible angle on this topic.

To see if one of these angles works, you should do some freewriting to get your ideas out on the screen. Freewriting involves opening a new page in your word processor and writing anything that comes to mind. Freewrite for about five minutes, and don't stop to correct or revise. If you run out of material, type and finish the phrases, "What I really mean to say is . . ." or "I remember . . ." Then, you will get rolling again.

Dating and mating in college is a very large topic—too large for a five- to ten-page paper. But if you decide to write a paper that explores a specific angle (e.g., the shift from a hooking-up culture to a culture of serial monogamous relationships), you can say something new and interesting about how people date and mate in college.

Purpose: What Should I Accomplish?

2.3 identify your purpose, or what you want to accomplish.

Your purpose is what you want to accomplish. Everything you write has a purpose, even informal kinds of writing like texting. Whenever you speak or write, you are trying to inform, ask a question, flirt, persuade, impress, or just have fun. When writing for college or the workplace, you should figure out the purpose of every document you create.

Your professor may have already identified a purpose for your paper in the assignment, so check there first. Assignments based on the topics given on page 11 might look like this:

> Your objective in this paper is to show how Martin Luther King, Jr.'s use of nonviolence changed the dynamics of racial conflict in the 1960s, undermining the presumption of white dominance among blacks and whites.

> Use close observation of students on our campus to support or debunk some of the common assumptions about dating and mating in college.

If you need to come up with your own purpose for the paper, ask yourself what you believe and what you would like to prove about your topic. For example, at the end of the freewrite in Figure 2.4, a purpose statement is starting to form:

> In my paper, I would like to argue that the hooking-up culture that existed a decade ago has changed into a culture of serial monogamy. It's still not ideal. My goal is not to defend or condemn what is going on. I simply want to explain a trend that I see here on campus and what I'm hearing about from my friends at other campuses.

This statement is still a bit rough and it lacks a clear focus, but the purpose of the project is starting to take shape.

Your purpose statement explains what you want your writing to do, and it also identifies the genre you are likely to follow. For example, the word "argue" in the rough purpose statement above signals that the author will likely be trying to persuade readers about an issue by writing an argument, a commentary, or a research report.

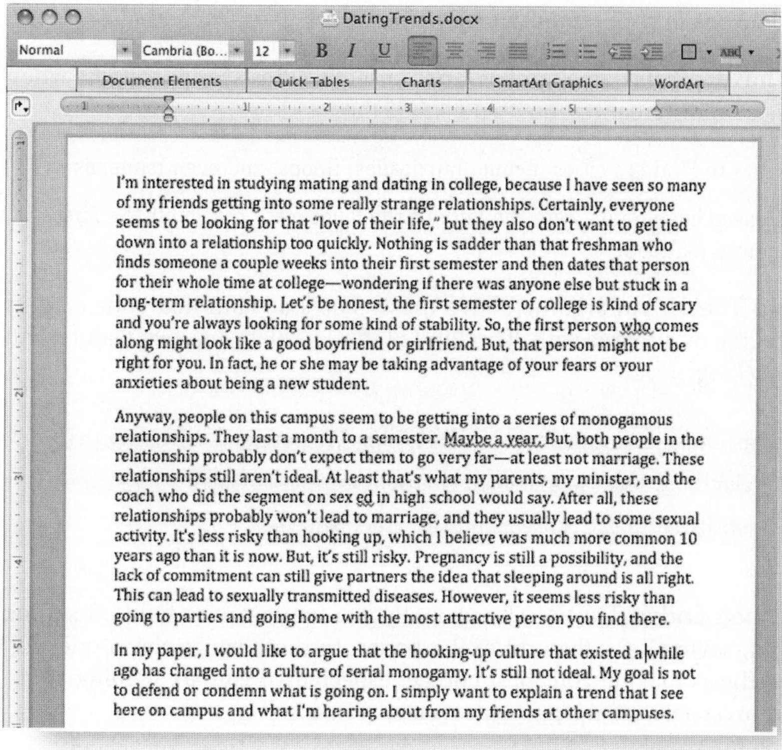

I'm interested in studying mating and dating in college, because I have seen so many of my friends getting into some really strange relationships. Certainly, everyone seems to be looking for that "love of their life," but they also don't want to get tied down into a relationship too quickly. Nothing is sadder than that freshman who finds someone a couple weeks into their first semester and then dates that person for their whole time at college—wondering if there was anyone else but stuck in a long-term relationship. Let's be honest, the first semester of college is kind of scary and you're always looking for some kind of stability. So, the first person who comes along might look like a good boyfriend or girlfriend. But, that person might not be right for you. In fact, he or she may be taking advantage of your fears or your anxieties about being a new student.

Anyway, people on this campus seem to be getting into a series of monogamous relationships. They last a month to a semester. Maybe a year. But, both people in the relationship probably don't expect them to go very far—at least not marriage. These relationships still aren't ideal. At least that's what my parents, my minister, and the coach who did the segment on sex ed in high school would say. After all, these relationships probably won't lead to marriage, and they usually lead to some sexual activity. It's less risky than hooking up, which I believe was much more common 10 years ago than it is now. But, it's still risky. Pregnancy is still a possibility, and the lack of commitment can still give partners the idea that sleeping around is all right. This can lead to sexually transmitted diseases. However, it seems less risky than going to parties and going home with the most attractive person you find there.

In my paper, I would like to argue that the hooking-up culture that existed a while ago has changed into a culture of serial monogamy. It's still not ideal. My goal is not to defend or condemn what is going on. I simply want to explain a trend that I see here on campus and what I'm hearing about from my friends at other campuses.

FIGURE 2.4 Freewriting to Find Your Angle

Freewriting about your topic helps you test your new angle. Just write freely for five to ten minutes without making revisions or corrections.

Sometimes, it helps to remember that papers in college and in the workplace tend to be written for two primary reasons: to *inform* and to *persuade*. So your purpose statement will usually be built around these kinds of verbs:

Informative Papers: inform, describe, define, review, notify, advise, explain, demonstrate.

Persuasive Papers: persuade, convince, argue, recommend, advocate, urge, defend, justify, support.

Thesis Statement (Main Claim)

2.4 use your identified purpose to develop a thesis sentence (or main point).

Closely related to your purpose statement is your *thesis statement* (also known as your "main point" or "main claim"). A purpose statement guides you, as the *writer,* by helping you develop your ideas and draft your paper. Your thesis statement guides your *readers* by announcing the main point or claim of the paper.

The thesis statement in your paper will usually first appear in your introduction (Figure 2.5). Then, it reappears, typically with more emphasis, in the conclusion.

In special cases, you may choose to use a "question thesis" or "implied thesis" in which a question or open-ended comment in the introduction sets up a thesis statement that appears only in the conclusion of the document.

There are four major types of thesis statements:

Informative Thesis. As its name implies, an informative thesis is appropriate when your purpose is to inform readers, not to persuade them:

> Natural threats to Florida's cities include hurricanes, floods, and even tsunamis.

> Irish and Chinese immigrants were the bulk of the labor force that built the First Transcontinental Railroad.

Argumentative Thesis. An argumentative thesis states a claim that your readers can choose to agree or disagree with. This kind of thesis usually has two features, an *assertion* and *backing*:

Assertion →

Backing →

> The Federal Communications Commission (FCC) should re-exert its authority over violence on television, because American children who watch violent shows are becoming desensitized to the consequences of cruel behavior.

Question or Open-Ended Thesis. Occasionally you may want to hold off stating your main point, saving it for the end of the paper. In these situations, a question or open-ended thesis may be your best choice, especially if you are arguing about something controversial or making a controversial point:

> What is the best way to ensure that guns are not used to commit crimes while also protecting the constitutional rights of gun owners?

> The question explored in this research paper is whether teachers' unions are beneficial or harmful to the American educational system.

The conclusion of your paper needs to clearly express your thesis statement. That way, the question or open-ended sentence you posed in your introduction is answered at the end of your paper.

Implied Thesis. In some situations, you might choose not to state your thesis explicitly. Genres that use the narrative pattern, such as memoirs, some profiles, and narrative argument papers, sometimes don't need an explicit thesis statement. In these situations, the author's purpose is to move readers toward thoughtful reflection rather than to inform or persuade them about a single specific point. Other times, the author might feel the overall message will be more powerful if readers figure out the main point for themselves. If you choose not to include a thesis statement, you need to make sure the message of your text comes through clearly for the readers, even though you aren't stating it explicitly.

Choosing the Appropriate Genre

2.5 choose the appropriate genre for your purpose.

Once you have sketched out your topic, angle, and purpose, you can choose which genre would be appropriate for your project. The appropriate genre depends on what

FIGURE 2.5
A Prominent Thesis Statement Orients Readers
Your thesis statement should help readers understand your main point or claim quickly and clearly.

Turnbow 1

Katelyn Turnbow

Professor Thompson

English 102

15 October 2014

Lives Not Worth the Money?

The outbreak and spread of Ebola has brought new attention to equally-lethal diseases that are often forgotten. The idea of a forgotten disease is almost absurd, a disease for which a cure is available but not given, effective, but never given a chance to work. We are often of the belief that human life is invaluable. In reality, however, the cures that do not make money for the manufacturer are simply not made at all. One need only look at African Sleeping Sickness (WHO). There is a cure, but the victims who would benefit from the drug are poor and considered "unprofitable" by the pharmaceutical industry. It remains, however, a drug company's ethical responsibility to care for the people that its drugs can save, even when helping others is not profitable.

West African Sleeping Sickness, also known as African Trypanosomiasis or HAT, was discovered in 1902 and it kills over 50,000 people a year. These victims,

you are trying to do and who you are writing for. Perhaps your professor has already identified the genre by asking you to write a "review," a "literary analysis," a "proposal," or a "research paper." If so, you can turn to that chapter in this book to learn about the expectations for that genre (Chapters 5–14).

If you are allowed to choose your own genre, or if you are writing something on your own, the best way to figure out which genre would work best is to look closely at your purpose statement. Your thesis sentence will signal which genre would be best for your paper. Look for verbs like "argue," "propose," "analyze," "explain," or "research" that signal which genre will work.

The genre that fits your purpose statement will help you make strategic decisions about how you are going to invent the content of your document, organize it, develop an appropriate style, and design it for your readers.

Ready to start right now? Here are some techniques and strategies for identifying your topic, angle, and purpose.

IDENTIFY Your Topic

Your topic will be assigned by your professor or you will need to come up with it yourself. Either way, figure out what interests you about the topic. Then, use a concept map to determine issues related to your topic.

NARROW Your Topic

Ask yourself whether the topic is appropriate for the amount of time you have available. If it seems too large, pick the most interesting ideas from your concept map and create a second map around them. This second map should help you narrow your topic to something you can handle.

DEVELOP Your Angle

Your angle is your unique perspective on the topic. A good way to develop an angle is to ask yourself, "What has changed recently about this topic that makes it especially interesting right now?" You might also ask what unique perspective you could offer on this issue.

WRITE Down Your Purpose

Your purpose is what you want to accomplish—that is, what you want to explain or prove to your readers. Decide whether you are *informing* or *persuading* your readers, or doing something else. Then, write a thesis statement that states exactly what you are going to do. Keep in mind that your thesis will probably change as you develop your drafts.

CHOOSE the Appropriate Genre

The best way to figure out which genre would work best for your project is to look closely at your purpose statement and thesis statement. In some cases, your professor will tell you which genre to use.

1. With a small group, list some topics that people often discuss and argue about. For example, what do people talk about on television or the radio? What do they argue about at local gathering places like cafés, restaurants, or bars? What are some things people discuss with their friends or families? Together, come up with ten things group members have discussed or argued about over the last few days.

2. Take a look at today's news on Web sites like CNN.com, FoxNews.com, or MSNBC.com. What are some of the topics in the news today? You will notice that new topics aren't all that common. However, reporters are developing new angles on topics all the time. With your group, discuss the new angles you notice on these topics. What changed recently that helped these reporters find new angles on existing topics?

3. Find an opinion piece in your local or campus newspaper or on the Internet. Examine the thesis. Does the author accurately and clearly announce the main point in a thesis statement? If the thesis is not stated, is it clear to you what point the author wanted to make? What kind of thesis is used—informational, argumentative, question, or implied? Do you think the author chose the best kind of thesis for this piece, or would a different kind of thesis statement have worked better?

1. List five topics that you might be interested in writing about this semester. They can include anything that captures your imagination. Then, for each of these topics, ask yourself, "What is new or has changed recently about this topic?" Using your answers to this question, write down two possible angles for each topic.

2. Think of a topic that catches your interest. For five minutes, create a concept map that includes everything you can think of about this topic. Now, look at your concept map and find a part of this topic that you would like to explore further. Next, freewrite on that part for five more minutes and see what kinds of ideas begin to emerge. Would this "narrower" topic be easier to write about than the topic you started with?

3. Pick a topic that interests you and develop a purpose statement for a paper about that topic. Your purpose statement doesn't need to be perfect right now, but try to describe what you want to achieve in your paper. Do you want to inform your readers about your topic or do you want to persuade them? Now, build your purpose statement around one of the words shown in the list on page 15.

4. Using the topic and purpose statement from the exercise above, identify which genre would be most appropriate for writing about this topic. Now, flip to that chapter in Part 2, "Using Genres to Express Ideas," to see what that genre usually involves.

5. Using the topic and purpose statement from Exercise 3, first decide what kind of thesis statement you think would work best (informative, argumentative, question, or implied). Now, write down your thesis statement. Try to come up with a thesis statement that captures your main point clearly and completely.

1. **Identify the topic, angle, and purpose of an assignment.** Choose a writing assignment from one of your professors. Using the steps and concepts discussed in this chapter, determine the topic you are being asked to write about and come up with a unique angle on it. Then, draft a purpose statement for your assignment. Write an e-mail to your professor in which you identify the topic, angle, and purpose of the paper you will be writing. Then, discuss which genre would be appropriate for this assignment and why.

2. **E-mail your professor about a new angle on a topic.** Pick any topic that interests you and find a new angle on that topic. Use concept mapping to explore and narrow your topic. Then, write a rough purpose statement that shows what you want to achieve in your paper.

   Choose a genre that would help you to say something meaningful and interesting about this issue. Turn to the chapter in Part 2 that discusses the genre you chose. Using the At-a-Glance diagram that appears early in the chapter, sketch a brief outline on this topic.

   Finally, write an e-mail to your professor in which you explain how you would go about writing an argument on this topic. Explain your topic, angle, and purpose, as well as the genre you would use. Tell your professor why you think your approach to the topic would be effective for your readers

> Go to **My WritingLab** to complete this chapter's
> exercises and test your understanding of its objectives.

Readers, Contexts, and Rhetorical Situations

In this chapter, you will learn how to—

3.1 profile your readers to understand their needs, values, and attitudes.

3.3 figure out how context—the place readers read and the medium you use—shapes your readers' experience.

3.3 use the rhetorical situation (topic, angle, purpose, readers, and context) to help you respond to any writing situation.

Writing doesn't happen in a vacuum. In college and your career, you will need to write to real people who are reading your work at specific times and in specific places. Your writing needs to inform them, persuade them, and achieve your purpose.

In the previous chapter, you learned how to identify your topic, angle, and purpose. In this chapter, you will learn how to achieve your purpose by developing *reader profiles* and sizing up the *contexts* in which people will read your work. Together, this information makes up the *rhetorical situation*—that is, the topic, angle, purpose, readers, and context.

Each rhetorical situation is unique, because every new situation puts into play a writer with a purpose, writing for specific readers who are encountering the work at a unique time and place. When you have sized up the rhetorical situation, you can figure out what genre will best help you accomplish what you want to achieve. Understanding your readers and the contexts in which they will experience your text will help you adjust the genre to fit both your needs and your readers' expectations.

Profiling Readers

3.1 profile your readers to understand their needs, values, and attitudes.

Before you start writing, you should develop a reader profile that helps you adapt your ideas to your readers' needs and the situations in which they will use your document.

A profile is an overview of your readers' traits and characteristics. At a minimum, you should develop a *brief reader profile* that gives you a working understanding of the people who will be reading your text. If time allows, you should create an *extended reader profile* that will give you a more in-depth view of their needs, values, and attitudes.

A Brief Reader Profile

To create a brief reader profile, you can use the Five-W and How questions to describe the kinds of people who will be reading your text (Figure 3.1).

Who Are My Readers? What are their personal characteristics? How young or old are they? What cultures do they come from? Do they have much in common with you? Are they familiar with your topic already or are they completely new to it?

What Are Their Expectations? What do they need from you and your document? What do they want, exactly? What ideas excite them, and what bores them? What information do they need to accomplish their personal and professional goals?

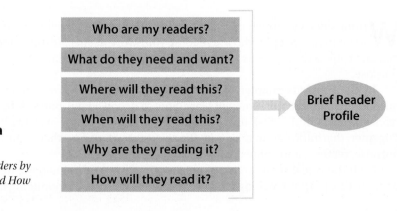

FIGURE 3.1 Elements of a Brief Reader Profile

You can quickly profile your readers by simply answering the Five-W and How questions about your readers.

Who are my readers?

What do they need and want?

Where will they read this?

When will they read this?

Why are they reading it?

How will they read it?

Brief Reader Profile

Where Will They Be Reading? In what locations might they read your document? Will your readers be sitting at their desks, in a meeting, or on an airplane? Will they be reading from a printed page, a computer screen, a tablet computer, or a small-screen device like a smartphone?

When Will They Be Reading? Will they be reading your work when the issue is hot and under discussion? Will they be reading it at a time when they can think about your ideas slowly and carefully? Does the time of day affect how they will read your document?

Why Will They Be Reading? Why will they pick up your document? Do their reasons for reading the document match your purpose for writing it? Do they want to be informed, or do they need to be persuaded?

How Will They Be Reading? Will they read slowly and carefully? Will they skip and skim? Will they read some parts carefully and other parts quickly or not at all?

Your answers to the Five-W and How questions will give you a brief reader profile to help you start writing. For simple documents, a brief profile like this one might be enough. For larger, more complex documents, you will need to dig a little deeper to develop a more thorough understanding of your readers.

An Extended Reader Profile

Keep in mind that your readers view issues differently than you do. Their needs, values, and attitudes will be unique to them and sometimes even conflict with yours.

To help you navigate these complex rhetorical situations, you might find it helpful to create an *extended reader profile* that goes beyond answering the Who, What, Where, When, Why, and How questions. An extended reader profile will help you to better anticipate what your readers expect, what they value, and what their attitudes are toward you and your topic.

What Are Their Needs? Your readers probably picked up your document because they *need* something. Do they need to know something specific? What do they need in order to do something or achieve a goal? What are their life goals, and what do they need to achieve them? Make a list of the two to five needs that your readers expect you to fulfill in your document for it to be useful to them.

You should also think broadly about what people in general need and why. An American psychologist, Abraham Maslow, developed a helpful tool for identifying people's needs. He suggested that human needs could be organized into five levels that move from lower-level *physiological needs* (food, air, sleep) to higher-level *self-actualization needs* (creativity, spontaneity, morality). Maslow's Hierarchy of Needs, as it is called, is often illustrated as a pyramid like the one in Figure 3.2.

Maslow's ranking of needs is culturally dependent, so people from different cultures may value some needs more than others. Also, high-stress situations like war or economic collapse can alter how people perceive their needs. Keeping these special cases in mind, if you can make reasonable guesses about your readers' needs, you are well on your way to knowing what to include in your document and how to present that information.

FIGURE 3.2 Maslow's Hierarchy of Needs

This pyramid is helpful toward figuring out how people rank what they need. Usually the needs at lower levels (physiological, safety) need to be satisfied before people are concerned about the needs at the higher levels (self-actualization) on the pyramid.

Source: Maslow, Abraham. (1943). "A Theory of Human Motivation". In *Psychological Review, 50* (4), 430-437.

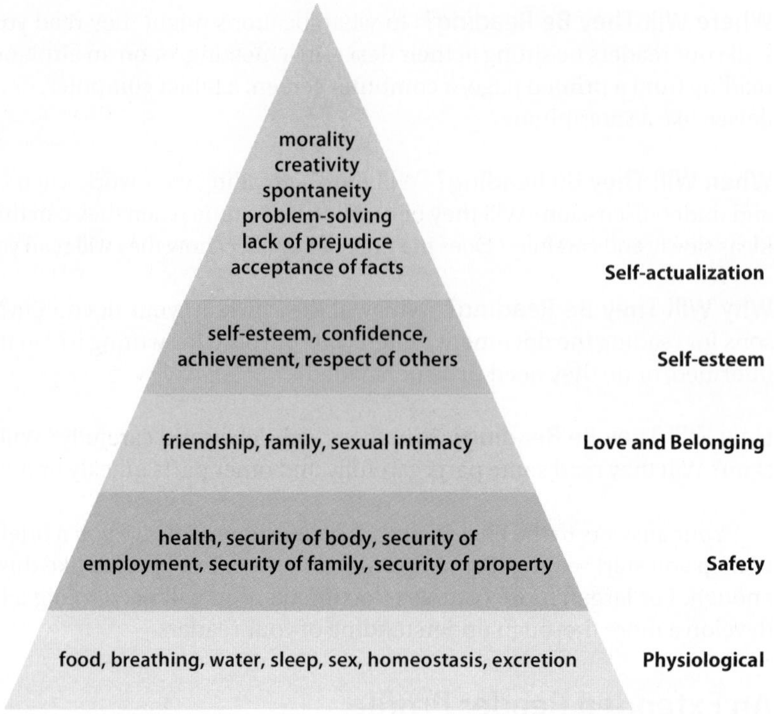

morality
creativity
spontaneity
problem-solving
lack of prejudice
acceptance of facts — **Self-actualization**

self-esteem, confidence, achievement, respect of others — **Self-esteem**

friendship, family, sexual intimacy — **Love and Belonging**

health, security of body, security of employment, security of family, security of property — **Safety**

food, breathing, water, sleep, sex, homeostasis, excretion — **Physiological**

What Are Their Values? *Values* involve personal beliefs, social conventions, and cultural expectations. Your readers' values have been formed through their personal experiences, family or religious upbringing, and social/cultural influences.

Personal values. Your readers' personal values can be hard to predict, but you should be able to take a few educated guesses. Think about your readers' upbringings and experiences. What are their core beliefs? What makes your readers and their values unique or different? What personal values do you and your readers likely hold in common?

Customs of their society. Think about how your readers behave among others in their own social circles. What expectations do their friends and family place on them? What traditions or codes govern their behavior?

Cultural values. Your readers' culture may influence their behavior in ways even they don't fully understand. What do people in their culture value? How are these cultural values similar to or different from your cultural values?

Mistakenly, writers sometimes assume that their readers hold the same values as them. Even people who seem similar to you in background and upbringing may have distinctly different ways of seeing the world.

What Is Their Attitude Toward You and the Issue? Your readers will also have a particular *attitude* about your topic and, perhaps, about you. Are they excited, or are they bored? Are they concerned or apathetic, happy or upset about your topic? Do you think they already accept your ideas, or are they deeply skeptical? Are they feeling positive toward you or negative? Will they welcome your views or be hostile toward them? Are they joyful or angry, optimistic or pessimistic?

If your readers are positive and welcoming toward your views, you will want to encourage their goodwill by giving them compelling reasons to agree with you. If they are negative or resistant, you will want to use solid reasoning, sufficient examples, and good style to counter their resistance and perhaps help them understand your point of view.

Using a Reader Analysis Worksheet

Anticipating all of your readers' needs, values, and attitudes can be especially difficult if you try to do it all in your head. That's why professional writers often like to use a Reader Analysis Worksheet like the one shown in Figure 3.3 to help them create an extended profile of their readers.

Using the Reader Analysis Worksheet is easy. On the left, list the types of people who are likely to read your document, ranking them by importance. Then, fill in what you know about their needs, values, and attitudes. If you don't know enough to fill in all of the squares on the worksheet, just put question marks (?) in those areas. Question marks signal places where you may need to do some additional research on your readers.

Types of Readers	Needs	Values	Attitudes
Most Important Readers:			
Second Most Important Readers:			
Third Most Important Readers:			

FIGURE 3.3 A Reader Analysis Worksheet

A Reader Analysis Worksheet is a helpful tool for understanding your readers and making good decisions about the content, organization, style, and design of your document.

An extended reader profile blends your answers to the Five-W and How questions with the information you added to the Reader Analysis Worksheet. These two reader analysis tools should give you a strong understanding of your readers and how they will interpret your document.

Analyzing the Context

3.2 figure out how context—the place readers read and the medium you use—shapes your readers' experience.

The *context* of your document involves the external influences that will shape how your readers interpret and react to your writing. You should keep in mind that readers react to a text moment by moment. So the happenings around them can influence their understanding of your document.

Your readers will be influenced by three kinds of contexts: place, medium, and social and political issues.

Place

Earlier, when you developed a brief profile of your readers, you answered the Where and When questions to figure out the locations and times in which your readers would use your document. Now go a little deeper to put yourself in your readers' place.

What are the physical features of this place?

What is visible around the readers, and what can they hear?

What is moving or changing in this place?

Who else is in this place, and what do they want from my readers?

What is the history and culture of this place, and how does it shape how people view things?

FIGURE 3.4 The Influence of Place

The place where your readers encounter your writing will strongly influence their interpretation of your ideas.

A place is never static. Places are always changing. So figure out how this place is changing and evolving in ways that influence your readers and their interpretation of your text (Figure 3.4).

The genre of your document may help you to imagine the places where people are likely to read it. Memoirs, profiles, reviews, and commentaries tend to be read in less formal settings—at home, on the bus, or in a café. Proposals and reports tend to be read in office settings, and they are often discussed in meetings. Once you know the genre of your document, you can make decisions about how it should be designed and what would make it more readable in a specific place.

Medium

The medium is the technology that your readers will use to interact with your document. Each medium (e.g., paper, Web site, public presentation, video, podcast) will shape how they interpret your words and react to your ideas:

Paper Documents. Paper documents are often read more closely than on-screen documents. With paper, your readers may be patient with longer paragraphs and extended reasoning. Document design, which is discussed in Chapter 18, "Designing," will make a paper document more attractive and help people read more efficiently. In print documents, graphics and photographs that enhance and reinforce the words on the page are appreciated by readers, but visuals aren't mandatory.

Electronic Documents. When people read text on a screen, as on a Web site or a blog, they usually "raid" it, reading selectively for the information they need. They tend to be impatient with a long document, and they generally avoid reading lengthy paragraphs. They appreciate informative and interesting visuals like graphs, charts, and photographs that will enhance their understanding. Typically, an electronic document will use a blend of written text and visuals. Chapter 29, "Writing with Social Networking," has more ideas about how to write for the screen.

Public Presentations. Presentations tend to be much more visual than on-screen and print documents. A presentation made with *PowerPoint* or *Keynote* usually boils an original text down to bullet points that highlight major issues and important facts. The people in your audience will focus on the items you choose to highlight, and they will rely on you to connect these items and expand on them. Turn to Chapter 32, "Presenting Your Work," for more ideas about how to make great presentations.

Podcasts or Videos. A podcast or video needs to be concise and focused. Hearing or seeing a text can be very powerful in this multimedia age; however, amateur-made podcasts and videos are easy to spot. The people listening to your podcast or watching your video will expect a polished, tight presentation that is carefully produced. Your work should get to the point and not waste their time, or they will turn to something else. Uploading podcasts and videos to the Web is not difficult. Websites like YouTube and Podcast Alley have easy-to-follow uploading directions. Turn to Chapter 29 for more information about making podcasts and videos.

Social and Political Influences

Now, think about the current trends and events that will influence how your readers interpret what you are telling them. Always keep in mind that your readers will encounter your writing in specific and real contexts that are always changing. These changes can be quick and dramatic, or they can be slow and almost imperceptible.

Social Trends. Pay attention to the social trends that are influencing you, your topic, and your readers. You originally decided to write about this topic because you believe it is important right now. What are the larger social trends that will influence how people in the near and distant future understand this topic? What is changing in your

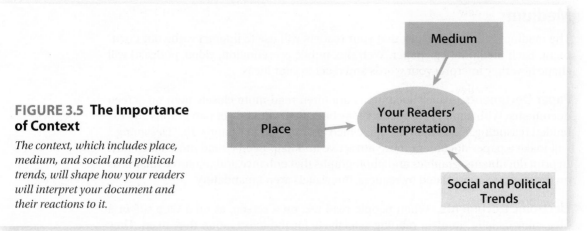

FIGURE 3.5 The Importance of Context

The context, which includes place, medium, and social and political trends, will shape how your readers will interpret your document and their reactions to it.

society that makes this issue so significant? Most importantly, how do these trends directly or indirectly affect your readers?

Economic Trends. For many issues, it all comes down to money. What economic factors will influence your readers? How does their economic status shape how they will interpret your arguments? What larger economic trends are influencing you and your readers?

Political Trends. Also, keep any political trends in mind as you analyze the context for your document. On a micropolitical level, how will your ideas affect your readers' relationships with you, their families, their colleagues, or their supervisors? On a macropolitical level, how will political trends at the local, state, federal, and international levels shape how your readers interpret your ideas?

Readers, naturally, respond to the immediate context in which they live (Figure 3.5). If you understand how place, medium, and social and political trends influence your readers, you can better adapt your work to their specific needs, values, and attitudes.

Genres and the Rhetorical Situation

3.3 use the rhetorical situation (topic, angle, purpose, readers, and context) to help you respond to any writing situation.

We threw quite a bit of material at you in this chapter and in the previous one. Here's our main point and a brief summary. Genres are used to respond to specific types of rhetorical situations. So when choosing the appropriate genre, you first need to completely understand the situation to which you are responding:

Topic. What is the exact topic your document is going to discuss? What information is "inside" the topic's boundaries and what is "outside" those boundaries? Have you sharpened your topic enough to handle it in the time and space you have available?

Angle. What is new or different about your approach to this topic? What has happened recently that makes your topic especially interesting to you and your readers right now? What makes your ideas about this topic different than the ideas of others?

Purpose. What exactly do you want to achieve in this document? What do you want your readers to believe or do after they are finished reading it? What are your goals in writing this text?

Readers. What are your readers' needs, values, and attitudes? How do these characteristics shape the content, organization, style, and design of your document?

Contexts. In what places do you expect your readers to encounter your document? How does the medium of your text shape how they will read it? What economic and social-political trends will influence how they react to what you are saying?

It might seem like a lot of work to figure all these things out, especially when the deadline is not that far away. In reality, though, analyzing the rhetorical situation only takes a few minutes for most documents. Once you have developed a full understanding of the rhetorical situation, you will find that writing the document goes more quickly and efficiently. In other words, you will save time because you won't hit dead ends or spend time collecting information you don't need. A few minutes invested at the beginning will pay off with better writing that takes less time and effort.

Need to quickly analyze your readers and the context for your document? Here are some steps to help you get started.

CREATE a Brief Profile of Your Readers

Using the Five-W and How questions, figure out *who* your readers are, *what* they need, *where* and *when* they will be reading the document, *why* they are reading it, and *how* they will be reading it. A sentence or two for each question should be enough to develop a brief profile.

KNOW Your Readers' Expectations

On a basic level, what are the two to five pieces of information your readers *expect* or *need* you to tell them for your document to be useful?

FIGURE OUT Your Readers' Values

Write down your readers' personal, social, and cultural values, and try to anticipate how these values will shape your document.

ANTICIPATE Your Readers' Attitudes About You and Your Topic

Try to figure out what your readers' mind-set will be. Will they be excited or bored, concerned or apathetic, happy or upset? Are they already convinced or deeply skeptical? Are they feeling positive toward you or negative? Will they welcome your views or be hostile toward them? Are they glad or angry, optimistic or pessimistic?

THINK About How Place and Medium Affect Your Readers

The physical place where they are reading may affect how closely they are reading and dictate what they need you to highlight for them. The medium of your document (e.g., paper, screen, presentation, podcast) will also shape how people interpret your ideas.

CONSIDER Social and Political Trends

Identify any current trends or events that might color your readers' understanding of your writing. What social trends affect your topic? How does money influence the situation? How does your project touch on micropolitical and macropolitical trends?

1. Choose an advertisement from a magazine or a newspaper. In a group, figure out the advertisement's purpose, target readers, and the contexts in which it was used. Be as specific and thorough as you can as you define the following:

   - *Purpose:* What is the advertisement trying to do? Use key words like *persuade, inform, entertain,* and others to describe its objectives.

   - *Readers:* What are the needs, values, and attitudes of the target readers? How does the advertisement try to use those needs, values, and attitudes to its advantage?

   - *Context:* Describe the place and medium of the advertisement as well as the social, economic, and political trends that might influence how it is interpreted. How do these contextual factors influence how readers respond to this ad?

   Finally, do you think the ad is effective in persuading or influencing its intended readers? For which readers would it be most effective, and for which ones would it be least effective?

2. Think of a time when you did not communicate effectively. With your group, discuss why the communication failed. What happened? Describe how you misread the situation, and why the audience or readers reacted as they did. How could you have handled the situation better if you had known the needs, values, and attitudes of the audience or readers? If you had better understood the social and political issues, how might your message have been more successful?

3. With your group, make a list of ten things that motivate people to agree with others or to take action. Discuss how these motives influence the ways people make decisions in real life. What are some ways you could use these motivations in your written work to persuade or influence people?

1. Imagine that you are an advertising specialist who has been asked to develop an ad campaign to sell "smart" eyewear like Google Glass to people over 60 years old. Figure out these customers' needs, values, and attitudes toward the product. Then take notes about how place and social and political factors shape their decisions about buying this kind of wearable technology. In a one-page memo to your professor, explain how you might use this knowledge to create an advertising campaign for this new market.

2. You have probably seen those electronic billboards that use light-emitting diodes (LEDs) to display content. These billboards offer more flexibility than traditional billboard media, because different advertisements can be displayed at different times of the day.

   Imagine that you are creating ads for these kinds of billboards. First, choose a product you want to advertise. Now create two thumbnail sketches (with images and words) for the billboard for two different contexts:

   - *Context A:* rush hour, when drivers are stopped at traffic lights in front of the billboard for as long as 90 seconds.

- *Context B:* normal drive time, when drivers may not stop at all, but drive by and have as little as two seconds to glance at the billboard. Write a one-page memo explaining how the two versions differ in response to the differing contexts. Explain why each version's design and content is right for the context.

3. For your next project in this class, do a brief reader analysis in which you answer the Five-W and How questions about your readers. Then, do an expanded reader analysis in which you explore their needs, values, and attitudes. In a one-page memo to your professor, explain the differences between your brief analysis and the extended analysis. What does the extended analysis reveal that the brief analysis didn't reveal? Would the brief analysis be enough for this project? Why? Or do you think the extended analysis would help you write a more effective document?

Write This

1. **Evaluate an argument.** Find an opinion article about an issue that interests you and write a two-page review in which you discuss how well the writer has adapted his or her article for its context. You can find a variety of opinion articles in your local or school newspapers (in the "opinion" section) or on the Internet (blogs, personal pages, online newspaper opinion sections and the responses to them). Mark up the text, paying attention to how the writer addresses the following contextual issues:

   - *Place:* How does the place in which the article was published influence how readers will interact with it? Where is someone likely to read this article and how does that physical place influence how readers will interpret its message?

   - *Medium:* How does the medium shape the way people read the text and what they will focus on?

   - *Social and Political Trends:* What have people been saying about the issue? If it's a hot topic, what makes it hot? What larger trends have motivated the writer to write this argument?

   In your evaluation, explain how the author of this opinion article adjusted his or her argument to the context in which it appears. Discuss whether you felt the opinion article succeeded. How might it be improved?

2. **Rewrite an online text for a different reader.** Find a brief document on the Internet that is aimed toward a specific kind of reader. Then, rewrite the document for a completely different type of reader. For example, if it was originally aimed at a young reader, rewrite it for an older reader.

   To complete this assignment, you will need to do a brief and extended reader analysis of your new readers.

   When you are finished rewriting the document, write a brief e-mail to your professor in which you explain how the change in readers altered the content, organization, style, and design of your rewrite. Attach your new version of the text to your e-mail.

> Go to **MyWritingLab** to complete this chapter's exercises and test your understanding of its objectives.

Reading Critically,
Thinking Analytically

In this chapter, you will learn how to—

4.1 "look through" and "look at" texts.

4.2 use seven strategies for reflecting on and responding to texts at a deeper level.

4.3 use critical reading to strengthen your writing.

Critical reading means analyzing a text closely through cultural, ethical, and political perspectives. Reading critically means adopting an inquiring and even skeptical stance toward the text, allowing you to explore beyond its apparent meaning.

Sometimes people mistakenly think critical reading is about discovering the so-called "hidden" or "real" meaning of a text. In reality, a text's meaning is rarely hidden, but it's not always obvious. As a critical reader, your job is to read texts closely and think about them analytically, so you can better understand their cultural, ethical, and political significance.

When reading a text critically, you are going deeper, doing things like:

- asking insightful and challenging questions

- figuring out why people believe some things and are skeptical of others

- evaluating the reasoning, authority, and emotion in the text

- contextualizing the text culturally, ethically, and politically

- analyzing the text based on your own values and beliefs.

Critical reading is a key component to good writing (Figure 4.1). In college courses and your career, you will be analyzing new and unfamiliar kinds of texts while interpreting thought-provoking images. In this chapter, you will learn a variety of critical reading strategies that will help you better understand words and images at a deeper level. You will learn strategies for analytical thinking, helping you look beyond the obvious meaning of texts to gain a critical understanding of what their authors are saying.

Looking Through and Looking At a Text

4.1 "look through" and "look at" texts.

When reading critically, you should think of yourself as interpreting the text in two different ways: *looking through* and *looking at*.[1]

Looking *through* a text.   Most of the time, you are *looking through* a text, reading the words and viewing the images to figure out *what* the author is saying. You are primarily paying attention to the content of each text, not its organization, style, or medium. Your goal is to understand the text's main points while gathering the information it provides.

FIGURE 4.1 Combining Critical Reading with Writing

As you improve your critical reading skills, you will also improve your ability to write effectively.

Looking *at* a text.   Other times, you are *looking at* a text, exploring *why* the author or authors made particular choices, including:

- *Genre:* choice of genre, including decisions about content, organization, style, design, and medium.

- *Persuasion strategies:* uses of reasoning, appeals to authority, and appeals to emotion.

- *Style and diction:* uses of specific words and phrasing, including uses of metaphors, irony, specialized terms, sayings, profanity, or slang.

Reading critically is a process of toggling back and forth between "looking through" and "looking at" to understand both *what* a text says and *why* it says it that way (Figure 4.2). This back-and-forth process will help you analyze the author's underlying motives and values. You can then better understand the cultural, ethical, and political influences that shaped the writing of the text.

[1]Richard A. Lanham, *Analyzing Prose* 2nd edition (New York: Continuum, 2003) 193–213.

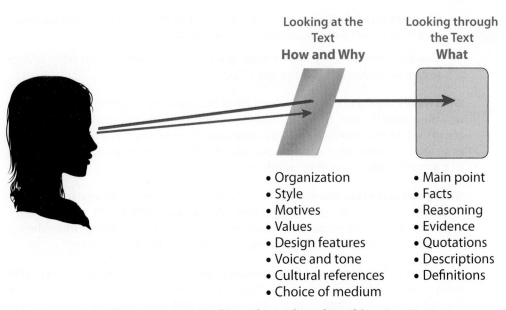

Looking at the Text
How and Why

- Organization
- Style
- Motives
- Values
- Design features
- Voice and tone
- Cultural references
- Choice of medium

Looking through the Text
What

- Main point
- Facts
- Reasoning
- Evidence
- Quotations
- Descriptions
- Definitions

FIGURE 4.2 Toggling Between *Looking Through* and *Looking At* a Text
Reading critically involves both looking through and looking at texts.

Reading Critically: Seven Strategies

The key to critical reading is to read *actively*. Imagine you and the author are having a conversation. Active reading means you should take in what the author is saying, but you also need to *respond* to the author's idea.

4.2 use seven strategies for reflecting on and responding to texts at a deeper level.

While you read, be constantly aware of how you are reacting to the author's ideas. Do you agree with these ideas? Do you find them surprising, new, or interesting? Are they mundane, outdated, or unrealistic? Are they making you angry, happy, skeptical, or persuaded? Does the author offer ideas, arguments, or evidence you can use in your own writing? What information in this text isn't useful to you?

Strategy 1: Preview the Text

When you start reading a text, give yourself a few moments to size it up. Ask yourself some basic questions:

What are the major features of this text?   Scan and skim through the text to gather a sense of the text's topic and main point. Pay special attention to the following features:

- **Title and subtitle**—make guesses about the text's purpose and main point based on the words in the title and subtitle.

- **Author**—on the Internet, look up the author or authors to better understand their expertise in the area as well as their values and potential biases.

- **Chapters and headings**—scan the text's chapter titles, headings, and subheadings to figure out its organization and major sections.

- **Visuals**—browse any graphs, charts, photographs, drawings, and other images to gain an overall sense of the text's topic.

What is the purpose of this text?   Find the place where the author or authors explain why they wrote the text. In a larger text like a book, the authors will often use the preface to explain their purpose and what motivated them to write. In a smaller text, such as an article or a report, the authors will usually tell you in the introduction or conclusion what they are trying to accomplish.

What genre is the text following?   Identify the genre of the text by analyzing its content, organization, style, and design. What do you expect from this genre? Is it the appropriate genre to achieve the authors' purpose? For this genre, what choices about content, organization, style, design, and medium would you expect?

What is my initial response?   Pay attention to your initial reactions to the text. What seems to be grabbing your attention? What seems new and interesting to you? What doesn't seem new or interesting? Based on your first impression, do you think you will agree or disagree with the authors? Do you think the material will be challenging or easy to understand?

Strategy 2: Play the Believing and Doubting Game

Peter Elbow, a scholar of rhetoric and writing, invented a close reading strategy called the "Believing and Doubting Game" that will help you analyze a text from different points of view.

> **The Believing Game**—Imagine you are someone who believes (1) *what* the author says is completely sound, interesting, and important and (2) *how* the author has expressed things is amazing or brilliant. You want to play the role of someone who is completely taken in by the argument in the text, whether you personally agree with it or not.

> **The Doubting Game**—Now pretend you are a harsh critic, someone who is deeply skeptical or even negative about the author's main points and methods for expressing them. Search out and highlight the argument's factual shortcomings and logical flaws. Look for ideas and assumptions that a skeptical reader would reject. Repeatedly ask, "So what?" or "Who cares?" or "Why would the author do *that*?" as you read and re-read.

Once you have studied the text from the perspectives of a "believer" and a "doubter," you can then create a *synthesis* of both perspectives that will help you develop your own personal response to the text (Figure 4.3). More than likely, you won't absolutely believe or absolutely reject the author's argument. Instead, your synthesis will be somewhere between these two sides.

Elbow's term, "game," is a good choice for this kind of critical reading. You are role-playing with the argument, first analyzing it in a sympathetic way and then

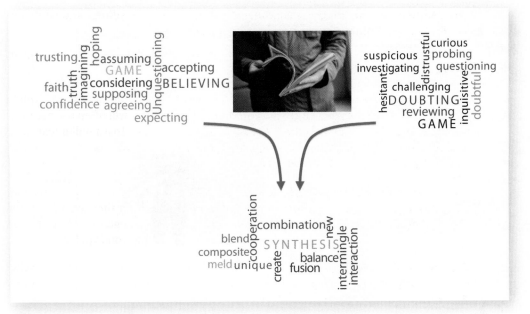

FIGURE 4.3 Playing the Believing and Doubting Game

Playing the Believing and Doubting Game allows you to see a text from completely opposite perspectives. Then, you can come up with a synthesis that combines the best aspects of each point of view.

scrutinizing it in a skeptical way. This two-sided approach will help you not only better understand the text but also figure out what you believe and *why* you believe it.

Strategy 3: Annotate the Text

As you are looking through and looking at a text, you should highlight important sentences and take notes on the items you find useful or interesting.

Highlight and annotate. While reading you should have a pencil or pen in your hand. If you are reading on screen, you should use the "review" or "comment" feature of your word processor or e-reader to highlight parts of the text and add comments. These highlights and notes will help you find and examine key passages later on.

Take notes. Write down longer notes about the text in your notebook or in a separate document on your computer. As you take notes, remember to *look through* and *look at* the text.

- Looking *through*: Describe *what* the text says, summarizing its main claims, facts, and ideas.

- Looking *at:* Describe *how* the author is using various strategies, such as style, organization, design, medium, and so forth to make the argument.

FIGURE 4.4 Using a Notetaking App

Evernote is one of the free notetaking apps that you might find useful.

You might find it helpful to use a notetaking app such as *Evernote, Google Keep, Memonic, OneNote,* or *Marky* (Figure 4.4). With these tools, your notes are stored "in the cloud," which means you can find your comments whenever you have online access. As more and more writing becomes electronic, notetaking with these kinds of online tools will become increasingly important.

Strategy 4: Analyze the Proofs in the Text

Almost all texts are argumentative in some way because most authors are directly or indirectly making claims they want you to believe. These claims are based on *proofs* that the author wants you to accept. Critical reading means challenging those claims and proofs to see if they make sense and are properly supported.

Arguments tend to use three kinds of proofs: appeals to reason, appeals to authority, and appeals to emotion. Rhetoricians often refer to these proofs by their ancient Greek terms: *logos* (reason), *ethos* (authority), and *pathos* (emotion).

- **Reasoning (*logos*)**—Analyze the author's use of logical statements and examples to support their arguments. Logical statements use patterns like: *if x then y; either x or y; x causes y; the benefits of x are worth the costs y;* and *x is better than y.* Meanwhile, reasoning through examples involves describing real or hypothetical situations by referring to personal experiences, historical anecdotes, demonstrations, and well-known stories.

- **Authority (*ethos*)**—Look at the ways the author draws ʋ
  authority or the authority of others. The author may appe
  tials, personal experiences, moral character, the expertise
  do what is best for the readers or others.

- **Emotion (*pathos*)**—Pay special attention to the author's ʒ
  to sway your opinion. He or she may promise emotional
  ple want, such as happiness, fun, trust, money, time, loˈ
  health, beauty, or convenience. Or the author may ˈ
  the readers uncomfortable, implying that they may beˈ
  cure, impoverished, stressed out, unliked, ignored,
  overworked.

Almost all texts use a combination of *logos, ethos,* and *pathos.* Advertising, oɪ ᴄ
relies heavily on *pathos*, but ads also use *logos* and *ethos* to persuade through reasoning and credibility. Scientific texts, meanwhile, are dominated by *logos*, but
occasionally scientists draw upon their reputation (*ethos*) and they will use emotion
(*pathos*) to add emphasis and color to their arguments (Figure 4.5).

You can turn to Chapter 22, "Using Argumentative Strategies," for a more detailed discussion of these three forms of proof.

FIGURE 4.5
**Using Emotion
in a Scientific
Argument**

*Scientists gener-
ally use reasoning
(logos) to support
their arguments, but
individuals like Bill
Nye, the Science Guy,
can often strengthen
their persuasive
impact with emo-
tion and appeals to
authority.*

tegy 5: Contextualize the Text

authors are influenced by the cultural, ethical, and political events that were happening around them when they were writing the text. To better understand these contextual influences, look back at what was happening while the text was being written:

Cultural context.   Do some research on the culture in which the author lived while writing the text. What do people from this culture value? What kinds of struggles did they face or are they facing now? How do people from this culture see the world similarly to or differently from the way you do? How is this culture different from your culture?

Ethical context.   Look for places in the text where the author is concerned about rights, legalities, fairness, and sustainability. Specifically, how is the author responding to abuses of rights or laws? Where does the author believe people are being treated unfairly or unequally? Where does he or she believe the environment is being handled wastefully or in an unsustainable way? How might the author's sense of ethics differ from your own?

Political context.   Consider the political tensions and conflicts that were happening when the author wrote the text. Was she or he trying to encourage political change or feeling threatened by it? In what ways were political shifts changing people's lives at the time? Was violence happening, or was it possible? Who were the political leaders of the time, and what were their desires and values?

Strategy 6: Analyze Your Own Assumptions and Beliefs

Reflecting on your own assumptions and beliefs is probably the toughest part of critical reading. No matter how unbiased or impartial you tried to be, you still relied on your own pre-existing assumptions and beliefs to decide whether or not you agreed with the text. Here are a few questions you can ask yourself:

- How did my first reaction influence my overall interpretation of the text?
- How did my personal beliefs influence how I interpreted and reacted to the author's claims and proofs?
- How did my personal values cause me to react favorably to some parts of the text and unfavorably to other parts?
- Why exactly was I pleased with or irritated by some parts of this text?
- Have my views changed now that I have finished reading and analyzing the text?

If an author's text challenges your assumptions and beliefs, that's a good thing. As an author yourself, you too will be trying to challenge, influence, inform, and entertain your readers. Treat other authors and their ideas with the same respect and open-mindedness that you would like from your own readers.

Even if you leave the critical reading process without substantially changing your views, you will come away from the experience stronger and better able to understand and explain what you believe and why.

Strategy 7: Respond to the Text

Now it's time to take stock and respond to the text. Ask yourself these questions, which mirror the ones you asked during the pre-reading phase.

Was your initial response to the text accurate?   In what ways did the text meet your original expectations? Where did you find yourself agreeing or disagreeing? In what ways did the author grab your attention? Which parts of the text were confusing, requiring a second look? Were you pleased with the text, or were you disappointed?

How does this text meet your own purposes?   In what ways did the author's purpose line up with the project you are working on? How can you use this material to do your own research and write your own paper? How did the author's ideas contrast or conflict with what you need to achieve?

How well did the text follow the genre?   After reading the text, do you feel that the authors met the expectations of the genre? Where did the text stray from the genre or stretch it in new ways? Where did the text disrupt your expectations for this genre?

How should you re-read the text?   What parts of the text need to be read a bit more closely? In these places, re-read the content carefully, paying attention to *what it says* and looking for ideas such as a key concept or some evidence that needs clarification.

Using Critical Reading to Strengthen Your Writing

Critical reading will be important throughout your time at college and your career. It is most important, though, when you are developing your own projects. Critical reading will help you write smarter, whether you are writing for a college course, your job, or just for fun. Here are some strategies for converting your critical reading into informed and persuasive writing.

4.3 use critical reading to strengthen your writing.

Responding *to* a Text: Evaluating What Others Have Written

When responding to a text, you should do more than conclude whether you "agree" or "disagree." All sides will have some merit—otherwise, the topic would not really be worth discussing. So, you need to explain your response and where your views align with or diverge from the author's views.

Ask yourself these questions to help develop a complete, accurate, and fair response.

Why should people care about what the author has written?   Explain why you think people should care about the issue and why.

_____ is an important issue because _____.

While _____ might not seem important on first glance, it has several important consequences, such as _____, _____, and _____.

Example Response: While the legal drinking age of 21 may seem like old news and a sensible federal law that saves lives, the issue demands further attention and public debate because, contrary to "common sense," many recent public health studies show that the law is not enforceable and only produces a culture of secret risky behavior, including binge drinking.

Where and why do you find the author's views compelling—or not?   Describe exactly where and why you agree or disagree with an author's conclusions or viewpoints.

At the heart of this debate is a disagreement about the nature of _____, whether it was _____ or _____.

While _____ contends that there are two and only two possibilities, I believe we should consider other possibilities, such as _____ or _____.

Admittedly, my negative reaction to _____'s assertion that _____ was influenced by my own beliefs that _____ should be _____

Example Response: While historian Jane Metzger mentions that some studies show that setting the legal drinking age at 21 reduces alcohol consumption and traffic fatalities, Jonah Wales, a sociologist, cites several studies that show just the opposite. I disagree with Metzger, who argues the law should remain unchanged, and also with Wales, who argues it should simply be reduced to 18 nationally. Instead of these either-or solutions, I believe colleges and communities can establish safe but open environments where underage drinkers are encouraged to drink responsibly.

Responding *with* a Text's Positions, Terms, and Ideas: Using What Others Have Written

You can now respond to the text by incorporating what the author has said into your writing. Joseph Harris offers a useful system of four "moves" for using what others have said to advance your own ideas and arguments.[2]

---

[2]Joseph Harris. *Rewriting: How to Do Things with Texts* (Logan: Utah State University Press, 2006).

Illustrating.   Use facts, images, examples, descriptions, or stories provided by an author to illustrate and explain your own views.

> As _____ summarizes the data on _____, there are three major undisputed facts: first, _____; second, _____; and third, _____.

> This problem is illustrated well by the example offered by _____, who explains that _____.

> **Example Illustration:** Sarah Jones, the Dean of Students, explained the negative consequences of the current law with the analogy of "forbidden fruit." "When you label alcohol as a forbidden fruit, it only becomes more attractive." It's human nature, she said, to desire what you can't have.

Authorizing.   Use the authority, expertise, or experience of the author to strengthen your own position or to back up a point you want to make without going into a lengthy explanation.

> As explained by _____, a recognized authority on the subject of _____, the most important features of a _____ are _____ and _____.

> Although _____ makes a valid point in arguing that _____, a more balanced and workable solution is offered by _____, who suggests we _____.

> **Example of Authorizing:** A new study, appearing in *The Journal on Studies for Alcohol and Drugs*, analyzed dozens of peer-reviewed scientific articles published since 2006 and concluded that the debate should cease because the "evidence is clear" that "lowering the legal drinking age would lead to a substantial increase in injuries, deaths, and other negative health-related consequences" (113).[3]

Borrowing.   Borrow a term, definition, or idea developed by the author for thinking about the issue you're writing about.

> _____ defines _____ as "_____."

> _____'s concept of "_____" is helpful for thinking through the complexities of this issue.

> **Example of Borrowing:** According to the National Institute on Alcohol Abuse and Alcoholism, alcohol use can be divided into three "drinking levels": "moderate or 'low-risk' drinking," "heavy or 'at-risk' drinking," and "binge drinking."

---

[3]William DeJong and Jason Blanchette, "Case Closed: Research Evidence on the Positive Public Health Impact of the Age 21 Minimum Legal Drinking Age in the United States," *Journal of Studies on Alcohol and Drugs* 17 (2014), 113.

Extending.   Extend the author's ideas in a new direction or apply them to topics and situations that the author did not consider.

> The successful model described by _____ could be implemented here with some modification, including _____, _____, and _____.

> While I agree generally with _____'s recommendations on this issue, I suggest they do not go far enough. For example, _____.

Example of Extending: Rather than employing the futile and unenforceable zero-tolerance policy currently in effect here at Farris College, I believe we would far more effectively discourage risky drinking behaviors if we employed the prevention, intervention, and treatment strategies described by the NIAAA.

Illustrating, authorizing, borrowing, extending. These four moves will help you become part of the larger conversation about your topic. By incorporating the ideas of others into your own work, you can support your own ideas while helping your readers understand where your ideas agree or contrast with the ideas of others.

Let's get started with critical reading and responding. Use these strategies to read texts closely.

TOGGLE Between *Looking Through* and *Looking at* the Text

Throughout the reading and writing process, combine *looking through* to understand *what* a text says with *looking at* the text to identify *how* it says it and *why*.

PREVIEW the Text to Size Up its Major Features

Rather than reading from the first word to the last, take a few minutes to scan and skim the text. Note its overall content, organization, genre, and your initial reactions.

VIEW the Text From Different Perspectives

Play the Believing and Doubting Game to interpret the text from different perspectives.

READ CLOSELY by Highlighting and Taking Notes

Focus your attention by reacting as you read, with a pencil in hand or an electronic notetaking tool.

ANALYZE the Proofs in the Text

Look closely at the authors' use of reasoning, authority, and emotion to support the text's argument.

CONTEXTUALIZE the Text Culturally, Ethically, and Politically

Pay attention to how cultural, ethical, and political issues might have influenced the authors or how people responded to the text.

RESPOND Critically with Reflection and Analysis

Challenge your own assumptions to gain a deeper understanding of the author's and your beliefs.

USE the Results of Your Critical Reading to Write Your Own Text

Now it's your turn. Put the authors' ideas, evidence, and strategies to use. Respond by using the text's ideas and evidence to advance your own ideas.

1. Think of a time when you needed to read and understand a difficult text. It may have been something you read for a high school or college class. Maybe it was something you read on the job or on your own. Discuss with your group the features that made the text challenging for you.

2. Ask each member of your group to bring in an article from the Internet that is interesting, puzzling, or infuriating. Ask all group members to briefly describe the articles they brought and explain why they thought their chosen texts were special in some way. Then, as a group, choose one article to analyze closely with the strategies described in this chapter. How do these critical reading strategies help you see things in the article that you had not seen before?

3. You have probably heard the term "critical thinking" throughout your high school and college career. Everybody agrees that being "critical" is supposed to be good for you, but it's hard to define exactly what it is. With your group, discuss the term "critical" and explain how it was defined for you in the past. As a group, using the ideas in this chapter, define "critical thinking" in your own words. Share your definition with the whole class.

1. Consider your major or a major that interests you. Using the Internet, identify the kinds of texts that a student pursuing this major would need to read critically and the kinds of texts people in this area need to write. Make a list of five kinds of texts these majors read and five kinds of texts they write. Then, use the Internet to explore the kinds of writing that people in this major might need to do in a future career. Write a brief paper in which you explain the kinds of writing people with this major do in their advanced courses and careers.

2. Think about a time when you read or viewed something that significantly changed your life or the way you see the world. Write a brief narrative about this experience. Describe the text and explain what you believed before and after reading. Explain also why you were "open" to changing your viewpoint. Try to go beyond explanations like "It was true" or "It made sense." Explain what the text *did* to you and why you were open to accepting this new viewpoint.

3. Find an article you completely disagree with on the Internet, in your local or campus newspaper, or in a magazine. Play the "Believing and Doubting Game" with this article. The hard part will be playing the "believing" part, but do your best to play the role of a complete true believer. Try to support the position you disagree with in a way that would make a supporter of that position say, "That's a fair way to describe what I believe and why I believe it." Then play the role of the complete skeptic. Finally, write a brief synthesis that explains what people on both sides believe and why they believe it.

1. **Create a "double-entry" notebook that *looks through* and *looks at* a text.** First, choose a text that you want to understand better. It could be an article, a textbook for one of your college courses, an argument on television, or just about any document. After previewing the text, closely read the text and take notes on two sides of the page or screen.

    a. **Left side: *Looking Through*.** Make longer notes that describe what the author is *saying*. Don't judge; focus just on the content.

    b. **Right side: *Looking At*.** Describe what the text is doing, focusing on genre, argumentative strategies, style, and rhetorical patterns. Describe *how* the author has chosen to express the content of the text. You should also speculate about *why* the author makes those particular choices and what those strategies *do to the reader*. You can ask questions, speculate, or explain why something confuses or puzzles you.

    When you are finished, write a brief reflection to your professor describing what you learned by *looking through* and *looking at* the text.

2. ***Look through* and *look at* a visual text.** Choose an advertisement that is visually rich and that you find interesting. First, *look through* the advertisement and describe it in vivid detail. If there's a story inside the ad, what is it (conflict → resolution → what was learned)? Now *look at* the ad and describe how it works and the strategies it uses to achieve its purpose. How does the ad use design, style, and rhetorical patterns to achieve its purpose? Does this ad belong to a specific genre of advertising? If so, what other ads fall into this genre?

Go to **My WritingLab** to complete this chapter's exercises and test your understanding of its objectives.

Write This

5

Memoirs

In this chapter, you will learn how to—

5.1 generate content for your memoir.

5.2 use the memoir genre to organize a story.

5.3 develop an engaging voice to tell your story.

5.4 design and add visuals to enhance the narrative.

The words *memoir* and *memory* come from the same root word. Memoirs, however, do more than allow writers to share their memories. Good memoirs explore and reflect on a central theme or question even though they rarely conclude with explicit answers to those questions. Instead, they invite readers to explore and reflect with the narrator to try to unravel the deeper significance of the recounted events.

People write memoirs when they have true personal stories that they hope will inspire others to reflect on intriguing questions or social issues. Readers expect memoirs to help them encounter perspectives and insights that are fresh and meaningful.

Today, memoirs are more popular than ever. They are common on best-seller lists of books with some recent memoirs selling millions of copies, such as Jeanette Walls' *The Glass Castle* about growing up in a dysfunctional family and Frank McCourt's *Angela's Ashes* about his childhood in Ireland. Meanwhile, blogs and social networking sites give ordinary people opportunities to post reflections on their lives.

In college, professors will sometimes ask you to write about your life to explore your upbringing and discern how you came to hold certain beliefs. In these assignments, the goal is not just to recount events but to unravel their significance and arrive at insights that help you explore and engage more deeply with the issues discussed in the class.

Memoirs

This diagram shows a basic organization for a memoir, but other arrangements of these sections will work, too. You should alter this organization to fit the features of your topic, angle, purpose, readers, and context.

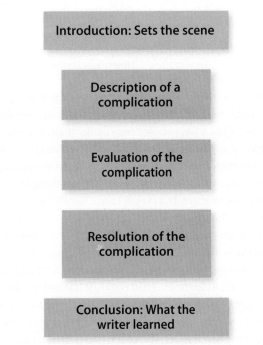

Introduction: Sets the scene

Description of a complication

Evaluation of the complication

Resolution of the complication

Conclusion: What the writer learned

Using rich detail, memoirs tell a personal story in which an event or series of events leads the writer to new insights about life. They tend to have these main features:

- **An engaging title** that hints at the memoir's overall meaning or "theme."
- **An introduction with a "lead"** that captures the reader's interest or sets a scene.
- **A complication** that must be resolved in some way—a tension or conflict between people's values and beliefs, or a personal inner conflict the author faces.
- **A plot** that draws the reader forward as the memoir moves through a series of scenes or stages.
- **Intimacy between the narrator and the reader,** allowing the writer to speak with readers in a personal one-on-one way.
- **Rich and vivid details** that give the story greater imagery, texture, and impact.
- **A central theme or question** that is rarely announced or answered explicitly but that the narrator explores and reflects on with the reader.
- **A new understanding or revelation** that presents a moment of growth, transformation, or clarity in the writer.

ONE STUDENT'S WORK
Memoirs

Visit **MyWritingLab** to explore an interactive version of this essay.

Engaging title that forecasts the subject of swimming and also hints at the memoir's theme.

Introduction starts fast with a lead that sets the scene, and it ends in a surprising way.

The complication is introduced, an inner struggle the narrator faces.

Background moves the plot forward.

Rich and vivid details give the story texture and intensify the complication.

Diving In

Helen Sanderson

Take your mark. Anticipation builds as I crouch and grip the edge of the rough plastic, ready to strike at any second. I finally hear the sound of the electronic starter just a few nanoseconds earlier than my competition. I hit a block of ice before I dive just below the surface. A few strong kicks and I'm taking my first stroke, and then another as fast as I can. Breathe as little as possible. By the time I'm on the second lap, I'm going nowhere. I am dying to take in gulps of air and rest for only a moment, but I know I can't. Surely this is almost over. My lungs and muscles burn for oxygen as I dig in for the final stretch; the end of the pool could not come soon enough. I look up to find that I have shaved a second off of my time and have achieved last place in my heat, as usual.

I have never been an athlete. My motions are awkward, uncoordinated, and uncertain. At fourteen, I had only just learned to swim the butterfly with a dozen eight year olds as my classmates. Deciding to try out for my high school swim team was the biggest challenge I had ever undertaken. I will never forget the day of my first tryouts. The coach had posted tryout times that were way beyond my reach: thirty-five seconds for fifty yards. I had never even come within twenty seconds of that time. All that time I had spent the summer before my freshman year swimming lap after lap, practicing for this day, seemed like wasted effort. I knew I could swim those fifty yards ahead of me, but only if I was given a full minute, not just thirty-five seconds. Holding back tears, I watched my classmates, fearless, dive into the water. Should I dive in behind them knowing I will fail?

It's not as though I've never failed before: a Latin test, a piano audition, or even as a friend. But I had personal experience behind me to reassure myself that I would get better. I started swimming with a stone cold slate and only a few months of summer training with a private instructor. No summer leagues or competitive teams. I just swam back and forth. Up to this point, I had never physically pushed myself so hard. All I wanted was to make the team.

Practices were much worse. Though no one was cut, I knew I was the slowest. My teammates passed me, and I always finished each set last. I can hear the coach yelling out the next set of drills: "Ten 100's! Ready … go!" Meanwhile I am still struggling to get to the end of the previous set, deprived of energy, oxygen, and morale. I cried countless times out of frustration and self-pity, wanting to quit. I had made the team, but I was failing my teammates. I cramped my team's efforts and embarrassed myself, but I swam every lap. I may have been the slowest, but I was going to work the hardest.

I improved tremendously after just a few weeks of rigorous practice. Although I was still the slowest, I was slower by a smaller margin. Fifty yards in thirty-nine seconds. No one else could say they had improved by seventeen seconds, a tremendous accomplishment. I persevered through every meet, practice, lap, and stroke. I had attained my goal: I was a swimmer.

> Narrator's personal tone is maintained throughout.

Swimming is the hardest challenge I have ever undertaken. I have always been very driven academically and socially, but I was very afraid to push myself to be an athlete because balance, endurance, and coordination were so unfamiliar to me. However, I did not allow myself to accept failure. Just dive in and keep swimming. There is only me and the pool, a full immersion of body and mind.

Take your mark. My muscles and mind lock into place, attentive and poised. I hear the starter sound and take a leap, already stretching toward the end of the pool. My strokes are fluid, deliberate, and quick. Breathe as little as possible. I do a flip turn, tight and well executed, as I push myself harder and faster. I don't think about the air I need to fill my lungs or the other girls in my race; I only concentrate on what I feel. This time as I reach the end of the pool, I look up to find that I have reached a new personal record of thirty-six seconds and have achieved next-to-last place in my heat. I have won.

> Conclusion resolves the conflict as narrator describes a newly gained clarity.

Inventing Your Memoir's Content

The aim of your memoir is to explore the meaning of an event or series of events from your past. When you start out, don't be too concerned about the point of your memoir. Instead, choose an interesting incident from your life that you want to explore in greater depth. You want to uncover the meaning of this event for your readers *and* yourself.

5.1 generate content for your memoir.

Inquiring: Finding an Interesting Topic

With your whole life as potential subject matter, deciding what to write about and narrowing your topic can be a challenge. Think about the times when you did something challenging, scary, or fun. Think about the times when you felt pain or joy.

Think about the times when someone or something important came into your life, helping you make a discovery about yourself.

Make a brainstorming list of as many of these events as you can remember (Figure 5.1). Don't think too much about what you are writing down. These events don't need to be earth shattering. Just list the stories you like to tell others about yourself.

Inquiring: Finding Out What You Already Know

Memoirs are about memories—of course—but they include your reflections on those memories. You need to do some personal inquiry to pull up those memories and then reflect on them to figure out what they meant to you at the time and what they mean to you now. Pick an event from your brainstorming list and use some of the following techniques to reflect on it.

Possible Topics for a Memoir

Breaking my leg skiing
Winning the clothing design competition
Failing that geometry class
The trip to Mexico
Death of Fred Sanders
Leaving home to go to college
Meeting Senator Wilkins
Discovering Uncle Jim is gay
When Bridgeport's downtown flooded
When the car broke down in Oklahoma
Going to the state volleyball finals
Not making the cheerleading team

FIGURE 5.1 Brainstorming to Find Topics

Brainstorming is a good way to list possible topics for your memoir. Try to think of moments when something important happened that changed your life or led to a new insight.

Make a Map of the Scene. In your mind's eye, imagine the place where the event happened. Then draw a map of that place (Figure 5.2). Add as many details as you can remember—names, buildings, people, events, landmarks. You can use this map to help you tell your story.

Record Your Story as a Podcast or Video. Tell your story into your computer's audio recorder or into a camcorder. Afterwards, you can transcribe it to the page or screen. Sometimes it's easier to tell the story orally and then turn it into written text.

Storyboard the Event. In comic strip form, draw out the major scenes in the event. It's fine to use stick figures, because these drawings are only for you. They will help you recall the details and sort out the story you are trying to tell.

Do Some Role Playing. Use your imagination to put yourself into the life of a family member or someone close to you. Try to work through events as that person might have experienced them, even ones that you were part of. Then compare and contrast that person's experiences with your own, paying special attention to any tensions or conflicts.

Researching: Finding Out What Others Know

Research can help you better understand the event or times you are writing about. For instance, a writer describing her father's return from a tour in the Iraq War

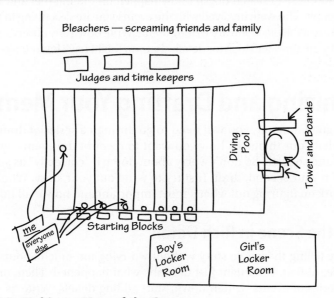

FIGURE 5.2 Making a Map of the Scene

Sometimes drawing a map of the scene where an event happened can help you reconstruct it and remember important details. Here is a map of the pool described in Helen Sanderson's memoir.

(2003–2011) might want to find out more about the history of this war. She could also find out about soldiers' experiences by reading personal stories at *The Library of Congress Veterans History Project* (loc.gov/vets). When researching your topic, you should try to find information from the following three types of sources:

Online Sources. Use Internet search engines to find information that might help you understand the people or situations in your memoir. Psychology Web sites, for example, might help you explain your own actions or the behavior of others that you witnessed. Meanwhile, historical Web sites might provide background information for an event. This knowledge would help you better recount an experience from a time when you were very young and had little or no awareness of what was happening in the world.

Print Sources. At your campus or public library, look for newspapers or magazines that might have reported something about the event you are describing. Or find historical information in magazines or a history textbook. These resources can help you explain the conditions that shaped how people behaved.

Empirical Sources. Research doesn't only happen on the Internet and in the library. Interview people who were involved with the events you are describing in your memoir. If possible, revisit the place you are writing about. Write down any observations, describe things as they are now, and look for details that you might have forgotten or missed.

Organizing and Drafting Your Memoir

5.2 use the memoir genre to organize a story.

To write a good memoir, you will need to go through a series of drafts in order to discover what your theme is, how you want to recount the events, what tone will work best, and so forth. So don't worry about doing it "correctly" as you write your first, or even your second, draft. Just try to write out your story. When you revise, you can work on figuring out what's most important and how it all holds together.

Setting the Scene in Rich Detail

Start out by telling the whole story without worrying too much about the structure you will use. At first, you might just describe what happened. Then, once you have the basic series of events written down, start adding details. Write as much as you can. Be sure to give rich descriptions of people, places, and things. Use dialogue to bring your readers into the story.

Main Point or Thesis

Memoirs explore and reflect on a central theme or question, but they rarely provide precise answers or explicit thesis statements early in the text. When writing a memoir, put your point in the conclusion, using an implied thesis. In other words, don't state your main point or thesis in your introduction unless you have a good reason for doing so.

Describing the Complication

The *complication* in your memoir is the problem or challenge that you or others needed to resolve. So pay special attention to how this complication came about and why you and others first reacted to it as you did.

Evaluating and Resolving the Complication

After describing the characters' initial reaction, you should show how you and others evaluated and resolved the complication. The complication isn't necessarily a problem that needs to be fixed. Instead, you should show how people tried to make sense of the complication, reacted to the change, and moved forward.

Concluding with a Point—an Implied Thesis

Your conclusion describes, directly or indirectly, not only what you learned but also what your reader should have learned from your experiences. Memoirs often have an "implied thesis," which means you're allowing readers to figure out the main point of the story for themselves. In some cases, though, it's fine to just tell your readers what you learned from the experience.

> Tearing an ACL my senior year was a major disappointment and the end of my dream of playing soccer in college. I learned, though, that when one dream ends, other dreams take its place.

Avoid concluding with a "the moral of the story is . . . " or a "they lived happily ever after" ending. Instead, you should strive for something that suggests the events or people reached some kind of closure. Achieving closure, however, doesn't mean stating a high-minded platitude or revealing a fairy tale ending. Instead, give your readers the sense that you and your characters are looking ahead to the future.

Whether you choose to state your main point directly or not, your readers should come away from your memoir with a clear sense of what the story meant to you.

Choosing an Appropriate Style

Your memoir's style and tone depend on how you want to portray yourself as the narrator of the story. Choose a style that works for you, your story, and your readers. If you want your narrator (you) to have a casual attitude, that's the style and tone you want to strive for. If the narrator's relationship to the story is more formal, then the style will be more formal.

5.3 develop an engaging voice to tell your story.

Evoking an Appropriate Tone or Voice

Tone or voice refers to the attitude, or stance, that you are taking toward your subject matter and your readers. That is, a certain "tone of voice" arises from the words on a page. Your tone or voice isn't something innate to you as a writer. Instead, it should fit your topic and readers.

Concept mapping is a useful tool for helping you set a specific tone and find your voice.

1. Think of a key word that describes the tone you want to set in your memoir.

2. Put that word in the middle of your screen or a piece of paper and circle it (Figure 5.3).

3. Around that key word, write down any words or phrases that you tend to associate with this tone word.

4. As you put words on the screen or paper, try to come up with more words that are associated with these new words. *Hint:* you can use your word processor's thesaurus to help you generate more words.

Eventually, you will fill the screen or sheet. Then, in the draft of your memoir, look for places where you can strategically use these words. If you use them consistently

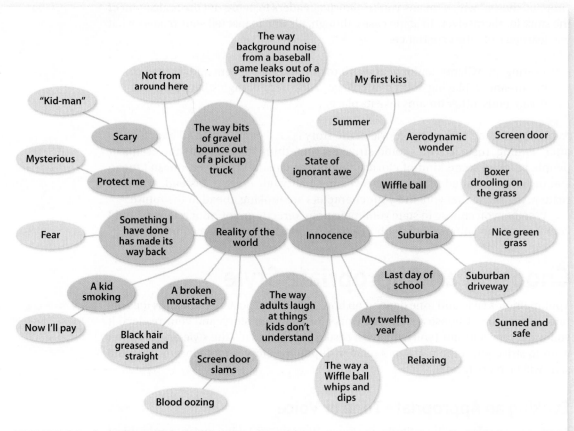

FIGURE 5.3 Creating a Tone with a Concept Map

A concept map is a good tool for helping you set a tone in your memoir. Simply choose the words or phrases that best describe the tone you are looking for and create a concept map around them. Here, a concept map has the ideas of "innocence" and "reality of the world" in the center, with other word and phrase clusters surrounding them.

throughout the memoir, your readers will sense the tone, or attitude you are trying to convey. This tone will help you develop your central "theme," the idea or question that the entire memoir explores.

You should use these words and phrases occasionally to achieve the effect you want. If you overuse these words, your readers will sense that you are overdoing it.

Using Dialogue

Allow the characters in your memoir to reveal key details about themselves through dialogue rather than your narration. Use dialogue strategically to reveal themes and ideas that are *key* to understanding your memoir. Here are some guidelines for using dialogue effectively:

Use Dialogue to Move the Story Forward. Dialogues between characters should be reserved for key moments that move the story forward in an important way.

Write the Way Your Characters Speak. People rarely speak in proper English. Take advantage of opportunities to show how people really talk.

Trim the Extra Words. In real dialogue, people often say more than they need to say. To avoid drawing out a conversation too much, craft your dialogue to be as crisp and tight as possible.

Identify Who is Talking. The readers should know who is talking, so make sure you use dialogue tags (e.g., *he said, she said, he growled, she yelled*). Not every statement needs a dialogue tag. If you leave off the tag, make sure it's obvious who is speaking.

Create Unique Voices for Characters. Each of your characters should sound different. You can vary their tone, cadence, dialect, or style to give them each a unique voice.

What if you cannot remember what people actually said? As long as you remain true to what you remember, you can invent some of the details of the dialogue.

Designing Your Memoir

Memoirs, like almost all genres today, can use visual design to reinforce the written text. You can augment and deepen your words with images or sound.

5.4 design and add visuals to enhance the narrative.

Choose the Medium. Readers might be more moved by an audio file of you narrating and enacting your memoir than by a written document. Or, perhaps a video or a multimedia document would better allow you to convey your ideas.

Add Visuals, Especially Photos. Use one or more photos to emphasize a key point, set a tone, or add a new dimension. Photos or drawings of specific places will help your readers visualize the places where the events in the memoir took place.

Find a Place to Publish. You might want to go a step further to get your story out there. Web sites, like *Teen Ink,* offer places where you can share your memories. Otherwise, you might consider putting your memoirs on a blog or on your *Facebook* page. Remember, though, to not reveal private information that might embarrass you or put you or others at any kind of risk. Save your most personal information and photographs for yourself.

The Literacy
Narrative

The literacy narrative and digital literacy narrative are memoirs that describe how the author learned to read and write or that focus on some formative experience that involved writing and speaking. Literacy narratives usually have all the elements of other memoirs. They don't just recount a series of events, but carefully work those events into a plot with a complication. Quite often, the author describes overcoming some obstacle, perhaps the quest for literacy itself or the need to overcome some barrier to learning. Digital literacy narratives are especially popular because they show how authors learned to use new technologies that helped them solve problems in their lives.

Literacy narratives are distinguished from other memoirs by a single feature: they focus on the author's experiences with reading and writing. Keep in mind that "literacy" encompasses more than learning to read and form letters on the traditional printed page. New writing situations are emerging due to new contexts, readers, purposes, and technologies. Learning to negotiate among these readers, situations, and technologies is the real challenge of becoming literate in today's world. The definition of literacy is constantly changing. New situations, technologies, and other changes require each of us to continually acquire new literacy skills. All of these challenges are fair game for a literacy narrative.

Literacy narratives should have all the features described in this chapter's At-a-Glance on page 49. Be sure to pay attention to the conflict or tension: What challenge did you face and how did you resolve it—or fail to resolve it? Also, how did the experience change you? What new understanding (positive or negative) did you come away with? And finally, think about the larger theme: What significance does your story have, and what does it tell readers about literacy or what questions does it encourage your readers to reflect on?

WRITE your own literacy narrative or digital literacy narrative. Remember
that "literacy" includes a broad range of activities, skills, knowledge, and technologies. Choose a significant incident or set of related incidents in your life that involved coming to terms with literacy. Write your literacy narrative or digital literacy narrative as a memoir, paying attention to the memoir's features. Possible subjects include:

- encountering a new kind of literacy, and the people involved
- working with or helping others with literacy issues
- encountering a new communication technology
- a situation where your literacy skills were tested
- a particular book, work of literature, or other communication that changed your outlook

Visit **MyWritingLab** to complete this exercise.

From *Narrative of the Life of Frederick Douglass*

Frederick Douglass

In the following excerpt from one of the best-known literacy narratives ever written, Douglass describes his determination as a young slave in America to become literate, even though the effort put him in grave personal danger.

I lived in Master Hugh's family about seven years. During this time, I succeeded in learning to read and write. In accomplishing this, I was compelled to resort to various stratagems. I had no regular teacher. My mistress, who had kindly commenced to instruct me, had, in compliance with the advice and direction of her husband, not only ceased to instruct, but had set her face against my being instructed by any one else. . . . The plan which I adopted, and the one by which I was most successful, was that of making friends of all the little white boys whom I met in the street. As many of these as I could, I converted into teachers. With their kindly aid, obtained at different times and in different places, I finally succeeded in learning to read. When I was sent on errands, I always took my book with me, and by going one part of my errand quickly, I found time to get a lesson before my return. I used also to carry bread with me, enough of which was always in the house, and to which I was always welcome; for I was much better off in this regard than many of the poor white children in our neighborhood. This bread I used to bestow upon the hungry little urchins, who, in return, would give me that more valuable bread of knowledge. I am strongly tempted to give the names of two or three of those little boys, as a testimonial of the gratitude and affection I bear them; but prudence forbids;—not that it would injure me, but it might embarrass them; for it is almost an unpardonable offence to teach slaves to read in this Christian country. It is enough to say of the dear little fellows, that they lived on Philpot Street, very near Durgin and Bailey's ship-yard. I used to talk this matter of slavery over with them. I would sometimes say to them, I wished I could be as free as they would be when they got to be men. "You will be free as soon as you are twenty-one, *but I am a slave for life!* Have not I as good a right to be free as you have?" These words used to trouble them; they would express for me the liveliest sympathy, and console me with the hope that something would occur by which I might be free.

[Margin annotations:]

Douglass introduces the complication.

The scene is set, while background information is provided up front.

Vivid descriptions of people and places.

Douglass shows how he resolved the conflict.

The conclusion reveals the larger point of the narrative: the injustice of slavery.

Here's one basic approach for creating an engaging memoir that makes a point.

CHOOSE the Event or Series of Events You Want to Write About

Use the brainstorming exercises to come up with a list of events and choose the one that could become an effective memoir.

QUESTION Your Memory About the Event(s)

Figure out what you know and what you can imagine about the event. What can you find out about the place, the objects in that place, and the people and what they did?

DO Some Research

If you want to find out more about the time, the place, or a person in your memoir, do some background research to find out what things were really like.

DRAFT the Story

Write the story, including all the events that relate to it. Describe people, their actions, and places with rich and vivid detail.

FIND the Theme

Reflect on what you've written and decide what "theme" you want this story to evoke for your readers. "Pets and people" is a topic, not a theme; "To what degree can pets replace people in our lives?" is a theme.

STATE the Message Directly or Indirectly

Whether you choose to make the main point directly or indirectly, your final paragraphs should provide a sense of closure that points readers to your overall message.

DEVELOP an Appropriate Tone or Voice

Develop your narrator's voice and use dialogue to add different voices to your story.

EDIT the Story to Its Essentials

When you ask yourself, *What is essential to the theme of my memoir?* you'll probably end up cutting a lot out of your original draft. Good memoirs are to the point; they should include only what is essential.

My Ex Went to Prison for Sex Crimes

JEAN ELLEN WHATLEY

In this memoir, Jean Whatley describes her reactions to discovering that her husband had become a pedophile. Memoirs like this one allow writers to better understand something that was once incomprehensible. Pay attention to the way she contrasts her original understanding of her ex-husband with the criminal that he had become.

People assume the wife knows. Not really. I found out about my former husband's descent into pedophilia at the same time the rest of the world did—on the 10 o'clock news.

My mind could not comprehend what my eyes were seeing. I studied his mug shot on TV. Here was the face of the man I had loved, the cleft in his chin, his square jaw, the soft, smooth skin just below his eyes, which I'd kissed a thousand times. Who was this broken man with the downcast eyes? Did he look away when the shutter closed because he was thinking of his children? What happened to the proud young father who cradled his newborns like fragile glass, the guy with a contagious laugh and shiny blue eyes, who owned any room he walked into? A hometown celebrity, a respected journalist, with a good wife and four great kids — now, reduced to this. Who *was* this man?

The kids in bed, I turned down the volume on the TV in a futile attempt to shield them for just one more day. My colleagues in the press, with whom I'd jockeyed for position at many a crime scene, were now covering a crime that would deal my kids a blow unimaginable. *"The accused is charged with three counts of statutory sodomy stemming from a series of sexual encounters with a teenage boy at a high school field house."* For years I'd been blase about broadcasting the worst day of someone else's life. In one minute, I knew what that felt like.

What would I say to my children? How could I prepare them? I had one son in college, a 17-year-old, a 14-year-old and my youngest, barely 13. How does a mother explain sodomy to a seventh grader? How does a mother suck back into the cylinder the toxic cloud that has just exploded all over her family? *How could he?*

Disbelief turned to maternal rage, like jet 5 fuel in my blood. I would *not* let him ruin my children's future. I would *not* let his indefensible addiction stain their beautiful lives. And in this flashpoint, I seized the strength of a righteous fury long trapped.

I had been one of those kids once, a victim kid. A little girl caught in a hopeless game of duck and cover. I remained silent for decades, until I simply couldn't hold down the bile of violation and secrecy any longer. I was in my 40s when I finally told my mother that my stepdad had molested me. By then he was dead. I'd even delivered the eulogy at his funeral, skipping over his ignoble deeds. Little did I know that the man I was married to—the man in the first pew, dabbing his eyes—would end up in prison years later for committing some crimes of his own.

I had no clue when I married him that the very thing I was running away from, I was actually running to. This happens sometimes to people who were sexually abused; we tend to behave like refugees. We don't assert our rights, because we're not sure we have any.

We lack confidence in scrutinizing others, because we feel like damaged goods ourselves.

But in time, I stood up for myself, challenging the endless hours he spent on the Internet, his increasing disengagement from our family. Backed into a corner, he told me he was gay. I told him to get out. But they don't lock people up for being gay anymore. No longer under the wary eye of a wife, or the threat of being discovered, he took greater risks. He was found out by a mother who made a painful discovery about what was keeping her son so busy on the computer.

After a 14-month IV drip of news coverage, my former husband was sentenced to seven years in prison for having sex with that teenage boy. I spent those seven years trying to convince my children that the sins of their father were not carried on their backs, seven years of trying to help them deflect the shame by association that I had endured firsthand. Seven years; I was like a widow with no death benefits, no child support, no moral support, no "every-other-weekend" relief, no one to call in the middle of the night to meet me at the hospital with a sick kid, nobody else to ante up for college or cars, braces or bail money. Nothing. We inherited nothing, except enough pain and financial hardship to throw us all into a bottomless well with no rope, just the bucket tossed in behind us, smackin' us on the head. But guess what?

We climbed out. We climbed out of that dark, slimy drowning hole by our bloody fingernails, each one, pushing up the next, back into the sunlight, where we sat on the side of the well, flicking off the mud. We made it. Three of my four kids are now out of college, the fourth will graduate next year. They're amazing: loving, resilient, remarkably well adjusted, and a funnier lot, I have never seen.

I just didn't realize how tired I was. It's hard to process stuff while you're holding up a car. When my brother died not long ago—the second of my brothers to die inside a few short years—I hit the mat. I couldn't rally. I found myself asking, *"Is this it? Really? Is this what my life is about?"* Have you ever felt that way? Like you just might lose it?

So I did something radical. I set the car down, got behind the wheel and drove—all across America. I blew off my soul-killing, 60-hour-a-week job, took every last dime I had in savings (which wasn't even enough to get back home on), loaded up my dog and more baggage than I realized and hit the road. We drove all over the country last summer, traveling through 21 states, from Missouri to New York to California and back again. I needed a defibrillator as big as a nation. I went to reconnect with every place and every person I had ever loved. I went to find a half-brother I had never seen. I went seeking solace.

What I got was healing. Eight weeks and more than 8,000 miles later, at a scenic overlook alongside a lonely, two-lane highway, it all got settled. Gazing out at the endless Utah desert, I sat on a huge, flat rock with my dog watching the sun go down. We were safe and dry, but out on the far horizon brewed a huge thunderstorm. Rain in the desert comes down in grey, vertical shafts from giant pink and purple clouds. Looking out at what felt like infinity, I was inspired to let it all go. I simply let it go.

All the egregious offenses that had been hurled my way—a betrayed wife, an abused child—over time, had ceased to matter. They were like a downpour on the desert, dark stabs into a porous surface. I absorbed them to make my life better, yes *better,* because along the way, I'd been blessed with the wisdom that there is far more surface than there is rain.

How quickly the pain can vanish if we are open to the healing. Mile by mile, house by house—at the end of this road trip in which I'd been embraced by friends, family, strangers on the highway, and yes, my found brother, I realized how fortunate I really am. The grimy corners of shame and bitterness had been scrubbed clean by love. Victim, no more.

We've heard a lot about victims in the news lately and the staggering abuse that came from people who were charged with helping them, not hurting them. Heads *should* roll.

But, in the cacophony of competing sound bites, with the accusations, denials, demands for retribution and pleas for justice, there is a vital message that isn't breaking through.

Healing is possible.

It takes time. It takes courage. It takes trusting another human being enough to open up your mind and your heart to speak your truth.

If I had a chance to yell from a mountain- 20 top to anyone whose life has been marred by sexual abuse, here's what I would say: There is a place where it's safe and dry. Come see how fleeting the rain can be.

A CLOSER LOOK AT
"My Ex Went to Prison for Sex Crimes"   MyWritingLab

1. In this memoir, Whatley uses metaphors (e.g. "toxic cloud," "jet fuel in my blood") to express thoughts that would be difficult to express in non-metaphorical terms. Find three other metaphors in this memoir. With your group, discuss the effects that these metaphors have on you as the reader.

2. When tragic things happen, people often go back over their history to rethink prior events and assumptions. Find three places in Whatley's mem-oir where she is rethinking her past. What kinds of conclusions does she reach?

3. At the end of this memoir, Whatley offers a lesson for the readers. Much of that lesson, however, seems directed at herself. With your group, discuss how memoirs like this one can help heal their authors. After reading this memoir, do you believe Whatley is fully healed?

IDEAS FOR
Writing and Discussion   MyWritingLab

1. Think of a moment when you made a painful discovery about yourself, someone you know, or something you cared about. In a memoir, tell this story of discovery and how it forced you to rethink much of what you thought you knew. Conclude with a lesson that you took away from the experience.

2. Find a memoir on the Internet or in a popular publication. Write a rhetorical analysis or literary analysis in which you explore how the memoir works. You might explain its content, organization, and style. Or, perhaps you might focus on its use of stylistic devices like metaphors and similes.

Slapstick

THADDEUS GUNN

In this memoir, author Thaddeus Gunn describes the physical abuse he and his siblings experienced from his mother. He discusses how this abuse shaped his life and the lives of others. Watch how he reveals the lesson of the narrative in a subtle way at the end.

I don't remember every beating mom gave us. I just remember that we named them after All Star wrestling moves. She had an extensive repertoire of techniques. The Half Suplex. The Full Suplex. The Spine Buster. Also the body part specific moves: the Wrist Lock, Atomic Knee Drop, and Corner Butt Slam. Some included hardware, like the Lasso from El Paso, which was a leather belt with a welt-inducing metal buckle, and The Board of Ed, a maple yardstick with steel end caps.

We six kids had our own repertoire of tortures as well, those we gave each other: the Irish Kiss, the Hertz Donut, the Purple Nerple, the Indian Burn, the Stop Hittin' Yourself, and the ever-popular Open Your Mouth and Close Your Eyes and You Shall Receive a Big Surprise.

It wasn't until my younger sister Emily was removed from custody that it stopped. The Board of Ed left marks where teachers could find them. But by then I was the only child left at home, and I was starting to grow muscles.

Years later, when my siblings and I were all grown and had kids of our own to beat, I accompanied my mother to the doctor's office to see the results of her CAT scan. He showed us an image of an enormous calcified tumor, an alabaster walnut that was crowding her right temporal lobe.

He asked her if she remembered ever [5] being hit in the head, ever receiving a blow to her temple hard enough that it would cause a sliver of her skull to separate inward, the same way a shard of glass separates from a windshield when it's been hit by a bb. He theorized that there was a shard of bone in the center of the mass, just as there is a grain of sand at the center of every pearl.

She said, "No, I can't remember anything. I can't even imagine what it would be."

He said, "Are you sure? Perhaps a car accident. It would have caused a concussion. You may have been knocked unconscious."

And again she said, "No, I don't remember anything."

But I remember perfectly well. My grandmother, proudly noting she was never one to spare the rod, told me herself what a bother my mother was: how she was sullen, how she burned the toast, spilled the juice, and failed in math. And for these infractions she was justly punished, with the rap on the knuckles, the slap on the jaw, the punch in the stomach, and the milk bottle to the side of the head.

A CLOSER LOOK AT
Slapstick   MyWritingLab

1. At the beginning of this memoir, Gunn uses names similar to those of professional wrestling moves to describe the kinds of physical abuses that his mother used on him and his siblings. How are these names descriptive, creating a visual image for the readers? With your group, use these names to imagine what each abuse might have actually been.

2. The tone of the narrative is rather flat, even though the subject is hurtful and emotional. With your group, discuss three strategies that Gunn uses to set this tone. Why do you think he chose this tone rather than an outwardly emotional tone?

3. Memoirs, like most narratives, offer a lesson. Where does the lesson in this memoir reveal itself? In one sentence, articulate that lesson and share it with your class. Did everyone come up with a similar understanding of the lesson?

IDEAS FOR
Writing   MyWritingLab

1. All parents make mistakes. Think back to a time when one of your parents or guardians made a mistake. Write a brief memoir in which you tell the story of that mistake. In your memoir, reveal the lessons that were learned or not learned from this mistake.

2. Do research on child abuse. Write a causal analysis in which you describe some of the reasons why child abuse exists in our culture. At the end of your paper, describe some of the effects of this abuse.

1. Ask each member of your group to tell a funny story about himself or herself (something PG-13 or milder, please). After each person tells his or her story, compare the organization of the story to the typical organization of a memoir. What are some of the similarities and differences between these funny stories and memoirs?

2. With a group of people in your class, talk about the physical space where you did a lot of your learning in elementary school. Is there a classroom or other space prominent in your memories? Describe sensory details: how the furniture was arranged, who sat or stood where, the background noises, perhaps even the smells of that place.

3. Do some people who don't really know you have a false idea about who you are? Perhaps it's an impression or image that you yourself have adopted, encouraged, or just never bothered to correct. Give your group a description of this mistaken or alternative impression that some people hold about you. Tell a story that illustrates the "you" others see, and how that image or impression just doesn't capture the real you.

1. All families have stories that have been told so often they have become "famous." Choose a story about you that stands out as especially celebrated in your family.

   a. Briefly relate that story. If you're writing the story, make it less than 300 words; if you're telling it in a small group, make it less than three minutes.

   b. Now explain (in writing or orally) *why* that story is a favorite. What does it *mean* to those who tell it? Does it mean the same thing for everyone involved? *When* is it told? What purpose does it serve? What *point* does it make about your family—what is its significance? Do different people draw different meanings from the story? What general *theme* does it evoke, and why is that theme important for your family?

2. Find a memoir in a book or magazine, or on the Internet. Think about how changing the intended audience and/or the medium might help the memoir reach a different set of readers. What other medium would you choose, and how would you alter the original memoir to adapt it to this medium?

3. Authors write memoirs because they have a point they want to get across to their readers. If you wanted to "repurpose" a memoir to, say, a profile, a proposal, or a research report, how might you do it? How would its angle and purpose change? When you change genres, the nature of the text changes. The readers themselves and their expectations may change significantly; tone needs to change, as do style and many other factors. List specifically what would change if you used a different genre to handle the subject of a memoir.

Explore This

Ready to search for your own microgenres? Here are some microgenres that are related to memoirs. Choose a microgenre from the list below and find three examples in print or on the Internet. Compare and contrast their content, organization, style, and design.

Manifesto—a statement of your personal beliefs based on your experiences

Confessional—a story about something you did wrong

"This I Believe"—a story that illustrates a belief or value you hold as true

Graphic-Novel Memoir—an illustrated memoir, designed like a comic or storyboard

Digital Literacy Narrative—a story about how you learned to use technology (e.g., texting, e-mail, mobile phone) to communicate with others

Write This

1. **Write a memoir.** Write a five-page memoir in which you explore your relationship with another member of your family. Choose an event or series of events that could illustrate that relationship and explore its tensions. Identify a complication or a struggle of values. Then show how you and this other family member evaluated the complication and resolved it. End your memoir by telling your readers what you learned from this experience.

2. **Create a map or a storyboard.** Create a map or a storyboard and write a three-page memoir about a specific event in your life. Develop your memoir by paying special attention to the scene, the people, and the events (actions, dialogue, thoughts) that make up the plot. Be sure that your memoir evokes some significant message or theme that you want your reader to understand.

3. **Write a "six-word memoir."** A six-word memoir tries to tell a story in just six words. For instance, when the famous writer Ernest Hemingway was challenged to tell a story in just six words, he responded: "For sale: baby shoes, never worn." *Smith Magazine* challenged famous and unknown writers to contribute and received over 11,000 responses, some of which were collected in *Not Quite What I Was Planning: Six-Word Memoirs by Writers Famous and Obscure*. Here are a few of them:

   - I'm ten, and have an attitude.
   - Anything's possible with an extension cord.
   - Revenge is living well, without you.
   - My reach always exceeds my grasp.
   - Never should have bought that ring.
   - Found true love after nine months.

Go to **MyWritingLab** to complete this chapter's exercises and test your understanding of its objectives.

Profiles

In this chapter, you will learn how to—

`6.1` invent the content of your profile.

`6.2` organize and draft your profile in an attention-grabbing way.

`6.3` choose a style that captures the essence of your topic.

`6.4` design your profile to fit the place where it will be used.

Profiles are used to describe interesting people, places, and events. Profiles create a snapshot of a person, place, or event by viewing the subject through a specific angle that reveals something essential—an insight, idea, theme, or social cause. Some of the best profiles focus on subjects that seem ordinary but are symbolic of larger issues.

Most profiles are written about people, but places and events can offer interesting topics, too. For example, you could profile a place in a city, a building, or a whole town, describing it as a living being. Or, you might write a profile of an event (e.g., a basketball game, a protest, a historical battle, an earthquake) in way that makes the subject come alive.

Profiles appear in a variety of print and online publications. They are common in magazines like *People, Rolling Stone*, and *Sports Illustrated*. They are regularly featured on Web sites like *Slate.com, National Review Online,* and *Politico*. Profiles are also mainstays on cable channels like ESPN, A&E, and the Biography Channel.

In college and in your career, you will write profiles for Web sites, brochures, reports, and proposals. Profiles are also called backgrounders and bios, and they appear under headings or links such as "About Us" or "Our Team." You will also write your own profile or bio for social networking sites like *Facebook, Instagram,* or *LinkedIn*.

Profiles

Here are two possible organizational patterns for writing a profile. The pattern on the left is good for describing your subject. The pattern on the right is best for telling a story about your subject. Other arrangements of these sections will work, too. You should organize your profile to fit your topic, angle, purpose, readers, and context.

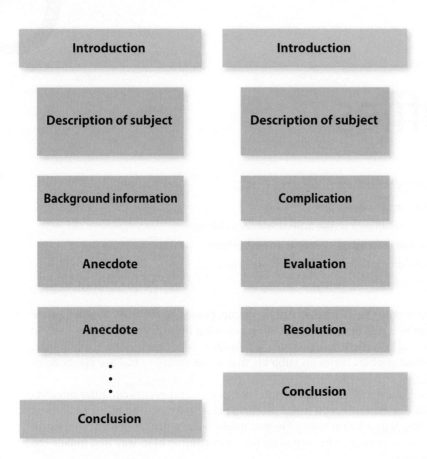

A profile can stick to the basic facts (as in a biographical sketch) or provide an intimate depiction of the subject. Profiles have some or all of these features:

- **A subject (a person, organization, place, or event)** that allows you to explore an issue, idea, or theme that is interesting to you and your readers.
- **An interesting angle** that captures a single dominant impression about the subject.
- **A description of the subject** that allows readers to visualize and imagine it.
- **Background information** that describes the setting or social context of the subject.
- **Anecdotes** that reveal the character of the subject through actions and dialogue.
- **A main point,** or central theme about the subject that goes beyond the surface and factual details to address larger questions.

ONE STUDENT'S WORK
Profiles

Visit **MyWritingLab** to explore an interactive version of this essay.

Brother, Life Coach, Friend

Katie Koch

On a spring morning at a Boston high school, Wyatt Posig, a caseworker in the Massachusetts Department of Youth Services, has some good news for Chris, an affable seventeen-year-old with a sleepy smile and an armed robbery conviction. Posig thinks he may have found Chris an office job for the summer.

The profile starts fast, setting a scene that shows the subject at work, what he *does*.

There's only one problem—the internship calls for business attire. Posig has been trying to get clothing vouchers for Chris, whose wardrobe runs to the type of oversized checked shirts and baggy pants he's wearing today. "I might have some ties for you," Posig says. Chris shrugs indifferently at the dilemma. (Some names and details have been changed.)

It wasn't too long ago that Posig was an intern himself. Now, just a year out of college, he is one of a handful of case-workers assigned to a pilot program designed to give Boston's juvenile offenders some much-needed support as they leave detention centers and reenter their communities. In search of a better way to cut recidivism, the state introduced the program last year, tweaking a model developed by the National Center on Addiction and Substance Abuse at Columbia University. Each of Boston's neighborhood community centers now has a dedicated caseworker to act as a consistent presence in these troubled kids' lives: an amalgam of older brother, life coach, negotiator, and friend. For Dorchester's teens, that person is Posig.

Photo by Kathleen Dooher.

Background information: where the subject came from, the context of his work.

He started prepping for the role years ago, studying sociology at BU and coordinating the Big Siblings program. He worked summer internships at the Department for Children and Families in his hometown of Burlington, Vermont. "I've always known I wanted to work with young people in this situation," Posig says. "I really thrive on being able to help them out. And for whatever reason, I've been able to connect with kids really easily my entire life."

continued

Physical description allows readers to visualize the subject.

Quotes and dialogue are used to bring the subject to life and develop the overall main point.

Anecdotes show readers who Posig is and the role he plays for the young men he works with.

Profile ends with a feeling of closure, *implying* rather than stating the main point (or thesis).

It helps that he could almost pass for a teenager. Tall and lanky, with a smattering of freckles and a dark red beard, he sticks to a uniform of loose shirts and jeans. He spends most of his day checking up on his clients, taking them to dental appointments, or letting the kids vent to him in his office. For the ten boys in his caseload, none of whom have fathers living at home, Posig is a role model, but not in the traditional sense.

"The other caseworkers are the parent figures," he says. "I'm more of a brother. The difficult part is that you want to be the kids' friend, but you also want to get that respect"—a hard thing to earn as the youngest guy in the office. But Posig brings a youthful energy to the Dorchester Community Reentry Center: he leads the daily staff meeting, chats up his coworkers, and—perhaps a first for world-weary social workers—does it all without caffeine. (He's never had a cup of coffee, he says.)

"I turned twenty-three yesterday," Posig says. "But none of the kids knows that."

Curtis, one of the center's charges, just celebrated a birthday as well. There were no parties, as Posig and coworker Sheila Cooper learn when they visit him that afternoon at Casa Isla, a lockup in Quincy for twenty boys ages eleven to seventeen. Curtis arrives in the visitors' room, and Cooper and Posig quickly assume their roles: Cooper, the tough-love veteran caseworker, and Posig, the tentative, encouraging upstart. "It's good to see you," Posig says. "It's not good to see you locked up, but it's good to see you."

Cooper starts to grill him: why did he call them down for a meeting? "I miss y'all," Curtis finally confesses. Just seven days away from his release, the fifteen-year-old is tense. "Don't tell the other kids you're waiting to get out," Posig advises, "or they'll test you." He later explains that it's not uncommon for an offender to slip up near the end of a sentence, back for a new crime just weeks after being let out. When Curtis is released, Posig's task will be to help him navigate the everyday challenges of school, family, and work that can make life on the inside seem relatively easy—even desirable.

Still, Posig is optimistic about Curtis's chances, perhaps more so than Curtis himself. In the year he's been on the job, he's witnessed success stories: one of his kids has never missed a day of work, and another recently made the honor roll. His attitude, he hopes, is contagious.

Inventing Your Profile's Content

Begin by choosing someone or something you can easily access. If you are profiling a person, choose someone you can shadow, interview, or research as your subject for the profile. If your subject is a place or event, choose something that you can portray as a living being that moves, has emotions, and is changing in an interesting way. The key is finding a subject that is fascinating to *you,* because if you are not interested, you will find it very difficult to spark your readers' interest.

6.1 invent the content of your profile.

Inquiring: Finding Out What You Already Know

Take some time to think about what makes this person, place, or event unique or interesting. Try to develop an angle that will depict your topic in a way that makes your profile thought provoking and meaningful. Use one or more invention methods to generate ideas for your profile. Here are a couple of especially good invention tools for profiles.

Answer the Five-W and How Questions.   Journalists often use the Five-W and How questions (who, what, where, when, why, how) to get started.

Who?   Who exactly is this person? Who influenced your subject, and who has your subject influenced? Who is regularly involved with your subject?

What?   What exactly is the person, place, or event you are profiling? What does the person, place, or event look like? What has your subject done that is especially interesting to you and your readers? What is unique about this person, place, or event?

Where?   Where did this person come from? Where did important events happen? Where did the events start and end? Where is this person now?

When?   When did the major events in the profile happen? When did the story begin? When did it end, or when will it probably end?

Why?   Why did this person or others behave as they did? Why has this person, event, or organization succeeded or failed? Why has your subject changed in a significant way?

How?   How did this person's background shape his or her outlook on life? How does your subject respond to people and events? How will this person, organization, place, or event be understood or misunderstood in the future?

Use Cubing.   Cubing allows you to explore your topic from six different viewpoints or perspectives (Figure 6.1). *Describe* your subject by paying attention to your senses. *Compare* your subject to someone or something else. *Associate* this subject with related issues or things you already know about. *Analyze* this subject, looking for any patterns, hidden questions, or unique characteristics. *Apply* your subject as a character by describing it in action. *Argue* for or against: Is this person or group of

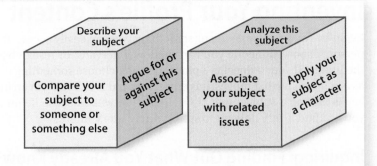

FIGURE 6.1 Using Cubing to Inquire About Your Subject

Cubing is a good way to study your topic from different viewpoints or perspectives. Each side of the cube urges you to see the person, place, or event you are profiling somewhat differently, generating new ideas and insights.

people right or wrong, a saint or a scoundrel, or has this place helped bring about good or bad results?

Researching: Finding Out What Others Know

Good research is essential to writing an interesting profile. You should begin by identifying a variety of online, print, and empirical sources.

Online Sources. Use an Internet search engine to gather biographical or historical information on this person, place, or event. Then gather background information on the time period you are writing about.

Print Sources. Consult newspapers, magazines, and books. These print sources are probably available at your campus library or a local public library.

Empirical Sources. Interview your subject and/or talk to people who can provide first-hand knowledge or experience about this person, place, or event. You might also ask whether you can observe or even shadow him or her. For a profile about a place or an event, you can interview people who live in the place you are profiling or who experienced the event you are writing about.

Interviewing. An interview is often the best way to gather information for a profile. If possible, meet people in person. If that not possible, phone calls or e-mails are often good ways to ask people questions about themselves or others.

Remember to script your questions before your interview. Then, while conducting the interview, be sure to *listen and respond*—asking follow-up questions that engage with what the interviewee has told you.

Shadowing. If the subject of your profile is a person, you could "shadow" him or her (with the person's permission, of course), learning more about that person's world, the people in it, and how he or she interacts with them. For a place or event profile, spend some time exploring and observing, either by visiting the physical location or examining pictures and firsthand accounts. Keep your notebook, a camera, and perhaps a digital recorder handy to capture anything that might translate into an interesting angle or a revealing quotation.

In Chapter 25, "Finding Sources and Collecting Evidence," you can learn more about interviewing and other empirical forms of research.

Organizing and Drafting Your Profile

A well-organized profile will capture the attention of readers and keep their attention. As you organize your ideas and write your first draft, you should keep a couple of key questions in mind:

6.2 organize and draft your profile in an attention-grabbing way.

> **What do you find most interesting, surprising, or important?** As you researched your subject, what did you discover that you weren't expecting? How can you make this discovery interesting for your readers?

> **What important conflicts does your subject face?** People are most interesting when they face important challenges. Similarly, places and events are scenes of conflict and change. What is the principal conflict for your subject?

Keep in mind that the profile is one of the most flexible genres. You can arrange the information you collected in a variety of ways to suit your topic, purpose, and readers and the contexts in which they will read the profile.

The Introduction

You want to start strong with a lead that hints at or captures the main point of the profile.

Identify Your Topic and Purpose. Your introduction should identify the subject of your profile, while directly or indirectly revealing your purpose. You might also want to show readers why the person, place, or event you are profiling is significant in some way.

State Your Main Point or Thesis. The placement of your main point (thesis) depends on the type of profile you are writing. In a descriptive profile, you can state your main point, or thesis, in the introduction. Tell your readers up front what you are trying to show about your subject. In a narrative profile, you probably won't state your main point or thesis in the introduction. Instead, you should wait until the conclusion to reveal your overall point.

The Body

In the body, you can include a variety of moves such as describing your topic, offering background information, recounting anecdotes, or revealing important ideas through dialogue.

Describe Your Topic. Use plenty of details to describe how your subject looks, moves, and sounds. In some situations, you might use your full senses to describe your subject's environment, including how things smell, sound, and feel.

Offer Background on the Topic. You can tell your readers something about the time periods and places in which your subject lived or lives now. Explore the circumstances that led to key events you describe in your profile.

Use Anecdotes to Tell Stories. An anecdote is a small story that reveals something important about a person or a place. Your anecdotes should also reflect the main point of your profile by revealing something important about your subject.

Reveal Important Information Through Dialogue or Quotes. Dialogue and quotes are often the best way to reveal something important about the topic of your profile without coming out and stating something directly. However, don't overuse dialogue or quotes. Because quotes receive special attention from readers, reserve them for insights or changes that are especially important.

The Conclusion

Profiles shouldn't just end; they should leave an impression. Because endings, like beginnings, get special attention from readers, your conclusion should include information, ideas, or images that leave readers with a sense of the point (or thesis) you want to make. Conclude with a strong impression that will stay with your readers.

Keep your conclusion brief. You should state or restate your main point (your thesis) with emphasis. If you have included a thesis statement in your introduction, phrase the main point differently here. Then, offer a look at the future in which you say something about what lies ahead for the person, place, or event you profiled.

Choosing an Appropriate Style

6.3 choose a style that captures the essence of your topic.

If possible, the style of your profile should reflect the essential character of the person, place, or event you are describing. If you are profiling an exciting or restless person, you want your tone or voice to be equally exciting and energetic. If you are profiling someone or something that is sad or dour, again, your profile's tone or voice should match that feeling.

Change the Pace. If you want to convey energy and spirit, speed up the pace by using abrupt, short sentences and phrases that will increase the heartbeat of the text. If you want your readers to sense a slower pace or thoughtfulness, you can use longer sentences that slow things down. All sentences, however, should be "breathing length," which means they can be read out loud comfortably in one breath.

Choose Words That Set a Specific Tone. Think of one word or phrase that captures the main feeling or attitude you want to express about the subject of your profile. Do you want to convey a sense of joy, sadness, energy, devotion, goodwill, seriousness, or anxiety? Pick a word and then use brainstorming or concept mapping to come up with more words and phrases that associate with that word. You can then seed those words and phrases into your profile to create this specific tone or feeling.

Get into Character. You might find the best way to develop a specific voice or tone is to inhabit the character of the person, place, or event you are profiling. Imagine you *are* that person (or at the place or event). From this different perspective, how would you describe the people, objects, and happenings around you? Are you amped up? Are you anxious or scared? Are you worried? Use words that fit this character.

Designing Your Profile

Profiles usually take on the design of the medium (e.g., magazine, newspaper, Web site, television documentary) in which they will appear. A profile written for a magazine or newspaper will look different than a profile written for a report or proposal. So as you think about the appropriate design for your profile, consider what will work with the medium in which it will appear.

6.4 design your profile to fit the place where it will be used.

Use Headings. Your readers may be looking for specific information about the person, place, or event you are profiling. Headings will allow you to reveal how your profile is organized, while helping your readers locate the information they need.

Add Photographs. When writing for any medium, consider using photographs, especially images that reflect the profile's main point. If possible, try to find photographs that capture the look or characteristic that you are trying to convey. Then, use captions to explain each picture and reinforce the profile's point.

Include Pull Quotes or Breakouts. Readers often skim profiles to see if the topic interests them. You want to stop them from skimming by giving them an access point into the text. One way to catch their attention is to use a pull quote or breakout that quotes something from the text. Pull quotes appear in a large font and are usually placed in the margins or a gap in the text. These kinds of quotes will grab the readers' attention and encourage them to start reading.

The Bio

A bio is used to describe a person's life and accomplishments. When you are applying for internships, scholarships, awards, and jobs, you will likely need to write a bio about yourself. A bio usually runs about 100–300 words, and it often takes up just one paragraph.

In your college classes, you may be asked to write bios of prominent people and fictional characters, such as famous scientists, presidents, social activists, protagonists, and villains. You may enjoy writing bios of musicians, sports figures, actors, and fictional characters for popular Web sites. A bio is a good way to explore a person's personality, characteristics, and motives.

When writing a bio about yourself or someone else, you should concentrate on your subject's personality, upbringing, education, career, relationships, memberships in organizations, awards, interests, and hobbies. You might also spend some time figuring out what makes you or the person you are describing unique and interesting. Here's how to write a bio:

Provide the basic biographical facts.   If appropriate, identify full name, date of birth, place of birth, date of marriage, and names of parents, spouse, and siblings. These personal facts would usually not be included in a professional bio.

Describe major life events.   Locate information about the places where the person lived, schools and colleges attended, awards received, disappointments, and special moments that have happened in his or her life.

Describe major interests and activities.   Look for information on this person's career, hobbies, religion, clubs, sports teams, volunteer work, pets, pleasures, and frustrations.

Tell one or two stories.   Use anecdotes to reveal this person's character or something interesting that this person has accomplished.

Organize these materials in a way that fits the bio's purpose.   If the bio is for a career-related purpose, such as a job, scholarship, corporate Web site, or internship, you should put career-related information early in the bio and any personal information that you feel is pertinent later. If you are writing a description of a person's life, including your own, then order the information chronologically.

WRITE **your retirement bio.** Imagine you are in your late 60s and getting ready to retire after a successful career and an enriched personal life. Write a 300-word bio in which you describe what you want said about you when people look back on your career and life.

Visit **MyWritingLab** to complete this exercise.

Stephanie Wilson, NASA Astronaut

Stephanie Wilson

After graduating from Harvard in 1988, Wilson worked for two years for the Martin Marietta Astronautics Group in Denver. As a Loads and Dynamics Engineer for Titan IV, Wilson was responsible for performing coupled loads analyses for the launch vehicle and payloads during flight events.

Title and first paragraphs provide an overall description of the bio's subject.

Wilson left Martin Marietta in 1990 to attend graduate school at the University of Texas at Austin. Following the completion of her graduate work, she began working for the Jet Propulsion Laboratory in Pasadena, California, in 1992. As a member of the Attitude and Articulation Control Subsystem for the Galileo spacecraft, Wilson was responsible for assessing attitude controller performance, science platform pointing accuracy, antenna pointing accuracy and spin rate accuracy.

Chronologically arranges information about subject's accomplishments and major life events.

Selected by NASA in April 1996, Wilson reported to the Johnson Space Center in August 1996. Wilson was initially assigned technical duties in the Astronaut Office Space Station Operations Branch to develop requirements for space station payload displays and procedures and to evaluate their user interfaces. She then served as a Capsule Communicator (CAPCOM), working in Mission Control as a prime communicator with several space shuttle and space station crews. Following her work in Mission Control, Wilson was assigned technical duties involving the space shuttle main engines, external tank and solid rocket boosters in the Astronaut Office Space Shuttle Operations Branch.

Offers details about specific activities and areas of expertise to show what distinguishes her from other astronauts.

In November 2004, Wilson was assigned to STS-121. Following STS-121, she served in the Astronaut Office Robotics Branch performing robotics procedure reviews and serving as a robotics Mentor and Instructor Astronaut. In November 2006, Wilson was assigned to STS-120.

Following STS-120 she was assigned joint duty in both the Astronaut Office Exploration and International Space Station Branches. Wilson served as the Astronaut Office primary representative to the generic joint Space Shuttle and Space Station Operations Panel. For the Exploration Branch, she was the Astronaut Office representative for the Orion Communications and Tracking System.

In May 2009, Wilson was assigned to STS-131. Following STS-131 she served as the Space Station Integration Branch Chief.

Concludes strongly with a distinctive and impressive achievement.

A veteran of three spaceflights, STS-121 in 2006, STS-120 in 2007 and STS-131 in 2010, Wilson has logged more than 42 days in space.

Need to get going with your profile? Here are some ideas to help you start.

CHOOSE an Interesting Subject

Find a person, group, place, or event that is fascinating to you and would be interesting to your readers. Choose someone or something that is unique or symbolic.

FIGURE OUT What You Already Know About Your Subject

Use invention tools like the Five-W and How questions, freewriting, and cubing to study your subject from a variety of perspectives.

RESEARCH Your Subject

Find information on the Internet or in print sources. Also, if possible, interview the individual you are writing about or visit the place. Talk to people who know your subject well.

DRAFT Your Profile

Start out strong by grabbing the readers in your introduction. Then, in the body, use detail to paint a portrait of your profile's subject. Avoid writing a complete history. Instead, pick an event or series of anecdotes that captures the essence of your subject.

DEVELOP an Appropriate Style

The appropriate style for your profile usually reflects the personality of your subject. You can use word choice and sentence length to portray a specific voice or tone.

LOCATE Some Photographs, If Available

Look for photographs that illustrate and reinforce what you want to say about your subject.

STRESS Your Main Point

You want your profile to do more than simply describe your subject. Use your subject's history and actions as a symbol of something larger or more significant. That's your point.

REVISE and Edit

Always remember that your profile needs to capture the essence of the person, place, or event you are describing. So clarify the content, straighten out the organization, and refine your writing style.

The Serial Rapist Is Not Who You Think

TIM MADIGAN

Tim Madigan is a journalist who writes for the Fort Worth Star-Telegram, *a daily newspaper. This is the second installment of a three-part investigative report. As you read, notice how he uses interviews and other research methods to establish credibility and authority. Notice also how he uses anecdotes, dialogue, and word choice to create a rich portrait of his subject, "the typical perpetrator of acquaintance rape."*

Dressed in a three-piece suit, Thomas is a well-spoken man of 32 who is clearly trying to make a good impression. He seems remorseful about the day a few years ago when he tried to rape his girlfriend's teenage daughter. That led to his conviction for attempted sexual assault, probation, a place on a sex offender registry and court-ordered therapy.

But most of a recent conversation in his therapist's office concerns the more distant past, the hundreds of sexual encounters with hundreds of girls and women. There was a time, he said, when he was hooking up at least once a week, often more than that.

"We'd just go out, me and my brother and my best friends, we'd go out and we'd just meet women at malls or driving down the road," Thomas said. "We had a competition to see who could pull the most tail."

How many conquests were too intoxicated to consent? How many did he hold down when they changed their minds?

"It's difficult to believe that some of them 5 didn't involve some twisting of arms," said his therapist, Ezio Leite.

Thomas said force wasn't necessary.

"Just using the silver tongue," he said. "Just persuasion. Conversation. Talking to a woman's emotional side. Romance. Just tell them what they want to hear. It gets you places."

Meet the typical perpetrator of acquaintance rape.

He is not who you think, experts say, not the drunken college boy who somehow misunderstood when she said no. Instead, more often than not, the acquaintance rapist is a serial hunter like Thomas—charming on the outside, hateful and manipulative within. He puts as much thought and planning into his crimes as a bank robber. And for him, women (or sometimes men) are little more than "tail."

"When they talk in front of juries, they 10 can convince them that they are just the little misunderstood college boy or workingman or whatever," said Fort Worth police Sgt. Cheryl Johnson, a veteran sex-crimes detective. "But they are predators. They are a wolf in sheep's clothing."

Some detectives and victim advocates have long been aware of that sinister portrait, one that has been confirmed by two major studies in the last decade. That portrait also punctures many stubborn myths about what is by far the most common form of sexual assault.

Acquaintance rape is not just "drunk sex" or "date rape." The perpetrator is not less guilty or destructive than the proverbial stranger who jumps out of the bushes.

In fact, stranger rapists and acquaintance rapists often share much, experts say, including a profound lack of empathy and a hatred of women. That's why detectives, prosecutors and researchers nationwide are developing new strategies to bring acquaintance rapists to justice, something that rarely happens now.

"It's essential, absolutely essential that we figure this out," said Russell Strand, a sex-crimes expert who trains military investigators and civilian detectives nationwide. "We can't get stuck on the old rape myths, continue to believe that this is just date rape. A date is nothing more than a tool for a sex offender. It might seem like a date, but they are being set up."

An Eye-Opening Study

Twelve years later, David Lisak remembers [15] his surprise when the results of his research first popped up on his computer screen.

"The data came out and my first reaction was 'Dammit, I've made a mistake somewhere. These numbers can't be,'" said Lisak, a psychologist and researcher at the University of Massachusetts.

In the late 1990s, Lisak administered a survey to 1,900 men at a midsize American university. Of them, 120 answered "yes" to one of the following questions. Have you had sex with someone too intoxicated to resist? Have you ever engaged in sex by threatening or using physical force, such as holding down a partner's arms?

Though the questions were careful not to characterize it as such, the men who answered in the affirmative had admitted committing rape. More than 60 percent of the admitted rapists in Lisak's study said they had done so more than once.

What shocked Lisak is what he learned from those men through follow-up questionnaires and interviews. The data showed that repeat rapists had not stopped with two. Each had committed an average of six sexual assaults. Seventy percent of their victims had been incapacitated by drugs or alcohol. Thirty percent of the time, their rapes had been committed with force or the threat of force.

"It was just the sheer number of violent [20] crimes committed by a very small number of serial rapists," Lisak said of his surprise. "And rapes and attempted rapes were just the beginning. There was domestic battery, child abuse. What I was having trouble with initially was that the men I was studying were college students. One doesn't think of college students as criminals."

Lisak's findings were published in 2002.

"How is it that they are escaping the criminal justice system?" he wrote then. "By attacking victims within their social networks—so-called acquaintances—and by refraining from the kind of violence likely to produce injuries, these rapists create 'cases' that victims are least likely to report."

His findings were replicated seven years later in a study done by the Navy. In that research, 2,900 male recruits were surveyed.

"That [Navy] study really confirmed for myself and a lot of other people what we had found," Lisak said. "It gives you a lot more assurance that your initial study was not some anomaly. We have two studies of men who commit rape and are not going to prison. A lot of people out there still refer to these guys as date rapists. It's a term I just loathe. It masks the reality and puts a kind of 'rape lite' label on it."

Lisak's term for them is "undetected rap- [25] ists." They are criminals who are often too aware that, in the unlikely event that a victim reports her assault, it will be his word against hers.

"We hear that when we interview them," Johnson said of acquaintance rape suspects questioned by Fort Worth police. "'It's my word against hers. There's nothing you can do.' I think that they know that as long as they draw it down to the line of consent, not whether sex happened, it's much harder for a case to be proven against them."

In that scenario, ironically, perpetrators often can come off as more believable, even more sympathetic than the victims.

"Victims often blame themselves, second-guess themselves about what they did or didn't do," Strand said. "They feel bad about what happened, while the suspect doesn't feel bad about it, other than being challenged or caught. The victim hasn't made sense of what has happened. There are fragmented memories or trauma issues. The suspect knows what happened and often makes more sense.

"We are trying to train law enforcement not to be fooled into thinking that credibility boils down to likeability," Strand said. "It's a trap we can fall into."

New Investigative Methods

His name was Sean Druktenis, a handsome 30 young man from a prominent family, accused by a woman in Albuquerque of acquaintance rape. That case in the late 1990s was not strong, said Claire Harwell, a prosecutor in the case.

"But the detective was struck by how the offender had controlled his victim so rapidly," Harwell said. "His methodology had seemed too practiced. It seemed so systematic. So the detective went to where this guy went, to his tanning salon, to his gym, to his clubs."

Nine additional victims were uncovered.

"The first case was not a case that we felt we could win," Harwell said. "But we explained to [the victim] how her disclosure had helped. When you have that many cases, you have a lot of authority. You can minimize the likelihood of having to take a case to trial, work toward getting a good plea and getting them on a sex offender registry."

Druktenis was sentenced to probation but was sent to prison after violating the terms.

The New Mexico case highlights the ne- 35 cessity of new investigative methods, experts say. One is to check out the haunts of the suspect as detectives did in Albuquerque. Another is to use unconventional interview techniques that play into a suspect's belief that he is a victim, falsely accused.

The goal is to get beneath the serial predator's carefully polished veneer.

"I do something when I teach classes," Strand said. "I usually dress in a nice suit and tie. After I explain [his theories] I'll take off my jacket and underneath I'll be wearing a shirt that will be dirty, torn, and has nasty words written all over it, like 'rapist.' Then I'll ask the class, 'Would any one of you have known I had this shirt on unless I showed it to you? We never know who that person is, under the jacket. All the [rape victim] saw was the jacket, and when the jacket comes off it will be too late. Then they put the jacket back on."

Thomas the hunter was literally wearing that nice jacket during that recent day in Fort Worth. Even in a confidential interview when he knew that his identity would be protected, he worked hard to conceal what was beneath. His therapist, for one, was not convinced that more women had not been victimized by the man in the three-piece suit with the silver tongue.

But admitting it, Ezio Leite said after Thomas was gone that day, "would mar the presentation."

"He would never tell you that he's a 40 monster," Leite said. "He's a nice guy. And when people talk to him, that's the perception they're going to have. That's the type that women will have a hard time knowing. They don't see him as a rapist until..."

Until it is too late.

A CLOSER LOOK AT
The Serial Rapist Is Not Who You Think

1. One of the main points in this profile is that serial offenders of acquaintance rape don't *appear* to be bad people. Find specific places where the author reinforces this point with disturbing anecdotes and quoted dialogue.

2. Profiles often use narrative to engage readers and make their points. A good narrative involves some kind of *conflict* between people. What exactly is the conflict here, and who is in conflict with whom? Is the conflict resolved in any sense?

3. Profiles often use design strategies such as photography and pull quotes. What kind of photography could have been used to augment this profile's effectiveness, and how would those photographs be captioned? Also, which two or three passages from the text would make the most effective pull quotes?

IDEAS FOR
Writing

1. This profile, like many good profiles, surprises readers by showing that their subjects are different from what you might expect. Write a profile that, like Madigan's, shows how a person, group, event, or place is not at all what it seems to be on the surface. Use quoted dialogue and rich description to reinforce your main point.

2. Write a brief commentary for your college newspaper or some other local publication that extends the findings of this profile to your local context. Do some research into the problem of acquaintance rape on your campus or in your community.

Hot for Creature

ERIC WILLS

Everyone knows that only gullible people believe in the existence of Bigfoot, right? Here Eric Wills profiles Bigfoot investigator William Dranginis and his quest to find answers to the mystery. As you read, notice how Wills uses narrative and research to persuade readers to reconsider their initial beliefs.

William Dranginis knows what you're thinking, so maybe it's best to get a few things straight right from the start. He's not crazy, delusional, some lunatic on the fringe. For the most part, he's your average suburban family man. Lives on a quiet street in Manassas. Has a great wife and two daughters; just became a grandfather. Has a good job designing surveillance equipment for the Windermere Group, an Annapolis-based technology firm that does contract work for the government.

He can't help that he saw Bigfoot in the woods near Culpeper, Va., on March 11, 1995. Two witnesses were with him, both FBI agents. It's not like he imagined the incident. In the 13 years since, he has spent more than

$50,000 trying to prove Bigfoot exists. He has created sophisticated surveillance systems—wait till you hear about his new Eye Gotcha system!—and even designed a tricked-out research van with parabolic microphones and thermal and night-vision cameras. So he's not exactly half-assing this quest.

Bigfoot, he wants you to know, are not just a bunch of pranksters running around in ape suits. Nor are Bigfoot the ghosts of some long-extinct creature, as some people claim. They're flesh and blood, and they don't just live in the Pacific Northwest. The creatures are here, within commuting distance of the nation's capital. Bigfoot is the "last greatest mystery on earth," Dranginis will tell you, so you may as well suspend your disbelief and come along for the ride.

A man in Chesterfield County claims he saw Bigfoot on his property. On a recent Saturday morning, Dranginis meets the man for the first time in a parking lot just south of Richmond. The subject is in his 20s, has close-cropped hair and the hint of a central Virginia drawl. He doesn't want his name in print because he's worried about losing his job as a public servant.

With his neatly trimmed beard and blue 5 eyes, Dranginis, 49, looks a little like Chuck Norris. He solicits reports of sightings on his Web site for the Virginia Bigfoot Research Organization—he's the president. He also places ads in *Northern Virginia Cooperative Living*, a magazine published by a local utility company. (Have you seen a Bigfoot or Sasquatch-type creature in Virginia? I have.) So far, he says, he has logged about 200 Bigfoot sightings in recent years, from southern Virginia to Bull Run Park just outside Fairfax, less than 35 miles from the District.

Now, Dranginis follows the man's truck along a rural road and begins to assess how genuine this individual is. "Usually I can look into people's eyes and tell whether they've had a real experience or not," he says.

Dranginis wants to believe that the man is telling the truth. Why would he risk his reputation and job to pull some sort of prank? But he has to be skeptical—after all, hoaxers are out there. I saw Bigfoot! He's 10 feet tall! Brown! He smells bad, like a skunk! The pranksters parrot all the descriptions they've read on Bigfoot Web sites. Pretty soon, though, they start contradicting themselves. Then they start looking for money. Sure, you can use my property for research. But it's going to cost you.

Dranginis once heard from a man who claimed to have casts of Bigfoot footprints. Only when Dranginis showed up did the man want money: $20 apiece. Dranginis studied a print: The toes were square and a faint but straight line ran along the edge of the foot, as if someone had pressed a wooden block into plaster. A fake. Dranginis bought a cast anyway. Figured, what the heck, may as well keep it as a memento.

Dranginis, driving his wife's Jeep instead of his own with the vabigft license plates, pulls into a dirt driveway behind the man's truck. The house is a one-story, concrete-block structure. Rusted lawnmowers, orange construction cones, even an old motorcycle are overgrown with weeds in the backyard. The house has been mostly vacant since his grandparents passed away, the man says. Dranginis, wearing dark green shorts and hiking boots with white socks, turns on a hand-held video camera.

Of all the stories the man tells—things 10 banging on the kitchen windows and crashing through the nearby woods—one stands out. About two years ago, he was working on his computer one night when he sensed something watching him. He turned and looked out the living room window and saw a creature at least 7 feet tall walk between his truck and a light post in the driveway: "I saw the silhouette real quick. It was shaped like a person," he says. "I could see a head and body. At first I thought someone was trying to break into my truck, so I ran and got my pistol, and when I came out here it was gone. Then I got around to thinking, What's that tall?"

From his truck he pulls out a white envelope that contains a clump of dark brown material, possible Bigfoot hair. He was cutting the bushes with a trimmer last fall when the clump stuck to the power cord. "I don't know if it's hair or what the heck it is," the man says. Dranginis studies it and concludes some of the strands resemble plant material. He'll take a look under a microscope later.

Dranginis ventures into the woods next to the house, looking for signs of Bigfoot activity: deer parts left over from a Bigfoot snack or maybe a stick structure. Bigfoot sometimes leans a bunch of long branches against a tree trunk, creating a tepee-like formation. Some Bigfoot researchers speculate it may be the creatures' way of marking their territory. Dranginis finds nothing.

Inside the house, the man shows off a faded portrait of his great-grandparents, tobacco farmers. Awards from his civil servant job line the walls. In the kitchen, Dranginis sets up a surveillance system using a digital video camera, a motion-detection device, and a black-and-white television that shows the area being monitored: the corner of the backyard. When something triggers the motion sensor, the camera records for 30 seconds.

Dranginis doesn't expect much from such a simple system, though it's better than nothing. When he has more time, he'll set up a trap to lure Bigfoot to the house. Maybe keep the kitchen lights on at night (Bigfoot are naturally curious) and conduct a stakeout. Or leave out food: deer corn in a large barrel or bacon grease in a garbage can. "Sometimes they can't resist that," he says. Dranginis drives off, optimistic that he's discovered a promising new research site.

Though you probably don't know it by name, chances are you've seen the Patterson/Gimlin film. On Oct. 20, 1967, in Bluff Creek, Calif., Roger Patterson and Robert Gimlin encountered a female Bigfoot (or, depending on whom you ask, a man in an ape suit). Search on YouTube, and you'll find 16mm footage of an apelike creature walking away from the camera, turning back for a second and seeming to meet your gaze before disappearing into the woods.

Interest in Bigfoot reached a frenzied pitch after the video got out. By the end of the 1970s, though, the enthusiasm had waned, in part because people increasingly faced ridicule when reporting their Bigfoot sightings.

Enter the Internet, a boon to anonymity and Bigfoot research. Also enter Jeffrey Meldrum, an associate professor of anatomy and anthropology at Idaho State University. In 1996, Meldrum discovered fresh tracks near Walla Walla, Wash., made by what he thought could be a Bigfoot. Intrigued in no small part because of his expertise in primate foot mechanics, he risked the scorn of fellow academics and began studying the creature.

In *Sasquatch: Legend Meets Science*, Meldrum argues that the circumstantial case for Bigfoot's existence is compelling. Meldrum has casts of Bigfoot prints from various years and locations that appear to be from the same creature. The prints, with dermal ridges similar to fingerprint whorls, would be nearly impossible to hoax, he says. Given that more than 200 new primate species were discovered in the last century, Meldrum argues, it's certainly possible that Bigfoot has managed to elude detection— even in Virginia, where Dranginis points out there's not only a history of sightings, there's more remote forest for the creatures to hide in than you realize.

If Meldrum is the unofficial director of Bigfoot research, Dranginis is a freelance assistant in the field, using his specific skill— surveillance—to find evidence that occasionally may interest his superior. They have exchanged a couple of e-mails and crossed

15

paths at a few conferences. "He's seems to be levelheaded and not prone to embellishing his stories," Meldrum says of Dranginis.

Which brings us to the story of Dranginis' sighting. In the mid-'90s, Dranginis had no idea that the Bigfoot movement was gaining momentum. He was simply looking for a hobby. The economy was booming, and he was finally making good money designing surveillance systems. His days of making ends meet by working a second job—in lawn maintenance and rental property management—were over. Friends had taken up metal-detecting and were finding Civil War belt buckles that they sold for $200, $300 apiece. Dranginis thought, Why not?

On the day his life changed, he went metal-detecting near an old gold-mining operations in the woods near Culpeper with his two friends, the FBI agents. They were walking down a logging road when one of the agents—a point man for three tours in Vietnam—spotted movement in his peripheral vision. He turned and made eye contact with something not quite human, not quite ape. "The expression on both of our faces was, Oh, shit," Dranginis remembers his friend saying.

(The agent didn't return phone calls. Daniel Perez, editor of *The Bigfoot Times*, a monthly newsletter, says he interviewed him and Dranginis separately and found their stories credible. He writes in an e-mail: "I've come to know Bill over the years as a dependable, honest and trustworthy individual.")

When the creature ducked behind a tree, the two agents drew their guns. Clearly, whatever it was, it had something to hide. A few seconds passed. A head poked out, assessing the situation. Jesus Christ, something's there, Dranginis thought.

And then the man-beast bolted, "started running from left to right, arms moving, muscles bulging," Dranginis says. "I could see its shoulders going back and forth like a football player wearing padding. The thing was

sailing through the woods." A man in an ape suit? Not a chance, Dranginis says. Even a 7-foot-tall man in a flawless costume couldn't imitate what he saw. The creature made a sharp right turn, bounded down a hill, and disappeared.

Dranginis returned the next day with the point man, who carried two sidearms and an AK-47. Dranginis brought plaster. He found a footprint in sand at the bottom of the hill and started to make a cast. Suddenly, leaves crunched nearby. Something started whistling. "There are two of them," Dranginis remembers his friend saying. "I survived Vietnam with my gut, and my gut is telling me to get the hell out of here." Something let loose a shrill scream as they retreated. "I'm never coming back, and neither should you," his friend told him.

Dranginis probably should have listened. But he can't help that he's so "damn inquisitive," and has been since childhood. When he thought about it, he realized that the perfect hobby had just fallen into his lap. Here he was a surveillance expert, and here was this elusive creature no one could capture. How could he pass up the chance to make history? Besides, how hard could it be to find a Bigfoot, look the creature in the eyes, and say, "Gotcha"?

The first challenge is convincing everyone that you aren't dropping acid. When Dranginis returned home right after the sighting, "he had an excitement that was different from anything I had ever seen," says his wife, Carol Dranginis. "His eyes were huge, like saucers." Carol knew the Vietnam point man, knew him to be credible, and he confirmed the story, she says. William, whom she had known since high school, was clearly a changed man.

On a recent Thursday evening, I met Carol at their two-story, gray-shingled house before Dranginis led me into the basement, his makeshift Bigfoot lab. Enough Bigfoot paraphernalia to start a museum lines the shelves: casts of Bigfoot prints (including the fake and copies of prints from the Patterson/ Gimlin sighting), Bigfoot action figures, Bigfoot newsletters, and Bigfoot books (including Roger Patterson's *Do Abominable Snowmen of America Really Exist?*).

Dranginis chuckles at his initial bravado as he sits in a swivel chair, a large American flag hanging over a computer behind him. Bigfoot have managed to elude capture for a reason, he discovered: The creatures are damn smart.

When Dranginis set up motion-activated cameras near his initial sighting, strange things happened, he says. Something threw sticks and rocks into the field of view, tapped the side of the camera at 1 or 2 in the morning, breathing heavily, and even placed an elm leaf in front of the lens. "These creatures are here. They're screwing with me, screwing with the camera system. They've outsmarted me," he thought. 40

One day, as he watched footage of a deer that had triggered the system, he had an epiphany. The deer looked up at the camera and started twitching its ears. Of course, Dranginis thought. The video equipment emits ultrasonic sound. Bigfoot, he concluded, can hear the cameras.

Dranginis gets up and walks over to a worktable filled with electronic equipment. He pulls out an ultrasonic leak detector and moves the device's microphone in front of a video camera. He turns the camera on, and a loud crackling noise confirms that it's producing ultrasonic sound. So much for installing cameras in trees.

And so began what Dranginis calls an epic game of cat-and-mouse. Every time he thought he was on the verge of cornering Bigfoot, the creature somehow escaped. In 2001, Dranginis bought a 24-foot mobile veterinary unit and converted it into a Bigfoot research center. On weekends, he traveled to areas with reported sightings and used parabolic microphones, night-vision cameras,

and a thermal camera that he attached to a 25-foot-tall crank-up mast to search for the creature. Countless weekends and sleepless nights later—nothing. He recently sold the van—another dead end.

He got a call a few years back from the owners of what he calls the Southern Virginia Research Location, not far from Richmond. They found possible Bigfoot hair. He gave it to a scientist at the National Museum of Natural History. "He's a sincere, honest guy, is genuine in what he believes, in what he thinks is true," says the scientist, who didn't want to be named. "That's why I helped him." The scientist was stumped by the hair, though—was it animal? human?—and sent it to another lab for analysis. The conclusion: llama hair.

Dranginis sent the hair to an Arizona lab for mineral analysis, which indicated it came from a human who ate red deer meat, plants, and clay—no processed foods. "I've never seen a llama eat deer meat," Dranginis says. He sent the hair to a lab in Copenhagen for DNA testing, and the results came back as wolf or dog. Three tests, three different results, and no closer to his goal. 45

Dranginis pulls out what looks like a suitcase and opens it to reveal a black tranquilizer gun with a DNA dart tip. His plan? Do a stakeout in a house at his so-called Southern Virginia Research Location. "I would be underneath a window in the crawlspace, see a leg, and pop! Hopefully he won't reach down and grab me and pull me out," he says. Dranginis would film the shot using a camera that he can connect to the gun, to show the dart tip snatching a sample of tissue and blood from the creature. Dranginis has practiced in his backyard shooting at a tree—he's accurate from 75 feet—but he has yet to take a shot at Bigfoot.

In the middle of his basement sits a stack of seven cases of Bigfoot ale, a special edition released annually by Sierra Nevada. Dranginis buys a case each spring hoping that he'll find Bigfoot during the year, that the beer will become a collector's item.

"Every year I buy it. Nothing happens. Next year I get another. Next year I get another. It's a real quick visual indicator that the thing's beating you," he says.

As Dranginis' respect for Bigfoot has grown, his patience for the upstarts joining the Bigfoot bandwagon has waned. "It does tick you off. The new guys come in, all jockeying for position, and the next thing you know everyone has sightings," he says. Barn owl call? Bigfoot! Coyote howl? Bigfoot! Falling branches? Bigfoot!

Wild tales circulate. Dranginis attended a recent Bigfoot conference in Ohio where some attendees floated far-fetched interpretations of the Patterson/Gimlin film. The two men, the story went, massacred a bunch of Bigfoot and fired bullets at the creature in their famous film clip. Look at this newly enhanced video! You can see a pool of blood here! Look, the creature's limping! They shot her in the leg!

Dranginis thinks such theories are ridic- 50 ulous. Here he is following scientific principles, and these conspiracy theorists are giving legitimate researchers like him a bad name. Did he ever think about quitting? "Yeah, I did a couple of times. Sort of just gave up and said forget it, screw this, I'm all done." But then damned if someone didn't contact him with an intriguing sighting, or damned if some world-famous primatologist didn't come along and lend her support. Enough coincidences, and Dranginis jumps back in, thinks he's destined to find Bigfoot.

Dranginis shows me a three-ring binder with postcards and letters from Jane Goodall tucked into plastic sleeves. In 2002, she declared in an NPR interview that she's sure Bigfoot exists. "I have talked to so many Native Americans who've all described the same sounds—two who have seen them," she said.

Dranginis says he met Goodall through another Bigfoot researcher soon after her NPR interview and gave her a tour of his Bigfoot research vehicle. They kept in touch. "I'm about to talk to a man who studies snow leopards in the Himalayas who doesn't rule out the possibility of a Yeti," he reads from one of her postcards. (A spokesperson confirmed that Goodall has corresponded with Dranginis but denied an interview request.)

Via all those slivers of wisdom accumulated over the years, Dranginis has developed what he thinks is the ideal system to capture Bigfoot. He pulls out a black plastic box slightly thicker than a briefcase: the Eye Gotcha. Inside is a small digital video recorder with a video card and space for enough batteries to keep the system running for at least a year. An armored steel cable runs from the box to a camera lens that Dranginis has concealed in a tree branch. A small motion-detection device works wirelessly.

Here's how he plans to nab Bigfoot: Bury the box, muffling any ultrasonic sound. Dig the armored wire into the ground and then plant the fake branch and camera lens in a pile of wood, up to 50 feet away. Install the motion detection device in a tree. With no ultrasonic sound or video equipment nearby, Bigfoot will be oblivious to the fact that he has walked into a camera trap.

Dranginis intends to sell the system— 55 about $900 fully loaded—at the upcoming East Coast Bigfoot Conference in Pennsylvania. But he also thinks he can generate interest in Eye Gotcha outside Bigfoot circles, from researchers hoping to get footage of other rare animals to park rangers worried about poaching. Many surveillance cameras are mounted visibly on trees and are often stolen. His will be safely hidden.

Before I go, Dranginis wants to show me one more gadget, his $15,000 thermal camera. It's 11 p.m., three hours after he first invited me into his basement, and we head outside. I hold the device—not much larger than a television remote—as Dranginis walks across his lawn, pretending to be Bigfoot. He appears on the small screen as a radiant blur of reds and yellows.

Dranginis ducks behind a pine tree and moves his arms and legs around in a makeshift Bigfoot dance. See, he calls out, the device is sensitive enough to detect a creature behind a tree. Sure enough, red splotches appear on the screen. I feel like a kid breaking curfew, playing with Dranginis' high-tech gadgets after the adults on the block have gone to sleep.

As I drive home, I remember the two images Dranginis showed me on his computer in the basement. In the first, a dark outline of a creature with a cone-shaped head that Dranginis estimates stood about 9 feet tall appears on the right edge of the frame. In the second photo, the thing—whatever it is—appears less distinct, more of a blur than anything else.

Dranginis captured the images at the Southern Virginia Research Location. When the creature triggered the motion sensor, an LED light blinked. (Dranginis thought he had turned it off.) He thinks the creature saw it, turned sideways, and then bolted.

Dranginis admits the pictures prove nothing. People may conclude it's an alien, or enhance the photos and make ridiculous claims: "Bigfoot had a knife! Or Bigfoot had a gun! Or There's a bat morphing out of its head!" Fair enough, but I must admit that in the quiet of Dranginis' basement, after hearing his various stories, I felt a slight shiver staring at the ghostly images on his screen.

"There was something standing, something huge standing in the middle of the road, just big enough that I could figure out it wasn't a human being," the man tells me. "I can't tell you exactly what it was. I can tell you it had very dark features from the head down. I don't know too many men that are 8 or 9 feet tall dressing up in black clothes and standing in the middle of the woods at 5:30 or 6 in the morning."

On a recent Saturday afternoon, I'm visiting the Southern Virginia Research Location with Dranginis. The man who owns the property doesn't want his name in print or his address revealed. Word leaked a few years back that Bigfoot lived here and intruders started

visiting at night, poking around. The last thing he wants is some gun-toting adventurer sneaking around trying to bag a Bigfoot.

At first, the man didn't believe what his wife and other visitors were telling him, that there were large, apelike creatures roaming around his property. His wife saw something black standing in the yard. Must be a bear on its hind legs, he thought. His dog came running out of the woods one day with some sort of mucus on its face, as if something had sneezed on it. "Hmm, that's strange," he said. Then he saw the beast standing on the road that morning as he was driving to work. "That kind of made a believer out of me."

Living so close to Bigfoot over the years, the husband and wife have learned a few things about the creature. "You call him, he calls you back. It sounds like three people talking three different languages at the same time with the same voice," the man says. Bigfoot likes singing, tends to come around when the wife's belting out church songs. He also likes peanut butter. They leave jars for him on branches of pine trees, and he's been known to lick the insides clean and replace the lids— only if the wife sets them out, though. A jar Dranginis left on a branch remains untouched, his initials and the date written on the plastic bottom in Magic Marker: wmd 9/4/04.

Come to think of it, Bigfoot's got a crush on the wife. "He's drawn to me," she says. "That's why I don't go over there too much," she says, pointing to the edge of their property. "What if he takes me into the woods?" She laughs. Bigfoot, the husband is quick to point out, has never shown the slightest inclination to hurt anyone.

Outside, Dranginis and the man lead me through rows of pine trees on the edge of the property and into a remote section of woods. "People think they migrate. I don't think they do. I think once they find an area with a good food source, water, shelter, they just stay put. Look at this place—this place is perfect. You've got a lake down here, feeder streams, got some farms locally, peanut butter on trees. It's Big Rock Candy Mountain," Dranginis says.

After listening to the stories, I'm primed for Bigfoot to appear. He doesn't, of course, but Dranginis thinks all hell is about to break loose. Developers have plans to build housing nearby, which will disturb Bigfoot's habitat and lead to Lord knows what (certainly an increase in sightings).

As Dranginis installs a surveillance system in a trailer on the property, the man excuses himself. "He's more interested in this than I am," he says, as Dranginis carries equipment to the trailer. The man finds Bigfoot fascinating, but he's never been tempted to do any research of his own: "My focus is elsewhere."

After 13 years of research and more than $50,000, Dranginis has some grainy video footage and photos, tracks he's discovered, eyewitness accounts—and still no hard evidence. He's posted this motto on a sheet of paper in his basement: absence of evidence is not evidence of absence.

Jane Goodall, in her NPR interview, ac- 70 knowledged that the lack of a body, of bones, remains problematic. But she also said something that captures the spirit of the chase: "I'm a romantic, so I've always wanted [Bigfoot] to exist."

As Dranginis drives home from the Southern Virginia Research Location, he acknowledges how difficult the journey has been. "My life is back and forth every weekend, trying to make something happen. Things just don't happen. You sort of look at it as a waste of a day out of your life," he says. "It's a roller coaster, up and down, and eventually you get what's called Bigfoot burnout."

Once, when he was flying out of BWI, he noticed imperfections in the mud at a construction site near his terminal. "I started looking at it like there were going to be Bigfoot prints right there in the middle of the airport." Time to take a break, he thought.

Lots of guys either quit or spend so many weekends in the woods they end up divorced,

he says. His wife, Carol, admits she had a few moments where she resented his hobby, but he always immediately pulled back and spent more time with his family, she says. A few years ago, they bought a cabin in West Virginia near reported Bigfoot sightings. Not only can they enjoy a weekend away together, he can also get in a few hours of research.

"I seem to keep coming back for more. I guess I'm just punch-drunk or something," says Dranginis. "But I think it's exciting, the cat-and-mouse thing. It's got me in its claws. I don't think there's anything wrong with that."

Carol says that since his sighting, a "dif- 75 ferent dimension" of her husband has emerged. "He's more motivated," she says, "more excited about everything in life." Not only has Dranginis invented a surveillance system, he also says he's developed newfound respect for nature after spending so much time in the woods. He came to realize how much we're polluting the planet. Dranginis once tried to rally support for legislation to have Bigfoot's habitat preserved. Of course, that requires proving the creature exists.

If Dranginis does find Bigfoot, the woods will be filled with hunters trying to take one down. So maybe it's not such a bad thing that the mystery persists. It will give a new generation of Bigfoot researchers a chance to make their mark.

We stop at a McDonald's, and a local strikes up a conversation with Dranginis as he waits for his burger and fries. Back in the car, Dranginis says he'll sometimes ask strangers in rural Virginia if they've ever seen a cougar, long thought to be extinct on the East Coast. It's a softball question before he asks what he really wants to know: Ever seen Bigfoot? Most times folks will chuckle and say no.

But sometimes they'll pull him aside and tell him about a sighting. Maybe one day, a farmer will tell him he found a body and has it in his barn. And the mystery of Bigfoot will be solved, not by fancy surveillance systems or DNA dart guns but by simple dumb luck.

A CLOSER LOOK AT
Hot For Creature
MyWritingLab

1. Write a 30- to 50-word summary of this profile that follows this template: "While most people _____, Eric Wills shows that _____.

2. How did your attitudes about Bigfoot and Bigfoot hunters change after you read this profile? What strategies does author Eric Wills use to suggest that the claims of Dranginis and other Bigfoot hunters should be considered seriously? Point out specific places in the text where Wills introduces people and ideas that would cause careful readers to reconsider their ideas.

3. This piece includes no headings and subheadings. Using the ideas in Chapter 20, "Developing Paragraphs and Sections," chunk this profile out into four to seven sections, each with a descriptive heading title that helps readers quickly perceive the main point of that section.

IDEAS FOR
Writing
MyWritingLab

1. All of us have experienced situations in which we tried to convince others that our beliefs should be taken seriously, even though others thought our ideas were outlandish. Write a brief memoir that recalls this situation, the complication that you and others were involved in, and how the complication was resolved (or was not).

2. Write a rebuttal to the article, "Hot for Creature." First review the argument in this article and challenge the assumptions, evidence, and logic used. Then write a solid counterargument that explains why this profile is misguided and why your counterargument makes more sense.

1. Pair off with a partner. Interview your partner about his or her life at college. Ask about his or her daily routine. Ask about what this person does that's unique or different from a typical college student. Find out what this person believes about life and the college experience.

Talk About This

2. With your group, discuss the portrait below, taken by Charles C. Ebbets (1905–1978) of workmen perched on a steel beam on the 69th floor of the Rockefeller Center in 1932. How are these workers portrayed? What word or phrase captures their attitude? Considering the historical context of this picture—the Great Depression—what message is conveyed about America at the time?

© Charles C. Ebbets/Ebbets Photo Graphics.

3. With your group, come up with five national issues that you all seem to care about. They don't have to be enormous issues. For each of these issues, pick a specific person, group, place, or event that is symbolic of that problem or its solution. Then talk about how a profile of these representatives could be used to help readers understand the issue you linked with them.

Try This Out

1. Choose one of the profiles included in this chapter and analyze it using the features listed in the At-a-Glance in this chapter. Does the profile adhere exactly to these features? List three ways the profile matches this description of the genre. Then list three ways the profile does not match the description.

2. On the Internet, find a profile of someone who interests you. Present this profile to your writing group, identifying its strengths and weaknesses. Then identify the main point of the profile and show your group how the author uses the profile to make a larger point.

3. With your group, list five places or buildings on campus that seem to come alive when people are in them. Pick one of these places and describe it as though it is a person or a living being of some kind. How can a place be similar to a person? How can personifying a place make it more interesting for readers?

Explore This

Go find your own examples of microgenres! Here are a few microgenres that are related to profiles. Choose a microgenre from the list below and find three examples in print or on the Internet. What are some common features of this microgenre?

Portrait—a short sketch that describes how another person looks and behaves

Snapshot—a description of a place or event as though everything has stopped

Social Networking Profile—a brief profile for a social networking site

Obituary—an end-of-life profile for a celebrity or someone you know

Personal Ad—a description of yourself for a dating Web site

Write This

1. **Profile someone you know.** Write a profile of someone you know well and like. Think about why you find this person interesting: they're quirky, hardworking, funny, unusual, and so on. Talk to others about this person to collect a variety of viewpoints and possibly gain new insights. Paint a verbal portrait of this person that views him or her from a specific angle and that captures something essential—an idea, social cause, insight, or theme.

2. **Create a profile with graphics or audio/video elements.** Write a profile about a historical figure or place from your state or country. Using the Internet and print sources, find out as much as you can. Then interview an expert who has studied this person or place in depth. Paint a verbal portrait, viewing your topic from a specific angle and capturing something essential—an idea, social cause, insight, or theme. Add pictures taken from the Internet or elsewhere.

3. **Write a profile of a person or group of people that is supposed to represent your generation.** Choose someone or something that is used as a cultural icon to explain young people in general and your generation in particular. What common experiences do you and your friends share with this person or group? What unique experiences or aspects of persona have made this person or group an icon (for better or worse) for your generation?

Go to **MyWritingLab** to complete this chapter's exercises and test your understanding of its objectives.

Reviews

In this chapter you will learn how to—

7.1 invent the content of a review.

7.2 organize a review and write a draft.

7.3 develop an appropriate style for a review.

7.4 create a design that fits the readers and context.

Writing a review is a good way to figure out and explain whether you thought something was successful or not. Reviews are written about movies, books, video games, software, music, consumer products, services, performances, and many other items. They help readers understand the strengths and limitations of the item being discussed.

In essence, a review gives you the opportunity to express your informed opinion about a product or performance and explain why you came to that conclusion. When writing a review, you need to do more than simply state whether you liked or didn't like something. Instead, you need to base your opinions on the *common expectations* that you share with your readers. When writing a review, your opinion is important, but it needs to be based on assumptions you share with your readers about what makes something successful or unsuccessful.

Reviews tend to be published in magazines and newspapers and on the Internet. You probably check the reviews before deciding to see a movie, buy a book, eat at a restaurant, go to a performance, or download some music. Reviews can help you determine whether you would enjoy something before you buy it. People also like to read reviews after they experience something to see if others agree with their opinion about it.

In college courses, professors will assign reviews to give you a chance to express your opinion about the arts, architecture, books, politics, education, fashion, and other issues. When assigning a review, professors are typically looking for your ability to support your opinions and to demonstrate your understanding of a subject, while also allowing you to express your opinion in an informed way.

Reviews

These diagrams show two possible organizations for a review, but other arrangements of these sections will work, too. You should alter these organizations to fit your topic, angle, purpose, readers, and context.

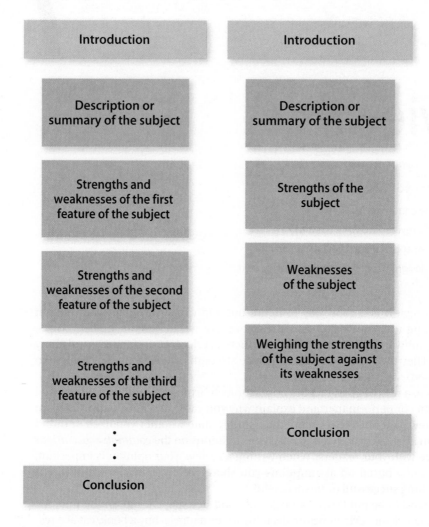

A review typically has the following features:

- **An introduction** that identifies the subject being reviewed and offers some background information on it.
- **A description** or summary of the subject.
- **A discussion** of the subject that determines whether it meets, exceeds, or falls short of common expectations.
- **A conclusion** that offers an overall judgment of the subject.

ONE STUDENT'S WORK
Reviews

Visit **MyWritingLab** to explore an interactive version of this essay.

Review: BB's Lawnside Blues & BBQ

Christina Lieffring

From the lopsided parking lot we could hear the harmonica wailin' and smell wood-smoke and spice. The low red-brick and wood building was packed with booths and long rows of tables with red and white checkered tablecloths inhabited by Johnson County teens in skinny jeans, a ponytailed senior donning a "Willie Nelson for President" t-shirt and everyone in between. BB's Lawnside Barbecue has the quintessential barbecue and blues joint vibe, but people from all over don't just come here for the ambiance; there is substance behind the style.

The Nick Moss Band was blasting down-home blues when we came in and local (and personal) favorite Trampled Under Foot was lined up to play the following Tuesday. Owner Lindsay Shannon's longtime presence in the KC blues scene means that any given night diners will be treated to quality local blues. However, since we valued conversation and our hearing, we opted to sit at the picnic tables on the patio and enjoy a reasonable decibel level.

The ribs were (and I am not hyperbole-prone) perfect. They were not covered in sauce because they didn't need to be—the meat was flavorful, moist, tender but not overcooked. Their sausage, linked at local meat legend McGonigles and smoked in-house, finds the right balance of sweet, smoke-y and savory. The pulled pork and beef were not especially flavorful and dry but that could be remedied by drowning it in BB's inhouse mild and spicy hot sauce. The extra kick in the spicy sauce brings out the sweet undertones without being so spicy you can't slather it on.

The BBQ Sunday is a combo of hickory smoked beans, coleslaw and pulled pork served out of a mason jar. But instead of the nicely defined layers we expected, we got a mason jar of brown goop with some coleslaw and a pickle on top. Once it was dumped out on a plate it tasted fine, but presentation matters. Our waitress recommended the meatloaf made of burnt ends but it was a little dry on the outside though the center was more flavorful. BB's also offers Louisiana-style fare, but the jambalaya was dry and nothing to write New Orleans about.

A nice surprise was the amount of care gone into the sides. Fries, coleslaw, green beans and smoked beans are standard barbecue sides, but BB's has tweaked them just enough to make them stand out. The fries are battered and fried, the coleslaw had less mayonnaise and more flavor, and green beans and smoked beans had an extra kick to them.

A scene-setter lead is used to bring the readers into the review.

The thesis statement states a point that the review will support.

Details allow the readers to imagine the writer's experience.

New or different experiences are often worth mentioning in reviews.

The reviewer mentions items that did not meet her expectations.

> Overall BB's provides a wide enough selection that each visit could bring something new. (After tasting their smoked ribs, I'm curious to try out their smoked chicken.) Combine that with their ribs, sauce, sides, atmosphere and music, and you've got a classic summer night out.

The thesis is restated with more emphasis.

Inventing Your Review's Content

7.1 invent the content of a review.

Of course, in order to write a review of something, you need to spend some time experiencing it. But wait. Before you see the movie, read the book, or make a trip to the restaurant, you should do some inquiry and background research to help you understand your subject from a critical perspective. Inquiry will help you determine what you and your readers expect of your subject. Background research will help you develop a fuller understanding of your subject's history and context.

Inquiring: Discovering Common Expectations

The foundation of a good review is the set of common expectations that you and your readers share about what makes something successful or unsuccessful. Those expectations are not usually stated directly in the review itself. Instead, the reviewer assumes that his or her readers share some assumptions about the qualities that make something successful.

For example, let's say you want to write a review of an action movie that just arrived in theaters. You might start by using an invention strategy like brainstorming to list all the things most people would expect from the kind of movie you are reviewing. As fast as you can, make a list like the one shown in Figure 7.1. Then put a star or asterisk next to the three to six items that are most important to you.

More than likely, if you asked a group of people to list their expectations for an action movie, they would produce lists similar to yours. They might use different words and they might put a star next to something you didn't, but most people would agree on what makes a good action film. That's what we mean by "common expectations." They are expectations that you and your readers already share.

Once you have identified the features you believe are most important, group the unstarred items on your list under the starred ones. For example, the list shown in Figure 7.1 could be sorted into six major categories: noble but flawed hero, complex and sinister villain, a romantic relationship, fast-paced plot, stunts and chase scenes, and music that enhances scenes.

Having created your list of common expectations, you will have a better idea about what you and your readers will be looking for in this kind of movie.

Researching: Gathering Background Information

Now you should do some background research that will help you better understand what you are reviewing.

Features of a Good Action Movie

*Great hero
  Memorable lines
*Love interest that doesn't sidetrack
  movie
  Real or potential victims of villain
  Character evolution, especially hero
  Suspense
  Interesting setting
  Something unexpected
  Chase scenes
  Use of weapons
*Complex and sinister villain
*Fast-paced plot
  Fighting scenes
  Some irony, but not too much
  Hero needs to be flawed in some way
  Mystery to be solved
*Amazing stunts

  Cool special effects
  Unexpected humor
  Intense music soundtrack
  Strong set of values
  Villain is brilliant
*Music that sets the moods for scenes
  Hero's desire for revenge
  Opening scene that grabs audience
  Social pressures on hero to give up
  Good friends for hero
  Low expectations for hero
  Recognizable actors
  Dark lighting
  Somewhat realistic, even if fantasy
  Characters worth caring about
  Rivalry between hero and villain
  Violence that has purpose and
  meaning

FIGURE 7.1
Using Brainstorming to List Common Expectations

Brainstorming is a good way to come up with a list of elements that you and your readers would expect the subject of your review to have.

Answer the Five-W and How Questions. You might start out with an Internet search, typing your subject's name or title into the search line. Look for answers to the Five-W and How questions:

- Who wrote it, developed it, or produced it?

- What is the genre of your subject, and what do people expect from that genre?

- When was it created?

- Where does it exist or where were the scenes set?

- Why was it created—for what purpose?

- How was it made?

Then follow up with print sources, which are available at your campus library. In magazines, newspapers, and academic journals, look for more background information on your subject and the people who created or participated in it.

Locate Other Reviews of Your Subject. You might also use an Internet search engine or newspaper indexes and databases to find other reviews about your subject.

While taking notes on these reviews, be very careful not to use the words or ideas from other reviews without citing them. In academic settings, borrowing ideas without citation is plagiarism. In professional settings, borrowing the words and ideas of others could violate copyright laws. Of course, it is not uncommon for reviews to arrive at similar conclusions and even to refer to each other, but your review needs to be original in wording and presentation.

Interview or Survey Others. On almost any college campus, someone is an expert about your subject. You could also survey others who have already seen the movie, eaten at the restaurant, listened to the music, and so on. What did they think of your subject? How did they react to it? What did they like and dislike about it?

Prepare to Do Field Observations. In a field observation, you would watch your subject closely *and* pay attention to how others react to it. For example, while watching an action movie, you should be prepared to take notes about how the audience reacted to particular scenes. You should be ready to answer these kinds of questions: Did they laugh? Did they groan? Did they seem to enjoy themselves, or were they dismissive of the film?

Researching: Go Experience It

Being critical means being aware of your own reactions to your subject. For example, when you are reviewing a movie, allow yourself to experience the movie as a regular moviegoer. But also step back and experience the movie critically as a reviewer. If something in the movie is funny, go ahead and laugh, but then ask yourself *why* you laughed. If you thought the food at a restaurant was bland, ask yourself *why* you had that reaction.

After you experience your subject, you might also spend some time playing the Believing and Doubting Game to draw out some ideas for your review.

Believing. First, imagine that you are going to write an overly positive review (i.e., a rave review). What did you like? What were your subject's strengths? What stood out as superior? How did your subject exceed your expectations?

Doubting. Now imagine that you are going to write a very negative review (i.e., a slam). What didn't you like? What didn't work? What were the weakest aspects of your subject? What annoyed or irritated you? What didn't fit your expectations or the subject's genre?

Synthesizing to Find Common Ground. Now examine what you wrote, both your positive and your negative comments. Which issues are most important to you and your readers? Where do your positive and negative analyses agree, and where do they strongly disagree? Which side do you think is stronger than the other?

Organizing and Drafting Your Review

7.2 organize a review and write a draft.

The organization of a review tends to be rather straightforward, so drafting this kind of argument is often easier than drafting in other genres.

The Introduction

Your introduction is the basis for the rest of the review. It will typically make some or all of these moves:

Identify Your Topic and Offer Background Information. Tell your readers your topic (the subject of your review) and offer enough background information to familiarize your readers with it.

State Your Purpose. You should also identify your purpose directly or indirectly. You don't need to say something like "My purpose is to review ..." but it should be clear to your readers that you are writing a review.

> When I decided to dine at Bistro 312, I was determined to arrive with an open mind and leave behind my usual biases against French food.

State Your Main Point or Thesis. Later in the introduction, you may want to tell your readers your overall assessment of your subject (your main point or thesis). Your main point or thesis statement should do more than say whether you liked or didn't like the subject of your review. You should be specific about what you liked or didn't like.

> **Weak:** *Halo: Spartan Assault* is an entertaining video game.

> **Stronger:** The storylines and characters in *Halo: Spartan Assault* are not original, but the combat scenarios are realistic, the soundtrack is engaging, and the new overhead perspective creates novel kinds of fighting sequences that make the game feel more intense.

Often, your main point or thesis statement will reveal the expectations on which you based your review.

Many reviewers prefer to use a "question thesis" in the introduction, which allows them to postpone giving their overall judgment until the conclusion. For example, you could ask, "Given the incredible success of the all-engrossing *Halo 4*, would it be possible for *Halo: Spartan Assault* to measure up?" Then, you can answer the question with a thesis statement in the conclusion.

Description or Summary of the Subject

Assume that your readers have not seen the movie, read the book, eaten at the restaurant, or gone to the performance. You will need to give them a brief description or summary of your subject. You have a couple of options:

Chronological Description or Summary. Describe or summarize your subject by leading your readers through the major scenes of the movie, book, or performance. At this point in your review, you should offer an objective description without making any evaluative comments.

Feature-by-Feature Description. Divide your subject into two to five major parts and then describe each part separately. Make sure you use your senses to include plenty of detail. What does it look like? How does it sound, taste, smell, and feel?

Discussion of Strengths and Shortcomings

Earlier, you generated a list of common expectations that you and your readers share about your subject. Point out the strengths of your subject for your readers and explain how the subject met these expectations. Then discuss any shortcomings—how the subject failed to meet these expectations—and explore why your subject came up short.

> The primary strength of the *The Bourne Identity* is the characters of Jason Bourne and his reluctant partner, Marie. Both Jason and Marie have typical desires and fears that make them very human. Jason seems like a regular guy, even though he discovers that he has unexplainable fighting abilities and expertise with weaponry. The audience wants Jason and Marie to survive and escape. . . .

> On the downside, the absence of a great villain means *The Bourne Identity* lacks some of the intensity of a typical action movie. The forces of evil in this movie are mostly faceless bureaucrats who send one-dimensional assassins to kill Jason Bourne. The audience has trouble focusing its anger on one person or a few people, because there is no single evil-doer in the movie. Instead. . . .

Early in each paragraph, make a direct claim about a strength or shortcoming of your subject. Then, in the rest of the paragraph, support that claim with reasoning, examples, quotes, facts, and any other evidence you need to prove your point.

In this part of the review, go ahead and express your opinion. That's what readers expect from you. They want you to tell them exactly how you felt about the movie, the book, the restaurant, or the performance.

Conclusion

The conclusion of your review will usually be brief, perhaps a few sentences. In your conclusion, you should state or restate your overall assessment of the subject. Then you might offer a look to the future.

> Overall, I found *The Bourne Identity* to be a thoroughly entertaining film, despite its few weaknesses. Matt Damon carries the film with one of his best performances. The film also leaves plenty of loose ends to be explored in its entertaining sequels, *The Bourne Supremacy, The Bourne Ultimatum,* and *The Bourne Legacy.* This movie certainly deserves to be listed among the classics of action movies.

Avoid introducing any new information about your subject in the conclusion. Your conclusion should bring readers around to your main point.

Choosing an Appropriate Style

7.3 develop an appropriate style for a review.

The style of your review depends on your readers and the places where they will encounter your review. A review written for a mainstream newspaper, magazine, or Web site should use a lively style that matches your overall reaction to the movie, book, or performance. An academic review, perhaps for a film studies or music appreciation course, might use a plainer or formal tone.

Use Plenty of Detail

If you are reviewing a movie, you want readers to be able to imagine what it actually looked and sounded like. Similarly, if you are reviewing a new restaurant, you want your readers to imagine the taste of the food, while hearing the same sounds you heard and smelling the same smells.

Add detail to your review by concentrating on your five senses (sight, hearing, taste, touch, smell). Of course, you don't need to include details from all five senses in your review. But keep all your senses open and take notes on what you detected. You never know what kinds of details might be useful as you draft and revise your review.

Set the Appropriate Tone

If you were really excited by the movie you saw, the tone of your review should reflect your excitement. If you thought a particular restaurant was disgusting, your readers should sense that disgust in the tone of your writing. You might find it useful to create a concept map around the word that best describes the tone you want to set. If you occasionally use words from your concept map in your writing, your readers will sense that tone.

Changing the Pace

You might also pay attention to pace in your review. Shorter sentences will make the pace of your writing feel faster, because they increase the heartbeat of the text. So if you are describing action scenes in a movie, you might try using shorter sentences to increase the intensity of your writing. If you want to describe a hectic day at a restaurant, shorter sentences will create a feeling of frantic chaos. Longer sentences slow the pace down. So if you are describing a calm, peaceful restaurant or a quiet scene in a movie, use longer sentences to match that slower pace.

Designing Your Review

7.4 create a design that fits the readers and context.

The format and design of your review will depend on where it will appear. A piece written for a movie review blog will be designed differently than one you are writing for a course in film studies.

Choose the Appropriate Medium. Paper is fine, but you should consider writing for other media, like a Web site, a blog, or even a podcast, so your review will be available to the public.

Add Photographs, Audio, or Video Clips. For some reviews, such as a movie review, you might be able to add in a link to a trailer or a clip from a scene (Figure 7.2). If you plan to publish your review or post it on a Web site, make sure you ask permission to use any photos or screenshots.

FIGURE 7.2 Adding a Still or Clip from a Movie

In your review, you might add a still from a movie or even a link to the trailer.

The Rave

Did you ever really like something? Did you really, really, really like it? Have you ever been completely blown away by a movie, song, play, novel, meal, or concert?

You should write a rave about it. A rave is an over-the-top review that is more about feelings and reactions than reason. In a rave, the reviewer suspends his or her ability to think rationally about the subject of the review. Instead, he or she shares that out-of-control feeling with the readers.

But how do you write a rave review without looking like you've lost it, gone off the deep end, drank the Kool-Aid? Here are some strategies:

Figure out what you liked best about it. There were probably one or two qualities that made this one "the best ever." What were those qualities and why did they make the experience so incredible?

Summarize it briefly. Summarize or describe your subject briefly, but use only positive terms and graphic details to illustrate your points.

Compare it favorably to the classics. Tell readers that your subject belongs with the classics and name those classics. Don't say it's better than the classics, because your readers will be skeptical. Instead, tell the readers it's just as good.

Use metaphors and similes to describe your experience. Metaphors and similes that use food and fighting work well: "It left us hungry for more." "The crowd was drooling with anticipation." "It was mind-blowing." "We were stunned." "It knocked me for a loop." "I felt like I had been elbowed in the head."

Tell the readers they *must* experience it. You're not just recommending they experience it; you're telling them they *must* do it.

Amplify and exaggerate. Liberally use words like "awesome," "incredible," "unbelievable," "fantastic," "amazing," and "astounding." Use the word "very" a little too often. Tell the readers it's one of the most important things ever written, filmed, created, cooked, played. Call it an instant classic.

Don't let up. In a rave review, there is no going halfway. This was the best thing that has happened to you in your life, this year, this month, this week, or at least today (pick one).

Have fun. Raves are about expressing your raw emotions about the things you love. You want readers to feel what you felt. They know you're being irrational. That's the best part about a rave.

WRITE your own rave. Think of a movie, television show, book, restaurant, or place that you really, really enjoyed. Then write a three-page rave review in which you share your enthusiasm with your readers. Let yourself go a little.

Visit **MyWritingLab** to complete this exercise.

The Hunger Games: Catching Fire Review

Haley Frederick

Like every other book-reading teen on the planet, I love the *Hunger Games* series. When the first movie rolled around, however, I left the midnight premiere majorly disappointed. I was unhappy with the casting, effects and disloyalty to the core of what our beloved story of *The Girl Who Was on Fire* is truly about.

Given my previous experience, I walked into the 8 p.m. showing of *The Hunger Games: Catching Fire* last night with low expectations. I heard rumors that this adaptation was more loyal to the book, but I wasn't sure that would be enough to win me over. To my delighted surprise, 30 minutes into the almost two and a half hour film, I was sure that this movie would live up to everything I wanted it to be.

Everything was how I imagined it reading the novel two years ago. The characters, the districts and the arena all immensely improved from the franchise's opening. It was much more focused on the twisted ways of the Capitol and the brewing rebellion than the love triangle the first film seemed to revolve around.

After *Hunger Games*, I wasn't sold on Jennifer Lawrence and Josh Hutcherson as District 12's tributes, Katniss and Peeta, but after their performances in *Catching Fire*, I could not be more pleased with the casting of these movies. Lawrence's portrayal of Katniss was true to her book equivalent. She had several intense scenes in this movie, and each was poignant and believable. Hutcherson's Peeta earned your sympathy, yet his strength was not lost in excessive pity. The new additions like Plutarch, Finnick and Johanna also did not disappoint in the slightest.

Another perfect thing about *Catching Fire* was the pacing. The victory tour, the preparations for the games and the time in the arena each had enough time to cover the important events, while nothing dragged on too long. The tributes' time in the arena kept you on the edge of your seat. Suspense and anticipation buzzed in the theater; my friends and I left with an adrenaline rush because of it.

The closing scene not only concluded the movie in a spectacular way, with amazing acting by J-law, but also set up the start of the next film, which we'll all be waiting for impatiently. All in all, my low expectations were blown away. I will definitely be going to see *Catching Fire* again.

Exaggeration is used to heighten the intensity.

Stronger words are used where milder ones would have worked.

Author overstates reaction to subject.

Physical reactions are played up.

Need to write a review? Here's what you need to get going.

FIND Something You Want to Review

Your professor may tell you what you should review. If not, choose something that you can analyze critically, not something you absolutely adore or detest. You want to pick something you can assess fairly.

FIGURE OUT Your and Your Readers' Common Expectations

List two to seven qualities that you and your readers would expect something like your subject to have.

GATHER Background Information on Your Subject

Using online and print sources, collect background information on your subject and read other reviews. You might also interview an expert.

GO Experience It

As you are experiencing your subject, pay attention to your own reactions as a regular participant and as a critical observer.

DRAFT Your Review

Introduce your subject and describe it. Figure out your main point or thesis statement. Then describe your subject's strengths and weaknesses. Finish with a conclusion that offers your overall judgment.

DEVELOP an Appropriate Writing Style

The style of your review depends on where it will appear and who will read it. Most reviews use a lively tone that is entertaining to readers.

ADD Graphics to Support Your Written Text

A few graphics, like photographs and movie stills, will help you to visually illustrate what you are talking about.

REVISE and Edit

Keep in mind that your opinion of the subject may have changed while you were reviewing it. If so, you may need to revise the whole argument to fit your current opinion.

The Lego Movie

CHRISTY LEMIRE

Christy Lemire is a movie critic who writes reviews on her own site. The Lego Movie was a surprising breakout film because audiences expected something childish and simple. They were treated to a so-called kid's movie with much more depth. Watch how Lemire explores these deeper levels in her review.

The Lego Movie: Merely a great film, or the greatest film ever in the history of cinema?

I ask this question—jokingly, rhetorically—but the more I think about it, the more in awe I am of the way *The Lego Movie* works on every level for every possible viewer. "Everything Is Awesome" isn't just an insanely catchy theme song, one that will be stuck in your head for days if not weeks afterward (and may even drive out "Let It Go" from *Frozen*, if you're lucky). It's a statement of fact. It may even be an understatement.

You know that old clichéd response after walking out of a movie or a play: "I laughed, I cried"? This time, it's really true. I laughed my ass off—and then I cried. A 3-D, animated movie about a bunch of tiny pieces of plastic made me cry. And you guys who have read me for a while know that I'm cold and soulless and not usually susceptible to the power of tearjerkery. But that's one of the many reasons I loved *The Lego Movie* so much: It kept surprising me.

It moves so beautifully, it has such irresistible humor and irrepressible energy, but always feels effortless. It's jammed with affectionate, cheeky pop-culture references but never seems hacky or strains for the laugh; so many of the jokes fly by at such a giddily frenzied clip, you'll probably have to go see the movie a second time just to catch them all. And you probably won't mind doing that; *The Lego Movie* is the rare film based on a toy or a game that truly feels like its own unique universe rather than a shameless, extended infomercial.

Did we mention the voice cast? We haven't even gotten to the exceptional voice [5] cast yet. So often with animated movies, the A-list stunt casting serves as a distraction and takes you out of the narrative. Here, it provides one of the many opportunities for directors and co-writers Phil Lord and Christopher Miller to take established genre conventions and turn them on their heads, similar to their inspired version of *21 Jump Street*. Morgan Freeman, for example, plays a blind mystic whose prophecy sends an ordinary guy on an extraordinary hero's journey. But in doing so, he knowingly pokes fun at his propensity for playing God-like figures, his rich voice providing both gravitas and goofy laughs.

The increasingly endearing Chris Pratt provides the voice of Emmet, a regular construction-worker drone who always follows the rules and does what's expected of him in his incessantly perky, if regimented, Lego town. Much of the humor comes from the way in which the characters' world mirrors ours, with its overpriced coffee, crowded commutes, idiotic sitcoms and overplayed radio tunes. Everything is awesome, as the song goes, but every day is exactly the same.

But one day, Emmet stumbles upon a random piece of red plastic that's unlike the rest of the interlocking bricks that surround him. It is the Piece of Resistance, a crucial component of the prophecy that Freeman's character, Vitruvius, told of at the beginning. And in finding it, Emmet becomes known as The Special—the one who will save the Lego universe from ultimate destruction. He gets help from a ragtag band of strangers including a bad-ass Goth chick who goes by the name Wyldstyle (an adorable Elizabeth Banks); Batman (Will Arnett, doing a Batman version of his pompous *Arrested Development* character, Gob); a makeshift pirate captain called Metal Beard (Nick Offerman); and the unflappably happy Unikitty (Alison Brie) which is—you guessed it—half unicorn and half kitty.

They must outsmart and outrun the evil President Business, better known as Lord Business, who wants the piece for himself to maintain order and separation between all the Lego realms. So yeah, he's kind of a fascist tyrant. But in the hands of Will Ferrell, he's also hilariously self-serious. President Business' right-hand man is the bi-polar Good Cop/Bad Cop (Liam Neeson), who dons whichever persona he must to get the job done and keep everyone in line.

The Lego Movie message of thinking for yourself and trying new things may sound a lot like the theme of *The Croods* last year, but it presents this notion in a much more lively and clever manner. A great deal of that has to do with the look of the animation, which is beautiful in its crudeness. While the images are computer-generated, they have the intentionally jumpy, rough-hewn look of stop-motion animation—as if the effects team had moved brick by brick painstakingly by hand to create the sensation of motion. Everything is made of Legos, from the people and vehicles to water and bullets. It is an endless joy to watch, and the fact that some of the pieces and characters' faces have a chip or a smudge here or there adds to the charm.

Just when you may start feeling like this [10] zippy thrill ride of a movie is exhausting you, it takes a third-act turn that you probably never would have seen coming. I wouldn't dream of giving anything away about it. But I will say that it's daring, profound and emotionally powerful in a way that caught me completely off guard—especially sitting in the theater with my 4-year-old son curled up in my lap.

A CLOSER LOOK AT
The Lego Movie   **MyWritingLab**

1. The reviewer, Lemire, summarizes the plot of the movie early in the review. What features of the movie does she decide to share or not share with the readers? What does she reveal, and what does she leave out of the summary? If you haven't seen *The Lego Movie,* did she offer you enough information to give you an overall sense of the plot?

2. With your group, discuss *The Lego Movie* if you have seen it. The movie met many common expectations of a typical movie for kids. But it also violated those expectations (in a good way) too. List three ways in which it met the typical expectations. Then, list three ways in which it bent the genre to be innovative.

3. Where would the ending of the movie appear if the reviewer decided to "spoil" it for the readers? How close does the reviewer get to giving it away, and how much did she reveal about the ending?

IDEAS FOR
Writing   **MyWritingLab**

1. Find three movie reviews on the Internet that show a mixture of responses to a particular movie. One should like the movie and another should dislike it. The third review can take a middle path. Then write a brief position paper in which you show both sides of the argument and express your opinion about whether the movie was award-winning caliber or not. You will need to see the movie to answer this question.

2. One of the interesting aspects of the movie *The Lego Movie* was the inability of critics to pin down its view of society. On one hand, the Lego world is the happy, bright place that most of us would expect in a movie marketed to kids (with an obvious toy tie-in). Yet, there's an undertone of skepticism and social critique, such as the ironic song "Everything is Awesome" and the instructions-governed universe of the Lego people. The movie becomes a criticism of some adults' desire to make everything perfect in their own lives and the lives of their children. Write a commentary in which you discuss the social tensions explored in this film. Do you think these kinds of social issues belong in a film marketed to children?

Sherlock Returns, Brilliant as Ever

MARGARET LYONS

In this review, Margaret Lyons discusses the popular British series Sherlock *that stars Benedict Cumberbatch as Sherlock Holmes and Martin Freeman as John Watson. In this review, watch how she critiques the show while also going deeper to discuss the impact that* Sherlock *has on its fans.*

It's been two years since we've had a new installment of *Sherlock*, so there's something extra thrilling about seeing that long coat billow anew behind Benedict Cumberbatch. When season three premieres on PBS Sunday night at 10, Sherlock's quips will seem quippier, his disdain for others more disdainful, and the bond between him and Watson even more powerful. Season two's "A Scandal in Belgravia" was about sex; "The Reichenbach Fall" about glory. The third season premiere, "The Empty Hearse," is about devotion. The people devoted to Holmes, the people to whom Holmes is devoted—and a little bit about fans who have devoted themselves to the show over the last four years.

At the end of "Reichenbach," we viewers knew Holmes had survived his supposed suicidal jump off a building (the only way to stop his foil Moriarty's evil schemes), but the grieving John Watson (Martin Freeman) knew no such thing. "Hearse" picks up two years later, with Watson still in a state of semimourning—as signified by a somewhat seedy mustache. He's also preparing to propose to his girlfriend, Mary (Amanda Abbington, Freeman's longtime companion), and one wonders if Watson would ever have been able to make room in his life for a significant relationship had Sherlock not been "dead." But the great detective is alive

(and the show has some fun teasing us with the hows and whys of his survival), and so the two of course must reunite—and there's a dazzling, Marx Brothers–esque sequence in a restaurant with Sherlock trying to surprise Watson by hiding in plain sight, even though this revelation will be quite painful for Watson, who struggled with issues of guilt and grief before he met Holmes. It's a quintessential Sherlock scene, one that uses a slapstick tone and impressive comic choreography to disguise the fact that something heavy is happening, like Moriarty's ringtone being the Bee Gees' "Staying Alive." Sherlock is all about how cleverness ameliorates cruelty. *Yes, I caused you tremendous and ultimately unnecessary emotional pain, but you gotta admit, I did it with style.*

That's the deal *Sherlock* strikes with its fans, too, and it's a deal most of us are more than willing to make. Sherlock (and *Sherlock*) is that good, we do forgive his callousness, and yeah, we'll wait for two years for his return and never let our fervor flag. In exchange, when the miracle happens and he (and the show) come back, he's as good or maybe better than ever.

Sherlock's two-year absence affected more than just Watson. Anderson, the Scotland Yard police officer who openly loathed Sherlock (and whom Sherlock loathed back), is now a major Sherlock conspiracy theorist, even organizing a group of fellow Holmes devotees who—before the presumed-dead detective reemerges—gather to share their occasionally crackpot ideas about how he could have faked his suicide. Given the group members' tendency to insert romantic moments into their stories, it's hard not to feel like this group is a stand-in for the show's actual obsessive fans who find moments of erotic significance in seemingly innocent gestures. (Or perhaps this club is meant to represent Tumblr in toto.) It's as if creator David Moffat is embracing and dismissing these fantasizing fans all at once—again, in keeping with *Sherlock* and Sherlock.

"The Empty Hearse" is funny and excit- 5 ing, heavier on the action than some other installments, but it also has a lot of work to do to move through Watson forgiving his best friend for faking his death. Freeman's performance has always been the emotional engine of the show, and in "Hearse" he's as powerful as ever. *Sherlock* can be a harsh and jagged show, with its zippy score, angry characters, jumpy editing, its perfect but almost-stressful use of technology (all those texts piling up on the screen), its sense of impending doom. The moments of softness or vulnerability tend to come from Watson, and that flips a little in "The Empty Hearse." Suddenly Sherlock is slightly vulnerable, and Watson's the one who's fed up. It's not a radical change, nor is it a permanent one, but it does add a richness to the season, another layer to Watson and Sherlock's deep relationship.

But there is one part of "The Empty Hearse" that threw me. In a moment of great distress (which I will not spoil here), Watson declares that Sherlock is the "best and wisest man" that he has ever known. Sherlock's certainly among the most interesting people one could know, the cleverest, and maybe the smartest. But Sherlock isn't wise. *Watson* is wise. Whether they realize it or not, Watson and Sherlock see themselves in each other throughout the show—what happens to one always happens to both, and Sherlock's death was in some ways Watson's death too. But, fortunately, now both are alive, and goddamnit, it's great.

A CLOSER LOOK AT
Sherlock Returns, Brilliant as Ever

MyWritingLab

1. In many ways, the BBC series, *Sherlock*, both satisfies and bends the mystery genre. In her review, Lyons points out how the audience's common expectations for the genre are met or challenged by this series. With your group, list three ways, according to Lyons, that *Sherlock* meets common expectations and two ways in which the series violates those expectations (in an innovative way).

2. As Lyons points out, any revival of the Sherlock Holmes mysteries lives and dies with the relationship between Holmes and Watson. With your group list five other mystery or crime movies in which the relationship between two characters is essential. Discuss why audiences like to see "buddy" relationships in these kinds of films.

3. Lyons' tone in this review is especially lively. With your group, identify five places where her voice seems especially strong. Discuss how she creates this voice in her review. You might use the "persuasive style" principles in Chapter 17 to help you figure out how she achieves this style.

IDEAS FOR
Writing and Discussion

MyWritingLab

1. Write a positive review of a television program that you enjoy. In your review, identify the genre of the program and figure out the common expectations that most people would have for this kind of program. Then, explain why you like the show and how it follows or bends the genre in new and satisfying ways.

2. On the Internet, find a negative review of a movie, restaurant, performance, or television show that you personally like. Write a refutation in which you argue against the reviewer's interpretation. Explain why you like this show, place to eat, or performance, even though it may not appeal to everyone.

1. With a group in your class, discuss a movie that you all have seen. What did you like about the movie, and what were some of its limitations? As you discuss the movie, take note of the issues that seem to be part of the discussion. What are some expectations that your group members seem to have in common? Are there any issues that some members seem to care about but others don't? When people disagree, what do they disagree about?

2. In class, discuss what you want a reviewer to talk about in a typical music or movie review. How much do you want the reviewer to reveal about the movie? What kinds of reviews do you find most helpful when you are considering whether to buy music? Do you like reviewers whose work reveals their personalities or do you prefer objective reviewers who seem to stick to the facts? Are there any movie, music, or book reviewers that you seem to trust more than others? Why?

3. Examine and critique the following passage, which is taken from a review of a Greek restaurant. Describe which aspects of the review work well. Explain how it could be improved so that it meets the expectations readers have for reviews.

   > Among the appetizers, everybody in the group agreed that the spanakopita was by far the best but that the hummus was not up to par. There was some disagreement about the entrees. Personally, I liked the chicken souvlaki and dolmades plate, but two members of the group preferred the "Greek Combo," which includes dolma, spanakopita, souvlaki, broiled scampi, and mousaka.

1. On the Internet, find a video advertisement that you can review. Most companies put their most recent advertisements on their Web sites, or you can find them on video sharing Web sites like *YouTube* or *Hulu*. Write a review of the advertisement in which you critique its effectiveness. Tell your readers why you thought it worked, failed, or just irritated you. Your review should run about two pages.

2. Choose a movie and write two one-page reviews for it. Your first review should be positive. Focus on your and your readers' common expectations and say mostly positive things about the movie. The second review should be negative. Focus on elements that would cast the movie in a negative light. Then, in a memo to your professor, explore how your shift from positive to negative changed your review and what you had to say about the movie. Could you reconcile these two reviews into one that is balanced?

3. Find a review on the Internet. The review can be about music, movies, television, or just about anything. In a one-page response to your professor, explain how the review works. Discuss its content, organization, style, and design. Did you find the review effective? What were its strengths, and how could it be improved?

Explore This

Now it's your turn to find some microgenres. There are several microgenres that are similar to reviews. Choose a microgenre from the list below and find three examples in print or on the Internet. How is the microgenre you studied similar to and different from a regular review?

Slam—a review of something you really disliked

Customer Review—a brief statement about a product you purchased

Complaint—a complaint to a company about a product or service

Synthesis—a review that summarizes what other reviewers have said

Star Rating—a rating for something (e.g., five stars, 1–10, thumbs up/thumbs down, rotten tomatoes) with a brief explanation of the rating

Write This

1. **Write a review for your campus newspaper.** Imagine that you are a reviewer for your campus newspaper or another local newspaper. You can review music, books, poetry, movies, video games, television, sports teams, or just about anything that you enjoy. Write a three- to four-page review of a subject you choose. Be sure to summarize your subject for your readers, who may not have seen, heard, or experienced it. Then discuss your subject based on expectations that you and your readers share. Explain to your readers why you are giving your subject a positive or negative review.

2. **Write an opposing review.** Find a review on the Internet that you disagree with. Then, write an opposing review. Your review should be written as a response to the original review, showing why you felt differently about the subject. Next, write a one-page cover memo to your professor in which you explain your strategy for rebutting the original review. Also, discuss why you believe someone might find your review of the subject stronger than the original one.

3. **Write a rave about something you *despise*.** Here's an opportunity to really challenge yourself. Think of something you have experienced recently that you absolutely loathed. You should choose something that other people would be able to experience for themselves—a book, a class, a sport, a restaurant, a vacation spot. First, as a brainstorming exercise, write down exactly what you hated about the experience, just to get it out of your system. Then put yourself in the position of someone who would have actually enjoyed the same thing. Write your rave from that imagined point of view, using as many details from your original brainstorming as possible. (However tempted you may be, don't get carried away by sarcasm or irony.)

Go to **MyWritingLab** to complete this chapter's exercises and test your understanding of its objectives.

Literary Analyses

In this chapter, you will learn how to—

`8.1`   invent the content of your literary analysis with critical reading strategies.

`8.2`   organize your literary analysis to highlight your interpretation of the text.

`8.3`   use an appropriate voice and quotations to add authority to your analysis.

`8.4`   create an appropriate design by following formatting requirements and adding visuals.

A literary analysis poses an *interpretive question* about a literary text and then uses that question to explain the text, its author, or the historical context in which the work was written. In a literary analysis, your purpose is to think critically about the text and offer your readers new and interesting insights into what the work means or what it represents.

Literary analyses interpret the text, analyze its structure and features, and examine it through the lenses of historical, cultural, social, biographical, or other contexts. An effective literary analysis helps readers understand what makes a literary work thought provoking, revealing, troubling, or enjoyable. These kinds of analyses also contribute to the larger scholarly conversation about the meaning and purpose of literature.

When writing a literary analysis, you shouldn't feel like you need to prove that you have the "right" interpretation. Instead, your literary analysis should invite your readers to consider the work from new and interesting angles, while showing them how a particular angle can lead to fresh insights.

Usually, you will write literary analyses for courses that feature creative works, such as English, language studies, cultural studies, gender studies, and history. However, other advanced courses, including those in the sciences, human sciences, and technology, are incorporating literature to help students better understand the ethical situations and cultures in which important historical or cultural shifts occurred.

Literary Analyses

These diagrams show two possible basic organizations for a literary analysis, but other arrangements will work, too. You should adjust these organizational patterns to fit your topic, angle, purpose, readers, and context.

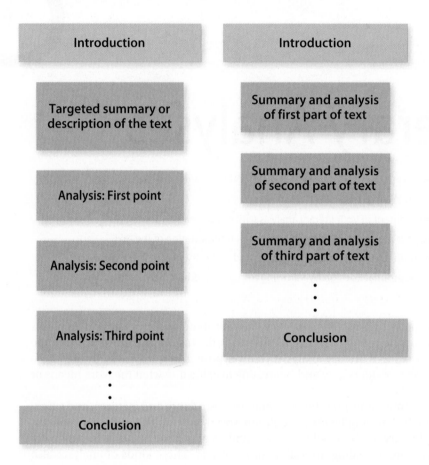

Literary analyses have these features:

- **An introduction** that identifies the literary work you are analyzing and its background. It should also state your interpretive question about the text and a main point (thesis statement) that answers the question.
- **Targeted summaries or descriptions of the text** that focus *only* on the events or features that play a key role in your interpretation.
- **Quoted material** taken directly from the text that moves your interpretation forward and illustrates your points.
- **Support for your interpretation** that shows how your interpretation makes sense and offers fresh insights into the interpretive question.
- **A conclusion** that discusses the significance of the interpretation.

ONE STUDENT'S WORK
Literary Analyses

Visit **MyWritingLab** to explore an interactive version of this essay.

Chalina Peña
Professor John Kutz
English 250
November 20, 2014

Making "The Story of an Hour" Make Sense

Surely, only a sick, ungrateful, and selfish person would ever find "monstrous joy" upon hearing about a loved one's death. In Kate Chopin's "The Story of an Hour," however, protagonist Louise Mallard is transformed, in the space of sixty minutes and few hundred words of narration, from a person who publicly experiences a "storm of grief" (128) to a person who alone in a room feels a "feverish triumph . . . like a goddess of Victory" (129). The *shortness* of Chopin's short story makes this transformation all the more surprising (and perhaps for some readers unrealistic), but it also invites us to read the work again and again, and then again. Some readers may find a simple, satisfying message to take away, but others will scour the story for answers that would explain why the transformation occurs. Is Louise is a monster or a reasonable and sane person, perhaps even a person like ourselves? Each time through the story, readers will recognize new details and clues, and perhaps will form new insights. However, with no completely satisfying answer emerging, many readers will ask, *why would Chopin choose to offer readers a narrative that clearly has a climax but no real resolution to the question about the main character?* Now, 120 years after its publication, the story still has the power to disturb us into considering the ways we judge and understand others and how we judge and understand ourselves.

If seen as a mere sequence of events, Chopin's story is pretty simple. A family friend and her sister Josephine understand Louise's frailty. Therefore, they try to break the news of her husband's death with care and tenderness. She reacts initially "not with a paralyzed inability to accept" things but with a "storm of grief" and an anguished "sudden, wild abandonment." Louise then retires upstairs alone and ponders the news, first sobbing "as a child who has cried itself asleep," then experiencing an "exalted perception" of newfound freedom to "live for herself" and "drinking in the very elixir of life" (129). Having composed herself,

> Begins with an intriguing feature of the work.

> Introduces the work and author with a very brief plot summary.

> States the interpretive question and places thesis statement at the end of the first paragraph.

continued

she returns downstairs and with the others only to experience another shock: Her husband has not died; he walks unaware through the front door. Then, she falls dead herself! For the characters in the story, the story is poignant but uncomplicated: "she had died of heart disease—of joy that kills" (129).

Readers, however, having witnessed the transformation process and knowing there's more to this story, try to find a reasonable interpretation. They know a "joy that kills" does not really explain what has occurred. But how do we explain what has occurred? We examine the story again to find an explanation that makes sense. This is something each of us human beings does when encountering a mystery: We try to figure out, for instance, why would a good and kind friend be unkind to you? Why did an international atrocity occur? Or, why does a character in a short story realize that her husband's death is a good thing? In fact, as brain scientist David Eagleman explains, we humans are hardwired to feel uncomfortable until we find explanations that makes sense.

> Minds seek patterns. . . . [Human beings] are driven to "patternicity"— the attempt to find structure in meaningless data. Evolution favors pattern seeking, because it allows the possibility of reducing mysteries to fast and efficient programs in neural circuitry. . . . [We are skilled] at spinning a single narrative from a collection of random threads. . . even in the face of thoroughly inconsistent data. (139–140)

Of course, Chopin knew nothing about the discoveries made by modern scientists, but she did understand human nature and how we are driven to search for meaning. I think she understood that even our own actions and motivations don't always make sense to us.

In our class discussions, many of my classmates hazarded interpretations that would make sense, but for some of us none of them was adequate. One classmate solved the mystery with "Chopin is just a lousy writer. She can't write a story that makes sense." Others concluded that Louise is an "ungrateful person . . . a *horrible* person. I hated her!" Still others suggested her transformation made perfect sense in the context of 1894: "In those days, women had no freedom and had to do whatever their husbands demanded. Of course women back then would want freedom from their husbands." "In *those* days," "back *then*"? More than a hundred years may have passed since this story was published, but human beings are still pretty much the same. We still strive to make sense of mysteries.

In fact, Louise herself struggles to understand what has happened to her. Her transformation comes from out of the blue. Even the narrator can't say what the "something" is that captures her:

Sidebar annotations (left margin):

Provides a summary of the key events.

Extends and deepens the interpretative question.

Includes concepts she has learned in her psychology course, quoting and citing the source.

Describes other possible interpretations and why they seem inadequate to her.

> There was something come to her and she was waiting for it, fearfully. What was it? She did not know; it was too subtle and elusive to name. But she felt it, creeping out of the sky, reaching toward her through the sounds, the scents, the color that filled the air. . . . She was beginning to recognize this thing that was approaching to possess her, and she was striving to beat it back with her will. (128–29)

Integrates quoted text and uses literary present tense.

Once captured by "this thing," Louise tries to understand what has happened to her. In her mind, she debates whether the "monstrous joy that held her" is justified, first acknowledging that her husband's face had "never looked [upon her] save with love upon her." In the end, though, she "abandons herself" to this mysterious feeling, not knowing and, it seems, not caring whether "this thing" comes from goodness and justice or ingratitude and selfishness. Louise, like the reader, has to figure that out.

A close reading of the story leaves us with no easy answers, and perhaps that is what Chopin wanted readers to ponder and remember from this vividly told and haunting story. As we try to make sense of others' motivations— whether close friends or figures in the news across the world—we are driven, as Eagleman explains, toward "spinning a single narrative" that will make sense. The same is true when we strive to understand our own private motivations and actions. Like Louise, I think, we are all "possessed," at least occasionally, by "somethings" that come from nowhere. We should search for answers, but Chopin's story reminds us that the things that motivate us are sometimes just mysterious.

Concludes by restating the thesis and then addressing broader issues that arise from her interpretation.

Works Cited

Chopin, Kate. "The Story of an Hour." *Writing Today*. 3rd ed., by Richard Johnson-Sheehan and Charles Paine, Pearson, 2016, pp. 128-129.

Eagleman, David M. *Incognito: The Secret Life of the Brain*. Pantheon, 2011.

Includes a Works Cited that identifies the sources she has consulted.

Inventing Your Literary Analysis's Content

The first challenge in writing a literary analysis is coming up with an interesting *interpretive question* about the work. As you read and research the text, look for evidence that might lead to insights that go beyond the obvious.

8.1 invent the content of your literary analysis with critical reading strategies.

Authors want their literary works to affect readers in a specific way. They rarely present straightforward simple lessons, but they do want to influence the way readers view the world. So as you are exploring the text from different angles, try to figure out what message or theme the author is trying to convey.

Read, Reread, Explore

If the literary work is a short story or novel, read it at least twice. If it is a poem, read it again and again, silently and aloud, to get a sense of how the language works and how the poem makes you feel. As you read the text, mark or underline anything that intrigues or puzzles you. Write observations and questions in the margins.

Inquiring: What's Interesting Here?

As you are reading and exploring the text, try to come up with a few interesting questions that focus on the work's genre, plot, characters, or use of language. The goal is to develop your interpretive question, which will serve as your angle into the text.

Explore the Genre. In your literature classes, your professors will use the term *genre* somewhat differently than it is used in this book. Literary works fall into four major genres: fiction, poetry, drama, and literary nonfiction.

Literary Genre	Subgenres
Fiction	short stories, novellas, novels, detective novels, science fiction, romance, mysteries, horror, fantasy, historical fiction
Poetry	limericks, sonnets, ballads, epic poems, haikus, ballads, villanelle, odes, sestinas, open verse
Drama	plays, closet dramas, comedies, tragedies, romances, musicals, operas
Literary nonfiction (or nonfiction prose)	memoirs, profiles (of people, places, events), biographies, histories, essays, nature writing, sports writing, religion, politics

While examining the text, ask yourself why the author chose this genre or subgenre of literature and not another one. Why a poem rather than a story? Why a short story rather than a novel?

Also, look for places where the author follows the genre or strays from it. How does the genre constrain what the author can do? How does she or he bend the genre to fit the story that he or she wants to tell? How does the author use this genre in a unique or interesting way?

Explore the Complication or Conflict. In almost every literary work, a key complication or conflict is at the center of the story. What are the complications or conflicts that arise from the narrative? How do the characters react to the complications? And how are these complications and conflicts resolved? Keep in mind that conflicts often arise from characters' values and beliefs and from the setting in which the characters reside. What conflicts do you sense in the story as you read? Are there conflicts between characters, between characters and their surroundings, between characters' aspirations, or between competing values and beliefs?

Explore the Plot. Plot refers not just to the sequence of events but also to how the events arise from the main conflict in the story. How do the events in the story unfold? Why do the events arise as they do? Which events are surprising or puzzling? Where does the plot seem to stray from a straight path? When studying the plot, pay special attention to the *climax,* which is the critical moment in the story. What happens at that key moment, and why is this moment so crucial? How is the conflict resolved, for better or worse?

Explore the Characters. The characters are the people who inhabit the story or poem. Who are they? What kinds of people are they? Why do they act as they do? What are their values, beliefs, and desires? How do they interact with each other, or with their environment and setting? You might explore the psychology or motives of the characters, trying to figure out the meaning behind their decisions and actions.

Explore the Setting. What is the time and place of the story? What is the broader setting—culture, social sphere, historic period? Also, what is the narrow setting—the details about the particular time and place? How does the setting constrain the characters by influencing their beliefs, values, and actions? How does the setting become a symbol that colors the way readers interpret the work? Is the setting realistic, fantastical, ironic, or magical?

Explore the Language and Tone. How does the author's tone or choice of words color your attitude toward the characters, setting, or theme? What feeling or mood does the work's tone evoke, and how does that tone evolve as the story or poem moves forward?

Explore the Use of Tropes. Also, pay attention to the author's use of metaphors, similes, and analogies. How does the author use these devices to deepen the meaning of the text or bring new ideas to light? What images are used to describe the characters, events, objects, or setting? Do those images become metaphors or symbols that color the way readers understand the work, or the way the characters see their world?

Researching: What Background Do You Need?

While most literary analyses focus primarily on the literary text itself, you can also research the historical background of a work and its author. The Internet and print sources are good places to find relevant facts, information, and perspectives that will broaden your understanding.

Research the Author. Learning about the author can often lead to interpretive insights. The author's life experiences may help you understand his or her intentions. You might study the events that were happening in the author's time because the work itself might directly or indirectly respond to them.

Research the Historical Setting. You could also do research about the text's historical setting. If the story takes place in a real setting, you can read about the historical, cultural, social, and political forces that were in play at that time and in that place.

Research the Science. Human and physical sciences can often give you insights into human behavior, social interactions, or natural phenomena. Sometimes additional research into psychology, sociology, biology, and other sciences can give you interesting insights into characters and events.

Organizing and Drafting Your Literary Analysis

8.2 organize your literary analysis to highlight your interpretations of the text.

So far, you have read the literary work carefully, taken notes, done some research, and perhaps written one or more responses. Now, how should you dive in and begin drafting? Here are some ideas for getting your ideas down on the page.

The Introduction: Establish Your Interpretive Question

Introductions in literary analyses usually contain a few common features:

Include Background Information That Leads to Your Interpretive Question. Draw your reader into your analysis by starting with an intriguing feature of the work. You can use a quote from the work or author, state a historical fact that highlights something important, or draw attention to a unique aspect of the work or author.

State Your Interpretive Question Prominently and Clearly. Make sure your reader understands the question that your analysis will investigate. If necessary, make it obvious by saying something like, "This analysis will explore why . . . ." That way, your readers will clearly understand your purpose.

Place Your Thesis Statement at or Near the End of the Introduction. Provide a clear thesis that answers your interpretive question. Since a literary analysis is academic in nature, your readers will expect you to state your main point or thesis statement somewhere near the end of the introduction. Here are examples of a weak thesis statement and a stronger one:

> **Weak:** Jane Austen's *Emma* is a classic early nineteenth-century novel that has stood the test of time.

Stronger: Jane Austen's **Emma** is especially meaningful now, because Emma herself is a complex female character whose passion for matchmaking resonates with today's socially networked women.

The Body: Summarize, Interpret, Support

In the body paragraphs, you should take your reader through your analysis point by point, showing them why your interpretation makes sense and leads to interesting new insights.

Summarize and Describe Key Aspects of the Work. You can assume that your readers will be familiar with the literary work, so you don't need to provide a complete summary or fully explain who the characters are. But you should describe the aspects of the work that are crucial to your analysis and that need to be brought to your readers' attention. You may wish to focus on a particular scene, or on certain features, such as a character, interactions between characters, setting, language, symbols, plot features, and so forth. Discuss *only* those aspects of the work that lay the foundation for your analysis.

Build Your Case, Step by Step. Keep in mind that the goal of a literary analysis is not to prove that your interpretation is correct but to show that it is plausible and leads to interesting insights into the text and related matters. Take your readers through your analysis point by point. Back up each key point with reasoning and evidence, and make connections to your interpretive question and thesis statement.

Cite and Quote the Text to Back Up and Illustrate Your Points. The evidence for your interpretation should come mostly from the text itself. Show your readers what the text says by quoting and citing it, or by describing and citing key scenes and events.

Include Outside Support, Where Appropriate. Other scholars have probably offered their own critical remarks on the text. You can use their analyses to support your own interpretations, or you can work against them by arguing for a different or new perspective. Make sure you cite these sources properly. Do not use their ideas and phrasings without giving them credit or quoting them. (Your professor, who is an expert in these literary works, will know what others have said about them.)

The Conclusion: Restate Your Thesis

Your conclusion should bring your readers' attention back to the thesis that you expressed in the introduction. Your conclusion should also point the reader in new directions. Up to this point in the literary analysis, your readers will expect you to closely follow the text. In the conclusion, though, they will allow more leeway. In a sense, you've earned the right to speculate and consider other ideas.

So, if you want, take on the larger issues that were dealt with in this literary work. What conclusions or questions does your analysis suggest? What challenges does the author believe we face? What is the author really trying to say about people, events, and the world we live in?

Choosing an Appropriate Style

8.3 use an appropriate voice and quotations to add authority to your analysis.

Literary analyses invite readers into a conversation about a literary work. Therefore, the style should be straightforward but also inviting and encouraging.

Use the "Literary Present" Tense

Describe the text, what happens, and what characters do as though the action is taking place at the present moment. Here are two examples that show how the literary present should be used:

> Louise Mallard is at first grief stricken by the news of her husband's death, but her grief fades and turns into a sense of elation.
>
> Many of Langston Hughes's poems recount the struggles of African Americans but are often tinged with definite optimism and hope.

When discussing the author historically, however, use the past tense.

> Of course, Chopin knew nothing about the discoveries made by modern scientists, but she did understand human nature and how we are driven to search for meaning.
>
> Langston Hughes was well known in his time as a Harlem Renaissance poet. He often touched on themes of equality and expressed a guarded optimism about equality of treatment for all races.

Integrate Quoted Text

Weave words and ideas from the literary text in with your words and ideas, and avoid quotations that are not directly related to your ideas. For example, you can include a quotation at the end of your own sentence:

> Louise reacts initially with an immense grief that conforms to what might be socially expected from any person who has just learned the death of a loved one: "She wept at once, with sudden wild abandonment, in her sister's arms" (652).

You could also take the same sentence from the story and weave a "tissue" of quotations into your words:

> Although Richards is "careful" and "tender" as when he "break[s] to her as gently as possible the news of her husband's death," Louise weeps "with sudden, wild abandonment," a reaction that conforms to society's expectations (69).

Make sure any sentences that include quotations remain grammatically correct. When you omit words from your quotation, use ellipses. Also, whenever you take a quote from the text, explain how the quotation supports the point you are trying to make. Don't leave your readers hanging with a quotation and no commentary. Tell them what the quote means.

Move Beyond Personal Response

Literary analyses are always partly personal, but your personal response is not enough. While your professor may encourage you to delve into your personal reactions in your response papers, your literary analysis should move beyond that personal response to a discussion of the literary work itself. In other words, describe what the text does, not just how you personally react to it.

Keep in mind that literary analyses are interpretive and speculative, not absolute and final. When you want your readers to understand that you are interpreting, use words and phrases such as "seems," "perhaps," "it could be," "may," "it seems clear that," and "probably."

> Louise seems to realize that her newly realized "exalted perception" would appear to others as "monstrous joy." That is why, perhaps, she chooses to remain behind closed doors until she can compose herself before opening "the door to her sister's importunities" to once again face her friends and family (653).

Designing Your Literary Analysis

Typically, literary analyses use a simple and traditional design, following the MLA format for manuscripts: double-spaced, easy-to-read font, one-inch margins, MLA documentation style (see Chapter 27). Always consult with your professor about which format to use.

8.4 create an appropriate design by following formatting requirements and adding visuals.

Headings and graphics are becoming more common in literary analyses. Before you use headings or graphics, ask your professor if they are allowed for your class. Headings will help you organize your analysis and make transitions between larger sections. In some cases, you may want to add graphics, especially if the literary work you are analyzing uses illustrations or if you have a graphic that would illustrate or help explain a key element in your analysis.

Design features like headers and page numbers are usually welcome, because they help professors and your classmates keep the pages in order. Also, if you are asked to discuss your work in class, page numbers will help the class easily find what is being discussed.

The Reading
Response

Here's something that happens more and more in courses in every college discipline. Your professor assigns a reading response as "informal writing." A literature professor might ask you to write about your first reaction to a poem to help you explore its meaning. An anthropology professor might ask you to describe your reactions to the rituals of a different culture. In the workplace, trainers and consultants often use informal writing exercises to help teams of employees explore ideas together—a kind of brainstorming.

Your professors may assign a wide variety of reading response assignments, but no matter what the specific assignment is, make sure you do the following:

Read the prompt carefully. Make sure you understand exactly what your professor wants you to do. Pay attention to the verbs. Are you supposed to summarize, explore, speculate, analyze, identify, explain, define, evaluate, apply, or something else?

Try out new ideas and approaches. Informal writing can be your chance to speculate, explore, and be creative. Be sure you understand and deliver what your professor expects, but be aware that reading responses can also provide opportunities to stretch your thinking into new areas.

Show that you have read, can understand, and can work with the material. Ground your response in the material you are being asked to discuss. When writing about a story or poem, come back to the text and provide quotes, summaries, and descriptions. If the reading involves a concept, make sure your response shows that you understand or can use the concept to address the prompt.

Branch out and make connections (if appropriate). Look for the broader implications and for connections with other issues from the course. With informal writing like reading responses, you're usually allowed to or even encouraged to take risks and speculate. If you're not sure whether your professor wants you to do this, ask.

WRITE your own reading response. Ground your response in the text itself by describing or summarizing aspects of the text or by quoting it. Then move to generating new ideas and insights, making connections between the text and something else (something you know about from personal experience). Because this is an informal response, speculate and take risks. Have fun exploring the text while you write your response.

Visit **MyWritingLab** to complete this exercise.

Reading response assignment

Here is an example of the kind of response prompt you might be assigned in a literature class. This prompt is about a poem written in 1896 by the African American writer Paul Laurence Dunbar (1872–1906). The professor's prompt follows the poem; the student's response is on the next page.

Paul Laurence Dunbar

We Wear the Mask (1896)

We wear the mask that grins and lies,
It hides our cheeks and shades our eyes,—
This debt we pay to human guile;
With torn and bleeding hearts we smile,   5

And mouth with myriad subtleties.

Why should the world be over-wise,
In counting all our tears and sighs?
Nay, let them only see us, while
      We wear the mask.   10

We smile, but, O great Christ, our cries
To thee from tortured souls arise.
We sing, but oh the clay is vile
Beneath our feet, and long the mile;
But let the world dream otherwise,   15

      We wear the mask!

Reading Response Prompt for "We Wear the Mask"

Specifies the use of at least two quotes.

Be sure to discuss concept of "mask" metaphor.

Write a response paper that is at least 400 words long and that incorporates at least two quotations from the poem. Paul Laurence Dunbar's poem renders a general social issue concrete and tangible with his central metaphor of "the mask." Examine this metaphor closely. Explain how it works in the poem and how it adds to the impact or meaning of the poem in terms of tone, theme, or overall message. Finally, speculate about whether you believe the metaphor is still appropriate in today's world, even though the poem was written over one hundred years ago.

The three key verbs are examine, explain, *and* speculate.

continued

A Student's Reading Response

Mateo Hernandez

When I first read this, it *sounded* kind of happy, almost like a nursery rhyme. So at first I thought the mask metaphor was kind of happy, because when you hear "mask," you think fun, childhood, and parties. And also there's the movie *The Mask* with Jim Carrey, which is pretty funny. But reading it a few more times, I noticed all those words that are the opposite of happy: "grins and lies," "human guile," "bleeding hearts," "tears and sighs," "tortured souls," and many others. So, this is not a happy mask at all. I also wondered

about who is the "We" in "We wear the mask." Then I noticed the picture of Dunbar and his life span. That made me think about my history class, where we're learning about the Jim Crow laws in America, from around 1875 to the 1960s, when whites passed laws that put blacks into incredibly brutal segregation. Bringing all these things together, the "We" and "the mask"

started to make sense. The "We" is "We black Americans" around 1896, when the poem was written. "The mask" is not a physical thing. It's a façade that blacks wear that makes whites *think* they're happy but really *hides* total despair: "But let the world dream otherwise, / We wear the mask." In 1896, blacks could not show even a hint of disobedience. So the black person, who has to act ignorant and happy, actually knows *more* than the white person who "dream[s] other-wise."

But why not just come out and say that racism and Jim Crow laws are hurting black Americans? With this metaphor, the poem is much more emotional and has more impact than just a straight argument. The message is more *memorable* because it gives us a human face. It's almost like a story inside the metaphor. The mask metaphor gives the poem more impact because it makes us see and feel something we might not have. It makes the message much more powerful.

But is the metaphor still appropriate today? You might say it's not appropriate because the Jim Crow laws aren't around anymore. Besides, everyone wears a mask sometimes because everyone faces situations where they can't show their real selves. But on the other hand, even today, certain groups have to pretend they're not angry about inequality and injustice because it makes some people say "Quit your complaining!" I know that this is true for Hispanics, and it's also true for other groups, like Muslims. People in power don't like to hear it. Sometimes it's still just the smart thing to do to wear "the mask," because most people just don't understand what it's like to walk in the shoes of someone else. Maybe they should read this poem. Maybe they're the ones Dunbar is talking to.

Here are some quick steps to get you going on your literary analysis.

READ the Literary Work at Least Twice and Narrow Your Topic

Make sure you're very familiar with the work you'll be analyzing so you can examine the text closely. If you have response papers or other notes, look at them closely, too.

STATE Your Interpretive Question

In one sentence, try to write down a few questions that you want to answer in your analysis. These will probably evolve as you draft your analysis and continue delving deeply into the text. This is just to get you started; you'll refine your question as you draft and revise.

INQUIRE and Do Some Research

Using your reading notes, decide what intrigues you most about the work. Then do some outside research on the text, its author, and the historical period in which it was written.

DEVELOP Your Thesis

Come up with a main point or thesis that answers your interpretive question. Your thesis will probably change and evolve, so just write down your best guess at this point.

DRAFT Your Analysis

Take your reader through the analysis step by step. Use targeted summaries and quotes to direct readers' attention to specific aspects of the text (not the whole text).

REVISIT Your Introduction and Conclusion

After drafting, go back to your introduction and refine your interpretive question and thesis. After reading through your analysis once more, go to your conclusion and make sure that it brings readers back to your thesis and then branches out in new directions.

DESIGN, Revise, and Edit

The design of a literary analysis is typically simple and straightforward. However, make sure you format the document the way your professor requests. Then revise by sharpening your topic sentences and making sure each paragraph stays focused on answering your interpretive question. Make sure you use the literary present tense and cite the text properly.

QUICK START GUIDE

The Story of an Hour

KATE CHOPIN

Kate Chopin (1851–1904), a writer of short stories and novels, wrote "The Story of an Hour" in 1894. During her lifetime, Chopin was sometimes criticized for writing "immoral" stories. More recent critics view her as an early feminist who explored themes of love, marriage, race, and the psychology of women. As you read, pay attention to the way Chopin paints a rich portrait of a character and works out a complete plot in a very short space.

Knowing that Mrs. Mallard was afflicted with a heart trouble, great care was taken to break to her as gently as possible the news of her husband's death.

It was her sister Josephine who told her, in broken sentences; veiled hints that revealed in half concealing. Her husband's friend Richards was there, too, near her. It was he who had been in the newspaper office when intelligence of the railroad disaster was received, with Brently Mallard's name leading the list of "killed." He had only taken the time to assure himself of its truth by a second telegram, and had hastened to forestall any less careful, less tender friend in bearing the sad message.

She did not hear the story as many women have heard the same, with a paralyzed inability to accept its significance. She wept at once, with sudden, wild abandonment, in her sister's arms. When the storm of grief had spent itself she went away to her room alone. She would have no one follow her.

There stood, facing the open window, a comfortable, roomy armchair. Into this she sank, pressed down by a physical exhaustion that haunted her body and seemed to reach into her soul.

5 She could see in the open square before her house the tops of trees that were all aquiver with the new spring life. The delicious breath of rain was in the air. In the street below a peddler was crying his wares. The notes of a distant song which some one was singing reached her faintly, and countless sparrows were twittering in the eaves.

There were patches of blue sky showing here and there through the clouds that had met and piled one above the other in the west facing her window.

She sat with her head thrown back upon the cushion of the chair, quite motionless, except when a sob came up into her throat and shook her, as a child who has cried itself to sleep continues to sob in its dreams.

She was young, with a fair, calm face, whose lines bespoke repression and even a certain strength. But now there was a dull stare in her eyes, whose gaze was fixed away off yonder on one of those patches of blue sky. It was not a glance of reflection, but rather indicated a suspension of intelligent thought.

There was something coming to her and she was waiting for it, fearfully. What was it? She did not know; it was too subtle and elusive to name. But she felt it, creeping out of the sky, reaching toward her through the sounds, the scents, the color that filled the air.

10 Now her bosom rose and fell tumultuously. She was beginning to recognize this thing that was approaching to possess her,

and she was striving to beat it back with her will—as powerless as her two white slender hands would have been.

When she abandoned herself a little whispered word escaped her slightly parted lips. She said it over and over under her breath: "free, free, free!" The vacant stare and the look of terror that had followed it went from her eyes. They stayed keen and bright. Her pulses beat fast, and the coursing blood warmed and relaxed every inch of her body.

She did not stop to ask if it were or were not a monstrous joy that held her. A clear and exalted perception enabled her to dismiss the suggestion as trivial.

She knew that she would weep again when she saw the kind, tender hands folded in death; the face that had never looked save with love upon her, fixed and gray and dead. But she saw beyond that bitter moment a long procession of years to come that would belong to her absolutely. And she opened and spread her arms out to them in welcome.

There would be no one to live for her during those coming years; she would live for herself. There would be no powerful will bending hers in that blind persistence with which men and women believe they have a right to impose a private will upon a fellow-creature. A kind intention or a cruel intention made the act seem no less a crime as she looked upon it in that brief moment of illumination.

And yet she had loved him—sometimes. 15 Often she had not. What did it matter! What could love, the unsolved mystery, count for in the face of this possession of self-assertion which she suddenly recognized as the strongest impulse of her being!

"Free! Body and soul free!" she kept whispering.

Josephine was kneeling before the closed door with her lips to the keyhole, imploring for admission. "Louise, open the door! I beg; open the door—you will make yourself ill. What are you doing, Louise? For heaven's sake open the door."

"Go away. I am not making myself ill." No; she was drinking in a very elixir of life through that open window.

Her fancy was running riot along those days ahead of her. Spring days, and summer days, and all sorts of days that would be her own. She breathed a quick prayer that life might be long. It was only yesterday she had thought with a shudder that life might be long.

She arose at length and opened the door 20 to her sister's importunities. There was a feverish triumph in her eyes, and she carried herself unwittingly like a goddess of Victory. She clasped her sister's waist, and together they descended the stairs. Richards stood waiting for them at the bottom.

Some one was opening the front door with a latchkey. It was Brently Mallard who entered, a little travel-stained, composedly carrying his grip-sack and umbrella. He had been far from the scene of the accident, and did not even know there had been one. He stood amazed at Josephine's piercing cry; at Richards' quick motion to screen him from the view of his wife.

But Richards was too late.

When the doctors came they said she had died of heart disease—of joy that kills.

A CLOSER LOOK AT
The Story of an Hour

1. What makes this a narrative and not just a sequence of events? In other words, explain how the plot moves from complication to conflict, tension, and resolution to hold the reader's interest. How would the reading experience and the story's significance have been different if the narrator had let it be known at the beginning that Louise Mallard dies at the end of the story?

2. Read the story again, this time highlighting those parts where the narrator provides details about Louise Mallard's character bit by bit. Notice where the disclosures of revealing details are placed. For example, we do not learn the main character's first name until close to the story's end. How does the author's sequencing of disclosures draw the reader into Louise's character?

3. Short stories often describe how characters change or come to a new understanding of themselves or their world. What does Louise Mallard learn in this story? How does her new understanding play a role in her death?

IDEAS FOR
Writing

1. Write a reading response in which you describe what you believe is the social or political message of "The Story of an Hour." Who were the readers that Chopin may have been writing for? What themes or questions did she want her readers to explore in the story and their own lives? What point do you think she was trying to make?

2. In a brief memoir, narrate and describe a significant experience in your life that you reacted to in an entirely unexpected way or in a way that others just couldn't understand. Within the memoir, explain what your reaction to this experience revealed or reveals about you.

An Enigma in Chopin's "The Story of an Hour"

DANIEL P. DENEAU

Daniel P. Deneau was a professor of English for many years. As you read his analysis of Chopin's short story, pay attention to the way he poses an interpretive question about the story and then carefully examines a single passage to help answer that question.

The much-anthologized "The Story of an Hour" (1894) is surely Kate Chopin's best-known piece of short fiction. Innumerable students, ranging from the very naive to the very sophisticated, must have grappled with the story in innumerable discussions and essays. As all readers should agree, Louise Mallard receives a great shock, goes through a rapid sequence of reactions, is in a sense awakened and then seems to drink in "a very elixir of life" (354), and finally receives another shock, a reversal, which proves lethal. Probably equally clear to all or to most readers are Chopin's economy, the significance of the open window and the spring setting, the power which she assigns to "self-assertion," and the bold dramatic irony with which the story concludes. About one issue, at least among readers of anthologies, there may be continuing debate: is Louise a normal, understandable, sympathetic woman, or is she an egocentric, selfish monster or anomaly? And, as more sophisticated readers may ask, is the degree of "self-assertion" or freedom that she thinks she has attained a real possibility in a world of normal human relationships? Obviously readers' preconceptions about love and marriage and independence will dictate different answers to these questions. At one crucial point, however, this relatively clear and realistic story becomes problematic, perhaps even enigmatic—that is, the passage in which Chopin attempts to account for the direct cause of Louise's awakening:

> There was something coming to her and she was waiting for it, fearfully. What was it? She did not know; it was too subtle and elusive to name. But she felt it, creeping[1] out of the sky, reaching toward her through the sounds, the scents, the color that filled the air.
>
> Now her bosom rose and fell tumultuously. She was beginning to recognize this thing that was approaching to possess her, and she was striving to beat it back with her will—as powerless as her two white hands would have been.
>
> When she abandoned herself [,] a little whispered word escaped her slightly parted lips. She said it over and over under her breath: "Free, free, free!" The vacant stare and the

look of terror that had followed it went from her eyes. They stayed keen and bright. Her pulses beat fast, and the coursing blood warmed and relaxed every inch of her body. (353)

This "something," this "it,"[2] which oddly arrives from the sky, exerts a powerful physical influence on Louise and leaves her with a totally new perspective on her self and her place in the scheme of things. In a limited space, and without the assistance of a psychological vocabulary, Chopin may have been forced to rely on the indefinite, the unidentified, which, as best we can judge, is some powerful force, something supernatural, something beyond the realm of mundane experience or the rule of logic.[3] If immediately after learning of the death of her husband Louise had gone through a rapid logical process leading to a celebration of her total freedom, she might have seemed to be a hard, calculating, and therefore unsympathetic woman. Or to put the point in another way: since she has neither the physical nor moral strength to "beat [. . .] back" her attacker, which she begins to recognize but sadly never names, her responsibility is abrogated. In addition, one of the problems presented by the passage is the fact that Louise meets the "something" with both fear and anticipation. Clearly what occurs is some type of sexual experience, one that at first seems, except for the anticipation, like a terrifying rape, but one that evolves into something sensually stimulating and relaxing, and, of course, spiritually illuminating. In short, a rape seems to have an ironic outcome.

There can be no doubt that the crucial passage becomes a fairly explicit description of a sexual union. One of the meanings of the verb "possess" is "to have sexual intercourse with (a woman)" (OED),[4] and this meaning was certainly known to Chopin, as illustrated by the climactic—that word, unfortunately, is inevitable—passage of "The Storm," the sexual union of Alcée and Calixta: "And when he possessed her, they seemed to swoon together at the very borderland of life's mystery" (595).[5] Moreover, the third paragraph quoted above does suggest coitus and post-coital reactions: the abandonment, the "slightly parted lips," the "keen and bright eyes," and especially the final sentence—"Her pulses beat fast, and the coursing blood warmed and relaxed every inch of her body."

With no male aggressor-partner named in the text, only a "something," readers naturally will speculate. For me, two possibilities exist—both supernatural—of which, time after time, I am reminded as I contemplate the passage: one is classical, pagan; the other, Christian. The former is Leda and the swan-Zeus, a potent, sinister force which creeps from the "sky," attacks, and engenders a world-shaking course of events.[6] But the passage is about more than fear, force, and sex; it is also about anticipation, pleasure, and ultimately enlightenment. Thus, I am also reminded of the descent of the Christian Holy Spirit,[7] who is associated with conception, renewal, empowerment, inspiration, enlightenment, and freedom.[8] Louise does indeed receive an infusion of knowledge from a source that seems beyond human understanding or even naming. Add to these subjective responses Chopin's "belief" that genuine sexual passion itself may help the blind see: after Edna Pontellier's first sexual union with Arobin, she has various reactions; however, "above all, there was understanding. She felt as if a mist had been lifted from her eyes, enabling her to look upon and comprehend the significance of life, that monster made up of beauty and brutality" (967).

"The Story of an Hour" lacks the kind of diagrammatic clarity that some readers may expect, mainly or even exclusively, as I have tried to suggest, because of one curious passage. Chopin's desire to transform her protagonist from a woman with a "dull stare in her eyes" (353) to one with "a feverish triumph in her eyes," a woman who carries

"herself unwittingly like a goddess of Victory" (354), required a force of exceptional intensity, a force as intense as a combination of a rape, a visitation by the Holy Spirit, and a sexual union—or, in short, a *deus ex machina*. It is no wonder that in a mere seven sentences this force remains perplexing, probably enigmatic. One final point, however, is perfectly clear: having experimented with one very condensed account of an awakening—the account of a mere hour—Chopin later proceeded to create one of the masterpieces of American Literature—the slowly paced, psychologically credible, many-staged awakening of Edna Pontellier.[9]

Notes

1. In one other notable place in her short fiction Chopin used the verb "creeping." See the sexually charged "The Night Comes Slowly" (366).

2. Madonne M. Miner recognizes the importance of the "something" passage (31), but she does not scrutinize it sufficiently. Mary E. Papke seems unclear to me: "The unnameable is, of course, her self-consciousness that is embraced once she names her experience as emancipation and not destitution" (63). Angelyn Mitchell observes that "freedom ravishes" Louise and, quite correctly, that the passage is "loaded with sexual imagery" (62).

3. Cf. "Athénaïse": "If she ever came to such knowledge [of her own mind], it would be by no intellectual research, by no subtle analyses or tracing of actions to their source. It would come to her as the song to the bird, the perfume and color to the flower" (433).

4. The editor of the *OED* adds a surprising note: "this sense [was] suggested in private correspondence in 1969 by Professor W. Empson." The meaning should have been commonly known much earlier.

5. Bert Bender finds the diction "wooden" and "ironically conventional" (266). I doubt that a similar charge could be

made about the crucial passage in "The Story of an Hour."

6. Recall Yeats' "Leda and the Swan," esp. 11.5 and 6: "How can those terrified vague fingers push/The feathered glory from her loosing thighs?"

7. Chopin would have been well aware of the Christian view of the Holy Spirit (Ghost). See in particular "At Chênière Caminada" (317) and *The Awakening* (893).

8. Various Epistles associate the Holy Spirit with freedom. See, for example, 2 Cor. 3.17, as well as Isa. 61.1.

9. After completing this paper, I was pleased to find Jacqueline Padgett's paragraph in which she refers to an "annunciation" (101) in "The Story of an Hour."

Works Cited

Bender, Bert. "Kate Chopin's Lyrical Short Stories." *Studies in Short Fiction*, vol. 11, 1974, pp. 257–266.

Chopin, Kate. *The Complete Works of Kate Chopin.* Edited by Per Seyersted, Louisiana State UP, 1969.

Miner, Madonne M. "Veiled Hints: An Affective Stylist's Reading of Kate Chopin's 'Story of an Hour.'" *The Markham Review* vol. 11, 1982, pp. 29–32.

Mitchell, Angelyn. "Feminine Double Consciousness in Kate Chopin's 'The Story of an Hour.'" *CEA Magazine*, vol. 5, no. 1, 1992, pp. 59–64.

Padgett, Jacqueline Olson, "Kate Chopin and the Literature of the Annunciation, with a Reading of 'Lilacs.'" *Louisiana Literature*, vol. 11, no. 1, 1994, pp. 97–107.

Papke, Mary E. *Verging on the Abyss: The Social Fiction of Kate Chopin and Edith Wharton.* Greenwood, 1990.

"Possess." Def. 3b. *The Oxford English Dictionary.* 2nd ed., Oxford UP, 1989.

A CLOSER LOOK AT
An Enigma in Chopin's "Story of an Hour"   MyWritingLab

1. What is the interpretive question that Deneau poses in this analysis? How does he set up this question?

2. What exactly does Deneau suggest happens to Louise? Do you find his interpretation persuasive? His interpretation certainly goes beyond the literal meaning of the text. Do you agree with him?

3. The author uses endnotes to make connections with other works by Chopin and with the comments of others who have written literary analyses about this short story. How do these endnotes help you understand Chopin's story or Deneau's analysis more fully? How do they enhance the author's authority or *ethos* as an interpreter of Chopin's short story?

IDEAS FOR
Writing   MyWritingLab

1. Write a rebuttal of Deneau's analysis. While it is true that there is no single correct interpretation of a literary work, any analysis needs to be supported and justified by the words in the literary text itself. Explain whether you think Deneau's analysis might be stretching too far to make its point.

2. Condense this literary analysis into a well-developed one-paragraph summary that provides an objective description of the question Deneau explores, how he explores it, and what he concludes. First, identify Deneau's interpretive question and restate it as clearly and directly as you can. Then describe Deneau's approach to exploring that question and his final conclusions.

1. In a group, consider how you could analyze a movie in the same way that you analyze a literary work. Start out by selecting a movie that most of you have seen or are familiar with. Then generate an "interpretive question" about the movie. Ask yourself, "What do I/we want to understand by going beneath the surface of the movie?" In a single sentence, write down your interpretive question, and in another single sentence, write down your thesis.

2. Ask each member of your group to bring in a short poem. Discuss the poem as a literary work by paying attention to its genre, plot, characters, setting, and use of language and tone. What intrigues you about each poem?

3. Find a literary analysis on the Internet. Point to specific places in the analysis where the author makes the following moves:

    a. Identifies an interpretive question
    b. States a thesis that addresses that question
    c. Examines the text itself to support the interpretation
    d. Goes outside the text (with information about the author, the social or historical setting, etc.) to develop the interpretation
    e. Provides insights that go beyond the obvious

1. Read Paul Laurence Dunbar's "We Wear the Mask" (page 125). Generate an "interpretive question" about the poem. Ask yourself, "What do I want to understand by going beneath the surface of the poem?" Focus on just one question.

    a. Address your interpretive question by discussing the specifics of the poem. Focus at first on the poem itself rather than what you might know about the author or the time it was written. Finally, come up with one aspect of the poem that makes a plausible case about its message, what makes it effective, thought provoking, revealing, or enjoyable.

    b. In a single sentence, write down your interpretive question. In another single sentence, write down your thesis.

2. Practice summarizing, describing, and quoting from Chopin's "The Story of an Hour." First, summarize that story as clearly and efficiently as possible in one paragraph. Second, rework what you've written to weave in quoted words and phrases that are particularly important to the summary. Be sure to use quotation marks and parenthetical citations to show which words are quoted.

3. Search the Internet to find literary definitions of the word "genre." Cut and paste those definitions into a single file. Now, look back at the definition of genre in Chapter 1, "Writing and Genres." How are the literary definitions of genre different than the one used in this book? Are there any similarities? In a response to your professor, try to reconcile these two definitions of genre in a way that makes both useful.

There are many microgenres that are similar to literary analyses. Choose a microgenre from the list below and find three examples in print or on the Internet. Using these examples, try to figure out the features common to this microgenre.

Explore This

Book Cover Blurb—a brief description that can run anywhere from one to five lines on the back of the book. A blurb tries to capture the spirit of the book, enticing potential readers to buy it

Movie or TV Episode Analysis—analysis of a movie or TV episode that uses the strategies and features of a literary analysis

Literary Review—a review that discusses the strengths and weaknesses of a literary work (novel, short story, or poem)

Imitation Piece—imitation of a literary work that uses the style, tone, themes, and structures of the original work (can be serious or humorous)

Literary Analysis Parody—a literary analysis of a literary work (or movie or TV show) that you really think is shallow and terrible but you have written it as if you think it's great art (using the conventions of literary analysis)

Write This

1. **Analyze a short story or poem.** Write a literary analysis of a short story or poem that poses an interesting interpretive question and offers an interpretive thesis that explains the work's message or significance or that analyzes its structure and features (character, symbol, setting, etc.). Be sure that you focus on the text itself for your interpretation.

2. **Create a multimedia literary analysis of a song or poem.** Drawing on a variety of media (images, sound, or text), create an electronic multimedia presentation of a song or poem. Choose whatever medium you are comfortable with (or that you want to learn), such as a podcast, Web page, or slide presentation. Combine these media to provide your audience with an experience that goes beyond the text and presents them with something new—a new insight, analysis, or interesting juxtaposition.

3. **Turn a review into a literary analysis.** Write an informal two-page review of a movie, a TV show, or a work in some other medium. Then transform the review into a more formal three- to four-page literary analysis using the strategies described in this chapter. Pose an interpretive question and state a thesis that answers the question. Quote and describe the text. Then explain the message or significance of the work you are analyzing.

Go to **MyWritingLab** to complete this chapter's exercises and test your understanding of its objectives.

9

Rhetorical
Analyses

In this chapter, you will learn how to—

`9.1` invent the content of a rhetorical analysis.

`9.2` organize and draft your rhetorical analysis.

`9.3` create a specific style that is descriptive and easy to read.

`9.4` develop a design with the use of visuals.

Rhetorical analysis is used to determine why some arguments are persuasive and why some are not. Advertisers, marketing analysts, and public relations agents use rhetorical analyses to understand how well their messages are influencing target audiences and the general public. Political scientists and consultants use rhetorical analyses to determine which ideas and strategies will be most persuasive to voters and consumers. Meanwhile, historians and rhetoricians use rhetorical analyses to study historic speeches and documents to discern why they were influential in their day and perhaps are still influential today.

Ultimately, the objective of a rhetorical analysis is to show why a specific argument was *effective* or *persuasive*. By studying arguments closely, you can learn how writers and speakers sway others and how you can be more persuasive yourself.

In your college courses, you may be asked to write rhetorical analyses that explore historical and present-day documents, advertisements, and speeches. These assignments are not always called "rhetorical analyses," but any time you are asked to analyze a nonfiction text, you are probably going to write a rhetorical analysis. Also, depending on your career after college, your supervisors may ask you to closely analyze your organization's documents, Web sites, marketing materials, and public messaging to determine their effectiveness. Your ability to do a rhetorical analysis will allow you to offer helpful insights and suggestions for improvement.

Rhetorical Analyses

Here are two possible organizations for a rhetorical analysis, but other arrangements of these sections will work, too. You should adjust these organizational patterns to fit your topic, angle, purpose, readers, and context.

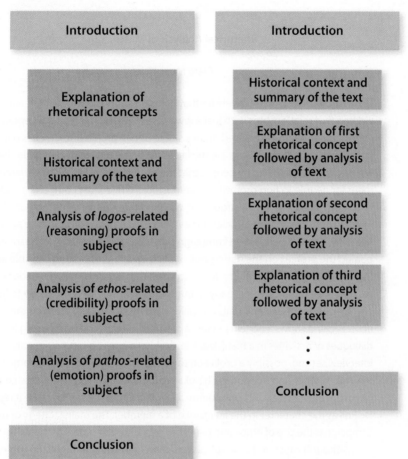

Rhetorical analyses can be written a variety of ways. Nevertheless, they tend to have some common features:

- **An introduction** that identifies the subject of your analysis, states your purpose and main point (thesis statement), offers background information on the subject, and stresses its importance.

- **An explanation of the rhetorical concepts** that you will use to analyze the subject.

- **A description or summary of your subject** that sets it in a historical context.

- **An analysis of the subject** through the chosen rhetorical concepts.

- **A conclusion** that states or restates your main point (thesis statement) and looks to the future.

ONE STUDENT'S WORK
Rhetorical Analyses

Visit **MyWritingLab** to explore an interactive version of this essay.

Rhetorical Analysis of Match.com

Clare Mengebier

Match.com is a dating website that helps thousands of single men and women find relationships with just a few clicks of the mouse. The concept of choosing people to date based off of a single online profile often makes people uneasy, yet 40 million people use these dating sites each year. So how do these websites persuade so many people that their service creates a relaxed environment for people to find promising relationships? While most companies such as eHarmony present a logical argument, claiming that there is a method used to match up couples based on scientific evidence, Match.com aims for the audience's heart. By creating a simple ad campaign that focuses on the unique personalities behind the profiles on the dating website as well as incorporating sensible advice from a familiar authority figure, Match.com creates a motto that persuades readers that even if they are not ready to put themselves out there, "It's okay to look."

Every advertisement in this campaign presents a simple picture for the audience. Each ad shows a certain person, a member of Match.com, engaging in various dialogues or activities in a blank black and white room. The setting appears to be an interview setting, possibly a profile on the website. The member's username is written in the corner and the slogan, "It's okay to look" is always present in the commercial or advertisement. Only one commercial differs from the rest because it replaces Dr. Phil as the character in the ad instead of a member. The main strategy of the campaign is the use of ethos and pathos to persuade customers to the website.

Although most of the people in this campaign show unfamiliar people, Dr. Phil is present in a few of the advertisements of the campaign, possibly as the informal "face" of Match.com. Dr. Phil has a high ethos because of his popular television show in which he gives advice to people about life and relationships. The creators of this commercial are assuming that the audience is familiar with Dr. Phil and assume that people rely on him to give the best advice to find love. By displaying his ethos, Dr. Phil is giving credibility to Match.com, unconsciously presenting the argument that if he is promoting the website as a reliable way to find love, then audiences will believe him.

Pathos seems to be the most important rhetorical strategy in a type of industry dominated by the main concepts of love and relationships. Match.com shows people that are vulnerable and are acting like themselves in order to kindle feelings of confidence to be themselves. Advertisers assume that people are nervous

---

The topic of the analysis and its importance are mentioned up front.

The thesis makes a claim that the remainder of the analysis will support or prove.

Examples and reasoning are used to support the analysis.

Topic sentences like this one make smaller claims that each paragraph will support.

or timid about entering this dating website, so confidence is considered as a vital aspect to persuade customers to go online. Match.com uses the phrase, "It's okay to look" to convince people that they can look at the possibilities without taking any risks and they do not necessarily have to dive into the process of searching for a long-term relationship just yet. Another tool that boosts the audience's confidence to become a member of Match.com is the process of showing people on the ads that are single members of the website, and they are all fun and attractive. This changes people's opinions about the type of single people one would usually expect to find on online dating websites. Match.com wants to convey the message that all types of people go onto the site looking for love and this concept is almost indistinguishable from the offline, dating world.

The perceived audience that the website is aiming at are single people of any age, gender, or culture. The large range of not only age and culture, but also personality types that Match.com is advertising to is evident in the sort of varying genders, races, ages, and personalities that the campaign includes. This tactic is used to reach out to all single members of society, one group at a time, and attract them to the type of personalities and faces that they would want to find on Match.com. However, advertisers must warrant that these types of people will actually be interested in finding members such as the ones shown in the advertisements, otherwise the entire function of the campaign is useless.

> Words like "tactic" and "campaign" are metaphors that suggest finding a spouse is a battle.

Match.com's main claim, "It's okay to look" uses a simple argument to persuade single people that taking the small risk of just browsing the website and trying something new could turn out to be a positive experience. This argument is backed up by the appearance of various fun, unique, and most importantly approachable characters included in the ad campaign. The underlying belief of the advertisers is that once the customers enter the site, they will find people they are interested in and proceed to join Match.com. The company recognizes that the biggest hurdle to attracting new members is simply getting people to browse their site in the first place. Once they are on the site and begin utilizing Match.com's matchmaking service, they are often hooked. The company's advertising campaign seeks to overcome fear potential customers have by demonstrating with a warm, well known television personality, Dr. Phil, and people with diverse backgrounds and warm personalities that Match.com is a comfortable place to seek companionship and a relationship. The campaign makes it easier for them to cross that invisible line separating those thinking about using an online dating service from those that actually do.

> The thesis is restated with more emphasis to bring closure to the argument.

Work Cited

Glasgow, Amanda. "Match.com Dedicates 2007 to Celebrating Member Individuality." Goliath Business News. 27 December 2006. The Gale Group. Web. 4 October 2009. http://goliath.ecnext.com/coms2/gi_0199-6093234/It-s-Okay-To-Look.html

Inventing Your Rhetorical Analysis's Content

9.1 invent the content of a rhetorical analysis.

When preparing to write a rhetorical analysis, the first thing you need to do is closely read the text you are analyzing. Read through it at least a couple of times, taking special note of any places where the author seems to make important points or perhaps misses an opportunity to do so.

Inquiring: Highlight Uses of Proofs

Now, do some analysis. When looking closely at the text, you will notice that authors tend to use three kinds of *proofs* to persuade you:

Reasoning (*logos*): appealing to readers' common sense, beliefs, or values

Credibility (*ethos*): using the reputation, experience, and values of the author or an expert to support claims

Emotion (*pathos*): using feelings, desires, or fears to influence readers

Rhetoricians often use the ancient Greek terms *logos, ethos,* and *pathos* to discuss these three kinds of proofs, so we have used them here. Let's look at these concepts more closely.

Logos: **Highlighting Uses of Reasoning.** The word *logos* in ancient Greek means "reasoning" in English. This word is the basis for the English word, *logic*, but *logos* involves more than using logic to prove a point. *Logos* also involves appealing to someone else's common sense and using examples to demonstrate a point. Here are some common ways people use reasoning to influence the beliefs and opinions of others:

If . . . then: "If you believe X, then you should believe Y also."

Either . . . or: "Either you believe X, or you believe Y."

Cause and effect: "X is the reason Y happens."

Costs and benefits: "The benefits of doing X are worth/not worth the cost of Y."

Better and worse: "X is better/worse than Y because . . ."

Examples: "For example, X and Y demonstrate that Z happens."

Facts and data: "These facts/data support my argument that X is true or Y is false."

Anecdotes: "X happened to these people, thus demonstrating Y."

As you analyze the text, highlight these uses of reasoning so you can figure out how the writer uses *logos* to influence people.

Ethos: **Highlighting Uses of Credibility.** The Greek word *ethos* means "credibility," "authority," or "character" in English. It's also the basis for the English word, *ethics*. *Ethos* could mean the author's credibility or the use of someone else's credibility to support an argument.

Highlight places in the text where the author is using his or her authority or credibility to prove a point:

Personal experience: "I have experienced X, so I know it's true and Y is not."

Personal credentials: "I have a degree in Z" or "I am the director of Y, so I know about the subject of X."

Good moral character: "I have always done the right thing for the right reasons, so you should believe me when I say that X is the best path to follow."

Appeal to experts: "According to Z, who is an expert on this topic, X is true and Y is not true."

Identification with the readers: "You and I come from similar backgrounds and we have similar values; therefore, you would likely agree with me that X is true and Y is not."

Admission of limitations: "I may not know much about Z, but I do know that X is true and Y is not."

Expression of good will: "I want what is best for you, so I am recommending X as the best path to follow."

Use of "insider" language: Using special terminology or referring to information that only insiders would understand.

When you are searching for *ethos*-related proofs, look carefully for places where the author is trying to use his or her character or experience to sway readers' opinions.

Pathos: **Highlighting Uses of Emotion.** Finally, look for places where the author is trying to use *pathos,* or emotions, to influence readers. The psychologist Robert Plutchik suggests there are eight basic emotions: joy, acceptance, fear, surprise, sadness, disgust, anger, and anticipation. As you analyze the text, highlight places where the author is using these basic emotions to persuade readers.

Promise of gain: "By agreeing with us, you will gain trust, time, money, love, advancement, reputation, comfort, popularity, health, beauty, or convenience."

Promise of enjoyment: "If you do things our way, you will experience joy, anticipation, fun, surprises, enjoyment, pleasure, leisure, or freedom."

Fear of loss: "If you don't do things this way, you risk losing time, money, love, security, freedom, reputation, popularity, health, or beauty."

Fear of pain: "If you don't do things this way, you may feel pain, sadness, grief, frustration, humiliation, embarrassment, loneliness, regret, shame, vulnerability, or worry."

Expressions of anger or disgust: "You should be angry or disgusted because X is unfair to you, me, or someone else."

Some other common emotions that you might find are annoyance, awe, calmness, confidence, courage, delight, disappointment, embarrassment, envy, frustration, gladness, grief, happiness, hate, hope, horror, humility, impatience, inspiration, jealousy, joy,

FIGURE 9.1 **Advertising and Emotions**

Advertising relies heavily on pathos *arguments, because there isn't much time available to persuade a customer to buy something.*

loneliness, love, lust, nervousness, nostalgia, paranoia, peace, pity, pride, rage, regret, resentment, shame, shock, sorrow, suffering, thrill, vulnerability, worry, and yearning.

Frequently, writers will not state emotions directly. Instead, they will inject feelings by using emotional stories about others or by incorporating images that illustrate the feelings they are trying to invoke. Advertisements, for example, rely heavily on using emotions to sell products (Figure 9.1).

Researching: Finding Background Information

Once you have highlighted the proofs (i.e., *logos, ethos, pathos*) in the text, it's time to do some background research on the author, the text, and the context in which the work was written and used.

Online Sources. Using Internet search engines and electronic databases, find out as much as you can about the person or company who created the text and any issues that he, she, or they were responding to. What historical events led up to the writing of the text? What happened after the text was released to the public? What have other people said about it?

Print Sources. Using your library's catalog and article databases, dig deeper to understand the historical context of the text you are studying. How did historical events or pressures influence the author and the text? Did the author need to adjust the text in a special way to fit the audience? Was the author or organization that published the text trying to achieve particular goals or make a statement of some kind?

Empirical Sources. In person or through e-mail, you might interview an expert who knows something about the author or the context of the text you are analyzing. An expert can help you gain a deeper understanding of the issues and people involved in the text. You might also show the text to others and note their reactions to it. You can use surveys or informal focus groups to see how people respond to the text.

Organizing and Drafting Your Rhetorical Analysis

At this point, you should be ready to start drafting your rhetorical analysis. As mentioned earlier, rhetorical analyses can follow a variety of organizational patterns, but those shown on page 137 are good models to follow. You can modify these patterns where necessary as you draft your ideas.

9.2 organize and draft your rhetorical analysis.

Keep in mind that you don't actually need to use rhetorical terms, such as *logos, ethos,* and *pathos*, in your rhetorical analysis, especially if your readers don't know what these terms mean. Instead, you can use words like "reasoning," "credibility," and "emotion," which will be more familiar to your readers.

The Introduction

Usually, the introduction to a rhetorical analysis is somewhat brief. In this part of your analysis, you want to make some or all of these moves:

Identify the Subject of Your Analysis and Offer Background Information. Clearly state what you are analyzing and provide some historical or other background information that will familiarize your readers with it.

State the Purpose of Your Analysis. Explain that the purpose of your analysis is to determine whether or not your subject was effective or persuasive.

State Your Main Point or Thesis Statement. Rhetorical analyses are usually used in academic settings, so they often include a clear main point or thesis statement in the introduction. Here are examples of a weak thesis statement and a stronger one:

> **Weak:** The advertisements for Buffalo Wild Wings are effective because they are funny.

> **Stronger:** Buffalo Wild Wings' "The Official Hangout of March Madness" campaign is successful because it humorously shows that B-Dubs is a place where funny, unexpected, and even magical things happen to the young people who are there.

Stress the Importance of the Text. Tell readers why your subject's rhetorical strategies are interesting or worth paying attention to.

Explanation of Rhetorical Concepts

After the introduction, you should define and explain the rhetorical concepts you are using to analyze the text. So if you are using *logos, ethos,* and *pathos*, you need to explain how these concepts are defined. For example, here is how a student defined *pathos* in her rhetorical analysis:

> *Pathos,* which involves using emotion to influence someone else, is a commonly used rhetorical tactic in advertisements aimed at teenage girls. Emotional scenes and images are used to grab the teen's attention and often make her feel something negative, like less confident, insecure, undesirable, unattractive, anxious, or dependent (Holt et al. 84).
>
> Of course, the product being pushed by the advertiser is then put forward as a solution to that supposed inadequacy in the teen's life. For example, as psychologist Tina Hanson points out, teenage girls don't really need a cabinet full of haircare products (73). The typical teenage girl's hair is already healthy, shiny, full, and rich in color. Yet, television and magazine advertisements from haircare companies, which make shampoo, conditioner, and dye, routinely show frustrated teens unsatisfied with their hair. Usually the message being sent to a teen is "You don't even know you need this product, but everyone else knows you do, especially guys." The images show a discouraged girl who risks losing friends or being embarrassed because her hair isn't perfect.

In your rhetorical analysis, you don't need to discuss all three of the rhetorical proofs mentioned in this chapter. Instead, you might decide to concentrate on just one of them, like *pathos,* so you can develop a fuller definition of that concept for your readers.

Also as mentioned earlier, keep in mind that other rhetorical concepts besides *logos, ethos,* and *pathos* are available. For instance, you could choose to study the metaphors used in a text, or perhaps its genre, style, or use of narrative. If you choose one of these other rhetorical concepts, you will need to define and explain that concept to your readers.

Provide Historical Context and Summary

To give your readers an overall understanding of the text you are analyzing, provide them with some historical background on it. Tell them who wrote it and where and when it appeared. Then summarize the text for them, following the organization of the text and highlighting its major points and features.

The aim of this historical context section is to give your readers enough background to understand the text you are analyzing. For example, here is the historical context and a summary of an advertisement for Red Bull:

> Advertisements for energy drinks rely heavily on emotion to make sales to college students. These unique soft drinks, which usually contain high amounts of caffeine and calories, began to grow in popularity in the late 1990s.
>
> Red Bull, one of the most popular brands, actually was invented in the 1970s in Thailand, and it was first exported to the United States in 1997 (FundingUniverse). From the beginning, Red Bull's advertising has been squarely aimed at college

Fig. 1. "Red Bull Gives You Wings."

students, telling them that they need to have extra energy to get through their hectic days. One of its recent advertising campaigns, which is called "Red Bull Gives You Wings," began in 2005 with simple hand-drawn movies like the one shown in Fig. 1.

In this advertisement, a bird relieves himself on a man who looks a lot like a professor. The man then drinks a can of Red Bull and sprouts wings. He flies above the bird, pulls down his pants, and proceeds to return the favor (offscreen, thankfully). The viewer hears the bird screech in horror as an image of a can of Red Bull fills the screen, but we can all imagine what happened.

During the span of the 30-second advertisement, the man transforms from being a seemingly helpless victim to a superheroic figure who can take vengeance on the bird. Drinking Red Bull is shown to be the way he gains this new power.

The length of your summary depends on your readers. If they are already familiar with the text you are analyzing, your summary should be brief. You don't want to bore your readers by telling them something they already know. If, however, they are not familiar with the text, your summary should be longer and more detailed.

Analysis of the Text

Now it is time to analyze the text for your readers. Essentially, you are going to interpret the text for them, using the rhetorical concepts you defined earlier in the rhetorical analysis.

There are two main ways to organize this section:

- You can follow the organization of the text you are analyzing, starting from the beginning and working to the end of the text. Apply the rhetorical concepts to each major section of the text.

- You can discuss the text through each rhetorical concept separately. For instance, if you are analyzing the uses of *logos*, *ethos*, and *pathos* in a text, you would separately discuss the text's use of each kind of proof.

For example, here is a discussion of *pathos* in the Red Bull advertisement:

Using Emotion to Sell Red Bull

Like much advertising aimed at young people, the Red Bull advertisement uses emotions to bring home its argument. In this advertisement, the use of humor is what gives the message its emotional punch.

Many young people feel like the professor in this advertisement, because they perceive that they are ultimately powerless in society. So when someone else treats them badly, young people usually assume they need to just take it. In this case, the Red Bull advertisement shows the bird relieving itself on the professor-like character. In most situations, the man would simply need to suffer that humiliation. But, he has a secret weapon, Red Bull. He drinks a can, sprouts wings, and humorously takes revenge on the bird.

The story itself is an emotional parable that reflects the life of most young people. The bird represents all the things in young peoples' lives that humiliate and embarrass them but that they cannot fix. The professor-like man, though not young, is a figure that students can relate to, because he is still in the educational system and seems powerless in his own way. So when he is able to actually use a product like Red Bull to take revenge, young people not only laugh but also feel an emotional release of their own frustration. The emotional message to young people is, "Drink Red Bull, and you can get back at all those people who crap on you."

The humor, coupled with the revenge theme, makes the advertisement's use of emotion very effective. According to Mark Jefferson, a professor at Penn State who studies advertisements, the use of revenge is very effective for reaching college students. "Students often feel powerless in a world that tells them they are adults but refuses to give them power. Advertisements that tap into that frustration in a humorous way are very powerful" (23).

In this discussion of emotion, the writer is applying her definition of *pathos* to the advertisement. This allows her to explain the use of emotion to sell Red Bull. She can now go on to discuss the use of *logos* and *ethos* in the ad. Or, if she has more to say about *pathos*, she might make her rhetorical analysis about the use of *pathos* alone.

The Conclusion

When you have finished your analysis, it's time to wrap up your argument. Keep this part of your rhetorical analysis brief. A paragraph or two should be enough. You should answer one or more of the following questions:

- Ultimately, what does your rhetorical analysis reveal about the text you studied?

- What does your analysis tell your readers about the rhetorical concept(s) you used to analyze the text?

- Why is your explanation of the text or the rhetorical concept(s) important to your readers?

- What should your readers look for in the future with this kind of text or this persuasion strategy?

Minimally, the key to a good conclusion is to restate your main point (thesis statement) about the text you analyzed.

Choosing an Appropriate Style

 create a specific style that is descriptive and easy to read.

The style of a rhetorical analysis depends on your readers and where your analysis might appear. If you are writing your analysis for an online magazine like *Slate* or *Salon*, readers would expect you to write something colorful and witty. If you are writing the argument for an academic journal, your tone would need to be more formal. Here are some ideas for using an appropriate style in your rhetorical analysis:

Use Lots of Detail to Describe the Text. In detail, explain the *who, what, where, when, why,* and *how* of the text you are analyzing. You want readers to experience the text, even if they haven't seen or read it themselves.

Minimize the Jargon and Difficult Words. Specialized terminology and complex words will unnecessarily make your text harder to read.

Improve the Flow of Your Sentences. Rhetorical analyses are designed to explain a text as clearly as possible, so you want your writing to flow easily from one sentence to the next. The best way to create this kind of flow is to use the "given-new" strategies that are discussed in Chapter 20, "Developing Paragraphs and Sections." Given-new involves making sure the beginning of each sentence uses something like a word, phrase, or idea from the previous sentence.

Pay Attention to Sentence Length. If you are writing a lively or witty analysis, you will want to use shorter sentences to make your argument feel more active and fast-paced. If you are writing for an academic audience, longer sentences will make your analysis sound more formal and proper. Keep in mind that your sentences should be "breathing length," neither too long nor too short.

Designing Your Rhetorical Analysis

9.4 develop a design with the use of visuals.

Computers make it possible to use visuals in a rhetorical analysis. Here are some things you might try:

Download Images from the Internet. If you are reviewing a book or a historical document, you can download an image of it to include in your rhetorical analysis. This way, readers can actually see what you are talking about.

Add a Screen Shot. If you are writing about an advertisement from the Internet, you can take a picture of your screen (i.e., a screen shot). Then you can include that screen shot in your analysis (Figure 9.2).

Include a Link to a Podcast. If you are analyzing a video or audio text (perhaps something you found on *YouTube*), you can put a link to that text in your analysis. Or you can include the Web address so readers can find the text themselves. If your analysis will appear online, you can use a link to insert the podcast right into your document.

Why not be creative? Look for ways to use technology to let your readers access the text you are analyzing.

"Red Bull Gives You Wings"

Energy drinks are a product that relies heavily on emotion for sales to high school and college students. These soft drinks, which usually contain high amounts of caffeine and calories, began to grow in popularity in the late 1990s. Red Bull, one of the most popular brands, actually was invented in the 1970s in Thailand, and it was first exposed to the United States in 1997 (FundingUniverse). From the beginning, Red Bull's advertising has been squarely aimed at college students, telling them that they need to have extra energy to get through their hectic days. It's current version of the "Red Bull Gives You Wings" slogan began in 2005 with simple hand-drawn movies like the one shown in Fig. 1.

Fig. 1. "Red Bull Gives You Wings."

In this advertisement, a bird relieves himself on a man who looks a lot like a professor. The man then drinks a can of Red Bull and sprouts wings. He flies above the bird, pulls down his pants, and proceeds to return the favor (offscreen, thankfully). The viewer hears the bird screech in horror as an image of a can of Red Bull fills the screen, but we can all imagine what happened.

During the span of 30-second advertisement, the man transforms from being a seemingly weak victim to a *superheroic* figure who can take vengeance on the bird. Drinking Red Bull is shown to be the way he gains this new power.

FIGURE 9.2 Adding a Screen Shot to Your Analysis

A screen shot is an easy way to put an image into your rhetorical analysis.

The Ad
Critique

An ad critique evaluates an advertisement to show why it was or was not effective. If the ad is persuasive, show the readers why it works. An ad critique can also help you explain why you like or dislike a particular type of advertisement. You should aim your critique at people like you who are consumers of mass media and products.

Today, ad critiques are becoming common on the Internet, especially on blogs. They give people a way to express their reactions to the kinds of advertisements being thrown at them. Here are some strategies for writing an ad critique:

Summarize the ad. If the ad appeared on television or the Internet, describe it objectively in one paragraph. Tell your readers the *who, what, where,* and *when* of the ad. If the ad appeared in a magazine or other print medium, you can scan it or download the image from the sponsor's Web site and insert the image into your document.

Highlight the unique quality that makes the advertisement stand out. There must be something remarkable about the ad that caught your attention. What is it? What made it stand out from all the other ads that are similar to it?

Describe the typical features of ads like this one. Identify the three to five common features that are usually found in this type of advertisement. You can use examples of other ads to explain how a typical ad would look or sound.

Show how this ad is different from the others. Compare the features of the ad to those of similar advertisements. Demonstrate why this ad is better or worse than its competitors.

Include many details. Throughout your critique, use plenty of detail to help your readers visualize or hear the ad. You want to replicate the experience of seeing or hearing it.

WRITE **your own ad critique.** While watching television or reading a magazine, find an ad that seems different. Then write a two-page critique in which you explain why it was or was not effective. Don't forget to scan, download, or take a picture of the ad so you can include it in your critique.

Visit **MyWritingLab** to complete this exercise.

The Axe Effect

Paloma Aleman

Axe Body Spray is known for its overly sexual ads that objectify women and insist that their products somehow build confidence in straight men. Now we are given their new campaign, which features five stereotypes of women that men supposedly have to deal with: Brainy Girl, High Maintenance Girl, Flirty Girl, Party Girl, and Sporty Girl. In the "flirty girl" ad, this stereotyped woman makes her boyfriend watch her flirt with people all night while he holds her things and is ignored. But it's alright folks: Axe knows a real man can handle anything that comes at him as long as he has his handy-dandy Axe products.

> Provides context by describing typical features of ads like this one.

The target audience for these ads, according to brand development director Mike Dwyer, is men ages 18 to 24. However, it appears that Axe is targeting a more specific group: *straight white men* between 18 and 24. We can see this because people of color are not featured or prominent in the ads, and the men only want women in these ads.

> The ad is summarized and shows how this ad is different from the others.

This ad uses pathos-based persuasion techniques. It uses humor by presenting a clearly outlandish situation. It also uses fear as the ad suggests to the male viewer he isn't a "real man" if he's not secure enough in his masculinity to keep his cool. Finally, it uses "promise of gain" too, implying that if you use Axe you will land gorgeous women and get lucky with the ladies.

> Describes the persuasive strategies used.

In the resolution of this Axe story, the "real man" is rewarded for keeping his cool in a way that Axe believes that any straight white man aged 18 to 24 would want to be rewarded—by going home with not one but two ladies. There's no danger in this adventure either, seeing as there is no possible way that two women could be attracted to each other or have the intention of being in a real relationship.

> Details help readers visualize the ad.

Through these advertisements, Axe is promoting the idea that they can help a straight white male aged 18 to 24 figure out his "lady problems" with stereotypes and body wash. However, their poor taste in humor is matched only by their poor judgment in marketing. Sure, men are their target audience for the product (and according to the commercial, getting rewarded for it), but let's get real. Women in the household are sometimes also going to be shopping for these products if the need arises. So even though Axe is obviously shooting for humor, shouldn't they consider that they might alienate a good part of their consumers?

> Offers an overall assessment of the ad's effectiveness, why it fails.

This humor tells us two things about Axe's way of thinking. First, Axe assumes that men make fun of women for their own amusement, and they believe that by doing the same they can connect better with their audience. Second, Axe sees women as mere objects rather than anything, or anyone for that matter, deserving of more attention than that which is sexual.

> Finishes strong with criticism of the ad's approach.

Need to write a rhetorical analysis? Here are some steps to get you going.

FIND a Text You Want to Analyze

Pick something you find intriguing. The best texts are ones that seem curiously persuasive to you (or not persuasive at all). You might also look for texts that are historically important.

HIGHLIGHT the Uses of *Logos, Ethos,* and *Pathos*

Read through the text, marking places in the text where the author uses reasoning (*logos*), credibility (*ethos*), or emotion (*pathos*).

RESEARCH the Context

Use a variety of sources to do background research on the text you are analyzing. Find out as much as you can about the author and the historical context in which he or she created the text. Use interviews or surveys to measure how others react to the text you are studying. Interview experts who know about this kind of text.

DRAFT Your Rhetorical Analysis

A rhetorical analysis typically has the following sections: Introduction (with a solid thesis statement), Definitions of Rhetorical Concepts, Historical Context and Summary, Analysis, and Conclusion. Draft each section separately.

CHOOSE an Appropriate Style

Your style depends on your readers, the place where your analysis will appear, and the text you are analyzing. Use ample details and good pacing to match your analysis's style with its potential place of publication.

DESIGN Your Rhetorical Analysis

Some graphics, especially screen shots, would make the text you are analyzing easier for readers to understand. If you want to do something more advanced, you might try creating a Web site or an audio or video podcast to an on-screen text.

REVISE and Edit

You have gone this far. Now finish the job. Do some revising and editing to make your rhetorical analysis shine. Look for any inconsistencies. Fill out places where more information might be helpful.

The Courage of Turtles

EDWARD HOAGLAND

On pages 156–158 below, you will find a rhetorical analysis of "The Courage of Turtles," an essay written by nature writer Edward Hoagland. The rhetorical analysis was written by Adam Regn Arvidson. You should read this essay first. Then, read Arvidson's analysis of it. As you are reading "The Courage of Turtles," pay attention to Hoagland's use of rhetorical strategies to persuade and move you. Then, when you read Arvidson's analysis, see if you agree with his interpretation of this classic essay.

Turtles are a kind of bird with the governor turned low. With the same attitude of removal, they cock a glance at what is going on, as if they need only to fly away. Until recently they were also a case of virtue rewarded, at least in the town where I grew up, because, being humble creatures, there were plenty of them. Even when we still had a few bobcats in the woods the local snapping turtles, growing up to forty pounds, were the largest carnivores. You would see them through the amber water, as big as greeny wash basins at the bottom of the pond, until they faded into the inscrutable mud as if they hadn't existed at all.

When I was ten I went to Dr. Green's Pond, a two-acre pond across the road. When I was twelve I walked a mile or so to Taggart's Pond, which was lusher, had big water snakes and a waterfall; and shortly after that I was bicycling way up to the adventuresome vastness of Mud Pond, a lake sized body of water in the reservoir system of a Connecticut city, possessed of cat-backed little islands and empty shacks and a forest of pines and hardwoods along the shore. Otters, foxes, and mink left their prints on the bank; there were pike and perch. As I got older, the estates and forgotten back lots in town were parceled out and sold for nice prices, yet, though the woods had shrunk, it seemed that fewer people walked in the woods. The new residents didn't know how to find them. Eventually, exploring, they did find them, and it required some ingenuity and doubling around on my part to go for eight miles without meeting someone. I was grown by now, I lived in New York, and that's what I wanted to do on the occasional weekends when I came out.

Since Mud Pond contained drinking water I had felt confident nothing untoward would happen there. For a long while the developers stayed away, until the drought of the mid-1960s. This event, squeezing the edges in, convinced the local water company that the pond really wasn't a necessity as a catch basin, however; so they bulldozed a hole in the earthen dam, bulldozed the banks to fill in the bottom, and landscaped the flow of water that remained to wind like an English brook and provide a domestic view for the houses which were planned. Most of the painted turtles of Mud Pond, who had been inaccessible as they sunned on their rocks, wound up in boxes in boys' closets within a matter of days. Their footsteps in the dry leaves gave them away as they wandered forlornly. The snappers and the little musk turtles, neither of whom leave the water except once a year to lay their eggs, dug into the drying mud for another siege of hot weather, which they were accustomed to doing whenever the pond got low. But this time it was low for good; the mud baked over them and slowly entombed them. As for the ducks,

a bin on the sidewalk to desiccate. Instead, he himself begins to find that turtle's "unrelenting presence exasperating" and he throws it into the Hudson. Hoagland describes how he comes to realize this will be certain death for the Diamondback, but he admits that "since, short of diving in after him, there was nothing I could do, I walked away."

Importantly, before that concluding statement, Hoagland describes the turtle as seeming "surprised when I tossed him in" and "afraid as he bobbed about on top of the water, looking up at me from ten feet below." Because of the personification, Hoagland's departure seems cruel, though he describes it in the same matter-of-fact way he describes snappers entombed in mud and baby turtles crushed by their own shells.

In all of these stories, Hoagland complicates who the villain is. There are plenty of people to indict—the developers, the water company, the artist, the arcade owner, the fish shop owner, himself—but Hoagland instead focuses on what happens to the turtles. By doing so, we readers are left to consider the rest, and to ask ourselves whether we care about what happens to turtles (and, by extension, other species), and to wonder how we might treat a turtle if and when we encounter one. The wrenching imagery is there (snapping turtles gradually suffocating in the mud, little painted babies stuck forever in baby-sized shells, a fully realized turtle individual abandoned under a pier in New York), but it is never accompanied by the implications of or reasons for those images. This is careful criticism of human actions, which leaves much up to the reader.

I love a good rant now and then. But the image of that little Diamondback looking pleadingly up at Mr. Hoagland as the man strides away—that sticks with me.

A CLOSER LOOK AT
Nature Writing in America: Criticism Through Imagery
MyWritingLab

1. Find the thesis statements in the introduction and conclusion of this rhetorical analysis. With your group, compare these two thesis statements and discuss whether they are effective. Do they establish a claim that the rhetorical analysis proves or supports? Does the concluding thesis statement express the analysis' main idea with more emphasis?

2. Arvidson believes that Hoagland's "The Courage of Turtles" is about turtles only on its surface. What does he think Hoagland's essay is really about?

With your group, find three places in the rhetorical analysis where Arvidson reveals what he believes is the underlying message in Hoagland's essay.

3. Arvidson uses stylistic techniques to establish his own tone, especially with words like "wrenching" and "suffocating." Underline the words that are related or synonyms to these words. With your group, discuss how Arvidson uses clusters of these words to create a consistent tone in this rhetorical analysis.

IDEAS FOR
Writing and Discussion
MyWritingLab

1. Write a rhetorical analysis of an argument of your choice. In your analysis, specifically pay attention to how the author is trying to influence your emotions (*pathos*). Explore at least three different emotions that play an important role in this argument.

2. Write a review of a book or movie that, as Arvidson says, "sticks with you." In your review explain why this particular text or film haunts you in some way.

1. With a group in your class, discuss the ways people try to persuade you. How do family members try to persuade you? How do your friends try to persuade you? In what ways do their persuasive strategies differ from the ways advertisers try to persuade people?

2. List some ways in which people try to use their credibility (*ethos*) or emotion (*pathos*) to persuade others. Supposedly, using reason (*logos*) is the most reliable way to persuade someone, and yet we use credibility and emotion all the time to get our points across. Why? When are arguments from credibility and emotion even more persuasive than arguments that rely on reason?

3. With a group, make a list of your favorite five commercials on television and a list of five commercials you cannot stand. Why do people in your group find some of these commercials interesting and worth watching? Why are some commercials so irritating that you want to turn the television off? As a group, create a list of ten do's and don'ts of advertising to college students.

1. Find an advertisement in a magazine that you think is persuasive (or not). Then write a one-page analysis of the advertisement in which you discuss why you think it is effective (or not). Look closely at its uses of reasoning, credibility, and emotion. What kinds of support does the advertiser rely on most? What do these rhetorical strategies say about the people the advertiser is targeting?

2. Imagine that a political candidate has hired you to explain how to persuade college students to vote for him or her. The candidate sees college students as very important, but is frustrated by some students' ability to see through the political spin. In a one- to two-page brief, explain what college students find persuasive these days and what kinds of message would get them to go to the polls.

3. Find a rhetorical analysis on the Internet that you can study. These documents are rarely called "rhetorical analyses." Instead, they tend to be critiques of advertisements, speeches, or documents. You can find good examples on Web sites like Slate.com or the *New York Times* Web site (nytimes.com). Write a one-page discussion in which you study the organization, style, and design of the rhetorical analysis. How does it work? What kinds of rhetorical elements does the reviewer pay attention to? Do you agree with the reviewer's analysis?

Hey. Go find your own microgenres. Choose a microgenre from the list below and find three examples in print or on the Internet. Use these examples to come up with your own guidelines for writing one of these microgenres, which are similar to a rhetorical analysis.

Ad Buster—demonstrates whether an ad's claims are true or false

Critique—brief discussion of a recent speech by a public figure

Song Analysis—exploration of the rhetorical meaning of a song

Ad Report Card—grading of advertisements with brief explanation of grade

Pundit's Response—partisan review of a speech by a candidate

1. **Analyze a text.** Choose a historical, nonfiction text you find interesting and write a rhetorical analysis of it. Your analysis should define the rhetorical concepts you will use to study the document. It should summarize the text and offer some historical background on it. Then offer a close analysis of the text, explaining why it is or is not effective.

2. **Analyze something else as a rhetorical text.** Find something other than a written text for your rhetorical analysis. You could study the architecture of a building, the design of a sculpture, the way someone dresses, or perhaps how someone acts. Using the rhetorical concepts of *logos*, *ethos*, and *pathos*, discuss how designs or people can be persuasive in nonverbal ways. Write a paper or create a web site in which you explain the ways in which reason, credibility, and emotion can be conveyed without using words.

3. **Critique an advertisement or advertising campaign.** Choose an advertisement or a series of advertisements that you enjoy or detest. Then write a rhetorical analysis in which you explain why the ad or series is effective or ineffective. You should embed a visual, like a screen shot, scan, or video, somewhere in your analysis so your readers can see what you are analyzing.

Go to **My WritingLab** to complete this chapter's
exercises and test your understanding of its objectives.

Commentaries

In this chapter, you will learn how to—

10.1 invent the content of your commentary by listening carefully.

10.2 organize your commentary to help the readers find important information.

10.3 use emotion and character to add style and energy to an argument.

10.4 design your commentary to enhance its message.

Commentaries are used to discuss issues and events that are currently in the news. They give you the opportunity to offer a new perspective about what is happening in the world around you.

When writing a commentary, you are usually trying to add something new to an ongoing public conversation. Your goal is to convince your readers to agree with you or at least understand your point of view. Meanwhile, readers of commentaries want to grasp the issue under discussion and understand the author's angle quickly and easily. They want to learn something new and figure out how someone else views an important issue. To catch their attention, a commentary needs to snap, making its point quickly and memorably.

Many college writing assignments are forms of commentary. Your professors will ask you to write your opinions about current events or describe your reactions to a reading. You may be asked to take a stand on an issue or consider opposing sides of a controversy. In upper-level courses, professors often assign opinion pieces so students can demonstrate that they have a firm grasp on a subject and are able to express what they believe.

You will likely find plenty of opportunities to write commentaries in your career. Editorials, op-ed essays, and letters to the editor are regular features of news Web sites, newspapers, and magazines. Meanwhile, blogs and social networking sites like Facebook, Instagram, and Tumblr allow people to write commentaries on current events and the world around them.

Commentaries

This diagram shows a basic organization for a commentary. When writing a commentary, you should explain the current event or issue. Then offer support for your opinion. Other arrangements can work well, too, so you should alter this organization to fit your topic, angle, purpose, readers, and context.

Introduction

Explain the current event or issue

Support for your argument

Support for your argument

⋮

Clarification of your argument

Conclusion

Commentaries take a new angle on a timely topic and back up claims with sound reasoning and solid evidence. They include some or all of these features:

- **A topic** based on current events or current issues.
- **An introduction** that immediately engages the reader by clearly announcing the *issue* under examination, the writer's thesis, and the angle he or she will take on this topic.
- **An explanation of the current event or issue** that reviews what happened and the ongoing conversation about it.
- **An argument for a specific position** that includes reasoning, evidence, examples, and observations.
- **A clarification** that qualifies the argument, avoiding the tendency to overgeneralize or oversimplify the topic.
- **A conclusion** that offers an overall assessment of the issue, highlights its importance to readers, and looks to the future.

ONE STUDENT'S WORK
Commentaries

Visit **MyWritingLab** to explore an interactive version of this essay.

Why My Generation Doesn't Care About Performance Enhancement

David Meany

Steroids in sports might come as a big shock to most of America, but not to my generation. Here's why. When it comes to sports stars, Hollywood celebrities, and political leaders, my generation (I'm 18 years old) has very low expectations. It's not that we're cynical or completely jaded; it's just that we don't hold these people up as role models. We don't really care if their morals are pure. We would say that we're simply realistic, that we see the world as it is. These celebrities— politicians, movie and TV stars, and, yes, sports figures—do whatever it takes to get ahead. The rest of us are different.

> Identifies the topic, purpose, angle, and thesis.

Let me back up just a little. I'm a huge baseball fan and always have been. I love baseball's history, in fact, all of sports history. Way back in grade school, when it was time to do a book report, I'd find a sports biography: Babe Ruth, Cal Ripken, Babe Didrikson, Roy Campanella, Joe Namath, Julius "Dr. J" Erving. Even nonhuman sports stars, like Sea Biscuit and Dan Patch, made great reads and reports. I grew up obsessed with Cal Ripken and his quest to break Lou Gehrig's record for consecutive games played. When I was younger and had more time, I could tell you the starting lineup and batting order for every Major League baseball team. So, yes, I was a total baseball nerd.

So now Barry Bonds and Roger Clemens have been caught shooting up, or creaming up, or doing whatever athletes do nowadays to get those steroids into their systems and build muscle, giving them strength and stamina that no steroid-free human could ever hope for. Talking heads on ESPN express outrage (Bryant and Quinn). Sports radio personalities howl in disgust. Even eggheads like commentator George Will moan about a "stain on baseball" (A31). Meanwhile, the Mitchell Report, a tell-all treatise written for the Commissioner of Baseball, says that investigations are "critical to effectively identifying and disciplining players who continue to violate Major League Baseball's rules and policies" (286).

> Explains the current issue and reviews the ongoing conversation.

And you know what, I don't care, and most of my generation doesn't care because we're more realistic than older generations. Some might say we're more cynical, but it's a question of expectations. We expect our celebrities and leaders to have low ethical standards.

continued

Uses reasoning and examples to support his argument.

Having low ethical standards, doing whatever it takes, that's how people get to be prominent figures in the first place. A person still has to work hard, but a person has to be willing to succeed "at any cost" if they want to really make it big. Look at our recent presidents and members of Congress. You can't stay out of the gutter and make it through an election successfully. Barack Obama and John McCain tried, but they ended up slinging the mud. Look at our Hollywood celebrities, like Paris Hilton, Justin Timberlake, and Lindsay Lohan. Sure, they have talent, but lots of people have talent, maybe even more talent than the stars who "make it." But not everyone has the will to succeed at any cost. That's how people get to be really successful. They're not normal people. Look what happens to celebrities between films or concerts: they're exposed as drug-using, law-breaking creeps. A little sunshine reveals some very dark corners.

I don't know if it's always been that way, or if scandals are just more out in the open these days. The Internet and other never-ending news shows have made it easier to uncover celebrity secrets, and harder to maintain the myth that those who have made it got there fair and square. We know better. I think we're just a little more realistic than people were a generation back.

Americans of my generation just don't expect their sports figures, Hollywood celebrities, and political leaders to be pure and free from the taint of scandal and unfair play. We know that these people probably abide by the credo that "If you're not cheatin', you're not trying." These people are not our heroes and don't deserve to be. They know it, and we know it.

Clarifies and qualifies his position.

I'm not saying we are a cynical generation, just that we are cynical about one thing in particular: celebrities of all kinds. When it comes to how we expect ourselves to behave, our standards are as high as any generation's. We expect ourselves, for the most part, to abide by common decency and commonsense values. My friends and I (and most of my generation) believe in fair play and honesty, and we expect the same from the people we have to deal with. For example, we play by the rules (most of us) when it comes to academics, too. Most of us don't cheat; most of us look down on people who do.

Concludes by restating the main point.

I'm talking about the people who really make it big. I don't trust them. I don't look up to them to help me figure out how to live my life. They're not my heroes, and that's just fine with me. It's just the way America works right now. We look elsewhere to find out how to live. We're pretty smart that way. I think we're a little more savvy about these things than previous celebrity-worshipping generations of Americans.

Works Cited

Bryant, Howard, and T.J. Quinn. "Has MLB Changed Since the Mitchell Report?" *ESPN*, 4 Mar. 2008, espn.go.com/videohub/video/clip?id=3765695&categoryid=0.

Mitchell, George. *Report to the Commissioner of Baseball of an Independent Investigation into the Illegal Use of Steroids and Other Performance Enhancing Substances by Players in Major League Baseball.* Office of the Commissioner of Baseball, 2007.

Will, George. "A Stain on Baseball." *The Washington Post*, 8 Dec. 2004, p. A31.

Inventing Your Commentary's Content

To start, you need a good topic. Commentaries are usually written in response to events that are currently happening. So watch the news, read Web sites, or search newspapers and magazines to find an event or issue that people are talking about. Choose a topic you personally care about so that you can contribute your own views to the general discussion.

10.1 invent the content of your commentary by listening carefully.

Inquiring: Finding Out What You Already Know

A great way to get your ideas out there is to play the Believing and Doubting Game, which can help you see different sides of an issue and find an angle that is uniquely your own:

Believing. Begin by studying one side of your topic from the perspective of a true believer. Assume that this side is completely correct and that all assertions—even if they are contradictory—are valid. Then freewrite or brainstorm for five minutes to figure out what kinds of arguments a true believer might come up with. What evidence might support this side of the argument? When would the believer's side make the most sense? Why is this argument so obvious to someone who already believes it to be true?

Doubting. Do another five-minute freewrite or brainstorm in which you look for weaknesses in the believer's argument that you could exploit. What are you most skeptical about? What kinds of weaknesses do people tend to overlook with this issue? If you wanted to undermine what others believe, what would you point to? What would be the worst possible aftereffects if people were wrong about this issue or they failed in some way? If you did exactly what the believers think should be done, what unintended consequences might occur?

Synthesizing. Finally, put the true believer and the true doubter at the two ends of a spectrum and figure out where you personally stand on this issue. After believing and then doubting, you will better understand both sides of the issue. You should also be able to figure out your angle on this topic—that is, your personal point of view. What are the major issues that separate the two sides? What are some of the assumptions and key terms that each side uses, and how do they use them differently? Also, is there any common ground that both sides share?

Researching: Finding Out What Others Know

A successful commentary needs to start with a foundation of solid research. As a writer, you are commenting about events that are still unfolding. Many of the facts are not known. So your goal is to figure out what others are saying and where their support comes from.

Electronic Sources. Because you are commenting on events that are happening right now, online sources may be your most useful resources for information. Using Internet search engines, collect other commentaries on your topic. Then try to sort these commentaries into two or more sides, and figure out where the sides disagree. Also, pay close attention to where these commentators found support for their arguments, so you can track down those sources yourself. Make sure you assess the bias and reliability of each source. All sources will be biased to some extent, but some will be better grounded in factual information than others.

Print Sources. Print sources are useful for doing background research on your topic. Articles in newspapers and magazines can give you a sense of the debate and who is involved. Books, meanwhile, will help you explore the history of the topic and develop a better understanding of the sides of the issue. Keep in mind that commentaries usually discuss issues that are happening in real time, so print sources will sometimes be outdated. Look for the most recent print sources on your subject.

Empirical Sources. Chances are good that someone on your campus is an expert on your topic. So find the faculty member or local expert on your campus who knows about this issue. Then set up an interview or correspond through e-mail. Other empirical methods you could use might include surveys or field observations, depending on your topic.

As always, you should triangulate your sources. For most commentary topics, you will likely collect primarily online sources, with print sources a distant second. Triangulating your sources should help you confirm facts and better understand all sides of the issue. For more on triangulation, see Chapter 25, "Finding Sources and Collecting Evidence."

Organizing and Drafting Your Commentary

10.2 organize your commentary to help the readers find important information.

As you organize and draft your commentary, think about what kinds of information would be most persuasive to your readers. You won't have time to explain everything, so figure out what kinds of information they need to know and what would help you make the strongest case.

The Introduction

While drafting your introduction, always remember that your readers will be interested in what you have to say only if you offer them something new and interesting they had not considered before.

State Your Topic, Angle, and Purpose. Up front, readers want to know your topic, your purpose, and the new angle you are bringing to the conversation. For example:

> In her recent commentary in the *New York Independent*, Brianna Hanson argues that parents should always have the right to decide whether their children will be vaccinated against illnesses like measles, whooping cough, and polio. However, with the severe outbreak of measles this year, which is quickly turning into a deadly epidemic, it's clear that that allowing uninformed parents to make these decisions could have devastating consequences.

State Your Main Point or Thesis Statement. Your introduction should also be clear about what you want to prove (your main point or thesis statement). Sometimes it is helpful to just come right out and state your position:

> **Weak:** People should be required to vaccinate their kids.

> **Stronger:** Only parents who have been fully educated on the benefits of vaccinations and the potentially deadly consequences of non-vaccination should be given the opportunity to opt their children out of common vaccinations.

A solid thesis statement gives your readers a good sense of where you are going with your commentary.

Explain the Current Event or Issue

Depending on your readers' familiarity with the topic, you should explain what has happened already and summarize the ongoing conversation about that event. If your readers are already familiar with the topic, you can keep this section of the commentary brief. If the topic is not familiar to your readers, you should provide enough background information to help them understand the event or issue. As much as possible, you should show them both sides (or all sides) of the issue. Summarize what others have said about this topic.

Besides educating your readers, the objective of this section is to show your readers that you understand the ongoing controversy and that you are able to see more than one side. You will have more credibility if your readers feel that you are considering all sides seriously and giving everyone a fair hearing.

Support Your Position

After explaining the current event or issue, it is time to present support for your side of the argument. Identify the strongest two to five major reasons behind your position.

In a brief commentary, each of these major reasons will likely receive a paragraph or two of coverage. State a claim (topic sentence) early in the paragraph and then use examples, details, reasoning, facts, data, quotations, anecdotes, and anything else you can think of to support that claim:

> The problem with the anti-vaxxer movement is that it's fronted by celebrities who can afford to cocoon their children from common diseases like measles, polio, and whooping cough. Jenny McCarthy, a television actress who has an autistic son, has long been a public face for the anti-vaccine movement, arguing (falsely, according to extensive medical research) that vaccines cause autism. Charlie Sheen and Bill Maher have both told the media that they would not let someone "stick" their kids or themselves because they don't trust the government. Recently, Kristin Cavallari, who is best known for her television work on *The Hills* and *Dancing with the Stars,* stated publicly that her children have not been vaccinated and that she believes vaccination is a "to each their own" kind of choice. Of course, wealthy celebrities live in a world that is completely different from the world of daycares, schools, and malls in which regular children live. Unlike regular people, celebrities have much more control over the kinds of people who come into contact with their children. Unfortunately, an alarming number of regular people view these celebrities as trendsetters or authorities on medical issues, and they have been misled into thinking their kids, too, won't come into contact with these deadly diseases.

Each major reason for your argument should support the main point, or thesis, you stated in the introduction. Your support needs to steadily build up your argument for your side of the issue.

Clarify Your Position

Before concluding your commentary, you might want to show readers that you are aware of the complexities of the issue. So you should clarify your argument by pointing out that new information or events might alter your ideas and approaches to the topic. Also, you can qualify your argument by conceding that the issue is not simple and the problem is not easy to solve. Writers often signal such clarifications with phrases like these:

> I'm not arguing here for a complete . . . , but only . . .
>
> I understand, of course, that . . .
>
> I'm only suggesting that . . .
>
> I recognize that the people on the other side want to do the right thing, too.

Typically a clarification needs only a small paragraph, depending on the length of your commentary.

Without this clarification, your readers might accuse you of "painting with too broad a brush"—that is, generalizing too far or failing to consider other perspectives.

The Conclusion

Your final words should leave readers with a clear statement of your position and a sense of your commitment to it. Restate your main point or thesis, preferably in stronger terms than you used in the introduction. You might also reemphasize the importance of the topic and offer a look to the future. Then finish the conclusion with a memorable anecdote, figure of speech, turn of phrase, or arresting image that will give readers something to think about. Here is a brief conclusion with all these moves:

> In America, we believe in freedom of choice—even the freedom to make stupid choices—but there comes a point where the choice of a few becomes a deadly threat to everyone. In those cases, the rights of the many need to be put ahead of the freedom of the few. Vaccines should be a choice, but people who choose not to vaccinate themselves or their children should be allowed to do so only after they have completed rigorous training that shows them the benefits of vaccination and explains the scientific truth about vaccines' miniscule risk. Freedom to remain ignorant is not a choice our children can live with.

In this four-sentence conclusion, the writer restates the issue and main point, stresses the importance of the topic, and finally offers a clever turn of phrase that gives the readers something to think about.

Choosing an Appropriate Style

The commentary genre tends to use a spirited style, which often sets it apart from other argumentative genres, such as argument papers or proposals. Catch your readers' attention by projecting a strong persona with a personal and lively style.

10.3 use emotion and character to add style and energy to an argument.

Get into Character

As you draft and revise your commentary, try to imagine yourself as an actor playing a role. If you want to sound angry, imagine being angry as you write. If you want to sound upbeat, imagine being in an upbeat mood.

Getting into character works because it allows you to write with less inhibition. You're playing a role, so you can freely let those emotions and that tone spill onto the screen or page. As you draft, explore the specific emotion or tone you are trying to project.

Imitate a Well-Known Writer

Find a few articles written by a person who uses a style similar to the one you want to use in your commentary. Look closely at how this person achieves that particular style or tone. Does he or she use details or words in a particular way? Are the sentences long or short? Does this author use analogies, metaphors, or similes to express complex thoughts? How does this writer convey excitement, anger, or other emotions you are seeking to express?

It's best if you *avoid* imitating the style of an article on the topic you are writing about. That way, you won't mistakenly plagiarize the writer's ideas or words.

Match Your Tone to Your Readers' Expectations

If your potential readers expect an informal, colloquial commentary, then you should adopt that informal style. For instance, if you're writing for an online discussion and the writers all speak in casual terms, you should probably do the same. On the other hand, if you're writing for a local newspaper or magazine with a more formal tone, then you should match that level of formality.

Use Analogies, Similes, and Metaphors

Since commentaries typically handle complex topics that can be difficult to understand, writers often turn to analogies, similes, and metaphors to make the unfamiliar seem more familiar. For example, note how this commentator uses a "shield" analogy to explain that refusing vaccinations is wrongheaded:

> We should remember that vaccinations are a shield that protects all of us, not just each individual. Each time someone decides not to vaccinate themselves or their child, a hole appears in that shield. If there are only a few holes, the rare infection that slips through the shield can be contained and dealt with. If there are many holes, though, the disease will evolve quickly and attack on many fronts, causing the shield to break down. Then, the whole population, not just individuals, are at risk from the epidemic.

Analogies, similes, and metaphors also have the benefit of adding a visual element to an argument. In the paragraph above, for example, it is easy to visualize a shield around the population that is damaged as more and more holes weaken it.

Designing Your Commentary

10.4 design your commentary to enhance its message.

Commentaries rarely appear in a stand-alone format. Instead, they appear within larger documents, like Web sites, newsletters, newspapers, and magazines. So as you are thinking about what design would be appropriate, pay attention to the place where your commentary is likely to appear.

Include Photography. Because commentaries address current events and issues, you may want to snap a few pictures or download photographs from the Internet to show what you are talking about (Figure 10.1). If you are using the picture for a strictly academic purpose (e.g., a paper for class), you don't need to ask permission to use it. However, if you are using the picture in a public way (e.g., on a Web site or blog, in a publication, on a poster, etc.), you will need to ask permission from the person who owns it.

Add Pull Quotes to Emphasize Important Points. You can use pull quotes to draw the readers' attention to a key sentence or short passage from the text that captures some essential point, question, or idea (Figure 10.1). Don't overdo it though. Reserve pull quotes for the important, attention-grabbing ideas. As a rule of thumb, use only one or two pull quotes per written page, and no more than one per screen.

The photo draws in the reader.

The pull quote highlights an important point in the article.

FIGURE 10.1 Using Photos and Pull Quotes

A photo or pull quote can capture an essential point, question, or idea from the text. They are helpful for drawing the readers' attention to the text.

Letter to
the Editor

A letter to the editor is a brief commentary that is written for the opinions section of a newspaper, magazine, or news Web site. Though addressed "to the editor," these letters are written for the larger readership. Letters to the editor usually respond directly to a specific news item or an opinion piece in the publication.

Letters to the editor often need to distill an argument to 250 words or fewer. Here's how to write a great one:

Address and summarize a specific issue, story, or opinion piece. Editors tend to publish only letters that respond directly to an issue or current event that was written about or reported in their publication.

State your purpose precisely. If you are challenging what was said previously, express concisely what you believe was inaccurate, misstated, or incomplete. If you are agreeing with the original text, explain why you agree with it.

Support your argument with personal experiences. Letters to the editor often use personal experiences to challenge or validate a story or opinion piece.

Support your argument with factual evidence. Back up your argument or challenge the text to which you are responding with carefully researched data, historical facts, quotations, and other details.

Recognize logical fallacies. Target logical fallacies in the text to which you are responding, and be careful not to use them yourself. See Chapter 22, "Using Argumentative Strategies."

Avoid condescension. When you disagree with a news story or opinion piece, it's tempting to be sarcastic or insulting. But if you keep your tone professional, readers will be open to your views, and your letter will have a better chance at publication.

WRITE **your own letter to the editor.** Find an article on a news Web site, in a magazine, or from a newspaper that is no more than a week old. Then write a letter to the editor that reacts in a positive or critical way. Give your professor contact information (address, e-mail address) for the editors to whom you could send your letter.

Visit **MyWritingLab** to complete this exercise.

Modern-Day Religious Climate on Campus Is Detrimental

Caroline Klinker

As I was reading the opinion piece "Come one, come all—It's just casual sex" in *The Badger Herald* last week, a particular comment caught my eye. "A student from the 19th century came back," it said, a reference, I suppose, to Ms. Cooley's Biblical references and religious perspective on sex.

> Identifies the piece the letter is responding to.

This brief comment illustrates quite well the current climate surrounding religion at UW-Madison; our highly secular campus views religion and the students who strive to live out their religious beliefs in their daily lives as backwards, old-fashioned and out-of-touch. I would like to propose, however that perhaps it is those who view religious students as artifacts of the past who align more closely with the 19th century than students like Ms. Cooley, who fearlessly live their faith each day.

> Further explains the issue at hand and the commentary's purpose.

Enter the Know Nothings, a mid-19th century American political movement fueled by nativism and anti-Catholicism. While the name of the Know Nothings is a reference to the secrecy of the organization (members who were questioned about its activities were instructed to reply "I know nothing"), it unintentionally reflects the reason behind the bigotry of its members: They knew nothing of the people they hated. They were ignorant, and perhaps innocently so; however, that ignorance spawned fear, which in turn fueled hatred and contempt.

> Supports the argument with a historical analogy that could inform the discussion.

To a large extent, a similar problem exists on our campus today. One need only look at the recent op-ed on Badger Catholic in *The Daily Cardinal* or *The Madison Misnomer's* pieces on Badger Catholic and St. Paul's University Catholic Center to see that anti-religious sentiment is alive and well on campus. As a Catholic, what pains me most about these articles is not the fact that somebody disagrees with me, mocks me or attempts to tear down my beliefs; it is that the faith and the Church I know and love are so grossly misrepresented. And why? It may be apathy, it may be fear, or it may be that we as Catholics have done a poor job showing the world who we truly are. However, the writers of these articles and many other students on campus remain largely unaware of what the Catholic Church is and believes. A quick scroll through the comments of these pieces only confirms the extent of the problem.

> Explains (plainly, without condescension) what she disagrees with and why she disagrees.

continued

Archbishop Fulton J. Sheen summarized the situation quite well when he said, "There are not a hundred people in America who hate the Catholic Church. There are millions of people who hate what they wrongly believe to be the Catholic Church—which is, of course, quite a different thing."

So what is the Catholic Church? What do we believe? Who are we? We are your friends, neighbors, roommates, classmates, TA's, and professors. We believe in God, in Jesus Christ and in the Holy Spirit. We want to be saints; our goal is Heaven. We pray, we adore, we praise, we worship. We strive to live lives of love and service. We sin and we fall. We seek God's forgiveness, are healed by his mercy, and get up to try again. We see all people as our brothers and sisters in Christ. We want to know you, and we want you to know us.

Finishes strong with a final clarifying main point.

Are you ready to start writing your commentary? Here are some ideas to help you do it.

FIND a Current Event or Current Issue That Interests You

Pay attention to the news or the events happening around you. Commentaries are typically written about events and issues that are current and hot.

FIND OUT What You Already Know and Believe About Your Topic

Use invention techniques like freewriting, brainstorming, or the Believing and Doubting Game to find out what you already know or believe about your topic.

RESEARCH the Event or Issue

Online sources are especially helpful when writing about current events or issues. Print and empirical sources are helpful for collecting background information on the topic.

DRAFT Your Commentary

Your introduction needs to grab the readers' attention. Then, in the body of your commentary, explain the current event or issue. Support your side of the argument and clarify your position. Use a brief conclusion to restate your main point (thesis statement), and try to end with a clever turn of phrase that gives the readers something to think about.

LIVEN UP Your Style

Commentaries are known for their lively and engaging style. People enjoy reading them for the content and the colorful way the ideas are expressed. So get into character and let your emotions show on the page.

CONSIDER the Design

Because they often appear in larger documents, commentaries tend to follow the design of the Web site, newspaper, or magazine in which they appear. Look for photography that will support or illustrate your argument. Pull quotes will allow you to highlight important ideas and quotes.

REVISE and Edit

Spend some time working and reworking your ideas. While revising and editing, pay special attention to your voice and tone. You want to polish your writing so that it stands out from the other commentaries available on the topic.

When May I Shoot a Student?

GREG HAMPIKIAN

In this op-ed published in the New York Times, *Boise State professor of biology and criminal justice Greg Hampikian offers a response to an issue that is current on his and many other campuses—allowing people to carry handguns. As you read, notice how the author uses a mocking and sarcastic tone but still addresses the main issues under discussion.*

BOISE, Idaho — TO the chief counsel of the Idaho State Legislature:

In light of the bill permitting guns on our state's college and university campuses, which is likely to be approved by the state House of Representatives in the coming days, I have a matter of practical concern that I hope you can help with: When may I shoot a student?

I am a biology professor, not a lawyer, and I had never considered bringing a gun to work until now. But since many of my students are likely to be armed, I thought it would be a good idea to even the playing field.

I have had encounters with disgruntled students over the years, some of whom seemed quite upset, but I always assumed that when they reached into their backpacks they were going for a pencil. Since I carry a pen to lecture, I did not feel outgunned; and because there are no working sharpeners in the lecture hall, the most they could get off is a single point. But now that we'll all be packing heat, I would like legal instruction in the rules of classroom engagement.

At present, the harshest penalty available 5 here at Boise State is expulsion, used only for the most heinous crimes, like cheating on Scantron exams. But now that lethal force is an option, I need to know which infractions may be treated as de facto capital crimes.

I assume that if a student shoots first, I am allowed to empty my clip; but given the velocity of firearms, and my aging reflexes, I'd like to be proactive. For example, if I am working out a long equation on the board and several students try to correct me using their laser sights, am I allowed to fire a warning shot?

If two armed students are arguing over who should be served next at the coffee bar and I sense escalating hostility, should I aim for the legs and remind them of the campus Shared-Values Statement (which reads, in part, "Boise State strives to provide a culture of civility and success where all feel safe and free from discrimination, harassment, threats or intimidation")?

While our city police chief has expressed grave concerns about allowing guns on campus, I would point out that he already has one. I'm glad that you were not intimidated by him, and did not allow him to speak at the public hearing on the bill (though I really enjoyed the 40 minutes you gave to the National Rifle Association spokesman).

Knee-jerk reactions from law enforcement officials and university presidents are best set aside. Ignore, for example, the lame argument that some drunken frat boys will fire their weapons in violation of best practices. This view is based on stereotypical depictions of drunken frat boys, a group whose dignity no one seems willing to defend.

The problem, of course, is not that drunken frat boys will be armed; it is that they are drunken frat boys. Arming them is clearly not the issue. They would cause damage with or without guns. I would point out that urinating against a building or firing a few rounds into a sorority house are both violations of the same honor code.

In terms of the campus murder rate— [10] zero at present—I think that we can all agree that guns don't kill people, people with guns do. Which is why encouraging guns on campus makes so much sense. Bad guys go where there are no guns, so by adding guns to campus more bad guys will spend their year abroad in London. Britain has incredibly restrictive laws—their cops don't even have guns!—and gun deaths there are a tiny fraction of what they are in America. It's a perfect place for bad guys.

Some of my colleagues are concerned that you are encouraging firearms within a densely packed concentration of young people who are away from home for the first time, and are coincidentally the age associated with alcohol and drug experimentation, and the commission of felonies.

Once again, this reflects outdated thinking about students. My current students have grown up learning responsible weapon use through virtual training available on the Xbox and PlayStation. Far from being enamored of violence, many studies have shown, they are numb to it. These creative young minds will certainly be stimulated by access to more technology at the university, items like autoloaders, silencers and hollow points. I am sure that it has not escaped your attention that the library would make an excellent shooting range, and the bookstore could do with fewer books and more ammo choices.

I want to applaud the Legislature's courage. On a final note: I hope its members will consider my amendment for bulletproof office windows and faculty body armor in Boise State blue and orange.

A CLOSER LOOK AT
When May I Shoot a Student?   **MyWritingLab**

1. Throughout this commentary, the author employs the rhetorical device of "irony," which means he states one perspective but actually wants to argue the opposite of that perspective. That is, although the author states that he wants "to applaud the Legislature's courage" for passing a "bill permitting guns on . . . campuses," he sends clear signals that he really opposes it. Choose three passages that use irony, and then describe the meaning that he actually wants readers to take away.

2. At what point do the author's actual beliefs come through? At what point should readers realize he is using irony to make his point?

3. If you were a person who believed that permitting guns on campus is a good idea, how would you react to Hampikian's argumentative strategies? In general, are such uses of irony a fair way to argue a point? Are they effective? Who would be most likely to be persuaded by an irony-filled argument like this one?

1. Choose a current issue that is highly controversial and about which you have strong beliefs. Write a commentary that uses Hampikian's ironic strategies to make its point by pretending on the surface to support the position you actually oppose. Pretend to defend the arguments for the position you oppose while showing how those arguments are absurd. Also, ridicule arguments against it but show how they make sense. Have fun with this.

2. Consulting Chapter 9, "Rhetorical Analyses," write a rhetorical analysis of "When May I Shoot a Student?" Summarize the commentary and describe how it uses the rhetorical strategy of irony to drive home its point. You'll need to define the term "irony" (perhaps consulting the Internet as your source) and then explain how the author employs it in various ways. Be sure to state your overall assessment of the commentary's effectiveness. Identify who would be persuaded by this commentary, and who would not.

Don't Click on Celebrity Nude Photos, ISIS Videos

SALLY KOHN

Sally Kohn is an activist, columnist, and television commentator. In this commentary, she pleads with people to stop doing exactly what hackers and terrorists expect them to do.

(CNN) — When you click on nude pictures of celebrities or ISIS videos of beheadings, you're part of the problem.

At the very least, you're complicit in the moral crime committed by those who post such pictures or videos. At worst, you're actively perpetuating the incentives behind posting such things in the first place. Want to be a responsible and considerate human being? Then for crying out loud, don't click on those things!

This week hackers released what they say are nude pictures of celebrity women, including Kim Kardashian, Vanessa Hudgens, Rihanna and Mary-Kate Olsen. These photos came on the heels of other leaked nude photos, also of celebrity women, which must have gotten enough attention to make the hackers want to do it again.

A week before, ISIS posted another video claiming to show the beheading of a British aid worker. The video—mind you, not just its existence but people actually seeing it—fueled the same sort of revenge mindset in Britain that previous such videos fueled in the United States.

President Obama himself has noted that 5 the videos in which ISIS beheads American journalists James Foley and Steven Sotloff "resulted in the American public's quickly backing military action." Yesterday, another such video was posted of ISIS supporters in Algeria beheading a French tourist.

Media outlets have struggled with whether to broadcast photos and videos that are on the one hand newsworthy—and incidentally, salacious and thus, traffic-generating—but on the other hand may perpetuate the harm or offense committed in the first place. For instance, CNN didn't air the Foley video, opting instead to show only a few images and audio. Some news organizations, however, were less restrained.

Speaking with Brian Stelter on "Reliable Sources" about the latest ISIS video showing British journalist James Cantlie speaking in captivity, CNN International managing director Tony Maddox said, "We know that ISIS wanted us to show it. And if we're in a situation where ISIS wants us to show anything, we should think really carefully about any way we can avoid doing that."

Let that sink in for a moment: ISIS wants you to watch those videos. The hackers who stole the celebrity pictures want you to look at them. When you click, you're doing precisely what the bad guys want you to do.

This summer, I gave a TED Talk about the changing landscape of American media and how we the consumers are becoming the new editors. Because online traffic performance drives media in the digital age, our clicks matter more than ever before. I used to think writing essays like this or going on television is a public act of making media, but that browsing the Web at home, clicking on this and that, is a private act of consuming media.

Wrong. Clicking is a public act of making 10 media because it feeds what gets attention. Your clicks matter.

I imagine that most Americans wouldn't buy things they knew had been stolen out of someone else's home. Isn't clicking on stolen photos the same thing? Or worse?

The *Guardian's* Van Badham writes that clicking on or sharing stolen celebrity nude photos is "an act of sexual violation" that in effect perpetuates the abuse of the theft in the first place. The *Daily Beast's* Marlow Stern writes that some actively spreading the pictures online feel so entitled to violate these celebrity women's privacy that they imply the celebrities might have leaked the pictures themselves—as though all the slut-shaming and misogyny would be an enjoyable PR boost.

Let's be clear, even if you aren't the scuz-bucket making rape jokes in chat rooms, just by curiously clicking on these nude celebrity pictures you're giving the hackers attention and the publishers traffic. You're basically encouraging them to keep doing it.

By the same token, I know most Americans would never want to support or encourage the murderous ISIS extremists. But does public obsession with and outrage around ISIS beheading videos do just that?

Analyzing the political and psychological 15 motives for beheadings, the *Boston Globe's* Jeff Jacoby writes, "Clearly the terrorists relish the horror beheading evokes in America and other Western democracies." Beheading Americans naturally provokes that very human reaction.

Still, if we had only heard about Foley and Sotloff being beheaded, would it have generated the same attention and outrage? Or was it the videos, or even just the still images from the videos, that incited and inflamed our anger?

According to a recent Wall Street Journal/NBC News poll, in 2013, 78% of Americans had heard about the Supreme Court's

Obamacare decision, 77% of Americans were aware of the debt ceiling fight in Congress, and 79% of Americans had heard about the alleged use of chemical weapons by Bashar al-Assad's regime in Syria. But fully 94% of Americans were aware that ISIS killed James Foley.

How much is the tail of these deeply vile and upsetting videos wagging the dog of our emotions and prompting us to military action?

In my TED Talk, I said that clicking on a train wreck "just pours gasoline on it and makes it worse." The result? "Our whole culture gets burned." If in our new media-driven universe, what gets the most clicks wins, "we have to shape the world we want with our clicks."

The good news there is that you—yes [20] you—have the power as just one individual to decide what we see more of or what we see less of in the media; to discourage disgusting videos and pictures and encourage positive, productive media coverage.

That is an incredible and important power. Use it wisely. Click responsibly.

A CLOSER LOOK AT

MyWritingLab

Don't Click on Celebrity Nude Photos, ISIS Videos

1. With your group, find three to five reasons in Kohn's commentary why she believes people should not click on illegally obtained photos or terrorist videos. Discuss whether you agree with her reasoning.

2. According to the U.S. Federal Bureau of Investigation, one aspect of terrorism is "(i) to intimidate or coerce a civilian population; (ii) to influence the policy of a government by intimidation or coercion; or (iii) to affect the conduct of a government by mass destruction, assassination, or kidnapping" (FBI.gov). In what ways could uploading murder videos be considered an act of terrorism?

3. Nude photos of celebrities seem like a completely different thing than videos of beheadings by terrorists. Yet, Kohn seems to be equating the two on some level. Do you agree with her? Why does your group think she links these two kinds of activities?

IDEAS FOR

MyWritingLab

Writing and Discussion

1. Imagine you are a government official who has been asked to develop a policy that explains when a terrorist video should not be shown by the news media. Of course, the Second Amendment gives the news media significant freedom of choice. However, such choices might play into the hands of terrorists while perhaps putting other innocent people at risk. Write a proposal in which you offer guidelines that clarify what the news media should or should not release to the public.

2. Write a memoir in which you describe how someone did something that embarrassed you. How did being exposed make you feel? How did you respond to this problem? What did you learn from this experience? Note: Keep your memoir PG-13 or milder, and don't write about anything that would cause you embarrassment again.

1. Ask each member of your group to describe a conversation he or she had with friends or family about a controversial current event or issue. What was the content and style of that discussion? How did the arguers try to get their ideas across to the others? Did any participant in the discussion become upset or stop listening? If so, what went wrong? Why couldn't friends or family get along well enough to discuss ideas in depth?

2. With your group, list seven issues or events being covered in the news right now. Pick two of these issues and discuss the different sides of the debate. Then go around the group and talk about how each member would approach writing a commentary about these two topics. What would your angle be? What could you add to the conversation about each topic?

3. Do you know someone whose participation in a discussion almost always results in discomfort, negative feelings, or anger? Do you enjoy conversing with this person, or do you avoid it? What does this person do that prompts such negative consequences? With your group, list five things that some people do to undermine discussions of important issues.

1. Listen to at least two news and opinion shows from different television or radio networks. Be attentive to how the pundits represent and exchange their differing viewpoints and (supposedly) try to influence each other as they attempt to persuade the audience. What do you notice about the "conversation" and its characteristics? Is there a reasonable exchange of ideas? Do the people in the discussion seem to want to persuade the other participants to adopt their viewpoints, or simply to dominate the others? Do they ever seem to really listen to each other?

2. Find an interesting opinion piece from a print or online magazine and bring it to class. With your group, talk about the written and visual features that make this piece effective. Then discuss the features that were not used that *could have* made it more effective. For instance, what is the writer's angle? What is he or she trying to achieve (purpose)? What is his or her main point? What does the commentary do to grab readers' attention and help them decide quickly whether it's worth reading?

3. Find a commentary in a newspaper or magazine, or on a news Web site. In a one-page analysis written to your professor, describe the commentary's content, organization, style, and design. What kinds of information does the writer use to support his or her points? Does the organization reflect the commentary organization described in this chapter? How would you describe the style, and how does the writer achieve this style? Finally, what design features are used to support the written text and make it more visually attractive?

The following microgenres are similar to commentaries but are different in important ways. Try your hand at one or two of these and notice how you need to reconsider features such as the writer-author relationship, angle, purpose, tone, and style.

Explore This

Rant—anger-fueled response about a current event

Believing/Doubting Game—discussion of both sides of an issue

Arguing the Opposite—brief argument for the side you disagree with

Call to Action—a rallying cry for your readers to take action on an issue

Mock Commentary—passionate argument about a silly issue (e.g., "the best flavor of gum," "which is better: pie or cake?")

Write This

1. **Express your opinion.** Imagine that you've been invited to write a weekly opinion piece (editorial) for your local community newspaper, campus newspaper, or some other regularly published venue that frequently carries commentaries. Pick an issue or current event that is in the news right now. Write a four-page commentary in which you express your own view on this issue. While inventing your argument, first figure out what you already know by using invention techniques, such as the Believing and Doubting Game. Then draft your argument, paying special attention to how you organize and support your ideas.

2. **Post your views on a Web site.** Most news Web sites allow readers to comment on the articles. Find one of these commentary areas and read the twenty most recent comments posted. What are some of the points of contention? Can you detect two or more sides to the debate? Write a contribution to the discussion. Be sure to respond to the original article as well as to what others have written. Hand in your commentary to your professor along with a one-page reflection in which you discuss the original article, the comments others have written, and the approach you took with your commentary.

3. **Start your own blog.** Blogs are popular places for writers to publish their commentaries on current events. Imagine that you would like to start your own blog. What topics would you write about? What angles would you take on them? Write a half-page description of your blog for your professor. Then write three 250-word entries, which you would publish on your blog. If you want, you could use this assignment to start your own blog on a free blogging service like *Blogger, Blogspot,* or *WordPress.*

Go to **MyWritingLab** to complete this chapter's exercises and test your understanding of its objectives.

11

Arguments

In this chapter, you will learn how to—

11.1 Invent the content of your argument, showing the major sides fairly.

11.2 organize and draft your argument as a debate.

11.3 use a style that will set your side apart from the others.

11.4 design your argument to create a favorable impression.

If you like to debate about issues and current events, you will enjoy writing arguments. The purpose of an argument is to explore two or more sides of a controversial topic and then to argue fairly and reasonably for one side over the others. Writing an argument helps you deepen your own understanding, and it might even influence how you think about your position. By fairly presenting all viewpoints, you will also strengthen your argument because readers will view you as fair minded and knowledgeable.

This balanced approach is what makes arguments different from commentaries, which usually express only the author's opinion. An argument describes other positions and discusses why one is stronger or better than the others.

In college, your professors will ask you to write argument papers that analyze and evaluate the different sides of an issue and then argue for one side or another. For example, you might be asked to write argument papers that explore controversial topics like climate change, texting while driving, immigration policies, or the costs of a higher education. You will likely write argument papers that discuss historical events, philosophical positions, religion, and ethics.

In the workplace, arguments are often called "position papers"; these documents are used to argue for or against business strategies or policies. Your supervisors will ask you to review the two or more sides of important issues and then express your own opinion on the best way to react or make progress.

The ability to argue effectively and persuasively is an essential skill that will help you throughout your life.

Arguments

This diagram shows two basic patterns for an argument, but other arrangements of these sections will work, too. In the pattern on the left, opposing positions are described up front; then your own position is explained. In the pattern on the right, you make a point-by-point comparison, explaining why your position is better than others. You should alter any pattern to fit your topic, angle, purpose, readers, and context.

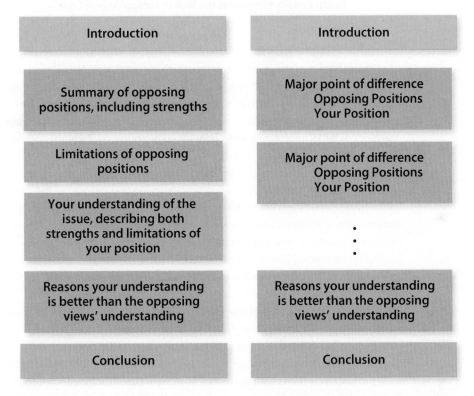

Arguing can be fun, but you need to argue fairly and reasonably if you want to win over your readers. The strongest arguments address differing viewpoints as objectively and fairly as possible and then persuade readers that one side is superior to the others. They tend to have the following features:

- **An introduction** that states the issue being debated, identifies the issue's two or more sides, and usually offers an explicit thesis that the argument will support.
- **An objective summary** of opposing views, including their strengths.
- **A point-by-point discussion** of the limitations of opposing views.
- **A summary** of your viewpoint and your understanding of the issue.
- **A point-by-point discussion** of both strengths and limitations of your position, arguing overall that yours is superior.
- **A conclusion** that drives home your thesis and looks to the future.

ONE STUDENT'S WORK
Arguments

Visit **MyWritingLab** to explore an interactive version of this essay.

Death Penalty Eliminates the Risk of Future Violent Crimes

Katlyn Firkus

The debate over the relevance of the death penalty has been resurrected in the U.S. According to CBC News, in the past six months there have been three "botched" executions of death row inmates across the country. Each of these cases involved prolonged suffering of the criminal due to error in administering the modern lethal injection cocktail, generating discourse over whether or not the current system of capital punishment is humane. Furthermore, it begs the question of the actual effectiveness of capital punishment as a whole.

There are thousands of competing articles online that debate the validity of the death penalty as a crime deterrent, which is one of its primary claims to purpose. Many argue that the threat of a death penalty will deter those willing to commit deadly crimes. Supporters of capital punishment reference similar studies completed by Emory in 2003, which determined with each execution of a violent criminal, between three and 18 additional murders are eradicated. Although antideath penalty advocates question the models and predictive methods used in these studies, the fact remains the deterrence, if not prevention, of violent crime is a definite benefit of capital punishment.

Both sides additionally argue over the fiscal nature of the death penalty. Generally, dissenters claim that sentences of life without parole (LWOP) are far less costly to taxpayers than death sentences. The Death Penalty Information Center has stated the average death penalty trial costs $1 million more than a comparable LWOP case. The costs continue to rise with the housing of these inmates at an average of $90,000 per year for the typical 20 year period while the sentence is being carried out. On average, a LWOP inmate only costs around $45,000 per year to house, making it a much more cost effective option.

However, many of these arguments fail to account for the lifespan and medical needs of LWOP inmates. Beginning at $45,000 per year, the cost rises with aging and associated medical needs to approximately $70,000 per year on average. Additionally, many LWOP inmates take part in various work and rehabilitation programs for any disorders, addictions, etc. they entered with. The costs of these are difficult to predict, but most certainly add to the LWOP inmate's average tab. Furthermore, a financial aspect of the death penalty that is rarely discussed is the monetary value of human life. The most conservative of government agencies

An open-ended thesis statement sets up the thesis in the conclusion.

Both sides of the issue are discussed in a factual way.

Discusses limitations of opposing view while supporting her own.

claims a human life to be worth around $6 million. Assuming that even one violent murder was deterred, much less the estimated three to 18, there is rarely a net loss in execution, but almost always in LWOP cases.

Many people hold strong opinions about the death penalty. Statistics can be found to support either side, but stronger arguments can be found in favor of it. When looking solely at the value of human life and the potential of the death penalty to deter subsequent murders of innocent people, there is no question that the risk of eliminating the death penalty entirely is not worth any potential reward.

> The thesis statement states the author's main point.

Inventing Your Argument's Content

11.1 invent the content of your argument, showing the major sides fairly.

When writing an argument, you need to understand the issue as thoroughly as possible. But here is the hard part: you must present all major sides of the controversy in a fair way. In other words, when reading your argument, a person with an opposing viewpoint would say, "Yes, that's a fair presentation of my view."

If your readers sense that you are distorting opposing positions or overlooking the weak points in your own position, they will question whether you are being fair and presenting the argument in an evenhanded way. So let your facts and reasoning do the talking for you. If your position is truly stronger, you should be able to explain all sides fairly and then demonstrate to your readers why your side is better.

Inquiring: Identifying Your Topic

When writing an argument, choose a topic (or question) that is narrow enough for you to manage, while allowing you to offer new insights. If you pick an overly broad or well-worn topic, such as gun control or abortion, you will find it difficult to say anything new or interesting. Instead, you should narrow your topic by asking what is new or what has changed about it recently.

Too Broad: Should we allow people to carry concealed handguns?

Better: Should students, faculty, and staff be allowed to carry concealed handguns on college campuses?

Even Better: Given the recent shooting at nearby Ridgeland University, should we allow students, faculty, and staff to carry concealed handguns on our college campus?

New topics for arguments are rare; however, new angles on topics are readily available. Pay attention to what has changed about your topic or how recent events have made your topic important today.

Inquiring: Identifying Points of Contention

To begin generating content for your argument, first identify the major points on which your side and opposing sides differ. A brainstorming list like the one shown in Figure 11.1 is often the best way to identify these major points.

When brainstorming, use two columns. In the left column, write "My position" and list all the arguments you can think of to support your case. In the right column, write "Opposing positions" and list the best arguments for the other sides of the controversy. When listing the ideas of people who disagree with you, try to see things from their perspective. What are their strongest arguments? Why do others hold these views or values? What goals are they trying to achieve that are different from yours?

When you have filled out your brainstorming lists, put checkmarks next to the two to five most important issues on which you disagree with the views of others. These are your argument's "major points of contention."

Researching: Finding Out What Others Believe and Why

You can use these major points of contention as a starting place for your research.

Begin by researching the opposing viewpoints first. By finding out what people who disagree with you believe, you can identify the strengths and weaknesses of your own position. And, if necessary, you can shift your position as you become more informed about the issue.

While researching the other side, imagine that you are arguing for these opposing positions. How would you build your argument? What would be your strongest points? What weaknesses would you point out in the other sides' positions? What kinds of sources would you use to support these positions? Your goal is to figure out why people hold viewpoints different than yours.

Then find sources that support your position. Your research on other viewpoints should help you pinpoint the kinds of sources that will support your side of the argument. You should look for credible sources that both support your position and answer the criticisms that individuals holding opposing positions might use against you.

Keep in mind that using a variety of sources will make your argument stronger. So you should look for a mix of online, print, and empirical sources that support all sides of the issue.

My position: Concealed weapons on campus are a greater risk than no handguns on campus.

Students, faculty, and staff will feel less safe on campus if guns are allowed.

✓ Alcohol could cause a lapse in judgment.

✓ Campus police don't want guns on campus.

✓ In a shooting incident, police cannot tell the criminals from the people defending themselves with guns.

Bullets from a defender's gun may strike innocent people in a classroom.

Students are less mature and may use their guns to threaten others or play games.

Some students will carry guns without a concealed- carry permit.

Guns on campus will cause parents to fear sending their students to our university.

✓ Guns locked in cars won't be any use in a shooting.

Less stable students are the ones most interested in carrying guns.

We can strengthen security if campus is thought to be unsafe.

Accidents do happen, and the university will be liable.

Opposing positions: Students, faculty, and staff should be able to carry concealed handguns on campus.

More shootings on college campuses have happened recently.

Gun-free campuses disarm citizens who could end campus shootings.

✓ Violent people would think twice about shooting at a campus.

More mentally ill students are going to college these days.

Universities would not be such easy targets for shooters.

A shooting could be ended quickly.

It may take minutes for security to arrive at the scene of a shooting.

Gun accidents are very rare.

✓ Gun ownership is a constitutional right.

People with guns would need to be licensed and weapons concealed.

People will carry guns anyway, so it's best to have it regulated.

Only way to stop someone with a gun is to use a gun.

✓ Guns on campus could be left in car.

People will feel more confident and less scared on campus.

People will be able to be on campus at night.

FIGURE 11.1 Brainstorming to Identify Major Points of Contention

When brainstorming about your topic, just write down anything about your topic that comes to mind.

Online Sources. The Internet can be helpful for generating content, but you need to be especially careful about your sources when you are preparing to write an argument. Countless people will offer their opinions on blogs and Web sites, but these sources are often heavily biased and may not cite support to back up their opinions. When researching, you should look for factual sources on the Internet and avoid sources that are too biased. Also, keep an eye out for credible television documentaries and radio broadcasts on your subject, because they will often address both sides of the issue in a journalistic way.

Print Sources. Print documents will likely be your most reliable sources of factual information. Look for magazines, academic journals, books, and other documents because these sources tend to be more careful about their facts than online sources and they usually have less bias. Through your library's Web site, try using the *Readers' Guide* to find magazine articles. Use periodical indexes to find academic articles. Your library's online catalog is a good place to search for books.

Empirical Sources. Facts you gather yourself will be very useful for backing up your claims about your topic. Set up an interview with an expert on your topic. You might find it especially helpful to interview an expert who holds an opposing view. This kind of interview will help you understand both sides of the issue much better. You can create a survey that will help you generate some data. You can also do field observations to study your topic in action.

Remember, you are looking for information that is credible and not too biased. It is fine to use sources that make a strong argument for one side or the other, but you need to make sure these sources are backed up with facts, data, and solid sources.

Organizing and Drafting Your Argument

11.2 organize and draft your argument as a debate.

The key to organizing an argument is to remember that you need to treat all sides of the issue fairly and thoroughly. As you are drafting your argument, imagine you are debating with another person or a group of people (Figure 11.2). If you were in a public debate, how would you express your best points and persuade the audience that yours is the most reasonable position? How would you counter criticisms of your position? Meanwhile, try to really understand and explain the opposing perspectives while countering their best arguments.

The Introduction

Your introduction should prepare readers for your argument. It will usually include some or all of these moves:

Start with a Grabber or Lead. Look for a good grabber or lead to catch readers' attention at the beginning of your introduction.

Identify Your Topic. State the controversial issue your argument will explore. You might express it as a question.

Offer Background Information. Briefly provide an overview of the various positions on the issue.

State Your Purpose. State your purpose clearly by telling readers that you will explain all sides of the issue and demonstrate why your position is stronger.

State Your Main Point or Thesis. State your main point or thesis clearly and completely. In most arguments, the main point or thesis statement typically appears at the end of your introduction. In some situations, you will want to save your main point or thesis statement for the conclusion, especially if you think readers might resist your argument. Your main point or thesis statement should be as specific as possible.

Weak: Only qualified police officers should be allowed to carry weapons on campus.

Stronger: Only qualified police officers should be allowed to carry weapons on campus, because the dangers of allowing students and faculty to carry weapons clearly outweigh the slight chance that a concealed weapon would be used in self-defense.

FIGURE 11.2 Imagining a Debate with the Opposing Side

When drafting an argument, imagine yourself debating people who hold positions that oppose yours. How would you win them over? Would they say you understand their perspective, even though you disagree with it?

Summary and Limitations of Opposing Positions

The body of an argument usually begins by explaining the other side or sides of the issue. Try to explain the opposing argument in a way that your readers would consider fair, reasonable, and complete. Acknowledge its strong points. Where possible, use quotes from opposing arguments to explain the other side's views. Paraphrasing or summarizing their argument is fine too, as long as you do it fairly.

Then, as objectively as possible, explain the limitations of the opposing positions. What exactly are they missing? What have they neglected to consider? What are they ignoring in their argument? Again, you want to highlight these limitations as fairly as possible. This is not the place to be sarcastic or dismissive. You want to point out the weaknesses in your opponents' argument in a straightforward way.

Your Understanding of the Issue

Now it's your turn. Explain your side of the argument by walking your readers through the two to five major points of contention, showing them why your side of the argument is stronger. Here is where you need to use your sources to back up your argument. You must use good reasoning, examples, facts, and data to show readers why your opinion is more credible.

Reasons Your Understanding Is Stronger

Before moving to your conclusion, you might spend some time comparing and contrasting the opposing views with your own. Briefly, compare the two sides head to head, showing readers why your view is stronger. At this point, it is all right to concede some points to your opponents. Your goal is to show your readers that your view is stronger *on balance.* In other words, both sides probably have their strengths and weaknesses. You want to show that your side has more strengths and fewer weaknesses than the opposing side.

Conclusion

Bring your argument to a close by stating or restating your thesis and looking to the future. Here is where you should drive home your main point or thesis by telling your readers exactly what you believe. Then show how your position leads to a better future. Overall, your conclusion should be brief (a paragraph in most arguments).

Choosing an Appropriate Style

11.3 use a style that will set your side apart from the others.

The style of your argument will help you distinguish your side from opposing sides. Even though your goal is to be *factually* fair to all sides, there is nothing wrong with using style to make your side sound more appealing and exciting.

Use Plain Style to Describe the Opposing Positions

When dealing with opposing perspectives, you should not be sarcastic or dismissive. Instead, describe opposing arguments as plainly as possible. In Chapter 17, "Choosing a Style," you will find helpful strategies for writing plainly, like putting the subjects of your sentences up front and using active verbs. You will also find techniques for writing better paragraphs that use clear topic sentences. By using these plain-style techniques to describe opposing perspectives, you will convey fairness and objectivity.

Use Similes, Metaphors, and Analogies When Describing Your Position

When you are describing your side of the argument, you want to present your case as visually as possible. Similes, metaphors, and analogies are a great way to help your readers visualize your argument and remember its key points.

Simile (X Is Like Y)

A college campus in which students carry guns would be like a tense Old West frontier town.

Downloading a movie is like borrowing a book from a library, not pirating a ship on the high seas.

Metaphor (X Is Y)

If a shooting incident did occur, the classroom could turn into a deadly crossfire zone, with armed students and police firing away at anyone with a gun in his or her hand. No one would be able to tell the difference between the "bad guy" and students who are defending themselves with their weapons drawn.

The purpose of the movie industry's lawsuits is to throw a few unfortunate college students to the lions. That way, they can hold up some bloody carcasses to scare the rest of us.

Analogy (X Is to Y Like A Is to B)

For some people, a gun has the same comforting effect as a safety blanket to a baby. Neither a gun nor a blanket will protect you from those imaginary monsters, but both can give you an imaginary feeling of security.

The movie industry's lawsuits are like your old Aunt Martha defending her tin of chocolate chip cookies at the church potluck. The industry offers a plate of delicious films, but only the "right people" are allowed to enjoy them. College students aren't the right people because we don't have enough money.

Try some of these "persuasive style" techniques to enhance the power of your argument. Similes, metaphors, and analogies will make your writing more visual and colorful, and they will also help you come up with new ways to think and talk about your topic. You can learn more about persuasive style in Chapter 17, "Choosing a Style."

Use Top-Down Paragraphs

Your argument needs to sound confident, and your readers should be able to find your major points easily. So, in your paragraphs, put each major point in the first or second sentence. Don't hide your major points in the middle of paragraphs because your readers won't find them easily. A top-down style will make you sound more confident, because you are stating your major claims and then proving them.

Define Unfamiliar Terms

Your readers may or may not be familiar with the topic of your argument. So if you use any specialized or technical terms, you should provide quick parenthetical or sentence definitions to explain them.

Sentence Definition

A conceal-carry permit is the legal authorization that allows private citizens to carry a handgun or other weapon on their person or in a secure place nearby.

Peer-to-peer file sharing involves using a network of computers to store and share files without charge.

Parenthetical Definitions

Colleges have traditionally invoked an "opt-out" statute, a law that allows the ban of weapons where posted, to keep concealed handguns off their campuses.

Movie sharing should become illegal when a person *commodifies* the files (i.e., sells them on a flash drive, CD, or Web site).

Designing Your Argument

11.4 design your argument to create a favorable impression.

Your readers will appreciate any helpful visuals and the use of good page design. If your work looks professional, they will likely have a more favorable impression of it.

Use Descriptive Headings. Each of the major sections in your argument should start with a clear heading that identifies what the section is about. For example, you could use headings like these:

> **The Case for Allowing Concealed Guns on Campus**
>
> **The Limitations of Allowing Guns on Campus**
>
> **Why Allowing Concealed Guns on Campus Is Dangerous**
>
> **Conclusion: The Risks of Concealed Weapons Aren't Worth It**

To help your headings stand out, use bold type and a larger font size where appropriate. Make sure your headings are formatted consistently.

Add Photographs and Illustrations. If you are writing about a local issue or an issue with a local angle, you can use your mobile phone or a digital camera to take a few pictures to include in your paper. The Internet is also a good place to find a few pictures and illustrations you can download to add a visual element to your text.

In your document, label your visuals with a number and title, and include a caption to explain them. If you download a photograph or other illustration from the Internet, you will need to cite your source in the caption and in your bibliography. If you want to put your argument on the Internet, you will need to ask permission from the owners of the photograph to use it on a public site.

Include Helpful Graphs, Diagrams, and Charts. Arguments often discuss trends in society, so look for ways to use graphs that illustrate those trends. If you collected data or found data on the Internet, you could create a graph or chart to present that data visually. Or, if you found a helpful graph on the Internet, you could use it in your own document, as long as you cite it properly. Graphs and charts should have a title, and you should use figure numbers in your written text to refer readers to the visual (e.g., "In Figure 2, the graph shows . . .").

Design the Page to Make It More Readable and Attractive. Let's be honest. A double-spaced paper with 1-inch margins just looks boring. Your readers will appreciate your efforts to design a document that is more readable and more attractive (Figure 11.3). A header or footer would be nice. Maybe you could use two columns instead of one. Your headings could be bolder and more colorful. Of course, if your professor asks for something specific, like "Your essay must use 12-point Times, be double-spaced, and use 1-inch margins," then you will need to format it that way. But if there are no guidelines, you might ask whether designing the document is acceptable.

Number the Pages. Page numbers might seem like a simple thing, but they are helpful when discussing your argument with other students or with your professor. Your word processor can add them automatically to the top or bottom of each page.

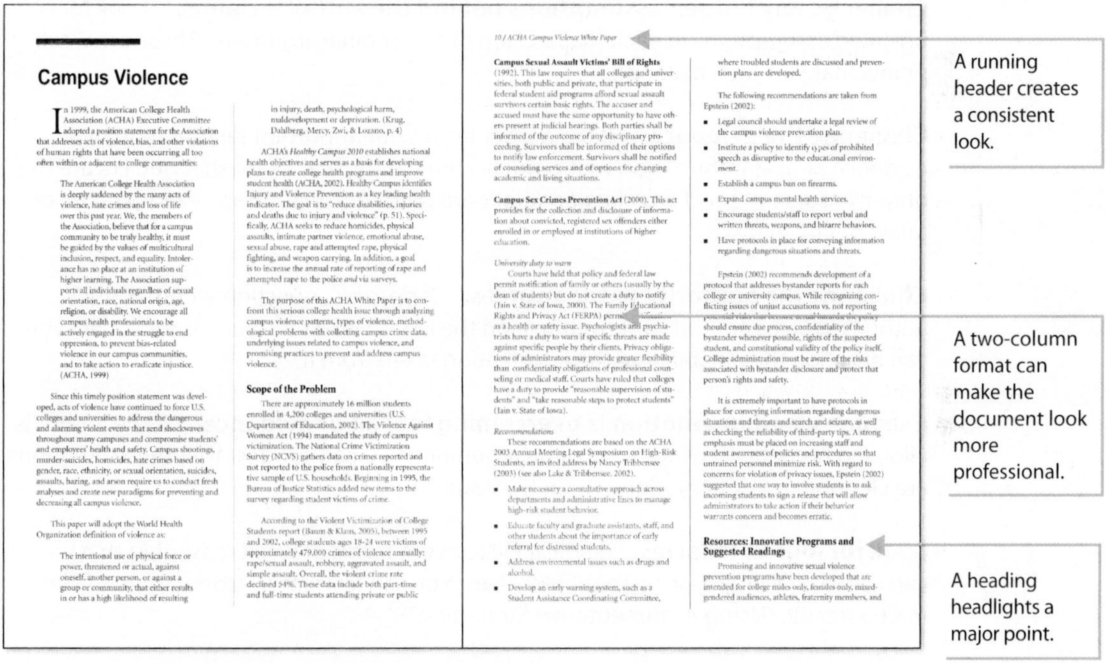

A running header creates a consistent look.

A two-column format can make the document look more professional.

A heading headlights a major point.

FIGURE 11.3 Designing an Argument

Your argument doesn't need to look boring or hard to read. The designers of this paper on campus violence used headings, bullets, indentation, and columns to make the text more accessible.

The Rebuttal

A rebuttal counters or refutes a specific argument. Rebuttals often appear as letters to the editor. They are also used in the workplace to argue against potentially damaging reviews, evaluations, position papers, and reports. Knowing how to write a rebuttal is an important part of defending your beliefs, projects, and research.

The main difference between a rebuttal and an argument is that a rebuttal responds directly to the points made in the original argument. After responding to that argument point by point, you then offer a better counterargument. Here are some strategies for writing a successful rebuttal:

Review the original argument briefly. Objectively summarize the original argument's thesis and its main points.

Challenge any hidden assumptions behind the author's claims. Look for unstated assumptions in each major claim of the original argument. These are weak points that you can challenge.

Challenge the evidence. If the author leaves out important facts and other evidence or uses information that is not accurate or typical, point that out. Locate the original source to see if any data or details are outdated, inaccurate, exaggerated, or taken out of context.

Challenge the authority of the sources. If possible, question whether the author's sources are truly authoritative on the issue. Unless a source is rock solid, you can question the reliability of the information taken from it.

Examine whether emotion is overcoming reason or evidence. If the author is allowing his or her feelings to fuel the argument, you can suggest that these emotions are clouding his or her judgment on the issue.

Look for logical fallacies. Logical fallacies are forms of weak reasoning that you can use to challenge your opponents' ideas. You can learn more about logical fallacies in Chapter 22, "Using Argumentative Strategies."

Offer a solid counterargument. Offer a different understanding of the issue supported by authoritative research.

WRITE your own rebuttal. Find an argument or similar document in a newspaper or on a Web site that you disagree with. Write a two-page rebuttal in which you refute the original argument and offer a counterargument. Your goal is to win readers over to your side.

Global Warming Most Definitely Not a Hoax—A Scientist's Rebuttal

Dr. John Abraham, School of Engineering, University of St. Thomas

LOS ANGELES, CA (Catholic Online) - In a recent Catholic Online interview, we heard from a seemingly reputable person (adjunct faculty member Mark Hendrickson) that global warming is a hoax "perpetrated by those who let a political agenda shape science". This is a very strong charge that cuts to the professionalism and competence of myself and my colleagues. As a scientist who carries out real research in this area, I can say Dr. Hendrickson is demonstrably wrong. Now, in his defense, Dr. Hendrickson admits he is not an expert although he "has followed it for over 20 years." In this field, expertise is judged by research accomplishments. On April 12, 2013, I performed a literature search on Dr. Hendrickson. I could not find a single study he has ever performed and published on any topic, let alone climate change. So, he is clearly not an expert. Of course, Dr. Hendrickson is entitled to his opinion; this is a free country. But to speak authoritatively about a subject he knows little about does a disservice to the readers.

> The author identifies the argument he is rebutting.

> The authority of the opposing side is challenged.

Dr. Hendrickson believes, erroneously, that climate science is like economics. Here he is wrong. Climate science is governed by physical laws (conservation of energy, conservation of mass, gravity, etc.) which have no corollary in economics. It is naïve to confuse economics and physical science disciplines.

> A false analogy used by the other side is revealed to the readers.

But what about his claims? Are they correct? Not hardly. In his interview, Dr. Hendrickson was asked to explain temperature changes that have already been observed. He responded by belittling computer models. His answer obviously confused past temperature measurements with future predictions of temperatures; they are not the same. The evidence from measurements clearly shows that temperatures have increased significantly over the past 150 years [. . .] and temperatures are currently higher than the past few thousand years [. . .]. These are but a few of the many studies that show the temperatures we are seeing now are out of the natural range that is expected.

He claimed that satellites have shown no warming in the last two or three decades. This is also false. In fact, even data from two of the most prominent climate skeptics (Dr. John Christy and Dr. Roy Spencer) show temperatures are clearly rising. Their results are confirmed by other satellite organizations that use other temperature measurement methods such as the Hadley Center, NOAA, and NASA. Even a Koch-brothers funded study has concluded that Earth temperatures are rising and humans are the principal cause.

> The author provides links to scientific studies that support his points.

> The author summarizes the position of the other side.

What about the claim that the Antarctic is gaining mass? Again not true, as shown by scientific articles published in *Science* (Shepherd et al., 2012) and *Geophysical Research Letters* (Rignot et al., 2012). What about the North Pole? There we have lost an astonishing 75% of the summer ice over the past four decades. Should we be concerned? Dr. Hendrickson is correct in stating that Arctic ice loss won't raise sea levels much because it is already floating in water. What he doesn't report is that Arctic ice loss is important for another reason. It helps keep the Earth cool by reflecting sunlight. The loss of this ice has led to an acceleration of the Earth's temperature rise. If you don't want to take my word for the importance of Arctic ice, perhaps we could listen to the Director of the National Snow and Ice Data Center (Mark Serreze). He has characterized Arctic is as in a "death spiral".

Dr. Hendrickson makes a series of other claims: the medieval times were warmer than today (false), there are 30,000 scientists with advanced degrees who have signed a petition to stop climate action (false), and that there are many scientists who have resigned from government research positions and begun speaking out against the science (he couldn't recall any names of such scientists).

So what can we make of all of this? First, it is obvious that non-experts like Dr. Hendrickson have every right to provide their opinion in any forum; however they must be held to the standards of truth and intellectual honesty. When someone makes serial and serious errors in his interpretations, those errors must be called out. Perhaps Dr. Hendrickson truly believes his statements are correct, but his belief does not make them so. This is why we defer to people who know what they are talking about. People who study this every day of their lives. Those people, the real scientists, clearly understand that climate change is a clear and present problem that will only get worse as we ignore it. Failure to deal with climate change will cost us tremendously, in dollars and lives. In fact, two recent studies [. . .] have shown that 97% of the most active climate scientists agree humans are a principal cause of climate change. Among the experts, there is strong agreement. It is up to each of us to decide who to believe (97% of the experts, or Dr. Hendrickson).

But this isn't all doom and gloom. The good news is there are solutions to this problem. Solutions we can enact today, with today's technology. If we make smart decisions, we can develop clean and renewable sources of energy. We can light our homes and power our cars while preserving this gifted Earth. Simultaneously, we can create jobs, diversify our energy supply, and improve our national security. Who can be against that? Failure to act is a choice. It is a choice with tremendous consequences. For me, the path forward is clear.

Uses credible sources to support major claims.

Concludes rebuttal by looking to the future.

Here are some quick steps for writing an argument.

IDENTIFY an Arguable Topic

An arguable topic has at least two sides. Choose the side that you agree with. Then narrow your topic to something suitable for an argument.

IDENTIFY the Points Separating Your Views from Opposing Views

Using brainstorming or another prewriting tool, put down everything you know about your topic. Then write down everything someone who holds the opposing view believes.

RESEARCH Both Sides of the Topic

Collect materials that support both (or all) sides of the issue, because you want to discover the best reasons for supporting opposing positions. You can then authoritatively counter these positions as you support your own.

DEVELOP Your Main Point or Thesis Statement

State the main point or thesis that you will be supporting in your argument. This main point or thesis statement will help you draft and revise your argument.

ORGANIZE Your Materials and Draft Your Argument

Arguments are organized to explain competing sides of an issue. Describe the strengths of the opposing positions fully and fairly before you challenge them.

CHOOSE Your Style

When explaining opposing positions, use a "plain style" with simple, clear sentences and paragraphs. When you explain your own position, add energy to your argument by using similes, metaphors, and analogies.

DESIGN the Document

Arguments tend to be rather plain in design. However, you might look for opportunities to add visuals to support your argument.

REVISE and Edit

As you draft your argument, your position may evolve. Give yourself time to modify your argument and refine your points. Proofreading is critical because readers will see errors as evidence that your argument has not been fully thought through.

Should College Football Be Banned?

TED MILLER

In this argument, a sportswriter for ESPN takes on the arguments against college football. While conceding many points to the opposing side, he still defends the sport against its critics. Observe how he shows both sides of the argument and reaches his final conclusion.

College football is too dangerous. College football subtracts from the academic mission of a university. It's hopelessly corrupt. There's too much money involved. And it's a travesty that the players aren't getting a fair share of the loot.

Those were the winning points put forward by writers Buzz Bissinger—yes, Mr. "Friday Night Lights" hates college football—and Malcolm Gladwell in an Intelligence Squared debate at New York University over whether college football should be banned. They bested sports columnist Jason Whitlock and author and former NFL/college player Tim Green.

It was an entertaining and interesting debate. These are smart men. The room was full of smart, engaged people.

Best line of the night? Said Bissinger, "A great country changes."

That is true. Great countries work to 5 solve social ills, particularly issues of inequality. Great countries work to create access to opportunity. Great countries aspire to create an ethical, ambitious, caring and intellectually active populace.

And great countries debate issues. That this debate will have less staying power in our culture than an average tweet from Lady Gaga—there is zero momentum behind the notion of banning college football—is not our present issue. Our present issue is whether you, fair college football fan, should feel a twinge of guilt over not caring why some intellectual types might think college football should be banned.

Yes, you should. So step out of the warm glow of your fandom for a moment.

Gladwell focused almost exclusively on head injuries suffered by players who were college students—officially amateurs—and not paid professionals. That should concern us all. Head injuries in football are serious business. The good news is that, after media pressure, the NCAA and NFL are taking head injuries seriously. There is reason to be optimistic that football can be made safer.

Bissinger, who at times channeled comedian Lewis Black with his sputtering passion, said football—and sports in general—had no place at universities that should be exclusively about higher learning. Of football, he said, "It sucks all the air out of the room." Not unreasonably, he pointed out that in a highly competitive world economy, education will become even more important, and U.S. universities that spend millions on football, football facilities and football coaches while cutting computer science departments are failing in their primary mission.

Everybody in the room lamented that 10 college players are not paid.

Green and Whitlock countered with the positives of football, including providing scholarships to young men who otherwise couldn't afford college, building character, promoting diversity and building a sense of community at a university and even within an entire state. Or, in the case of the SEC, an entire region.

And both, not unreasonably, pointed out that once you start banning things, you step onto a slippery slope. Said Whitlock of living with freedom, "You can't have the free without the dumb."

Perhaps it's a facile point, but we could make America better by banning a lot of popular things: cigarettes, booze, fast food, sugar and reality TV. Without those, we'd be healthier and smarter. We could go further with our Utopian vision and make a law that politicians must go to jail for a week every time they willfully mislead the public with a false statement about themselves or their opponents. We could require all Americans to go to the theater weekly and read all of Jonathan Franzen's novels.

Of course, then we wouldn't be America. Freedom and capitalism and the messiness they sometimes create inexorably spiral through the circulatory system of our nation. It is often for better and sometimes for worse, but it's who we are. "Football has to be tolerated, just like Ronald McDonald," Whitlock opined.

There was some garbling of facts on the 15 ban football side. Talking about chronic traumatic encephalopathy (CTE), a progressive degenerative disease of the brain found in people with a history of repetitive brain trauma, can scare an audience. Yet it's also critical to note that concussions and anecdotal evidence about debilitated former football players have not been causally connected by scientific research, as Gladwell repeatedly implied. We know a concussion is bad and multiple concussions are worse, but it's irresponsible to point to Junior Seau's suicide and say, "See!" (No one specifically did that Tuesday night, by the way.)

Now I'll make note of a quibble that is also the basis for my position. Neither Bissinger nor Gladwell know much about college football. It's not just that they haven't played, it's that they aren't educated on the subject. That is where most critics of college football come from: the ignorant. I've been around college football much of my life, and professionally since 1997. My take on the sport, and the take of most folks who have been around the sport for a good deal of time, is that the good far outweighs the bad. If the sport is far from pure, it's also far from impure. And I'd be glad to debate that point with anyone. They'd lose.

A CLOSER LOOK AT
Should College Football Be Banned?   MyWritingLab

1. Miller concedes several points to the opposing point of view. Find three concessions that he makes in this argument. With your group, discuss whether making these concessions was a good strategy on his part.

2. As Miller points out, Americans would be better off banning many things that aren't good for us.

Yet we don't. With your group, discuss the point at which harmful things should be banned. When should harmful activities be allowed?

3. Miller claims that critics of college football are wrong because they are "ignorant." Why does he believe they don't understand the importance of football as a sport?

1. As Miller points out, Americans do many things that aren't good for us. Write an argument in which you defend a practice or habit that most people would consider harmful.

2. Miller published this argument on the ESPN website, so his readers are probably already inclined to agree with him. Let's imagine he wants to write a version of this article for college presidents who are growing increasingly concerned about football injuries and potential legal liability. Write an e-mail in which you offer Miller advice about how to revise his argument for this new group of readers. Send this e-mail to your instructor.

Friends with Benefits: Do *Facebook* Friends Provide the Same Support as Those in Real Life?

KATE DAILEY

Social networking sites like Facebook and Instagram have challenged our ideas about what it means to be a "friend." Today, people can keep in touch with others who might otherwise have faded into the past. Also, we can be "friends" with people we barely know who share common interests or backgrounds. In this argument, pay attention to how Dailey builds her case and notice where she summarizes the other side of the debate.

I have a friend named Sue. Actually, "Sue" isn't her real name, and she isn't really a friend: she's something akin to a lost sorority sister—we went to the same college, participated in the same activities and had a lot of mutual respect and admiration for one another. But since graduation, we've fallen out of touch, and the only way I know about Sue, her life and her family is through her *Facebook* updates. That's why I felt almost like a voyeur when Sue announced, via *Facebook*, the death of her young son. I was surprised she had chosen to share something so personal online—and then ashamed, because since when did I become the arbiter of what's appropriate for that kind of grief?

The more I thought about it, the more I realized *Facebook* might be the perfect venue for tragic news: it's the fastest way to disseminate important information to the group without having to deal with painful phone calls; it allowed well-meaning friends and acquaintances to instantly pass on condolences, which the family could read at their leisure, and it eliminated the possibility that were I to run into Sue in the supermarket, I'd ask unknowingly about her son and force her to replay the story over again.

Numerous studies have shown that a strong network of friends can be crucial to getting through a crisis, and can help you be healthier in general. But could virtual friends, like the group of online buddies that reached out to Sue, be just as helpful as the flesh-and-blood versions? In other words, do *Facebook* friends—and the support we get from them—count? These questions are all the more intriguing as the number of online social-network users increases. *Facebook* attracted 67.5 million visitors in the U.S. in April (according to ComScore Inc.), and the fastest-growing demographic is people over 35. It's clear that connecting to friends, both close and distant, via the computer will become more the norm than novelty.

Researchers have yet to significantly study the social implications of *Facebook*, so what we do know is gleaned from general studies about friendship, and some of the emerging studies about online networking. First, a definition of "friend": In research circles, experts define a friend as a close, equal, voluntary partnership—though Rebecca G. Adams, a professor of sociology at the University of North Carolina, Greensboro, says that in reality, "friendships don't have to be equal or close, and we know from research that friendships aren't as voluntary as they seem," because they're often constricted by education, age and background. Friends on *Facebook* seem to mimic, if not replicate, this trend—there are people online that you are more likely to chat with every day, while others only make an appearance once or twice a year, content to spend the rest of the time residing silently in your friend queue. (Though the *Facebook* friends with whom you have frequent social interaction might not be people you interact with often in "real life.")

In life, having 700 people in your circle of 5 friends could get overwhelming, but that's less of an issue online. "Research suggests that people are only intermittently in touch with many of their online 'friends' but correspond regularly with only a few good friends," says Shelley E. Taylor, professor of psychology at The University of California, Los Angeles. "That said, creating networks to ease the transition to new places can be hugely helpful to people, offsetting loneliness until new friends are made."

In other words, *Facebook* may not replace the full benefits of real friendship, but it definitely beats the alternative. I conducted a very informal poll via my *Facebook* status update, asking if *Facebook* makes us better friends. A high-school pal, with whom I haven't spoken in about 10 years, confessed that since she had her baby, corresponding via *Facebook* has been a lifeline—and even if she wasn't actively commenting, it was nice to know what people were up to. "Any electronic communication where you don't have to be in the same physical space is going to decrease feelings of isolation," says Dr. Adams.

Several people in my online network admit that *Facebook* doesn't make them a better friend, but a better acquaintance, more likely to dash off a quick happy birthday e-mail, or to comment on the photo of a new puppy. But that's not a bad thing. Having a large group of "friends" eager to comment on your daily life could be good for your self-esteem. When you get a new job, a celebratory lunch with your best friends will make you feel good and make for a fantastic memory. But the boost you get from the 15 *Facebook* friends who left encouraging comments can also make you happy.

"The way to think of this is before the Internet, we wouldn't see our acquaintances very often: every once in a while, we might show up at a wedding and suddenly have 100 of our closest friends around," says James Fowler, associate professor of political science at the University of California, San Diego. "With *Facebook*, it's like every day is a wedding." And just like leaving a wedding may leave you feeling energized and inspired by reconnecting to old pals, so can spending time on *Facebook*, says Fowler.

While Fowler's research also shows that bad habits like smoking and weight gain can be contagious among close friends, emotions like happiness and sadness are easily transferable through acquaintances. The good news? "Because happiness spreads more easily than unhappiness, getting positive comments from your *Facebook* friends is more likely to make you happy than sad," he says.

Shy people who may not always be able to engage friends in the real world are finding solace in the structure of *Facebook*. Though people who identify as shy have a smaller circle of *Facebook* friends than those who don't, they are better able to engage with the online friends they do have. "Because people don't have to interact face-to-face, that's why we're seeing them having relationships: they can think more about what they have to say and how they want to say it," says Craig Ross, a graduate student in psychology at the University of Windsor who studies online social networks.

And what of my "friend" "Sue"? Can the support she received from *Facebook* friends upon learning about the death of her son replicate the support that would come from friends stopping by the house? It's impossible to replace the warm feelings—or brain-boosting endorphins—that come from human-on-human contact, and you can't send someone a casserole through *Facebook*. But grieving online can have powerful and productive benefits. Diana Nash, professor of psychology at Marymount Manhattan College, who has studied how college students use *MySpace* to deal with grief, notes that, "One of the primary desires that we all have is for someone to really listen to us in a deep kind of way. They want to be listened to," she says. Her research shows that by sharing their grief on *MySpace*, her subjects

felt more listened to and more visible, and doing so helped them heal.

Posting personal experiences, no matter how painful, also allows acquaintances who have lived through similar experiences to reach out, either with information about support groups or just an empathetic ear. "The idea of sharing a commonality helps make it a little more bearable. You're not alone, and there are others going through what you went through," says Nash. "It doesn't take away the pain, but it can lessen the pain and make you feel not so alone."

The majority of times we reach out on *Facebook*, however, it's not about a tragedy, but a smaller problem for which we need advice: good movers in the San Francisco area, a copy of yesterday's newspaper, answers to a question about taxes. This is another place where the large *Facebook* networks come in handy. In real life, people tend to befriend people who think thoughts and live very similar lives to their own, but because on *Facebook* people often "friend" classmates, people met at parties, and friends-of-friends, the networks include individuals who wouldn't make the "real friend" cut. Having that diversity of opinion and experience available online increases the diversity of responses received when posting a question, which allows you to make a better-informed decision.

Still, there are experts who worry that too much time online keeps us from living satisfying lives in the real world. "It's great to have a lot of *Facebook* friends, but how many of those friends will show when you're really in trouble?" asks Michael J. Bugeja, a professor of communications at Iowa State University of Science and Technology and author of *Interpersonal Divide: The Search for Community in a Technological Age*. He notes the world of difference between someone typing a frowny emoticon upon hearing that you've been in a car crash and showing up to help you get home. He also says that *Facebook*, with its focus on existing relationships—and its ability to codify and categorize those relationships—in some ways belies the promise of the Internet. "Rather than opening us up to a global community, it is putting us into groups," he says.

That's why *Facebook* works best as an amplification of a "real life" social life, not a replacement—even as time and technology progress and the lines between online interactions and real-world experiences continue to blur. 15

A CLOSER LOOK AT
Friends with Benefits

MyWritingLab

1. In this argument, the definition of the word "friend" seems open for debate. Dailey offers a couple of different definitions of a friend, a traditional definition and a social-networking site definition. How are these two types of friends similar, and how are they different?

2. This argument talks about how habits can be contagious among friends, like smoking and weight gain. Bailey, however, sees this kind of contagiousness as a good thing because of *Facebook*. Why?

3. A good argument fairly describes the other side of the debate, usually early in the argument. However, in this one, Dailey waits until the end to clearly state the opposing argument. What do these people find wrong with calling people on *Facebook* "friends"?

IDEAS FOR
Writing

MyWritingLab

1. Write a three-page commentary in which you discuss the future of friendships in an electronically networked world. Do you think people will lose touch with each other because they are mostly interacting through texting, social networking sites, or e-mail? Or do you think electronic networking is actually making relationships stronger? What are some of the benefits of friendships through electronic networking? What are some of the downsides?

2. Find one of your childhood friends on *Facebook, Instagram*, or another social networking site. Write a two-page profile of your friend using only evidence drawn from his or her page. On his or her page, your friend has tried to project a particular image. What is that image? How is that image similar to or different from the person you know or knew personally?

1. With a small group, make a list of some challenging issues facing our society to-day. Pick an issue and explore both sides. What are the two to five major points of contention between the two sides of the issue? What are the strengths of each side? What are the limitations of each side?

2. With your class, list ten effective and ineffective ways to argue. What is the best way to get your point across to someone else? What are your most effective strate-gies? Then list some of the worst ways to argue. What are some of the annoying ways in which other people have tried to persuade you? How did you react to some of these less effective methods?

3. Think about arguments you have had with friends, family members, and other people you care about. With a small group, discuss why these arguments are sometimes more difficult than arguments with people who are not so close to you. Do you have any strategies for arguing effectively with people you care strongly about? Do you avoid these kinds of arguments? If so, why?

1. Look at the opinions section of your local or campus newspaper. Pick an issue that is being discussed in the editorials, commentaries, or letters to the editor. On your screen or a piece of paper, list the positions and the kinds of support offered by one of the writers. Then list the points opponents might make to counter these positions and support their own opinions. In a memo to your professor, explain both sides of the argument as fairly as possible. Then show why you think one side or the other has the stronger argument.

2. Find an argument on the Internet. You might look for arguments in the online versions of newspapers or magazines. In a two-page memo to your professor, an-alyze the argument and explain whether you think the author is arguing effec-tively or not. Did the author fairly represent both sides of the issue? Is the author too biased, or does he or she neglect any strengths of the opponents' position or limitations of his or her own position?

3. Pick a topic that you feel strongly about. Create a two-column brainstorming list that explores the issues involved with this topic. Then identify the two to five main points of contention that separate you from someone who disagrees with you about this topic. In a one-page memo to your professor, discuss the strengths and limitations of your side of the issue and that of your opponents. Explain what kinds of information you would need to collect to support your best arguments and highlight the limitations of your opponents' views.

Working with one or two of the microgenres listed below can be fun and instructive about arguments generally. If you are working in a group, write just the introduction and conclusion and report back to the class. If you are doing an informal writing assignment, include a memo to your professor that describes how the microgenre differs from the basic argument.

Explore This

Mock Argument—a parody that pretends to argue seriously about a silly (or nonarguable) issue

Argumentum Ad Absurdum—an argument taken to ridiculous extremes

Devil's Advocate—argument for the side you or a friend disagrees with

Debate Dialogue—imagined dialogue between two people on opposite sides of an issue

You're Doing It All Wrong—an argument in which the author argues that people should be doing something a better way

Write This

1. **Write an argument about a local issue.** Write a five-page argument in which you explore both sides of a contentious local issue. Pick an issue that affects you directly and try to fairly represent both sides. Explain opposing sides of the issue as clearly and fairly as possible. Then point out their limitations. Explain your side of the issue and concede any limitations. Then persuade your readers that your understanding of the issue is stronger and more reasonable than your opponents' understanding.

2. **Create a multimedia presentation.** Illegal downloading of music or movies has been an important issue on college campuses for some time. Some students are being sued by the music industry, and they are being forced to pay thousands of dollars in damages and fines. Create a ten-slide presentation in which you state your opinion about downloading music and movies "illegally" off the Internet. Explain how people with opposing perspectives understand the issue. Then explain your side and show why you think your understanding is stronger. Your presentation could be made with *PowerPoint*, *Keynote*, or any other presentation software. Try adding photographs, charts, video, and audio, where appropriate.

3. **Argue that something bad for people is really good for them.** In a five-page argument, make and support the claim that something people traditionally assume is "bad" (e.g., playing video games, being overweight, seeing violence in movies, watching television, cramming for an exam) is actually good. Summarize the conventional assumptions about why something is bad. Then use research to show that it is actually good for people.

> Go to **MyWritingLab** to complete this chapter's exercises and test your understanding of its objectives.

Proposals

In this chapter, you will learn how to—

12.1 use invention to understand problems and develop solutions.

12.2 organize a proposal by drafting the major sections separately.

12.3 choose a style that will be persuasive to your readers.

12.4 create a design that will make your proposal attractive and accessible.

Proposals help people explore problems and devise plans for solving those problems. In your advanced college courses, your professors will ask you to write proposals that describe new technologies, develop strategies, pitch new products, and improve your community. In the workplace, proposals are used to develop marketing campaigns, design new products, take advantage of new opportunities, and plan new projects.

The aim of a proposal is twofold. First, a proposal helps readers understand a problem's *causes* and *effects*. Second, it tries to persuade the readers that a specific step-by-step plan offers the best solution for that problem. Your readers will expect your proposal to be clearly written and persuasive. They expect you to try to win them over with strong reasoning, good examples, and appropriate appeals to authority and emotion.

Proposals tend to come in three basic forms.

Internal Proposal—used within a company or organization to plan projects and pitch new ideas.

External Proposal—used to conduct business between two different companies or organizations.

Grant Proposal—used by non-profit organizations and researchers to request funding for projects.

In this chapter, you will learn strategies that will help you write all three of these kinds of proposals.

Proposals

This diagram shows a basic pattern for a proposal, but other arrangements of these sections will work, too. You should alter this organization to fit your topic, angle, purpose, readers, and context.

Introduction

Problem analysis
Major causes
Evidence
Effects of the problem

Plan for solving the problem
Major steps
Support
Deliverables

Benefits of the plan
Costs-benefits analysis

Conclusion

A proposal is one of the more complicated genres you will be asked to write. Here are a proposal's typical features:

- **An introduction** that defines a problem, stresses its importance, and offers a brief description of the proposed solution (the thesis).
- **An analysis** of the problem that discusses its causes and its effects.
- **A detailed plan** that shows step by step how to solve the problem.
- **A costs-benefits analysis** that measures the benefits of the plan against its costs.
- **A conclusion** that looks to the future and stresses the importance of taking action.

ONE STUDENT GROUP'S WORK
Proposals

Visit **MyWritingLab** to explore an interactive version of this essay.

This proposal was written by Matthew Steele and the Associated Students of the University of Washington (Seattle Campus). Responding to a request for proposals (RFP) soliciting ideas for replacing an underused café space, they suggest a new food-services facility that offers healthy and local alternatives.

Descriptive title tells readers what the proposal is about.

Descriptive headers and table of contents help readers see the big picture.

Color and images attract readers' attention.

The purpose of the proposal is stated here.

Introduction defines the topic and links it to larger campus issues.

SCC Café Proposal

Spring 2010

Proposed by the ASUW Food Cooperative Task-Force

Contents

1 Executive Summary
2 Background
2 Problem Statement
3 Proposed Solution
    Info on the Co-op &
    How It Will Address
    these Problems
4 Vision for Café Space
    Sample Menu
4 Recommendations

Appendices

Appendix A: Café Floor Plan
Appendix B: Statement of Support (I)
Appendix C: Statement of Support (II)
Appendix D: Health Sciences Student Petition

Executive Summary

The UW Student Food Cooperative proposes operating a food Café offering a local, healthy, and affordable menu in the former SCC café space. The need for food service was identified as a significant concern of students in a 2006 report created by a taskforce of health sciences administrators and students. The low traffic that the building currently receives makes a food enterprise difficult to financially sustain. However, the co-op caters to a niche market and thus has magnet market qualities that will be able to pull traffic to the site.

We believe this niche market makes the co-op uniquely able to sustain itself in that space. Furthermore, the food co-op has similar goals as those stated by the School of Public Health and its department of Nutritional Sciences. The co-op will support the SCC as a hub for health and food interests, both for its students and staff and the campus at large. The enterprise will provide healthy, sustainable, and affordable eating options while utilizing student participation and creating opportunities for collaboration, education, and leadership.

1

ASUW | THE ASSOCIATED STUDENTS OF THE UNIVERSITY OF WASHINGTON

Background

The South Campus Center (SCC) was originally built by funds from UW students in the 1970s. Generally its use has waned in recent years and since 2004 both the Café space and the industrial kitchen have not been operating. Traffic for food service was absorbed by the creation of the Rotunda in the main Health Sciences building. Due to its under-use by the student body at large, daily operational responsibilities will appropriately transfer to Health Sciences Administration on July 1st, 2010.

The idea of the food co-op has developed out of the growing excitement and interest in food issues on campus evidenced by the proliferation of food-related curriculum and public events on campus, the influx of applications for the graduate department of Nutritional Sciences, and the envisioning of an interdisciplinary program collaborating across the fields of Anthropology, Public Health, Biology, Geography, the Program on the Environment, Urban Horticulture and Urban Planning. Campus activities around food have also expanded, for example, the UW Farm has grown substantially over the last few years to a community of over 400 students with various projects constantly underway. Due to the student interest in urban agriculture, the UW Farm is poised to expand to a full acre plot on campus.

The food co-op will be supported by students and their concern for issues of health, environmental degradation, loss of biodiversity, and exploitation of workers' rights implicated by large-scale industrial farming practices, the corporate dominance of food choices, and the far-flung transportation of food. As a solution to these issues, the café will source organic food exclusively from local farmers and producers, including the UW farm. The café's commitment to sustainability, which will be extended to include waste recycling practices, will create awareness of issues surrounding the food system at every level. Student demand for healthy and sustainable options is overwhelming. Recently, café s with comprehensive approaches to healthy food and sustainability have opened and enjoyed overwhelming success like the vegetarian café Chaco Canyon on 50th and 12th and Thrive raw food café in Ravenna. UW students, especially those in residence halls who are required to purchase HFS meal plans, suffer from the lack of organic, vegetarian, and vegan food options. Currently, healthy on-campus venues that accept husky cards are limited.

In January 2010, the Associated Students of the University of Washington (ASUW) formed a taskforce to research the formation of a food co-op, similar to the entities that exist at University of British Columbia, University of California Berkeley, Evergreen State College, Puget Sound University, and many other universities around the United States. The ASUW Food Co-op Taskforce's conclusion is that the former SCC café space would meet the need for food service by students, draw more foot traffic to the area, and provide local, healthy, affordable food.

Problem Statement

In 2006 a taskforce of university administrators and students produced a report for Provost Phyllis Wyse on the current and potential Health Sciences uses of the South Campus Center (SCC). The specific conclusions of 2006 SCC Taskforce Report were that "food service, at least on a small scale, was a major priority and would be needed in order to revitalize the usage of the SCC." Specifically, they recommended a "small specialty food service that would offer something different such as an emphasis on a healthy menu." In addition, they wanted to fully utilize the beautiful views of Portage Bay. Based on a student survey the taskforce sent, 70.7% of the comments were related to the availability of food service in the building. In particular, specific comments from the students expressed their desire for food options that were healthy, local, affordable, and provided an alternative to what is currently offered at the Rotunda. The closure of the newspaper and candy stand on June 18, 2010 will further limit the food options in the SCC and make the concern of providing healthy, affordable food in SCC more pressing. Though the transfer of the building to Health Sciences Administration will more fully utilize the space, the lack of food traffic and food service will persist until another food provider is identified.

The background explains the current situation.

The benefits of implementing the plan are described up front.

The problem and its causes are described.

Proposed Solution

Based on findings of the 2006 SCC taskforce, the reopening of the SCC Café space would help to address the lack of alternative and affordable food choices. A food cooperative would provide excellent food service to the SCC, while catering to a growing niche market of those concerned with nutrition, sustainability, affordability, and democratic business structures. The opening of a Café focused on these priorities and values will attract a community of conscientious eaters and will bring additional foot traffic to the SCC as well as spread awareness of food-related topics.

Spring 2010 Food Survey - Conducted by ASUW Food Cooperative Task-Force

(1250 total students surveyed)

20% of students responded: "I can't get food on campus that meets my dietary preferences – I eat off campus or pack food"

35% of students responded: "I'd like to eat more local and organic produce, but am limited by budget"

18% of students identified as vegetarian (almost 100% of diet), 13% identified vegan food as at least a large portion of their diet

53% of students expressed interest in participating in working for the Co-op, in exchange for meal credits.

Intro on the Food Co-op

UW students are following the models of prominent universities across the nation in creating a student food cooperative whose purpose is to achieve food sovereignty on campus and address food justice issues through the affordable provision of healthy and organic high-quality prepared foods that are locally sourced and sustainably grown and produced, possibly right on the UW campus. The UW Farm is currently undergoing major visioning and administrative partnering as it embarks on an expansion to an acre of land on the campus. If their current production capabilities are any indicator of what they will be able to do with that acre, they will be a major producer of food for students in years to come. Working directly with the UW Farm, the idea is to create a localized food system where students can gain an understanding of not only what real food is, but also where it comes from. In addition to sourcing locally and establishing partnerships with the UW Farm, the student-run food co-op will further create a localized and contextualized food system on campus through projects such as a bulk-buying club, a CSA program, and the operation of the cooperative for food credit.

We are seeking a collaborative partnership with the department of Nutritional Sciences. The Nutritional Sciences wants to expand their undergraduate program and the number of classes offered and students served. A Student Food Co-op will aid in these efforts. Specifically, the department of Nutritional Sciences will repurpose the SCC commercial kitchen into a gastronomy teaching laboratory.

The cooperative could prove instrumental to engage students in the cooking classes that the department hopes to conduct and be involved in the activities occurring there. The food co-op will link Nutritional Sciences and all the Health Sciences Schools with the sustainability movement at this university.

How a Student-Run Food Cooperative Addresses These Problems

The 2006 SCC taskforce specifically identified "the need to provide a magnet use in the SCC that will bring students to the facility." As previously mentioned, interest in food issues as it relates to urban agriculture, social and food justice, environmentalism, and alternative agrifood movements are quickly building momentum on campus. Thus, by addressing popular food-related issues on campus, the cooperative can be a magnet for student activity and presence along with the repurposing of the building to teaching spaces and student lounge/study areas. This emphasis, in addition to providing students with healthy and affordable food and an extraordinary, waterfront study and meeting space, will meet the goal from the 2006 Task Force report that a unique Café will be able to pull traffic past the Rotunda and E Court Café. Our plans will revitalize the SCC space, while functioning largely with the existing plans for the building.

Opening for plan section.

The benefits are discussed at the end of the plan.

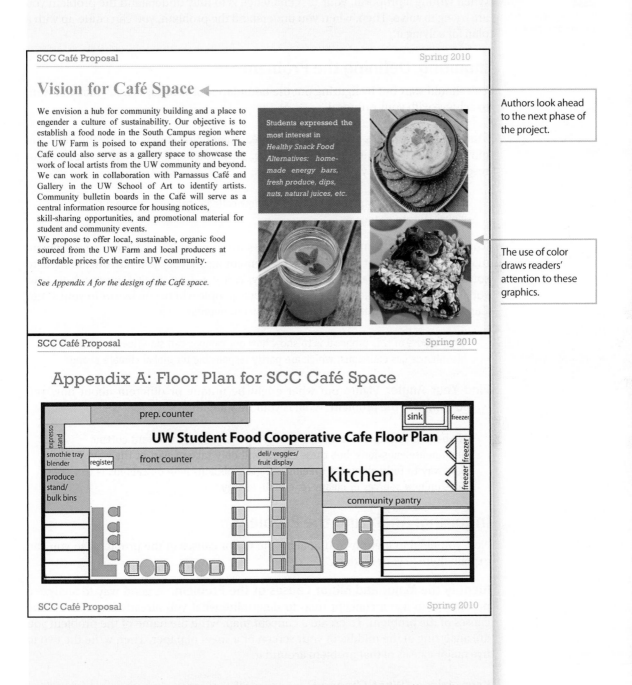

SCC Café Proposal   Spring 2010

Vision for Café Space

We envision a hub for community building and a place to engender a culture of sustainability. Our objective is to establish a food node in the South Campus region where the UW Farm is poised to expand their operations. The Café could also serve as a gallery space to showcase the work of local artists from the UW community and beyond. We can work in collaboration with Parnassus Café and Gallery in the UW School of Art to identify artists. Community bulletin boards in the Café will serve as a central information resource for housing notices, skill-sharing opportunities, and promotional material for student and community events.

We propose to offer local, sustainable, organic food sourced from the UW Farm and local producers at affordable prices for the entire UW community.

See Appendix A for the design of the Café space.

Students expressed the most interest in *Healthy Snack Food Alternatives: homemade energy bars, fresh produce, dips, nuts, natural juices, etc.*

Authors look ahead to the next phase of the project.

The use of color draws readers' attention to these graphics.

SCC Café Proposal   Spring 2010

Appendix A: Floor Plan for SCC Café Space

UW Student Food Cooperative Cafe Floor Plan

expresso stand

prep. counter

sink   freezer

smothie tray blender   register   front counter   deli/ veggies/ fruit display   kitchen

produce stand/ bulk bins

freezer freezer

freezer

community pantry

SCC Café Proposal   Spring 2010

Inventing Your Proposal's Content

12.1 use invention to understand problems and develop solutions.

When writing a proposal, your first challenge is to fully understand the problem you are trying to solve. Then, when you understand the problem, you can come up with a plan for solving it.

Inquiring: Defining the Problem

You should start out by figuring out the boundaries of your topic and what you want to achieve with your proposal.

State Your Proposal's Topic and Purpose. A good first step is to state the topic and purpose of your proposal in one sentence. This statement will help you focus your research and will save you time.

> The purpose of this proposal is to show how college students can help fight global climate change.

Narrow Your Topic and Purpose. Make sure you aren't trying to solve a problem that is too big. Look at your purpose statement again. Can you narrow the topic to something more manageable? Specifically, can you take a local approach to your subject by discussing how the problem affects people where you live or in your state? Can you talk about your topic in terms of recent events?

> The purpose of this proposal is to show how our campus can significantly reduce its greenhouse gas emissions, which are partly responsible for global climate change.

Find Your Angle. Figure out what might be unique or different about how you would approach the problem. What is your new angle?

> We believe attempts to conserve energy offer a good start toward cutting greenhouse emissions, but these efforts will only take us part of the way. The only way to fully eliminate greenhouse gas emissions here on campus is to develop new sources of clean, renewable energy.

Inquiring: Analyzing the Problem

Now you need to identify and analyze the major causes of the problem, so you can explain them to your readers.

Identify the Major and Minor Causes of the Problem. A good way to analyze a problem is to use a concept map to determine what you already know about the causes of the problem. To create a concept map, write the name of the problem you are analyzing in the middle of your screen or a sheet of paper. Then write the two to five major causes of that problem around it.

Keep Asking "What Changed?" As you fill out your concept map, keep asking yourself, "What has changed to create this problem?" If you pay attention to the aspects that are changing about your topic, you will find it easier to identify what is causing the problem itself.

Analyze the Major and Minor Causes. Once you have identified two to five major causes, find the minor causes of these main issues. Ask yourself, "What are the two to five minor causes of each major cause? What has changed recently that created each of the major causes or made them worse?"

Researching: Gathering Information and Sources

Your concept map will give you a good start, but you also need to do some solid research on your topic. When doing research, collect information from a variety of sources. You should then "triangulate" your research by drawing material from online, print, and empirical sources.

Online Sources. Choose some keywords from your concept map, and use one or more Internet search engines to gather background information on your topic. Pay special attention to Web sites that identify the causes of the problem you are exploring. Also, look for documentaries, podcasts, or broadcasts on your subject. You might find some good sources on *YouTube, Hulu,* or the Web sites of television networks.

Print Sources. For proposals, your best print sources will usually be newspapers and magazine articles, because most proposals are written about current or local problems. You can run keyword searches in newspaper and magazine archives on the Internet, or you can use the *Readers' Guide* at your library to locate magazine sources. On your library's Web site, you can use research indexes to find articles in academic journals. These articles tend to offer more empirically grounded discussions of issues.

Empirical Sources. Set up interviews, do field observations, or survey people to gather empirical evidence that supports or challenges your online and print sources. Someone on your campus, perhaps a professor or a staff member, probably knows a great deal about the topic you have chosen to study. So send that person an e-mail to set up an interview. If you aren't sure who might know something about your topic, call over to the department that seems closest to your topic.

Inquiring: Planning to Solve the Problem

With your preliminary research finished, you are ready to start developing a plan to solve the problem. A plan is a step-by-step strategy for getting something done.

List a Few Possible Solutions. Usually, there are at least a few different ways to solve the problem. List the possible solutions and then rank them from best to worst. Keep in mind that some of the "best" solutions might not work due to how much they cost.

Map Out Your Plan. Again, a concept map is a useful tool for figuring out your plan. Start out by putting your best solution in the middle of your screen or a piece of paper. Then ask yourself, "What are the two to five major steps we need to take to

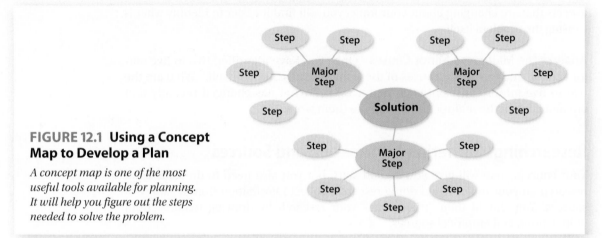

FIGURE 12.1 Using a Concept Map to Develop a Plan

A concept map is one of the most useful tools available for planning. It will help you figure out the steps needed to solve the problem.

achieve this solution?" Write those major steps around your solution and connect them to it with lines (Figure 12.1).

Explore Each Major Step. Ask yourself, "What are the two to five steps we need to take to achieve each of these major steps?" For example, if one of your major steps is "develop alternative sources of energy," what steps would your university need to take to do that?

1. The university might look for grants or donations to help it do research on converting its campus to renewable energy sources like wind power or solar energy.

2. The university might explore ways to replace the inefficient heating systems in campus buildings with geothermal heating and cooling systems.

3. The university might convert its current fleet of buses and service vehicles to compressed natural gas or plug-in hybrids.

Each major step can be broken down further into minor steps that offer more detail.

Figure Out the Costs and Benefits of Your Plan. With your plan mapped out, you should now identify its costs and benefits. You want to prove to your readers that the benefits are worth the costs. When figuring out the costs and benefits, brainstorming is an especially helpful tool. You can use it to list all the costs of your plan and then all the benefits (Figure 12.2).

Researching: Find Similar Projects

Now that you have developed your plan, do some more research to find projects similar to yours. Of course, you don't want to copy their solution—their plan probably won't work for your situation anyway—but you might learn what others have tried before, what has worked, and what hasn't worked.

> **Benefits of My Plan to Make Our Campus Carbon Neutral**
>
> Help save humanity from apocalyptic end (!)
>
> Reduce this university's dependence on foreign oil
>
> Help clean up local air, water, and soil
>
> Widely distributed power sources, which will make us less vulnerable to energy system failures
>
> Not contribute to ecological destruction involved with mining coal and drilling for oil
>
> Help create more local jobs for a "green economy"
>
> Millions of dollars in energy savings, starting in 10 years
>
> Be ahead of energy policy changes that are coming anyway
>
> Make our campus modern and forward thinking, which is attractive to top students
>
> **Costs of My Plan**
>
> Transformation costs will be high, perhaps even $100 million
>
> University will need to invest in energy research and training
>
> Need to retrain current power plant employees
>
> University will need to stress energy conservation as system evolves

FIGURE 12.2 Costs and Benefits of Your Plan

Brainstorming can help you list the costs and benefits of your plan. Your goal is to show your readers that the benefits of your plan outweigh the costs.

Organizing and Drafting Your Proposal

Proposals are typically larger documents, so organizing and drafting these texts can be challenging. The best way to draft a proposal is to write each of its major sections separately. In other words, draft each major section as though it is a small argument on its own.

> **12.2** organize a proposal by drafting the major sections separately.

The Introduction

An introduction to a proposal will typically make up to five moves, which can be arranged in just about any order:

State the topic. Tell your readers what the proposal is about.

State the purpose. State the purpose of your proposal in one or two sentences.

Provide background information. Give readers just enough historical information to understand your topic.

Stress the importance of the topic to the readers. Tell readers why they should care about this topic.

State your main point (thesis). Offer a straightforward statement that summarizes your plan and explains why it will succeed.

Weak: We think our campus should convert to alternative energy.

Stronger: We propose the "Cool Campus Project" that replaces our campus's existing coal-fire plant with a local electricity grid that combines an off-campus wind farm with a network of solar panels on all campus buildings.

In the introduction to a proposal, you should almost always state your topic, purpose, and main point (thesis). The other two moves are optional, but they become more important and necessary in larger proposals.

Description of the Problem, Its Causes, and Its Effects

You should now describe and analyze the problem for your readers, showing them its causes and effects. Look at your concept map and your research notes to identify the two to five major causes of the problem. Then draft this section of the proposal around those causes (Figure 12.3).

Opening Paragraph. Use the opening paragraph to clearly describe the problem and perhaps stress its importance.

> The problem we face is that our campus is overly dependent on energy from the Anderson Power Facility, a 20-megawatt coal-fired plant on the east side of campus that belches out many tons of carbon dioxide each year. At this point, we have no alternative energy source, and our backup source of energy is the Bentonville Power Plant, another coal-fired plant 50 miles away. This dependence on the Anderson Plant causes our campus's carbon footprint to be large, and it leaves us vulnerable to power shortages and rising energy costs.

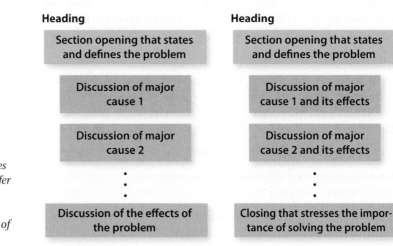

FIGURE 12.3 Drafting the Problem Section

An effective analysis of the problem will discuss its causes and effects. Make sure you offer good support for your statements. Here are two possible ways to organize this section of the proposal.

Heading

Section opening that states and defines the problem

Discussion of major cause 1

Discussion of major cause 2

⋮

Discussion of the effects of the problem

Heading

Section opening that states and defines the problem

Discussion of major cause 1 and its effects

Discussion of major cause 2 and its effects

⋮

Closing that stresses the importance of solving the problem

Body Paragraphs. Explain the causes of the problem, providing plenty of support for your claims. Here is an example discussion of one cause among a few others that the writers want to include.

> The primary reason the campus is so reliant on coal-fired energy is the era when the campus was built. Our campus is like many others in the United States. The basic infrastructure and many of the buildings were built in the early twentieth century when coal was cheap and no one could have anticipated problems like global warming. A coal-fired plant, like the one on the east side of campus, seemed like the logical choice. As our campus has grown, our energy needs have increased exponentially. Now, on any given day, the campus needs anywhere from 12 to 22 megawatts to keep running (Campus Energy Report, 22).

Closing Paragraph. You might consider closing this section with a discussion or summary of the effects of the problem if no action is taken. In most cases, problems grow worse over time, so you want to show readers what will happen if they choose not to do anything.

> Our dependence on fossil fuels for energy on this campus will begin to cost us more and more as the United States and the global community are forced to address global climate change. More than likely, coal-fired plants like ours will need to be completely replaced or refitted with expensive carbon capture equipment (Gathers, 12). Also, federal and state governments will likely begin putting a "carbon tax" on emitters of carbon dioxide to encourage conservation and conversion to alternative energy. These costs could run our university many millions of dollars. Moreover, the costs to our health cannot be overlooked. Coal-fired plants, like ours, put particulates, mercury, and sulfur dioxide into the air that we breathe (Vonn, 65). The costs of our current coal-fired plant may seem hidden now, but they will eventually bleed our campus of funds and continue to harm our health.

Figure 12.3 shows two of the more common patterns for the Problem section, but other patterns will work, too. You can use whichever pattern helps you best explain the causes and effects of the problem to your readers.

Description of Your Plan

Draft the Plan section next. In this section, you want to describe step by step how the problem can be solved (Figure 12.4). The key to success in this section is to tell your readers *how* you would solve the problem and *why* you would do it this way.

Opening Paragraph. The opening paragraph of this section should be brief. Tell the readers your solution and give them a good reason why it is the best approach to the problem. Give your plan a name that is memorable and meaningful. For example:

> The best way to make meaningful cuts in greenhouse gas emissions on our campus would be to replace our current coal-fired power plant with a 12-turbine wind farm and install solar panels on all campus buildings. The Cool Campus

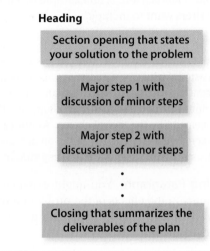

Heading

Section opening that states your solution to the problem

Major step 1 with discussion of minor steps

Major step 2 with discussion of minor steps

⋮

Closing that summarizes the deliverables of the plan

FIGURE 12.4 Drafting the Plan Section

A Your Plan section should walk readers through your solution step by step. After you state each major step, discuss the minor steps and explain why they are needed.

Project would cut greenhouse gas emissions by half within ten years, and we could eliminate all greenhouse emissions within twenty years.

Body Paragraphs. The body paragraphs for this section should tell the readers step by step how you would carry out your plan. Usually, each paragraph will start out by stating a major step.

Step Three: Install a 12-Turbine Wind Farm at the Experimental Farm

The majority of the university's electricity needs would be met by installing a 12-turbine wind farm that would generate 18 megawatts of energy per day. The best place for this wind farm would be at the university's Experimental Farm, which is two miles west of campus. The university already owns this property, and the area is known for its constant wind. An added advantage to placing a wind farm at this location is that the Agriculture Department could continue to use the land as an experimental farm. The turbines would be operating above the farm, and the land would still be available for planting crops.

Closing Paragraph. In the closing paragraph of this section, you should summarize the *deliverables* of the plan. Deliverables are the things the readers will receive when the project is completed:

When the Cool Campus Project is completed, the university will be powered by a 12-turbine wind farm and an array of solar panels mounted on campus buildings. This combination of wind and solar energy will generate the 20 megawatts needed by the campus on regular days, and it should be able to satisfy the 25 megawatts needed on peak usage days.

Don't get locked into the pattern shown in Figure 12.4. It's a useful pattern, but you might find other, more effective patterns for describing your plan, depending on the solution you are proposing.

Discussing the Costs and Benefits of Your Plan

A good way to round out your argument is to discuss the costs and benefits of your plan. You want to show readers the two to five major benefits of your plan and then argue that these benefits outweigh the costs.

> In the long run, the benefits of the Cool Campus Project will greatly outweigh the costs. The major benefits of converting to wind and solar energy include—
>
> > A savings of $1.2 million in energy costs each year once the investment is paid off.
> >
> > The avoidance of millions of dollars in refitting costs and carbon tax costs associated with our current coal-fired plant.
> >
> > The improvement of our health due to the reduction of particulates, mercury, and sulfur dioxide in our local environment.
> >
> > A great way to show that this university is environmentally progressive, thus attracting students and faculty who care about the environment.
>
> We estimate the costs of the Cool Campus Project will be approximately $60 million, much of which can be offset with government grants. Keep in mind, though, that our coal-fired plant will need to be refitted or replaced soon anyway, which would cost millions. So the costs of the Cool Campus Project would likely be recouped within a decade.

> Costs do not always involve money, or money alone. Sometimes, the costs of the plan will be measured in effort or time.

The Conclusion

Your proposal's conclusion should be brief and to the point. By now, you have told the readers everything they need to know, so you just need to wrap up and leave your readers in a position to say yes to your plan. Here are a few moves you might consider making in your conclusion:

- **Restate your main point (thesis).** Again, tell the readers what you wanted to prove in your proposal. Your main point (thesis) first appeared in the introduction. Now bring the readers back around to it, showing that you proved your argument.

- **Restress the importance of the topic.** Briefly, tell the readers why this topic is important. You want to leave them with the sense that this issue needs to be addressed as soon as possible.

- **Look to the future.** Proposal writers often like to leave readers with a description of a better future. A "look to the future" should only run a few sentences or a brief paragraph.

- **Offer contact information.** Tell readers whom to contact and how to contact that person if they have questions, want more information, or are interested in discussing the proposal.

Your conclusion should not take up more than a couple brief paragraphs, even in a large proposal. The goal of your conclusion is to wrap up quickly.

Choosing an Appropriate Style

12.3 choose a style that will be persuasive to your readers.

Proposals are persuasive documents by nature, so your style should be convincing to match your proposal's content. In Chapter 17, "Choosing a Style," you can learn about how to use persuasive style techniques. For now, here are some easy strategies that will make your proposal sound more convincing:

Create an Authoritative Tone. Pick a tone that expresses a sense of authority. Then create a concept map around it. You should weave these terms from your concept map into your proposal, creating a theme that sets the desired tone.

Use Metaphors and Similes. Metaphors and similes allow you to compare new ideas to things that are familiar to your readers. For example, calling a coal-fired plant a "dirty tailpipe" will make it sound especially unattractive to your readers, making them more inclined to agree with you. Or, you might use a metaphor to discuss your wind turbines in terms of "farming" (e.g., harvesting the wind, planting wind turbines in a field, reaping the savings) because farming sounds more natural.

Pay Attention to Sentence Length. Proposals should generate excitement, especially at the moments when you are describing your plan and its benefits. To raise the heartbeat of your writing, shorten the sentences at these key places in your proposal. Elsewhere in the proposal, keep the sentences regular length (breathing length). See Chapter 17, "Choosing a Style," for more on sentence length and style.

Minimize the Jargon. Proposals are often technical, depending on the topic. So look for any jargon words that could be replaced with simpler words or phrases. If a jargon word is needed, make sure you define it for readers.

Designing Your Proposal

12.4 create a design that will make your proposal attractive and accessible.

Your proposal needs to be attractive and easy to use, so leave yourself some time to design the document and include graphics. Good design will help your proposal stand out, while making it easy to read. Your readers will also appreciate graphics that enhance and support your message.

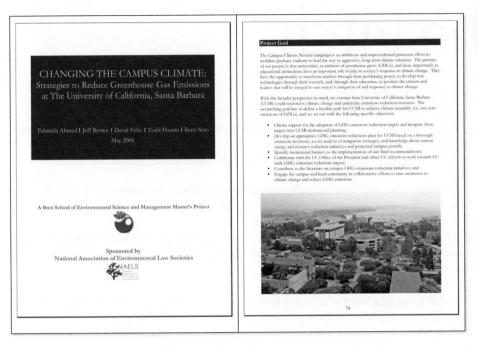

FIGURE 12.5
Setting a Proposal's Tone with Design

Your proposal shouldn't look boring. Instead, use design to create a tone for your proposal and make it easier to read. The photographs, bulleted lists, graphic icons, and color used in this proposal set a professional tone that gives the authors credibility and engages the readers.

Create a Look. Figure out what visual tone your proposal should project to the readers. Do you want it to appear progressive or conservative? Do you want it to look exciting or traditional? Make choices about fonts, columns, and photographs that reflect that tone (Figure 12.5).

Use Meaningful Headings. When your readers first pick up your proposal, they will likely scan it before reading. So your headings need to be meaningful and action oriented. Don't just use headings like "Problem" or "Plan." Instead, use headings like "Our Campus's Global Warming Problem" or "Introducing the Cool Campus Initiative."

Include Relevant, Accurate Graphics. Proposals often talk about trends, so you should look for places where you can use charts or graphs to illustrate those trends. Where possible, put data into tables. Use photographs to help explain the problem or show examples of your solution.

Use Lists to Highlight Important Points. Look for places in your proposal where you list key ideas or other items. Then, where appropriate, put those ideas into bulleted lists that are more scannable for readers.

Create White Space. You might want to expand your margins to add white space. Readers often like to take notes in the margins of proposals, so a little extra white space is useful. Also, extra white space makes the proposal seem more welcoming and easier to understand.

The Pitch

Pitches are brief proposals made to people who can offer their support (usually money) for your ideas. Pitches tend to be about one minute long, which means you need to be focused, concise, and confident. You're promoting yourself as much as you are selling your idea.

Here are some good strategies for making a persuasive one-minute pitch:

Introduce yourself and establish your credibility.   Remember that people invest in other *people,* not in projects. So tell them *who* you are and *what* you do.

Grab them with a good story.   You need to capture your listeners' attention right away, so ask them, "What if _____?" or explain, "Recently, _____happened and we knew there must be a better way."

Present your big idea in one sentence.   Don't make them wait. Hit them with your best idea up front in one sentence.

Give them your best two or three reasons for doing it.   The secret is to sell your idea, not explain it. List your best two or three reasons with minimal explanation.

Mention something that distinguishes you and your idea from the others.   What is unique about your idea? How does your idea uniquely fit your listeners' prior investments?

Offer a brief cost-benefits analysis.   Show them very briefly that your idea is worth their investment of time, energy, or money. If relevant, tell them what you need to make this project a reality.

Make sure they remember you.   End your pitch by telling them something memorable about you or your organization. Make sure you put your contact information in their hand (e.g., a business card or résumé). If they allow it, leave them a written version of your pitch.

The pitch shown here was written by Hans Fex, an entrepreneur with an exciting product idea that he pitched on Kickstarter, a crowdfunding website.

WRITE your own pitch.   Think of an original product, company, service, or idea that you can offer (please keep it PG-13). Then write a one-minute pitch that sells your idea to someone who can say yes and give you the resources to make it a reality.

Elevator Pitch: Mini Museum

Hans Fex

What exactly is the mini museum?

The mini museum is a portable collection of curiosities where every item is authentic, iconic and labeled. It's been carefully designed to take you on a journey of learning and exploration. The idea is simple. For the past 35 years I have collected amazing specimens specifically for this project. I then carefully break those specimens down into smaller pieces, embed them in resin, and you end up with an epic museum in a manageable space. Each mini museum is a handcrafted, individually numbered limited edition. And if you consider the age of some of these specimens—it's been billions of years in the making. The majority of these specimens were acquired directly from contacting specialists recommended to me by museum curators, research scientists and university historians.

I've been working on this pocket-sized collection of rare specimens for most of my life...

Now all I need to bring it to the world is your support!

The collection starts with some of the oldest matter ever collected in the known Universe—matter collected from carbonacious chondrites. These meteorites contain matter that is over 4 billion years old. Other meteors include some that have skimmed off the surface of Mars or the moon and then landed on Earth—each of those containing matter from those celestial bodies.

What's next? Specimens from the strelly pool stromatolites that contain the earliest evidence of life on Earth. Also, a piece of a palm tree from Antarctica—yes Antarctica. Everybody loves dinosaurs and the mini museum contains plenty of unique specimens from hundreds of millions of years ago including favorites like the T-Rex and Triceratops. Even dinosaur poop.

As we migrate from the beginning of the Universe to early life on Earth, we discover Homo Sapiens. Naturally, the Mini Museum also has many amazing and rare specimens documenting human history and culture. Mummy wrap, rocks from Mt. Everest, Trinitite, coal from the *Titanic*, and even a piece of the Apollo 11 command module to name just a few.

It's space and time in the palm of your hand. There is nothing else quite like it.

The Universe is amazing. I really wanted to remind people of that with this collection. How awesome would it be to own a group of rare meteorites, dinosaur fossils and relics of some of the most talked about places and events in human history? All in the palm of your hand?

Rex identifies the product right away.

He grabs them with an interesting story.

He uses examples to illustrate the unique nature of his product.

He concludes strong with excited statements and an intriguing question.

Here are some quick steps to get you working on your proposal.

IDENTIFY the Problem You Want to Solve

In one sentence, write down the topic and purpose of your proposal. Then narrow the topic to something you can manage.

ANALYZE the Problem's Causes and Effects

Use a concept map to analyze the problem's two to five major causes. Then use another concept map to explore the effects of the problem if nothing is done about it.

DO Your Research

Search the Internet and your library to collect sources. Then use empirical methods like interviews or surveys to help support or challenge the facts you find.

DEVELOP Your Plan for Solving the Problem

Using a concept map, figure out the two to five major steps needed to solve the problem. Then figure out what minor steps will be needed to achieve each of these major steps.

FIGURE OUT the Costs and Benefits of Your Plan

Look at your Plan section closely. Identify any costs of your plan. Then list all the benefits of solving the problem your way. You want to make sure the benefits of your solution outweigh the costs.

DRAFT the Proposal

Try drafting each major section separately, treating each one like a small document on its own. Your introduction should include a main point or thesis statement that expresses your solution to the problem in a straightforward way.

DESIGN Your Proposal

Your proposal needs to look professional and easy to read. Make choices about fonts, graphics, and document design that best suit the materials you are presenting to your readers.

REVISE and Edit

Proposals are complicated documents, so you should leave plenty of time to revise and edit your work.

How to Fix Grade Inflation at Harvard

SAMUEL GOLDMAN

In this proposal, Samuel Goldman explains why grade inflation is a problem at universities, especially elite universities. Then, he offers an intriguing solution. Watch how he blames the changing nature of higher education, not people, for this problem.

Reports [1] that A- is the median grade in Harvard College have reopened the debate about grade inflation. Many of the arguments offered in response to the news are familiar. The venerable grade hawk Harvey "C-" Mansfield, who brought the figures to public attention, describes the situation as an "indefensible [2]" relaxation of standards.

More provocative are defenses of grade inflation as the natural result of increased competition for admission to selective colleges and universities. A new breed of grade doves point out that standards have actually been tightened in recent years. But the change has been made to admissions standards rather than expectations for achievement in class.

According to the editorial board [3] of the Harvard Crimson, "high grades could be an indicator of the rising quality of undergraduate work in the last few decades, due in part to the rising quality of the undergraduates themselves and a greater access to the tools and resources of academic work as a result of technological advances, rather than unwarranted grade inflation." Matt Yglesias, '03, agrees [4], arguing that "it is entirely plausible that the median Harvard student today is as smart as an A-minus Harvard student from a generation ago. After all, the C-minus student of a generation ago would have very little chance of being admitted today."

There's a certain amount of self-congratulation here. It's not surprising that Harvard students, previous and current, think they're smarter than their predecessors—or anyone else. But they also make an important point. The students who earned the proverbial gentleman's Cs are rarely found at Harvard or its peers. Dimwitted aristocrats are no longer admitted. And even the brighter scions of prominent families can't take their future success for granted. Even with plenty of money and strong connections, they still need good grades to win places in graduate school, prestigious internships, and so on.

The result is a situation in which the majority of students really are very smart and very ambitious. Coursework is not always their first priority. But they are usually willing to do what's necessary to meet their professors' expectations. The decline of core curricula has also made it easier for students to pick courses that play to their strengths while avoiding subjects that are tough for them. It's less common to find Chemistry students struggling through Shakespeare than it was in the old days. [5]

According to the Harvard College Handbook for Students, an A- reflects [5] "full mastery of the subject" without "extraordinary distinction". In several classes I taught as an instructor and teaching fellow at Harvard and Princeton, particularly electives, I found that around half the students produced work on this level. As a result, I gave a lot of A-range grades.

Perhaps my understanding of "mastery" reflects historically lower demands. For example, I don't expect students writing about Aristotle to understand Greek. Yet it's not my impression that standards in my own field of political theory have changed a lot in the last fifty years or so. In absence of specific evidence of lowered standards, then, there's reason to think that grade inflation at first-tier universities has some objective basis.

But that doesn't mean grade inflation isn't a problem. It is: just not quite the way some critics think. At least at Harvard and similar institutions, grades are a reasonably accurate reflection of what students know or can do. But they are a poor reflection of how they compare to *other students in the same course*. In particular, grade inflation makes it difficult to distinguish truly excellent students, who are by definition few, from the potentially much larger number who are merely very good.

Here's my proposal for resolving that problem. In place of the traditional system, students should receive two grades. One would reflect their mastery of specific content or skills. The other would compare their performance to the rest of the class.

For example, a student might receive an A- for content, but a B for comparison. That wouldn't necessarily indicate low standards. It might just as easily mean that the class was unusually strong. Contrary to the assumption that they hand out praise like candy, professors make this kind of distinctions all the time. It's just that they do so privately in letters of recommendation, which are now more necessary than ever to make sense of inflated transcripts. [10]

In general, you'd expect to see greater divergence between the two grades in upper division courses for which students self-select by interest and ability than you would in general education requirements or introductory surveys that attract a more mixed group. There, a high content grade would be likely to correspond to high comparative grade.

Mark Bauerlein has suggested [6] a similar policy, in which a student's grade is listed alongside the average grade in the course. That's not a bad idea, but does little to prevent the confusion between objective and comparative measures that encourages grade inflation. After all, noting that a student received a B+ in a course with an average grade of B doesn't provide much information about what the instructor thinks a B means.

My proposal is also different from Mansfield's practice of giving students an inflated formal grade and a "real" grade given in private. Evaluations of content or skill mastery and comparisons to the rest of the class are equally real. They just measure different things. Moreover, secret grades, like sealed letters of recommendation, offer students little help in determining where they stand relative to their classmates.

The approach would increase the burden on professors to think about how they grade. In particular, we would have to be much more specific about their standards for the content grade than we often are under the current arrangement.

That's a good thing in an educational [15] system characterized by increasing diversity of preparation and expectations. No grading policy can restore the consensus about the meaning of an A that may (or may not) have existed half a century ago. But we can be reflective and transparent about what we're looking for—and about the information that our evaluations are intended to convey.

URLs in this post:

[1] Reports: http://www.thecrimson.com/article/2013/12/3/gradeinflationmodea/

[2] indefensible: http://www.bostonglobe.com/metro/2013/12/03/harvardprofessorraisesconcernsaboutgradeinflation/McZHfRZ2RxpoP5Xvwged1N/story.html

[3] editorial board: http://www.thecrimson.com/article/2013/12/4/gradeinflationharvard/

[4] agrees: http://www.slate.com/blogs/moneybox/2013/12/05/harvard_grade_inflation_the_real_problem_is_admissions.html

[5] reflects: http://isites.harvard.edu/icb/icb.do?keyword=k79903&tabgroupid=icb.tabgroup125605

[6] suggested: http://www.mindingthecampus.com/forum/2013/12/a_solution_to_galloping_grade_.html

A CLOSER LOOK AT
How to Fix Grade Inflation at Harvard   MyWritingLab

1. With your group, identify the causes of the grade inflation problem, according to Goldman. Which of these causes seems the most important to you? Are there other causes for the problem that you might add to your list?

2. Come up with another solution to the grade inflation problem. If you were in charge of a university, how might you change the grading system to (a) better reflect the efforts or mastery of students, or (b) present a wider range of scores to distinguish the high performers and the lower performers in a class?

IDEAS FOR
Writing and Discussion   MyWritingLab

1. Now it's your turn. Write a proposal that offers a better way to grade students at your university. You can propose to improve the current system or start completely over. If you want, you could even write a proposal in which you argue that the grading system is unnecessary and should be dispensed with.

2. Write a brief memoir about a time when you failed at something or fell short of a goal. Describe what happened at the time and how you felt about it. Did you learn anything from this moment? If so, explain that lesson to your readers. Or, was it just a bad experience from which nothing was learned?

A Rebirth of "We the People"

JIM ROUGH

Jim Rough, like many people, is concerned about the future of American democracy. In this proposal, he suggests that a constitution written in the 18th century may not be able to govern a modern society like the one we live in today. Pay attention to how he presents a new approach to self-government by arguing for a different way of interacting with other citizens.

A good system of governance needs to work for both individuals and society as a whole. In the eighteenth century, the old forms of governance headed by a king and hereditary aristocracy were not working to the benefit of most people, and a new system was needed. Through processes like the U.S. Constitutional Convention, state ratifying conventions, and the enactment of the Bill of Rights, "We the People" of the former colonies transformed their system. This transformation renewed politics, economics, and the social paradigm, creating a new version of the "Good Society."

The limitations of this eighteenth century system are now becoming apparent in this very different world of the twenty-first century. This article suggests how we might simply and safely revamp that old system to help us solve many of today's most pressing problems by creating a modern version of We the People.

The Underlying Problem

Our constitutional, rule of law, adversarial, majority-voting, competitive free market system faces grave challenges. It is based on the premise that when each of us pursues our own selfish interests, the "invisible hand" will make things better for everyone, that if we each seek our own private goals, the "general interest" will take care of itself. Growing economic inequality, inattention to macro problems, and eroding citizen involvement make it clear that the general interest is languishing.

For our competitive game-like system to work properly, the players must be largely independent, like small farmers or shopkeepers, on a level playing field. All must be small enough that none can manipulate the market, or have enough political power to unduly influence the rules. As we confront the limits of planetary resources and as corporations seize control of our global systems, our fates become linked together, dependent on decisions made in corporate boardrooms. By design, these ultimate decision-makers are not concerned with what's best for human beings but with the score of the game.

In order to make our system work, we buy bigger cars, take more pills, fly more miles, eat more food, and sell more weapons than we want, or is healthy for us—or than we can afford. In this context we tell ourselves that we "can't afford" to educate our children, or to sustain our environment, or maintain community infrastructures. We have allowed ownership of our media to be concentrated in so few hands that collectively we don't even know what's going on.

We have made these decisions because of the way our system is designed, not because of the failings of individuals. Our system forces each of us to direct our attention, energy and talents to serving competing special interests, letting it take care of the big picture.

Our political system doesn't even recognize the possibility of a "general-interest" viewpoint. It presumes that each voice is a "special interest," pursuing personal gain. So, if you are an environmentalist or a social activist, you must adopt a competitive stance and do battle against well-organized, well-funded competitors who really are special interests. If you persist in trying to serve the whole, you must live in poverty or make a small fraction of what you could earn.

Because we live within a competitive structure, our ability to think and converse is compromised. We have learned to think in sound bites, and to accept simple answers instead of seeking the underlying causes and finding real solutions. We are more comfortable blaming individuals like "greedy" CEO's, "lazy" welfare recipients, "bureaucratic" civil servants, "corrupt" politicians, or "apathetic" citizens than looking for the systemic conditions that encourage them to act the way they do. For real change to happen We the People, all of us together, must reawaken, determine what kind of world we want, and take charge of our system.

We the People

"We the People" is a phrase that describes much more than "lots of people eager for positive change" or even "all of us." There are six characteristics of a legitimate We the People:

1. *Inclusiveness* . . . Everyone participates
2. *Unanimity'* . . . We express one viewpoint.

3. *Autonomy* . . . We choose the issues to address, determine solutions, and act.

4. *Authority* . . . We are ultimately in charge. We provide direction to government, not the other way around.

5. *Intelligence* . . . We have all the expertise there is and we can use it to make good decisions.

6. *Creativity* . . . We can solve impossible problems.

Does this sound impossible? It's not. Many think poorly of "the people." They see what appears to be citizen apathy, narrow mindedness, and self-interest, and assume that these are characteristic of the ordinary person. But these are largely effects of our system's design. An adversarial, majority-rule voting structure, for example, practically guarantees right/wrong arguing rather than a genuine search for answers. It also guarantees a minority of people will seem apathetic because they know their voices don't matter.

Many people do not believe that a meaningful consensus among all of us is possible, yet we have already reached meaningful consensus in many areas. It's just that we are not structured to take advantage of it. For example, I've asked many people, "Which set of values should have priority? Corporate values or human values?" It's unanimous—human values should predominate. But our system keeps us busy arguing, so that collectively we do the opposite of what we really want.

The Solution: A Wisdom Council

How might a real "We the People" with all six characteristics come into being? How might all of us call "time out" from the competitive, adversarial aspects of society to face the big issues, dialogue creatively, develop new options, and reach consensus on a shared vision? If we can do this, many of today's problems would just go away. Our competitive political and economic systems would morph into the cooperative ventures they need to

be. This voluntary "pulling together to create what is best for all" would seem like a transformation of human nature.

There is a new social invention, called the "Wisdom Council," that promises to help us gather into this kind of We the People. A growing body of tests in organizations and communities indicates that it works.

Here's how it would work for the nation: Every three months or so, there is an officially sanctioned, nationwide public lottery, in which twelve participants are randomly selected to meet for a few days, assisted by a specially trained facilitator. This person dynamically facilitates the group to determine key issues of their choice, to work on them creatively, and to develop consensus statements. These "Statements of the People" have no coercive authority, but are offered to the larger community in a ceremony similar to the "State of the Union" message. Everyone in the nation is invited and encouraged to gather with others to hear this report in local face-to-face settings. Those attending these sessions visit in small groups for a short time to consider the Statements, and to report their conclusions back through the media or the Internet. In our experiments, we've generally found that each small group is supportive of both the statements and the process.

Assume for a moment that the Wisdom Council process is well known among all citizens. After the Wisdom Council presents its results, many people will participate in the official dialogues and practically all will discuss the issues and recommendations with someone at some time, extending their individual perspectives. They can respond through the Internet, or through letters to the editors of papers. If some disagree with the Wisdom Council's statements, people will be interested to hear why, and the media will seek them out. In this way the Wisdom Council sparks a whole-system conversation that listens to and celebrates diverse viewpoints, seeking consensus.

This conversation continues until the next randomly selected group meets and picks up these (or other) issues, and makes new Statements. Eventually, Statements of the People are developed which almost everyone supports. When there is wide consensus, action may happen voluntarily through individuals or groups, or through policy decisions by elected officials. Elected officials are part of the conversation. Voters assess them on their ability to implement the building consensus.

To achieve the promised benefits, a Wisdom Council must have all of the following twelve features:

1. The Wisdom Council must be chartered by We the People—This is a paradoxical requirement since without the Wisdom Council there is no possibility for a "We the People" to exist. However, experience indicates that just a few dedicated people can initially convene a Wisdom Council. This Wisdom Council expresses a "We the People" viewpoint which is not widely known, but which gathers support for the next Wisdom Council. Each successive cycle is a more accurate approximation of We the People, which can "charter" the next Wisdom Council. Ultimately as interest and involvement build, there is enough support for an "official" marking of this charter, which might take the form of a U.S. Constitutional amendment.

2. It is a microcosm, composed of randomly selected people—The people on a Wisdom Council are not self-selected, or elected, or appointed by any authority. They are randomly chosen, and each member speaks only for him or her self and not for any constituency like women, Democrats, poor people—or for a geographical region.

3. It is empowered to select and frame the issues it addresses—Because the Wisdom Council symbolizes We the People, there is

no higher authority. As boss of the system, symbolically speaking, the Wisdom Council chooses the issues it will consider, frames them as it wishes, and works towards solving them.

4. The members are chosen in a ceremony: a lottery—In the annual, semi-annual, or quarterly lottery, each registered voter has an equal chance to be selected.

5. It is non-coercive—No one is forced to serve on a Wisdom Council and its results have no coercive power. The Wisdom Council just presents its conclusions, and then it disbands.

6. It operates in a fishbowl—Once Wisdom Council members have been publicly selected, they are isolated from the influence of others, but everyone knows they are meeting.

7. It is facilitated dynamically—(See below.)

8. It generates unanimous statements—Unlike the world of agree/disagree meetings, the Wisdom Council strives to reach conclusions that everyone—not just those on the Wisdom Council—can fully support.

9. The results are presented in a ceremony—When the Wisdom Council concludes its work, there is an immediate presentation of the final results, as well as stories of the Council's experience. Everyone in the system is part of the extended audience to whom the Wisdom Council speaks.

10. Small group dialogues are convened—Everyone in the system (nation, state, community, organization) is invited to participate in small group dialogues in town halls, cafes, churches, community centers, individual homes, and the internet, and to voice their responses.

11. The process is ongoing—Each Wisdom Council articulates interim conclusions in an ongoing dialogue that involves everyone. The

Councils' Statements provide a way to track progress on the issues.

12. The process operates in parallel with normal governance structures—The Wisdom Council does not change existing structures—it merely adds a periodic short-term, small-group meeting and presentation.

Action happens through existing structures or through direct citizen action.

The Magic of Choice-creating

The Wisdom Council's benefits come largely from the magical quality of talking and thinking it establishes—both among its members and throughout the larger population. This quality of thinking, known as choice-creating, is different from normal political decision-making, where people agree and disagree on topics, trying to gain influence. It is similar to dialogue because it is a deep open-minded exploration of issues and similar to deliberation because groups reach conclusions. But with choice-creating the emphasis is not on people carefully weighing different options and negotiating an agreement. It is oriented toward reaching unanimity via breakthroughs of both head and heart.

Experience tells us that a breakthrough is the best way for any group to reach unanimity on a difficult issue. Then consensus happens naturally and quickly, and all feel motivated to help implement the result. This is not a rational phenomenon. In fact, the use of rational, deliberative modes of talking and thinking make breakthroughs unlikely. Even consensus-building, where people are expected to suppress their own individuality for the benefit of the group, stifles the possibility for consensus via breakthroughs.

Choice-creating is what happens when a [20] community or organization faces and overcomes a survival challenge. People put aside their normal prejudices and come together like a family, rising to the occasion to do what is necessary. Each person's contribution is valued and the process builds an exhilarating sense of "We."

The Wisdom Council is structured to elicit choice-creating in all of us, and to build this sense of "We." It is a "time out" from the usual back and forth political conversation, for a different kind of conversation where people address the big issues and seek consensus on what's best for everyone. This new conversation is open-minded, creative and thoughtful, where people speak from the heart.

Through experience, we've discovered that the best way to assure choice-creating is through Dynamic Facilitation. Unlike traditional facilitators who orient to extrinsic factors like goals, agendas and guidelines, the dynamic facilitator orients to intrinsic factors like the energy of passion or fear. She or he uses charts of Solutions, Data, Concerns, and Problem-statements to capture comments as they come up. This approach honors and acknowledges each comment, letting each participant know they are heard, and encouraging new ideas. Different kinds of breakthrough happen in this process, like when the "real" problem is identified, or new solutions emerge, or when people realize they no longer feel about an issue as they once did.

As an example, one dynamically facilitated group achieved consensus on the issue of abortion. At first, the usual pro-life and pro-choice positions were expressed and people talked about those. Then someone asked, "How frequent are abortions anyway?" and the group wondered if there wasn't some way to eliminate abortions altogether. After about thirty minutes, the group's consensus was: "How can we achieve a society where all children are conceived and born into families that want and love them?"

When people hear this story they sometimes express concern that this consensus avoids the issue. But in fact, it's the opposite. This answer ends the longstanding avoidance by identifying the real issue, which neither the pro-life nor the pro-choice position addresses. It was a breakthrough because it freed people from the argument, so they can start thinking and solving the real problem.

Tom Atlee, the author of *The Tao of* [25] *Democracy: Using Co-Intelligence to Create a World That Works for All* says, "Part of why I love Dynamic Facilitation (DF) so much is that it works with people AS THEY ARE. It doesn't require that they buy into a set of rules about how they're going to talk together. They can be [jerks] and the facilitator makes sure (a) that they don't get shut down because of that, (b) that the people they target—and the group as a whole—continue to feel safe and (c) that whatever gift they bring gets heard and made available to the group mind. This alone makes DF incredibly useful in a pluralistic democracy. Add to that its power to metabolize conflict into useful insights and to engender co-creativity among diverse people, and it's a real treasure."

A Wisdom Council Example

The Wisdom Council is a new concept, which can be difficult to understand from a description. It can best be appreciated when it is experienced. The concept has been tested with citizens in cities, with students in schools, with homeless people, and with employees in government agencies and corporations. The most comprehensive experiment so far was initiated by three citizens in the Rogue Valley of Oregon, who separately heard an interview describing it on National Public Radio. They met each other and convened a Wisdom Council experiment in their area (www.rvwc.org). That successful experience taught us how a Wisdom Council can charter itself, that Dynamic Facilitation is crucial to establishing the spirit of choice-creating, and that onlookers 'get it' from seeing the presentation.

The best example to illustrate how a nationally chartered Wisdom Council might transform society is from American history—the U.S. Constitutional period of 1787-1791. This was very much a Wisdom Council-like process.

The delegates to the U.S. Constitutional Convention acted outside of their assigned level of responsibility in the name of "We the People." They didn't want to use that phrase because to them it was really the states that were ordaining and establishing the Constitution. But since they had decided that the Constitution would go into effect as soon as it was ratified by nine of the thirteen states, and no one knew which states would adopt it first, the document couldn't start with a list of states. Instead, the delegates came up with "We the People" as a grammatically convenient phrase.

The Constitutional delegates were not democratic in their intentions. They wanted a republic rather than a democracy. Most believed that only property-owning males had sufficient gravitas and investment in society to make sound decisions, so they excluded slaves, women, Native Americans, and those who had no property from participating in government. But the fortuitous use of the phrase "We the People," and the way they conducted their meetings, set the stage for a real We the People to emerge.

This process foreshadowed the Wisdom [30] Council. Just a small group of people took "time out" from the normal course of politics—and life—for a "fishbowl" meeting. They addressed the big issues of the day using a higher than normal quality of conversation, seeking consensus rather than a majority. In the end, they spoke as We the People, issuing a near-unanimous proposal signed by 39 of 42 present. Then they disbanded.

You might have asked of the Constitutional Convention, just as people often ask of the Wisdom Council today, "How could there be real change without any power of coercion or follow-up process?" The Constitutional Convention just presented its conclusions and disbanded. Action happened because its conclusions sparked a widespread conversation throughout the land and set off a self-organizing dynamic of change. Ratifying conventions were organized, the Constitution was implemented, and thanks to a disagreement among many in the general public, the Bill of Rights was added.

The whole process took only one Wisdom Council-like meeting, plus four and a half years of talking and thinking. In the end, there was a consensus voice of all, a We the People that really did "ordain and establish" a new system, which transformed human expectations and actions. No longer did people blindly grant authority to those in charge. They were empowered to self-govern and became more entrepreneurial, independent and self-reliant.

Going Forward

Our current system is designed like a machine based on eighteenth-century assumptions about who we are and what is needed in the world. There is no one in charge of it. It is in charge of us. Without a We the People, it is on automatic pilot taking us mindlessly toward a future no one would choose. We all keep our heads down, focused on improving special interests and ignoring our collective situation.

Thomas Jefferson described the problem in a letter he wrote to his friend, James Madison. Consulting actuarial tables of his time, he calculated that the majority of any given generation would be dead after about nineteen years. With this statistic in mind, he wrote: "It may be proved that no society can make a perpetual constitution, or even a perpetual law. The earth belongs always to the living generation. . . . Every constitution, then, and every law naturally expires at the end of 19 years. If it be enforced longer, it is an act of force and not of right."

The Wisdom Council offers a simple, practical, risk-free way to add the missing element—a wise and responsible We the People—to our system. Recent experiments give reason to be optimistic: The Wisdom Council seems to engender a genuine We the People; it can be initiated by just a few people while it honors and includes everyone; when people experience the process (and perhaps only then) they 'get' its potential to help us solve today's most pressing issues; and momentum is gathering.

There is a new non-profit organization [35] helping to bring Wisdom Councils to communities and the nation, the Center for Wise Democracy. One current strategy is to convene a gathering of many public service organizations from both left and right to charter the first national Wisdom Council, followed by a national day of dialogue. You are invited to become involved with these efforts or to explore the Wisdom Council further by conducting your own experiments.

A CLOSER LOOK AT
A Rebirth of "We the People"   MyWritingLab

1. Many people believe that the United States government is no longer functioning properly. Some people, like Rough, say that the problem is caused by an outmoded constitution. Others would say that the problem has come about because Americans have strayed from the Constitution. With your group, discuss both sides and decide which one you find more believable.

2. Rough is proposing a "Wisdom Council" that is chosen randomly to work on social issues and come up with solutions to problems. With your group, list ten pros and five cons to this proposal. You can use some of the pros and cons mentioned by Rough, but come up with a few of your own.

3. Though attractive, it is highly unlikely a proposal like this one would be adopted, even if the ideas it offers are very good. With your group, list five barriers to major constitutional changes, such as the ones proposed by Rough.

IDEAS FOR
Writing and Discussion   MyWritingLab

1. Write a profile of one of the people who founded the country in which you grew up. In your profile, explain how this founder's personal beliefs and convictions eventually shaped the nation's constitution.

2. Fictional utopias and dystopias are common ways to imagine societies and governments that are different from current ones. Write a literary analysis of a utopian or dystopian novel that you have read. In your literary analysis discuss whether you think the government in the novel could actually exist.

1. What are some of the problems on your college's campus? With a group in your class, list them and pick one that seems especially troublesome. What do you think are the causes of this problem? What has changed recently to bring this problem about or make it worse? Discuss this problem with a group of other people in your class.

2. Now try to figure out a way to solve this campus problem. What would be a good solution to this problem? Can you think of a few other solutions? With a small group, discuss the costs and benefits of solving the problem in different ways.

3. With a group in class, find a proposal on the Internet that you can discuss. Look closely at the proposal's content, organization, style, and design. Do you think the proposal is effective? What are its strengths? What are its weaknesses? If you were going to revise this proposal, what are some of the things you would change?

Talk About This

1. Find a proposal on the Internet by entering the keyword "proposal" and a problem that interests you into a search engine. Write a one-page analysis of the proposal, describing how it explains the problem and offers a plan for solving it. In your analysis, tell your readers whether you think the proposal is or is not effective. Explain why you think so, and offer suggestions about how the proposal could be improved.

2. List five problems that are facing our society right now. Pick one that interests you and then try to narrow the topic down to something you can manage in a small proposal. Use a concept map to explore what you already know about the problem, its causes, and its effects. Then do research on the subject by collecting online and print sources on it. Draft a one- or two-page causal analysis of the problem that does not offer a solution.

3. Find a proposal on the Internet that is badly designed. Do a makeover of the design to improve the look and usability of the proposal. What would make it more appealing to readers? How could design techniques be used to make it simpler to scan or easier to understand? You should create two sample pages that illustrate your design.

Try This Out

Here are some other microgenres that are similar to proposals. Choose a microgenre from the list below and find three examples in print or on the Internet. Create your own set of guidelines for writing one of these microgenres.

Ridiculous-invention proposal—a "mock proposal" for an outrageous invention (perhaps an overly complex solution to a simple problem)

Marriage (or date) proposal—a proposal of marriage (or a romantic date) with someone using all the features of a formal proposal

Assignment prospectus—description of your proposed approach to a particular writing or other assignment, addressed to a professor

Job application letter—a letter that describes how you can help a business or organization solve its problems

Letter to politician or campus leader—a proposed solution to a pressing national, local, or campus problem

Write
This

1. **Propose your own solution.** Write a proposal that solves a problem in our society or in your life. Explore the causes of the problem and come up with a plan that solves it. Then identify all the benefits that would come about if the problem were solved according to your plan. The best topics for proposals are ones that affect your life in some way. Pick a problem that you feel strongly about or something that affects your everyday life. Your proposal should run about seven to ten pages. Include graphics and make sure the document is well designed.

2. **Remake a proposal into a multimedia presentation.** Using a search engine, find a proposal on the Internet. Transform the proposal into a presentation that incorporates multimedia features. You can use presentation software, overhead projector slides, flipcharts, or posters. Then write a one-page rhetorical analysis for your professor that introduces the proposal and describes how you altered the original proposal's content, organization, style, and design to make it work as a multimedia presentation.

3. **Propose something absurd.** One of the most famous "proposals" is Jonathan Swift's "A Modest Proposal" in which he suggests consuming Irish children as a way to solve a famine. Swift's intent was to draw attention to the desperation of the Irish, while shaming absent English landlords. Write an ironic five-page proposal like Swift's that proposes an absurd solution for an important problem. Remember that the key to irony is to bring about a positive change by shaming the people who are at fault.

> Go to **MyWritingLab** to complete this chapter's
> exercises and test your understanding of its objectives.

13

Analytical Reports

In this chapter, you will learn how to—

13.1 invent the content of your analytical report with solid research.

13.2 use the report genre's pattern to organize your document.

13.3 develop a writing style that is neutral and sounds objective.

13.4 create a design that makes your analytical report easy to use.

Analysis involves studying a subject closely by examining its features, movements, or trends. Analytical reports help you explain how you studied something, what you discovered, and what you learned from the information you collected. They are used to explain trends, explore causes and effects of problems, study natural and social phenomena, present research findings, and make recommendations. In an analytical report, you need to do more than present the results from research. You also need to interpret those results to help your readers better understand the information you collected.

In college, your professors will ask you to write reports about local, national, and international problems and trends. You might study an uptick in crime on campus or do research on recent flooding in the area. You might analyze a new fashion trend or explain the results of a scientific experiment. In advanced courses in your major, analytical reports will grow larger and more complex as class projects become more complicated, inventive, and collaborative. You and teams of others will use analytical reports to study problems and trends and then present your findings to your readers.

In the workplace, the analytical report genre has many versions, including *research reports, recommendation reports, completion reports, feasibility reports,* and *scientific reports.* They are used to explain accidents, investigate business opportunities, explore trends, and offer recommendations to supervisors, clients, and customers.

Because analytical reports are so important in the workplace, college is the best place to learn how to write these complex documents. Once you know how analytical reports work, you will be able to write them more effectively and efficiently.

Reports

To help you remember this structure, you might memorize the acronym IMRaD, which is widely used by professional researchers. IMRaD stands for Introduction, Methods, Results, and Discussion.

Summary or abstract

Introduction

Methods

Results

Discussion

Conclusions/
Recommendations

End Material: References
and Appendices

A typical report tends to have the following features:

- **Executive summary or abstract** that summarizes the major sections of the report.
- **Introduction** that defines a research question or problem and explains why it is important to the reader. The introduction clearly states the purpose and main point of the report, while offering background information on the topic.
- **Methods section** that describes how the research was carried out.
- **Results or Findings section** that presents the results of the research objectively.
- **Discussion section** that analyzes the results and explains what they mean.
- **Conclusion/Recommendations** section that restates the main point of the report and offers specific recommendations.
- **End Material: References** section that provides a list of references or works cited. **Appendices** that offer additional sources and other materials.

ONE STUDENT GROUP'S WORK
Analytical Reports

Visit **MyWritingLab** to explore an interactive version of this essay.

College Students' Attitudes on the Causes of Infidelity

Kaisa Lee and Jamie Koss, Undergraduate Students,
Human Development and Family Studies

Abstract

Infidelity is a problem in today's society associated with instability in relationships and the high divorce rate. The study consisted of 23 male and female students at a Midwestern university. It was hypothesized that males would perceive sexual attraction as a primary cause of infidelity while females would perceive relationship dissatisfaction as a primary cause. Survey data was statistically analyzed using frequencies, cross-tabulations and a reliability analysis. Findings supported the literature and hypothesis in that more males viewed sexual attraction as a primary cause of infidelity and more females viewed relationship dissatisfaction as a primary cause. It is important for practitioners to be aware of the problems infidelity causes in relationships and further researchers could investigate root causes for preventative and proactive actions.

The abstract offers an overview of the analytical report.

Introduction

Roughly 50% of individuals in married relationships engage in some form of infidelity at some point in their marriage (Drigotas, Safstrom, & Gentilia, 1999). It is no wonder researchers are studying this serious relationship transgression more to better understand the root of the problem. In several studies, more than fifty percent of both men and women in college dating relationships have been involved in some form of infidelity behavior (Lewandowski & Ackerman, 2006). Infidelity can be portrayed differently in society and between men and women. It causes a great deal of distress, turmoil, and often termination of the relationship. Society's high rate of divorce and infidelity in the relationship indicates the need for this problem to be more widely researched and addressed. In this study infidelity refers to a violation in trust or a breaking of understanding about the sexual monogamy of the relationship (Pittman & Pittman Wagners, 1995). Male and female college students were surveyed on their attitudes on the causes of infidelity in committed relationships.

The authors identify the topic and stress its importance.

continued

Literature Review

It was found that there are definite differences and similarities between males and females regarding their attitudes towards causes of infidelity. Predicting infidelity has various components such as composite, physical, and emotional infidelity. It was found that when there is commitment, satisfaction, fewer alternatives, and a strong investment in the relationship, there are considerably fewer infidelity behaviors. Females were found to view emotional infidelity as more upsetting and males found sexual infidelity to be more upsetting. Jealousy is found to be a key result and trigger of infidelity. One study found that the plausible reasoning for causes of infidelity varied among genders. Legitimacy, seduction, sexuality, sensation seeking, normalization, and social background make up the six component model of infidelity, used to measure such behavior in this study. Males were found to view seduction as the major cause while women were found to view social background as a major cause of betrayal. Cross-cultural research is important in finding similarities and differences. When need-fulfillment and self-expansion were looked into they found that lower levels of each of these pieces led to higher susceptibility for infidelity. Very little research was found on the causes of infidelity according to the views of each gender. All the information found regarding infidelity is supportive in regards to linking gender differences with infidelity (Drigotas et al., 1999; Harris, 2003; Yeneceri & Kokdemir, 2006; Lewandowski & Ackerman, 2006).

When predicting infidelity behavior, three main types were found: composite infidelity, physical infidelity, and emotional infidelity (Drigotas et al., 1999). Within those three topics, the researchers measured commitment, satisfaction, alternative quality and investment. Those individuals that were studied who were more satisfied and committed, had fewer alternatives, and were invested in their relationships more were less likely to have infidelity behaviors. The findings of this article suggested that women were more likely to engage in such behaviors. Overall, individuals who engaged in infidelity behaviors reported less satisfaction and commitment.

When looking at infidelity in relationships, undoubtedly jealousy comes to mind as an outcome of this behavior. Harris (2003) has taken a closer look at gender differences in jealousy as a result of infidelity. Social-Cognitive Theory was used to look into these differences of male and female variables comparing emotional infidelity and sexual infidelity. A survey was administered to assess college students' attitudes towards actual infidelity, hypothetical infidelity, which type of infidelity would be worse: emotional infidelity or sexual infidelity, as well as the relationship experiences of the participants. The results of the study showed that forced-choice hypothetical infidelity supported the notion that women view emotional infidelity as the worse form of infidelity. Another discovery to the study was that men placed higher importance on sex which was a stronger predictor for

---

A literature review is used to provide background information on the topic.

Three different types of infidelity are defined for the readers.

sexual jealousy over women. A trigger to jealousy for males was the perception that females' sexual act is driven by love. However a woman's trigger was shown to be emotional involvement. More females were found to believe that if a male is either emotionally involved or in love with another, then sex would also be involved. Jealousy is a significant component to infidelity in relationships especially when viewed via a social-cognitive perspective. Jealousy as looked at in this study is a major component of both the causes and results of infidelity. Emotional and sexual infidelities are the two types that decipher between the two genders.

Yeniceri and Kokdemir (2006) conducted a cross–cultural study investigating possible reasons for infidelity behavior, broken into six components. This study concluded that males rated seduction as the primary cause of infidelity more so than females did. Females perceived social background as a major cause more often than men did. Seduction was viewed as the major cause of infidelity when it was the male partaking in the behavior. Conversely, if the female is to blame for infidelity then legitimacy was perceived as a more reasonable cause.

Lewandowski and Ackerman (2006) reported that the lack of need fulfillment and self-expansion were additional predictors of susceptibility of infidelity. A group of college students were surveyed on five types of need-fulfillment (intimacy, companionship, sex, security, and emotional involvement). Three types of self-expansion were assessed such as self-expansion, inclusion of the other in the self, and potential for self-expansion. Susceptibility to infidelity was the last variable in the study to be evaluated connecting with need fulfillment and self-expansion. Their hypothesis predicted that gender, relationship length, need fulfillment, and self expansion will contribute a major increase to the overall variance in susceptibility to infidelity. The results to their study supported their hypothesis. In fact, lower satisfaction in need fulfillment and lower levels of self-expansion lead to higher susceptibility to infidelity. A significant finding to the research was that gender plays a large role in susceptibility to infidelity. The results showed that males are more susceptible to infidelity than women. This study focused on the prediction of infidelity as well as the beliefs of college students on the sole causes of infidelity.

It has been found across studies that there are definite variables among the two genders regarding the reasons for and views toward infidelity (Yeniceri & Kokdemir, 2006). Research has discovered differences between males and females regarding emotional and sexual infidelity (Harris, 2003). It also has defined some possible reasons for such behaviors. Models have been created to measure infidelity amongst couples and theories have been made regarding the susceptibility (Lewandowski & Ackerman, 2006). Most of the research that has been conducted addresses many forms of infidelity, predictions for the relationship as well as socialization components (Drigotas et al., 1999). While many studies on infidelity were found, only the study conducted in Turkey pertained directly to our topic. The Social Learning Theory

continued

was used as a framework for the causes of infidelity. There is little research that has related this theory to the two genders' views on the causes of betrayal within a relationship; this is the gap in the family social science literature that we hope to fill.

Theoretical Framework

Bandura's Social Learning Theory indicates that by observing behaviors that are modeled one tends to then imitate or match performances (Mihalic & Elliott, 2005). Humans learn and comprehend attitudes and behaviors as a result of the social interactions they have with other people (Strong, DeVault, Cohen, 2005). Bandura said that human nature is formed by the connections between the individual. Bandura further stressed the importance of learning by observation of others instead of solely from oneself. As applied to our study, this theory would predict that by observing infidelity behavior by one's peers, media, or family, one would deem such actions as acceptable in their dating relationships.

Purpose Statement

The purpose of this study was to examine the attitudes of a group of Midwestern University male and female students' perceptions on the causes of infidelity. The central research question in this study was, "What are the comparable attitudes of a Midwestern state university sample of male and female students regarding the causes of infidelity behavior in committed relationships?" It was hypothesized that the males would rate sexual attraction as the primary cause for infidelity and females would rate relationship dissatisfaction as the primary cause.

> The research question is stated for the readers.

Methods

Participants

This study was done at a small Midwestern university. There were 14 female and nine male college student participants. Participants' ages ranged from 18–25. In regards to the academic status of females, two were sophomores, two were juniors, and 10 were of senior status or higher. Of the male participants, there was one freshman, two juniors, five were at senior status or higher, and there was one graduate student. There were 11 females and eight males that had previously been in a committed relationship and of those who were currently in a committed relationship, 12 were females and three were males. Three females and one male had not previously been in a committed relationship but were currently in one. Two females and six males were single.

> The authors describe their research methods.

Research Design

The design is most appropriately described as the cross-sectional design type. The form of data collection was self-administered surveys. The population was the university student body. The sample consisted of males and females ages

> Major step

18–25 that were currently in or previously in a committed relationship. The sampling design type used was the nonrandom snowball design type because this type allowed researchers to search within their personal networks to obtain those individuals who were in the types of relationships needed for this research. The primary reason snowball type and nonrandom were used was we were accessing an inaccessible population. In order to ethically protect our human subjects, we completed the Human Subjects Institutional Review Board (IRB) training and then were approved by the IRB to begin data collection.

Data Collection Instrument

A survey was designed to collect data about the attitudes of students regarding the causes of infidelity in committed relationships. The survey contained a cover letter and an implied consent form that described what the study entailed. A definition of any terms that would not be universally known, risks and benefits, time commitment, confidentiality, voluntary participation, instructions for completing the survey and contact information of the researchers, as well as the supervisor was also included.

Age, gender, academic status, and relationship status made up the demographic questions. Based on a five point Likert scale, the survey contained nine closed-ended questions regarding what the participants thought was the primary cause of infidelity. The scale ranged from one being strongly disagree, to five being strongly agree. Questions were created from infidelity literature. The survey instrument has both face validity and content validity.

Major step

Procedure

Our participants were selected from each of our social networks. This ensured they had had a personal experience with a committed relationship at some point. We contacted participants via phone, email, or in person and worked out a time that worked best for them to take the survey. Since the topic could potentially be uncomfortable for some of our participants, extra care was used to make sure they knew that the survey was voluntary and that they did not have to participate if they did not feel comfortable. We asked them to choose a setting that would best suit them to take the surveys; most of which was at their home or on campus. With each participant we distributed the survey and read the survey verbatum. We instructed them to place their completed surveys in the envelope provided. We stepped out of the room or area in which they took the survey so they would not feel rushed or pressured to answer questions in a way they thought would be socially acceptable. We also made sure they were taking it in separate areas if they were taking the survey simultaneously with another person, such as their significant other. This ensured that there was no pressure to answer the questions in a biased manner. Our survey instruments were kept in a large sealed envelope at one of the researcher's homes in a locked closet.

Major step

continued

Data Analysis Plan

Data was first "cleaned" and checked for any missing data. The surveys were then "coded" using acronyms for each of the demographic and dependent variables. The demographic variables were: Academic status (STAT), gender (GEN), and age (AGE), with gender being an independent variable. The other two demographic variables were if they had previously been in a committed relationship (PCR) or if they were currently in a committed relationship (CCR). To determine which dependent variables the participant felt to be the primary cause of infidelity, they were asked about: lack of personal accountability (LPA), relationship dissatisfaction (RDS), lack of security in relationships (SEC), lack of attention from partner (ATN), sexual attraction (SXA), sexual dissatisfaction (SDS), revenge on partner (RVG), being exposed to infidelity in one's group of friends, peers, or media (EXP), or alcohol consumption (ALC). The level of analysis was the individual. To analyze the data, the data-analyzing computer program called Statistical Package for the Social Sciences (SPSS), was used. Given the fact we were comparing groups based on gender, our data analysis included: Frequencies, cross-tabulations, mean-comparisons, and a reliability analysis called Chronbach's Alpha.

Results

The results are presented in a straightforward way.

A frequency distribution analysis indicated that there was no data missing from our surveys. The Chronbach's Alpha measure of reliability was .780 in this analysis. This indicates that the survey items were a reliable index of our major concept on college students' attitudes on the causes of infidelity.

Table 1: Crosstabs

Tables help present data in an accessible way.

Gender	SD	D	U	A	SA	Total
LPA						
Female	0.0%	21.4%	21.4%	35.7%	21.4%	100.0%
Male	0.0%	11.1%	33.3%	44.4%	11.1%	100.0%
RDS						
Female	0.0%	14.3%	7.1%	50.0%	28.6%	100.0%
Male	0.0%	0.0%	11.1%	66.7%	22.2%	100.0%
SEC						
Female	7.1%	0.0%	14.3%	57.1%	21.4%	100.0%
Male	11.1%	11.1%	11.1%	44.4%	22.2%	100.0%
ATN						
Female	0.0%	7.1%	0.0%	57.1%	35.7%	100.0%
Male	0.0%	0.0%	0.0%	77.8%	22.2%	100.0%

Table 1: *Continued*

Gender	SD	D	U	A	SA	Total
			SXA			
Female	7.1%	7.1%	28.6%	28.6%	28.6%	100.0%
Male	0.0%	33.3%	0.0%	44.4%	22.2%	100.0%
			SDS			
Female	0.0%	21.4%	21.4%	21.4%	35.7%	100.0%
Male	11.1%	22.2%	22.2%	44.4%	0.0%	100.0%
			RVG			
Female	0.0%	21.4%	28.6%	42.9%	7.1%	100.0%
Male	0.0%	22.2%	22.2%	44.4%	11.1%	100.0%
			EXP			
Female	14.3%	21.4%	21.4%	42.9%	0.0%	100.0%
Male	11.1%	11.1%	44.4%	22.2%	11.1%	100.0%
			ALC			
Female	0.0%	7.1%	21.4%	35.7%	35.7%	100.0%
Male	11.1%	0.0%	33.3%	44.4%	11.1%	100.0%

Note. (GEN) = Gender of participant; (LPA) = Lack of personal accountability is a primary cause of infidelity; (RDS)=Relationship dissatisfaction is a primary cause of infidelity; (SEC)=Lack of security in relationships is a primary cause of infidelity; (ATN) = Lack of attention from partner is a primary cause of infidelity; (SXA) = Sexual attraction is a primary cause of infidelity; (SDS) = Sexual dissatisfaction is a primary cause of infidelity; (RVG) = Revenge on partner is a primary cause of infidelity; (EXP) = Being exposed to infidelity in one's group of friends, peers, or media has a lot to do with the cause of infidelity; (ALC) = Alcohol consumption has a great deal to do with the cause of infidelity

Discussion

Overall, results supported the hypothesis by demonstrating that the majority of males thought sexual attraction was a primary cause of infidelity. Results also demonstrated that the majority of female participants thought that relationship dissatisfaction was a primary cause of infidelity. In our study, our hypothesis using the Social Learning Theory was supported because both male and female responses were evenly distributed along the Likert scale on the exposure to one's peers, friends, or media being the primary cause of infidelity. This shows that neither males nor females viewed this as a primary cause of infidelity. Lack of attention from one's partner had 100% of males and 92.9% of females agree that this was a primary cause of infidelity. This variable was rated the highest compared to all the others between both genders.

The authors interpret and discuss the results for the readers.

continued

The majority of our results were also supported by our literature. Regarding relationship dissatisfaction, the literature supported the idea that the more dissatisfied you are in your relationships, the more likely you are to have infidelity behaviors (Drigotas et al., 1999). The work done by Harris (2003) supported our hypothesis that females view relationship dissatisfaction as the primary cause of infidelity while men view sexual attraction as the primary cause of infidelity. She found that women view emotional infidelity as a worse form of infidelity while men view sexual infidelity as a worse form. The emotional dimension relates to females' view of relationship dissatisfaction while the sexual dimension relates to males' view of sexual attraction.

Literature that supported our results the strongest was the study done by Yeniceri and Kokdemir (2006). Their six components related closely to the variables in our survey. Their results were similar to ours in saying that they found men to view seduction as a major cause of infidelity as we found the sexual attraction component with males. They also found females to view legitimacy as a major cause of infidelity as we found the relationship dissatisfaction and lack of security in the relationship components with females. Their study also found that women view social background to be a major cause of infidelity. Our study also found women to view the exposure to infidelity in one's group of friends, peers, or media as a major cause of infidelity. Lewandowski & Ackerman's (2006) found that lower satisfaction in need fulfillment and lower levels of self-expansion lead to higher susceptibility to infidelity. Their results supported our findings that 100% of males and 92.9% of females agreed with the statement that lack of attention from one's partner was a primary cause of infidelity. The variable lack of personal accountability (LPA) was also highly rated by both genders. Overall, our literature supported our results and our hypothesis.

The Social Learning Theory assumes that by observing behaviors that are modeled, one tends to then imitate or match performances (Mihalic & Elliott, 2005). This theory relates to the variable statement that exposure to infidelity in one's group of friends, peers, or media can be a cause of infidelity (EXP). This supports what we predicted to find through our research; the majority of males were undecided at 44.4% and the majority of females agreed with this statement at 42.9%. Our theory could explain more females agreeing with this statement because of females having a higher awareness of infidelity in their peer groups than males may have. Females may discuss personal issues and also do this in groups more than males, leading to an increased likelihood of these behaviors being imitated. The difference in responses could also be explained due to societal gender role constraints that males may consider infidelity a "rite of manhood" and not think about how another man's infidelity could impact his own behavior.

Limitations

A limitation to our study was that we had a small sample size to compare, contrast, and generalize to a larger population of male and female college students. Time constraints also limited us to the number of participants and the lack of diversity in our sample population. Being at a smaller Midwestern university also limited us to a less diverse population. We used the nonrandom sample method which limited the study to a certain population chosen by the researchers. This was due to the fact the participants had to previously or currently be in a committed relationship and to do this we had to select the participants ourselves. The fact that the survey participants were selected by the researchers may have limited the diversity and variance among groups of students that were involved in the study.

The limitations of the research methods are discussed.

Implications for Practitioners

Findings can be applied by counselors, especially those at a university working with dating relationships among college students. Family practitioners can best use our findings by applying them to marriages, committed dating relationships, and for their own understanding of this problematic issue. Marriage and family therapists need to have the knowledge of this issue to further help those affected by infidelity. The high divorce rates indicate the need for those working in the field to understand some of the problems within relationships. Students can also apply our research findings for their own knowledge and understanding. It is important to be aware of the information available to benefit one's own relationships.

Implications for Future Research

Future research could use a larger sample population and try to randomize the sampling by having a longer period of time to distribute surveys. A further step that could be taken would be to survey those that have experienced infidelity first-hand. Another way to get first-hand been affected by infidelity personally. This would make the study even more plausible by increasing the richness and purity of first-hand account perspectives. Another implication for future research could be to have more variables to the survey related to the Social Learning Theory. This would provide further possible explanations to the findings.

continued

Conclusion

It is hoped that the issue of infidelity will be looked into further and taken into account when dealing with committed relationships. Counselors, family practitioners, marriage and family therapists, and those in relationships themselves need to address this issue with importance and awareness. We want people to recognize that infidelity is a big problem in today's society and to understand how music, TV, movies, and other forms of media play into and normalize this issue. Relating to our theory, we want greater awareness that being around those involved in infidelity behaviors can affect the way one views the issue and behaves in relationships. Infidelity has not been highly researched and the causes have not been looked into thoroughly by other researchers out there in the field. Our study filled some of the gaps concerning the possible causes to this problem in relationships. Infidelity is a problematic issue in relationships that needs to be looked into and recognized when working with couples.

In the conclusion, the authors re-stress the importance of the topic and look to the future.

References

Drigotas, S., Safstrom, A., & Gentilia, T. (1999). An investment model prediction of dating infidelity. *Journal of Personality and Social Psychology, 77*(3), 509–524.

Harris, C. R. (2003). Factors associated with jealousy over real and imagined infidelity: An examination of the social-cognitive and evolutionary psychology perspectives. *Psychology of Women Quarterly, 24*(4), 319–330.

Lewandowski Jr., G. W., & Ackerman, R. A. (2006). Something's missing: Need fulfillment and self-expansion as predictors of susceptibility to infidelity. *Journal of Social Psychology, 146*(4), 389–403.

Pittman, F., & Pittman Wagners, T. (1995). Crises in infidelity. In N. Jacobson & A. Gurman (Eds.), *Clinical Handbook of Couple Therapy* (p. 295). London, UK: Guilford Press.

Strong, B., DeVault, C., & Cohen, T. (2005). *The marriage and family experience: Intimate relationships in a changing society* (9th ed.). Belmont, CA: Wadsworth.

Mihalic, S. W., & Elliott, D. (2005). A social learning theory model of marital violence. In T. Chibucos & R. Leite (Eds.), *Readings in Family Theory* (p. 98). London, UK: Sage, Inc.

Yeneceri, Z., & Kokdemir, D. (2006). University students' perceptions of, and explanations for, infidelity: The development of the infidelity questionnaire (INFQ). *Social Behavior and Personality: An International Journal, 34*(6), 639–650.

Inventing Your Analytical Report's Content

The content of an analytical report describes your research methods, presents your findings, analyzes those findings, and makes recommendations. To gather this information, though, you first need to identify your research topic, develop an angle, form a research question, and state your hypothesis.

13.1 invent the content of your analytical report with solid research.

Topic. Define your topic and then narrow it down to something you can handle in the time you have available. You might be tempted to take on a large topic, but a narrower topic will allow you to focus your research and get the project done.

Angle. The best way to narrow down your topic is to find the *angle* you want to pursue. Completely new topics are rare, but there are always new angles you can explore on existing topics. To help you find your angle, ask yourself: What has changed about this topic recently? What makes this topic especially interesting right now? How does this topic affect us locally?

Research Question. Now, it's time to develop your *research question*. Your research question should state the unknown or intriguing issue that your research will address. As discussed in Chapter 24, "Starting Research," your research question also needs to be as focused as possible.

Too Broad: Why do people eat so much fast food?

Focused Research Question: Do college students turn to fast food as a way to help them handle stressful situations?

Too Broad: Why do crows on campus behave the way they do?

Focused Research Question: Why do crows tend to live here on campus in the winter and how can we encourage them to go somewhere else?

Too Broad: Are children becoming more violent?

Focused Research Question: Do violent video games cause children to act out more violently in their everyday lives?

Hypothesis. Once you have figured out your research question, you should turn it into a *hypothesis* that will guide your research. Your hypothesis is your best guess—for the moment—about how your research question will be answered.

> My hypothesis is that fast food contains ingredients like salt, protein, carbohydrates, and fat that give human bodies short-term fuel for overcoming threatening moments. Our minds, when anxious or stressed, start thinking about the needs of short-term survival, not long-term health.
>
> My hunch is that crows congregate on our campus in the winter because there is ample food available and sources of warmth. Also, they are intelligent birds and they have strong social bonds, so campus provides a consistently safe place for them to live together through the winter.
>
> My hypothesis is that today's children fantasize more about violence due to video games, but these games actually make children less violent because kids can work through their aggression in a virtual environment.

Your hypothesis serves as your analytical report's "working thesis." You're not committed to proving it. Instead, your hypothesis gives your research a starting point, and you should expect to modify it as you find evidence that supports or goes against it. You can turn to Chapter 24, "Starting Research," for help with creating a good hypothesis.

Inquiring: Finding Out What You Already Know

There is a good chance you already know quite a bit about your topic. That's why you or your professor chose it in the first place. So your first task is to discover what is already stored away in your gray matter about your topic.

Begin by brainstorming about your topic (Figure 13.1). Put your topic at the top of a piece of paper. Then list everything you know about that topic. Do this for five minutes or more. When you are finished brainstorming, identify two to five major *issues* on your list that you could explore further in your research. Circle these issues or make a special mark next to them. At this point, you could do some freewriting or Internet research to see which issue would offer the most interesting topic for your analytical report.

Researching: Creating a Research Plan

When you are finished writing down what you already know, you will have a good idea about where your research project is going. Now it's time to figure out which methods you are going to use to test your hypothesis (i.e., how you are going to do your research).

A concept map is an especially useful tool for developing your research methods because it will help you figure out the steps needed for your research (Figure 13.2). You can map out your research methods like this:

Why Fast Food When We're Stressed?

Tastes good, so it comforts us.

Fast food has salt, protein, fat, and carbs, which we do need.

Our bodies can't tell the difference between threats that are physical and psychological, so it reacts to stress the same way by seeking fuel.

Bodies need quick fuel to handle stressful situations.

Survival now, deal with consequences later.

Survival requires more short-term fuel, so the body expects to burn it off.

Your body is telling you to eat!

It's in your head. Your body isn't hungry. It's just getting ready for "fight or flight." It's anticipating that you're going to need to move quickly.

Constant stress causes obesity, which can lead to diabetes (?).

Refined foods, like sugar and white flour, are like rocket fuel. They are easier to process, and our bodies are very efficient at using and storing them.

Lack of sleep puts stress on the body, causing us to crave junk food.

High-stress situations, like exams, cause us to look for "comfort food." Mentally, an exam is treated as a threat, much like a fight with another person or getting away from a dangerous animal.

Ironically, the fast food leads to higher stress, because the temporary high turns into a crash. That's fine in the wild, where threats tend to be brief. ("Oh good, you survived. Now rest for a moment.")

But, in the modern world, stress can continue for a long time, so more junk food is needed to satisfy the craving and avoid the crash.

We need to plan our eating for stressful situations.

What kinds of healthy foods will help us cope without also adding to our waists?

Exercise might be a way to satisfy that "fight or flight" urge and overcome stressful moments.

Issue 1: Craving these ingredients is a natural response.

Issue 2: Body treats stressful situations as physical threat.

Issue 3: Desire to "fight or flight" causes cravings.

Issue 4: Planning eating will help avoid coping with junk food.

Issue 5: Exercise helps cope with fight or flight feeling.

FIGURE 13.1 Brainstorming on Your Topic

A brainstorming list is a great way to put your ideas on the screen or a piece of paper. It will also help you identify the two to five major issues you will probably explore as you do research for your analytical report.

1. In the middle of the screen or page, write down your research question.

2. Write down the two to five *major steps* you will need to take to answer that research question. Circle them.

3. For each major step, write down two to five *minor steps* needed to achieve that major step. Circle them and draw lines to connect each one to a major step.

FIGURE 13.2
Inventing Your Methods with a Concept Map

Even the most experienced researchers find it difficult to develop their research methods. Making a concept map allows you to get your thoughts down in front of you and to organize them spatially.

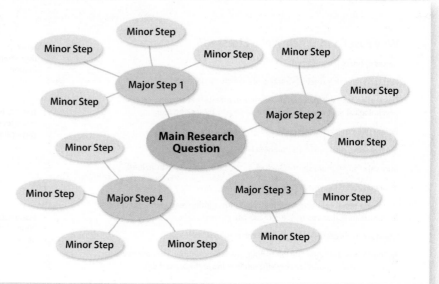

While you are creating your concept map, you should keep asking yourself, "How?" "*How* am I going to answer that question?" "*How* am I going to find that information?" "*How* am I going to generate that data?" Chapter 24, "Starting Research," can give you some helpful ideas about how to do your research.

You can then turn your concept map into an outline, as shown in Figure 13.3.

Researching: Gathering Sources and Revisiting Your Hypothesis

Your research will inevitably turn up new ideas, concepts, and evidence that you didn't expect. That's good. Your objective is *not* to simply find sources that prove your hypothesis. Instead, your objective is to do open-ended inquiry into your topic, letting the facts *lead* you to answers.

As you do research for your analytical report, you will also find information and facts that challenge your hypothesis. That's not a bad thing. Your original hypothesis was only your best guess when you began your research. Now that you know more about your topic, you should be willing to modify or even completely change your hypothesis to fit the evidence you've collected.

Good research is a cyclical process (Figure 13.4). Periodically, you should return to your hypothesis to see if you have changed your mind about how you will answer

FIGURE 13.3
Outlining a Methodology

A concept map can easily be turned into an outline like the one shown here. List your major steps and then arrange the minor steps beneath them.

Research Question: Why Do Stressed Out People Eat So Much Fast Food?

Major Step 1: Search for Online Sources

- Review hospital Web sites for information about fast food
- Look on *WebMD* and other medical Web sites
- Find documentaries about fast food at library or through Netflix
- Search fast food companies' Web sites for nutrition information

Major Step 2: Find Print Sources

- Visit the Student Health Center to collect pamphlets on stress and diet
- Use *Readers' Guide* to find articles in health magazines
- Find articles in medical journals at library
- Check out nutrition and health textbooks in library
- Go to bookstore to browse books that discuss stress and food

Major Step 3: Do Empirical Research

- Interview nutritionist here on campus or in the community
- Create survey for college students
- Observe stressed people at the Student Union
- Interview spokesperson for McDonalds, Taco Bell, or Arby's

your research question. Your ideas will evolve as you figure things out and gain a better understanding. Eventually, your hypothesis will solidify and become the main point (or thesis) of your report.

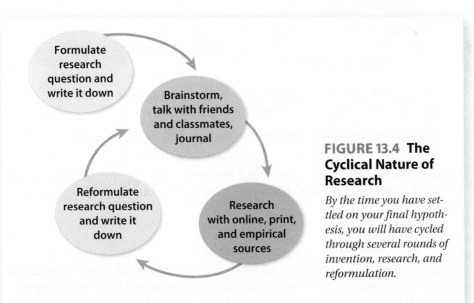

FIGURE 13.4 **The Cyclical Nature of Research**

By the time you have settled on your final hypothesis, you will have cycled through several rounds of invention, research, and reformulation.

Organizing and Drafting Your Analytical Report

13.2 use the report genre's pattern to organize your document.

The best way to draft an analytical report is to write each major section separately. If you concentrate on one section at a time, you will avoid feeling overwhelmed by the size of the report.

Executive Summary or Abstract

Executive summaries usually devote a small paragraph to each major section of the report. Abstracts tend to be only one paragraph, devoting a sentence or two to each section of the report. The executive summary or abstract should be written after you have finished drafting the rest of the report.

Introduction

An introduction in a report will typically make up to five moves.

State the topic. Tell your readers what the report is about.

State the purpose. In one or two sentences, explain what the report is going to do or achieve.

State the main point or thesis of the report. State the overall conclusion of your report (i.e., what you discovered in your research).

> **Weak:** Our research has turned up some interesting reasons why first-year college students gain weight.

> **Stronger:** Based on our research, we have found that stress often causes first-year students to turn to fast food, which is in part responsible for their "freshman fifteen" weight gain.

Provide background information. Briefly, give readers enough historical information about your topic to help them understand it.

Explain why the topic is important to readers. Tell readers why they should care about this topic.

These moves can be made in just about any order, and they are not all necessary. Minimally, your introduction should tell your readers the report's topic, purpose, and main point.

Methods Section

Explain your research methods step by step in a way that would allow your readers to replicate your research. Each major step will usually receive at least one paragraph of coverage (Figure 13.5). Explain *how* you did each step and *why* you did it that way.

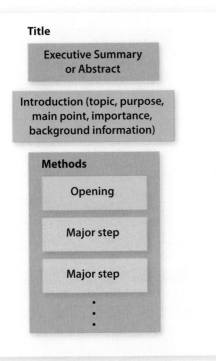

FIGURE 13.5 First Half of a Report

In the first half of a report, include an executive summary or abstract, an introduction, and a detailed description of your research methods.

Findings or Results Section

Choose the two to five most important findings or results from your research. In larger reports, each major finding should at least receive its own paragraph. Your job in this section is to describe what you found. Where possible, use graphics, such as charts, graphs, and tables, to present the data you've collected.

Discussion Section

Discuss your results and what they mean. Show how your results answer your research question. Researchers often boil their results down to two to five "conclusions." In most reports, each conclusion will need a paragraph to discuss how it supports the hypothesis and its implications. As shown in Figure 13.6, the Discussion section can be merged with the Findings/Results section if the findings and discussion of those findings can be handled together.

Conclusion/Recommendations

The conclusion of your analytical report should be brief. It should make all or some of the following moves.

Restate your main point. One more time, state the analytical report's overall main point or discovery.

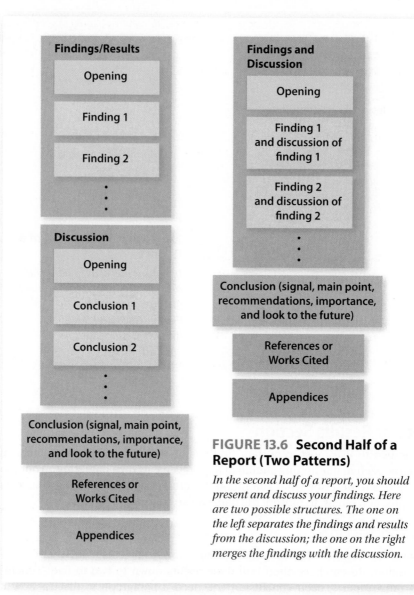

FIGURE 13.6 Second Half of a Report (Two Patterns)

In the second half of a report, you should present and discuss your findings. Here are two possible structures. The one on the left separates the findings and results from the discussion; the one on the right merges the findings with the discussion.

Make two to five recommendations. Using the results of your research, offer some recommendations about what should be done about this problem, issue, or trend. Analytical reports often present these recommendations in a list.

Reemphasize the importance of the topic. Explain briefly why your readers should care about this topic and take action.

Look to the future. Analytical reports often end with a small paragraph that describes what will happen with this topic in the near and distant future.

Your conclusion should be brief, perhaps only two or three paragraphs. You want to leave your readers with a clear sense of what you discovered and what should be done about it. Your conclusion should not summarize your whole report, nor should it add new evidence that was not addressed in the report's introduction or body.

References or Works Cited

Provide bibliographic information for any sources you have cited. For APA style, they should be listed under the title "References." For MLA style, call them "Works Cited." Turn to Chapters 27 and 28 for help with your references.

Appendices

In the appendices, put any other materials you used or created to collect information such as surveys and questionnaires. Appendices might also contain data charts, graphs, previous reports, or other documents that your readers might find useful.

Choosing an Appropriate Style

For most analytical reports, you should try to adopt a neutral and objective tone, providing information in a straightforward way. For this reason, analytical reports are usually written in a plain style. Here are some plain style techniques that work particularly well with the analytical report genre.

13.3 develop a writing style that is neutral and sounds objective.

Use Top-Down Paragraphs. Consistently put each paragraph's main claim or statement in the first or second sentence (i.e., the topic sentence). Then use the remainder of the paragraph to prove or support that claim or statement. Putting topic sentences at the top of each paragraph will help your readers locate the most important information. Moreover, if your readers only have limited time to skim your report, they can get an overall understanding by reading only the topic sentences.

Use Plain Sentences. Your sentences should be simple and straightforward. In each sentence, move your subject (i.e., what the sentence is about) to an early position, and use active verbs where possible. Look for ways to minimize your use of excessive prepositional phrases. Make sure sentences are "breathing length"—able to be said out loud in one breath, not more.

Use Active Voice Where Possible. Passive voice is common in reports (e.g., "These field observations were reinforced by our survey."), especially in scientific reports. However, active voice is often stronger and easier to read, so you should look for places where you can turn passive sentences into active sentences. Active voice will help your readers understand who or what did the action (e.g., "Our survey results confirmed these field observations.").

Get Rid of Nominalizations. Because analytical reports are usually technical, they sometimes overuse nominalizations, which can cloud the meaning of sentences. A nominalization happens when the action in the sentence is expressed as a noun rather than a verb. *Hint:* Look for words that end in "-tion" or "-sion."

> **Nominalization:** This report offers a presentation of our findings on the consumption of fast food by Clemson students.

> **Revised:** This report presents our findings on the amount of fast food consumed by Clemson students.

> **Nominalization:** We made a decision to focus our attention on junk food consumption in the dorms, especially during mid-terms.

> **Revised:** We decided to focus our attention on junk food consumption in the dorms, especially during mid-terms.

Nominalizations make your writing less clear because they hide the action in a noun. If you move the action into the sentence's verb, your meaning will be much clearer to your readers.

Define Jargon and Other Technical Terms. In research reports, jargon words and technical terms are common and often unavoidable. When you use a jargon word or a technical term for the first time, give your readers a sentence definition or parenthetical definition to clarify its meaning.

> **Sentence Definition:** Low-density lipoprotein cholesterol (LDL) is a waxy substance that causes fat to build up in the walls of larger arteries.

> **Parenthetical Definition:** The extreme amount of salt in most fast food can cause hypertension, a condition in which a person's blood pressure rises to an abnormally high level and potentially does damage to the heart.

In moderation, jargon and technical terms are fine. Define these specialized words so your readers understand what you are talking about. Where possible, though, use simpler words that your readers will find easier to understand.

Designing Your Analytical Report

13.4 create a design that makes your analytical report easy to use.

Analytical reports usually aren't flashy documents, but they should still look attractive and easy to read. Your report's page design and graphics will often determine whether your readers actually read your report and whether they can quickly find the information they are looking for.

Design a "Raidable" Page Layout. People rarely read reports from front to back. Instead, they "raid" reports, looking for the information they need. So you should use clear headings to highlight key sections and important information. Put critical pieces of information in lists, tables, or graphics to make them easy to find. Figure 13.7 shows a report that uses an attractive, raidable page layout. The headings help

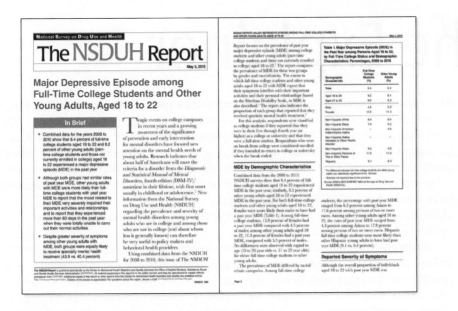

FIGURE 13.7 A Raidable Page Layout

The design of a report needs to be attractive and accessible to readers. In this report, the authors use headings, graphics, color, and boxes to highlight important information.

readers locate key information, and the graphics support the written text. The use of color attracts the reader to the text. In other words, there are plenty of *access points* to begin reading this document.

Use Meaningful Headings. Your analytical report's headings should give readers a clear idea about what is in each section of the report. You don't need to use *Methods, Results, Discussion,* and *Conclusion* as headings. Instead, you can give readers a sense of what they will find in each section with descriptive and interesting headings:

> Our Research Methods: Going Undercover in the World of Fast Food

> Our Findings: Stress Drives People to Fast Food

> Our Recommendations: Battling the Expanding Waistline with Good Information

Use Tables, Graphs, and Charts to Reinforce Written Text. Where possible, find ways to put your data and other facts into tables, graphs, and charts. Your graphics should reinforce the written text, not replace it.

Use Photographs to Illustrate or Emphasize Key Points. With the availability of digital cameras and mobile phones, photographs are now common in analytical reports. If you find something is difficult to describe, perhaps you can take a picture of it and add it to your report.

Insert a Table of Contents. If your report is over six pages long, insert a table of contents to help readers gain an overview of its contents and locate specific information easily. Most word-processing programs can generate a table of contents for you.

The Explainer

An "explainer" is a very brief report that addresses a specific question that your readers want to understand. The question might be one that people are curious about—"Does truth serum really work?" "Why do school grades go from *A* to *F* with no *E*?" Or it could be used to inform people about a local issue—"How do you apply for student financial aid on our campus?" Or it could be used to inform an organization's management or other group about an important issue—"How are businesses using social networking to increase sales?" "How does a student apply for financial aid on our campus?" The ability to write explainers is a valuable skill in the workplace, and it's becoming increasingly important in college as well.

Assignments similar to the explainer are becoming more popular in advanced college courses and on the Internet. Your professors may ask you to examine a very specific question that leads into a larger project. News Web sites publish briefs that offer factual information on important stories. For example, *Slate.com* publishes "The Explainer" to address questions that are in the news. Think tanks, like the Pew Foundation and the Brookings Institution, publish in a related genre called "The Brief" on their Web sites to influence public policy. Briefs are miniature reports that include most of a regular report's features.

Here is how to write an explainer:

Use a title that asks your question.   Introduce your topic and purpose in the title itself.

Explain why the topic is interesting, important, or timely.   Relate your question to current events or to issues that your readers are interested in.

Provide context for your topic.   If readers don't know about your topic, define it, explain its function, or briefly review the history of your topic's origins and how it changed over the years.

Do your research and state the facts.   As objectively as possible, state the facts that you have collected. You should cite any sources you have collected, but you don't need to explain fully how you collected the facts you are providing.

Add a graphic.   If possible, put your data into a graph, chart, or table. Add a photograph if it would help illustrate your point or draw your readers in.

WRITE **your own explainer.** Choose a question related to an issue on your campus that interests you. Write a two-page explainer in which you objectively answer that question. Keep your opinions to a minimum.

What Is Parkour?

World Freerunning Parkour Federation

The word comes from the French "parcours," which literally means, "the way through," or "the path." What we now all know as "Parkour" with a "k" had its origins in a training program for French Special Forces known as "Parcours du combattant" or "The Path of the Warrior." It was David Belle, a French dude, son of a Parcours Warrior and the "inventor" of Parkour, who changed the "c" to a "k" and, along with his comrades, the Yamakazi, began the worldwide movement you are now officially a part of and which also includes the phenomenon known as Freerunning (confused yet? Don't give up! You're almost there!)

According to the strictest definition, Parkour is the act of moving from point "a" to point "b" using the obstacles in your path to increase your efficiency. Sounds like a fun game, right? A basic repertoire of moves developed over the years, like the "tic-tac," the "kong vault" and the "gap jump" that make Parkour immediately recognizable to most people who see it, even if they don't know what it's called!

> The topic is identified and defined up front.

> A formal one-sentence definition is provided.

continued

But a funny thing happened on the way to Point B. The cool, super-creative moves that the Yamakazi came up with started morphing, and since there was no one chasing them (most of the time) the efficiency part got less and less important to some of the Yamakazi, who decided they wanted to start throwing flips and stuff, and just generally expressing themselves through movement. The leader of that splinter group was named Sebastian Foucan, the guy from the beginning of CASINO ROYALE. David Belle decided he wanted to stick with the efficiency program, so he and Sebastian kind of went their separate ways, and the "two" sports started developing along separate but parallel paths.

The author uses a narrative to explain the origin of the sport.

For a long time, people argued about which was which (and which was better!) but while they were busy doing that a whole bunch of new guys (and some girls) came along and just started training, together or separately, picking up the skills they saw on YouTube, coming up with their own that played to their unique strengths and interests, and then sharing them through their own vids. Some liked to time themselves, some were just out to express. Some did it in urban environments, some in the forest. Some thought it should never be competitive or commercialized in any way. Some were anxious to compete, cause that was more in THEIR nature. And what do all these busy people call what they do? In the end, most of them decided it was all just movement, and more importantly, it was all just play.

The facts are stated in a straightforward way.

So what do we here at the WFPF believe Parkour (and Freerunning) to be? Haha! You're not going to get us on that one! I will tell you what we know, though, and that is that Parkour, fundamentally, is a philosophy, and a way of life. It's a way of looking at any environment and believing in your heart that there is no obstacle in life that cannot be overcome. Everyone is a unique individual, so no two people will come up with the exact same solution, but there is a "way through" for us all.

Little kids all learn to walk at their own pace and in their own way; they don't start by jumping off rooftops, and no matter how many times they fall, they never give up. The basic fact never changes. We just need to pick ourselves up and start to play with whatever is challenging us right now, and to hold to the motto that to Know Obstacles is to Know Freedom!

The explainer ends with a thesis statement.

Here are some quick strategies to get you going on that analytical report.

DEVELOP Your Research Question and Hypothesis

Write down an interesting research question about your topic—a question you would like to answer with some research. Then turn that question into a hypothesis (your best guess about how that research question will be answered).

FIND Out What You Already Know

Use prewriting tools to get your ideas out on the screen or a piece of paper. Star or highlight your best ideas. Then share your ideas with your friends and classmates.

FIND Out What Others Know

Develop a research plan that uses a combination of online, print, and empirical sources to find information. Interview experts on campus to find out more.

REVISIT Your Hypothesis

After you have done a good amount of research, look at your hypothesis again. Does it need to be modified or refined?

ORGANIZE and Draft Your Analytical Report

Organize your draft into sections and write one section at a time. The most common organization for an analytical report is this: Executive Summary/Abstract, Introduction, Methods, Findings/Results, Discussion, Conclusion/Recommendations, References, and Appendices.

CHOOSE an Appropriate Style

Analytical reports are almost always written in plain style, because this style sounds objective and authoritative. Use plain sentences and top-down paragraphs with solid topic sentences. The best style is one that sounds neutral and objective.

DESIGN the Document

Create an attractive and accessible page layout. Use active headings to help readers locate important information. Put your data and facts into tables, graphs, and charts, so your readers can see how they support the written text.

REVISE and Edit

Revise headings so they clearly state the points you want to make. Edit your paragraphs to make them easy to scan.

"How Many Zombies Do You Know?" Using Indirect Survey Methods to Measure Alien Attacks and Outbreaks of the Undead

ANDREW GELMAN AND GEORGE A. ROMERO

Andrew Gelman, a respected and award-winning professor of statistics and political science at Columbia University, wrote on his blog that he created this unpublished paper to do some "humorous fun-poking" but also to illustrate how a very real cutting-edge survey method could be used for solving difficult research problems. As you read this, notice how the authors use the conventions of the scientific-article genre.

1 Introduction

Zombification is a serious public-health and public-safety concern (Romero, 1968, 1978) but is difficult to study using traditional survey methods. Zombies are believed to have very low rates of telephone usage and in any case may be reluctant to identify themselves as such to a researcher. Face-to-face surveying involves too much risk to the interviewers, and internet surveys, although they originally were believed to have much promise, have recently had to be abandoned in this area because of the potential for zombie infection via computer virus.

In the absence of hard data, zombie researchers[1] have studied outbreaks and their dynamics using differential equation models (Munz et al., 2009, Lakeland, 2010) and, more recently, agent-based models (Messer, 2010). Figure 1 shows an example of such work.

But mathematical models are not enough. We need data.

2 Measuring zombification using network survey data

Zheng, Salganik, and Gelman (2006) discuss how to learn about groups that are not directly sampled in a survey. The basic idea is to ask respondents questions such as, "How many people do you know named Stephen/ Margaret/etc." to learn the sizes of their social networks, questions such as "How many

---

[1] By "zombie researchers," we are talking about people who research zombies. We are not for a moment suggesting that these researchers are themselves zombies. Just to be on the safe side, however, we have conducted all our interactions with these scientists via mail.

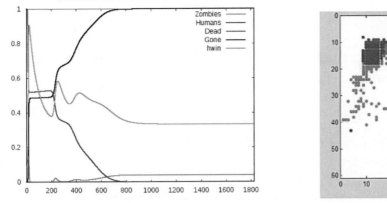

Figure 1: From Lakeland (2010) and Messer (2010). There were other zombie graphs at these sites, but these were the coolest.

lawyers/teachers/police officers/etc. do you know," to learn about the properties of these networks, and questions such as "How many prisoners do you know" to learn about groups that are hard to reach in a sample survey. Zheng et al. report that, on average, each respondent knows 750 people; thus, a survey of 1500 Americans can give us indirect information on about a million people.

This methodology should be directly applicable to zombies or, for that matter, ghosts, aliens, angels, and other hard-to-reach entities. In addition to giving us estimates of the populations of these groups, we can also learn, through national surveys, where they are more prevalent (as measured by the residences of the people who know them), and who is more likely to know them.

A natural concern in this research is potential underreporting; for example, what if your wife[2] is actually a zombie or an alien and you are not aware of the fact. This bias can be corrected via extrapolation using the estimates of different populations with varying levels of reporting error; Zheng et al.

(2006) discuss in the context of questions ranging from names (essentially no reporting error) to medical conditions such as diabetes and HIV that are often hidden.

3 Discussion

As Lakeland (2010) puts it, "Clearly, Hollywood plays a vital role in educating the public about the proper response to zombie infestation." In this article we have discussed how modern survey methods based on social networks can help us estimate the size of the problem.

Other, related, approaches are worth studying too. Social researchers have recently used Google Trends to study hard-to-measure trends using search volume (Askitas and Zimmerman, 2009, Goel, Hofman, et. al., 2010); Figure 2 illustrates how this might be done in the zombie context. It would also make sense to take advantage of social networking tools such as Facebook (Goel, Mason, et. al., 2010) and more zombie-specific sites such as ZDate. We envision vast unfolding vistas of funding in this area.

---

[2] Here we are choosing a completely arbitrary example with absolutely no implications about our marriages or those of anyone we know.

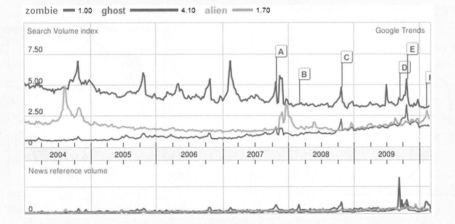

Figure 2: Google Trends report on "zombie," "ghost," and "alien." The patterns show fascinating trends from which, we feel, much could be learned if resources were made available to us in the form of a sizable research grant from the Department of Defense, Department of Homeland Security, or a major film studio. Please make out any checks to the first author or deposit directly to his PayPal account. *Source:* Google and the Google logo are registered trademarks of Google Inc., used with permission.

4 References

Askitas, N., and Zimmermann, K. F. (2009). Google econometrics and unemployment forecasting. *Applied Economics Quarterly*, 55, 107–120.

Goel, S., Hofman, J. M., Lahaie, S., Pennock, D. M., & Watts, D. J. (2010). What can search predict? Technical report, Yahoo Research.

Goel, S., Mason, W., & Watts, D. J. (2010). Real and perceived attitude homophily in social networks. Technical report, Yahoo Research.

Lakeland, D. (2010). Improved zombie dynamics. Models of Reality blog, 1 March. http://models.street-artists.org/?p=554

Messer, B. (2010). Agent-based computational model of humanity's prospects for post zombie outbreak survival. The Tortise's Lens blog, 10 March. http://thetortoiseslens.blogspot.com/2010/03/agent-based-computational-model-of.html

Munz, P., Hudea, I., Imad, J., & Smith, R. J. (2009). When zombies attack!: Mathematical modelling of an outbreak of zombie infection. In *Infectious Disease Modelling Research Progress*, ed. J. M. Tchuenche and C. Chiyaka, 133–150. Hauppage, New York: Nova Science Publishers.

Romero, G. A. (1968). *Night of the Living Dead*. Image Ten.

Romero, G. A. (1978). *Dawn of the Dead*. Laurel Group.

Zheng, T., Slaganik, M., & Gelman, A. (2006). "How many people do you know in prison?": Using overdispersion in count data to estimate social structure in networks. *Journal of the American Statistical Association*, 101, 409–423.

A CLOSER LOOK AT
How Many Zombies Do You Know?   **MyWritingLab**

1. How well does this mock scientific-research report use the features (organization, feature, style, etc.) of the report genre? Where does it differ from the typical report genre?

2. All of the books and articles cited are real. Some are serious articles written by scientists and some are added for humorous effect. Run through the References section and try to predict which are

serious and which are silly. Use Google or another search engine to actually find these articles and test the accuracy of your predictions.

3. The introduction of a report should define a research question and explain why it is important to the reader. What is the question defined here? Does the author explain its importance?

IDEAS FOR
Writing

MyWritingLab

1. Write a mock research report in the style of Gelman and Romero's article. Choose a silly topic and write a report similar to this one. Be sure to follow the analytical report genre. Try to make the moves they make, and try to come up with a few of your own moves.

2. Write a bio of Andrew Gelman. Using Google or another search engine, find Gelman's professional page at Columbia University and take a look at his papers and some of his blog entries. Do Internet research into his areas of specialization. Try to capture what distinguishes the work that he does and how he approaches his work. We usually think of the scientist as a very, very serious, almost non-human figure who is devoted to seeking the scientific truth. How is Gelman different?

The Rising Cost of *Not* Going to College

PEW RESEARCH CENTER

In this report, researchers at a "think tank" share their research on the advantages of going to college. Pay attention to their use of plain style to explain their methods and findings.

Overview

For those who question the value of college in this era of soaring student debt and high unemployment, the attitudes and experiences of today's young adults—members of the so-called Millennial generation—provide a compelling answer. On virtually every measure of economic well-being and career attainment—from personal earnings to job satisfaction to the share employed full time—young college graduates are outperforming their peers with less education. And when today's young adults are compared with previous generations, the disparity in economic outcomes between college graduates and those with a high school diploma or less formal schooling has never been greater in the modern era.

These assessments are based on findings from a new nationally representative Pew Research Center survey of 2,002 adults supplemented by a Pew Research analysis of economic data from the U.S. Census Bureau.

The economic analysis finds that Millennial college graduates ages 25 to 32[1] who are working full time earn more annually—about $17,500 more—than employed young adults holding only a high school diploma. The pay gap was significantly smaller in previous

---

[1] The Millennial generation includes those born after 1980 (which would include adults ages 18 to 32 in 2013). Unless otherwise noted in the text, references in this report to the economic outcomes of Millennials are based only on those ages 25 to 32, a period in which most young adults have completed their formal education and have entered the workforce.

generations.[2] College-educated Millennials also are more likely to be employed full time than their less-educated counterparts (89% vs. 82%) and significantly less likely to be unemployed (3.8% vs. 12.2%).

Turning to attitudes toward work, employed Millennial college graduates are more likely than their peers with a high school diploma or less education to say their job is a career or a steppingstone to a career (86% vs. 57%). In contrast, Millennials with a high school diploma or less are about three times as likely as college graduates to say their work is "just a job to get [them] by" (42% vs. 14%).

The survey also finds that among employed Millennials, college graduates are significantly more likely than those without any college experience to say that their education has been "very useful" in preparing them for work and a career (46% vs. 31%). And these better educated young adults are more likely to say they have the necessary education and training to advance in their careers (63% vs. 41%).

But do these benefits outweigh the financial burden imposed by four or more years of college? Among Millennials ages 25 to 32, the answer is clearly yes: About nine-in-ten with at least a bachelor's degree say college has already paid off (72%) or will pay off in the future (17%). Even among the two-thirds of college-educated Millennials who borrowed money to pay for their schooling, about nine-in-ten (86%) say their degrees have been worth it or expect that they will be in the future.

Of course, the economic and career benefits of a college degree are not limited to Millennials. Overall, the survey and economic analysis consistently find that college graduates regardless of generation are doing better than those with less education.[3]

Disparity among Millennials Ages 25-32 By Education Level in Terms of Annual Earnings ...

(median among full-time workers, in 2012 dollars)

Bachelor's degree or more	$45,500
Two-year degree/ Some college	$30,000
High school graduate	$28,000

Unemployment Rate ...

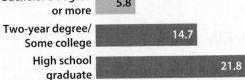

Bachelor's degree or more	3.8
Two-year degree/ Some college	8.1
High school graduate	12.2

And Share Living in Poverty ...

Bachelor's degree or more	5.8
Two-year degree/ Some college	14.7
High school graduate	21.8

Notes: Median annual earnings are based on earnings and work status during the calendar year prior to interview and limited to 25- to 32-year-olds who worked full time during the previous calendar year and reported positive earnings. "Full time" refers to those who usually worked at least 35 hours a week last year. The unemployment rate refers to the share of the labor force (those working or actively seeking work) who are not employed. Poverty is based on the respondent's family income in the calendar year preceding the survey.

Source: Pew Research Center tabulations of the 2013 March Current Population Survey (CPS) Integrated Public Use Micro Sample

---

[2] Throughout this report, references to those who are "high school graduates" or who have a diploma refer to those who have attained a high school diploma or its equivalent, such as a General Educational Development (GED) certificate.

---

[3] For a detailed look at economic outcomes by education, see the Pew Research Center blog post "The growing economic clout of the college educated" by Richard Fry.

Education and Views About Work

% of employed adults ages 25 to 32 with each level of education saying...

■ Bachelor's degree or more
■ Two-year degree/Some college
■ High school grad or less

...they have a career/career-track job

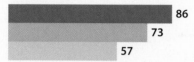

86
73
57

...they have enough education and training to get ahead in their job

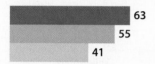

63
55
41

...they are "very satisfied" with current job

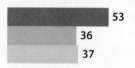

53
36
37

...their education was "very useful" in preparing them for a job or career

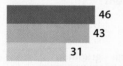

46
43
31

Notes: Based on currently employed 25- to 32-year-olds (n=509).

But the Pew Research study also finds that on some key measures, the largest and most striking disparities between college graduates and those with less education surface in the Millennial generation.

For example, in 1979 when the first wave of Baby Boomers were the same age that Millennials are today, the typical high school graduate earned about three-quarters (77%) of what a college graduate made. Today, Millennials with only a high school diploma earn 62% of what the typical college graduate earns.

To be sure, the Great Recession and the subsequent slow recovery hit the Millennial generation particularly hard.[4] Neither college graduates nor those with less education were spared. On some key measures such as the percentage who are unemployed or the share living in poverty, this generation of college-educated adults is faring worse than Gen Xers, Baby Boomers or members of the Silent generation when they were in their mid-20s and early 30s.

But today's high school graduates are doing even worse, both in comparison to their college-educated peers and when measured against other generations of high school graduates at a similar point in their lives.

For example, among those ages 25 to 32, fully 22% with only a high school diploma are living in poverty, compared with 6% of today's college-educated young adults. In contrast, only 7% of Baby Boomers who had only a high school diploma were in poverty in 1979 when they were in their late 20s and early 30s.

To examine the value of education in today's job market, the Pew Research Center drew from two complementary data sources. The first is a nationally representative survey conducted Oct. 7–27, 2013, of 2,002 adults, including 630 Millennials ages 25–32, the age at which most of these young adults will have completed their formal education and started their working lives. This survey captured the views of today's adults toward their education, their job and their experiences in the workforce.

---

[4] For a detailed look at the impact of the Great Recession on various demographic groups, see the Pew Research Center report "How the Great Recession Has Changed Life in America"

Rising Earnings Disparity Between Young Adults with And Without a College Degree

Median annual earnings among full-time workers ages 25 to 32, in 2012 dollars

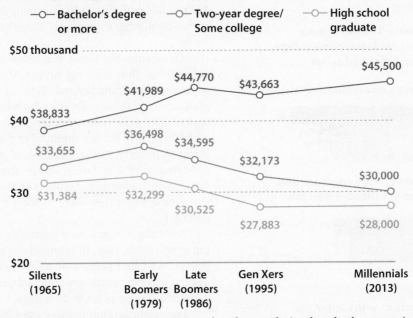

—○— Bachelor's degree or more   —○— Two-year degree/ Some college   —○— High school graduate

Notes: Median annual earnings are based on earnings and work status during the calendar year prior to interview and limited to 25- to 32-year-olds who worked full time during the previous calendar year and reported positive earnings. "Full time" refers to those who usually worked at least 35 hours a week last year.

Source: Pew Research Center tabulations of the 2013, 1995, 1986, 1979 and 1965 March Current Population Survey (CPS) Integrated Public Use Micro Samples

Percentage of Generation in Poverty, by Educational Attainment

	All	College graduate	Two-year Degree/ Some college	High school-graduate
Millennials in 2013	16	6	15	22
Gen Xers in 1995	13	3	10	15
Late Boomers in 1986	12	4	8	12
Early Boomers in 1979	8	3	6	7

Notes: "All" includes those who are not high school graduates. Poverty is based on the respondent's family income in the calendar year preceding the survey. Silent generation not shown because poverty measures are not available before 1968.

To measure how the economic outcomes of older Millennials compare with those of other generations at a comparable age, the Pew Research demographic analysis drew from data collected in the government's Current Population Survey. The CPS is a large-sample survey that has been conducted monthly by the U.S. Census Bureau for more than six decades.

Specifically, Pew analysts examined CPS data collected last year among 25- to 32-year-olds and then examined data among 25- to 32-year-olds in four earlier years: Silents in 1965 (ages 68 to 85 at the time of the Pew Research survey and Current Population Survey); the first or "early" wave of Baby Boomers in 1979 (ages 59 to 67 in 2013), the younger or "late" wave of Baby Boomers in 1986 (ages 49 to 58 in 2013) and Gen Xers in 1995 (ages 33 to 48 in 2013).

The Rise of the College Graduate

Today's Millennials are the best-educated generation in history; fully a third (34%) have at least a bachelor's degree. In contrast, only 13% of 25- to 32-year-olds in 1965—the Silent generation—had a college degree, a proportion that increased to 24% in the late 1970s and 1980s when Boomers were young adults. In contrast, the proportion with a high school diploma has declined from 43% in 1965 to barely a quarter (26%) today.

At the same time the share of college graduates has grown, the value of their degrees has increased. Between 1965 and last year, the median annual earnings of 25- to 32-year-olds with a college degree grew from $38,833 to $45,500 in 2012 dollars, nearly a $7,000 increase.

Taken together, these two facts—the growing economic return to a college degree and the larger share of college graduates in the Millennial generation—might suggest that the Millennial generation should be earning more than earlier generations of young adults.

The Generations Defined

The Millennial Generation
Born: After 1980
Age of adults in 2013: 18 to 32*

Generation X
Born: 1965 to 1980
Age in 2013: 33 to 48

The Late Baby Boom Generation
Born: 1955 to 1964
Age in 2013: 49 to 58

The Early Baby Boom Generation
Born: 1946 to 1954
Age in 2013: 59 to 67

The Silent Generation
Born: 1928 to 1945
Age in 2013: 68 to 85

* The youngest Millennials are in their teens. No chronological end point has been set for this group.

Note: The "Greatest Generation," which includes those born before 1928, is not included in the analysis due to the small sample size.

But they're not. The overall median earnings of today's Millennials ($35,000) aren't much different than the earnings of early Boomers ($34,883) or Gen Xers ($32,173) and only somewhat higher than Silents ($30,982) at comparable ages.

The Declining Value of a High School Diploma

The explanation for this puzzling finding lies in another major economic trend reshaping the economic landscape: The dramatic decline in the value of a high school education. While earnings of those with a college degree rose, the typical high school graduate's earnings fell by more than $3,000, from $31,384 in 1965 to $28,000 in 2013. This decline, the Pew Research analysis found, has

While Education Levels of 25- to 32- year-olds Have Risen Dramatically Across the Generations ...

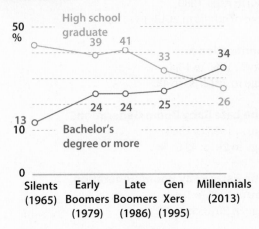

... Median Annual Earnings Have Remained Relatively Flat

(among full-time workers, in 2012 dollars)

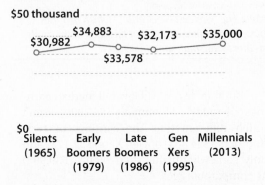

Notes: The Census Bureau altered the educational attainment question in 1992. See Appendix B for details on comparability. Median annual earnings are based on earnings and work status during the calendar year prior to interview and limited to 25- to 32- year-olds who worked full time during the previous calendar year and reported positive earnings. "Full time" refers to those who usually worked at least 35 hours a week last year.

Source: Pew Research Center tabulations of the 2013, 1995, 1986, 1979 and 1965 March Current Population Survey (CPS) Integrated Public Use Micro Samples

been large enough to nearly offset the gains of college graduates.

The steadily widening earnings gap by educational attainment is further highlighted when the analysis shifts to track the difference over time in median earnings of college graduates versus those with a high school diploma.

In 1965, young college graduates earned $7,499 more than those with a high school diploma. But the earnings gap by educational attainment has steadily widened since then, and today it has more than doubled to $17,500 among Millennials ages 25 to 32.

Other Labor Market Outcomes

To be sure, the Great Recession and painfully slow recovery have taken their toll on the Millennial generation, including the college-educated.

Young college graduates are having more difficulty landing work than earlier cohorts. They are more likely to be unemployed and have to search longer for a job than earlier generations of young adults.

But the picture is consistently bleaker for less-educated workers: On a range of measures, they not only fare worse than the college-educated, but they are doing worse than earlier generations at a similar age.

For example, the unemployment rate for Millennials with a college degree is more than double the rate for college-educated Silents in 1965 (3.8% vs. 1.4%). But the unemployment rate for Millennials with only a high school diploma is even higher: 12.2%, or more than 8 percentage points more than for college graduates and almost triple the unemployment rate of Silents with a high school diploma in 1965.

The same pattern resurfaces when the measure shifts to the length of time the typical job seeker spends looking for work. In 2013 the average unemployed college-educated Millennial had been looking for work for 27 weeks—more than double the time it took an unemployed college-educated 25- to

The Widening Earnings Gap of Young Adults by Educational Attainment

The difference in median annual earnings of college and high school graduates when members of each generation were ages 25 to 32

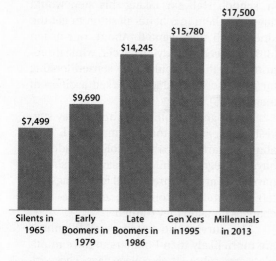

Notes: *Median annual earnings are based on earnings and work status during the calendar year prior to interview and limited to 25- to 32-year-olds who worked full time during the previous calendar year and reported positive earnings. "Full time" refers to those who usually worked at least 35 hours a week last year. "College graduates" are those with a bachelor's degree or more.*

Source: Pew Research Center tabulations of 2013, 1995, 1986, 1979 and 1965 March Current Population Survey (CPS) Integrated Public Use Micro Samples

32-year-old in 1979 to get a job (12 weeks). Again, today's young high school graduates fare worse on this measure than the college-educated or their peers in earlier generations. According to the analysis, Millennial high school graduates spend, on average, four weeks longer looking for work than college graduates (31 weeks vs. 27 weeks) and more than twice as long as similarly educated early Boomers did in 1979 (12 weeks).

Similarly, in terms of hours worked, likelihood of full-time employment and overall wealth, today's young college graduates fare worse than their peers in earlier generations. But again, Millennials without a college degree fare worse, not only in comparison to their college-educated contemporaries but also when compared with similarly educated young adults in earlier generations.

The Value of a College Major

As the previous sections show, having a college degree is helpful in today's job market. But depending on their major field of study, some are more relevant on the job than others, the Pew Research survey finds.

To measure the value of their college studies, all college graduates were asked their major or, if they held a graduate or professional degree, their field of study. Overall, 37% say they were social science, liberal arts or education majors, a third (33%) say they studied a branch of science or engineering and a quarter (26%) majored in business. The remainder said they were studying or training for a vocational occupation.

Overall, those who studied science or engineering are the most likely to say that their current job is "very closely" related to their college or graduate field of study (60% vs. 43% for both social science, liberal arts or education majors and business majors).

At the same time, those who majored in science or engineering are less likely than social science, liberal arts or education majors to say in response to another survey question that they should have chosen a different major as an undergraduate to better prepare them for the job they wanted.

According to the survey, only about a quarter of science and engineering majors regretted their decision (24%), compared with 33% of those whose degree is in social science, liberal arts or education. Some 28% of business majors say they would have been better prepared for the job they wanted if they had chosen a different major. (Overall, the survey found that 29% say they should

Usefulness of Major, by Field of Study

% of majors in each area who say their current job is ... related to their major in college or graduate school

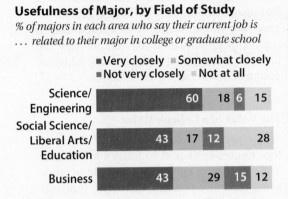

Note: Based on those with at least a bachelor's degree who are employed full time or part time (n=606). "Don't know/Refused" responses not shown.

have chosen a different major to better prepare them for their ideal job.)

Major Regrets

In addition to selecting a different major, the Pew Research survey asked college graduates whether, while still in school, they could have better prepared for the type of job they wanted by gaining more work experience, studying harder or beginning their job search earlier.

College Days, Reconsidered

% who say doing each of the following while they were undergraduates would have better prepared them to get the job they wanted

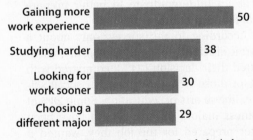

Note: Based on those with at least a bachelor's degree (n=790). Voluntary responses of "Maybe" not included.

About three-quarters of all college graduates say taking at least one of those four steps would have enhanced their chances to land their ideal job. Leading the should-have-done list: getting more work experience while still in school. Half say taking this step would have put them in a better position to get the kind of job they wanted. About four-in-ten (38%) regret not studying harder, while three-in-ten say they should have started looking for a job sooner (30%) or picked a different major (29%).

When analyzed together, the survey suggests that, among these items tested, only about a quarter (26%) of all college graduates have no regrets, while 21% say they should have done at least three or all four things differently while in college to enhance their chances for a job they wanted.

The survey also found that Millennials are more likely than Boomers to have multiple regrets about their college days. Three-in-ten (31%) of all Millennials and 17% of Boomers say they should have done three or all four things differently in order to prepare themselves for the job they wanted. Some 22% of Gen Xers say the same.

Definitions and Methods

Throughout the chapter, "young adults" refers to those ages 25 to 32 (inclusive). Unless noted, all figures refer to 25- to 32-year-olds.

Consistent with earlier Pew Research definitions, Millennials were born after 1980. Gen Xers were born from 1965 to 1980, Baby Boomers from 1946 to 1964 and Silents from 1928 to 1945.

Labor market and economic outcomes are examined in 2013, 1995, 1986, 1979 and 1965 (when available). Young adults in 2013 were Millennials. Most young adults in 1995 were Gen Xers. Young adults in 1986, 1979, and 1965 capture late Boomers, early Boomers and the Silents, respectively.

The 2013 data were collected in March of 2013 and (according to the official National

Observing 25- to 32-year-olds in National Economic Context

	Year observed	Prior economic trough	National unemployment rate	Real to potential GDP	Capacity utilization
Millennials	2013	Jun 2009	7.6%	97.7	78.2
Largely Gen Xers	1995	Mar 1991	5.4%	100.7	84.4
Late Boomers	1986	Nov 1982	7.2%	100.6	78.4
Early Boomers	1979	Mar 1975	5.8%	101.6	86.2
Silents	1965	Feb 1961	4.7%	103.1	NA

Notes: National unemployment rate is the civilian unemployment rate in March. The unemployment rate refers to the share of the labor force (those working or actively seeking work) who are not employed. Real to potential GDP compares the quarterly real GDP to FRED's estimated quarterly potential GDP (in the first quarter). Capacity utilization is estimated monthly and is used by corporations and factories to describe the ratio of how much is actually being produced to the amount that could potentially be produced within resource constraints if there was market demand for the goods. Figure shown is for March. Capacity utilization is not available before 1967.

Source: Unemployment rate and real to potential GDP downloaded from FRED (Federal Reserve Economic Data), Federal Reserve Bank of St. Louis. Capacity utilization is published by the Board of Governors of the Federal Reserve system.

Bureau of Economic Research business cycle dating) captures economic outcomes four years into the economic recovery. The Great Recession officially ended in June 2009.

The 1995, 1986, 1979 and 1965 time points are comparable to 2013 in that they also represent a point in time four years into an economic recovery. NBER designates bottoms of economic recessions occurring in March 1991, November 1982, March 1975, and February 1961, respectively.

Though the five time points examined mark years that were four years into an economic recovery, national macroeconomic conditions were not identical in the five years. Prominent macroeconomic indicators suggest that the aggregate economy was less vigorous in 2013 than the earlier comparison points.

Common wisdom also suggests 2013 marks a distinct period. After all, the Great Recession is coined the Great Recession.

Though aggregate economic conditions may be weaker in 2013 than earlier years, this does not necessarily imply that Millennials are worse off than earlier generations. That depends on how they are faring in the labor market and their particular circumstances, the subject of this chapter.

References

Aguiar, Mark, and Erik Hurst. 2007. "Measuring Trends in Leisure: The Allocation of Time Over Five Decades," *The Quarterly Journal of Economics,* August, vol. 122, no. 3, pp. 969–1006.

Bell, Lisa, Gary Burtless, Janet Gornick, and Timothy M. Smeeding. 2007. "Failure to Launch: Cross-National Trends in the Transition to Economic Independence," in *The Price of Independence: The Economics of Early Adulthood,* edited by Sheldon Danziger and Cecilia Rouse. New York: Russell Sage Foundation.

DeNavas-Walt, Carmen, Bernadette D. Proctor, and Jessica C. Smith. 2013. "Income, Poverty, and Health Insurance Coverage in the United States: 2012." Current Population Reports, Consumer Income, P60-245. Washington, DC: U.S. Census Bureau, September

Fry, Richard, D'Vera Cohn, Gretchen Livingston, and Paul Taylor. 2011. *The Rising Age Gap in Economic Well-being.* Washington, DC: Pew Research Center Social & Demographic Trends project, November. http://www.pewsocialtrends.org/2011/11/07/the-rising-age-gap-in-economic-well-being/

Fry, Richard, and Kim Parker. 2012. *Record Shares of Young Adults Have Finished Both High School and College.* Washington, DC: Pew Research Center Social & Demographic Trends project, November. http://www.pewsocialtrends.org/2012/11/05/record-shares-of-young-adults-have-finished-both-high-school-and-college/

Fry, Richard. 2013. *A Rising Share of Young Adults Live in Their Parents' Home.* Washington, DC: Pew Research Center Social & Demographic Trends project, August. http://www.pewsocialtrends.org/2013/08/01/a-rising-share-of-young-adults-live-in-their-parents-home/

Gottschalck, Alfred O. 2008. *Net Worth and the Assets of Households: 2002.* Current Population Report P70-115. Washington, DC: U.S. Census Bureau, April. http://www.census.gov/prod/2008pubs/p70-115.pdf

King, Miriam et al. *Integrated Public Use Microdata Series, Current Population Survey: Version 3.0.* [Machine-readable database]. Minneapolis: University of Minnesota, 2010.

Mykyta, Laryssa. 2012. "Economic Downturns and the Failure to Launch: The Living Arrangements of Young Adults in the U.S. 1995-2011." U.S. Census Bureau Social, Economic and Housing Statistics Division (SEHSD) Working Paper 2012-24. https://www.census.gov/hhes/www/poverty/publications/WP2012-24.pdf

Pew Research Center. 2010. *Millennials: Confident. Connected. Open to Change.* Washington, DC: Pew Research Center, February. http://www.pewsocialtrends.org/2010/02/24/millennials-confident-connected-open-to-change/

Thomas, Adam, and Isabel Sawhill. 2005. "For Love and Money? The Impact of Family Structure on Family Income," *The Future of Children,* vol. 15, no. 2, Fall.

A CLOSER LOOK AT
The Rising Cost of *Not* Going to College   MyWritingLab

1. The Pew Research Center concludes rather definitively that going to college is a good investment and "worth it." Find five pieces of evidence in this report that allow them to make that conclusion. With your group, discuss whether this evidence is persuasive or not.

2. Some famous college dropouts include successful people like Bill Gates, Ellen DeGeneres, Oprah Winfrey, and Mark Zuckerberg. Do these exceptions undermine the Pew Research Center's conclusions in this report? With your group, discuss whether these kinds of exceptions are challenges to the research in this report or whether they are simply exceptions.

3. Make a list of ten reasons why you decided to go to college instead of stopping with your high school diploma. Then, compare your list with the lists of people in your group. Are your lists similar? What are some of the other reasons people go to college that you didn't put on your own list?

IDEAS FOR
Writing   MyWritingLab

1. Choose a successful person who did not go to college. This person could be famous or someone you know personally. Write a profile in which you describe her or his career. Then, discuss why college was not part of this person's career path and why they found success despite not going to college.

2. Some of the major complaints about college are the expense, the time, and the irrelevance of some courses to students' futures. Write a proposal in which you come up with a new kind of college experience. What are some things about college that you would keep the same? What would you change?

1. With your group, brainstorm all of the different "reports" that you can think of—lab reports, research reports, recommendation reports, police reports, credit reports, and other report types that you might have come across. Come up with five characteristics that all these reports have in common. Then list one thing about each kind of report that makes it unique.

2. Find and download a report from the Internet. To find a report, put "Report" and a topic that interests you into an Internet search engine like *Google, Bing, Yahoo!,* or *Ask.* (You might include ".pdf" or ".doc" in the search line to narrow the search.) A list of reports should pop up. With your group, discuss whether the report's topic, purpose, and main point are clearly stated in the introduction.

3. After reading the student group example in this chapter, discuss with your group how well this report follows the genre of the research report. Separately, consider its content, organization, and style. What could be improved?

1. Make a list of five topics on which you might want to do research. Then pick three of these topics, choose an angle, and narrow them down to something that you could handle in an analytical report. When choosing an angle, try to figure out why this issue is interesting right now. Share your topic ideas with your group.

2. Devise a research question that interests you. Then turn it into a hypothesis. Using a prewriting tool, such as brainstorming or a concept map, sketch out a research methodology that would allow you to answer this question and prove or disprove your hypothesis. Turn your methodology into an outline. Then write a one-page memo to your professor that reviews your outline and discusses why you would pursue your research question this way.

3. Use an Internet search engine to find a report on the issue you are or will be investigating. Write a one-page analysis of the report. Does the report have all the elements described in this chapter? Were there gaps in the report? Was the report organized well? Is the style and design appropriate for the topic?

There are many, many microgenres related to the analytical report. Choose a microgenre from the list below and find three examples in print or on the Internet. Then, come up with your own guidelines that explain how to write one of these microgenres.

Primer—a brief report about a well-understood issue but addressed to an outsider (e.g., older person, foreigner, extraterrestrial being) who is unfamiliar with it

Incident report—description of an event (an accident or unusual occurrence) that you witnessed or experienced

White Paper—a brief factual report about an issue or trend that informs people about problems, issues, and trends.

Consumer report—a report describing head-to-head testing of two or more products

Research-activity report—a report describing how you conducted your print, online, and empirical research (listing search engines, search terms, etc.) and how you assessed the reliability of those sources (consult Chapters 24 and 25)

Write This

1. **Turn a print report into a multimedia presentation.** On the Internet, find a report and transform it into a multimedia presentation that has ten to fifteen slides. Use presentation software like *PowerPoint* or *Keynote* to help organize the information and make it attractive to an audience. Where possible, add graphs, charts, photographs, and other visuals that will help explain the topic.

2. **Write a field research report.** A field research report gives you a chance to collect data about local issues in your community or on campus. To write one, you need to pose a research question, devise a method for answering it, do the research, and interpret your findings. With a small group, do these activities:

   a. Make a list of interesting or urgent issues or questions that your community or campus faces. What are some of the more annoying problems on your college's campus that you know about or that are in the news?

   b. Choose one that seems especially annoying. What has changed recently to bring this problem to a head?

   c. Discuss this problem with a group of other people in your class.

   d. Choose one angle of that issue and turn it into a research question that could be answered by doing field research (interviews, surveys, observations). State that research question briefly but clearly and thoroughly.

   e. Turn your research question into a hypothesis.

   Show your research question and hypothesis to your professor. If he or she approves it, begin your research. Write an eight-page report on your topic.

3. **Answer an eccentric question in an experimental report.** Pose an odd question that you would like to answer (e.g., "How big are the splatters from eggs dropped from different heights?" "How do people react when they see a strangely worded sign?"). Then devise a research methodology and come up with some results. Write a report that presents your findings. Include pictures or other graphics.

> Go to **My WritingLab** to complete this chapter's exercises and test your understanding of its objectives.

14

Research Papers

In this chapter, you will learn how to—

14.1 invent the content of your research paper with a wide range of sources.

14.2 develop an organization that fits the content of your research paper.

14.3 determine whether a plain or persuasive style is best to achieve your purpose.

14.4 add design elements and visuals to enhance your argument.

The research paper is one of the most common large assignments you will write in college, but it is also one of the most misunderstood. Research papers, which are also called "term papers," are typically assigned in the last month of a semester and they involve doing substantial research at the library and on the Internet. They are used to explain historical periods or events, study social trends or natural phenomena, or argue about culture, art, science, technology, or religion.

When a professor assigns a research paper, he or she is most likely asking you to do a substantial amount of investigation about a subject, synthesize the results of your research, and explain your subject in a clear and engaging way. Research papers tend to be around ten double-spaced pages with a list of "Works Cited" or "References" at the end. Your professors may ask for research papers that are longer or shorter, depending on the course and the subject matter.

Research paper assignments can be confusing because professors often have different ideas about their content, organization, style, and format. For example, some professors have an "expository" research paper in mind. An expository research paper explains an issue without making an overt argument for one side or the other. Other professors will want an "argumentative" research paper in which you take a side on an issue and use your research to support your position. So, when you are assigned a research paper, one of your first tasks is to find out what kind of research paper—expository or argumentative—your professor expects.

Outside of college, you probably won't be asked to write something called a "research paper." In the workplace, you will be asked to write *white papers* and *research reports,* which are very similar to research papers.

Research Papers

Research papers can be organized a variety of ways. These models show two basic patterns that you can adjust to fit your topic, angle, purpose, readers, and context.

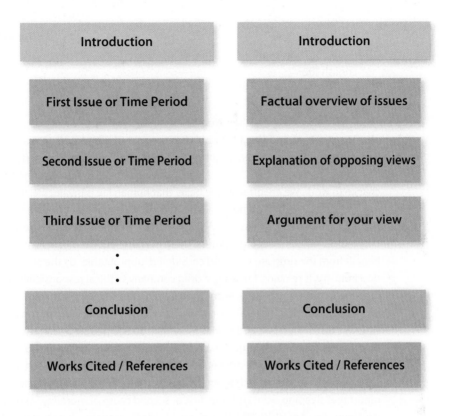

Effective research papers use sources to explain an issue or argue for a position. They tend to have the following major features:

- **An introduction** that identifies the research paper's topic and purpose, while clearly stating a thesis or main point that you will support or prove; the introduction should offer background information and explain why the topic is important.

- **Body paragraphs** that use an issue-by-issue or chronological pattern to present the results of your research; the body is divided into sections with headings.

- **A conclusion** that restates the thesis or main point of the research paper and summarizes your major points.

- **A References or Works Cited** section that includes a list of references or works cited in a standardized citation style (usually MLA or APA style).

ONE STUDENT'S WORK
Research Paper

Visit **MyWritingLab** to explore an interactive version of this essay.

Katelyn Turnbow   Turnbow 1
Professor Thompson
English 102
15 October 2014

Lives Not Worth the Money?

The outbreak and spread of Ebola has brought new attention to equally-lethal diseases that are often forgotten. The idea of a forgotten disease is almost absurd—a disease for which a cure is available and effective but never given a chance to work. We are often of the belief that human life is invaluable. In reality, however, the cures that do not make money for some manufacturer are simply not made at all. According to the World Health Organization (WHO), one need only look at African sleeping sickness. There is a cure, but the victims who would benefit from the drug are poor and considered "unprofitable" by the pharmaceutical industry. It remains, however, a drug company's ethical responsibility to care for people its drugs can save, even when helping them is not profitable.

African sleeping sickness, also known as Human African Trypanosomiasis or HAT, was discovered in 1902 and kills more than 50,000 people a year. These victims, however, are often forgotten because they are poor and live in sub-Saharan Africa, not a prosperous Western nation (see fig. 1). The disease is caused by a parasite and transmitted to humans by the Tsetse fly. Some villages in the region report that sleeping sickness is the "first or second cause of mortality," and that it is "even ahead of HIV/AIDS" (World, par. 10). WHO estimates that on top of the 9678 cases reported in 2009, about 20,000 cases were never diagnosed (par. 10).

> Specific statistics from credible sources provide credibility for the paper's arguments.

Sleeping sickness manifests in two distinct stages. The haemolymphatic stage (blood-lymph node) occurs shortly after exposure to the parasite and causes headache, fever, joint pain, and itching (World). The neurological stage follows, occurring months or even years after initial infection (see fig. 2). This phase begins when the deadly parasite invades its host's central nervous system (CNS) and is accompanied by a large array of neurological symptoms including confusion, loss or disturbance of the senses, personality changes, and decreased coordination as well as the "disturbance of the sleep cycle which gives the disease its name" (par. 17). Sleeping sickness is always fatal if not treated, and by the time the disease reaches its neurological stage, it is usually too late (par. 15).

Turnbow 2

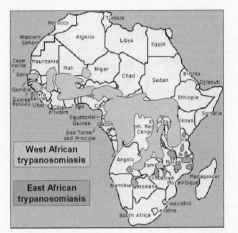

FIGURE 1. **Distribution of West African or Gambian Sleeping Sickness and East African or Rhodesian Sleeping Sickness.**
University of South Carolina, School of Medicine; Parasitology; Microbiology and Immunology Online, 24 Feb. 2014; Fig. 2E, www.microbiologybook.org/parasitology/blood-proto.htm.

Effective treatments for sleeping sickness have been available since 1921, but they are dangerous and extremely painful. If diagnosed and treated in the early stages, sleeping sickness responds well to Pentamidine or, in extreme cases, Suramin. Both drugs, while sometimes accompanied by serious side effects such as heart and kidney failure, are fairly safe and inexpensive (World). Victims in the CNS stage of HAT, however, have for a long time been treated with a drug called Melarsoprol. Melarsoprol is widely available and cheap, but is derived from arsenic, and, acting as the potent poison that it is, can kill 5-20 percent of patients. The drug is also excruciatingly painful, described by many victims as "fire in the veins" ("Sleeping Sickness"). Although Melarsoprol "wouldn't pass a single ethical or drug-safety test" in the developed world, it is still used in Africa because it is the only treatment readily available to victims of this fatal but neglected disease (Gombe).

It is surprising, then, to learn that a new and highly effective treatment was developed almost 40 years ago. The chemotherapy drug, defluoro-methyl-ornithine (DFMO), was developed in the 1970s but failed as a cancer treatment, causing only hair loss in patients (Wickware 908-09). It would have been the end of the pharmaceutical, but in 1983, New York parasite biologist Cyrus Bacchi discovered DFMO's effectiveness on the later stage of sleeping sickness (Shah 22). Shortly after this discovery, Belgian doctor Henri Taelman used DFMO to treat

Maps, illustrations, and photographs should be placed in the paper where they provide the most support for in-text arguments.

When there is no author, use an abbreviated title of the article.

continued

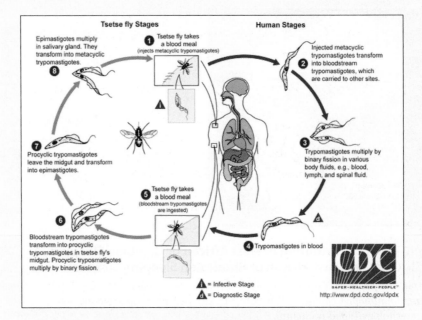

FIGURE 2. Life Cycle of *T.b. gamienese* and *T.b. rhodesiense*.

Alexander J. da Silva and Melanie Moser; Centers for Disease Control Public Health Image Library, 18 Mar. 2005; phil.cdc.gov/phil/details.asp?pid=3405.

an infected woman who had already fallen into a coma, and, almost miraculously, DFMO brought the woman out of her coma within 24 hours. Dr. Taelman renamed the drug eflornithine, but it quickly became known as the "resurrection drug" because it was "so effective at reviving even comatose patients" (Wickware 909; McNeil A1). Other than the highly toxic Melarsoprol, eflornithine is the only drug effective against late-stage Trypanosomiasis (McNeil A1). In addition to a much lower drug-induced mortality rate, eflornithine has fewer and milder side effects than Melarsoprol, and patients who receive eflornithine are more than twice as likely to survive the year following treatment as those treated with the older drug (Chappuis et al. 748-50).

It is clear that the drug is sorely needed by those who suffer the formidable symptoms of sleeping sickness. Despite this, eflornithine was very short-lived. The pharmaceutical company, Sanofi-Aventis, halted production of the resurrection drug in 1995 along with two other antitrypanosome drugs (Wickware 909). A drug aimed toward treatment of diseases in poor countries was simply not

When quoting more than one author, separate the citations with a semicolon.

When a work has more than three authors, use the name of the first author listed followed by "et al." meaning "and others."

State Your Main Point or Thesis Statement. In a research paper, your main point or thesis should be clearly stated somewhere in the introduction.

> **Weak:** King George III's mistakes were partially responsible for the American Revolutionary War.

> **Stronger:** The United States would have eventually gained its independence through peaceful means, but King George III's ill-conceived economic sanctions sparked a violent revolt among the American colonists, igniting an expensive and humiliating war for the British Empire.

Offer Background Information on the Topic. Give the readers just enough historical information or factual evidence to familiarize themselves with the topic.

Stress the Importance of the Topic to the Readers. Briefly mention why this topic is significant, especially to the readers. You might also consider using a grabber or a lead to catch the readers' attention at the beginning of your research paper. In Chapter 20, you can learn more about using grabbers or leads to spark the readers' interest in your topic.

These five introductory moves can be made in almost any order. Many research papers, for example, start out with some background information to catch the readers' attention. Others begin by identifying the topic and stressing its importance. If you make these five moves, you will probably have a good start to your research paper.

The Body

The body of your research paper can be organized in a variety of ways. Here are a few common ways to organize your draft:

Issues Divide your information into two to five major issues that you want to discuss in your research paper. Specifically, pay attention to issues on which people tend to disagree. List the major points that people often discuss when they consider this topic.

Chronological Divide your information into two to five historical time periods (e.g., 1980s, 1990s, 2000s; or before the event, start of the event, during the event, end of the event, aftermath of the event). Then, arrange your information by sorting out what happened in each of those time periods.

Argumentation Divide your information into three categories: Review of the facts; discussion of how others, especially people with opposing views, interpret the facts; discussion of how you and people who agree with you interpret the facts.

Carving the Body into Sections. Each section in your research paper can follow a variety of patterns. The following organizational strategies can be helpful for arranging the material in each section:

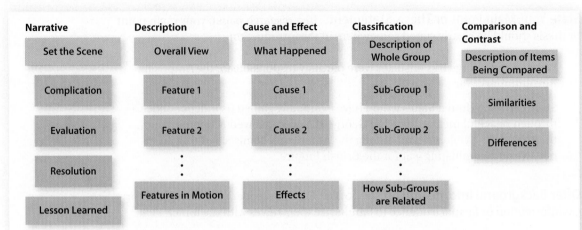

FIGURE 14.1 Organizing Sections in a Research Paper
Each section in your research paper should have its own organization. These diagrams show a few possibilities.

Narrative—Use true stories and anecdotes to illustrate your points in a chronological way.

Description—Divide something into its major parts and describe them separately.

Cause and Effect—Explain the causes of a problem and the effects.

Classification—Divide something into major and minor categories.

Comparison and Contrast—Identify similarities and differences between two things.

Figure 14.1 shows some models for how sections might be organized.

Using and Citing Your Sources.   While drafting the body of your research paper, you need to carefully quote and thoroughly cite your sources.

In-Text Parenthetical Citations—Each time you take an idea or quote from a text, you need to use an in-text citation to signal where it came from. Chapters 27 and 28 on using MLA and APA styles will show you how to use in-text citations.

Quotations—Using quotes from experts is encouraged in research papers. Brief quotations can appear within a sentence and are marked off by quotation marks. Longer quotations (more than three lines of text) should be put into block quotes that are indented.

Paraphrasing and Summarizing—You can also paraphrase or summarize your sources. When paraphrasing, you should follow the structure of the source, putting the ideas or information in your own words. When summarizing, you should re-organize the information from most important to least important, using your own words.

The Conclusion

The conclusion of your research paper should be similar in many ways to your introduction. When concluding, you should restate your main point (thesis) and stress the importance of your subject one final time. You should also briefly discuss the future of your topic.

Your research paper's conclusion should make up to five moves:

- Make an obvious transition from the body to the conclusion.
- State your main point, or thesis statement.
- Stress again the importance of the topic to the readers.
- Call your readers to action (in an argumentative research paper).
- Briefly discuss the future of this topic.

The transition to your conclusion should be obvious to the readers. A heading like "Conclusion: A New Nation Is Born" will signal that you are concluding. Otherwise, you can start your conclusion with a transitional phrase like "In conclusion," "In summary," or "In closing" to signal that you are making your final points.

Your main point or thesis statement should be similar to the sentence you used in your introduction, but not exactly the same. State your main point in different words, perhaps with a little more emphasis.

Finally, you should end your research paper by discussing the future of the topic. If you're arguing for a specific point, call the readers to action (e.g., "Now is the time to do something about this problem"). You can also discuss what you think will happen in the near future. If you're writing an expository research paper, you can briefly discuss what happened next with this topic (e.g., "The American Revolution sparked a wave of revolutions throughout the world").

Your conclusion should be brief, perhaps one or two paragraphs. Once you signal that you are concluding, your readers will expect you to wrap up in a short amount of time.

Works Cited or References

The final page(s) of your research paper will be your list of Works Cited (MLA) or References (APA). You should turn to Chapter 27, "Using MLA Style," or Chapter 28, "Using APA Style," to determine how to format your list of sources.

Choosing an Appropriate Style

Expository research papers tend to be written in the plain style, while argumentative research papers use both plain and persuasive styles. The plain style is especially helpful for explaining the facts about your topic and discussing what happened. The persuasive style should be used when you are trying to influence the readers to accept your point of view.

14.3 determine whether a plain or persuasive style is best to achieve your purpose.

Use Doers as the Subjects of Your Sentences. When drafting a research paper, writers tend to use passive voice (e.g., "In a 2011 study, brain-enhancing drugs were given by scientists to 200 college students"). When revising, change this kind of sentence into active voice by moving the doers into the subject of your sentence (e.g., "In a 2011 study, scientists gave brain-enhancing drugs to 200 college students"). Active voice will make your research paper sound more authoritative.

Avoid Weak Sentence Constructions. Where possible, avoid starting sentences with "It is . . . ," "There are . . . ," and "This is . . . ." You can strengthen these sentences by using real subjects and active verbs, such as "Students know . . . ," "Researchers discovered . . . ," and "This experiment demonstrated. . . ."

Keep Sentences Breathing Length. Research papers are often plagued with long, overly complex sentences that are difficult to read. As you revise, look for sentences that are longer than breathing length. Then, cut them down or divide them into two sentences.

Use Similes and Analogies to Explain Difficult Concepts. If you are trying to explain something complicated to your readers, try using a simile or analogy. For example, you might use a simile like "After the skirmish at Concord, the American Revolution spread like a wildfire throughout the colonies." You could also use analogies, such as "Using brain-enhancing drugs to study for an exam is like putting rocket fuel in your car. The benefits are noticeable but also short-lived and dangerous."

Designing Your Research Paper

14.4 add design elements and visuals to enhance your argument.

More than likely, your professor will give you specific guidelines about how the research paper should be formatted. In some cases, your professor may ask you to follow MLA or APA style, which are the formats spelled out in the *MLA Handbook for Writers of Research Papers* or the *Publication Manual of the American Psychological Association*. These handbooks, which should be available at your library or on the Internet, offer clear guidelines about how to format research papers.

You should also look carefully at the assignment sheet to determine exactly what kind of design or format your professor requires. Part of your grade, after all, may be based on whether you followed the assignment's formatting directions. If your professor does not spell out a specific format or design, you should ask for some guidance.

If you are given flexibility to choose your own design, here are some design features you might consider:

Include a Cover Page. A cover page, like the one shown in Figure 14.2, can add a professional touch to your research paper. Your cover page should include the title of your paper, your name, your professor's name, and the date the research paper was submitted. An appropriate image on the cover can also set a specific tone for the paper.

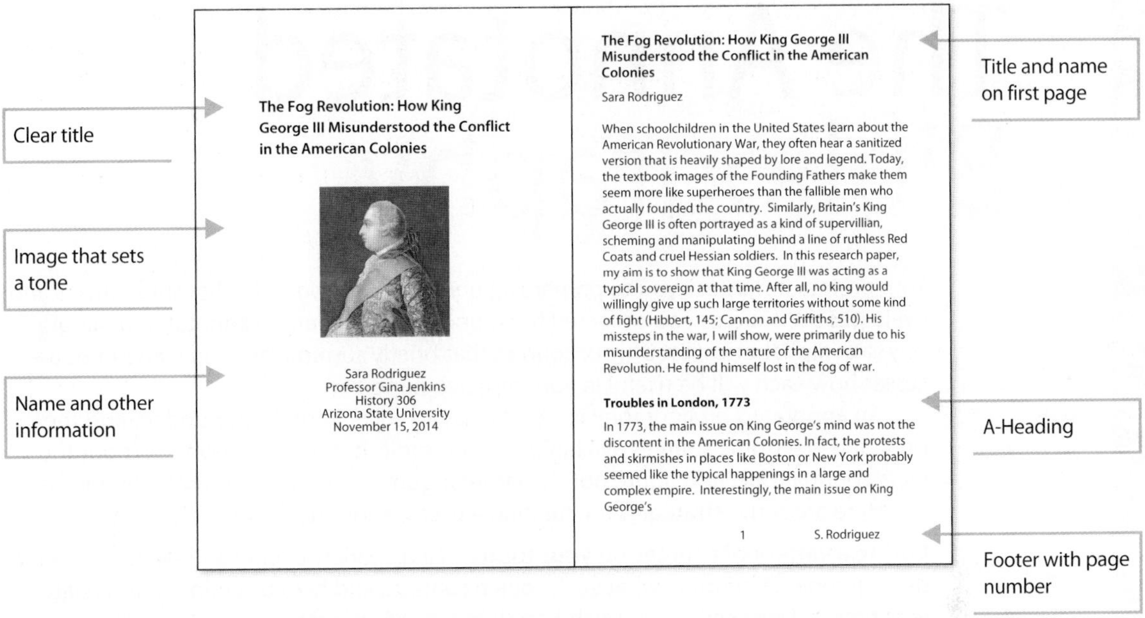

FIGURE 14.2 Designing a Research Paper

Even a traditional design for a research paper, like the one shown here, can be attractive.

Use Meaningful Headings. The headings in your research paper should be descriptive and accurate but not boring. For example, instead of "Start of Revolutionary War," you might use "The Shot Heard Around the World." Your headings should offer the readers an overall view of your paper, while giving them good reasons to read each section.

Add in Graphs, Charts, and Images. Look for ways to use graphs and charts to reinforce your major points. Photographs and other images can also enhance the readers' understanding and add some visual appeal.

Use Page Numbers and Perhaps a Header or Footer. All multi-page documents should have page numbers, but this guideline is especially true with research papers. Due to their length, research papers need page numbers to make them easier to discuss. You might also consider adding in a footer or header that includes your name.

Pay Attention to Paragraph Length. In a research paper, you don't want your paragraphs to be too short or too long. Short, choppy paragraphs (only two or three lines) signal to your readers that your topic sentences probably lack sufficient support. Long paragraphs (over one page) can signal a tendency toward rambling or a lack of focus. In some cases, short or long paragraphs are appropriate, but you should make sure they are necessary.

The Annotated
Bibliography

Your professor may ask you to prepare an *annotated bibliography* that summarizes and evaluates the sources you collected for your research paper. An annotated bibliography is an alphabetical list of your sources that briefly summarizes and sometimes assesses how each will be useful in your research paper.

An annotated bibliography is a great way to collect and better understand the print and electronic sources available for your topic. It is a good way to sort out the facts about a topic and figure out the larger arguments and trends that influence it.

Here are some strategies for creating a useful annotated bibliography:

Locate a variety of sources on your topic.   Find a variety of print and electronic sources on your topic. Determine what each source contains and how this information relates to your project. Don't collect only web-based sources. You need to go over to the library, too.

Don't include sites like Wikipedia as sources.   Wikipedia and similar Web sites can give you an overview of your topic and help you locate sources. However, since the entries on these Web sites are written anonymously and can be altered by the public, you should not consider them authoritative.

Format your sources accurately.   List your sources and format them in MLA or APA style. If you format them properly as you are creating your annotated bibliography, they will be easier to include at the end of your research paper.

Offer a brief summary or commentary on each source.   Your summary should run the length of a typical paragraph. The first line should state the main point of the text. The remaining sentences should each express the major points of the source.

Consider each source in depth and figure out how it fits into your research project.   Your professors will also use your annotated bibliography to review the kinds of sources you have collected and make suggestions about other possible sources. At the end of each source in your list, write a couple sentences about how it might be used in your research paper.

Be careful not to plagiarize your sources.   If you take a quote or ideas from a source, carefully label these items with page numbers and the necessary quotation marks. This labeling is especially important while writing a research paper, because as you draft your text, you may forget which words and ideas originally came from your sources.

WRITE **your own annotated bibliography.** Create an annotated bibliography for the research paper you have been assigned to write. Your annotated bibliography should include at least ten sources from a variety of print and electronic texts.

Visit **MyWritingLab** to complete this exercise.

Annotated Bibliography: The Fog of Revolution

Sara Rodriguez

Allen, Thomas. "One Revolution, Two Wars." *Military History*, **vol. 27, 2011, pp. 58-63.**

This article points out that the American Revolution was in many ways a civil war between Patriots, who wanted revolution, and Loyalists who supported King George III. As Allen points out, "the signers [of the Declaration of Independence] knew they did not speak for 'one people' but for a people including Americans who opposed the Revolution" (58). Many members of established families acted as informants for the British. Many Loyalists would join the British forces in battles against the Patriots. These divisions led to much distrust among the Patriots, because they weren't certain who was on their side and who was against them (61).

My assessment: This article can be helpful for my argument. Part of my argument is that we are given a rather cleaned-up version of the American Revolution in our classes and textbooks. This article demonstrates that the war was not one that pitted American patriots against British oppressors. Instead, there were many factions in the colonies who had reasons to support or fight against independence.

Bonwick, Colin. *The American Revolution.* **U of Virginia P, 1991.**

This book suggests that the American Revolution is often misunderstood by the general public. Typically, Bonwick argues, the American Revolution is portrayed as an uprising among colonists who were seeking their freedom from Britain. This revolutionary narrative glosses over the many "internal debates and processes which gave birth to the United States from 1776 onwards" implying they "were little more than necessary consequences of independence" (1). The book steps back and shows that each colony had its own reasons for seeking independence. Overall, though, much of the tension between the colonies and Britain was due to economic rather than ideological reasons (56). The final move toward Revolution was more about preserving economic strength rather than freeing people from any kind of bondage.

My assessment: This book makes a similar argument to the one I am making. I'm arguing that King George III's actions, especially increased taxation, made the economic situation in the colonies more difficult, which made it easier for arguments for independence to take hold.

Full citation in MLA style.

Summary of the article.

Explains how the source might be used in the research paper.

Summary of the book.

Interpretive comments that explain how the source might fit into the research project.

Here are some quick strategies to get you going on your research paper.

DEFINE Your Research Topic and Find a New Angle

Your professor may have given you a topic or asked you to find one of your own. You should first narrow your topic to something specific that you can handle in about a ten-page paper. Then, look for an angle on that topic that is new or different.

STATE Your Purpose

In one sentence, state exactly what you want to achieve in your research paper. Your purpose statement will evolve as you do research and draft.

STATE Your Main Point or Thesis Statement

In one sentence, state exactly what your research paper will demonstrate or prove. An expository research paper will offer a thesis that guides the discussion. An argumentative research paper will state a thesis that you intend to prove.

RESEARCH Your Topic

Research papers rely heavily on print and electronic sources. Use your computer to access databases at your campus library. If you use sources from the Internet, make sure they are reliable. Go to the library!

ORGANIZE Your Research Paper

A variety of organization styles are available for your research paper. They almost always include an introduction and conclusion. The body should be organized in a way that allows you to present your research in a logical way.

CHOOSE an Appropriate Style

The style of a research paper tends to be straightforward and formal. You can use stylistic devices like similes, metaphors, and analogies. For the most part, though, a plain style is best.

DESIGN and Format the Document

Your professor will likely have some specific guidelines for how to format your paper (e.g., double-spaced, one-inch margins, 12-point font). You should ask if you can include images and if there is any flexibility in designing the document.

REVISE and Edit Your Writing

Pay special attention to your paragraphs, especially the topic sentences. Also, your research paper needs to be error-free if you want your readers to take your work seriously.

Drones in U.S. Airspace: Principles for Governance

PAUL ROSENZWEIG, STEVEN P. BUCCI, PhD, CHARLES D. STIMSON, AND JAMES JAY CARAFANO, PhD

In this research paper, experts from the Heritage Foundation, a think tank, review the constitutional and privacy issues involving the use of drones in United States airspace. Watch how they use their understanding of today's drone technology to think about future potential problems involving drones.

Abstract

Flying drones—unmanned aerial vehicles—have been made famous by their use in the war on terrorism, notably in operations in Iraq and Afghanistan, but such military drones are a small fraction of those used by the United States today. Thousands of drones are used for a wide variety of purposes, from scientific research to military operations. Both government and the private sector use drones mostly without weapons capabilities. Because of their wide-reaching surveillance capabilities, however, even unarmed drones could threaten personal privacy and civil liberties. As the Federal Aviation Administration develops regulations for the operation of drones in domestic skies, it should consider constitutional concerns and privacy rights.

Rapidly advancing technology has made it possible to employ pilotless aircraft "drones" for public missions (such as countersurveillance and strikes on enemy targets) as well as private purposes (such as crop dusting). As new technologies present these options to policymakers, it is an opportune time to establish general principles and legal guidelines for the government's use of drones in domestic airspace. These guidelines should go beyond safety and transit issues that are addressed by the Federal Aviation Administration (FAA), the agency that oversees regulation of civil aviation, and should define the scope of permissible federal activities. Congress should play an active role in establishing the guidelines.

It is no accident that questions of law and policy relating to the domestic use of drones have moved to the front burner in Washington. The saliency of the issue was heightened by a little-noticed provision in the congressional bill reauthorizing the Federal Aviation Administration. A much wider-ranging bill (dealing with funding questions and modernization of the air traffic control system) contains one little-noticed section directing the FAA to develop and promulgate a series of regulations that would establish the rules of the road (or, more accurately, the rules of the airspace) for the operation of drones in domestic skies.[1] As framed in the FAA reauthorization bill, the presumption was, broadly speaking, that domestic drone use is appropriate and that the only real questions were technical, relating, for example, to delineating air corridors for drones and standards of reliability for ensuring their safe operation.

Understanding Drones

For most people, the word "drone" conjures up an image of a lethal, missile-armed "Predator" or "Reaper" unmanned aerial vehicle (UAV) like those used in the Iraq and Afghanistan campaigns. Yet they are a small fraction of the types of drones used by the United States today.

The use of drones is not new. Israelis [5] designed the modern, glider-type drone in the 1970s to be lightweight and small, making it inexpensive to build and difficult to shoot down. After the United States produced the Predator, UAVs became an indispensable military tool.

Today, there are thousands of drone platforms that are used for a wide variety of purposes, from scientific research to military operations. Drones are employed by governments and by the private sector. The drones themselves are entirely unmanned and are controlled by a human operator. The remote operators of drones are highly skilled and must be trained not only to carry out intelligence, surveillance, and reconnaissance missions, but also to conduct or respond to electronic attacks, implement strike missions, conduct search and rescue operations, and many other tasks. Such remote piloting greatly reduces the risks to the drone operator and makes the vehicles cheaper to produce.

The Pentagon currently controls some 7,000 military-grade drones—up from fewer than 50 drones just a decade ago.[2] The drones have been used increasingly in military missions overseas, first running reconnaissance and then targeting al-Qaeda operatives in Afghanistan, Iraq, Pakistan, Somalia, Yemen, and elsewhere.

Domestically, different types of drones are now being used on a non-controversial limited basis for border patrol, biological and chemical air testing, geological surveys, livestock and wildlife monitoring, crop dusting, wildfire containment, and search and rescue operations.[3, 4] These drones are not armed with weapons, nor are they capable of carrying any. Their use will only increase as drones become smaller and more sophisticated and their cost plummets. Non-governmental entities, as well as individuals, can purchase a wide variety of drones for their own use.

Because of their surveillance capabilities, however, without proper legal guidelines and oversight, drones could threaten personal privacy and civil liberties. Therefore, as the FAA develops regulations for the operation of drones in domestic skies, it must also take into account constitutional concerns and privacy rights. To date, the FAA has interpreted its mandate to focus solely on technical issues, such as delineating air corridors for drones, and instituting standards for safe operation.

General Principles

Any guidelines must ensure appropriate pro- [10] tections of the freedoms guaranteed to U.S. citizens under the Constitution. The general rule balancing security and freedom is to be found, in large part, in the structure of American constitutional government itself. The protections codified in the Bill of Rights are an additional firewall against any intrusions on liberty that would unravel the checks in the Constitution. The Fourth Amendment's prohibition against unlawful search and seizure is the right most directly implicated by unbounded and unrestrained use of domestic drones.

Now is the time to return to first principles of individual liberty in a free society and assess their interaction with technology and governance in an age of domestic drones. There are basic first principles that underlie any use of new technology and the existing constitutional limitations that might apply to drones. An assessment of these principles suggests that there are:

- Substantial liberty interests;

- Acceptable domestic uses of drone technology that should be permitted and in fact fostered, such as the use of drones to search for survivors after a disaster; and

- Prohibited uses of drone technology that raise significant questions of law and policy—such as the deployment of drones operated by the military within U.S. borders in a manner that violates existing rules (such as Posse Comitatus) on the use of military force domestically.

Beyond these uses, the challenge for the Administration and Congress is to define strict, appropriate implementation policies and oversight structures that can protect individual liberties while allowing appropriate uses of domestic drones with appropriate oversight.

First Principles and Drones

As a practical matter, the FAA has expertise in and is the appropriate forum for considering safety and technical questions, but other governmental bodies have expertise in and are better suited to address privacy and civil liberties concerns. Given the potentially wide range of uses for drones in U.S. territory, resolving air-traffic safety and security issues alone is inadequate. Washington needs a more comprehensive and thoughtful framework.

Fundamentally, these are questions of law and policy. The issue is not whether the use of drones is technically feasible: Obviously, it is and will be increasingly so. Nor is it a question of legality: Most current uses are lawful, and most future uses are likely to be. Rather, the proper subject for discussion is the extent to which society wants to provide tools to the state that have beneficial uses and are also susceptible to abuse.

This question is not a new one; it is one that has been a tension point within American society since the Founding. Americans want a

government that fosters liberty and freedom and that provides security. Americans want a constrained government that is subject to checks and balances and one that has "energy in the executive" (to quote Hamilton) to achieve legitimate governmental objectives. As always, striking the proper balance is both difficult and essential.

As a first step, several first principles [15] should guide the analysis[5]:

- No fundamental liberty guaranteed by the Constitution can be breached or infringed upon.

- Any increased intrusion on American privacy interests must be justified through an understanding of the particular nature, significance, and severity of the threat addressed by the program. The less significant the threat, the less justified the intrusion.

- The full extent and nature of the intrusion worked by any new technology must be understood and appropriately limited. Not all intrusions are justified simply because they are effective. Strip searches at airports would certainly prevent people from boarding planes with weapons, but they would do so at too high a cost.

- Whatever the justification for the intrusion, if there are less intrusive means of achieving the same end at a reasonably comparable cost, the less intrusive means ought to be preferred. There is no reason to erode Americans' privacy when equivalent results can be achieved without doing so.

- Any new system that is developed and implemented must be designed to be tolerable in the long term. The war against terrorism, uniquely, is one with no foreseeable end. Thus, excessive intrusions may not be justified as emergency measures that will lapse upon the termination of hostilities. Policymakers must be restrained in their actions; Americans might have to live with their consequences for a long time.

From these general principles one can derive certain other, more concrete conclusions regarding the development and construction of any new technology—principles that are directly relevant to the deployment of drones domestically:

- No new system should alter or contravene existing legal restrictions on the government's ability to access data about private individuals. Any new system should mirror and implement existing legal limitations on domestic or foreign activity, depending on its sphere of operation.

- Similarly, no new system should alter or contravene existing operational system limitations. Development of new technology is not a basis for authorizing new government powers or new government capabilities. Any such expansion should be justified independently.

- No new system that materially affects citizens' privacy should be developed without specific authorization by the American people's representatives in Congress and without provisions for their oversight of the operation of the system.

- Finally, no new system should be implemented without the full panoply of protections against its abuse. As James Madison told the Virginia ratifying convention in 1788, "There are more instances of the abridgment of the freedom of the people by gradual and silent encroachments of those in power than by violent and sudden usurpations." [6]

Legal Guidelines and Limits on Use

While wide-scale domestic drone usage is an emerging phenomenon, the Administration and Congress are not without legal guidance. There are likely to be few direct constitutional limits on the domestic use of drones. The nearly parallel case, *Dow Chemical Co. v. United States*,[7] involved the use of helicopters to survey the walled compound of a chemical facility. The Supreme Court concluded that the use of helicopters in this manner did not require a warrant.

This is a natural extension of the general rule that law enforcement does not need a warrant to examine conduct that is exposed to public view—at least in part because by performing one's actions in public, one has manifested the absence of a reasonable expectation of maintaining his privacy. Hence, as someone walks down the street, the police need no warrant to follow him. Likewise, in pursuit of an escaping criminal, police may follow him by car, and police helicopters may monitor traffic without a warrant. Extending the warrant requirement to drone activity would therefore be novel and a significant dislocation of current practice.

Nevertheless, it is also likely that outer limits on the use of drones domestically may exist if the drones are equipped with advanced sensor technology. In the case of *Kyllo v. United States*,[8] the Supreme Court considered the use of infrared sensing devices to obtain the heat signature inside a house. (The signature was indicative of plant-growing lamps used to cultivate marijuana.) The Court concluded that the use of novel sensors, not generally available to the public, would implicate the reasonable expectation of privacy. The Court held that a warrant was required to use an infrared sensor to monitor the heat signature of a house.

One can suggest that *Kyllo* would support the broader conclusion that placing unusual sensor arrays on drones (say, a millimeter-wave ground-penetrating radar) might require

20

a warrant in situations where a more common sensor (such as a camera) would not.

Limits on domestic drone use may also arise when and if drones proliferate such that widespread and large-scale observation and data-collection mechanisms are enabled. Here, the Supreme Court doctrine is still in development, but the Court has sounded a cautionary note. This past term, in *United States v. Jones*,[9] Justice Samuel Alito wrote a concurrence (speaking for only four Justices) in which he posited that even though the collection of an individual piece of data might be lawful without a warrant, the collection of numerous such pieces of data to form a larger mosaic picture would raise constitutional concerns. Under this so-called mosaic theory, limits on the collection of routine images throughout a city—linked to a facial recognition program, for instance—might exist.

As mentioned, this legal doctrine has yet to be adopted by the Supreme Court, but it, too, sounds a cautionary note: Certainly, the routine and systematic use of drones for widespread surveillance and analysis is likely to be suspect on constitutional grounds.

These precedents clearly suggest a "sweet spot" for lawful domestic drone activity. Camera-equipped drones used for routine purposes, such as observing public activity, will likely pass constitutional muster. Legal limits on such use, if any, will come from policy development or statutory enactments.

Striking the Right Balance

Given these guidelines, acceptable uses that (safety considerations permitting) ought to have sensible and minimal restrictions, are:

- Border Patrol Security
  1. Long-term surveillance of a specified area or route
  2. Criminal personnel search and/or pursuit
  3. Personnel search and rescue
  4. Monitoring of "blind spots"

5. Communications augmentation (e.g., hosting flying cell phone towers[10])

- Emergency Preparation and Disaster Response
  1. Planning routes and anticipating vulnerabilities
  2. Long-term surveillance of a specified area or route
  3. Catastrophic effects and remediation planning
  4. Criminal personnel search and/or pursuit
  5. Personnel search and rescue
  6. Emergency cell coverage restoration
  7. Deterrence of criminal behavior in unpatrolled areas

- Agriculture
  1. Crop dusting (pesticides) or infestation eradication
  2. Monitoring of soil moisture levels and crop growth

- Cargo Delivery (private sector)
  1. Long-haul trips
  2. Transporting hazardous materials
  3. Deliveries during hazardous flying conditions and emergencies

- Maritime Domain Awareness
  1. Long-term surveillance of a specified area or route
  2. Criminal personnel search and/or pursuit
  3. Personnel search and rescue
  4. Identification and surveillance of low observable vessels (semi-submersibles) and small craft (under 300 tons)

- Environmental Monitoring
  1. Long-term surveillance of a specified area or route
  2. Wildlife tracking
  3. Monitoring droughts and flooding
  4. Monitoring locks, dams, and levees in remote areas

- Law Enforcement
  1. SWAT team reconnaissance
  2. Long-term surveillance of a specified area or route
  3. Criminal personnel search and/or pursuit
  4. Personnel search and rescue
  5. Communication augmentation

25

There are, of course, some clear "red lines" where domestic drone use should be prohibited. The use of drones in a military capacity (while armed) should be severely restricted to situations of actual invasion or insurrection; the use of drones for domestic surveillance of First Amendment activity is fundamentally at odds with U.S. constitutional principles; drones equipped with novel sensor arrays ought not to be permitted absent a clearly demonstrated need and a careful consideration of countervailing privacy and civil liberties concerns; and drones should not be used as a platform for the collection of massive unstructured data sets that could form the basis for sophisticated tracking and behavioral analytics.

Finally, drones are unsuitable for use as a routine means of surveillance in non-threatening situations. Certainly, one can envision the utility of deploying drones to monitor the progress of a peaceful protest march on Washington, D.C., but the idea of a watchful "eye in the sky" for basic crowd control of peaceful activity crosses an indefinable line—at least in part because the cheapness of drone resources (compared to the deployment of police) would make their ubiquitous use far more likely.

The notion of imposing a warrant requirement on the use of drones is likely a categorical mistake, as it would involve the application of a Fourth Amendment concept to an area where the Fourth Amendment simply does not apply. Congress cannot and should not avoid the hard task of sorting permissible uses from impermissible uses on its own; it is likely that many of the uses envisioned would not fit in the warrant construct at all. Many of the

prohibitions recommended are independent of the existence or lack of probable cause.

Next Steps for Congress

Congress and the executive branch have yet to do the hard work of determining precisely what those limits on drone use ought to be, and this paper's outline suggests that the lack of thought in some of the blunt instrument proposals currently pending might very well throw the baby out with the bath water.

The way forward, however, is reasonably clear. Congress should:

- Permit the FAA to continue with its rulemaking regarding the domestic use of drones but make clear that the rulemaking is limited to issues of safety and airspace use that are squarely within the FAA's expertise;

- Condition further expansion of the domestic use of drones in accordance with the FAA's rulemaking on the development of clear guidelines on permissible uses for drones and the development of an oversight and audit mechanism; and

- Task the Administration with the development of guidelines that, at a minimum:
  1. Recognize and authorize legitimate uses of drones that pose no appreciable risk to privacy or civil liberties;
  2. Prevent the militarization of the domestic drone air fleet;
  3. Prohibit the use of drones to monitor constitutionally protected First Amendment expression; and
  4. Ensure that drones do not become another comprehensive platform for the collection of large data sets of unstructured surveillance data.

30

In the absence of congressional action, the executive branch should reluctantly proceed independently with the development of its own privacy and civil liberties policies for the use of drones. What should not happen—what cannot be allowed to happen—is that domestic drones continue to proliferate without any consideration of privacy and civil liberties. What also must not happen is that Americans allow an unreasoned fear of hypothetical abuse to stampede the country into a blanket prohibition on the use of drones for domestic purposes, depriving all Americans of a wide range of benefits.

Notes

1. Ben Wolfgang, "FAA Chief Says Drones Will Force Change at Agency," *The Washington Times*, August 7, 2012, http://www.washingtontimes.com/news/2012/aug/7/faa-chief-says-drones-will-force-change-at-agency/ (accessed August 17, 2012).

2. U.S. Government Accountability Office, *Unmanned Aircraft Systems: Comprehensive Planning and a Results-Oriented Training Strategy Are Needed to Support Growing Inventories*, GAO-10-331, March 2010, http://www.gao.gov/new.items/d10331.pdf (accessed August 29, 2012).

3. Chad C. Haddal and Jeremiah Gertler, "Homeland Security: Unmanned Aerial Vehicles and Border Surveillance," Congressional Research Service *Report for Congress*, July 8, 2010, http://assets.opencrs.com/rpts/RS21698_20100708.pdf (accessed August 29, 2012).

4. Brian Bennett, "Drones Tested as Tools for Police and Firefighters," *Los Angeles Times*, August 5, 2012, http://www.latimes.com/news/nationworld/nation/la-na-drones-testing-20120805,0,6483617.story (accessed August 29, 2012).

5. These principles first appeared in Paul Rosenzweig, "Principles for Safeguarding Liberty in an Age of Terrorism," Heritage Foundation Executive Memorandum No. 854, January 31, 2003, http://www.heritage.org/research/reports/2003/01/principles-for-safeguarding-civil-liberties.

6. James Madison, Speech in the Virginia Ratifying Convention on Control of the Military, June 16, 1788, in History of the Virginia Federal Convention of 1788, Vol. 1, p. 130 (H.B. Grigsby ed. 1890).

7. 476 U.S. 227 (1986).

8. 533 U.S. 27 (2001).

9. No. 10-1259, __ U.S. __ (2012).

10. See, for example, "Flying Cell Towers," DailyWireless.org, March 6, 2012, http://www.dailywireless.org/2012/03/06/flying-cell-towers/ (accessed September 7, 2012).

A CLOSER LOOK AT   MyWritingLab
Drones in U.S. Airspace: Principles for Governance

1. List three of the constitutional and privacy issues involved in the domestic use of drones, according to the authors of this report. With your group, discuss whether you believe these issues are serious problems or issues that will be resolved as people grow more familiar and comfortable with drones as a technology.

2. The authors make some specific recommendations to legislators about how the use of drones should be governed. What are the five most important recommendations? Do you agree with all of these recommendations, or do you believe the authors are recommending too much government interference in the development and use of a new technology?

3. With your group, come up with five ways that drones could be used on your college campus. Discuss the pros and cons of using drones in these ways. Present your ideas to the class.

IDEAS FOR
Writing

MyWritingLab

1. The authors of this report argue that drones should not be used in any way that violates the U.S. Constitution. However, there is no way the framers of the U.S. Constitution could have anticipated new technologies like drones. Write a commentary in which you discuss how the U.S. Constitution should be flexible (or not flexible) when it comes to new technologies.

2. This Heritage report is about the use of drones in the United States. However, drones are actively used throughout the world by the United States for surveillance and military purposes. These kinds of activities would, of course, be unconstitutional in the United States. Write a research paper in which you discuss whether you believe the rights afforded by the U.S. Constitution should be extended to people around the world. How does your opinion shape your views on the use of drones outside of the United States?

Serial Murder: A Forensic Psychiatric Perspective

JAMES KNOLL, MD

TV shows and magazine articles about serial killers are common in today's media, but what do we really know about serial murder? To answer that question, forensic psychiatrist James Knoll reports on the available scientific and medical research and reveals what we know and what we need to find out through further research. As you read, pay attention to Knoll's exploration of myths and misconceptions about serial murder.

'You feel the last bit of breath leaving their body. You're looking into their eyes. A person in that situation is God!'

—Ted Bundy

Ressler: "Do you have any idea at all, of what would start bringing this type of fantasy to mind . . .?"

Dahmer: "It all revolved around having complete control. Why or where it came from, I don't know."

—How to Interview a Cannibal
Robert K. Ressler

When law enforcement apprehends a serial murderer, the event is consistently the focus of unswerving media coverage. For local communities, the ordeal can be particularly shocking and upsetting. Residents living in a community that is exposed to serial murder may even experience posttraumatic stress disorder symptoms for varying periods of time (Herkov and Beirnat, 1997).

Over the past three decades, our society has become fascinated by the phenomenon of serial murder as evidenced by the numerous books, movies and television shows on the subject. Yet, despite the high level of interest, there is no current theory that adequately explains the etiology of serial murder (Holmes et al., 2002). This is primarily due to the fact that serial murder is an event with an extremely low base rate and therefore is difficult to study via rigorous scientific methods (Dietz, 1986).

While serial murder is a universally terrifying concept, it is an extraordinarily rare event. In a study of the frequency of serial sexual homicide, McNamara and Morton (2004) found that it accounted for only 0.5% of all homicides over a 10-year period in Virginia. In contrast to the sensationalized perception that serial murder is a growing epidemic, there is no solid evidence that this is the case. An analysis of homicide victims from 1960 to 1998 indicated that the percentages of female homicide victims have actually decreased (Schlesinger, 2001a). Because the victims of serial murderers are overwhelmingly female, these data fail to support the notion that serial murder is increasing in frequency.

Historically, the term serial murder may be relatively new, but its occurrence is not. In the United States alone there have been documented cases as far back as the 1800s. In 16th-century France, it is likely that myths such as "werewolves" were used to explain the deeds of serial murderers that were too horrifying to attribute to human beings (Everitt, 1993). In all likelihood, serial murderers have always been among us.

In 1886, psychiatry professor Richard von [5] Krafft-Ebing wrote the classic *Psychopathia Sexualis,* in which he described the characteristics of individuals who appeared to obtain sexual gratification from acts of sadistic domination. The next major psychiatric contribution to our understanding of serial murderers was in 1970 when forensic psychiatrist Robert Brittain produced detailed descriptions of sadistic murderers he had encountered over his career. Beginning in the early '70s, media coverage of notorious cases such as Ted Bundy and the Hillside Strangler produced a sense of urgency to study and explain the phenomenon.

Thus far, the study of serial murder has been somewhat hampered by lack of a unanimously agreed upon definition. However, most experts agree on the criteria that the offender must have murdered at least two victims in temporally unrelated incidents. This phenomenon usually involves a cooling off or refractory period between killings that varies in duration for each individual offender. To date, our greatest source of knowledge and data on serial murder has come from experts working in the Federal Bureau of Investigation's Behavioral Science Unit, now called the Behavioral Analysis Unit. To emphasize the sexual nature of the crimes, and to distinguish these offenders from others who murder serially for other reasons (e.g., contract killers), Douglas et al. (1997) have used the term sexual homicide. For each individual serial sexual homicide offender, the performance and meaning of the sexual element may vary.

Researchers at the FBI gathered data from detailed interviews of 36 convicted serial murderers and were able to extract and analyze important personality and behavioral characteristics that helped distinguish different types of serial murderers. For ease of communication and conceptualization, the offenders were categorized into either "organized" or "disorganized" types (Table 1). These terms were initially meant to help law enforcement interpret crime scenes and can be understood as generally applicable concepts. They may also have appeal to forensic mental health professionals in that they provide illustrative descriptors of personality and behavior. The term mixed sexual homicide is used to describe the offender whose crime scene reflected aspects of both the organized and disorganized types. Finally, the term sadistic murderer describes the offender who is primarily a sexual sadist and derives the greatest satisfaction from the victim's response to torture.

TABLE 1 Offender Traits

Organized	Disorganized
Good verbal skills, socially adept	Poor verbal and social skills
May live with spouse	Loner or lives with parents
Reasonably intelligent	Low intelligence
Usually employed	Under- or unemployed
Planning of crime	Little to no planning of crime
Ruse or con to gain control of victim	Blitz or surprise attack of victim
Targeted victim	Victim of opportunity
Crime scene: suggests control, order	Crime scene: disarray
Crime scene and death scene not the same	Crime scene and death scene often the same
Movement of body	Body left at death scene
Attempts to conceal evidence	Little to no attempts to conceal evidence

Source: Knoll J (2006)

Meloy (2002) has advanced a similar typology, but with a clinical emphasis. Sexual homicide perpetrators may be described as either "compulsive" or "catathymic." The compulsive perpetrators are similar to the FBI's organized killers. They leave organized crime scenes and can be diagnosed with sexual sadism and antisocial/narcissistic personality disorders. The catathymic perpetrators leave disorganized crime scenes and may be diagnosed with a mood disorder and varying personality traits. While the compulsive type display emotional detachment and autonomic hyporeactivity, the catathymic type are less psychopathic. In contrast, the catathymic type are autonomically hyperreactive and may have histories of abuse. Again, these types were intended to be generalities, and any individual case is likely to fall on a continuum between the two.

Psychiatric Findings

In terms of formal psychiatric diagnoses, most data come from individual case studies and retrospective analyses. When these studies are reviewed, they do suggest a common collection of diagnoses: psychopathy, antisocial personality, sexual sadism and other paraphilias (voyeurism, fetishism and sometimes necrophilia). The sexual sadism seen in serial murderers must be distinguished from sexual sadism between consenting adults that would not be considered criminal. The variant of sexual sadism seen in serial murderers is at the extreme end of the spectrum. Dietz et al. (1990) have provided an analysis of individuals who engaged in torturing victims to the point of death to obtain the "pleasure in complete domination" over them.

Paraphilias, particularly voyeurism and fetishism, have been described in many serial murderers. In fact, over 70% of sexual murderers had these paraphilias in Ressler et al.'s 1988 study. Schlesinger and Revitch (1999) have suggested that some individuals with voyeurism and fetishism may engage in burglaries that actually serve the purpose of gratifying these two paraphilias.

Focusing on the compulsive nature of the offenses, researchers have speculated on the significance of the seemingly obsessive qualities of the serial murderer, particularly the organized type. These individuals demonstrate a tendency toward orderliness, obsessive fantasy and ritualistic behavior (e.g. posing the body, biting, inserting objects and so forth) during their murders that suggest compulsive qualities. Experts believe that these obsessive and compulsive traits, combined with higher than average intelligence, permit organized offenders to improve their predatory skills and ability to avoid apprehension over time.

There is a notable absence of psychosis among serial murderers, and approximately half of perpetrators report substance use prior to their offenses (Ressler et al., 1988). At the present time, there is no conclusive evidence that specific organic factors play a causal role in the creation of a serial murderer. However, studies have found right temporal lobe abnormalities (Hucker et al., 1988) and other neurological abnormalities (Gratzer and Bradford, 1995) in sexual sadists.

Silva and colleagues (2004, 2002) have used neuropsychiatric concepts to approach the study of serial murderers, most notably Jeffrey Dahmer. They describe an association between autism spectrum disorders and a subgroup of serial murders, and propose that Dahmer may have suffered from Asperger's syndrome. Along these lines, it is interesting to note that after exhaustive interviews with Dahmer, legendary FBI profiler Robert Ressler was impressed by the peculiar nature of Dahmer's presentation. In fact, Ressler held the opinion that Dahmer should have been sent to a psychiatric hospital instead of prison (Ressler, 2004a).

One of the most reliable psychological findings in the mental lives of serial murderers is the presence of violent fantasy. Convicted serial murderers have consistently described a high frequency of violent fantasies that are both persistent and arousing (Brittain, 1970; Johnson and Becker, 1997; Warren et al., 1996). Behavioral theorists have speculated that an early developmental pairing of sexual arousal with aggression is responsible for the deviant fantasy life seen in serial murderers.

Developmental Theories

Over the past several decades, there have [15] been a number of different psychosocial theories put forth on the etiology of serial murder. Investigators with significant experience interviewing serial murderers have speculated that the behavior may result from a deadly convergence of: 1) early childhood attachment disruptions; 2) psychopathy; and 3) early traumatogenic abuse (Myers et al., 2005).

However, there is conflicting evidence on the presence of child abuse in the development of serial murderers. When the FBI studied 36 serial murderers, many of them had a history of either abuse or neglect: 43% reported a history of childhood sexual abuse, and 74% reported a history of psychological abuse that typically involved humiliation (Ressler et al., 1988). In contrast, other studies have found that the majority of sexually sadistic murderers had no evidence of childhood abuse (Dietz et al., 1990; Gratzer and Bradford, 1995). One possibility accounting for these differences may be due to heterogeneity in the populations studied.

When sexual murderers with a history of sexual abuse were compared to murderers without such a history, Ressler et al. (2004) found significant differences. Sexual murderers with a history of early sexual abuse were significantly more likely to begin fantasizing about rape earlier, in addition to developing more severe sexual deviancy. In addition to abuse, the family histories of many sexual murderers reveal unstable environments that may predispose them to disordered early life attachments. In one study, 70% of the sexual murderers' families had histories of alcohol abuse, and about 50% had family members with criminal histories (Ressler, 2004b). It is hypothesized that parental neglect from either absence or preoccupation with their own problems might have further exacerbated these men's ability to form healthy attachments.

Animal cruelty appears to be a common finding in the childhood and adolescent developmental stages of many serial murderers. The link between animal cruelty during childhood and subsequent physical violence during adulthood has been demonstrated in a number of studies (Kellert and Felthouse, 1985; Tingle et al., 1986), leading animal cruelty to be added to the DSM III-TR as a symptom under the diagnosis of conduct disorder in 1987. In keeping with the developmental theme of conduct disorder symptoms, researchers have also commented on a possible link between childhood fire setting and adult serial murder (Singer and Hensley, 2004).

Obviously, children who are diagnosed with conduct disorder or engage in animal cruelty do not all go on to become serial murderers. Nevertheless, it is thought that in the cases of those who do, an early "practicing" of violent and/or sadistic behavior on a living creature plays a role in desensitizing the individual to violence against humans. This notion has been termed "the graduation hypothesis" (Wright and Hensley, 2003). Indeed, some individuals progress past mere desensitization and actually derive pleasure and satisfaction from acts of animal cruelty.

Psychodynamically oriented investigators have theorized that a sexually provocative mother may contribute to the formation of a serial murderer (Fox and Levin, 1994; Meloy, 2002). It is important to note that this premise is far from another "blaming of the mother" theory. Rather, investigators point to

documented instances of strikingly inappropriate sexual behavior on the part of the mother that in some cases would easily qualify as sexual abuse. Evaluations of some convicted serial murderers suggest that a displacement of aggression from their mothers onto to their female victims was present during their offenses.

In summarizing both developmental theories and individual case studies of serial murderers, some relatively consistent traits are observed: a strong need for control/domination, an active deviant fantasy life, deviant sexual interests and psychopathic traits. Upon synthesizing these traits into a gestalt, the following picture emerges: an individual who spends excessive time in a reverie of deviant fantasy and has a tendency toward isolation, a need for totally submissive partners and a preference for autoerotic pleasure (Grubin, 1994). As can be imagined, such an individual will have a lack of healthy relationships and subsequently must depend on fantasy for gratification.

At some point, mere fantasy becomes an insufficient source of pleasure for the potential offender. It is theorized that a gradually progressive series of "tryouts" occur where he attempts to turn his fantasies into reality. For example, an offender may begin by simply following a potential victim. This may next progress to voyeurism or breaking into victims' homes as suggested by Schlesinger and Revitch (1999).

During a burglary, the offender may steal fetishistic items for sexual pleasure, such as undergarments. When this fails to provide sufficient satisfaction, the offender may progress to rape and ultimately murder. Such [20] behavior is positively reinforced over time through paired association with masturbation, making the deviant fantasies extremely refractory to extinction (Prentky et al., 1989). Each time the serial murderer takes a victim, there is further stimulation of fantasy and an overall reinforcement of the cycle.

Assessment and Prevention

Forensic assessments of suspected serial murderers are best done by those with experience evaluating psychopathic and serial sexual offenders. Dishonesty and underreporting of deviant fantasies and offenses are commonplace, and a meticulous review of collateral data prior to the evaluation is necessary. Individuals who have already confessed to murders may nevertheless be unwilling to discuss the sexual nature of their offenses for a variety of reasons, the most common being the fact that sex offenders are severely harassed by other inmates in prison.

In an effort to help guide forensic risk assessments, Schlesinger (2001b) has put forth a list of 10 ominous signs (Table 2). The list consists of traits, characteristics and behaviors that were frequently found in the backgrounds of perpetrators of sexual homicides. It is suggested that when these signs are seen in combination, the individual may be predisposed to committing sexual homicides.

Most experts believe that the prognosis for individuals who have committed serial murder is extremely poor (Douglas and Olshaker, 1995; Revitch and Schlesinger, 1989). At the present time, a preventive approach is most widely endorsed. Children and adolescents who demonstrate sexually sadistic fantasies or other ominous signs should be followed closely by mental health professionals who can direct efforts toward extinguishing the reinforcing cycle and conducting periodic risk assessments (Johnson and Becker, 1997).

Conclusions

Regarding the origins of serial murder, Park Dietz, MD (1986), arguably forensic psychiatry's leading expert on the subject, cautioned us:

> The tendency of the press, public and public officials to regard such individuals as mad solely on the basis of their crimes reflects the widespread needs to attribute such behavior to alien forces.

As difficult as it is to fathom, serial murder may "simply be part of the spectrum of human possibility, a brutal dark side of man, not representing demons or disease" (Drukteinis, 1992).

It is important to recognize how limited our present understanding is in terms of the etiology and development of serial murder, so that erroneous conclusions are not drawn. While researchers have identified traits and abnormalities common to serial murderers, there are many who possess these traits and do not go on to become serial murderers. What is it then that leads some to act on their deviant fantasies while others do not? Until future research can help further clarify this question, Dietz suggested that, in his experience, "the leap from fantasy to action has much to do with character and the vicissitudes of life" (Simon, 1996).

TABLE 2 Ominous Signs (When Seen in Combination) Indicate Risk for a Potential Sex Murderer

1. Childhood abuse
2. Inappropriate maternal (sexual) conduct
3. Pathological lying and manipulation
4. Sadistic fantasy with a compulsion to act
5. Animal cruelty, particularly against cats
6. Need to control and dominate others
7. Repetitive firesetting
8. Voyeurism, fetishism, and (sexual) burglary
9. Unprovoked attacks on females, associated with generalized misogynous emotions
10. Evidence of ritualistic (signature) behavior

Source: Schlesinger LB (2001), The potential sex murderer: ominous signs, risk assessment. *Journal of Threat Assessment* 1(1):47-62. Reprinted with permission from The Haworth Press, Inc.

References

Brittain RP (1970), The sadistic murderer. Med Sci Law 10(4):198–207.

Dietz PE (1986), Mass, serial and sensational homicides. Bull NY Acad Med 62(5): 477–491.

Dietz PE, Hazelwood RR, Warren J (1990), The sexually sadistic criminal and his offenses. Bull Am Acad Psychiatry Law 18(2): 163–178.

Douglas JE, Burgess AW, Burgess AG, Ressler R, eds. (1997), Crime Classification Manual: A Standard System for Investigating and Classifying Violent Crimes. San Francisco: Jossey Bass Publishers.

Douglas JE, Olshaker M (1995), Mind Hunter: Inside the FBI's Elite Serial Crime Unit. New York: Scribner.

Drukteinis AM (1992), Serial murder—the heart of darkness. Psychiatr Ann 22(10):532–538.

Everitt D (1993), Human Monsters: An Illustrated Encyclopedia of the World's Most Vicious Murderers. Chicago: Contemporary Books.

Fox JA, Levin J (1994), Overkill: Mass Murder and Serial Killing Exposed. New York: Plenum Press.

Gratzer T, Bradford JM (1995), Offender and offense characteristics of sexual sadists: a comparative study. J Forensic Sci 40(3):450–455.

Grubin D (1994), Sexual sadism. Criminal Behavior and Mental Health 4:3–9 [editorial].

Herkov MJ, Biernat M (1997), Assessment of PTSD symptoms in a community exposed to serial murder. J Clin Psychol 53(8): 809–815.

Holmes ST, Tewksbury R, Holmes RM (2002), Fractured identity syndrome: a new theory of serial murder. In: Current Perspectives on Sex Crimes, Holmes RM, Holmes ST, eds. Thousand Oaks, Calif.: Sage Publications.

Hucker SJ, Langevin R, Wortzman G et al. (1988), Cerebral damage and dysfunction in sexually aggressive men. Annals of Sex Research 1:33–47.

Johnson BR, Becker JV (1997), Natural born killers?: the development of the sexually sadistic serial killer. J Am Acad Psychiatry Law 25(3):335–348.

Kellert SR, Felthouse AR (1985), Childhood cruelty toward animals among criminals and noncriminals. Human Relations 38(12):1113–1129.

McNamara JJ, Morton RJ (2004), Frequency of serial sexual homicide victimization in Virginia for a ten-year period. [Published erratum J Forensic Sci 49(5):1148.] J Forensic Sci 49(3):529–533.

Meloy JR (2002), The nature and dynamics of sexual homicide: an integrative review. Aggression and Violent Behavior 5(1):1–22.

Myers WC, Gooch E, Meloy JR (2005), The role of psychopathy and sexuality in a female serial killer. J Forensic Sci 50(3): 652–657.

Prentky RA, Burgess AW, Rokous F et al. (1989), The presumptive role of fantasy in serial sexual homicide. Am J Psychiatry 146(7):887–891.

Ressler RK (2004a), How to interview a cannibal. In: Profilers: Leading Investigators Take You Inside the Criminal Mind, Campbell JH, DeNevi D, eds. Amherst, N.Y.: Prometheus Books.

Ressler RK (2004b), The men who murdered. In: Profilers: Leading Investigators Take You Inside the Criminal Mind, Campbell JH, DeNevi D, eds. Amherst, N.Y.: Prometheus Books.

Ressler RK, Burgess AW, Douglas JE (1988), Sexual Homicide: Patterns and Motives. Lexington, Mass.: Lexington Books.

Ressler RK, Burgess AW, Hartman CR et al. (2004), Murderers who rape and mutilate. In: Profilers: Leading Investigators Take You Inside the Criminal Mind,

Campbell JH, DeNevi D, eds. Amherst, N.Y.: Prometheus Books.

Revitch E, Schlesinger LB (1989), Sex Murder and Sex Aggression: Phenomenology, Psychopathology, Psychodynamics and Prognosis. Springfield, Ill.: Charles C. Thomas.

Schlesinger LB (2001a), Is serial homicide really increasing? J Am Acad Psychiatry Law 29(3):294–297.

Schlesinger LB (2001b), The potential sex murderer: ominous signs, risk assessment. Journal of Threat Assessment 1(1):47–62.

Schlesinger LB, Revitch E (1999), Sexual burglaries and sexual homicide: clinical, forensic, and investigative considerations. J Am Acad Psychiatry Law 27(2):227–238.

Silva JA, Ferrari MM, Leong GB (2002), The case of Jeffrey Dahmer: sexual serial homicide from a neuropsychiatric developmental perspective. J Forensic Sci 47(6):1347–1359.

Silva JA, Leong GB, Ferrari MM (2004), A neuropsychiatric developmental model of serial homicidal behavior. Behav Sci Law 22(6):787–799.

Simon RI (1996), Bad Men Do What Good Men Dream: A Forensic Psychiatrist Illuminates the Darker Side of Human Behavior. Washington, D.C.: American Psychiatric Press, Inc., p312.

Singer SD, Hensley C (2004), Applying social learning theory to childhood and adolescent firesetting: can it lead to serial murder? Int J Offender Ther Comp Criminol 48(4):461–476.

Tingle D, Barnard GW, Robbins L et al. (1986), Childhood and adolescent characteristics of pedophiles and rapists. Int J Law Psychiatry 9(1):103–116.

Warren JI, Hazelwood RR, Dietz PE (1996), The sexually sadistic serial killer. J Forensic Sci 41(6):970–974.

Wright J, Hensley C (2003), From animal cruelty to serial murder: applying the graduation hypothesis. Int J Offender Ther Comp Criminol 47(1):71–88.

A CLOSER LOOK AT

MyWritingLab

Serial Murder: A Forensic Psychiatric Perspective

1. According to Knoll's findings in the medical research, why do psychiatrists and other forensic experts still know so little about serial murder?

2. This paper was originally published in a magazine, *Psychiatric Times*. With your group, discuss how Knoll adjusts the purpose of this research paper to fit the needs of his readers.

3. Highlight or make a list of the myths and misconceptions about serial murder that Knoll addresses.

4. After reading Knoll's report on the scientific research about serial murder, in what ways have your views on the topic changed?

IDEAS FOR

Writing

MyWritingLab

1. Write a 200-word abstract for this research report. Be sure to explain what topic and question is addressed, the main findings, and implications.

2. Search the Internet for a report or article about serial killers that takes a more "sensational" angle.

Using what you know from Knoll's article, write a rhetorical analysis of that sensational article. How does it seek to excite and shock its readers? Does it succeed in informing them as well as exciting them?

1. Using an Internet search engine, find a research paper written by a college student. With your group, discuss the strengths and weaknesses of this research paper. Determine whether this research paper is an expository research paper or an argumentative one. Can you find a clear purpose statement or thesis? Do you think the writer covered the topic in enough depth, or can you find gaps in his or her research?

2. The research paper is often criticized as a genre that is mostly used in school. With your group, come up with five ways in which a research paper could be used outside of college. What kinds of readers would find a research paper interesting and worth reading?

3. With your group, discuss the student example of a research paper included at the beginning of this chapter. How well does the student follow the research paper genre, as described in this chapter? Where does she deviate from the genre? How is she creative with the content, organization, style, and design of the document?

1. More than likely, your professor has asked you to write a research paper. With your group, read through the assignment sheet carefully. List ten topics that would be appropriate for this assignment. Then, identify a new angle for each of these topics. A good way to find a new angle is to ask, "What is new or has changed recently about this topic?"

2. Find an annotated bibliography on the Internet. What kinds of sources did the author include in the bibliography? Do you find the summaries of the sources helpful, or could the writer have described the sources in more depth? Using your library's Web site, find five additional sources that could have been included in this bibliography.

3. Even a brief search on the Internet will turn up many of those "Buy a Research Paper" Web sites. Looking at these Web sites, write down ten ways that would help you detect whether a research paper was bought or plagiarized. Do these Web sites promise results that they cannot possibly deliver?

Here's your chance to play around with some other microgenres. Choose a microgenre from the list below and find three examples in print or on the Internet. Use these examples to come up with your own guidelines for writing one of these microgenres, which are similar to a research paper.

Brief—answers a simple scientific or historical question with a factual response

Abstract—a one-paragraph summary of a book or article, using the original wording from the source

White Paper—a brief report that explains an important concept or event with factual research

Overview—a concise explanation of an event or phenomenon that gives readers some helpful background on that subject

Q&A—in a question and answer format, addresses potential questions that might be asked by readers or an audience about a specific topic

Write This

1. **Collect sources and create an annotated bibliography.** For a research paper you are writing, collect ten documents from a variety of print and electronic sources. Read these sources and create an annotated bibliography. Each source should be put into MLA or APA bibliographic format. Include a three-sentence or more summary for each entry.

2. **Write a research paper.** Research papers can be written on a variety of topics. More than likely, your professor has asked you to write one for the course you are taking. Working on your own or in a small group, do these activities:

   a. Identify a topic that you would be interested in writing about and come up with a new angle.

   b. In one sentence write down a statement of purpose that describes what you want the research paper to demonstrate or prove.

   c. Write down two possible thesis statements that could be used to guide this research paper. Which one is stronger? Why?

   d. Create an outline of your research paper. Start out with the diagrams shown in the At-A-Glance at the beginning of this chapter. Which of these patterns will be most useful for your project? How can this pattern be modified to fit your topic's needs?

   e. Find at least ten items from print and electronic sources. Create a Works Cited or References list from these sources. Then, use them as support in your research paper.

3. **Invent an electronic research paper.** Research papers have traditionally been handed in on paper. If you were to completely rethink the research paper as an electronic document, what would it look like and how would it work? Write a two-page proposal for a new kind of research paper that is multimedia-based. Your proposal should describe how written text, images, audio, and video could be used make a more dynamic document for the readers.

> Go to **MyWritingLab** to complete this chapter's exercises and test your understanding of its objectives.

15

Inventing Ideas
and Prewriting

In this chapter, you will learn how to—

15.1 use prewriting techniques to get your ideas flowing.

15.2 develop your ideas with heuristics.

15.3 reflect on your ideas with exploratory writing and extend them in new directions.

Coming up with new ideas is often the difficult part about writing. You stare at the page or screen, and it blankly stares back.

Writers use a variety of techniques to help them "invent" their ideas and view their topics from new perspectives. In this chapter, you will learn about three types of invention strategies that you can use to generate new ideas and inquire into your topic:

Prewriting uses visual and verbal strategies to put your ideas on the screen or a piece of paper, so you can think about them and figure out how you want to approach your topic.

Heuristics use time-tested strategies that help you ask good questions about your topic and figure out what kinds of information you will need to support your claims and statements.

Exploratory writing uses reflective strategies to help you better understand how you feel about your topic. It helps you turn those thoughts into sentences, paragraphs, and outlines.

Some of these invention strategies will work better for you than others. So try them all to see which ones allow you to best tap into your creativity.

Prewriting

Prewriting helps you put your ideas on the screen or a piece of paper, though usually not in an organized way. Your goal while prewriting is to figure out what you already know about your topic and to start coming up with new ideas that go beyond your current understanding.

15.1 use prewriting techniques to get your ideas flowing.

Concept Mapping

One of the most common prewriting tools is *concept mapping*. To create a concept map, write your topic in the middle of your screen or a piece of paper (Figure 15.1). Put a circle around it. Then write down as many other ideas as you can about your topic. Circle those ideas and draw lines that connect them with each other.

The magic of concept mapping is that it allows you to start throwing your ideas onto the screen or a blank page without worrying about whether they make sense at the moment. Each new idea in your map will help you come up with other new ideas. Just keep going. Then, when you run out of new ideas, you can work on connecting ideas into larger clusters.

For example, Figure 15.1 shows a concept map about the pitfalls of male fashion on a college campus. A student made this concept map for an argument paper. She started out by writing "Male Fashion Don'ts on Campus" in the middle of a sheet of paper. Then she began jotting down anything that came to mind. Eventually, the whole sheet was filled out. She then linked ideas into larger clusters.

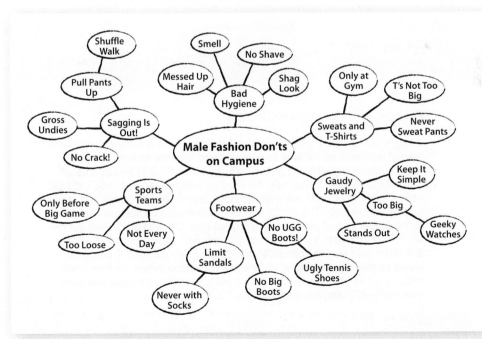

FIGURE 15.1
Using a Concept Map

A concept map will help you get your ideas onto the screen or a piece of paper. Write down your ideas and then draw lines to connect larger clusters of ideas.

With her ideas in front of her, she could then figure out what she wanted to write about. The larger clusters became major topics in her argument (e.g., sweats and T-shirts, jewelry, footwear, hygiene, saggy pants, and sports uniforms). Or she could have picked one of those clusters (e.g., footwear) and structured her entire argument around that narrower topic.

If you like concept mapping, you might try one of the free mapping software packages available online, including *Compendium, Free Mind, Connected Mind, MindMeister,* and *VUE,* among others.

Freewriting

When *freewriting,* all you need to do is open a page on your computer or pull out a piece of notebook paper. Then write as much as you can for five to ten minutes, putting down anything that comes into your mind. Don't worry about making real sentences or paragraphs. If you find yourself running out of words, try finishing phrases like "What I mean is. . . ." or "Here's my point. . . ."

When using a computer, try turning off the monitor or closing your eyes as you freewrite. That way, the words you have already written won't distract you from writing down new ideas. Plus, a dark screen will help you avoid the temptation to go back and fix those typos and garbled sentences.

Figure 15.2 shows an example freewrite. The text has typos and some of the sentences make no sense. That's fine.

When you are finished freewriting, go through your text, highlighting or underlining your best ideas. Some people find it helpful to do a second, follow-up freewrite that focuses just on the best ideas.

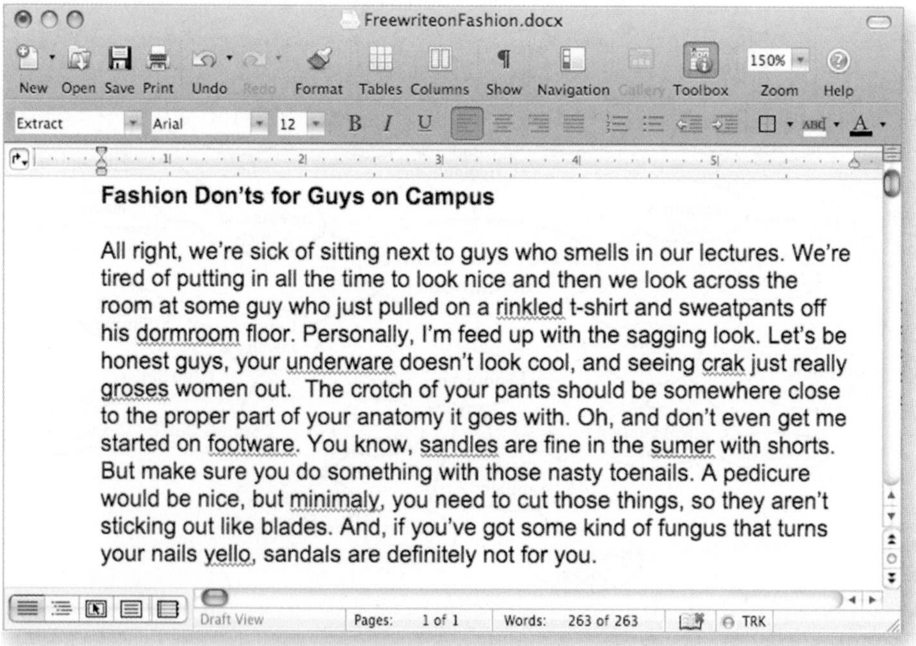

FIGURE 15.2
Freewriting

When you are freewriting, just let the ideas flow and see where they lead you. In this sample, the writer didn't stop to correct typos. She just moved from one topic to the next. The result is a little chaotic, but now she has several new ideas to work with.

Fashion Don'ts for Guys on Campus

All right, we're sick of sitting next to guys who smells in our lectures. We're tired of putting in all the time to look nice and then we look across the room at some guy who just pulled on a rinkled t-shirt and sweatpants off his dormroom floor. Personally, I'm feed up with the sagging look. Let's be honest guys, your underware doesn't look cool, and seeing crak just really groses women out. The crotch of your pants should be somewhere close to the proper part of your anatomy it goes with. Oh, and don't even get me started on footware. You know, sandles are fine in the sumer with shorts. But make sure you do something with those nasty toenails. A pedicure would be nice, but minimaly, you need to cut those things, so they aren't sticking out like blades. And, if you've got some kind of fungus that turns your nails yello, sandals are definitely not for you.

Brainstorming or Listing

To brainstorm about your topic, open a new page on your screen or pull out a piece of paper. Then list everything that comes to mind about your topic. As in freewriting, you should just keep listing ideas for about five to ten minutes without stopping.

Next, pick your best idea and create a second brainstorming list on a separate sheet of paper. Again, list everything that comes to mind about this best idea. Making two lists will help you narrow your topic and deepen your thoughts about it.

Storyboarding

Movie scriptwriters and advertising designers use a technique called *storyboarding* to help them sketch out their ideas. Storyboarding involves drawing a set of pictures that show the progression of your ideas. Storyboards are especially useful when you are working with genres like memoirs, reports, or proposals, because they help you visualize the "story."

The easiest way to storyboard about your topic is to fold a regular piece of paper into four, six, or eight panels (Figure 15.3). Then, in each of the panels, draw a scene or a major idea involving your topic. Stick figures are fine.

Storyboarding is similar to turning your ideas into a comic strip. You add panels to your storyboards and cross them out as your ideas evolve. You can also add dialogue into the scenes and put captions underneath each panel to show what is happening. Storyboarding often works best for people who like to think visually in drawings or pictures rather than in words and sentences.

FIGURE 15.3
A Storyboard That Illustrates the Major Parts of a Text

Some writers find it helpful to draw out their ideas as a storyboard. Each scene in the storyboard becomes a major part of the text.

Using Heuristics

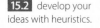 develop your ideas with heuristics.

You already use heuristics, but the term is probably not familiar to you. A *heuristic* is a discovery tool that helps you ask insightful questions or follow a specific pattern of thinking. Writers often memorize the heuristics that they find especially useful. Here, we will review some of the most popular heuristics, but many others are available.

Asking the Journalist's Questions

The most common heuristic is a tool called the *journalist's questions*, or sometimes called the "Five-W and How questions." Writers for newspapers, magazines, and television use these questions to help them sort out the details of a story.

Who was involved?   **When** did it happen?

What happened?   **Why** did it happen?

Where did the event happen?   **How** did it happen?

Write each of these questions separately on your screen or a piece of paper. Then answer each one in as much detail as you can. Make sure your facts are accurate, so you can reconstruct the story from your notes. If you don't know the answer to one of these questions, put down a question mark. A question mark signals a place where you might need to do some more research.

When using the Five-W and How questions, you might also find it helpful to ask, "What has changed recently about my topic?" Paying attention to change will also help you determine your "angle" on the topic (i.e., your unique perspective or view).

Using the Five Senses

Writers also like to use their five senses as a heuristic to explore a topic and invent their ideas. When trying to describe something to your readers, concentrate separately on each of your senses:

Sight What can you see? What does it look like? What colors or shapes do you see?

Hearing What sounds can you hear? What do people or objects sound like?

Smell What can you smell? Does anything have a distinctive scent?

Touch What do things feel like? Are they rough or smooth? Are they cold or hot?

Taste Are there any tastes? If so, are they sweet, salty, sour, delicious?

Using all five senses will help you (and your readers) experience your topic from various standpoints. These sensory descriptions will also give you and your readers a richer understanding of your subject.

Investigating *Logos, Ethos, Pathos*

Aristotle, a philosopher and rhetorician, realized that arguments tend to draw on three kinds of proof: reasoning (*logos*), authority (*ethos*), and emotion (*pathos*). Today, writers still use these Greek terms to remind themselves to gather evidence from all three kinds of proof. This heuristic works especially well for persuasive texts, such as commentaries, argument papers, and proposals.

Logos. *Logos* includes any reasoning and examples that will support your claims. You can use logical statements to prove your points, or you can use real or realistic examples to back up your claims. Here are some basic strategies that you can use to support your ideas with *logos*:

If . . . then: "If you believe X, then you should believe Y also."

Either . . . or: "Either you believe X, or you believe Y."

Cause and effect: "X is the reason Y happens."

Costs and benefits: "The benefits of doing X are worth/not worth the cost of Y."

Better and worse: "X is better/worse than Y because . . . "

Examples: "For example, X and Y demonstrate that Z happens."

Facts and data: "These facts/data support my argument that X is true (or Y is false)."

Anecdotes: "X happened to these people, thus demonstrating Y."

Ethos. *Ethos* involves information that will help you build your authority and reputation with readers. If you are an expert on a particular topic, you can use your own experiences to support your argument. For example, on the topic of clothing, someone majoring in fashion design would have more *ethos* than most others. If you are not an expert on your topic, then you can draw from sources written by experts to add *ethos* to your writing. Here are a few ways to use *ethos* in your writing:

Personal experience: "I have experienced X, so I know it's true and Y is not."

Personal credentials: "I have a degree in Z" or "I am the director of Y." "So I know a lot about the subject of X."

Good moral character: "I have always done the right thing for the right reasons, so you should believe me when I say that X is the best path to follow."

Appeal to experts: "According to Z, who is an expert on this topic, X is true and Y is not true."

Identification with the readers: "You and I come from similar backgrounds and we have similar values; therefore, you would likely agree with me that X is true and Y is not."

Admission of limitations: "I may not know much about Z, but I do know that X is true and Y is not."

Expression of goodwill: "I want what is best for you, so I am recommending X as the best path to follow."

Use of "insider" language: Using jargon or referring to information that only insiders would understand.

Pathos. *Pathos* relates to emotional support for your argument. Think about the aspects of your topic that make people happy, mad, sad, anxious, concerned, surprised, disgusted, joyful, or fearful. You can appeal to these emotions to persuade people to see things your way. Here are some strategies for using emotion:

Promise of gain: "By agreeing with us, you will gain trust, time, money, love, advancement, reputation, comfort, popularity, health, beauty, or convenience."

Promise of enjoyment: "If you do things our way, you will experience joy, anticipation, fun, surprises, enjoyment, pleasure, leisure, or freedom."

Fear of loss: "If you don't do things this way, you risk losing time, money, love, security, freedom, reputation, popularity, health, or beauty."

Fear of pain: "If you don't do things this way, you may feel pain, sadness, grief, frustration, humiliation, embarrassment, loneliness, regret, shame, vulnerability, or worry."

Expressions of anger or disgust: "You should be angry or disgusted because X is unfair to you, me, or others."

Emotion alone usually won't create the strongest arguments. Instead, you should use emotion to support your *logos*-based or *ethos*-based arguments. Emotion will add power and feeling to your argument, while heightening the intensity for your readers. Figure 15.4 shows the introduction to a first draft in which the author uses emotion to support her *logos* and *ethos* arguments.

Cubing

A cube has six sides, and cubing asks you to explore your topic through six "sides" or angles.

1. **Describe it.** What does your topic look like? What are its color and shape? How big or small is it? What is it made of?

2. **Compare it.** What is it like? What is it *not* like? In what ways is it similar to or different from things that are more familiar to your readers?

As a fashion design major (and a woman), let me offer you guys a little helpful advice about attracting women on campus. College women view campus differently than most men. Guys see campus as a place to go to class and study, perhaps throw a frisbee. So, showing up in a faded t-shirt, sweatpants, and flipflops might seem all right. Quite differently, women see campus as a place to socialize and meet friends, in addition to doing class-related stuff. For women, campus is a place to see people and be seen. Consequently, women don't like to be seen with guys who look like they were just shot out of a wrinkle gun. But, if you guys make a few simple wardrobe changes, women are going to notice you.

Ethos

Logos

Pathos

Ethos

Pathos

FIGURE 15.4
A First Draft That Uses *Logos, Pathos,* and *Ethos* for Support

In this first draft of an essay's introduction, the author uses a combination of reasoning, authority, and emotional appeals to persuade her readers.

3. **Associate it.** What does it remind you of? What other topics is it related to that you know something about?

4. **Analyze it.** What patterns run through your topic? What are its hidden questions or meanings? Who created it? What has changed that makes it important?

5. **Apply it.** How could you or someone else use it? Who would use it? What good would it do them? What harm might it do?

6. **Argue for or against it.** What arguments could you or someone else make for or against your topic?

Exploratory Writing

Exploratory writing helps you reflect on your ideas and get your thoughts on paper or screen for further consideration. Essentially, it is "writing about writing" that allows you to examine your writing projects from a little more distance.

15.3 reflect on your ideas with exploratory writing and extend them in new directions.

Journaling, Blogging, or Microblogging

Some writers find it helpful to keep a regular journal or blog to reflect on their experiences and generate new ideas. In these forums, you can write down your opinions and think about your experiences without the pressure of drafting the full argument.

Journaling. This kind of exploratory writing can be done in a notebook or on your computer. The key to successful journaling is to add something new every day. You can talk about the things that happen to you and what is going on in your world.

Blogging. Blogging is very similar to journaling, but blogs are public texts (Figure 15.5). You can sign up for a blog at several blogging Web sites, usually for free. You may not

FIGURE 15.5
A Blog

Journals or blogs can be helpful for coming up with new ideas and reflections. Some blogs have evolved into full websites like this one.

Source: College Fashion, http://www.collegefashion.net

want everyone to read your innermost ideas—but then, of course, you might! Some personal blogs develop their own cult followings. For more on blogging, see Chapter 29, "Writing with Social Networking."

Microblogging. You can use a microblog like *Twitter, Tumblr, Plurk, Qaiku, BrightKite, identi.ca,* and others to describe what is happening to you. Besides keeping your friends informed about where you are and what you are doing, your microblog can track your thoughts and experiences.

Before writing a new entry into your journal or blog, go back and read what you wrote previously. That way, you can build from your previous thoughts or use them as a springboard for coming up with new ideas.

Writing an Exploratory Draft

Sometimes it is helpful to write an "exploratory draft" before you begin trying to write a rough draft. In an exploratory draft, write about how you feel about the topic and what you already know about it. Write down some of the main points you want to make in your paper and what kinds of information or examples you will need to support your points. Your exploratory draft is also a good place to express your concerns about the project and come up with some strategies for handling them.

In this paper, I want to argue that guys should dress nicer on campus. But I don't want to come off as some kind of fashion snob or diva. I also don't want to give the impression that I think everyone has enough money to buy designer clothes. I strongly believe that looking good is not a matter of money or being physically attractive. It's about making good choices and taking a few minutes to think about what looks good to others. I guess my main goal in this paper is to give guys good reasons to dress nicer on campus. Yeah, I'll need to tweak them a little to get their attention. My writing style will probably need to be funny or even teasing. If they get a little angry, maybe they'll think a little more about how they look. It would be nice if I could find some pictures that demonstrate good fashion choices. Nothing GQ. Just normal guys on campus making good choices about clothing. That would help me show my readers what I mean.

The purpose of an exploratory draft is not to write the paper itself but to use writing to help you explore your topic and sort out your ideas.

Exploring with Presentation Software

Presentation software can be a powerful tool for doing exploratory writing about your subject. There are many software packages, such as Microsoft's *PowerPoint*, Apple's *KeyNote*, and free programs like *Prezi, SlideRocket, PowToon,* and OpenOffice's *Impress*. The software can help you create slides, making a bulleted list of your major subjects and key points. Then you can fill out the slides with details, pictures, and graphs. Try this:

1. Create a new page in your favorite presentation software.

2. On the title slide, type a title for your paper that identifies your topic. In the subtitle area, type in your angle on that topic.

3. Think of two to five major topics that will be discussed in your argument. Create a separate slide for each major topic.

4. On the slide for each major topic, list two to five issues that you might need to talk about in your paper.

5. As you fill in each slide, look for opportunities to add visuals, such as photographs, charts, and graphs.

If you don't have information about one of your major topics, just leave that slide blank for now. These gaps in slides signal places where you need to do more exploration or research.

When you are finished filling in the slides as best you can, you might find it helpful to change your screen to Slide Sorter View, so you can see an overview of your whole text (Figure 15.6). The Slide Sorter is usually under the "View" menu of your presentation software. It will allow you to move slides around to figure out the best way to organize your ideas.

FIGURE 15.6
Outlining with Presentation Software

Presentation software can help you make a quick outline of your argument and insert graphics.

When you are finished exploring your topic with the presentation software, you will have a good outline for writing your paper. Plus, you will have collected the photographs, charts, and other visuals you need for designing the document.

Taking Time to Invent and Prewrite

When writing a paper, it is tempting to jump straight to the drafting stage of the writing process. After all, time spent prewriting, using heuristics, and doing exploratory writing might seem like time away from your real task—getting that assignment finished. In reality, though, inventing and prewriting will save you time because you will be more creative and won't find yourself staring at a blank screen.

Above all, think of "invention" as a separate stage in your writing process. Set aside some time to discover and form your ideas before you start trying to draft your paper.

Start developing the content of your document. Here are some techniques for prewriting, using heuristics, and doing some exploratory writing.

DO Some Prewriting to Get the Ideas Flowing

Prewriting uses visual and verbal strategies to help you figure out what you already know about your topic and how you want to approach it. Try making a concept map, freewriting, doing some brainstorming, or making a storyboard on your topic.

USE Heuristics to Draw Out Your Ideas

A heuristic is a discovery tool that helps you ask insightful questions or follow a specific pattern of thinking. Some of the common heuristics are the Five-W and How questions, the five human senses, *logos/ethos/pathos*, and cubing.

REFLECT on Your Topic with Exploratory Writing

Exploratory writing is "writing about writing" that allows you to think about your writing projects from a little more distance. You can do some journaling or blogging. Or you can write an exploratory draft that lets you talk through what you want to write about. Presentation software can be a useful tool for putting your ideas on the screen in an organized way.

GIVE Yourself Time to Invent Your Ideas

It's tempting to jump right to the drafting stage. That deadline is looming. But you will find that you write more efficiently and better if you give yourself time to sort through your ideas first.

1. List three times in your life when you have been especially creative or innovative. Why did you decide to take the more creative path rather than the ordinary path? Tell your group about these creative moments and how they came about.

2. With your group, list five celebrities, artists, or professional athletes whom you think are especially original and innovative. What unique characteristics make each of them creative? Can you find any common characteristics that they all share?

3. What kinds of invention strategies have you learned previously, and what has worked for you in the past? With your group, talk about methods you have used in the past to come up with new ideas for projects.

1. Create a concept map about a topic that interests you. Then, identify the one or two most interesting issues in your concept map. Put one of those issues in the middle of your screen or a piece of paper and create a second concept map on this narrower version of the topic. Ask yourself, "What has changed to make this topic interesting right now?" Doing so will help you find a new angle on your topic.

2. For about five minutes, freewrite about a topic for your next paper in this class. When you are finished, pick your best idea and freewrite for another five minutes. This second freewrite will help you develop a solid understanding of the topic, purpose, and angle for your paper.

3. Check into some of the free blogging services available online. What are some of the pros and cons of each blogging site? If you don't have a blog of your own, what kind of blog might you enjoy keeping?

1. **Invent with presentation software.** For your next project in this class, start out by creating a version of your document with presentation software. Begin with a title slide that includes your title and main point. Then create slides for the major points in your paper. Add a slide for the conclusion. Then go back and fill in the bullet points for each of your major points. Find any graphics you can and add them to the slides. When you have finished creating your "presentation," use the slide sorter feature to move slides around. When you are finished, talk through your presentation with your group.

2. **Start keeping a journal or blog.** For the next two weeks, keep a journal or a blog. Each day, spend a few minutes writing something about the topic of your next paper. Then, as you draft, design, and edit your paper, describe your successes and challenges while developing the document. Hand in your journal or your blog's URL with the final draft of your paper.

> Go to **My WritingLab** to complete this chapter's exercises and test your understanding of its objectives.

16

Organizing and Drafting

In this chapter, you will learn how to—

16.1 sketch out how your paper will be organized.

16.2 draft an introduction that catches your readers' attention.

16.3 support your thesis in the body of your paper.

16.4 develop a conclusion that ends your paper on a strong note.

I n the previous chapter, you learned how to "invent" the content of your paper by using prewriting, heuristics, and exploratory writing to be creative and develop your ideas. In this chapter, you will learn about the second stage in the writing process: how to use genres to organize your ideas and compose a draft with a solid introduction, body, and conclusion.

To begin, think about which genre fits your purpose and how that genre is typically organized. Genres are not formulas to be followed mechanically. However, they do offer useful patterns that will help you arrange your ideas into a structure that is familiar to you and your readers. Keep in mind that genres follow flexible patterns that reflect how people act, react, and interact in the real world. Since no two writing situations are ever exactly the same, you should alter, bend, and stretch the genre to fit your particular needs.

Fortunately, the genres used in college and the workplace have some common organizational features that you can commit to memory right now. Almost all genres, for example, will include an introduction, body, and conclusion. To help you remember this three-part pattern, keep the time-tested speechwriter's pattern in mind: "Tell them what you're going to tell them. Tell them. Then tell them what you told them."

Sketching Out Your Paper's Organization

16.1 sketch out how your paper will be organized.

For larger papers, most writers find it helpful to sketch out a rough outline or diagram to help them sort out their ideas or to get input from others. In the workplace, teams often use a white board or a glass wall to create an outline or draw a diagram. Increasingly, people are also using presentation software, like *PowerPoint*, *Keynote*, or *Prezi* to outline their project as slides (Figure 16.1). The presentation software allows them organize their ideas as bullet points and rearrange the slides as needed.

As shown in Figure 16.1, your outline, diagram, or presentation doesn't need to be formal, unless your professor wants a formal outline. Minimally, it should identify

FIGURE 16.1 Three Ways to Outline a Paper

To sketch out the organization of your paper, you can use a traditional outline, a diagram, or presentation software.

the major parts of your paper and fill in some of the details. Your outline, diagram, or presentation will then serve as map that guides your drafting of the paper.

Using the Genre to Create a Basic Outline

To start, figure out which genre you are using for your paper. Then, turn to that chapter in Part 2 of *Writing Today*. At the beginning of each genre chapter, you will see an "At a Glance" diagram illustrating one or more organizational patterns that the genre tends to follow. These patterns should give you an overall idea about the kinds of sections that could be included in your outline.

Here's an easy way to get your outline started. Type or write "I. Introduction" on your screen or a piece of paper. Then type or write "X. Conclusion" at the bottom. Why? Because you already know your document will need an introduction and a conclusion. For now, use an "X" with the conclusion, because you don't know yet how many sections will be needed for the body of your paper.

If you are using presentation software to outline your project, create an "Introduction" slide and a "Conclusion" slide.

Filling Out Your Outline

Now you're ready to start listing the major sections that will appear in your document. Give each one an uppercase roman numeral (e.g., II, III, IV, V, VI, VII, etc.). The genre you are following should give you a good idea about how many sections you will need (Figure 16.2). *Hint:* If your roman numerals are nearing X (that's ten sections), you probably have too many sections. If that's the case, some of your sections should be combined or removed.

If you are using presentation software, create a separate slide for each section of your paper. Include a title for each slide that describes what that section will be about.

After you have identified the sections, think about each one separately and list the issues that might be discussed. Each section should include about two to five issues for discussion.

In some situations, you may be asked to hand in a more formal outline for your paper, so your professor can look it over before you begin drafting. The "Starter Outline" in Figure 16.2 shows how you can use roman numerals (I, II, III, IV) and uppercase letters (A, B, C, D) to sort out the items you will discuss in your paper.

Drafting Your Introduction: Tell Them What You're Going to Tell Them

You may have been told not to draft the introduction first. Some writers find that advice helpful, and others don't. If you have identified your topic, purpose, and main point, you should be able to draft your introduction as soon as you feel ready.

16.2 draft an introduction that catches your readers' attention.

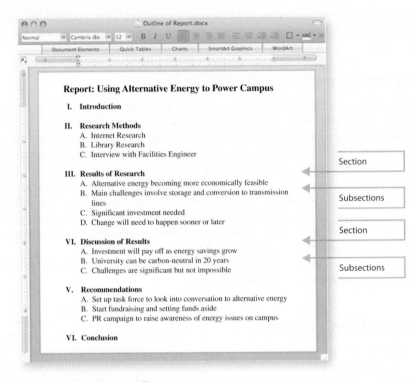

FIGURE 16.2 A Starter Outline

Sometimes professors and supervisors will ask you for a starter outline that describes the major sections and topics you will discuss in your paper.

As you begin drafting the introduction, put yourself in your readers' place. As a reader, you would have some questions you want answered when you start: "What is this?" "Why was this sent to me?" "What is this writer trying to get me to believe or do?" "Is this important?" "Do I care about this?" Try to anticipate who your readers will be and address the questions they will have.

Five Introductory Moves

Your introduction should answer your readers' questions up front by making some or all of the following five introductory moves:

Move 1: Identify your topic.

Move 2: State your purpose.

Move 3: State your main point, thesis statement, or a question you will answer.

Move 4: Offer background information on your topic.

Move 5: Stress the importance of the topic to your readers.

These opening moves can be made in just about any order. The first three are the most important, because they tell readers (a) what you are writing about, (b) why you are writing, and (c) what you want to explain or prove. The other two will help your readers familiarize themselves with your topic. This sample introduction uses all five moves:

Streets of Death: The Perils of Street Racing

That night, Davey Yeoman hadn't planned on almost killing himself. He was out cruising with a couple of friends in his blue turbo-charged Honda Accord. The other guy was in a yellow Pontiac GTO with katana rims. The driver of the GTO asked if Davey wanted to race. He said yeah. So they agreed to meet at 11:00 that night on a two-laner outside town. It was a popular place for street racing.

When the stoplight changed, Davey hit 120 mph almost right away. The GTO was running beside him, a little off his right quarter panel. His Accord was shaking, and its engine was screaming. Suddenly, ahead, Davey saw the headlights of a semitrailer turning into his lane from a side road. The last thing Davey remembered thinking was, "Not me, God, not me." He knew he was dead.

Street racing is a craze that has grown steadily in the last decade. Last year, over two hundred young people were killed in street racing incidents (FARS). Some of the dead and maimed were the drivers or their passengers, and some were people who just got in the way. Street racing has turned some of our roads into deadly places. These street racers need to understand the deadly dangers of turning our roads into racetracks.

> Topic identified.

> Background information.

> Importance of the topic stressed.

> Purpose identified in thesis statement.

> Main point (thesis) stated.

In this introduction, the author *identifies the topic* (street racing) and then offers some *background information.* Then he *stresses the importance of the topic* with some data. Then he finishes by stating his *purpose* and *main point.*

Generally, your paper's main point, or thesis statement, should arrive near the end of the introduction, but you don't need to put it there. In the sample introduction above, for example, the writer could move the sentences and paragraphs around to put the main point earlier if that seemed to work better.

Using a Grabber to Start Your Introduction

To catch readers' attention, some writers use a *grabber* or *hook* at the introduction's beginning. A grabber can gently spark your readers' curiosity. Or, your grabber can shout, "Listen to me!" Here are some good grabbers you can use:

Ask an Interesting Question. A question draws readers into the text by prompting them for an answer.

Have you ever thought about becoming a professional chef? The training is rigorous and the work can be difficult, but the rewards are worth it.

State a Startling Statistic. An interesting statistic can immediately highlight the importance of the topic.

> A shocking survey recently showed that 73 percent of teens in Bloomington have smoked marijuana, and 23 percent report using it at least once a week ("Weed" A3).

Make a Compelling Statement. Make a statement that challenges readers at the beginning of the text.

> Unless we take action now on climate change, we are likely to see massive storms and rising ocean levels that will drown coastal cities.

Begin with a Quotation. A quote is a good way to pique your readers' curiosity.

> That great American Ben Franklin once said, "They who would give up an essential liberty for temporary security deserve neither liberty nor security." Today, it seems like our fellow citizens are more willing than ever to make this trade.

Use Dialogue. Dialogue can quickly bring readers into the story you are telling.

> One morning at breakfast, I heard a couple of other students from my dorm talking about the terrorist attacks on September 11th. One of them said, "September 11th was just like when the Germans bombed Pearl Harbor." The other gave a confused look and asked, "You mean the Chinese, right? They're the ones who bombed Pearl Harbor." That's when I came to the troubling conclusion that many people my age have a dangerously flawed understanding of American history.

Address Readers as "You." Addressing the readers directly with "you" is a good way to get their attention.

> Has this ever happened to you? You finally have a chance to take your significant other out for a night out on the town. You're dressed up, and you're dining at one of the finest restaurants in the city. But then, the maître d' escorts you to the worst table in the place, right next to the swinging doors to the kitchen or the station where they fill the water glasses. Right away, you realize that you're being discriminated against because you're young.

The best grabber is one that (1) identifies your topic, (2) says something that intrigues your readers, and (3) makes the point of your paper in a concise way.

Using a Lead to Draw in the Readers

You can also use a lead (sometimes spelled "lede") to introduce your text. The lead is the first one or two paragraphs of a news story in a magazine, newspaper, or Web site. Like a grabber, the aim of a lead is to capture the readers' attention while giving them good reasons to continue reading. Here are some commonly used types of leads:

Scene Setter. A scene setter describes the place in which something important or interesting happened.

> The young men wade through thigh-high grass beneath the firs and ponderosa pines, calmly setting the forest on fire. With flicks of the wrist, they paint the landscape in flame. The newborn fires slither through the grass and chew into the sagging branches. Every few minutes a fire ignites, flames devouring it in a rush of light, the roar of rockets. It is over in seconds. Only a smoking skeleton remains. (Neil Shea, "Under Fire")

Anecdote. An anecdote starts out the introduction with an interesting true story that happened to the author or someone else.

> My parents didn't know, once again, that I was wide awake at 4:00 in the morning on a school night, inside an enormous and beautiful world, chatting and playing with twenty of my closest friends. Sometimes, I'd stay there for two or three days without a break. Yes, *World of Warcraft* is addictive, and you could say I was one of its countless victims.

Case Histories. A case history tells two to three very short true stories about different people who have had similar problems or experiences.

> Fred Jenkins never thought he was the kind of person to declare bankruptcy. He was a successful businessman with money in the bank. When his wife discovered she had ovarian cancer, though, his bank accounts were soon emptied by the costs of treatment. Mira Johanson took a different path to bankruptcy. She racked up $24,000 in credit card debt, because she bought a house she couldn't afford. When she was laid off at Gerson Financial, she could no longer make the minimum payments on her credit cards. Then, with her credit in ruins, she could not refinance her mortgage. Her personal finances collapsed, causing her to lose everything.

Personal Sketch. Articles that are about a person often begin with a description of the person and a small biography.

> In mid-January 1959, Fidel Castro and his comrades in revolution had been in power less than a month. Criticized in the international press for threatening summary justices and execution for many members of the government of ousted dictator Fulgencio Batista, Castro called on the Cuban people to show their support at a rally in front of Havana's presidential palace.

Castro, 32, wore a starched fatigue cap as he faced the crowd. With him were two of his most trusted lieutenants, Camilo Cienfuegos, unmistakable in a cowboy hat, and Ernesto (Che) Guevara in his trademark black beret. (Guy Gugliotta, "Comrades in Arms")

The lead comes before your main point (i.e., your thesis) in the introduction. Its job is to draw your readers into your paper and encourage them to keep reading.

Drafting the Body of Your Paper: Tell Them

16.3 support your thesis in the body of your paper.

The body of your paper will likely include between two to five paragraphs (shorter paper) or two to five sections (longer paper). Chapter 20, "Developing Paragraphs and Sections," shows you how to write paragraphs and sections.

Your challenge at this point is getting your ideas onto the screen or paper. As you start drafting each paragraph, ask yourself, "In this paragraph, what statement do I want to support, or what claim do I want to prove?" Write that sentence down. Then, begin writing down everything you can think of that supports that statement or claim.

Sometimes it helps to think of each paragraph as a container that you are filling up with examples, details, reasoning, facts, data, quotations, anecdotes, definitions, descriptions, and anything else you need to support that statement or claim. When you run out of things to say, start a new paragraph.

Freewriting is often a good way to get the words flowing. Just write down everything that comes to mind without stopping. You can revise the sentences and move them around after you have them on the screen or page.

Overcoming Writer's Block

The body is usually the place where you will experience some difficulty putting words and sentences on the screen or paper. Writer's block happens to everyone, including the most experienced writers. Here are some strategies for keeping the words flowing, and for working through those moments of writer's block.

Drafting (Almost) Every Day. The worst thing you can do is start drafting the night before your paper is due. You will often hear people say things like, "I write best under pressure" or "I need to figure out what I'm going to say before I start writing." They're fooling themselves. These kinds of statements are warning signals that the writer is procrastinating. People don't really write well under pressure, and the best way to figure out what you have to say is to *get started and write something down*.

The best strategy is to draft for a half hour every day. Each day, set aside a regular time in the morning or evening to work on your writing assignments. Writing is like exercising at the gym. If you exercise for a half hour every day, you will improve steadily—much more than exercising four hours only one day once a week. In the same way, if you say, "I'm setting aside Sunday afternoon to write that paper," you are not going to do your best work. But if you write for a half hour every day, you will write better and faster. Try it, and you'll see that it makes a big difference.

Getting Past Writer's Block. Almost all writers find themselves blocked at some point. Here are some techniques for overcoming writer's block:

"What I really mean is. . . ."   Whenever you are blocked, finish the sentence "What I really mean is. . . ." You will discover that simply finishing this sentence will help you get past the temporary block.

Lower your standards while drafting.   Stop trying to get it right on the first try. Instead, put your ideas on the screen or paper without worrying about whether they are intelligent or grammatically correct. Then spend extra time during the revision phase turning those ideas into a document that has the high quality you expect.

Talk it out.   Professional writers can often be found talking to friends about their work or even talking to themselves. Sometimes it helps to just say out loud what you want to write—to yourself or someone else who is willing to listen. Then, after you have rehearsed the text a few times, you should find it easier to write your ideas down.

Change how and where you write.   If you normally draft on a computer, try switching over to pen and paper for a little while. If you normally write in your dorm room, try a change of scenery by going over to the library or out on central campus. Sometimes the change in medium or location will help you loosen up.

Use both sides of your brain.   The right side of your brain is more visual than the left. So, use invention techniques like concept mapping, freewriting, and cubing to tap into that visual creativity. These techniques will help you put your ideas on the screen or paper. Then, the left side of your brain can organize them into sentences and paragraphs.

Write an e-mail.   Start writing your document as an e-mail to a friend. E-mail is often a more familiar writing environment, allowing you to relax as you write.

Talk to your professors.   Your professors probably have some helpful ideas about how to draft your papers. Visit your professors during office hours. They are there to help you.

Go to the writing center.   If your campus has a writing center, you should drop by for some help. You can talk your ideas over with an experienced writer who can offer you some advice and strategies.

Stop procrastinating. Procrastination is the usual culprit behind writer's block. The pressure of a deadline can cause your brain to freeze. So, start each project early, and write a little every day. Your writer's block will evaporate.

Your first year of college is the best time to develop good writing habits. Don't wait until your advanced courses or your first job to form these habits, because it will be too late.

Drafting Your Conclusion: Tell Them What You Told Them

16.4 develop a conclusion that ends your paper on a strong note.

What happens when one of your professors says, "In conclusion . . . ," or "Finally," or "Here is what I really want you to take away from today's lecture"? Everyone in the class wakes up and starts paying close attention. Why? Because everyone knows the professor is going to state his or her main points.

The same is true of the conclusion at the end of your document. When your readers realize they have arrived at the conclusion, they will start paying closer attention because they know you are going to state your main points.

Here are five moves that you could make in your conclusion:

Move 1: Signal clearly that you are concluding.

Move 2: Restate your main point or thesis statement with added emphasis.

Move 3: Stress the importance of your topic again.

Move 4: Call your readers to action (if needed).

Move 5: Look to the future.

Your conclusion should be as short as possible, and it should be similar to your introduction in content and tone. In your conclusion, you need to bring readers back around to the beginning of your argument, showing them that you have achieved your purpose. For example, consider the following conclusion:

Street Racing Must Stop

> Signal conclusion.

> Importance of topic.

In the end, street racing just isn't worth it. A few seconds of thrill can cause a lifetime of suffering or even get someone killed—maybe you. Davey Yeoman found that out the hard way, and he wants his wrecked life to be an example to others. He's paralyzed and eats through a straw. The Accord he once loved is a mangled heap that is towed around to local high schools as a warning to others. Davey hopes he can use his destroyed life to save the lives of others.

> Call to action.

> Look to the future.

> Main point.

The laws against street racing are already on the books. We don't need more laws. What we need is more education and tougher enforcement to stop street racing. Only then will we be able to end this dangerous craze that leaves so many lives destroyed. Only then will our streets be safe again.

This conclusion makes all five concluding moves in two brief paragraphs. First, the author *signals that he is concluding* in the first sentence with the phrase "In the end."

Phrases that signal a conclusion include the following:

In conclusion,	Put briefly,	Ultimately,
To sum up,	In brief,	Overall,
In summary,	Finally,	As a whole,
In closing,	To finish up,	On the whole,

Then the author stresses the *importance of the topic* by returning to the story of Davey Yeoman, which started the introduction. By returning to this story, the author also brings the reader around to the beginning of the argument, making it feel whole.

A *call to action* and the *main point* appear in the final paragraph. Pairing the main point (thesis statement) with a call to action gives it more power because the author is stating it directly and telling readers what should be done.

Finally, the conclusion ends with a *look to the future* in which the author looks beyond the boundaries of the argument to talk about what should happen or will happen in the future.

You don't need to include all five moves in your conclusion, and they don't need to appear in any specific order. However, if you find yourself writing a conclusion longer than one or two paragraphs, you should consider moving some of the information into the body of the paper.

Knowing the appropriate genre for your paper is a good way to organize and draft it. Here is what you need to know.

USE Genres to Organize Your Ideas

Genres are not formulas, but they do offer helpful patterns for organizing the content of your document. Chapters 5–14 show how various genres are organized.

DIVIDE Your Document into an Introduction, Body, and Conclusion

Almost all nonfiction genres include an introduction, body, and conclusion. The introduction "tells them what you're going to tell them." The body "tells them." And the conclusion "tells them what you told them."

SKETCH an Outline

Outlines may seem a bit old-fashioned, but an informal outline is often a good way to sort your ideas into sections of a document.

DRAFT Your Introduction

A typical introduction includes up to five moves: (1) identify your topic, (2) state your purpose, (3) state your main point or thesis, (4) stress the importance of the topic, and (5) provide background information on the topic.

DEVELOP a Good Grabber or Lead for Your Introduction

Your introduction needs to capture the readers' interest right away. So use a question, intriguing statistic, compelling statement, interesting story, or quotation to hook them.

OVERCOME Writer's Block

It happens to everyone. The techniques discussed in this chapter should help you get through those moments.

DRAFT Your Conclusion

A conclusion should make up to five moves: (1) signal that you are concluding, (2) restate the main point or thesis with more emphasis, (3) reemphasize the importance of the topic, (4) call for action, and (5) look to the future.

VERIFY That Your Introduction and Conclusion Work Together

The introduction and conclusion should work together, containing similar information, restating your main point, and using a similar tone.

1. With a group, discuss how you were taught to outline papers in high school. Do you think outlining works well for you? In which situations do outlines seem to work best?

2. Find a document on the Internet and identify its introduction and conclusion. With a group of people in your class, talk about whether you think the introduction and conclusion are effective and how they could be improved.

3. When does writer's block happen most frequently to you? Can you think of ways to avoid writer's block in the first place? When writer's block happens, which strategies have you used to get writing again?

1. As you draft your next paper, keep a log of how much time you spend drafting. When you hand your paper in, look at your log. Where have you devoted more or less time to the project? How can you spread your time out better on the next project to strengthen your writing?

2. Find a text that you think has a weak introduction and/or conclusion. Write a one-page rhetorical analysis in which you diagnose the structural problems with the text's introduction and conclusion. What could the author have done better to build a stronger introduction and/or conclusion?

1. **Analyze your writing process.** In a brief report, describe how you currently draft your documents. How much time do you usually devote to drafting? Which strategies or routines help you draft a paper? Next, offer some ideas for improving how you draft documents. Which techniques for overcoming writer's block in this chapter would be most helpful for you?

2. **Interview a professional via e-mail.** Set up an e-mail interview with a professional in your desired career or a professor in your major. Ask that person about his or her writing process and pay special attention to what he or she says about organizing ideas and drafting documents. Ask how documents are organized in his or her field. Ask how he or she learned how to write those kinds of documents. In a brief profile, describe how your subject uses writing in his or her personal life.

> Go to **My Writing Lab** to complete this chapter's exercises and test your understanding of its objectives.

17

Choosing a Style

In this chapter, you will learn how to—

17.1 use plain style to write clearly and confidently.

17.2 establish a voice or tone in your papers.

17.2 use persuasive style to add energy and impact to your writing.

Style is the way you express yourself or your distinctive way of doing something. In writing, style is a way of revealing your attitude and feelings about your topic. It is a way of establishing your character and a sense of authority with your readers. In a word, style is about the quality of your writing.

Style is *not* flowery language or fancy words. It's *not* about sprinkling in a few adjectives to make dull sentences more interesting or colorful. Style is also not something you either have or you don't. Just as anyone can be stylish with their clothing or manner, anyone can write with good style—with a little thought and practice.

Sometimes inexperienced writers will talk about "my style," as though each writer possesses one unique voice or way of writing. In reality, the best style for your document depends on your topic, the rhetorical situation, and the genre that you are using.

There is no correct style for a particular genre; however, some genres are associated with specific styles. Scientific reports, for example, tend to be written in a plain, objective style. Movie reviews are often colorful and upbeat. In some circumstances, though, a scientific report could use an upbeat style, and a movie review could be serious. Ultimately, the style you choose depends on what you are trying to achieve with your writing.

Writing in Plain Style

17.1 use plain style to write clearly and confidently.

Plain style is the foundation for all other writing styles. The usual advice given is to "write clearly" or "write in concrete language," as though making up your mind to do so is all it takes. Actually, using plain style is a skill that requires some practice. Once you learn a few basic guidelines, writing plainly will become a natural strength.

Guideline 1: Clarify Who or What the Sentence Is About

Often, difficult sentences simply lack a clear subject. For example, consider the following sentence, which is difficult to understand:

Original:

Seven months after our Spring Break trip to Vail in which a bunch of us travelled around the front range of the Rockies, my roommates' fond memories of the trip were enough to ignore the nagging reality that the trip itself had yet to be fully paid for.

Who or what is this sentence about? The word "memories" is currently in the subject position, but the sentence might also be about "months," "vacation," "bunch of us," "my roommates," or "trip." A sentence like this one is difficult to understand because readers cannot easily locate the subject.

You first need to decide what the sentence is about. Then you can move that topic into the subject position of the sentence. For example, when this sentence is reconstructed around a clear subject, "my roommates and I," it is much easier to understand.

Revised:

Seven months after our Spring Break trip to Vail, my roommates and I still have fond memories of travelling around the front range of the Rockies, which helps us ignore the nagging reality that we haven't paid for the trip yet.

This revised sentence is still difficult to read, but it is clearer because the noun is in the subject position ("my roommates and I" is what the sentence is about).

Guideline 2: Make the "Doer" the Subject of the Sentence

Readers tend to focus on who or what is doing something in a sentence, so whenever possible, try to move the "doer" into the subject position. For example, which of the following sentences is clearer?

On Monday morning, the semester project was completed just in time by Sarah.

On Monday morning, Sarah completed her semester project just in time.

Most readers would say the second sentence is clearer, because Sarah, who is the subject of this sentence, is doing something. Meanwhile, the subject of the first sentence, the report, is just sitting still, not doing anything.

Guideline 3: Put the Subject Early in the Sentence

Subconsciously, your readers start every sentence looking for the subject. The subject is the anchor of the sentence, so the longer you make them wait for it, the harder the sentence will be to read.

Original:

If the Sandia Mountains ecosystem experiences another drought like the one observed from 2000–2009, black bears will suffer severely from a lack of available food and water.

Revised:

Black bears will suffer severely from lack of available food and water if the Sandia Mountains ecosystem experiences another drought like the one from 2000–2009.

The second sentence is easier to read, because the subject appears early in the sentence. When readers find that anchor, they know how to read the sentence.

Guideline 4: State the Action in the Verb

In each sentence, ask yourself what the doer is doing. Then move that action into the verb position and put the verb as close to the subject as possible.

Original:

The detective is the person who conducted an investigation into the homicide that happened last night on 4th Avenue.

Revised:

The detective investigated last night's homicide on 4th Avenue.

The original sentence is harder to understand because the action (investigation) is not a verb, and it's buried later in the sentence. The revised sentence is easier to understand because the action (investigate) is a verb, and it's close to the subject.

Guideline 5: Eliminate Nominalizations

Nominalizations are perfectly good verbs and adjectives that have been turned into awkward nouns.

Original:

Students have an expectation that all professors will be rigorous and fair in the assignment of grades.

Revised:

Students expect all professors to be rigorous and fair when assigning grades.

Original:

Our discussion about the matter allowed us to make a decision to go to Florida for spring break this year.

Revised:

We discussed our spring break options and decided to go to Florida this year.

With the nominalizations ("expectation," "discussion") turned into verbs ("expect," "discuss"), the revised sentences are shorter, simpler, and active.

Guideline 6: Boil Down the Prepositional Phrases

Prepositional phrases follow prepositions, such as *in, of, by, about, over,* and *under.* These phrases are necessary in writing, but they can be overused.

Original:

This year's increase *in* the success *of* the basketball team called the Hokies *of* Virginia Tech offered a demonstration *of* the importance *of* a coach *with* a national reputation *for* the purposes *of* recruiting.

Revised:

This year's successful Virginia Tech Hokies basketball team demonstrated the importance *of* a nationally known coach *for* recruiting.

In the examples above, the prepositions have been italicized and the prepositional phrases are highlighted in green. Notice how the prepositional phrases can create "chains" of phrases that make these sentences harder to read.

Try turning some of them into adjectives. For example, "in the success of the basketball team called the Hokies of Virginia Tech" was boiled down to "successful Virginia Tech Hokies basketball team." You don't need to eliminate all prepositional phrases, but you can simplify a sentence by eliminating some of them.

Guideline 7: Eliminate Redundancies

To stress an important idea, some writers mistakenly use redundant phrasing. For example, they might say "unruly mob" as though some mobs are controlled and orderly. Or, they might talk about "active participants" as though people can participate without doing anything.

Original:

We are demanding important, significant changes to university policies.

Revised:

We are demanding significant changes to university policies.

Original:

The London plague of 1665 was especially deadly and lethal for the poor, who could not escape to the countryside.

Revised:

The London plague of 1665 was especially deadly for the poor, who could not escape to the countryside.

Redundancies should be eliminated because they use two or more words to do the work that can be done with just one word.

Guideline 8: Use Sentences That Are Breathing Length

You should be able to read a sentence out loud in one comfortable breath. If one of your sentences runs on and on—even if it is grammatically correct—your readers will feel like they are mentally holding their breath. They will be more concerned about when the sentence will end than what it means.

On the other hand, if you use only short sentences, your readers will feel like they are breathing too quickly. Each period signals, "Take a breath." Many short sentences together will make readers feel like they are hurrying.

Here are two ways to make your sentences breathing length:

- Sentences that cannot be said out loud comfortably in one breath should be shortened or cut into two sentences. (Don't asphyxiate your readers with overly long sentences!)

- Sentences that are too short should be combined with other short sentences around them. (Don't hyperventilate your readers, either!)

Plain style takes some practice, but writing clearly is not that hard to master. These eight guidelines will help you transform your writing into something that is easy to read. This is the essence of plain style.

Establishing Your Voice

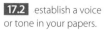 **17.2** establish a voice or tone in your papers.

When reading to ourselves, all of us, including your readers, hear a voice that sounds out the words. The best way to create a specific voice in a text is first to decide what *tone* you want your readers to hear as they read your writing.

In other words, think about how you want your voice to sound. Do you want to sound excited, angry, joyful, sad, professional, disgusted, objective, happy, compassionate, surprised, optimistic, aggressive, regretful, anxious, tense, affectionate, or sympathetic?

After you choose a specific tone, you can create your voice by creating a tone, getting into character, or imitating other writers.

Set a Specific Tone

One of the easiest ways to establish your voice is to come up with a list of words associated with the tone you want. What is the one word that best describes how you feel about your topic? Are you excited? Are you disgusted? Are you angry? Are you delighted?

Write or type that one word at the top of a blank sheet of paper, and brainstorm a list of twenty other words or phrases that are usually associated with that word (Figure 17.1). *Hint:* As shown in Figure 17.1, the thesaurus feature of your word processor can be especially helpful for coming up with these words or phrases.

Then, while you are drafting or revising your work, look for opportunities to use these words in your text. If you selectively weave them into sentences throughout your paper, your readers will subconsciously sense the tone you are trying to create in your writing. For instance, if you want your argument to sound "optimistic," keep using words and phrases associated with optimism and confidence. When people read your writing, they will hear that optimistic tone.

Don't overdo it, though. If you use these words too often, the tone will become too obvious and even tedious to the readers. Remember that some seasoning makes food taste better, but too much seasoning is overwhelming.

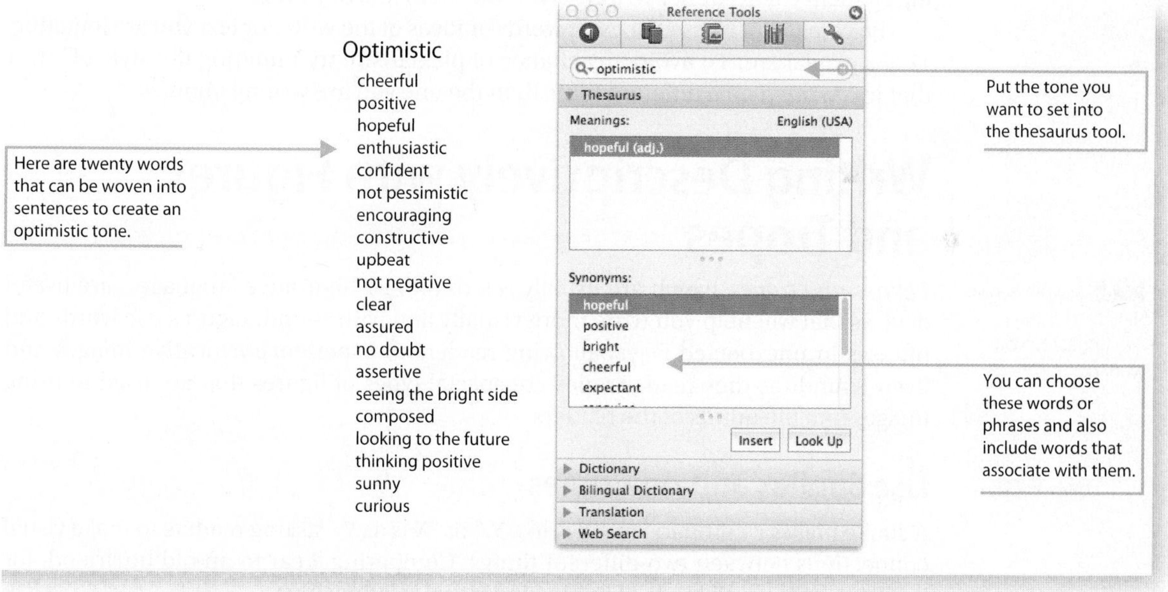
Here are twenty words that can be woven into sentences to create an optimistic tone.
Optimistic
cheerful
positive
hopeful
enthusiastic
confident
not pessimistic
encouraging
constructive
upbeat
not negative
clear
assured
no doubt
assertive
seeing the bright side
composed
looking to the future
thinking positive
sunny
curious
Reference Tools
optimistic
Thesaurus
Meanings:
English (USA)
hopeful (adj.)
Synonyms:
hopeful
positive
bright
cheerful
expectant
Insert
Look Up
Dictionary
Bilingual Dictionary
Translation
Web Search
Put the tone you want to set into the thesaurus tool.
You can choose these words or phrases and also include words that associate with them.

FIGURE 17.1 Using Brainstorming to Create a Tone

You can set a specific tone in your writing by using brainstorming to create a list of words that are associated with the tone you want to establish.

Get into Character

While drafting, one easy way to establish your voice is to imagine yourself playing a role, as in a movie or a play. You need to get into character before you start drafting.

For instance, you might need to write about a topic that is serious or tragic, but you happen to be in a good mood that day. Or perhaps you are writing about something that should be exciting, but you just aren't feeling thrilled.

The best way to handle these situations is to pretend that you are feeling "serious" or "excited" while you are working on the first draft of your document. You might even imagine that you are someone else who is serious or excited about your topic. Get into character, and then let that character compose from his or her point of view.

Imitate Other Writers

Imitation was once a common way for people to learn how to improve their voice and tone. Teachers of speech and writing would regularly ask their students to imitate the style of well-known speakers and writers to practice new stylistic techniques.

Imitation is not widely used to teach writing today, but it's still a useful way for improving your own style. Choose an author whose work you enjoy. Pay close attention to his or her style. How does the choice of words shape what the writer says? How do the writer's sentences convey his or her meaning? As you are drafting or revising your next paper, use some of those word choices and sentence strategies to convey your own ideas. When imitating someone else, you will usually end up blending elements of his or her writing style with elements of yours.

Be careful not to use the exact words or ideas of the writer or text you are imitating. That's plagiarism. To avoid any chance of plagiarism, try imitating the style of a text that was written on a different topic than the one you are writing about.

Writing Descriptively with Figures and Tropes

17.3 use persuasive style to add energy and impact to your writing.

Figures and tropes, which are usually referred to as "figurative language," are useful devices that will help you write more visually and with sound. Figures use words and phrases in unexpected ways, allowing readers to experience evocative images and lively sounds as they read. Tropes are special types of figures that are used to bring images into the minds of the readers.

Use Similes and Analogies

A simile makes a comparison, "X is like Y," or "X is as Y," asking readers to make visual connections between two different things. Comparing a car to an old boyfriend, for instance, calls up all kinds of interesting visual relationships.

> My car is like an old boyfriend. I still love it and we've had some great times together, but it's becoming unreliable and a little clunky. For now, I'm hanging on to it until something sleeker and sportier comes along.

Up ahead, two dozen white pelicans were creating a spiral staircase as they flew. It looked like a feathered DNA molecule. Their wings reflected the sun. The light shifted, and they disappeared. (Terry Tempest Williams, *Refuge*)

Analogies are similes that work at two levels. When using an analogy, you are saying, "X is like Y, as A is like B."

Like police keeping order in a city, white blood cells patrol your body's bloodstream, controlling viruses and bacteria that want to do you harm.

In the 17th century, England's reliance on imported salt was similar to the United States' dependence on foreign oil today. England's Queen Elizabeth I was especially anxious about her nation's reliance on salt from France, her nation's old enemy (Kurlansky, *Salt*, 195). So, she pushed hard for increased domestic production and sought to open other, more dependable sources of salt. England's navy was built in part to protect its salt supply, much as the United States' navy is responsible for ensuring the flow of oil.

Analogies are used to highlight and explain complex relationships. A good analogy allows readers to visualize similar features between two things.

Use Metaphors

Metaphors, which are also tropes, are much more powerful than similes and analogies because they tend to work at a deeper level. There are two types of metaphors that you can use to add power and depth to your writing: simple metaphors and cultural metaphors.

A *simple metaphor* states that one thing is something else, "X is Y."

Mr. Lewis's face is an aged parchment, creased and wrinkled from his years of sailing.

Vince, our boss, threw one grenade after another in our meeting.

This year, my bike is my car—because I can't afford gas anymore!

On the surface, these metaphors say something obviously false (i.e., a face is a parchment, the boss threw grenades in the meeting, a bike is a car). Their falseness on the surface urges readers to figure out an alternative meaning.

A simple metaphor can be extended:

Mr. Lewis's face is an aged parchment, creased and wrinkled from his years of sailing. In his bronze skin, you can see months spent sailing in the Caribbean. The wrinkles around his eyes reveal many years of squinting into the wind. His bent nose and a scar on his chin bear witness to the storms that have thrown him to the deck. His bright eyes peer out from beneath his white brow, hinting at memories that nonsailors like me will never have.

In this example, you can see the power of a fertile metaphor. A good metaphor can be used to create a perspective or a unique way of "seeing" something.

There are also larger *cultural* metaphors that shape the way people think about issues. For example, here are some common cultural metaphors that we almost take for granted:

> Time is money (e.g., spend time, waste time, saved time, lost time).
>
> Thought is light (e.g., he is bright, she was in the dark, they enlightened me).
>
> Argument is war (e.g., she defended her argument, she attacked my claims).

Cultural metaphors like the "war on cancer" or the "war on drugs" have become so ingrained that we rarely challenge them. And yet, the "war on X" metaphor urges us to think of a subject in a certain way that may not be beneficial. It suggests, for example, that we need to respond to illegal drug use or cancer with weapons and surveillance rather than managing them as diseases.

Use Personification

Personification is a trope that uses human qualities to describe something that is not human. It uses human characteristics to make something appear to be more familiar, personal, friendly, or threatening.

> The building scowled at me, daring me to enter.
>
> Finally, winter released us from its icy grasp, and spring called us out to dance.
>
> The wolf stared at us, irritated that we were interrupting her hunt but also knowing we would be gone soon.
>
> The tree groaned in agony as the storm heaved it back and forth.

Use Onomatopoeia

Onomatopoeia uses words that sound like the things being described.

> The fire *crackled* in the fireplace.   She *hissed*, "I hate this class!"
>
> He *shuffled* down the hallway.   The leaves *fluttered* in the wind.

Using onomatopoeia isn't difficult. Think about the sounds that are associated with your subject. Then look for words that capture those sounds.

Use Alliteration and Assonance

Alliteration is a figure that uses repeated consonant sounds, such as *s, c, t, d, g,* usually within neighboring words. Assonance is the repeated use of the same vowel sounds, such as *a, o, oo, i.* When used correctly, alliteration and assonance will make your writing sound more intense. Here is an example of alliteration from author Annie Dillard:

> It is possible, in deep space, to sail on solar wind. Light, be it particle or wave, has force: you rig a giant sail and go. The secret of seeing is to sail on solar wind. Hone and spread your spirit till you yourself are a sail, whetted, translucent, broadside to the merest puff. (33)

The repeated use of the "*s*" sound in this passage weaves this text together, giving it a consistent tone. The recurrence of "*s*" words also intensifies the tone by establishing a consistent sound that the readers can hear.

Here is an example of assonance, also from Dillard:

> A male English sparrow, his mouth stuffed, was hopping in and out of an old nest in a bare tree, and sloshing around in its bottom. A robin on red alert in the grass, trailing half a worm from its bill, bobbed three steps and straightened up, performing unawares the universal robin trick. (113)

The "*o*" sound is repeated here in words that are near each other, such as *hopping*, *sloshing*, *bottom*, *robin*, and *bobbed*. Again, this repeated use of a vowel sets a particular sound or tone in the text. Assonance is more subtle than alliteration because vowels lack the sharp qualities of consonants. But both techniques can be used effectively to weave the text together with sound.

Improving Your Writing Style

With a little practice, you can dramatically improve the power and intensity of your writing by simply choosing a style and keeping it in mind as you compose and revise. You can help your readers "see" and "hear" what you are writing about.

If you practice these techniques, they will become a natural part of your writing skills. Then, after deciding on the tone and style you want, you can project it to your readers with just a little effort.

Remember that style is a choice that you can and should make. Style is a way to express your attitude and feelings about a topic, while establishing your character and a sense of authority.

USE Plain Style

Plain style is the basis of all other writing styles. By choosing an appropriate subject for each sentence and moving it to an early position in the sentence, you can clarify what or who the sentence is about. Put the action of the sentence in the verb. Then eliminate nominalizations, boil down prepositional phrases, and eliminate redundancies.

ESTABLISH Your Voice

Think of a voice or tone that would be appropriate for your text. Then put that voice into your writing by setting a specific tone, getting into character, or imitating other writers.

USE Similes, Analogies, Metaphors, and Personification

Similes, analogies, metaphors, and personifications highlight relationships among different things and ideas. They allow readers to see your topic in new and interesting ways.

EXPLORE and Challenge Cultural Metaphors

Pay attention to the cultural metaphors that shape how we think. You can use those cultural metaphors or challenge them.

EVOKE Atmosphere with Sound

You can also describe something by using sound. An onomatopoeia is a word that sounds like the thing it is describing (e.g., *crackling* fire, *shuffling* walk, *hissing* voice). Alliteration and assonance can add intensity and sound to your writing by combining consonants and vowels in original ways.

1. With a group of people from your class, make a list of ten people whom you consider stylish. What about them signals that they have good style?

2. With your group, talk about the ways people adopt a particular style or voice. Are there situations in your life when you need to adopt a different style or voice than you normally would?

3. Find three texts on the Internet that demonstrate three different styles. Have each member of your group explain why he or she likes or dislikes the style of each document. How does the style of each document fit or not fit the needs of its readers and contexts?

1. Find a text or author that you would like to imitate. Then, with that text on your desk or screen, try to write about a different topic, but use the style of that text. Try to match that author's use of tone, metaphors, similes, detail, and sentence length.

2. Search the Internet to explore the different uses of a common cultural metaphor. What does this metaphor say about how we think about these subjects in our culture?

3. Come up with your own simile or metaphor—perhaps something absurd. Pick any metaphor that comes to mind. Try freewriting for three minutes with your simile or metaphor in front of you. Does the simile or metaphor give you any new insights? At what point does the simile or metaphor become far-fetched or absurd?

1. **Analyze a cultural metaphor.** Find a common cultural metaphor and write an analysis in which you discuss its strengths and weaknesses. Where does the metaphor fail to capture the full meaning of its subject?

2. **Review the style of an online document.** Choose a document on the Internet that exhibits good style and write a review of the document's use of any figurative language, rich descriptions, or other stylistic strategies.

> Go to **MyWritingLab** to complete this chapter's
> exercises and test your understanding of its objectives.

Designing

In this chapter, you will learn how to—

18.1 use principles of design to lay out a document.

18.2 use photography and images to illustrate ideas.

18.3 enhance and reinforce written text with graphs and charts.

I magine your own reaction to a document with no pictures, no headings, no graphics, and no lists. Every page looks like a brick wall of words, page after page. If you are like most people, you wouldn't even want to start reading.

Document design has two primary purposes: (1) to make the information more accessible, so readers can locate what they need, and (2) to make the document more attractive so people want to read it. If your paper looks difficult and unattractive, they might not read it. However, if your writing looks accessible and attractive, readers are going to want to spend more time reading it.

18.1 use principles of design to lay out a document.

Good design creates a sense of order and gives your readers *access points* to help them locate the information they need. The five principles discussed in this chapter are based on the Gestalt theory of design, which is followed by many graphic designers, clothing designers, architects, and artists. Once you learn these principles, you should find it easy—and even fun—to design your documents.

Design Principle 1: Balance

To balance a text, imagine that a page from your document has been placed on a point, like a pencil point. Everything you add to the left side of the page needs to be balanced with something on the right. For example, if you add a picture to the left side, you will need to add text or perhaps another picture on the right.

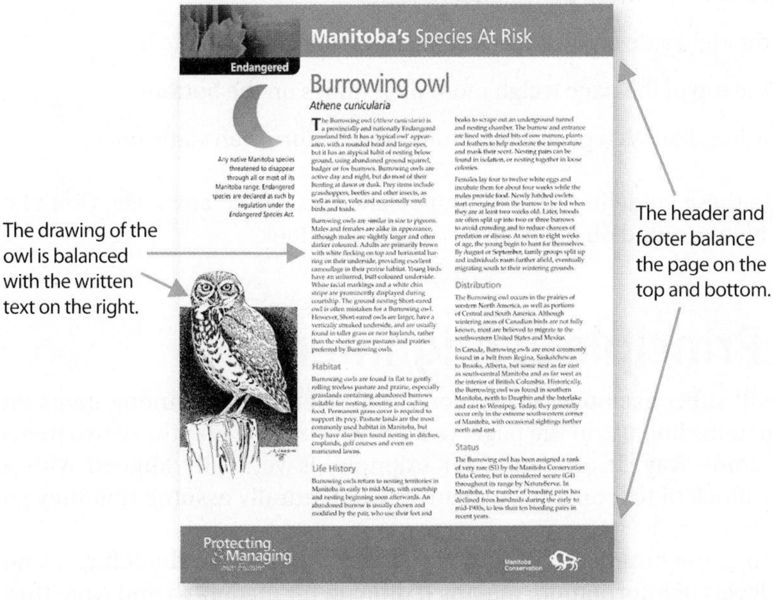

FIGURE 18.1 A Balanced Design

Balance creates a sense of order in documents. This page is balanced both left to right and top to bottom.

The drawing of the owl is balanced with the written text on the right.

The header and footer balance the page on the top and bottom.

To illustrate, look at the page from a report shown in Figure 18.1. On this page, the drawing of an owl on the left has what graphic designers call "weight." This drawing strongly attracts the readers' eyes to it. So to offset this drawing, the designers decided to put a large block of two-column text on the right. Meanwhile, the heavy green borders at the top and bottom of the sheet balance each other, making the page feel stable and steady from top to bottom.

Balance is not a matter of making the page look symmetrical (the same on the left and right). The items should balance, but they shouldn't simply mirror each other.

Balancing a Page

When graphic designers talk about how much the items on the page "weigh," they are talking about how strongly these elements will attract the readers' eyes to them. For example, on a Web page, animated images weigh more than images that don't move. (That's why advertisers often use dancing people in their Internet ads.)

Here are some guidelines for balancing the features on a page:

- Pictures weigh more than written text.

- Color items weigh more than black and white items.

- Big items weigh more than small ones.

- Strange shapes weigh more than standard shapes.

- Things on the right side of the page weigh more than things on the left.

- Things on the top of the page weigh more than things on the bottom.

- Moving features, like Web page animations, weigh more than static ones.

You can use these guidelines to help you balance just about any page. Don't be afraid to move items around on the page to see how they look.

Design Principle 2: Alignment

Your readers will subconsciously search for visual relationships among items on the page. If two items line up on the page, readers will assume that those two items are related in some way. If a picture, for example, is vertically aligned with a caption, list, or block of text on a page, readers will naturally assume that they go together.

In Figure 18.2, the absence of alignment means the page on the left gives no hint about the levels of information, making it difficult for readers to find what they are looking for. The page on the right, on the other hand, uses vertical alignment to highlight the levels in the text. Most readers would find the text on the right page easier to read, because they immediately understand how the information is structured.

To create vertical alignment in your page design:

- Use margins and indentation consistently to highlight the hierarchy of the information.

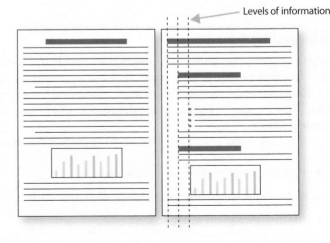

FIGURE 18.2 Using Vertical Alignment

Aligning text vertically allows you to show different levels of information in the text, making the document easier to read and scan. The page on the left is harder to read because it has minimal alignment. The page on the right uses alignment to signal the levels of information in the text.

- Use bulleted lists or numbered lists to set off related information from the main text.

- Adjust the placement of any photographs or graphics to align vertically with the text around them, so readers see them as belonging together.

Design Principle 3: Grouping

The design principle "grouping" takes advantage of your readers' tendency to see any items on a page that are close together as belonging to a group. If a photograph appears near a block of text, your readers will naturally assume that the image and text go together. Similarly, if a heading appears near a block of written text, the readers will see the heading as belonging with the written text.

Figure 18.3 shows a page design that uses grouping well. The "BioGems Facts" on the top left of the page is put close to the picture of mountains on the top right, creating a group. The three logos in the bottom left are grouped together, forming another unit. Also, the picture and the green headline, "Stop Electrocuting Patagonia," can be seen as one group because they appear close together. Finally, the columns of text are naturally seen as a group, too, because they are so close together on the page.

One key to using grouping well is to be aware of the *white spaces*, areas where no text or images appear. When areas are left blank, they frame graphics and written words and catch readers' eyes.

Look again at Figure 18.3. Notice how the white space in the left margin creates a frame for the "BioGems Facts" and the three logos. The white space draws the readers' attention to these visual elements by creating a frame around them.

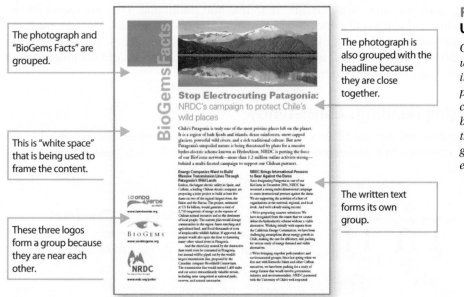

The photograph and "BioGems Facts" are grouped.

This is "white space" that is being used to frame the content.

These three logos form a group because they are near each other.

The photograph is also grouped with the headline because they are close together.

The written text forms its own group.

FIGURE 18.3
Using Grouping

Grouping is a good way to help readers put items together on the page. In this page, you can see four distinct blocks of information that are grouped together, making the text easier to read.

Design Principle 4: Consistency

The principle of consistency suggests that design features should be used predictably throughout the document:

- Headings should be used in a predictable and repeatable way.

- Pages should follow a unified and predictable design pattern.

- Lists should use consistent bullets or numbering schemes.

- Headers, footers, and page numbers should be used to help make each page look similar to the others.

Consistency creates a sense of order, so your readers know what to expect. If the page design or features like headings or images are used consistently, your readers will find it easier to understand how your document is structured.

Choosing Typefaces

A good first step toward consistency is to choose appropriate typefaces. A typeface is the design of the letters in your written text (e.g., Times Roman, Arial, Bookman, Helvetica). As a basic guideline, you should only choose one or two typefaces for your document. To add contrast, you might choose one typeface for the headings and a different typeface for the main text.

There are two basic types of typeface: serif and sans serif. A serif typeface, like Times Roman, New York, or Bookman, has small tips (serifs) at the ends of the main strokes in each letter (Figure 18.4). Sans serif typefaces like Arial and Helvetica do not have these small tips. ("Sans serif" means "without serifs" in French.)

Serif fonts are considered more formal and traditional. They are useful for the main text and parts of a document where readability is important. Most people think sans serif fonts, like Helvetica and Arial, look more modern. These modern fonts are especially useful for titles, headings, footers, captions, and parts of a document where you want to catch the reader's eye.

Using Headings Consistently

Headings are very useful visual elements in any kind of document, but you need to use them consistently. Make some choices up front about the levels of headings you will use.

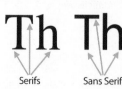

FIGURE 18.4 Serif vs. Sans Serif Typefaces
Serif fonts, like Times Roman on the left, have serifs, while sans serif fonts, like Arial on the right, do not have them.

Title. The title of the document should be sized significantly larger than other headings. You might consider using color to set off the title, or you could center it.

First-Level Headings ("A Heads"). These are the most common headings. They divide your text into its major sections. First-level headings are often bold and are larger than the text used in the body of the document.

Second-Level Headings ("B Heads"). These are used when you need to divide a large section in your document into even smaller parts. These headings tend to use italics and are often slightly larger than the body text.

Third-Level Headings ("C Heads"). These are usually the smallest level of headings. They are often italicized or boldfaced and placed on the same line as the body text.

Headings help readers in a few important ways. First, they offer access points into the text, giving readers obvious places to locate the information they need. Second, they highlight the structure of the text, breaking the larger document down into smaller blocks of information. Third, they give readers places to take breaks from reading sentence after sentence, paragraph after paragraph.

Headings are also beneficial to you as the writer, because they help you make transitions between large sections of the document. Instead of a clumsy statement like, "And now, let me move on to the next issue," you can use a heading to quickly and clearly signal the transition to a new subject.

Design Principle 5: Contrast

The fifth and final design principle is *contrast*. Using contrast means making different items on the page look significantly different. Your headings, for example, should look significantly different than the main text (Figure 18.5).

There are a variety of ways to create contrast in your document's design. You can change the size of the font, add color, use shading, and use highlighting features like boldface, italics, or underlining. The sample report shown in Figure 18.5 uses contrast in several important ways:

- The blue banner across the top, "Geothermal Technologies Program, Colorado," clearly contrasts with the rest of the items on the page because it uses big lettering and a bold color.

- Below the banner, the italicized text contrasts sharply with the body text, helping it stand out on the page.

- The blue heading "Current Development" is easily distinguishable from the body text because it is larger and uses color.

- In the blue screened box on the right of the page, the use of a sans serif font helps to distinguish this text from the body text just to its left.

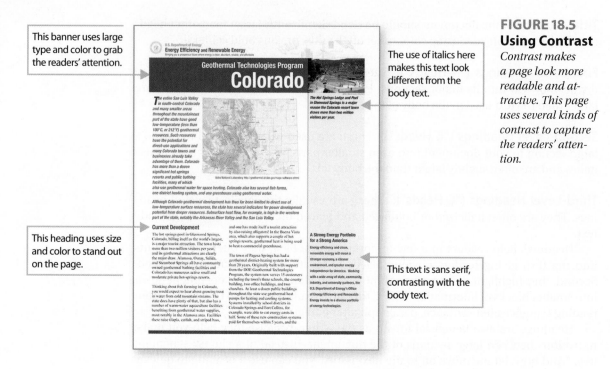

This banner uses large type and color to grab the readers' attention.

The use of italics here makes this text look different from the body text.

This heading uses size and color to stand out on the page.

This text is sans serif, contrasting with the body text.

FIGURE 18.5
Using Contrast
Contrast makes a page look more readable and attractive. This page uses several kinds of contrast to capture the readers' attention.

The secret to using contrast is experimenting with the page design to see how things look. So be daring and explore how items on the page look when you add contrast. Try making visual features larger, bolder, more colorful, or different.

Using Photography and Images

18.2 use photography and images to illustrate ideas.

With the capabilities of today's computers, it's easy to add photographs to your document. To add a picture, you can use a digital camera or a mobile phone to snap the picture, or you can download a picture from the Internet.

You should label each photograph or image by giving it a figure number and a title (Figure 18.6). The figure number should then be mentioned in the written text, so your readers know when to look for the photograph.

Captions are not mandatory, but they can help your readers understand how the image relates to the written text and what they should notice.

Using Graphs and Charts

18.3 enhance and reinforce written text with graphs and charts.

Graphs and charts can also be helpful additions to your documents, especially if you are presenting data to your readers. Some genres, such as reports and proposals, routinely use graphs and charts to illustrate data. These graphics can also be useful in evaluations and position papers to provide support for claims you make in the written text.

FIGURE 18.6 Labeling a Photograph

Proper labeling will help readers understand how the graphic supports the written text.

Figure number and title.

Fig. 1: A Tiktaalik

The Tiktaalik was a prehistoric fish that had four legs. Paleontologists think this creature fills the fossil gap between fish and early limbed animals.

Caption and source information.

Source: Natl. Sci. Found., Oct. 2008; Web; 19 Mar. 2009.

Creating a Graph or Chart

Your best option for making a visual might be to use the spreadsheet program, such as *Excel* or *Quattro Pro,* that came with your word-processing software (Figure 18.7). Simpler graphs can be made in presentation software, like *PowerPoint* or *Keynote.*

These spreadsheet and presentation software packages can help you create quick graphs and charts from a data set. Then, you can insert the graphic right into your document. (Your word processor will probably have a Chart feature that will take you to the spreadsheet program.) Once you have created the graph, you should add a title and label the horizontal x-axis and vertical y-axis (Figure 18.7).

Make sure you have labeled your graph properly and provided a citation for the source of the data. To label the graph, give it a number or letter and a title. For example, the graph in Figure 18.8 is called "Figure A: Obesity Rates (Percentage) By County." After you have labeled the graph, include your source below or beside the graph using a common citation style (e.g., MLA, APA).

In the written part of your document, refer to the graphic by its number, so readers know when to look at it. When you want the readers to consider the graph, write something like, "As shown in Figure A, the local obesity rate. . . ." Or, you can simply put "(Figure A)" at the end of the sentence in which you refer to the graph.

Choosing the Appropriate Graph or Chart

You can use various kinds of graphs and charts to display your data. Each type of graph or chart allows you to tell a different story to your readers.

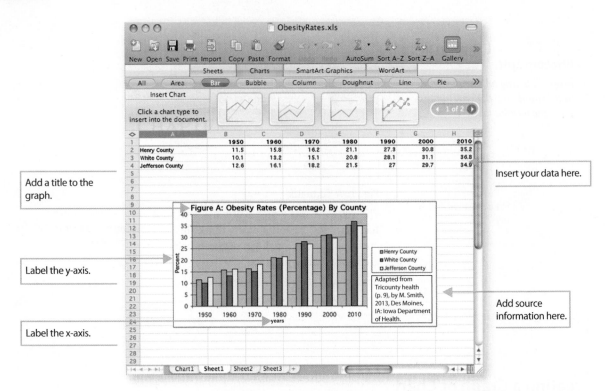

Add a title to the graph.

Label the y-axis.

Label the x-axis.

Insert your data here.

Add source information here.

FIGURE 18.7 Using Spreadsheet Software to Make a Graph

A spreadsheet is a helpful tool for creating a graph. Enter your data and then click the graphing button to create a graph. Then you can insert the graph into your document.

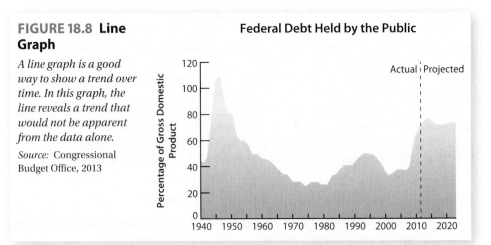

FIGURE 18.8 Line Graph

A line graph is a good way to show a trend over time. In this graph, the line reveals a trend that would not be apparent from the data alone.

Source: Congressional Budget Office, 2013

Federal Debt Held by the Public

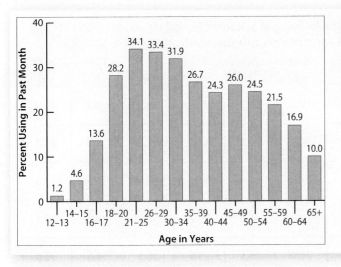

FIGURE 18.9
Bar Chart

A bar chart allows you to illustrate and compare quantities.

Source: 2012 National Survey on Drug Use and Health, U.S. Department of Health and Human Services

Line Graph. A line graph is a good way to show measurements or trends over time. In a line graph, the vertical axis (y-axis) displays a measured quantity, such as temperature, sales, growth, and so on. The horizontal axis (x-axis) is usually divided into time increments such as years, months, days, or hours. See Figure 18.8.

Bar Chart. Bar charts are used to show quantities, allowing readers to make visual comparisons among different amounts (Figure 18.9). Like line graphs, bar charts can be used to show fluctuations in quantities over time.

Pie Charts. Pie charts are useful for showing how a whole quantity is divided into parts. These charts are a quick way to add a visual element into your document, but you should use them sparingly. They take up a lot of space in a document while presenting only a small amount of data. See Figure 18.10.

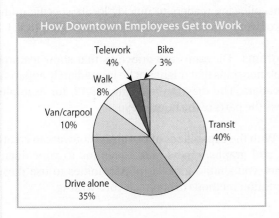

Source: Seattle Department of Transportation, 2011.

FIGURE 18.10 Pie Chart

A pie chart is a good way to show how a whole is divided into parts. When using a pie chart, you should label the slices of the pie and add the numerical information that was used to create the chart.

Source: Seattle Department of Transportation, 2011

Table 3. Percentage of Youth Reporting Bullying at School or Sexual Harassment on the Internet in the Past Year, Pennsylvania Statewide 2011	Female %	Male %	6th %	8th %	10th %	12th %	Overall %
Been hit, kicked, pushed, or shoved around	12.5	19.5	20.0	21.5	13.2	9.4	15.9
Been called names, made fun of, or teased	43.7	39.8	39.1	48.4	43.2	35.9	41.7
Been left out of things on purpose	38.2	27.7	30.4	36.2	33.4	31.5	32.9
Other students telling lies or spreading false rumors	54.6	45.8	45.3	55.7	50.9	48.8	50.3
Other students taking money or damaging your things	18.7	20.9	16.3	23.6	20.3	18.6	19.8
Other students threatening or forcing you to do things	11.4	11.9	11.4	15.0	11.5	8.9	11.7
Other students using the Internet or a cell phone to threaten or embarrass you	15.6	8.6	7.3	14.7	13.3	13.0	12.1
Sexual harassment on the Internet	15.5	9.0	6.1	13.9	15.0	13.4	12.3

FIGURE 18.11 Table

A table offers a great way to quickly and clearly summarize a large amount of data in a small space.

Source: 2011 Pennsylvania Youth Survey Report, Pennsylvania Commission on Crime and Delinquency

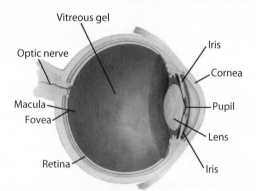

FIGURE 18.12 A Diagram

A diagram is only partially realistic. It shows only the most important features and concentrates on relationships instead of showing exactly what the subject looks like.

Tables. Tables provide the most efficient way to summarize data or facts in a small amount of space. In a table, information is placed in horizontal rows and vertical columns, allowing readers to quickly locate specific numbers or words that address their interests (Figure 18.11).

Diagrams. Diagrams are drawings that show features or relationships that might not be immediately apparent to readers. The diagram in Figure 18.12, for example, shows the parts of the human eye.

With the capabilities of computer software to create and add graphs, charts, and diagrams to your documents, you should look for opportunities to use these illustration methods to enhance your writing.

Now it's time to make your document look more accessible and attractive. Here are some basic strategies for adding design to your writing.

REVIEW Your Genre, Purpose, Readers, and Context

Your document's design should reflect and reinforce the genre and the overall purpose of your text. Design features should also be appropriate for your readers and the contexts in which your document will be used.

BALANCE the Text

Use design features to balance elements on the left and right as well as on the top and bottom of the page.

ALIGN Items Vertically on the Page

Look for opportunities to vertically align items on the page. Indenting text and aligning graphics with text will help create a sense of hierarchy and structure in your document.

GROUP Related Items Together

Put items together that are meant to be viewed together. Photos should be near any text they reinforce. Headings should be close to the paragraphs they lead off. Use white space to frame items you want to be seen as a group.

CHECK the Document for Consistency

Your headings and other design features should be used consistently throughout the document. Make sure you use a consistent design for lists, headings, images, and other design features.

ADD Some Contrast

Items on the page that are different should look significantly different. Use color and font size to make written text stand out.

INCLUDE Photographs, Graphs, and Charts

Add your own photographs or images downloaded from the Internet to your document. Create graphs or charts to illustrate data and complex ideas. Number, title, and caption these visuals so readers understand how they connect to your text.

1. Ask each member in your group to bring a favorite magazine to class. Discuss the magazines' full-page advertisements and their use of design features. Pay special attention to the use of balance, alignment, grouping, consistency, and contrast.

2. Discuss the design of your favorite Web site. What kinds of design features make it interesting or fun to read? What design features help you access information more easily?

3. On campus or in the community, find a flyer or brochure that you think is a design failure. With your group, discuss how the document could be redesigned to make it more accessible and attractive.

Try This Out

1. Find a document on the Internet, on campus, or at your workplace that shows minimal attention to design. Then do a "design makeover" to make the document more accessible and attractive to readers.

2. Write a brief critique of the visual elements of a document you found on campus or at your workplace. Show how each of the five design principles makes the document's design effective or ineffective.

3. Get some practice downloading photographs and images and inserting them into a document. Add figure numbers and titles to the images. Include captions that explain the images and their relevance to your document.

Write This

1. **Review the design of a document.** Write an evaluation in which you discuss the visual design of a document of your choice. Your analysis should consider whether the design is appropriate for the document's topic, purpose, readers, and context.

2. **Redesign a document on a computer.** Choose a document you wrote earlier in the semester or in another class. Redesign the document using your computer's word-processing and graphics software, employing some of the concepts and principles discussed in this chapter. Then write a brief review in which you discuss your design decisions.

> Go to **My Writing Lab** to complete this chapter's exercises and test your understanding of its objectives.

Revising and
Editing

In this chapter, you will learn how to—

19.1 revise globally to shape a document's overall approach.

19.2 edit the content, organization, and design of your paper.

19.3 copyedit paragraphs and sentences to make them clearer.

19.4 proofread your work carefully and quickly.

Now it's time to take your draft from "good" to "excellent." This chapter shows you how to revise and edit your work at four different levels, moving from global issues to small details.

Level 1: Global Revision. Adjust your document's overall approach, using genre to sharpen the topic, angle, purpose, thesis, and appropriateness for the readers and for context.

Level 2: Substantive Editing. Focus on your document's content, organization, and design.

Level 3: Copyediting. Revise the style for clarity, persuasion, and consistency, paying close attention to paragraphs and sentences.

Level 4: Proofreading. Inspect your document's surface features, such as grammatical correctness, spelling, and usage.

As shown in Figure 19.1, you should work from the "global level" (global editing) to the "local level" (proofreading). That way, you can start out making large-scale changes. Then, as you move closer to finishing the final draft, you can focus exclusively on style and correctness.

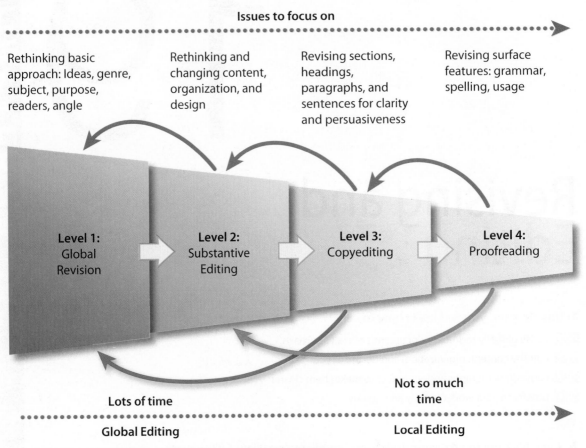

FIGURE 19.1 The Four Levels of Revising and Editing

Whether you are revising and editing your own work or helping others revise and edit their work, the process can be broken down into four levels. The idea is to progress toward a final, polished draft efficiently, first addressing the big issues (purpose, audience) and then moving toward final editing and polishing.

Level 1: Global Revision

19.1 revise globally to shape a document's overall approach.

Let's start with your first draft. When revising globally, it's time to reexamine and reconsider your project's topic, angle, and purpose, and your understanding of the readers and the context.

Figure 19.2 shows an excerpt from a student's first draft of a proposal. Figure 19.3 (on page 371) shows how Zoe's original notes helped her challenge her ideas and rethink how she could persuade her readers to agree with her.

Binge Drinking by College Students

Let's face the fact that the majority of college students drink and that most college students are underage and are therefore breaking the law. Too often on college campuses across the country, this leads to "binge drinking." Some people say that we can solve this problem by encouraging total abstinence or scaring them away from drinking through education. Others argue that a better strategy is to simply lower the drinking age to 18, as it was in many states 30 years ago. Neither of these proposed solutions will work: Young people naturally resist authority, and there is simply no way that politicians today will pass a law lowering the legal drinking age. There must be a better way.

I think my experience with alcohol education and socializing with friends is probably typical. During orientation, there was a whole one-hour session dedicated to scaring us away from drinking on campus. They showed us statistics about the rise in binge drinking, followed by pictures of passed-out students lying on a couch and drooling all over themselves. They told us about the zero-tolerance policy that would be strictly enforced. Most of the people around responded with snickers and snarky remarks under their breath. Then, just a few hours after this session, I went to my first campus party, and yes there was alcohol—a *lot* of alcohol and a *lot* of drunk people. Then again, people were having fun, shaking off their inhibitions, relaxing, laughing a lot. The real lesson I learned by the end of that long day was that the campus authorities talked a big game, but the reality was far different. So much for their scare tactics, I thought.

Now, months later, I realize binge drinking really is a problem that needs to be addressed because people are getting hurt. Their grades suffer, many are driving while very drunk, and it's leading to unsafe sex and even sexual assault. I've personally witnessed all this, which makes

FIGURE 19.2
Rough Draft

With global revision, you need to look at the big picture and rethink your basic approach. Here is an excerpt from student writer Zoe's rough draft of a proposal. Figure 19.3 shows part of her global revision.

Zoe realizes her title is too broad and doesn't forecast her angle or thesis (see her notes in Figure 19.3).

Zoe realizes that her introduction doesn't match up with the issue she really wants to address. She is addressing the issue of improving the way students are educated about alcohol and zero-tolerance policies, not the legal drinking age. She decides she needs to completely rewrite this.

(continued)

FIGURE 19.2
Rough Draft
(continued)

She recognizes that hidden here in the middle of a paragraph is her angle and thesis. She decides to focus on this in the next draft.

She realizes that although the zero-tolerance policy might be an important issue, she needs to focus more closely on the education aspect.

Zoe likes this figure of speech and realizes it could be used as a grabber or even part of her title.

She sees that her proposed plan needs expanding.

me realize that they were making a good point after all. They failed to make a dent in our behaviors, however, because their persuasion strategies were all wrong. Basically, they took a "scared straight" approach, which they seemed to think would turn us into Puritans who would never touch the "demon rum." This strategy, of course, only made alcohol seem *more* interesting and alluring because they portrayed it as "forbidden fruit." Their intentions were good, and their message was important, but they didn't understand their audience. In all, their education achieved exactly the opposite of what they wanted.

Also, our supposed zero-tolerance policy fails to prevent anyone from drinking. Instead, it only drives student drinking underground, into dorm rooms, off campus, or wherever they think they're safe from the authorities. These environments encourage students to binge. Basically, they were telling us that the problem was alcohol, and there was one and only one sane choice: total abstinence. Alcohol is not the problem, however. The problem is too much consumption of alcohol, but they never entertained the idea that underage drinkers could in fact enjoy alcohol if they consumed it in moderation.

But what would be more effective? First, those who are trying to educate us need to understand who they are talking to and how we think. You don't scare young people away from something by portraying it as an absolute evil. You will never succeed in "scaring them straight," but you do need to *be straight* with them. They need to acknowledge that the students they are addressing are going to drink. They're going to at least try the "forbidden fruit." Yes, they should make students aware that drinking can be dangerous, but they need to stress that these dangers result almost entirely from drinking in *excess*, not from alcohol. Few of us are choosing total abstinence, so we would be better served with strategies for drinking moderately and responsibly.

FIGURE 19.3
Global Revision

Zoe's professor asked her to reflect on her first draft. In these notes, Zoe examines what she hopes to accomplish and how she will accomplish it with a global revision of her draft.

Notes on First Draft (Global Revision)

I'm writing a proposal about the ineffective way our college tries to reduce excessive alcohol consumption.

Topic: My topic is how college authorities talk to us students about alcohol. That's what I need to focus on, not on the zero-tolerance policy, or the legal drinking age, which are also important but not something I can address well here or persuade my audience to change. I don't want to suggest alcohol is not actually a problem. It is. I need to propose how education about this problem can be done more *effectively*.

Angle: My angle hinges on the word "straight." Currently, they are using a "scared straight" strategy, but instead they should just "be straight with us," because students see right through the exaggerations and then dismiss this important message completely. I can use my own experiences as a first-year student to show why that doesn't work.

Purpose: I don't think my purpose is clearly stated in this draft, but I do finally get around to it in the middle of the third paragraph. Here it is in one sentence: The purpose of my proposal is to argue that the college should change the way they frame the issue of excessive alcohol consumption, from urging total abstinence to a more realistic and effective message about responsibility and moderation.

Thesis statement: The thesis statement has to be placed earlier in the proposal and needs more punch. They need to stop using the "scared straight" approach and treat us like adults they can "be straight with." That could also be a good title that tells readers up front what I'm arguing for.

Readers: I guess I was writing to other students in this draft, but writing to them would just be complaining because they can't do anything about this. I'm going to change the audience to campus officials, maybe the dean of students. These are the people who need to be convinced.

    Needs—First my readers need to understand that the real problem is that their message is not working and might even be doing more harm than good. They need to understand that when they simply demonize alcohol, telling us abstinence is the only path, students just roll their eyes. Instead, they need to be frank with us, stop exaggerating, and give us strategies for moderate and responsible alcohol use. So they need a clear strategy for solving that problem from someone who understands how students really think.

    Values—Even though I disagree with their strategy, their values are really pretty much the same as my own. They care about student safety and well-being, but I think they also understand that abstinence, which might be ideal, is just not realistic. They want to do what's best. They really do care about us.

    Attitudes—They are probably frustrated and disgusted by binge drinking as much as I am. They're trying to do what's right and I'm sure they understand their approach is not working. If I just rant and complain about how stupid they've been, they won't listen, but they'll be open to my argument if I show that I understand and respect their values and needs, and that in the end we both want the same thing.

Here are Zoe's notes to help her with the global revision process.

She realizes she needs to narrow her topic, which means editing out some of the content and extending other parts.

Here Zoe locates her hidden purpose statement, which will guide her as she writes her next draft. As Chapter 2 explains, "the purpose statement guides you, as the *writer*…. Your thesis statement guides your *readers*."

Zoe analyzes her readers to figure out how she can use their expectations, values, and attitudes to persuade them.

Challenge Your Draft's Topic, Angle, and Purpose

You need to challenge your first draft to make sure it's doing what you intended. Reread your draft, paying special attention to the following global issues:

Topic. How has your topic evolved since you started? Do you now have a better understanding of the boundaries of your topic? Can you sharpen the topic, or does it need to be broadened a little and extended in new directions? Can you find any places where your paper strays from the topic? Can you find any gaps in coverage where you don't address a key issue about your topic?

Angle. Have you shown what is new about your topic or what has changed recently? Have you connected your paper to any recent events or changes in our culture? Have you uncovered any unexpected issues that complicate or challenge your own views?

Purpose. Is your purpose clear in the introduction of your paper, and have you achieved that purpose by the conclusion? Does your purpose need to be more focused?

Thesis Statement. If you are writing in a genre that calls for an explicit thesis statement, have you announced your thesis clearly and prominently? Have you considered what kind of thesis statement to use: informative, argumentative, question/open-ended, or implied?

Think About Your Readers (Again) and the Context

As you drafted your paper, chances are good that you gained a better understanding of your readers' needs, values, and attitudes. Now try to put yourself in your readers' place to imagine how they will react to your ideas and the way you have expressed them.

Needs. Have you considered how the genre and topic will lead readers toward certain expectations and needs? Have you given readers all the information they require to make a decision? What additional information do they need if they are going to agree with you? Are they expecting an explicit thesis statement?

Values. Are your readers' values different from yours? If so, have you anticipated how their values might cause them to react to your ideas differently than you would? Can you add anything that would help build trust between you and them?

Attitudes. Have you adjusted the text to fit your primary readers' attitude about your topic? If they have a positive attitude about your topic, have you reinforced that attitude? If they have a negative attitude, have you given them good reasons to think differently about your topic?

Now look at the context for your document to check whether you have addressed issues of place, medium, and social and political influences.

Place. How will the physical place in which readers experience your document shape how they read it? What will they see, hear, and feel? How will the history and culture of this place shape how readers will interpret what you are saying?

Medium. How will the medium (e.g., paper, podcast, presentation) influence how people react to your message or interpret what you have to say?

Social and Political Influences. How will current social, economic, and political trends influence how your readers feel about what you have to say?

If you need more help profiling your readers, turn to Chapter 3, "Readers, Contexts, and Rhetorical Situations."

Level 2: Substantive Editing

When doing "substantive editing," you should look closely at the content, organization, and design of your paper.

19.2 edit the content, organization, and design of your paper.

Determine Whether You Have Enough Information (or Too Much)

Your paper should have enough information to support your claims and explain your ideas to readers, but you don't want to include more content than you need.

- Does your thesis statement and main claim (usually in the introduction and/or the conclusion) describe what you're trying to achieve in this paper?

- Are your claims in the body of the paper expressed completely and accurately? Could you express them in a more prominent, precise, or compelling way?

- Can you find any places where your ideas need more support or where your thesis and claims need more evidence drawn from sources?

- Are there any digressions you can remove? Can you trim the text down?

If you need more information or sources to back up your ideas, turn to Chapter 25, "Finding Sources and Collecting Evidence."

Reorganize Your Work to Better Use the Genre

Your readers will expect your document to conform to the genre's typical organizational pattern. This does not mean mechanically following a formula. It does mean that your document should reflect the features that readers expect to find in a document that uses this genre.

- Does your draft have each of the sections included in this genre? If not, are you making a conscious choice to leave out a section or merge it with something else?

- Does your introduction do its job according to the conventions of the genre? Does it draw your readers in, introduce them to the topic, state the thesis and main claim, and stress the importance of the subject?

- Are your main ideas prominent enough? If not, can you move these main ideas to places where your readers are more likely to see them?

- Does the conclusion do its job according to the conventions of the genre? Does it restate the thesis or main point, reemphasize the importance of the topic, and offer a look to the future?

- Do the introduction and conclusion echo each other? If not, can you adjust them so they reflect the same topic, angle, purpose, and thesis?

Chapter 16 offers strategies for writing good introductions and conclusions, and Chapter 20 discusses paragraphing and sections.

Look for Ways to Improve the Design

Review how your document looks, focusing on whether the design is a good fit for your readers. The design should make your text easier to read and more attractive.

- Does the design of the document match your readers' expectations for the genre? Is the visual "tone" of the design appropriate for this genre?

- From a distance, does the text look inviting, interesting, and easy to read? Can you use page design, images, or color to make it more attractive and inviting to your readers?

- Have you used the design principles of balance, alignment, grouping, consistency, and contrast to organize and structure the page layout?

- Have you used graphics and charts to reinforce and clarify the written text, while making your text more visually interesting?

Chapter 18, "Designing," offers some helpful strategies for improving the design of your document.

Ask Someone Else to Read Your Work

Substantive editing is a good time to ask others to review your work. Ask a friend or classmate to read through your paper. Tell him or her to concentrate on content, organization, and design. Your editor can ignore any typos or grammatical errors, because right now you need feedback on higher-level features and problems.

Figure 19.4 shows some helpful substantive editing comments from Cruz, a fellow student in Zoe's class, on her second draft. Zoe has made significant improvements to her first draft. Cruz's thorough comments will help her improve it even more, because they highlight the proposal's weaknesses in content, organization, and design.

Rethinking How We Frame the Problem of Binge Drinking:

A Proposal for a More Effective Approach

On our campus, like most every campus nationwide, binge drinking remains a significant problem. The National Institute on Alcohol and Alcoholism (NIAA) explains that college drinking affects all students, not just those who drink. In fact, according to the NIAA, 80% of college students consume some alcohol, and 40% of all college students engage in binge drinking. This results in drunk driving, physical injuries and mental-health problems, poor grades, and even sexual assault. Judging from what we have seen in our college newspaper and from the experiences of most students here, the students here also suffer these consequences. I recognize that our campus leaders take this issue very seriously and have devoted a great deal of effort into addressing the problem. I believe, however, that we could address the problem more effectively by changing the way we talk to students about this issue.

During orientation, we all were exposed to the same "Alcohol Awareness" message. Frankly, that one-hour session was not effective. In some places, graphs and statistics were dry and boring. In other places, it felt like you were trying to scare us away from using alcohol altogether, arguing that abstinence was the only sane path. I remember looking around and seeing everyone rolling their eyes, smirking, and making snarky comments. Honestly, I feel the session had zero impact, because we felt you were talking at us, not to us. In fact, because the issue was presented in black-and-white terms, it felt completely unrealistic to every single person there. Also, just a few hours later, many of us went to parties and witnessed binge drinking firsthand. There, we saw students drinking a great deal and having fun. With all due respect to your intentions, at the end of that day, our experiences did not match up with the exaggerations we heard at the session. By stigmatizing alcohol as the problem, the

Cruz
I like how you explain this problem and connect our problems to national problems. I think you could start faster with a grabber, maybe a "scene setter" describing the passed-out kids you saw during the party. Also, don't forget to cite your source and maybe even quote from it.

Cruz
It seems like you're stating your thesis here, but it's stated more strongly and specifically below. It might work better placed here.

Cruz
You're making a good point about how the session and approach are ineffective, but you say in your reflection you need to show them you respect their efforts if they're going to be open. I agree. But when you say things like "every single person," "completely unrealistic," and "zero impact," that sounds disrespectful. Can you use words like "many of us," "may have," and "perhaps"?

Cruz
This would be a good place to include some empirical research, maybe an interview with students. Then you could quote them and show this is what others think, not just you.

(continued)

FIGURE 19.4 Substantive Editing

Zoe revised her first draft for a peer review session the next day. Here is the second draft and substantive editing comments from Cruz, a classmate in her writing group.

session leaders only portrayed alcohol as "forbidden fruit," and we all know how young people are attracted to anything that is forbidden. I agree that binge drinking is a serious problem on our campus. Since that day, I've been to parties where I saw disgusting and destructive behaviors.

> **Cruz**
> I'd like to hear more about this. This could be a new paragraph where you describe what you've seen in more detail. This would show them that you share their concerns and values.

I respectfully suggest students would respond more positively if you abandoned the "scared straight" approach and adopted an approach that showed you were "being straight" with us. Yes, we understand drinking alcohol is illegal and is a drug. We've heard that message many times before. I am sure that you share my belief that there is simply no way that you will succeed in persuading students that they should completely stop drinking alcohol.

> **Cruz**
> These two sentences sound like your main point, your thesis. Could you state this succinctly and place it at the end of the first paragraph?

I believe students would respond more positively to a frank, honest conversation that shows you value both total abstinence and drinking in moderation by discussing with us realistic and useful strategies for either abstaining or drinking in moderation. I think you'll agree that alcohol itself is not the problem; excessive drinking is the problem. Would it be possible for you to frame the problem and solutions this way instead? Students are going to drink alcohol. Let's help them understand that they can still enjoy alcohol by drinking moderately.

> **Cruz**
> I think your readers would like to hear about some more specific strategies. You could also bring in your research from the NIAA and other experts that describe these educational programs and how they work at other colleges. Then you could explain how to use those strategies here.

Thank you for considering my ideas for more effectively addressing this very serious problem on our campus. I would be happy to meet with you to discuss my ideas further.

> **Cruz**
> Perhaps you can say more here about the benefits of your plan. This might help win over your readers.

> OVERALL COMMENT: I love this idea, Zoe, and I'm convinced your plan would be a much better way to talk to us.
> But sometimes I got confused by your organization, which could be clearer, perhaps using headings. First describe the PROBLEM nationally and here. Then do your ANALYSIS (ineffective message), followed by your DETAILED PLAN backed up by further research. Finally, don't forget to stress the BENEFITS.
> Also, your tone wanders from respectful in places to disrespectful. Tone down the criticism and highlight the positive aspects of your solution. I hope they consider your ideas because they're important and realistic. Good luck with this! -- Cruz

FIGURE 19.4 Substantive Editing *(continued)*

Level 3: Copyediting

Copyediting involves improving the "flow" of your text by making it *clear, concise, consistent,* and *correct* (sometimes called the "Four Cs"). When copyediting, you should focus exclusively on your document's title and headings, paragraphs, and sentences. Your ideas need to be as clear as possible and stated as concisely as possible. Also, make sure your ideas are consistent and that your facts are accurate.

19.3 copyedit paragraphs and sentences to make them clearer.

Review Your Title and Headings

Your title should grab the readers' attention, and the headings in your document should help them quickly grasp your ideas and understand how the document is structured.

- Is the title unique, and does it grab the readers' attention? If your readers saw the title alone, would they be interested in reading your paper?

- Do the headings accurately reflect the information that follows them?

- Do the headings grab the readers' attention and draw them into the text?

- Are the headings consistent in grammar and parallel to each other in structure?

You can learn more about using effective titles and headings in Chapter 16, "Organizing and Drafting," and Chapter 18, "Designing."

Edit Paragraphs to Make Them Concise and Consistent

Work through your document paragraph by paragraph, paying attention to how each one is structured and how it works with the paragraphs around it.

As you read through each paragraph, ask yourself these questions:

- Would a transition sentence at the beginning of the paragraph help make a bridge from the prior paragraph?

- Is each paragraph unified? Does each sentence in the paragraph stick to a consistent topic? Do any sentences seem to stray from the paragraph's claim or statement?

- Does each paragraph logically follow from the paragraph that preceded it, and does it prepare readers for the paragraph that follows?

- If the paragraph is long or complex, would it benefit from a "point sentence" at its end that states or restates the paragraph's overall point?

You can learn more about writing better paragraphs in Chapter 20, "Developing Paragraphs and Sections."

Revise Sentences to Make Them Clearer

After you reshape and refine each paragraph, focus your attention on the clarity and style of individual sentences.

- Are the subjects of your sentences easy to locate? Do they tend to be placed early in the sentences where your readers can easily find them?

- Do the verbs express the action of the sentence? Can you remove any passive verbs (e.g., *is, was, be, has been*) by replacing them with active verbs?

- Can you eliminate any unnecessary prepositional phrases?

- Are your sentences breathing length? Are any sentences too long (i.e., do they take longer than one breath to say out loud)?

In Chapter 17, "Choosing a Style," you can find some "plain style" techniques for improving the clarity of your sentences while making them more concise.

Revise Sentences to Make Them More Descriptive

Now, work on giving your sentences more impact and power.

- Do your sentences use vivid detail to help readers see, hear, touch, taste, and smell what you are writing about?

- Would any similes, metaphors, or analogies help your readers to understand or visualize what you are talking about?

- Do your sentences generally use a consistent tone and voice? Can you describe in one word the tone you are trying to set in your paper?

Level 4: Proofreading

19.4 proofread your work carefully and quickly.

Proofreading is the final step in editing your document, during which you should search for any typos, grammatical errors, spelling mistakes, and word usage problems. Proofreading takes patience and practice, but it is critical to successful writing.

Read Your Writing Out Loud

Your ear will often detect problems that slip past your eyes. Read your work out loud to yourself or have someone else read it to you.

Read Your Draft Backwards

Aloud or silently, read the last sentence, then the next-to-last, all the way through to the first. Reading "backwards" helps you focus on sentence constructions and misspelled words rather than their meaning.

Read a Printed Copy of Your Work

If you have been drafting and editing on your screen, reading a print copy will help you to see your writing from a fresh perspective. You might even try changing the font or line spacing to give the text a different look.

Know Your Grammatical Weaknesses

If you know you tend to make certain grammatical mistakes, devote one proofreading pass to those problems alone. For instance, if you tend to use run-on sentences, devote one entire proofreading session to looking only for that kind of mistake.

Use Your Spellchecker and Grammar Checker

Spellcheck has become a reliable tool over the years. A spellchecker can flag most of those annoying typos and spelling errors. (Look for the squiggly red lines that highlight potential problems.) You should not, however, rely exclusively on your spellchecker or grammar checker for proofreading. Spellcheckers sometimes flag technical terms that are not included in their spelling dictionaries. Grammar checkers sometimes flag constructions such as passive voice that may be appropriate for the genre. Unlike these electronic tools, you are able to exercise judgment and take into account the genre, purpose, and context of your project.

Instead, read through your document looking for *possible* spelling and grammar issues. If you aren't sure about a flagged word or sentence, use your best judgment, consulting a dictionary or a usage guide for help. You can use online dictionaries and usage guides to find quick answers about spelling, grammar, and word usage.

Peer Review: Asking for Advice

The keys to productive peer review are focus and honesty. As the writer, you need to tell your reviewers specifically what kind of help you need. For example, you might say:

- "This is an early draft, so don't pay any attention to the grammar and wording. Look at my ideas and my thesis. Could they be stronger or sharper?"

- "My readers are high school students who are considering skipping college. Do you think this draft addresses their needs and answers the questions they would have?"

- "My thesis is X. What can I do to make sure that it comes through clearly and persuasively?"

- "Please look at the introduction closely. Do I introduce the topic clearly and grab the readers' attention?"

Encourage your reviewers to be honest about your draft. You need them to do more than say "I like it," "It looks good," or "I would give it an A." Ask them to be as tough as possible, so you can find places to improve your writing.

When you are editing someone else's paper, write your comments and suggestions for improvements on a sheet of paper or in an e-mail, so the author has something concrete to work with while revising the draft. Also, make sure you tell the author what you liked about his or her paper, not just the negative stuff. Authors need to know what they are doing well.

Ready to finish your document? Use the "Four Levels of Editing" to revise and edit your text like a professional.

REVISE Globally (Level 1)

Revision means "re-visioning" the text from a fresh perspective. Challenge your draft's topic, angle, purpose, and thesis. Then think further about your readers and the contexts in which they will read or use your document.

EDIT the Content, Organization, and Design (Level 2)

Substantive editing involves looking closely at the content, organization, and design of your document. Determine whether you have enough (or too much) content. Then make sure the organization of your document highlights your major ideas. Also, look for ways you can improve the design.

COPYEDIT Paragraphs and Sentences (Level 3)

Copyediting involves improving the "flow" of your text by making it *clear, concise, consistent,* and *correct*. Review your title and headings to make sure they are meaningful and consistent. Work paragraph by paragraph to make the text concise and consistent. Then revise the style of your sentences to make them clear and descriptive.

PROOFREAD Your Work (Level 4)

As a last step, proofreading is your final opportunity to catch any errors, including typos, grammatical errors, spelling mistakes, and word usage problems. To help you proofread, try reading your document out loud, reading the draft backwards, and reading a hard copy of your work. Be aware of your grammatical weaknesses and look for those specific errors. Meanwhile, your computer's grammar and spelling checkers can detect smaller errors, but always double-check these tools to make sure they are flagging real errors.

ASK Someone Else to Review Your Work

As the author of your document, you may no longer be able to view it objectively. So have someone else look over your work and give you an honest assessment. Your professor may even give you and the members of your group time to "peer review" each other's writing.

1. On the Internet, find a document that seems to be poorly edited. With your group, discuss the impact that the lack of editing has on you and other readers. What do the errors say about the author and perhaps the company or organization he or she works for?

2. Choose a grammar rule with which you have problems. Explain in your own words what the rule is. Use an online writing lab (like the Purdue OWL) or the "Handbook" section of this book for help. Then explain why you have trouble with it. Why do you have trouble remembering to follow it during composing?

3. Find a text on the Internet that you think is pretty strong but that lacks a clearly stated thesis statement. As a group, write a few thesis statements that could help guide readers about the main claim. Try the different kinds of thesis statements described in Chapter 2: an informative, argumentative, or question/open-ended thesis. Discuss which would work best for this text and explain your reasons.

Talk About This

1. On your own or with a colleague, choose a draft of your writing and decide which level of revising and editing it needs. Then, using the appropriate section in this chapter, walk through the steps for editing the document at that level.

2. Write a brief e-mail explaining the main differences between the levels of revising and editing to someone unfamiliar with the concept.

3. Find a text on the Internet that you think is poorly written. Using the four levels of editing, read through the text four separate times. Each time, explain what you would need to do to revise the text to make it stronger.

Try This Out

1. **Edit a text from someone in your class.** Exchange drafts with another person or within a small group during peer review. In addition to the draft, write a memo to your reviewers telling them exactly what you'd like them to focus on. Use the language from this chapter ("level 1," "level 2," "global," "local," etc.) and define as precisely as you can what you think might be an issue.

2. **Copyedit a text onscreen with Track Changes.** Find a rough draft (one of your own, a colleague's, or something from the Internet) and use Track Changes to do a level 3 edit (copyediting) on it. When you have finished, write an e-mail to your professor explaining your edits.

Write This

Go to **MyWritingLab** to complete this chapter's exercises and test your understanding of its objectives.

20

Developing Paragraphs and Sections

In this chapter, you will learn how to—

`20.1` write a paragraph with an effective topic sentence and support.

`20.2` get paragraphs to flow from one sentence to the next.

`20.3` make sections out of related groups of paragraphs.

Paragraphs and sections divide your papers into building blocks of ideas that help your readers quickly understand how you have structured your paper. They also help your readers figure out your main points and how you are supporting them.

A paragraph's job is actually rather straightforward: A paragraph presents a statement or a claim and then supports or proves it with facts, reasoning, examples, data, anecdotes, quotations, or descriptions. A paragraph isn't just a bunch of sentences that seem to fit together. Instead, a solid paragraph works as a single unit that is built around a central topic, idea, issue, or question.

A section is a group of paragraphs that supports a larger idea or claim. A section offers a broad claim and includes a series of paragraphs that support or prove that claim. Longer college-length papers and most workplace documents are typically carved up into a few or several sections to make them easier to read.

In this chapter, you will learn how to develop great paragraphs and sections that will help you organize your ideas and strengthen your writing.

Creating a Basic Paragraph

Paragraphs tend to include up to four kinds of sentences: a *transition sentence*, a *topic sentence, support sentences,* and a *point sentence.* The diagram in Figure 20.1 shows where these kinds of sentences usually appear in any given paragraph. Here is a typical paragraph with these four elements highlighted.

20.1 write a paragraph with an effective topic sentence and support.

> Of course, none of this happened overnight (transition). In fact, more important than the commercialization of rap was the less visible cultural movement on the ground in anyhood USA (topic sentence). In rap's early days, before it became a thriving commercial entity, dj party culture provided the backdrop for this off-the-radar cultural movement (support). What in the New York City metropolitan area took the form of dj battles and the MC chants emerged in Chicago as the house party scene, and in D.C. it was go-go (support). In other regions of the country, the local movement owed its genesis to rap acts like Run DMC, who broke through to a national audience in the early 1980s (support). In any case, by the mid-1980s, this local or underground movement began to emerge in the form of cliques, crews, collectives, or simply kids getting together primarily to party, but in the process of rhyming, dj-ing, dancing, and tagging (support). Some, by the early 1990s, even moved into activism (support). In large cities like Chicago, San Francisco, Houston, Memphis, New Orleans, Indianapolis, and Cleveland and even in smaller cities and suburban areas like Battle Creek, Michigan, and Champaign, Illinois, as the '80s turned to the '90s, more and more young Blacks were coming together in the name of hip-hop (point sentence). (Bakari Kitwana, *Hip Hop Generation*)

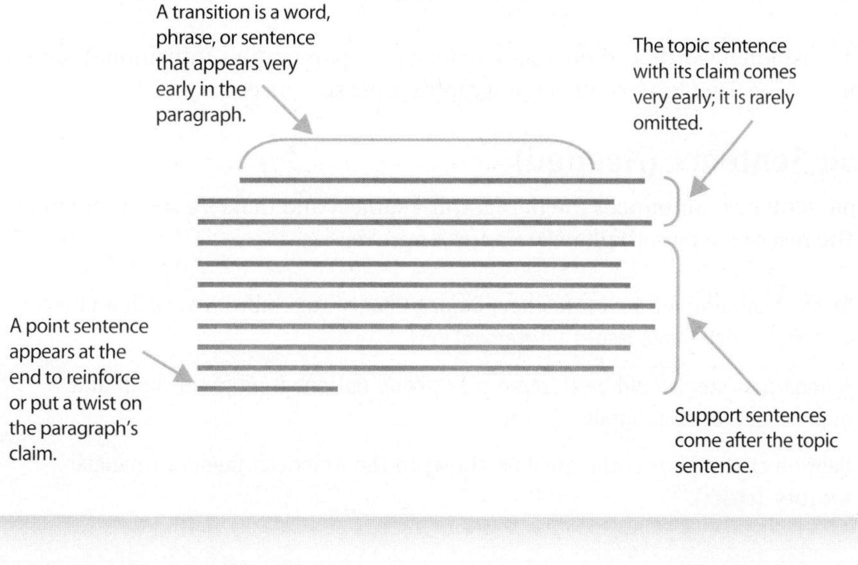

A transition is a word, phrase, or sentence that appears very early in the paragraph.

The topic sentence with its claim comes very early; it is rarely omitted.

A point sentence appears at the end to reinforce or put a twist on the paragraph's claim.

Support sentences come after the topic sentence.

FIGURE 20.1
The Shape of a Paragraph

Although paragraphs vary in terms of function and structure, the core of a paragraph includes the topic sentence with a claim followed by support sentences. Transition and point sentences can, in many cases, improve the flow of the paragraph.

Transition or Transitional Sentence (Optional)

The purpose of a transition or transitional sentence is to make a smooth bridge from the prior paragraph to the current paragraph. Transitions are especially useful when you want to shift or change the direction of the discussion.

A transition, if needed, should appear at the beginning of the paragraph. It might be as brief as a single word or phrase (e.g., *finally, in the past*) or as long as a complete sentence. A transitional sentence might ask a question or make an obvious turn in the discussion:

> If fast food is responsible for America's expanding waistlines, what can we do to change how much fast food young people eat?

A question like this one sets up the topic sentence, which usually follows immediately. Here is a transitional sentence that makes an obvious turn in the discussion:

> Before moving ahead, though, we first need to back up and discuss some of the root causes of poverty in the United States.

A transitional sentence often redirects the readers' attention to a new issue while setting up the paragraph's claim (topic sentence).

A transitional word or phrase can also make an effective bridge between two paragraphs. Here are some transitional words and phrases that you can try out:

For example	The next step	Specifically
To illustrate	In any event	On the contrary
For this reason	On the whole	Nevertheless
As an illustration	Likewise	To summarize
Besides	Accordingly	Equally important
Of course	In conclusion	As a result
In the past	More specifically	Consequently
In the future	In other words	Meanwhile

Transitional words and phrases can lead off a paragraph's transitional sentence, or they can be used to start out a paragraph's topic sentence.

Topic Sentence (Needed)

A topic sentence announces the paragraph's subject and makes a statement or claim that the rest of the paragraph will support or prove.

> At the beginning of his presidency, Barack Obama was confronted with a number of pressing economic issues (statement).

> A good first step would be to remove fast food options from junior high and high school lunch programs (claim).

> Debt on credit cards is the greatest threat to the American family's financial security (claim).

The topic sentence will be the first or second sentence in most paragraphs. You have probably been told that a topic sentence can be put anywhere in a paragraph. That's true. But you should put the topic sentence early in the paragraph if you want your readers to understand the paragraph's subject and be able to identify its key statement or claim quickly. Putting the topic sentence in the middle or at the end of a paragraph will make your main ideas harder to find.

Of course, any guideline has exceptions. For example, if you are telling your readers a story or leading them toward a controversial or surprising point, your topic sentence might be better placed at the end of the paragraph.

Support Sentences (Needed)

Support sentences will make up the body of your paragraphs. These sentences back up each paragraph's topic sentence with examples, details, reasoning, facts, data, quotations, anecdotes, definitions, descriptions, and anything else needed to provide support. Support sentences usually appear after the topic sentence.

> With over 4,210 acres of both natural chaparal-covered terrain and landscaped parkland and picnic areas, Griffith Park is the largest municipal park with urban wilderness area in the United States (topic sentence). Situated in the eastern Santa Monica Mountain range, the Park's elevations range from 384 to 1,625 feet above sea level (support). With an arid climate, the Park's plant communities vary from coastal sage scrub, oak and walnut woodlands to riparian vegetation with trees in the Park's deep canyons (support). The California native plants represented in Griffith Park include the California species of oak, walnut, lilac, mountain mahogany, sages, toyon, and sumac (support). Present, in small quantities, are the threatened species of manzanita and berberis (support). ("Griffith Park," par. 3)

Point Sentence (Optional)

Point sentences state, restate, or amplify the paragraph's main point at the end of the paragraph. A point sentence is especially useful in longer paragraphs when you want to reinforce or restate the topic sentence of the paragraph in different words.

> That early anti-commercial intent symbolized the ethos of the alternative music scene (topic sentence). In 1990, Grohl became the drummer for Seattle-based band Nirvana, which had been formed by singer Kurt Cobain and bass player Krist Novoselic in 1987. Nirvana had already released a debut album, *Bleach* (1989), and the three-piece—Cobain, Novoselic and Grohl—toured small venues in a tiny van. It was a love of music that fuelled them, not the desire to become rich, famous rock stars (point sentence). (Wilkinson, "David Grohl")

As shown in the paragraph above, a point sentence is a good way to stress the point of a complex paragraph. The topic sentence at the beginning of the paragraph states a claim and the point sentence drives it home.

Getting Paragraphs to Flow (Cohesion)

20.2 get paragraphs to flow from one sentence to the next.

Getting your paragraphs to flow is not difficult, but it takes a little practice. Flow, or *cohesion*, is best achieved by paying attention to how each paragraph's sentences are woven together. You can use two techniques, *subject alignment* and *given-new chaining*, to achieve this feeling of flow.

Subject Alignment in Paragraphs

A well-written paragraph keeps the readers' focus on a central subject, idea, issue, or question. For example, the following paragraph does not flow well because the subjects of the sentences are inconsistent:

> Watching people at the park on a Saturday afternoon is a true pleasure. Frisbee golf is played by a group of college students near the trees. Visiting with each other are dog owners with their pets running around in playful packs. Picnic blankets have been spread out, and parents are chatting and enjoying their lunch. The playground is full of children sliding down slides and playing in the sand.

One way to get a paragraph to flow is to align the paragraph's sentences around a common set of subjects.

> Watching people at the park on a Saturday afternoon is a true pleasure. Near the trees, a group of college students play frisbee golf. Off to the side, dog owners visit with each other as their pets run around in playful packs. Parents chat and enjoy their lunch on spread-out picnic blankets. On the playground, children slide down slides and play in the sand.

This paragraph flows better (it is coherent) because the subjects of the sentences are all people. The paragraph is *about* the people at the park, so making people the subjects of the sentences creates the feeling that the paragraph is flowing.

Given-New in Paragraphs

Another good way to create flow is to use something called "given-new chaining" to weave together the sentences in a paragraph. Here's how it works.

Each sentence starts with something that appeared in a prior sentence (called the "given"). Then the remainder of the sentence offers something that the readers didn't see in the prior sentence (called the "new").

Recently, an art gallery exhibited the mysterious paintings of Irwin Fleminger, a modernist artist whose vast Mars-like landscapes contain cryptic human artifacts. One of Fleminger's paintings attracted the attention of some young schoolchildren who happened to be walking by. At first, the children laughed, pointing out some of the strange artifacts in the painting. Soon, though, these artifacts in the painting drew the students into a critical awareness of the painting, and they began to ask their bewildered teacher what they meant. Mysterious and beautiful, Fleminger's paintings have this effect on many people, not just schoolchildren.

In this paragraph, the beginning of each sentence takes something from the previous sentence or an earlier sentence and then adds something new. This creates a given-new chain, causing the text to feel coherent and flowing.

A combination of subject alignment and given-new chaining will allow you to create good flow in your paragraphs.

Organizing a Section

A section is a group of paragraphs that supports a major point in your text. When used properly, sections break a larger document into manageable portions. They also provide readers with a bird's-eye view of the document, allowing them to take in the gist of a longer document at a glance.

20.3 make sections out of related groups of paragraphs.

Opening, Body, Closing

A section supports or proves a major statement or claim. This statement or claim tends to be placed at the beginning of the section, often in a brief *opening paragraph*. Then the *body paragraphs* in the section each contribute something to support that statement or claim. Finally, an optional *closing paragraph*, which tends to be shorter, can be used to restate the major statement or claim that the section was supporting or trying to prove.

Organizational Patterns for Sections

When organizing a section, begin by asking yourself what you want to achieve. Then identify a pattern that will help you structure and fill out that space. Figure 20.2 (page 388) shows a variety of patterns for organizing sections in your text. These are some of the most common patterns, but others, including variations of the ones shown here, are possible.

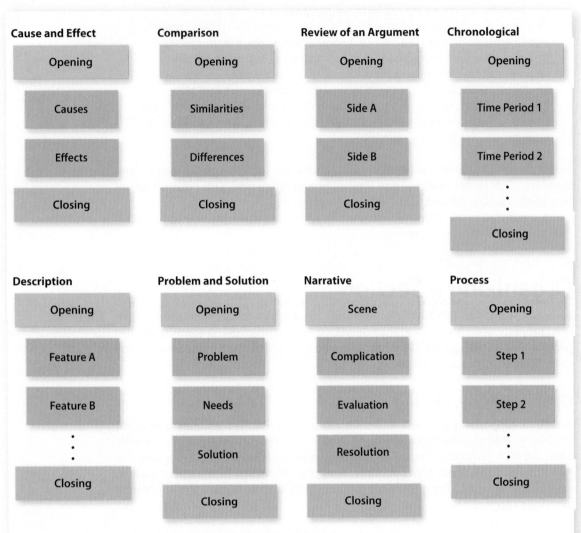

FIGURE 20.2 Organizational Patterns for Sections

Simple patterns like these can help you organize sections in your document. These patterns should not be followed mechanically, though. You should adapt them to suit your purpose.

Here are some basic strategies for creating clear, logical paragraphs and sections in your documents.

IDENTIFY the Four Kinds of Sentences in a Paragraph

A typical paragraph has a *topic sentence* and *support sentences*. As needed, a paragraph can also include a *transition sentence,* phrase, or word and a *point sentence*.

STATE Each Paragraph's Topic Sentence Clearly

A topic sentence announces the paragraph's subject—the central idea or issue covered in the paragraph. Your topic sentences should make a statement or claim that the rest of the paragraph will support or prove.

DEVELOP Support Sentences for Each Paragraph

Support sentences make up the body of most paragraphs. These sentences provide examples, details, reasoning, facts, data, anecdotes, definitions, descriptions, and anything else that backs up the paragraph's topic sentence.

DECIDE If a Transition Sentence or Transition Is Needed

If the prior paragraph is talking about something significantly different from the current paragraph, you might consider using a transition sentence or a transitional word or phrase to bridge the gap.

DECIDE If a Point Sentence Would Be Helpful

In a longer paragraph, you might decide to use a point sentence to state or restate the paragraph's main point. Usually, the point sentence makes a claim that is similar to the topic sentence at the beginning of the paragraph.

REVISE Paragraphs So They Flow

Use subject alignment and given-new techniques to help paragraphs flow better.

COMBINE Paragraphs into Sections

Larger documents should be carved into sections. A typical section has an opening paragraph and body paragraphs. A closing paragraph is optional.

Talk About This

1. In studies of high school students' writing, researchers have found that inexperienced writers tend to place topic sentences at the end of their paragraphs, not the beginning. With your group in class, come up with two or three theories about why inexperienced writers would tend to put their topic sentences late in paragraphs.

2. In this chapter, you learned that topic sentences should usually appear at the beginning of a paragraph and occasionally at the end. Can you think of any situations in which burying the topic sentence in the middle of a paragraph would be a good idea?

3. With your group, choose a reading in this book and analyze five of its paragraphs, identifying their topic sentences, support sentences, transition sentences, and point sentences.

Try This Out

1. Collect some interesting paragraphs from the Internet. Identify the topic sentence and support sentences in each paragraph. If transition sentences and point sentences are used, highlight them, too. In a presentation to your class, choose one of your paragraphs and show how it works.

2. Find a badly written paragraph in a printed or online text. First, improve the flow of the paragraph by aligning the subjects of the sentences. Second, use given-new strategies to revise the paragraph's sentences. Finally, use a combination of subject alignment and given-new strategies to improve its flow. Which of these methods (subject alignment, given-new, or a combination) worked best?

3. On the Internet or on campus, find a document that is divided into sections. Look at each section carefully to determine what patterns are used. Which patterns for sections described in this chapter are most common? Are the sections following any patterns that aren't shown in this chapter?

Write This

1. **Diagnose and solve a paragraph's organizational problems.** Find a paragraph that has a confusing organization (one of your own, a colleague's, or something from the Internet). Diagnose the paragraph's problems using the guidelines given in this chapter. Then write a one-page analysis of the paragraph in which you explain its problems and offer two to five suggestions for improving it.

2. **Use a computer to revise the structure of a section.** Find a poorly organized multiple-page document on the Internet that is divided into sections. Revise the organization of one section so that it includes a clear opening paragraph and body paragraphs. Write an e-mail to the document's author (but don't actually send it) in which you discuss the problems with the original section and describe your strategy for improving it.

> Go to **MyWritingLab** to complete this chapter's exercises and test your understanding of its objectives.

Using Basic
Rhetorical
Patterns

In this chapter you will learn how to—

21.1 use rhetorical patterns to organize your ideas.

21.2 organize paragraphs and sections into familiar patterns.

21.3 combine rhetorical patterns to make sophisticated arguments.

Rhetorical patterns can help you to organize information into patterns that your readers will find familiar and easy to understand. Ancient rhetoricians called these patterns *topoi*, which meant "places" or "commonplaces." Rhetorical patterns are familiar places (*topoi*) that can help you develop and organize your ideas.

A variety of rhetorical patterns are available, but the most common are—

Narrative	Classification
Description	Cause and Effect
Definition	Comparison and Contrast

21.1 use rhetorical patterns to organize your ideas.

You may already be familiar with these patterns because they are often used to teach high school students how to write essays, such as *cause and effect* essays or *comparison and contrast* essays.

Keep in mind, though, that rhetorical patterns are not formulas to be followed mechanically. You can alter, bend, and combine these patterns to fit your text's purpose and genre. When drafting and revising, writers will often use rhetorical patterns to help them construct well-written paragraphs and sections.

21.2 organize paragraphs and sections into familiar patterns.

Narrative

A narrative describes a sequence of events or tells a story in a way that illustrates a specific point.

Narratives can be woven into just about any genre. In reviews, literary analyses, and rhetorical analyses, narratives can be used to summarize or describe the work you are examining. In proposals and reports, narratives can be used to recreate events and provide historical background on a topic. Some genres, such as memoirs and profiles, often rely on narrative to organize the entire text.

The diagram in Figure 21.1 shows the typical pattern for a narrative. When telling a story, writers will usually start out by *setting the scene* and *introducing a complication* of some kind. Then the characters in the story *evaluate the complication* to figure out how they are going to respond. They then *resolve the complication*. At the end of the narrative, the writer *states the point* of the story, if needed.

Consider, for example, the following paragraph, which follows the narrative pattern:

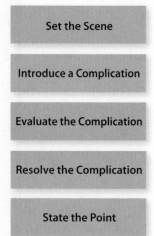

FIGURE 21.1 The Narrative Pattern

Narratives tend to have these five parts, but parts can be moved or removed to fit the rhetorical situation.

Yesterday, I was eating at Gimpy's Pizza on Wabash Street (scene). Suddenly, some guy started yelling for everyone to get on the floor, because he was robbing the restaurant (complication). At first, I thought it was a joke (evaluation). But then everyone crawled under the tables. I saw the guy waving a gun around, and I realized he was serious. I got down, too. Fortunately, the guy just took the money and ran (resolution). That evening, on the news, I heard he was arrested a couple of hours later. This brush with crime opened my eyes about the importance of personal safety (point). We all need to be prepared for the unexpected.

The narrative pattern is probably already familiar to you, even if you didn't know its name before. This is the same pattern used in television sitcoms, novels, jokes, and just about any story. In nonfiction writing, though, narratives are not "just stories." They help writers make specific points for their readers.

Description

Descriptions often rely on details drawn from the five senses—seeing, hearing, touching, smelling, and tasting. You can also use rhetorical devices, like metaphor, simile, and onomatopoeia, to deepen the readers' experience and understanding.

Describing with the Senses

When you need to describe a person, place, or object, start out by considering your subject from each of the five senses:

What Does It Look Like? What are its colors, shapes, and sizes? What is your eye drawn toward? What makes your subject visually distinctive?

What Sounds Does It Make? Are the sounds pleasing, sharp, soothing, irritating, metallic, or erratic? What effect do these sounds have on you and others?

What Does It Feel Like? Is it rough or smooth, hot or cold, dull or sharp, slimy or firm, wet or dry?

How Does It Smell? Does your subject smell fragrant or pungent? Does it have a particular aroma or stench? Does it smell fresh or stale?

How Does It Taste? Is your subject spicy, sweet, salty, or sour? Does it taste burnt or spoiled? Which foods taste similar to the thing you are describing?

Describing with Similes, Metaphors, and Onomatopoeia

Some people, places, and objects cannot be fully described using the senses. Here is where tropes like similes, metaphors, and onomatopoeia can be especially helpful. These stylistic devices are discussed in depth in Chapter 17, "Choosing a Style," so we will only discuss them briefly here.

Simile. A simile ("X is like Y"; "X is as Y") helps you describe your subject by making a simple comparison with something else:

> Directing the flow of traffic, the police officer moved as mechanically and purposefully as a robot on an assembly line.

Metaphor. A metaphor ("X is Y") lets you describe your subject in more depth than a simile by directly comparing it to something else.

> When the fall semester starts, a college campus becomes a colorful bazaar with strange new people, cars stuffed with clothes, and merchants hawking their wares.

Onomatopoeia. Onomatopoeia uses words that sound like the thing being described.

> The flames crackled and hissed as the old farmhouse teetered on its charred frame.

Description is commonly used in all genres. Where possible, look for ways to use combinations of senses and tropes to add a visual element to your texts.

Definition

A definition states the exact meaning of a word or phrase. Definitions explain how a particular term is being used and why it is being used that way.

Sentence definitions, like the ones in a dictionary, typically have three parts: the term being defined, the category in which the term belongs, and the distinguishing characteristics that set it apart from other things in its category.

Category

Term

Distinguishing characteristics

Cholera is a potentially lethal illness that is caused by the bacterium, *Vibrio cholerae,* with symptoms of vomiting and watery diarrhea.

An *extended definition* is longer than a sentence definition. An extended definition usually starts with a sentence definition and then continues to define the term further. You can extend a definition with one or more of the following techniques:

Word Origin (Etymology). Exploring the historical origin of a word can provide some interesting insights into its meaning.

> According to the *Online Etymology Dictionary,* the word *escape* comes from the Old French word "eschaper," which literally meant "to get out of one's cape, leave a pursuer with just one's cape."

Examples. Giving examples can put a word's meaning into context.

> For example, when someone says she "drank the Kool-Aid" for Barack Obama, it means she became a mindless follower of him and his ideas.

Negation. When using negation, you explain something by telling what it is not.

> St. John's Wort is not a stimulant, and it won't cure all kinds of depression. Instead, it is a mild sedative.

Division. You can divide the subject into parts, which are then defined separately.

> There are two kinds of fraternities. The first kind, a "social fraternity," typically offers a dormitory-like place to live near a campus, as well as a social community. The second kind, an "honorary fraternity," allows members who share common backgrounds to build networks and support fellow members.

Similarities and Differences. When using similarities and differences, you can compare and contrast the item being defined to other similar items.

> African wild dogs are from the same biological family, *Canidae,* as domestic dogs, and they are about the same size as a labrador. Their coats, however, tend to have random patterns of yellow, black, and white. Their bodies look like those of domestic dogs, but their heads look like those of hyenas.

Analogy. An analogy compares something unfamiliar to something that readers would find familiar.

Your body's circulatory system is similar to a modern American city. Your arteries and veins are like roads for blood cells to travel on. These roadways contain white blood cells, which act like police officers patrolling for viruses and bacteria.

Classification

Classification allows you to divide objects and people into groups, so they can be discussed in greater depth. A classification can take up a single paragraph, or it might be used to organize an entire section. Here are a few steps to help you use classification to organize a paragraph or section.

Step One: List Everything That Fits into the Whole Class

List all the items that can be included in a specific class. Brainstorming is a good tool for coming up with this kind of list.

Step Two: Decide on a Principle of Classification

The key to classifying something is to come up with a *principle of classification* that helps you do the sorting.

For example, let's suppose you are classifying all the ways to stop smoking. You would list all the methods you can find. Then you would try to sort them into categories:

Lifestyle changes—exercise daily, eat healthy snacks, break routines, distract yourself, set up rewards, keep busy

Smoking-like activities—chew gum, drink hot tea, breathe deeply, eat vegetables, eat nuts that need to be shelled

Nicotine replacement—nicotine patch, nicotine gum, sprays, inhalers, lozenges, nicotine fading

Medical help—acupuncture, hypnosis, antidepressants, support group

Step Three: Sort into Major and Minor Groups

You should be able to sort all the items from your brainstorming list cleanly into the major and minor categories you came up with. In other words, an item that appears in one category should not appear in another. Also, no items on your list should be left over.

Here is a classification that was written by someone trying to stop smoking:

I really want to quit smoking because it wastes my money and I'm tired of feeling like a social outcast. Plus, someday, smoking is going to kill me if I don't stop. I have tried to go cold turkey, but that hasn't worked. The new e-cigarettes are too expensive and just make me want to start smoking again. So, I began searching for other ways to stop. While doing my research, I found that there are four basic paths to stopping smoking:

Lifestyle Changes. The first and perhaps easiest path is to make some lifestyle changes. Break any routines that involve smoking, like smoking after meals or going outside for a smoke break. Start exercising daily and set personal rewards for reaching milestones (e.g., dinner out, treat, movie). Mostly, it's important to keep yourself busy. And, if needed, keeping pictures of charcoal lungs around is a good reminder of what happens to people who don't give up smoking.

Smoking-Like Activities. For many of us, the physical aspects of smoking are important, especially doing something with the hands and mouth. Some people keep a bowl of peanuts around in the shells, so they have something to do with their hands. Drinking hot tea or breathing deeply can replicate the warmth and sensation of smoking on the throat and lungs. Healthy snacks, like carrots, pretzels, or chewing gum, will keep the mouth busy.

Nicotine Replacement. Let's be honest—smokers want the nicotine. A variety of products, like nicotine gum, patches, sprays, and lozenges can hold down those cravings. Also, nicotine fading is a good way to use weaker and weaker cigarettes to step down the desire for nicotine.

Medical Help. Medical help is also available. Here on campus, the Student Health Center offers counseling and support groups to help people stop. Meanwhile some people have had success with hypnosis and acupuncture.

My hope is that a combination of these methods will help me quit this habit. This time I'm going to succeed.

The author of this classification has found a good way to sort out all the possible ways to stop smoking. By categorizing them, she can now decide which ones will work best for her.

Cause and Effect

Exploring causes and effects is a natural way to discuss many topics. Identifying causes is the best way to explain why something happened. Exploring the effects is a good way to describe what happened afterward. When explaining causes and effects, identify both causes and effects and then explain *how* and *why* specific causes led to those effects.

Some cause-and-effect explanations simply point out the causes and effects of a particular event. Other cause-and-effect explanations are *arguable,* especially when people disagree about what caused the event and its effects (Figure 21.2).

Even when describing a complex cause-and-effect scenario, you should try to present your analysis as clearly as possible. Often, the clearest analysis will resemble a narrative pattern, as in this analysis of tornado formation:

Although scientists still do not completely understand the causes behind the formation of tornadoes, most agree on this basic pattern. Three ingredients must be present: a large mass of warm moist air, a large mass of cold dry air, and a violent collision between the two. During springtime in the central United States, enormous masses of warm moist air can move rapidly northeastward from the Gulf of Mexico into what has become known as "tornado alley." When the warm air collides with the cold air, thunderstorms are almost always produced. However, if the rapidly moving warm air slides *under* the cold air and gets trapped beneath, that's when a tornado can occur. Because warm air is lighter than cold air, the warm-air mass will try to form something like a "drain" in the cold-air mass that would allow the warm air to shoot through. If this happens, a vortex of air develops, sucking everything on the ground upward at enormous velocities, causing the strongest winds produced anywhere in nature, up to 300 miles per hour. These powerful winds sometimes accomplish the unbelievable, such as uprooting enormous trees and driving pieces of straw through wooden planks.

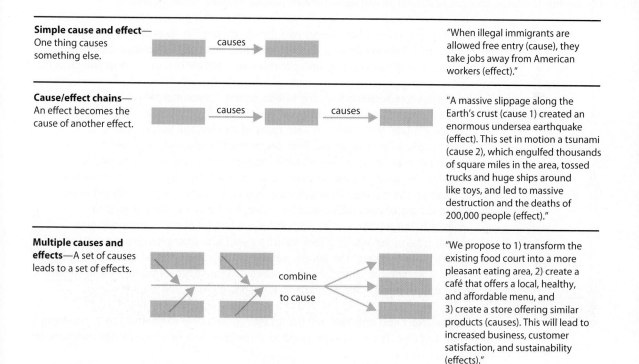

FIGURE 21.2 Three Kinds of Cause and Effect

Comparison and Contrast

Comparison and contrast allow you to explore the similarities and differences between two or more people, objects, places, or ideas. When comparing and contrasting, you should first list all the characteristics that the two items have in common. Afterward, list all the characteristics that make them different.

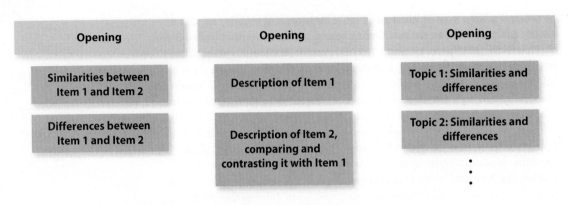

FIGURE 21.3 Three Patterns for Comparison and Contrast

Comparing and contrasting can be done in several ways. Here are three of the more common patterns.

You can then show how these two things are similar to and different from each other. Figure 21.3 shows three patterns that could be used to organize the information in your list. The following paragraph provides an example of comparison and contrast:

> The differences between first-degree and second-degree murder can seem subtle. Both are forms of homicide, which is "the act of taking someone's life through murder" ("Homicide"). Also, in both types of murder, the perpetrator intentionally killed the victim. First-degree murder happens when the perpetrator planned in advance to kill someone. He or she wanted to murder someone else, made a plan, and carried out the act. Usually, he or she then tried to cover up the murder. Second-degree murder happens when the alleged killer was in the act of committing another crime, but he or she did not plan in advance to murder the victim. For example, a burglar commits second-degree murder if he intentionally kills a security guard who discovers him committing the crime. In this case, the burglar did not set out to kill the security guard, but he did it on purpose when he was discovered. Second-degree murder might occur as a result of arson, rape, robbery, or kidnapping.

Comparison and contrast is a useful way to describe something by comparing it to something else. It can also be used to show how two or more things measure up against each other.

Combining Rhetorical Patterns

21.3 combine rhetorical patterns to make sophisticated arguments.

Rhetorical patterns can be combined to meet a variety of purposes. For example, you can embed a comparison and contrast within a narrative. Or you can use a classification within a description. In other words, you shouldn't get hung up on a particular pattern as *the* way to make your point. You can mix and match these rhetorical patterns to fit your needs. All of the readings in *Writing Today* use combinations of rhetorical patterns, so you should turn to them for examples.

Here are some easy ways to start using and combining basic rhetorical patterns in your writing.

NARRATE a Story

Look for places in your writing where you can tell a story. Set the scene and then introduce a complication. Discuss how you or others evaluated and resolved the complication. Then tell readers the main point of the story.

DESCRIBE People, Places, or Objects

Consider your subject from your five senses: sight, sound, touch, smell, and taste. Pay attention to movement and features that make your subject unique or interesting.

DEFINE Your Words or Concepts

Look for important words or concepts that need to be defined. A sentence definition should have three parts: the term, the category, and distinguishing characteristics. To extend the definition, describe the word's history, offer examples of its usage, use negation to show what it isn't, divide the subject into two or more parts, or discuss its similarities and differences with other things.

CLASSIFY Items by Dividing Them into Groups

If you are discussing something large or complex, list all its parts. Then use a principle of classification to sort that list into two to five major groups. Each group can be divided further into minor groups.

USE CAUSE AND EFFECT to Explain What Causes What

Examine your subject in terms of causes and effects. When analyzing a problem, explain what has changed to cause it. When pitching a solution, describe how your plan will lead to good results.

COMPARE AND CONTRAST Things

Find something that is similar to your subject. List all the similarities between the two items. Then list all the differences. Describe their similarities and differences.

MIX It Up!

Rhetorical patterns are not recipes or formulas to be mechanically followed. You should combine these patterns in ways that enhance their strengths.

1. Have each member of your group find two print examples of each of the basic rhetorical patterns discussed in this chapter. Give a brief presentation in which each person shows how the examples illustrate the patterns.

2. Make a list of ten slang words or phrases. With your group, come up with definitions for each of these words in which you identify the term, the category, and the distinguishing characteristics.

3. Basic rhetorical patterns are sometimes used as structures for essays. For example, you have probably heard of "cause and effect" essays or "comparison and contrast" essays. With your group, discuss and list the advantages and disadvantages of using these patterns to learn how to write whole documents.

Try
This
Out

1. Pick a place where you can sit undisturbed for half an hour. Write down everything you hear, feel, smell, and taste. Do *not* write down what you see. Then try to write a one-page description of the place where you were sitting without including any visual elements. Use only your other senses to describe the place.

2. Pick two things that are similar in most ways but different in some important ways. Write three one-paragraph comparison and contrasts of these things using each of the patterns shown in Figure 21.3. Which pattern worked best for your comparison and contrast, and why?

3. With your group, create a concept map that classifies the men and women at your university. When you are finished, discuss whether it is possible to appropriately sort people into groups without resorting to stereotypes.

4. In a group or on your own, think of a major problem that your university, community, or nation faces. What are the two to five major causes of this problem? What are the two to five major effects of this problem? Would everyone agree completely with your cause-effect analysis? If not, how would others analyze the issues?

Write
This

1. **Examine something using six basic rhetorical patterns.** Think of something you know well but about which others are unfamiliar. Using the six basic rhetorical patterns (narrative, description, definition, classification, cause and effect, comparison and contrast), help someone who knows little about your topic to understand it.

2. **Find rhetorical patterns on the Internet.** Write a two-page rhetorical analysis of a Web site in which you identify these basic rhetorical patterns and discuss how they are used on the site.

> Go to **MyWritingLab** to complete this chapter's exercises and test your understanding of its objectives.

22

Using Argumentative Strategies

In this chapter, you will learn how to—

`22.1` determine the source and nature of an arguable claim.

`22.2` use reasoning, authority, and emotion to support your argument.

`22.3` identify and avoid logical fallacies.

`22.4` rebut and refute the arguments of others.

For some people, the word *argument* brings up images of fingerpointing, glares, out-bursts, or quiet resentment. Actually, when people behave like this, they really aren't arguing at all. They are quarreling. And, when people quarrel, they are no longer listening to or considering each other's ideas.

An argument is something quite different. Arguments involve making reasonable claims and then backing up those claims with evidence and support. The objective of an argument is not necessarily to "win" or prove that you are right and others are wrong. Instead, your primary goal is to show others that you are *probably* right or that your beliefs are reasonable. When arguing, both sides attempt to convince others that their position is stronger or more beneficial, thus striving for an agreement or compromise.

In college and in the professional world, people use argument to think through ideas and debate uncertainties. Arguments are about getting things done by gaining the cooperation of others. In most situations, an argument is about agreeing as much as disagreeing, about cooperating with others as much as competing with them. Your ability to argue effectively will be an important part of your success in college courses and in your career.

What Is Arguable?

22.1 determine the source and nature of an arguable claim.

Let's begin by first discussing what is "arguable." Some people will say that you can argue about anything. And in a sense, they are right. We *can* argue about anything, no matter how trivial or pointless.

"I don't like chocolate."	"Yes, you do."
"The American Civil War began in 1861."	"No, it didn't."
"It really bugs me when I see a pregnant woman smoking."	"No way. You think that's cool."

These kinds of arguments are rarely worth your time and effort. Of course, we can argue that our friend is lying when she says she doesn't like chocolate, and we can challenge the historical fact that the Civil War really started in 1861. However, debates over *personal judgments,* such as liking or not liking something, quickly devolve into "Yes, I do." "No, you don't!" kinds of quarrels. Meanwhile, debates about *proven facts,* like the year the American Civil War started, can be resolved by consulting a trusted source. To be truly arguable, a claim should exist somewhere between personal judgments and proven facts (Figure 22.1).

Arguable Claims

When laying the groundwork for an argument, you need to first define an arguable claim that you want to persuade your readers to accept as probably true. For example, here are arguable claims on two sides of the same topic:

> **Arguable Claim:** Marijuana should be made a legal medical option in our state because there is overwhelming evidence that marijuana is one of the most effective treatments for pain, nausea, and other symptoms of widespread debilitating diseases, such as multiple sclerosis, cancer, and some kinds of epilepsy.

> **Arguable Claim:** Although marijuana can relieve symptoms associated with certain diseases, it should not become a legal medical option because its medical effectiveness has not been clinically proven and because legalization would send a message that recreational drugs are safe and even beneficial to health.

These claims are "arguable" because neither side can prove that it is factually right or that the other side is factually wrong. Meanwhile, neither side is based exclusively on personal judgments. Instead, both sides want to persuade you, the reader, that they are *probably* right.

When you invent and draft your argument, your goal is to support your position to the best of your ability, but you should also imagine views and viewpoints that disagree with yours. Keeping opposing views in mind will help you to clarify your ideas, generate support, and identify any weaknesses in your argument. Then, when you draft your argument, you will be able to show readers that you have considered both sides fairly.

Personal
Judgments   **Arguable Claims**
                                                              Proven Facts

I don't like   *The American Civil War*
chocolate.   *began in 1861.*

FIGURE 22.1 The Region of Arguable Claims

People can argue about anything, of course. However, "arguable" claims exist somewhere between personal judgments and proven facts.

On the other hand, if you realize that an opposing position does not really exist or that it's very weak, then you may not have an arguable claim in the first place.

Four Sources of Arguable Claims

Once you have a rough idea of your arguable claim, you should refine and clarify it. Arguable claims generally arise from four sources: issues of definition, causation, evaluation, and recommendation (Figure 22.2).

Issues of Definition. Some arguments hinge on how to define an object, event, or person. For example, here are a few arguable claims that debate how to define something:

> Animals, like humans, are sentient beings who have inalienable rights; therefore, killing and eating animals is an unethical act.

> The terrorist acts of September 11, 2001, were an unprovoked act of war, not just a criminal act. Consequently, the United States was justified in declaring war on Al-Qaeda and its ally, the Taliban government of Afghanistan.

> A pregnant woman who smokes is a child abuser who needs to be stopped before she further harms her unborn child.

Issues of Causation. Humans tend to see events in terms of cause and effect. Consequently, people often argue about whether one thing caused another.

> The main cause of boredom is a lack of variety. People become bored when nothing changes in their lives, causing them to lose their curiosity about the people, places, and events around them.

> Advocates of gun control blame the guns when a school shooting happens. Instead, we need to look at the sociological and psychological causes of school violence, such as mental illness, bullying, gang violence, and the shooters' histories of aggression.

> Pregnant mothers who choose to smoke are responsible for an unacceptable number of birth defects in children.

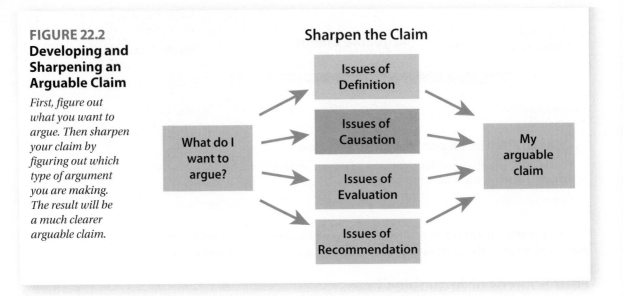

FIGURE 22.2
Developing and Sharpening an Arguable Claim

First, figure out what you want to argue. Then sharpen your claim by figuring out which type of argument you are making. The result will be a much clearer arguable claim.

Sharpen the Claim

What do I want to argue? → Issues of Definition · Issues of Causation · Issues of Evaluation · Issues of Recommendation → My arguable claim

Issues of Evaluation. We also argue about whether something is *good* or *bad, right* or *wrong,* or *better* or *worse.*

> Usually, the "threequel" of a movie series is awful, but *Toy Story 3* is arguably the best animated film of all time with its thrills, heartbreaks, and moments of redemption.

> The current U.S. taxation system is unfair, because the majority of taxes fall most heavily on people who work hard and corporations who are bringing innovative products to the marketplace.

> Although both are dangerous, drinking alcohol in moderation while pregnant is less damaging to an unborn child than smoking in moderation.

Issues of Recommendation. We also use arguments to make recommendations about the best course of action to follow. These kinds of claims are signaled by words like "should," "must," "ought to," and so forth.

> Tompson Industries should convert its Nebraska factory to renewable energy sources, like wind, solar, and geothermal, using the standard electric grid only as a backup supply for electricity.

> The meat industry is heavily subsidized by the American taxpayer; therefore, we recommend removing all subsidies, making vegetarianism a financially viable choice.

> We must help pregnant women to stop smoking by developing smoking-cessation programs that are specifically targeted toward this population.

To refine and sharpen your arguable claim, you should figure out which type of claim you are making, as shown in Figure 22.2. Then revise your claim to fit neatly into one of the four categories.

Using Reason, Authority, and Emotion

Once you have developed an arguable claim, you can start figuring out how you are going to support it. A solid argument will usually employ three types of "proofs": reason, authority, and emotion (Figure 22.3).

22.2 use reasoning, authority, and emotion to support your argument.

Greek rhetoricians like Aristotle originally used the words *logos* (reason), *ethos* (authority), and *pathos* (emotion) to discuss these three proofs.

Reason (*Logos*)

Reasoning involves appealing to your readers' common sense or beliefs.

Logical Statements. Logical statements allow you to use your readers' existing beliefs to prove they should agree with a further claim. Here are some common patterns for logical statements:

If . . . then. "If you believe X, then you should also believe Y."

Either . . . or. "Either you believe X or you believe Y."

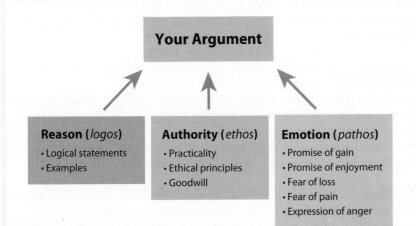

FIGURE 22.3 Three Types of Proofs for Supporting an Argument

Three types of proofs can be used to support an argument: reason, authority, and emotion.

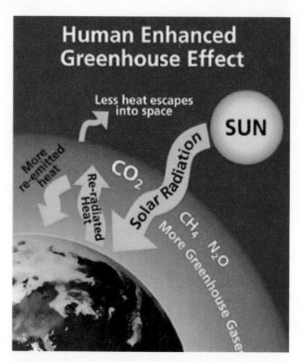

FIGURE 22.4 A Cause and Effect Proof

In this diagram, the causes and effects of the greenhouse effect are explained. Human-added greenhouse gases cause excessive solar radiation to be trapped in the atmosphere. The effect is that the atmosphere grows warmer over time.

Cause and effect. "X causes Y." or "Y is caused by X." (See Figure 22.4.)

Costs and benefits. "The benefits A, B, and C show that doing X is worth the costs."

Better and worse. "X is better than Y." or "X is worse than Y."

Examples. The second type of reasoning, examples, allows you to illustrate your points or demonstrate that a pattern exists.

"For example." "For example, in 1994 . . . ." "For instance, last week . . . ." "To illustrate, there was the interesting case of . . . ." "Specifically, I can name two situations when . . . ."

Personal experiences. "Last summer, I saw . . . ." "Where I work, X happens regularly."

Facts and data. "According to our survey results, ..." "Recently published data show that . . . ."

Patterns of experiences. "X happened in 2004, 2008, and 2012. Therefore, we expect it to happen again in 2016." "In the past, each time X happened, Y has happened also."

Quotes from experts. "Dr. Jennifer Xu, a scientist at Los Alamos National Laboratory, recently stated . . . ." "In his 2013 article, historian George Brenden claimed . . . ."

Authority (*Ethos*)

Authority involves using your own experience or the reputations of others to support your arguments. Another way to strengthen your authority is to demonstrate your practicality, ethical principles, and goodwill (Figure 22.5). These three types of authority were first mentioned by Aristotle as a way to show your readers that you are fair and therefore credible. These strategies still work well today.

Practicality. Show your readers that you are primarily concerned about solving problems and getting things done, not lecturing, theorizing, or simply winning.

Where appropriate, admit that the issue is complicated and cannot be fixed easily. You can also point out that reasonable people can disagree about the issue. Being "practical" involves being realistic about what is possible, not idealistic about what would happen in a perfect world.

Ethical Principles. Demonstrate that you are arguing for an outcome that meets a specific set of ethical principles. An ethical argument can be based on any of three types of ethics:

- *Rights:* Using human rights or constitutional rights to back up your claims.

- *Laws:* Showing that your argument is in line with civic laws.

- *Utilitarianism:* Arguing that your position is more beneficial for the majority.

In some situations, you can demonstrate that your position is in line with your own and your readers' religious beliefs or other deeply held values.

Goodwill. Demonstrate that you have your readers' interests in mind, not just your own. Of course, you may be arguing for something that impacts you personally or something you care about. So show your readers that you care about *their* needs and interests, too. Let them know that you understand their concerns and that your position is fair or a "win-win" for both you and them.

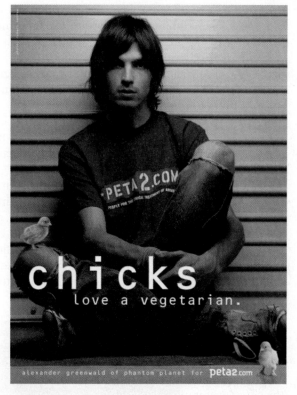

FIGURE 22.5 Building *Ethos*

Celebrities are often used to promote causes and products because they have credibility with the public.

Source: People for the Ethical Treatment of Animals

Emotion (*Pathos*)

Using emotional appeals to persuade your readers is appropriate if the feelings you draw on are suitable for your topic and readers. As you develop your argument, think about how your emotions and those of your readers might influence how their decisions will be made.

Begin by listing the positive and negative emotions that are associated with your topic or with your side of the argument.

Promise of Gain. Demonstrate to your readers that agreeing with your position will help them gain things they need or want, like trust, time, money, love, loyalty, advancement, reputation, comfort, popularity, health, beauty, or convenience.

Promise of Enjoyment. Show that accepting your position will lead to more satisfaction, including joy, anticipation, surprise, pleasure, leisure, or freedom.

Fear of Loss. Suggest that not agreeing with your opinion might cause the loss of things readers value, like time, money, love, security, freedom, reputation, popularity, health, or beauty.

Fear of Pain. Imply that not agreeing with your position will cause feelings of pain, sadness, frustration, humiliation, embarrassment, loneliness, regret, shame, vulnerability, or worry.

Expressions of Anger or Disgust. Show that you share feelings of anger or disgust with your readers about a particular event or situation.

Use positive emotions as much as you can, because they will build a sense of goodwill, loyalty, or happiness in your readers (Figure 22.6). Show readers that your position will bring them respect, gain, enjoyment, or pleasure.

Negative emotions should be used sparingly. Negative emotions can energize your readers or spur them to action (Figure 22.7). However, be careful not to threaten or frighten your readers, because people tend to reject bullying or scare tactics. These moves will undermine your attempts to build goodwill. Any feelings of anger or

FIGURE 22.6
Using Emotions in an Argument

This advertisement uses the emotion of loyalty to persuade its readers.

Source: United States Army. Use of U.S. Department of Defense (DoD) visual information does not imply or constitute DoD endorsement.

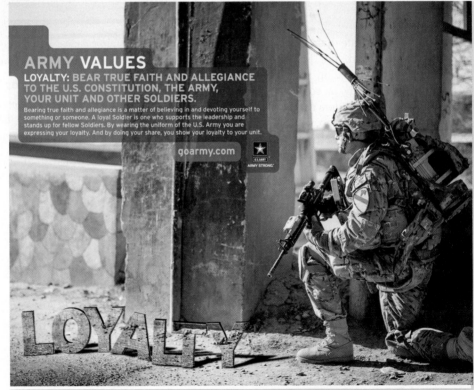

disgust you express in your argument must be shared by your readers, or they will reject your argument as unfair, harsh, or reactionary.

Avoiding Logical Fallacies

A logical fallacy is an error in reasoning. You should avoid logical fallacies in your own writing because they tend to undermine your argument. Plus, they can keep you from gaining a full understanding of the issue because fallacies usually lead to inaccurate or ambiguous conclusions.

22.3 identify and avoid logical fallacies.

Figure 22.8 defines and gives examples of common logical fallacies. Watch out for them in your own arguments. When an opposing viewpoint depends on a logical fallacy, you can point to it as a weakness.

Fallacies tend to occur for three primary reasons:

False or Weak Premises. In these situations, the author is overreaching to make a point. The argument uses false or weak premises (bandwagon, *post hoc* reasoning, slippery slope, or hasty generalization), or it relies on comparisons or authorities that are inappropriate (weak analogy, false authority).

Irrelevance. The author is trying to distract readers by using name calling (*ad hominem*) or bringing up issues that are beside the point (red herring, *tu quoque, non sequitur*).

Ambiguity. The author is clouding the issue by using circular reasoning (begging the question), arguing against a position that no one is defending (straw man), or presenting the reader with an unreasonable choice of options (either/or).

Logical fallacies do not prove that someone is wrong about a topic. They simply mean that the person is using weak or improper reasoning to reach his or her conclusions. In some cases, logical fallacies are used deliberately. For instance, some advertisers want to slip a sales pitch past the audience. Savvy arguers can also use logical fallacies to trip up their opponents. When you learn to recognize these fallacies, you can counter them when necessary.

FIGURE 22.7 Using Emotions in an Argument

This advertisement uses a "fear of loss" emotional appeal to influence readers.

Source: Ferdi Rizkiyanto

Logical Fallacy	Definition	Example
Ad Hominem	Attacking the character of the arguer rather than the argument.	"Mary has no credibility on the smoking ban issue, because she was once a smoker herself."
Bandwagon (*Ad Populum*)	Suggesting that a person should agree to something because it is popular.	"Over one thousand people have decided to sign up, so you should, too."
Begging the Question	Using circular reasoning to prove a conclusion.	"Conservatives believe in hard work and strong values. That's why most Americans are conservative."
Either/Or	Presenting someone with a limited choice, when other choices are possible.	"We either buy this car now, or we spend the rest of the year walking to school."
Straw Man	Arguing against a position that no one is defending.	"Letting children play soccer on a busy highway is wrong, and I won't stand for it."
Weak Analogy	Making an improper comparison between two things that share a common feature.	"Paying taxes to the government is the same as handing your wallet over to a mugger in the park."
Post Hoc Reasoning	Arguing that one event caused another when they are unrelated.	"Each time my roommate is out of town, it causes my car to break down and I can't get to work."
Hasty Generalization	Using a part to make an inaccurate claim about a whole.	"The snowboarder who cut me off proved that all snowboarders are rude."
Slippery Slope	Suggesting that one event will automatically lead to a chain of other events.	"If we allow them to ban assault weapons, soon handguns, rifles, and all other guns will be banned, too."
Red Herring	Saying something that distracts from the issue being argued about.	"Of course, people who live in the suburbs don't believe racism and sexism exist."
False Authority	Defending a claim with a biased or untrustworthy source.	"My mother read my paper, and she thinks it deserves an A."
Non Sequitur	Stating a conclusion that does not follow from the premises.	"Watching *The Big Bang Theory* each week will make you smarter and more popular."
Tu Quoque	Improperly turning an accusation back on the accuser.	"If you cared about global warming, as you claim, you wouldn't have driven a car to this meeting."

FIGURE 22.8 Common Logical Fallacies

Rebuttals and Refutations

Because you will argue *with* others in an effort to gain their understanding and cooperation, you need to understand opposing viewpoints fully. You also need to anticipate how your readers will respond to your claims and your proofs. After all, something that sounds like a good reason to you may not seem as convincing to readers who do not already share your views.

22.4 rebut and refute the arguments of others.

Summarize Your Opponents' Position Objectively

If you're discussing something "arguable," then there must be at least one other side to the issue. Show your readers that you understand those other sides before you offer a rebuttal or counter it. If you ignore the opposing viewpoints, your readers will think either you are unfairly overlooking potential objections or you just don't understand the other side of the argument.

You can show readers that you do understand by summarizing other viewpoints objectively early in your argument. Try to frame their argument in a way that makes your readers say, "Yes, that's a fair and complete description of the opposing position."

Summarizing opposing viewpoints strengthens your argument in three ways. First, it lays out the specific points that you can refute or concede when you explain your own position. Second, it takes away some of your opponents' momentum, because your readers will slow down and consider both sides of the issue carefully. Third, it will demonstrate your goodwill and make you look more reasonable and well informed.

Recognize When the Opposing Position May Be Valid

The opposing viewpoint probably isn't completely wrong. In some situations, other views may be partially valid. For example, let's say you are arguing that the U.S. automobile industry needs to convert completely to manufacturing electric cars within twenty years. Your opponents might argue that this kind of dramatic conversion is not technically or economically feasible.

To show that you are well informed and reasonable, you could name a few situations in which they are correct.

> Converting fully to electric vehicles within twenty years may not be possible in some circumstances. For example, it is unlikely that large trucks, like semitrailers, will be able to run on electricity two decades from now because batteries will not be strong enough to provide the amount of energy required to move their weight for long distances. Furthermore, even if we stopped manufacturing gasoline-powered vehicles immediately, they would still be on the road for decades, and they will require gas stations and spare parts. We cannot, after all, ask all drivers to immediately switch over to electric vehicles, especially if they cannot afford it.

By identifying situations in which the opposing position may be valid, you give some ground to the opposing side while limiting the effectiveness of their major points.

Concede Some of the Opposing Points

When you concede a point, you are acknowledging that some aspects of the opposing viewpoints or objections are valid in a limited way. It's true that you will be highlighting potential weaknesses in your own position but you will strengthen your argument by candidly acknowledging these limitations and addressing them fairly.

For instance, if you were arguing that the federal government should use taxpayer money to help the auto industry develop electric cars, you could anticipate two objections to your argument:

> As X points out, production of electric cars cannot be ramped up quickly because appropriate batteries are not being manufactured in sufficient numbers.

> It is of course true that the United States' electric grid could not handle millions of new electric cars being charged every day.

These objections are important, but they do not undermine your argument entirely. Simply concede that they are problems but demonstrate that they can be fixed or do not matter in the long run.

> It is true that the availability of car batteries and the inadequacy of the United States' electricity grid are concerns. As Stephen Becker, a well-respected consultant to the auto industry, points out, "car manufacturers are already experiencing a shortage of batteries," and there are no plans to build more battery factories in the future (109). Meanwhile, as Lauren King argues, the United States' electric grid "is already fragile, as the blackouts a few years ago showed. And there has been very little done to upgrade our electric-delivery infrastructure." King states that the extra power "required to charge 20 million cars would bring the grid to a grinding halt" (213).
>
> However, there are good reasons to believe that these problems, too, can be dealt with if the right measures are put in place. First, if investors had more confidence that there would be a steady demand for electric cars, and if the government guaranteed loans for new factories, the growing demand for batteries would encourage manufacturers to bring them to market (Vantz, 12). Second, experts have been arguing for years that the United States needs to invest in a *nationalized* electricity grid that will meet our increasing needs for electricity. King's argument that the grid is "too fragile" misses the point. We already need to build a better grid, because the current grid *is* too fragile, even for today's needs. Moreover, it will take years to build a fleet of 20 million cars. During those years, the electric grid can be rebuilt.

By conceding some points, you weaken their effectiveness. By anticipating your readers' doubts or the other side's arguments, you can minimize the challenge to your own argument.

Refute or Absorb Your Opponents' Major Points

In some situations, your opponents will have one or two major points that cannot be conceded without completely undermining your argument. In these situations, you should study each major point to understand why it challenges your own argument. Is there a chance your opponents have a good point? Could your argument be flawed in some fundamental way? Do you need to rethink or modify your claims?

If you still believe your side of the argument is stronger, you have a couple of choices. First, you can refute your opponents' major points by challenging their factual correctness. It helps to look for a "smoking gun" moment in which the opposing side makes a mistake or overstates a claim.

> Critics of electric cars argue that the free market should determine whether electric cars and the infrastructure to support them should be built. They argue that the government should not determine which automotive technologies survive and thrive. However, this kind of argument goes against the historical record. The US government has always been involved in building roads, railways, and airports. For decades, it has given tax breaks to support the manufacturing of gasoline vehicles. We are simply asking for these supports to be shifted in ways that will meet future needs, not the needs of the past.

In other situations, you can absorb your opponents' arguments by suggesting that your position is necessary or is better for the majority.

> The skeptics are correct that the conversion from gasoline cars to electric cars will not be easy and may even be economically painful. At this point, though, we have little choice. Our dependence on foreign oil, which is something we all agree is a problem, is a threat to our economic and political freedom. Moreover, our planet is already experiencing the negative effects of global climate change, which could severely damage the fragile ecosystems on which we depend for food, air, and water. We aren't talking about lifestyle choices at this point. We are talking about survival.

When absorbing opposing points, you should show that you are aware that they are correct but that the benefits of your position outweigh the costs.

Qualify Your Claims

You might be tempted to state your claims in the strongest language possible, perhaps even overstating them.

Overstatement. The government must use its full power to force the auto industry to develop and build affordable electric cars for the American consumer. The payoff in monetary and environmental benefits will more than pay for the investment.

Qualified Statement. Although many significant challenges must be dealt with, the government should begin taking steps to encourage the auto industry to develop and build affordable electric cars for the American consumer. The payoff in monetary and environmental impact could very well pay for the effort and might even pay dividends.

When qualifying your claims and other points, you are softening your position a little. This softening gives readers the sense that they are being asked to make up their own minds. Few people want to be told that they "must" do something or "cannot" do something else. If possible, you want to avoid pushing your readers into making an either/or, yes/no kind of decision, because they may reject your position altogether.

Instead, remember that all arguments have gray areas. No one side is absolutely right or wrong. Qualifying your claims allows you to show your readers that your position has some flexibility. You can use the following words and phrases to qualify your claims:

unless	would	in all probability
except	perhaps	usually
if	maybe	frequently
even though	reasonably	probably
not including	plausibly	possibly
aside from	in most circumstances	conceivably
in some cases	almost certainly	often
although	most likely	may
could	if possible	might
should		

You can also soften your claims by acknowledging that you are aware of the difficulties and limitations of your position. Your goal is to argue reasonably while strongly advocating for your side of the argument.

Here are some strategies for becoming more effective at argument.

DEVELOP an "Arguable Claim"

An arguable claim is a statement that exists between personal judgments and proven facts. It should also be a claim that others would be willing to dispute.

IDENTIFY the Source of Your Arguable Claim

Arguable claims tend to emerge from four types of issues: issues of definition, causation, evaluation, and recommendation. You can sharpen your claim by figuring out what kind of issue you are arguing about.

FIND Reason-Based Proof to Back Up Your Claims

Reasoning (*logos*) consists of using logical statements and examples to support your arguments.

LOCATE Authoritative Support to Back Up Your Claims

You can use your own experience if you are an expert, or you can draw quotes from other experts who agree with you. You should also build up your authority (*ethos*) by demonstrating your practicality, ethical principles, and goodwill toward readers.

USE Emotional Proofs to Back Up Your Claims

Identify any emotions (*pathos*) that shape how your readers will be influenced by your argument. You can use promise of gain, promise of enjoyment, fear of loss, fear of pain, and expressions of anger and disgust to influence them.

AVOID Logical Fallacies

Look for logical fallacies in your argument and locate them in the opposing position's arguments. A logical fallacy is a weak spot that should be addressed in your own work and can be exploited as you counter the opposing sides' arguments.

COUNTER the Claims of the Opposing View

There are a variety of ways to counter or weaken the opposing argument through rebuttal and refutation including (a) summarizing the position objectively, (b) identifying limited situations in which the opposing position may be valid, (c) conceding your opponents' minor points, (d) refuting or absorbing your opponents' major points, and (e) qualifying your claims.

Talk About This

1. With a group of people from your class, talk about how you usually argue with your friends and family. When are arguments productive? At what point do they become quarrels?

2. Discuss whether each of the following claims is "arguable." Explain why each is or is not arguable. For claims that are not arguable, alter them enough to make them arguable.

   a. I much prefer reading on a tablet or computer rather than from a book.

   b. Childhood obesity is one of the most important issues facing the United States.

   c. The increase in school violence and bullying is due to the popularity of violent video games.

3. With your group, identify five reasons why arguing can be useful, productive, and even entertaining.

Try This Out

1. On the Internet, find a fairly short opinion article about an issue that interests you. Identify its main claim and determine which kind of proof (*logos, ethos,* or *pathos*) is most dominant.

2. Find three different Web sites that attempt to persuade people to stop smoking. Compare and contrast their argument strategies. In a presentation, show why you think one Web site is more persuasive than the others.

3. With a group of three or four people from your class, divide up the list of fallacies in Figure 22.8 (on page 410). Then find or create examples of these fallacies. Share your examples with other groups in your class.

Write This

1. **Generate four claims and four counterclaims.** Choose an issue that you care about and develop an "arguable claim" from each of the sources of arguable claims discussed in this chapter (i.e., definition, causation, evaluation, recommendation). Then, for each of these arguable claims, develop a counterclaim that an opposing arguer might use against your positions.

2. **Find the fallacies in an advertisement.** Find an advertisement on television or on YouTube that uses one or more logical fallacies to support its points. In a two-page ad critique, draw attention to the logical fallacies and use them as weak spots to undermine the advertisement.

> Go to **MyWritingLab** to complete this chapter's exercises and test your understanding of its objectives.

23

Collaborating
and Peer Response

In this chapter, you will learn how to—

23.1 work successfully with peers and workplace colleagues in groups.

23.2 work successfully in teams by doing good planning and managing conflict.

23.3 use peer response to offer and receive helpful feedback.

In college and throughout your career, your ability to work in teams will be an important asset. With a team, you can combine your ideas and personal strengths with the ideas and strengths of others, so you can be more creative and take on larger and more complex projects. Plus, working in a team can be satisfying and fun.

Collaborating with others is also useful at every stage of the writing process. Early in the writing process, you and your team can brainstorm ideas, work on outlines, and do research together. Later, you can help each other improve the organization, style, and design of your drafts. And when your papers are almost finished, you can use *peer-response* strategies to edit each other's work and offer useful suggestions for improvement.

In advanced classes and the workplace, computers and the Internet have made working in teams a common and essential part of writing. You probably already use social networking, e-mail, texting, mobile phones, and tablets to keep in touch with your friends and family. In your career, you will use these tools to interact with your colleagues and clients, whether you are collaborating face to face or working together in virtual meetings.

Your professors and supervisors will ask you to work collaboratively in three ways:

- **Group Work**—In college classes, you will be asked to discuss readings in groups, work on in-class group activities, and update each other about your current projects. In the workplace, groups often meet to share information, brainstorm, and develop new products and services.

- **Team Work**—In college and the workplace, you will work with teams on larger projects, submitting one document or project for the whole team (Figure 23.1).

- **Peer Response and Document Cycling**—In small groups, you will need to revise, edit, and proofread the writing of others, giving them advice and suggestions for improvement. In the workplace, peer response is called "document cycling" because important texts are routed through multiple people at the organization for revision, editing, and proofreading.

To this point in your academic life, you have mostly been asked to write alone and hand in work you completed by yourself. So, writing alone probably feels normal. However, in your career, you will need to write and edit with others in teams. In surveys, employers rate the ability to "work well in teams" as one of the most important skills they are looking for in new employees. College is a good time to develop those collaboration skills.

Working Successfully in Groups

23.1 work successfully with peers and workplace colleagues in groups.

In college, you will be working in small groups regularly. Your professors will ask you and a group of other students to:

- Discuss readings

- Generate new ideas for projects

- Offer feedback on the ideas and works of others

- Work together on in-class tasks and assignments

Group meetings are also important in the workplace. Weekly and sometimes daily, work groups will meet in person or virtually to brainstorm new concepts, discuss current progress, share concerns, and solve everyday problems.

In the workplace, your role will usually be defined by your position at the company, but in college classes your role in a group isn't always clear. So, choosing roles up front helps members sort out who is doing what. Here are some common roles:

Facilitator. The facilitator is responsible for keeping the group moving forward. The facilitator's main job is to keep the group on task, making sure that everyone has a chance to contribute. When the group goes off on a tangent or becomes distracted, the facilitator should remind the group members what they are trying to achieve and how much time is left to complete the task. If a member of the group has not said much, the facilitator should make room for that person to contribute.

Scribe. The scribe takes notes on what the group discusses or decides. These notes should be reviewed periodically, helping everyone remember what has been talked

FIGURE 23.1 Working Collaboratively in College and Career

Whether collaborating face to face or virtually, the ability to work with others is essential.

about and decided. The scribe may also check in with the group to ensure that the notes accurately and completely reflect the decisions that were made.

Spokesperson. The spokesperson is responsible for reporting about the group's progress to the class or professor. While the group is discussing a reading or doing an activity, the spokesperson should take notes and think about what she or he is going to say to the class.

Innovator. The innovator should feel free to come up with new and unique ideas that allow the group to see the issue from other perspectives. The innovator should look for ways to be creative and different, even if he or she might suggest something that the rest of the group will resist or reject.

Designated Skeptic. The designated skeptic's job is to help the group resist group-think and push beyond simplistic responses to the issues under discussion. The skeptic should bring up concerns that a critic might use to raise doubts about what the group members have decided.

These roles can be combined. For instance, one person might serve as both the scribe and designated skeptic. These roles should also be rotated throughout the semester so that everyone has a chance to be a facilitator, scribe, spokesperson, innovator, and skeptic.

Working Successfully in Teams

23.2 work successfully in teams by doing good planning and managing conflict.

Teaming involves working collaboratively on a project that you and others will hand in together. Working with a team allows you to take on larger, more complex projects, while blending your unique abilities with those of others.

But, let's just admit something up front. Working in teams doesn't always work out. Sometimes, slackers don't get their work done. Sometimes, members of your team waste time chatting about what they are doing this weekend. One member keeps checking his phone for text messages. In some cases, you end up doing more than your share of the work, and that can be frustrating.

There are slackers out there, even in the workplace, but most people want to do their best and want to do their share of the work. When groups don't work well, it's usually because the team doesn't have a plan and people don't know what they are supposed to do. That's why successful groups need to spend some time up front planning out the project and defining each person's role. Only then are they able to get down to work.

Planning the Project

During the planning phase, you and your team members should set goals, figure out the deadlines, and divide up the work. While planning, you should also talk about how you are going to resolve any disagreements that will arise during the project.

One helpful way to plan a team project is to use the "Four Stages of Teaming" developed by management guru Bruce Tuckman (Figure 23.2). Tuckman noticed that teams tend to go through four stages when working on a project:

Forming. Getting to know each other, defining goals and outcomes, setting deadlines, and dividing up the work.

Storming. Experiencing disagreements, sensing tension and anxiety, doubting the leadership, facing conflict, and feeling uncertain and frustrated.

Norming. Developing consensus, revising the project's goals, refining expectations of outcomes, solidifying team roles.

Performing. Sharing a common vision, delegating tasks, feeling empowered, and resolving conflicts and differences in constructive ways.

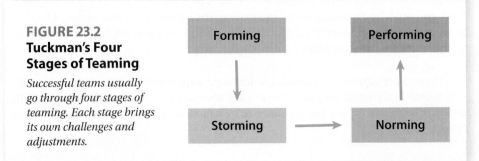

FIGURE 23.2
Tuckman's Four Stages of Teaming

Successful teams usually go through four stages of teaming. Each stage brings its own challenges and adjustments.

The secret to working in teams is recognizing that these stages are foreseeable and almost predictable—including the storming stage. Good planning helps teams work through these stages effectively.

Forming: Setting Goals, Getting Organized

When a new team is formed, the members should first get to know each other and discuss the expectations of the project.

Hold a Planning Meeting. At a planning meeting, do some or all of the following:

- Ask all team members to introduce themselves
- Define the purpose of the project and its goals
- Describe the expected outcomes of the project
- Identify the strengths and interests of each team member
- Divide up the work
- Create a project calendar and set deadlines
- Agree on how conflicts will be solved when they arise (because they will)

Choose Team Responsibilities. Each member of the team should take on a specific role on the project. When working on a project, your group might consider assigning these four roles:

Coordinator. This person is responsible for maintaining the project schedule and running the meetings. The coordinator is not the "boss." Rather, she or he is responsible for keeping people in touch and maintaining the project schedule.

Researchers. One or two group members should be assigned to collect information. They are responsible for digging up material at the library, running searches on the Internet, and coordinating any empirical research.

Editor. The editor is responsible for the organization and style of the document. He or she identifies missing content and places where the document needs to be reorganized. The editor is also responsible for creating a consistent voice, or style, in the document.

Designer. The designer sketches out how the document will look, gathers images from the Internet, creates graphs and charts, and takes photographs.

Notice that there is no "writer" in this list. Everyone on your team should be responsible for writing a section or two of the document. Everyone should also be responsible for reading and responding to the sections written by others.

Storming: Managing Conflict

Conflicts will happen. They are a normal part of any team project, so you need to learn how to manage any conflicts that come up. In fact, professors divide classes into teams because they want you to learn how to manage conflict in constructive ways. Here are some strategies and tips for managing conflict:

Run Efficient Meetings. Before each meeting, the coordinator should list what will happen, what will be achieved, and when the meeting will end. In the workplace, this list of meeting topics is called an "agenda." At the end of each meeting, each team member should state what she or he will do on the project before the next meeting. Write those commitments down and hold people to them.

Encourage Participation from Everyone. During each meeting, each team member should have an opportunity to contribute ideas and opinions. No one should be allowed to sit back and leave the decisions to others. If a team member is not participating, the coordinator should ask that person to offer his or her opinion.

Allow Dissent (Even Encourage it). Everyone should feel welcome to disagree or offer alternative ideas for consideration. In fact, dissent should be encouraged, because it often leads to new and better ways of completing the project. If team members are agreeing on everything too easily, you might ask, "What would a critic or skeptic say about our project?" "How might someone else do this project?"

Mediate Conflicts. People will become irritated and even angry with each other. When conflicts surface, give each side time to think through and state their position. Then identify the two to five issues that the sides disagree about. Rank these issues from most important to least. Address each of these issues separately, and try to negotiate a solution to the conflict.

Motivate the Slackers. Slackers can kill the momentum of a team and undermine its ability to finish the project. If someone is slacking, your team should make your expectations clear to that person as soon as possible. Often, slackers simply need a straightforward list of tasks to complete, along with clear deadlines. If a slacker refuses to participate, you might ask the professor to intervene or even to remove that person from the team.

Always remember that conflict is normal and inevitable in teams. When you see conflict developing in your team, remind yourself that the team is just going through the storming stage of the teaming process (that's a good thing). While in college, you should practice managing these kinds of uncomfortable situations so you can better handle them in your career.

Norming: Getting Down to Work

Soon after the storming stage, your team will enter the norming stage. Norming gives your group an opportunity to refine the goals of the project and complete the majority of the work.

Revise Project Goals and Expected Outcomes. At a meeting or in a Web conference, your team should look back at the original goals and outcomes you listed during the planning stage. Sharpen your goals and clarify what your team will accomplish by the end of the project.

Adjust Team Responsibilities. Your team should redistribute the work so the burden is shared fairly among team members. Doing so will raise the morale of the group and allow the work to get finished by the deadline. Also, if everyone feels the workload is fairly divided, your team will usually avoid slipping back into the storming stage.

Revise the Project Calendar. Unexpected challenges and setbacks have probably already put your team a little behind schedule, so spend some time working out some new deadlines. These dates will need to be firmer than the ones you set in the forming stage because you are getting closer to the final deadline.

Use Online Collaborative Tools. You can't always meet face to face, so you should agree to work together online. Online collaborative sites such as *Google Docs* allow team members to view the document's editing history, revert to previous versions of a document, and even work on the same document simultaneously. A voice connection is helpful when you are working on a document together.

Keep in Touch with Each Other. Depending on the project deadline, your group should be in touch with each other daily. Texting, social networking, and e-mailing work well for staying connected. If you aren't hearing regularly from someone, call, text, or e-mail that person. Regular contact will help keep the project moving forward.

Performing: Working as a Team

Performing usually occurs when teams are together for a long time, so it's rare that a team in a one-semester class will reach the performing stage. During this stage, each team member recognizes the others' talents, abilities, and weaknesses. While performing, your team is doing more than just trying to finish the project. At this point, everyone on the team is looking for ways to improve how the work is getting done, leading to higher-quality results (and more satisfaction among team members).

This is as much as we are going to say about performing. Teams usually need to be together for several months or even years before they reach this stage. If your team in a college class reaches the performing stage, that's fantastic. If not, that's fine, too. The performing stage is a goal you should work toward in your advanced classes and in your career, but it's not typical in a college writing course.

Using Peer Response to Improve Your Writing

Peer response is one of the most common forms of collaboration in college. By sharing drafts of your work with others, you can receive useful feedback while also helping yourself and others succeed on the assignment. Critiquing others' drafts will help you improve your own writing skills because you will be able to see what works and doesn't work in the writing of others.

23.3 use peer response to offer and receive helpful feedback.

Types of Peer Response and Document Cycling

Peer response can be used at any stage during the writing process but it usually happens after a good draft has been completed. The most common peer response strategies include:

Rubric-Centered Editing The professor provides the rubric that he or she will be using to evaluate the paper. In groups of three or four, responders use the rubric to highlight places where their peers' drafts can be improved. In some cases, your professor might ask you to score each other's papers according to the rubric.

Analysis with a Worksheet The professor provides a worksheet that uses targeted questions to draw the responders' attention to key features of the paper (Figure 23.3). The worksheet will often ask responders to highlight and critique specific parts of the paper, such as the thesis sentence and topic sentences in paragraphs.

Read-Aloud In a group of three to four people, the draft's author stays silent as another person reads the draft out loud. The others in the group listen and take notes about what they hear. Then the members of the group discuss the draft's strengths—while the author stays silent—and make suggestions for improvement. Afterward, the author can respond to the group's comments and ask follow-up questions.

Round Robin A draft of the paper is left on a desk or on a computer screen. Then, readers rotate every 15–20 minutes to a new desk or workstation, offering written suggestions for improving each paper. At the end of the class, each paper will have received comments from three or more different readers. *Hint: In a computer classroom, the "Review" function of a word processor is a great way to add comments in the margins of papers.*

Document Cycling Each paper is shared through a common storage site like *Google Drive* or *Dropbox* or it is sent to two or three other people via e-mail. Each person is then responsible for offering critiques of two or three papers from other members of the group.

Keep in mind that peer response isn't just about helping others improve their papers. By paying attention to what works and doesn't work in the writing of others, you will improve your own skills.

Responding Helpfully During Peer Response

While offering a peer response, you are engaging with both the paper and the author. Here are five guidelines to follow when responding to someone else's draft:

Peer Response Worksheet for _____

Writer's Name _____　　**Reader's Name** _____

Each paper will be read and reviewed by two readers. Reader A will focus on three issues/concerns that the author wants him/her to focus on. Reader B will respond to the questions under "Response from Reader B."

From the Author to Reader A: Please read my draft and look for—

1. _____
2. _____
3. _____

From Reader A to the Author: Here's what I noticed—

1. _____
2. _____
3. _____

Response From Reader B

1. Read the introduction and conclusion together. Underline the thesis statements in both. Then, read the whole paper one time through without marking anything. How well are the thesis statements articulating the paper's main argument?

   Here's what you did well:

   Here's how I would improve your thesis sentences:

2. Read through the draft and underline the topic sentence of each paragraph. Write a comment about the topic sentences and the supporting evidence used in each paragraph. In general, how well are the topic sentences working in this argument?

   Here's what you did well:

   Here's how I would improve your topic sentences:

3. Read through the draft paying special attention to style. Mark the places where the author's voice seems especially effective and clear. Also, mark the places where the author's voice changes or seems less effective or unclear. In general, describe the strengths of the author's voice and the places that need improvement.

   Here's what you did well:

   Here's how I would improve your style:

4. Look at the paper's use of images, graphs, charts, and visual design. In what ways has the author used visual elements effectively to make the text more engaging and meaningful? What visuals or design features could be added or changed?

   Here's what you did well:

   Here's how I would improve your document's visual features:

FIGURE 23.3 Sample Peer Response Worksheet

Your professor may guide your responses with a worksheet like this one, which asks you to focus on specific issues. In this worksheet, there is a place for the author to request specific kinds of feedback.

Guideline One: Read the Entire Paper Before Responding. First, you should gain a sense of the whole paper before offering comments to the author. You can take notes while you are reading the draft for the first time, but refrain from inserting comments until a second reading. That way, you can respond to the most important issues in the paper rather than reacting sentence by sentence. A few broader suggestions for improvement are always better than several scattered or disjointed comments about usage, grammar, and typos.

Guideline Two: Read Like a Reader. Read the paper again. This time, you should "read like a reader," responding to each paragraph as a normal reader would. Write a comment next to each paragraph, describing how the text is affecting you. To avoid sounding too negative, use "I" or "me" in your comments rather than "you" or "this." For example, you might write first-person comments such as, "I like this straightforward claim" or "The meaning of this sentence isn't clear to me." Avoid writing comments directed at the author like, "You aren't making sense in this paragraph," or "This is confusing."

Guideline Three: Identify Strengths as Well as Weaknesses. Always try to balance criticism with praise and advice. Of course it's your job to help other writers identify what is not working in their papers and what is unclear. Keep in mind, though, that it's just as important to highlight what works well. Explain what you liked and didn't like, what you agreed with and disagreed with, what came through clearly and what you found confusing and or undeveloped.

Guideline Four: Offer Specific Criticism and Advice. Every comment should be directed toward a specific sentence or paragraph. If you are making a suggestion for improvement, start out by explaining why something doesn't work. Then, follow through with specific strategies for solving the problem. No matter how polite you are, a vague comment won't help a writer improve his or her draft. So, be as specific as possible about what could be improved.

Guideline Five: Use Genre and Writing-Specific Terminology. In this class and this book, you are learning a set of helpful terms about genres and writing that you and your classmates share. Use those terms to frame your responses. That way, you and the others will use a common vocabulary to talk about how to improve drafts.

Students and even workplace colleagues sometimes hesitate to offer honest critiques of others' writing. They are concerned about hurting another person's feelings or giving bad advice. In truth, your classmates would rather receive your honest feedback and do well on an assignment than hear your praise and then do poorly.

If you are uncomfortable or unsure about giving advice, try this trick: Say, "This is good, and here's how I would make it better." In other words, start out by reassuring the author that the paper is interesting and valued. Then, offer some ideas about how you would improve it. Framing your comments in terms of "improvement" will give both you and the author more confidence.

Here are some useful strategies and tips that will help you succeed on collaborative activities like group work, teaming, and peer response.

UNDERSTAND the Value of Collaboration

At all stages in the writing process, from invention to proofreading, collaborating with peers allows you to see your ideas through the eyes of others, combine your skills, and handle larger and more complex projects.

CHOOSE Group Member Roles

A group works best when each person plays a specific role. Some common roles include facilitator, scribe, spokesperson, innovator, and designated skeptic.

PLAN the Team Project

While forming, hold a planning meeting and have each team member choose his or her responsibilities on the project.

WORK Through Any Conflicts

When the team reaches the storming phase, work on running good meetings, encouraging participation from everyone, allowing dissent, mediating conflict, and motivating any slackers.

USE Online Tools for Virtual Collaboration

For small-group work, peer response, and team writing, there are many free and easy-to-use tools, such as *Google Docs* and *Dropbox*. The ability to use these tools effectively has become an essential skill for college and the workplace.

USE Peer Response to Improve Your Writing

By sharing and reviewing drafts, you and your peers can help each other improve the papers you are working on. By learning to respond meaningfully to others' writing, you will develop your ability to identify writing problems and improve your own skills.

RESPOND to Peers' Writing in Helpful Ways

Writers will gain the greatest benefit from your responses when you offer respectful and specific criticism that notes both strengths and weaknesses and offers suggestions for improvement.

1. With a group in class, discuss the positive and negative experiences you have had while working in groups or teams. Consider experiences in school and other settings, such as sports, clubs, and other organizations. Identify two or three specific problems that can make a collaborative project go badly. Then, identify two or three ways members can get a project back on track.

2. In your group, each person should discuss an instance when someone tried to offer him or her advice that ended up being unhelpful, or even making things worse. As a group, identify three kinds of advice that are unhelpful or harmful. Then, describe three or four ways that advice givers and advice receivers can provide and accept better advice.

3. With your group, discuss some of the qualities of a successful competitive team. How do the leaders of the team behave? How do the others on the team contribute? How do the team members resolve conflicts and disagreements?

1. Use the Internet to research the career field you want to enter. Then, list five ways you will need to use collaborative skills to be successful in your chosen career path. Write a brief report in which you discuss the kinds of collaborative projects that happen in your field.

2. With a team of people in your class, pick a topic that you are all interested in. Then, in less than an hour, put together a visual report on that topic. While your team is working, pay attention to how each person contributes to the project. Before your next class, each person in the group should write two to three brief paragraphs describing (a) what happened, (b) what went well, and (c) what could have gone better. Compare experiences with your team members.

3. Research the future of virtual offices, telecommuting, and teleworking. In a brief report, explain how new media and technology will change the way people communicate and collaborate. Describe how people in your career path will work collaboratively in the future with new media.

1. **Imagine that your classroom is a virtual workplace.** With a group in your class, come up with ways you could convert your class into a completely virtual workplace (i.e., you only meet through the Internet or by phone). Then, write a brief proposal for restructuring the classroom as a virtual workplace. How would lectures be given? How would group discussions work? How would papers be submitted, graded, and returned? In your report, explain both the positive and negative aspects that would result from this kind of change and finally explain whether the change would be a good idea overall.

2. **Use an online collaborative tool for peer response.** For the paper you are working on right now, use a file-sharing service like *Google Drive* or *Dropbox* to share documents online with at least two other people in your class. Read the papers and respond to them online. Write an e-mail to your instructor in which you describe how the peer response session went and some of the ways these kinds of file-sharing sites might make classwork and workplace collaboration easier (or perhaps harder).

> Go to **My**WritingLab to complete this chapter's exercises and test your understanding of its objectives.

Starting Your Research

In this chapter, you will learn how to—

24.1 develop your own dependable "research process" that will help you inquire into topics that interest you.

24.2 assess whether sources are reliable and trustworthy.

24.3 devise a "research plan" for your project that allows you to stay on schedule and keep track of sources and evidence.

Research allows you to systematically explore topics by collecting factual evidence, consulting secondary sources, and using your hands-on experiences. Research allows you to do three important things in college and the workplace:

- **Inquire:** You can gather evidence to investigate an issue and explain it to other people.

- **Acquire knowledge:** You can collect and analyze facts to increase or strengthen your knowledge about a subject. In some cases, research can allow you to add knowledge to what is already known.

- **Support an argument:** You can use research to persuade others and support a particular side of an argument while gaining a full understanding of the opposing view.

Doing research requires more than simply finding books or articles that agree with your preexisting opinion. It also requires you to look beyond the first page of hits from an Internet search engine like *Google*. Instead, research is about pursuing the truth and developing knowledge, whether the facts agree with your opinion or not.

In this chapter, you will learn how to develop your own *research process*. A dependable research process allows you to write and speak with authority, because you will be more confident about the evidence you collect and the reliability of your sources. Following a consistent research process will save you time while helping you find more useful and trustworthy sources of evidence.

Starting Your Research Process

A reliable research process, as shown in Figure 24.1, is "recursive," which means the researcher collects evidence and then repeatedly tests it against a *working thesis*. This cyclical process ends when the working thesis fits the evidence you collected.

24.1 develop your own dependable "research process" that will help you inquire into topics that interest you.

Step One: Define Your Research Question

Your research question identifies specifically what you want to discover about your topic. Name your topic and then write down a question your research will try to answer:

Topic: The anti-vaccine movement in the United States.

Research Question: Why are some people, including celebrities, choosing not to vaccinate their kids against common illnesses like measles, mumps, and whooping cough?

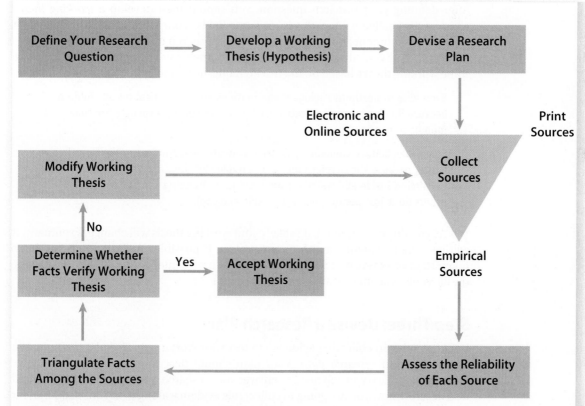

FIGURE 24.1 Following a Research Process

A reliable research process will save you time and energy. Each source you collect will lead you to other sources. Keep looping until you collect the evidence you need to draft your paper.

Topic: The oddity of wearing shorts and flip-flops in wintertime.

Research Question: Why do some college students wear shorts and flip-flops in the middle of the winter?

Once you have drafted a research question, you should spend some time sharpening it to a topic that you can answer in a college-length paper. The research questions mentioned above, for example, are too broad for a typical college paper. Here are sharper versions of those questions:

> Is the anti-vaccine movement a real national threat, or is it primarily a problem for people who live in places like California with dense populations and many unvaccinated people?

> Why do some students at Falls County Community College always wear shorts and flip-flops, even in the middle of the winter?

Step Two: Develop a Working Thesis

After defining your research question, you should then develop a *working thesis*, which is also called a "hypothesis" in some fields. Your working thesis is your best guess at this moment about the answer to your research question.

Try to boil your thesis statement down to one sentence. For example, here are some working theses based on the research questions above:

> Even here in northern Michigan, vaccinations are still critical for all children because illnesses spread quickly over the winter since we spend more time indoors in confined spaces.

> Some Falls County Community College students wear shorts and flip-flops in the winter because they prefer light, comfortable clothing, and they can keep warm by staying inside and walking from building to building across campus, but others do it just because it's fashionable and cool.

As you do your research, it is likely your working thesis will change. Eventually, it will become the main claim for your project. If possible, boil your working thesis down to one sentence. If you require two or three sentences to state your working thesis, your topic may be too complex or broad.

Step Three: Devise a Research Plan

Before you begin collecting evidence to test your working thesis, take some time to sketch out your *research plan*. Your plan should describe the kinds of evidence, including sources, you will need to answer your research question. Your plan should also describe how you are going to collect this evidence along with your deadlines for finding sources. A typical research plan has these elements:

- Research question
- Working thesis

- Description of available sources about the topic, including print and electronic sources
- Schedule for conducting and completing the research
- Bibliography

Creating a research plan will save you time by helping you identify the evidence you need and streamline your research.

Doing Start-Up Research

Now that you have figured out your research question, working thesis, and research plan, you're ready to start tracking down evidence and collecting sources. Some researchers find it helpful to begin by doing an hour of "start-up" research. This kind of research will help you to gain an overall view of the topic, figure out its various sides, and identify the kinds of sources available.

In Chapter 25, "Finding Sources and Collecting Evidence," we will talk about doing formal research, which is much more targeted and structured than start-up research. For now, though, let's look at some good ways to do start-up research:

Search the Internet. Put your research question or its keywords into *Google, Yahoo!, Bing,* or *Ask.com.* See what pops up. Jot down notes about the kinds of evidence you find. Identify some of the major issues and people involved with your topic and take note of any key sources of evidence that you might want to look up later. Bookmark any Web sites that seem especially useful.

Look Through Online Encyclopedias. Major online encyclopedias include *Wikipedia, MSN Encarta,* and *Encyclopaedia Britannica Online.* Again, note the major issues and people involved with your topic. Identify key terms and any controversies about your topic.

One note: Professors probably won't let you cite online encyclopedias like *Wikipedia* or *Encyclopaedia Britannica* as authoritative sources, because the entries are often written anonymously or by non-experts. Nevertheless, online encyclopedias are useful for gaining a quick overview of your topic and finding sources that are authoritative.

Search Your Library's Catalog. Use the online catalog to search for materials available in your campus library. Write down the names of any authors and titles that look like they might be helpful. In some cases, your library's catalog can e-mail your selections to you.

Start-up research should take you an hour or less. Your goal is to gain an overall sense of your topic, not form your final opinion. Keep your options open and don't become too occupied by one source or perspective.

Assessing a Source's Reliability

All information is not created equal. Some people who claim to be "authorities" can be wrongheaded or even dishonest. In some situations, people who have agendas or biases stretch the truth or selectively use facts to support their positions. To assess the reliability of your sources, consider these questions:

24.2 assess whether sources are reliable and trustworthy.

FIGURE 24.2
Using Online Sources for Start-Up Research

Even though popular Web sites like eHow are not always authoritative, they are helpful for start-up research because they can help you understand trends, identify different sides of the issue, and locate sources.

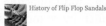

Is the Source Credible?

To determine whether a source's author and publisher are trustworthy, you should use an Internet search engine to check out their backgrounds and expertise. If you cannot find further information about the author or publisher—or if you find questionable credentials or reputations—you should look for other sources that are more credible.

Is the Source Up to Date?

Depending on your topic, sources can quickly become obsolete. In some fields, like cancer research, a source that is only a few years old might already be out of date. In other fields, like geology or history, data that is decades old might still be relevant today. So pay attention to how rapidly the field is changing. Consult your professor or a research librarian about whether a source should be considered up to date.

How Biased Are the Author and the Publisher?

All sources have some bias because authors and publishers have their own ideas and opinions. When you are assessing the bias of a source, consider how much the author or publisher *wants* the evidence to be true. If it seems like the author or publisher would only accept one kind of answer from the outset (e.g., "climate change is a liberal conspiracy"), the evidence should be considered too biased to be reliable. On the other hand, if the author and publisher were open to a range of possible conclusions, you can feel more confident about using the source.

Can You Verify the Evidence in the Source?

You should be able to confirm your source's evidence by consulting other, independent sources. If just one source offers a specific piece of evidence, you should treat it as unverified and use it cautiously, if at all. If multiple sources offer the same or similar kinds of evidence, then you can rely on those sources with much more confidence.

How Biased Are You?

As a researcher, you need to keep your own biases in mind as you assess your sources. Try viewing your sources from alternative perspectives, even perspectives you disagree with. Knowing your own biases and seeing the issue from other perspectives will help you gain a richer understanding of your topic.

Evaluating Your Sources: A Checklist

☐ Is the source reliable and credible?

☐ Is the source up to date?

☐ How biased are the author and the publisher?

☐ Can you independently verify the evidence in the source?

☐ How biased are you?

Managing Your Research Process

When you finish your start-up research, you should have enough information to finalize a schedule for completing your research. At this point, you should also start a bibliographic file to help keep track of your sources.

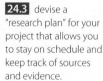

24.3 devise a "research plan" for your project that allows you to stay on schedule and keep track of sources and evidence.

Finalizing a Research Schedule

You might find "backward planning" helpful when finalizing your research schedule. Backward planning means working backward from the deadline to today, filling in all the tasks that need to be accomplished. Here's how to do it:

1. On your screen or a piece of paper, list all the tasks you need to complete.

2. On your calendar, mark a final deadline for finishing your research. Then, fill in your deadlines for drafting, designing, and revising your project.

3. Work backwards from your research deadline, filling in the tasks you need to accomplish and identifying the days on which each task needs to be completed.

Online calendars like those from *Google, Mozilla,* or *Yahoo!* are great tools for creating research schedules. A low-tech paper calendar still works well, too.

Starting Your Bibliography File

One of the first tasks on your research schedule should be to set up a file on your computer that holds a working bibliography of the sources you find. Each time you find a useful source, add it to your bibliography file.

As you collect each source, record all the information for a full bibliographic citation (you will learn how to cite sources in Chapters 27, "Using MLA Style," and 28, "Using APA Style").

Following and Modifying Your Research Plan

You should expect to modify your research plan as you move forward with the project. In some cases, you will find yourself diverted from your research plan by interesting facts, ideas, and events that you didn't know about when you started. That's fine. Let the facts guide your research, even if they take you in unexpected directions.

Also, check in regularly with your research question and working thesis to make sure you are not drifting too far away from your original idea for the project. In some cases, you might need to adjust your research question and working thesis to fit some of the sources or new issues you have discovered.

When Things Don't Go as Expected

Research is a process of inquiry—of exploring, testing, and discovering. You are going to encounter ideas and issues that will require you to modify your approach, research question, or working thesis. Expect the unexpected, make the changes, and then move forward.

Roadblocks to Research. You may not be able to get access to all the sources you had planned on using. For example, you might find that the expert you wanted to interview is unavailable, or that the book you needed is checked out or missing from the library, or that you simply cannot find the data or evidence you expected to find. Don't give up. Instead, modify your approach and move around the roadblock.

Evidence and Ideas That Change Your Working Thesis. You might find something unexpected that completely changes how you view your topic. For instance, the evidence you collect might not support your working thesis after all. Or, you might find that a different, more focused working thesis is more interesting to you or relevant for your audience. Rather than getting distracted or disappointed, consider this an opportunity to discover something new. Modify your research question or working thesis and move forward.

These temporary roadblocks can be frustrating, but following unexpected paths can also make research fun. They can lead you to new breakthroughs and exciting innovations.

Let's get started. Use these guidelines to begin your research process.

UNDERSTAND Why Writers Do Research

Keep in mind that the purpose of research is to inform and support your ideas. Research is not just a regurgitation of others' ideas.

DEFINE Your Research Question

Name your topic and state your research question as specifically as possible. Improve the efficiency of your research by sharpening that research question as much as possible.

DEVELOP a Working Thesis

In a single sentence, write down your working thesis. This is your best guess, or "hypothesis," for what you think will be your main claim.

DO Some "Start-Up" Research

Take half an hour to an hour to scan the kinds of sources available and get an overall sense of the various views on your research question.

ASSESS the Reliability of Your Sources

Determine whether the sources you have collected are credible, up to date, and reasonably unbiased. Also, verify the evidence behind each source.

DEVISE Your Research Plan

Avoid the temptation to just dive in. Take a little time to make a written plan that describes your research question, working thesis, start-up research results, schedule, and an early bibliography.

CREATE a Schedule

Use "backward planning" to break your research into manageable chunks. After listing all the tasks you will need to complete, work backward from your deadline, filling in the tasks and the days they need to be completed.

KEEP a Bibliography File

Keep a computer file of your working bibliography and maintain it. Your readers will need this bibliographic information to see where your sources can be found.

EXPECT the Unexpected

As you find new evidence, you will want to modify your research approach, research question, and working thesis. This is all part of the research process.

Talk About This

1. List five possible research questions about a topic that you find personally interesting. Then turn each of your research questions into a working thesis. With a small group, talk about these research questions and your working theses. Ask your group members to help you sharpen your working thesis into something you can successfully pursue.

2. With a small group, develop a research question on a topic that is interesting to all of you. Go online and use a variety of keywords to explore that topic. What are some possible answers to the research question?

3. In class, discuss the kinds of sources you think are most reliable. Do you believe online sources can be as reliable as print sources? When are hands-on empirical sources, like interviews or surveys, better than online and print sources?

Try This Out

1. Do about 30 minutes of start-up research on something that interests you. In an e-mail, describe to your professor what kinds of issues you will face if you decide to do some formal research on this topic.

2. In a brief memo to your professor, describe your research plan for your next project. Explain why you think specific types of sources will be most helpful and why other kinds of sources probably will not be helpful.

3. On the Internet, find three sources of evidence that you would consider "heavily biased." Write an evaluation of these sources, explaining why you consider them biased and perhaps unreliable as sources.

Write This

1. **Create a research plan.** Write a full research plan. Identify your research question and your working thesis. Then, identify the kinds of evidence you expect to find and the kinds of sources you plan to target.

2. **Start a research journal.** Keep a journal while you do research for your next paper. Keep track of the kinds of research you did and the amount of time you devoted to those activities. Determine what kinds of research yielded the most useful evidence and what kinds of research cost you too much time.

Go to MyWritingLab to complete this chapter's exercises and test your understanding of its objectives.

Finding Sources
and Collecting
Evidence

In this chapter, you will learn how to—

25.1 recognize the differences between primary and secondary sources.

25.2 triangulate your research by collecting evidence from electronic, print, and empirical resources.

25.3 use reliable strategies to find and evaluate electronic sources.

25.4 collect evidence from a variety of print sources.

25.5 do your own empirical research with interviews, surveys, and field observations.

Now that you have figured out your working thesis and research plan, you are ready to start collecting sources. In this chapter, you will learn how to find a variety of *primary* and *secondary* sources that will help you research your topic and uncover useful evidence.

Using Primary and Secondary Sources

Researchers tend to distinguish between two types of sources: *primary sources* and *secondary sources*. Both kinds are important for doing dependable research.

25.1 recognize the differences between primary and secondary sources.

Primary Sources. Primary sources are the actual records or artifacts, such as letters, photographs, videos, memoirs, books, or personal papers, that were created by the people involved in the issues and events you are researching (Figure 25.1). These sources can also include any data, observations, or interview answers that you or others collected from empirical methods.

KENEDY COUNTY SHERIFF'S DEPARTMENT
TX 1310000
INCIDENT REPORT
02/11/2006

NUMBER: 06020136   REPORT DATE: 02/15/2006   ORI: TX1310000
LOCATION: ARMSTRONG RANCH   ZONE: ARMSTRONG

At approximately 1830 hrs on Saturday February 11, 2006, Kenedy County Sheriff Ramon Salinas contacted me, Chief Deputy Gilberto San Miguel Jr. The phone call was in reference to a hunting accident that occurred on the Armstrong Ranch. I was told by Sheriff Salinas to report to the main house on the Armstrong Ranch on Sunday February 12, at 0800 hrs and I would receive more information when I got there.

On Sunday, February 12, 2006, at approximately 0805 hrs, I Chief Deputy Gilberto San Miguel Jr., arrived at the bump gate to the Armstrong Ranch. This ranch is located approximately twenty-one miles south of Sarita, Texas in Kenedy County. There at the bump gate, Secret Service and Border Patrol personnel met me. I identified myself and told everyone I was to report to the main house. I was instructed to park my vehicle so it could be inspected before I could proceed to the main house. While my vehicle was getting inspected, a Secret Service agent approached me and he advised me he would be riding with me to the main house. As I was approaching the main house, I was instructed to park my vehicle by the cattle guard. There I walked across the cattle guard and was turned over to another agent who identified himself to me as Michael A. Lee, Special Agent in charge with the Secret Service.

As we entered the main house, Mr. Lee introduced me to Vice President Cheney. Mr. Cheney shook my hand and told me he was there to cooperate in any way with the interview. As I got comfortable at a table inside the main house, I asked Mr. Cheney if he could explain to me what had happened the day of the incident.

Mr. Cheney told me that on Saturday, February 11, 2006 at approximately 5:30 pm on the Armstrong Ranch there was a three vehicle hunting party that consisted of himself, Bo Hubert, Pam Willeford, Jerry Medellin, Katharine Armstrong, Sarita Armstrong Hixon, Harry Whittington, and Oscar Medellin. Mr. Cheney told me the sun was setting to the west when the dogs had located a covey. Around the same time, Oscar Medellin notified the hunters he had also located a covey. After the group shot at the first covey he and Pam Willeford proceeded to the second covey because Harry Whittington was looking for his downed birds. Mr. Cheney told me he and Pam Willeford had walked approximately 100 yards from the first location and met up with Oscar Medellin and the hunting guide Bo Hubert. There was a single bird that flew behind him and he followed the bird by line of sight in a counter clockwise direction not realizing Harry Whittington had walked up from behind and had positioned himself approximately 30 yards to the west of him. Mr. Cheney told me the reason Harry Whittington sustained the injuries to his face and upper body was that Mr. Whittington was standing on ground that was lower than the one he was standing on. Mr. Cheney told me if Mr. Whittington was on the same ground level the injuries might have been lower on Mr. Whittington's body.

STATUS: CLOSED   STATUS DATE: 02/15/2006
OFFICER: SAN MIGUEL, GILBERTO JR.   502

02/15/2006 16:00 P.M.   1

FIGURE 25.1 **Primary Sources of Evidence**

Primary sources have been created by the people involved in the events you are studying or through empirical research.

Secondary Sources. Secondary sources are the writings of scholars, experts, and other knowledgeable people who have studied your topic. Scholarly books and articles by historians are secondary sources because their authors analyze and reflect critically on past events. Secondary sources also include books, academic journals, magazines, newspapers, and blogs.

You will usually rely on secondary sources for most college papers. However, you should always look for opportunities to collect evidence from primary sources, such as archives, interviews, surveys, and observations. Collecting your own evidence allows you to confirm or challenge the information you find in secondary sources.

Evaluating Sources with Triangulation

When doing any kind of research, you should try to collect evidence from a variety of sources and perspectives. If you rely on just one type of source, especially the Internet, you risk developing a limited or inaccurate understanding of your topic. To avoid this problem, you should *triangulate* your research by looking for evidence from three different types of sources:

25.2 triangulate your research by collecting evidence from electronic, print, and empirical resources.

Electronic and online sources: Web sites, podcasts, videos, DVDs, listservs, television, radio, and blogs.

Print sources: Books, journals, magazines, newspapers, government publications, reference materials, and microform/microfiche.

Empirical sources: Personal experiences, archives, field observations, interviews, surveys, case studies, and experiments.

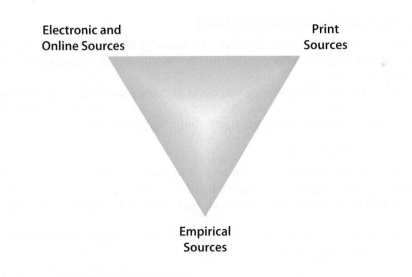

Electronic and Online Sources

Print Sources

Empirical Sources

FIGURE 25.2 The Research Triangle
Triangulating your sources is a good way to ensure that you are drawing evidence from a variety of places. If you find similar evidence from all three corners of the triangle, it is probably reliable.

Together, these three types of sources are called the *research triangle* (Figure 25.2). Here's how the research triangle works.

- **Probably Reliable:** If you collect similar evidence from all three kinds of sources, the evidence you found is probably reliable.

- **Somewhat Reliable:** If you gather comparable evidence from only two points of the triangle, your findings are probably still reliable but are open to some doubt.

- **Unreliable:** If you can only find comparable evidence from one point on the triangle, then you probably need to do more research to back up your findings.

Of course, finding similar evidence in all three types of sources doesn't make something true. It just means the evidence is *probably* trustworthy. Triangulation is a good way to evaluate your sources and corroborate the facts you uncover about your topic.

Also, remember that there are always at least two sides to any issue. So don't just look for sources that support your working thesis. Even if you completely disagree with one of your sources, the argument it makes might give you a stronger understanding of your own position.

Finding Electronic and Online Sources

25.3 use reliable strategies to find and evaluate electronic sources.

The Internet is a good place to start researching your topic. Keep in mind, though, that the Internet is not the *only* place to do research. You should use print and empirical sources to triangulate the evidence you find on the Internet.

Using Internet Search Engines

Search engines let you use keywords to locate information about your topic. If you type your topic into *Google, Bing,* or *Yahoo!,* the search engine will return many thousands of sites.

With a few easy tricks, though, you can target your search with some common symbols and strategies. For example, let's say you are researching how sleep deprivation affects college students. You might start by entering the phrase:

sleep and college students

With this generic subject, a search engine will pull up millions of Web pages that might refer to this topic. Of course, there is no way you are going to have time to look through all those sites to find useful evidence, even if the search engine ranks them for you.

So you need to target your search to pull up only the kinds of materials you want. Here are some tips for getting better results:

Use Exact Words. Choose words that exactly target your topic, and use as many as you need to sharpen your results. For example,

sleep deprivation effects on students test taking

Use Quotation (" ") Marks. If you want to find a *specific phrase*, use quotation marks to target those phrases.

"sleep deprivation" effects on students and "test taking"

Use the Plus (+) Sign. If you put a plus (+) sign in front of a word the search engine will only find pages that have that exact word in them.

sleep +deprivation effects on +students +test +taking

Use the Minus (–) Sign. If you want to eliminate any pages that refer to words or phrases you don't want to see, you can use the minus sign to eliminate pages that refer to them.

sleep deprivation +effects on students +test +taking –insomnia –apnea

Use Wildcard Symbols. Some search engines have symbols for "wildcards," such as ?, *, or %. These symbols are helpful when you know most of a phrase, but not all of it.

"sleep deprivation" +effects on students and "test taking" neural* behavioral* –insomnia –apnea

These search engine tips will help you pull up the pages you need. Figure 25.3 shows the results of a *Bing* search using the phrase

"sleep deprivation" effects on students "test taking" –insomnia –apnea.

Note that the first items pulled up by some search engines may be *sponsored links*. In other words, these companies paid to have their links show up at the top of your list. Most search engines highlight these links in a special way. You might find these links useful, but you should keep in mind that the sponsors are biased because they probably want to sell you something.

Using the Internet Cautiously

Many of the so-called "facts" on the Internet are really just opinions and hearsay with little basis in reality. Also, many quotes that appear on the Internet have been taken out of context or corrupted in some way. So you need to use information from the Internet critically and even skeptically. Don't get fooled by a professional-looking Web site, because a good Web designer can make just about anything look professional.

In Chapter 24, "Starting Research," you learned some questions for checking the reliability of any source. Here are some additional questions you should use to assess whether an Internet source is reliable:

FIGURE 25.3
Targeting Your Search

In this search, the use of symbols has helped narrow the search to useful pages.

- Can you identify and verify the author(s) of the source?

- What organization is this author and source associated with and why is it publishing this information?

- What does the author or organization behind the source have to gain from publishing this information?

- Does the source clearly distinguish between opinions and independent facts?

- Does the source fairly discuss two or more sides of the issue?

- Does the source use other independent sources to back up claims, and can you access those sources?

- Does the information seem farfetched, too terrible, or too good to be true?

- Has the Web site been updated recently?

The Internet will help you find plenty of useful, reliable evidence, but there is also a great amount of junk. It's your responsibility as a researcher to critically decide what is reliable and what isn't.

Using Documentaries and Television/Radio Broadcasts

Multimedia resources such as television and radio broadcasts are available online through network Web sites as well as sites like *YouTube* and *Hulu*. Depending on who made them, documentaries and broadcasts can be reliable sources. If the material is from a trustworthy source, you can take quotes and cite these kinds of electronic sources in your own work.

Documentaries. A documentary is a nonfiction movie or program that relies on interviews and factual evidence about an event or issue. A documentary can be biased, though, so check into the background of the person or organization that made it.

Television Broadcasts. Cable channels and news networks like CNN, HBO, the History Channel, the National Geographic Channel, and the Biography Channel are producing excellent broadcasts that are reliable and can be cited as support for your argument. However, programs on news channels that feature just one or two highly opinionated commentators are less reliable because they tend to be sensationalistic and biased.

Radio Broadcasts. Radio broadcasts, too, can be informative and authoritative. Public radio broadcasts, such as those from National Public Radio and American RadioWorks, offer well-researched stories on the air and at their Web sites. On the other hand, political broadcasts like *The Sean Hannity Show, The Rush Limbaugh Show, The Rachel Maddow Show,* and *The Ed Schultz Show* are notorious for slanting the news and playing loose with the facts. You probably cannot rely on these biased broadcasts as factual sources in your argument.

Using Wikis, Blogs, and Podcasts

In the past, wikis, blogs, or podcasts were often considered too opinionated or subjective to be usable as sources for academic work. However, they are becoming increasingly reliable because reputable scholars and organizations are beginning to use these kinds of new media to publish research-based information. These electronic sources are especially helpful for defining issues and helping you locate other sources.

Wikis. You already know about *Wikipedia,* the most popular wiki, but a variety of other wikis are available, like *WikiHow, Wikibooks,* and *Wikitravel.* Wikis allow their users to add and revise content, and they rely on other users to back-check facts. On some topics, such as popular culture (e.g., television programs, music, celebrities), a wiki might even be the best or only source of up-to-date information. On more established topics, however, you should always be skeptical about the reliability of the information because these sites are written anonymously and can be changed frequently. Your best approach is to use these sites primarily for start-up research on your topic and to find leads that will help you locate other, more reliable sources.

Blogs. Blogs can be helpful for exploring a range of opinions on a particular topic. However, even some of the most established and respected blogs like *Daily Kos, Power Line,* and *Wonkette* are little more than opinionated commentaries on the day's events. Blogs can help you identify the topic's issues and locate more reliable sources; however, most blogs cannot be considered reliable sources themselves. If you want to use a blog as a source, you should explain in your paper why the author of the blog is a trusted source who is supporting the argument with reliable evidence.

Podcasts. Most news Web sites offer podcasts and vidcasts, but the reliability of these sources depends on who made the audio or video file. Today, anyone with a mobile phone, digital recorder, or video camera can make a podcast, even a professional-looking podcast, so you need to carefully assess the credibility and experience of the person who made it.

On just about every topic, you will find plenty of people on the Internet who have opinions. The problem with online sources is that just about anyone can create or edit them. That's why the Internet is a good place to start collecting evidence, but you need to also collect evidence from print and empirical sources to triangulate what you find online.

Finding Print Sources

25.4 collect evidence from a variety of print sources.

With such easy access to electronic and online sources, people sometimes forget to look for print sources on their topic. That's a big mistake. Print sources are typically the most reliable forms of evidence on just about any subject.

Locating Books at Your Library

You can easily find useful books at your campus or local public library. More than likely, your university's library Web site has an online search engine that you can access from any networked computer (Figure 25.4). This search engine will allow you to locate books in the library's catalog. Meanwhile, your campus library will likely have research librarians who can help you find useful print sources. Ask for them at the Information Desk.

FIGURE 25.4 Searching Your Library's Catalog

Your library's catalog is easy to search online. Here is the Georgia Tech library's Web page for searching its catalog. Finding books is almost as easy as using a search engine to find evidence on the Internet.

Books. The most reliable information on your topic can usually be found in books. Authors and editors of books work closely together to check their facts and gather the best evidence available. So books are usually more reliable than Web sites. The downside of books is that they tend to become outdated in fast-changing fields.

Government Publications. The U.S. government produces an amazing amount of printed material on almost any topic you could imagine. Government Web sites, like *The Catalog of U.S. Government Publications,* are good places to find these sources. Your library probably collects many of these materials because they are usually free or inexpensive.

Reference Materials. The reference section of your library collects helpful reference tools, such as almanacs, directories, encyclopedias, handbooks, and guides. These reference materials can help you find facts, data, and evidence about people, places, and events.

Right now, entire libraries of books are being scanned and posted online. Out-of-copyright books are appearing in full-text versions as they become available. Online versions of copyrighted books are searchable, allowing you to see excerpts and identify pages on which you can locate the specific evidence you need.

Finding Articles at Your Library

At your library, you can also find articles in academic journals, magazines, and newspapers. These articles can be located using online databases or periodical indexes available through your library's Web site. If your library does not have these databases available online, you can find print versions of them in your library's "Reference" or "Periodicals" areas.

Academic Journals. Articles in journals are usually written by scientists, professors, consultants, and subject matter experts (SMEs). These journals will offer some of the most exact information available on your topic. To find journal articles, you should start by searching in a *periodical index* related to your topic. Some of the more popular periodical indexes include:

> *ArticleFirst.* Business, humanities, medicine, popular culture, science, and technology
>
> *EBSCOhost.* Academic, business, science, psychology, education, and liberal arts
>
> *ERIC.* Education research and practice
>
> *Humanities Index.* Literature, history, philosophy, languages, and communication
>
> *LexisNexis.* News, business, medical, and legal issues
>
> *OmniFile.* Education, science, humanities, social science, art, biology, and agriculture
>
> *PsycINFO.* Psychology and related fields
>
> *Web of Science.* Physics, chemistry, biology, and life sciences
>
> *IEEE Xplore.* Engineering and science

Magazines. You can find magazine articles about your topic in the *Readers' Guide to Periodical Literature* (also called simply the *Readers' Guide*), which is likely available through your campus library's Web site. Print versions of the *Readers' Guide* should be available in your library's periodical or reference rooms. Other useful online databases for finding magazine articles include *Find Articles, MagPortal,* and *InfoTrac.*

Newspapers. For research on current issues or local topics, newspapers often provide the most recent information. At your library or through its Web site, you can use newspaper indexes to search for information. Past editions of newspapers are often stored on microform or microfiche, which can be read on projectors at your campus library. Some of the more popular newspaper indexes include *ProQuest Newspapers, Chronicling America, LexisNexis, New York Times Index,* and *EBSCOhost.*

Doing research at your campus or local public library is almost as easy as doing research on Internet search engines. You will find that the librarians working there can help you locate the materials you need. While at the library, you will likely find other useful materials you didn't expect, and the librarians might be able to help you find additional materials you would never have found on your own.

Using Empirical Sources

Empirical sources include observations, experiments, surveys, and interviews. They are especially helpful for confirming or challenging the claims made in your electronic, online, and print sources. For example, if one of your electronic or online sources claims that "each day, college students watch an average of five hours of television but spend less than one hour on their homework," you could use observations, interviews, or surveys to confirm or debunk that statement.

25.5 do your own empirical research with interviews, surveys, and field observations.

Interviewing People

Interviews are a great way to go behind the facts to explore the experiences of experts and regular people. Plus, interviewing others is a good way to collect quotes that you can add to your text. Here are some strategies for interviewing people:

Prepare for the Interview

1. **Do your research.** You need to know as much as possible about your topic before you interview someone about it. If you do not understand the topic before going into the interview, you will waste your own and your interviewee's time by asking simplistic or flawed questions.

2. **Create a list of three to five factual questions.** Your research will probably turn up some facts that you want your interviewee to confirm or challenge.

3. **Create a list of five to ten open-ended questions.** Write down five to ten questions that cannot be answered with a simple "yes" or "no." Your questions should urge the interviewee to offer a detailed explanation or opinion.

4. **Decide how you will record the interview.** Do you want to record the interview as a video or make an audio recording? Or do you want to take written notes? Each of these methods has its pros and cons. For example, audio recording captures the whole conversation, but interviewees are often more guarded about their answers when they are being recorded.

5. **Set up the interview.** The best place to do an interview is at a neutral site, like a classroom, a room in the library, or perhaps a café. The second best place is at the interviewee's office. If necessary, you can do interviews over the phone.

Conduct the Interview

1. **Explain the purpose of your project.** Start out by describing your project to the interviewee and describe how the information from the interview will be used. Also, tell the interviewee how long you expect the interview will take.

2. **Ask permission to record.** If you are recording the interview in any way, ask permission to make the recording. First, ask if recording is all right before you turn on your recorder. Then, once the recorder is on, ask again so you record the interviewee's permission.

3. **Ask your factual questions first.** Warm up the interviewee by asking questions that allow him or her to confirm or deny the facts you have already collected.

4. **Ask your open-ended questions next.** Ask the interviewee about his or her opinions, feelings, experiences, and views about the topic.

5. **Ask if he or she would like to provide any other information.** Often people want to tell you things you did not expect or know about. You can wrap up the interview by asking, "Is there anything else you would like to add about this topic?"

6. **Thank the interviewee.** Don't forget to thank the interviewee for his or her time and information.

Interview Follow-Up

1. **Write down everything you remember.** As soon as possible after the interview, describe the interviewee in your notes and fill out any details you couldn't write down during the interview. Do this even if you recorded the interview.

2. **Get your quotes right.** Clarify any direct quotations you collected from your interviewee. If necessary, you might e-mail your quotes to the interviewee for confirmation.

3. **Back-check the facts.** If the interviewee said something that was new to you or that conflicted with your prior research, use electronic, online, or print sources to back-check the facts. If there is a conflict, you can send an e-mail to the interviewee asking for clarification.

4. **Send a thank-you note.** Usually an e-mail that thanks your interviewee is sufficient, but some people prefer to send a card or brief letter of thanks.

Using an Informal Survey

Informal surveys are especially useful for generating data and gathering the views of many different people on the same questions. Many free online services such as *SurveyMonkey, Survey Gizmo,* and *Zoomerang* allow you to create and distribute your own surveys. They will also collect and tabulate the results for you. Here is how to create a useful, though not a scientific, survey:

1. **Identify the population you want to survey.** Some surveys target specific kinds of people (e.g., college students, women from ages 18–22, medical doctors). Others are designed to be filled out by anyone.

2. **Develop your questions.** Create a list of five to ten questions that can be answered quickly. Surveys typically use four basic types of questions: rating scales, multiple choice, numeric open-ended, and text open-ended. Figure 25.5 shows examples of all four types.

3. **Check your questions for neutrality.** Make sure your questions are as neutral as possible. Don't lead on the people you are surveying with biased or slanted questions that fit your own beliefs.

Rating Scales

Going skiing is a good Spring Break activity.

Strongly Agree	Agree	Disagree	Strongly Disagree	No Opinion
☐	☐	☐	☐	☐

Multiple Choice

In what region did you spend most of your childhood?

☐ Northeast States   ☐ Mountain Western States
☐ Midwest States   ☐ West Coast States
☐ Southern States   ☐ Other

Numeric Open-Ended

How many times have you gone downhill skiing in your life? _____

Text Open-Ended

What do you enjoy most about skiing in Minnesota?

_____
_____
_____
_____

FIGURE 25.5
Types of Survey Questions

Make sure your questions are easy to understand to help your survey takers provide answers quickly and accurately.

4. **Pilot-test your questions for clarity.** Make sure your questions won't confuse your survey takers. Before distributing your survey, ask a classmate or friend to take it and watch as he or she answers the questions. Questions that are clear to you may not be clear to someone else.

5. **Distribute the survey.** Ask a number of people to complete your survey, and note the kinds of people who agree to do it. Not everyone will be interested in completing your survey, so remember that your results might reflect the views of specific kinds of people.

6. **Tabulate your results.** When your surveys are returned, convert any quantitative responses into data. In written answers, pull out phrases and quotes that seem to reflect how the people you surveyed felt about your topic.

Professional surveyors will point out that your informal survey is not objective and that your results are not statistically valid. That's fine, as long as you are not using your survey to make important decisions or support claims about how people really feel. Your informal survey will still give you some helpful information about the opinions of others.

Doing Field Observations

Conducting a field observation can help you generate ideas and confirm facts. Field observations involve watching something closely and taking detailed notes.

1. **Choose an appropriate location (field site).** You want to choose a field site that allows you to see as much as possible, while not making it obvious that you are watching and taking notes. People will typically change their behavior if they think someone is watching them.

2. **Take notes in a two-column format.** A good field note technique is to use two columns to record what you see. On the left side, list the people, things, and events you observed. On the right side, write down how you interpret what you observed.

3. **Use the Five-W and How questions.** Keep notes about the *who, what, where, when, why,* and *how* elements that you observe. Try to include as much detail as possible.

4. **Use your senses.** Take notes about the things you see, hear, smell, touch, and taste while you are observing.

5. **Pay attention to things that are moving or changing.** Take special note of the things that moved or changed while you were observing, and what caused them to do so.

When you are finished taking notes, spend some time interpreting what you observed. Look for patterns in your observations to help you make sense of your field site.

Reliable research involves collecting sources from a variety of electronic, online, print, and empirical sources.

KNOW the Difference between Primary and Secondary Sources

Primary sources are the artifacts that were used or created by the people you are researching. Secondary sources are the writings of experts on your topic.

TRIANGULATE Your Sources

Make sure your research plan will allow you to triangulate your sources. Collect electronic, print, and empirical sources that will allow you to confirm or challenge any facts or evidence you find.

SEARCH Online Sources

Use Internet search engines, listservs, podcasts, and other online sources to collect evidence on your subject. As you are searching, consider the reliability of each source. A professional-looking Web site does not mean the source is reliable.

FIND Documentaries or Broadcasts about Your Topic

You can download documentaries and broadcasts online. Your library may have documentaries you can borrow as well.

READ Books on Your Topic

You can access many books through your library's online catalog. Books are often the most reliable sources of information.

USE Indexes and Databases to Find Articles

Access indexes and databases through your library's Web site to find articles in academic journals, magazines, and newspapers.

TRY Empirical Methods to Gather Evidence

You can interview experts, conduct surveys, or do field observations to confirm or challenge the online and print sources you have gathered about your topic.

LOOK for Gaps in Your Evidence

Each source you find will raise more questions. When you notice gaps, do some more research to fill them.

- **Quoting sources** allows you to use key words, phrases, or passages taken directly from the works of others. A direct quote conveys the original text's immediacy and authority while capturing its tone and style.

- **Paraphrasing sources** helps you explain a source's specific ideas or describe its major points using your own words and sentence structures. Typically, a paraphrase will be about the same length as the material in the source.

- **Summarizing sources** allows you to condense a source down to just its major ideas and points. Summaries often describe *what* authors say and also *how* they say it. They can also describe an author's underlying values, reasoning processes, or evidence.

This chapter will show you how to incorporate the ideas and words of others into your work while giving appropriate credit. Chapters 27 and 28 will show you how to cite your sources properly using MLA and APA documentation styles.

Citing

26.1 cite sources to give credit to other authors and researchers.

Whenever you integrate the ideas, findings, or arguments of others into your own writing, you need to give them credit by citing them with a *parenthetical citation*. This citation should correspond to a full citation in your paper's Works Cited or References list. In most situations, a parenthetical citation will include an author's name and the page number of the page on which the information appeared. In some situations, the year of the source is also included.

Here are a few examples of parenthetical citations that follow the MLA and APA styles. More examples and guidelines appear in Chapter 28, "Using MLA Style," and Chapter 29, "Using APA Style."

	MLA Style	**APA Style**
Single Author	(Mitchell 93)	(Mitchell, 2010, p. 93)
Two Authors	(Lopez and Green 72-76)	(Lopez & Green, 2014, pp. 72-76)
Three Authors	(Johnson et al. 23)	(Johnson, Baker, & Han, 2011, p. 23)
Corporate Author	(NRA 23)	(National Rifle Association [NRA], 1998, p. 23)
Unknown Author	("Frightening" 23)	("Frightening," 2009, p. 23)

Note: In some situations, APA style does not require a page number from the source in a parenthetical citation. If you are using APA style, check with your professors about whether they want you to include the page numbers in every parenthetical citation.

Typically, a parenthetical citation will appear at the end of the sentence. In some situations, the citation should appear in the middle of a sentence if the ideas in the remainder of the sentence are not attributable to the source:

MLA Style

Economists have long questioned whether tax cuts, especially tax cuts for the wealthy, truly stimulate growth (Mitchell 93).

Economists have long questioned whether tax cuts, especially tax cuts for the wealthy, truly stimulate growth (Mitchell 93), but politicians are still making that old "trickle down" argument today.

APA Style

Economists have long questioned whether tax cuts, especially tax cuts for the wealthy, truly stimulate growth (Mitchell, 2010, p. 93).

Economists have long questioned whether tax cuts, especially tax cuts for the wealthy, truly stimulate growth (Mitchell, 2010, p. 93), but politicians are still making that old "trickle down" argument today.

If you use the author's name within the sentence, the parenthetical citation at the end of the sentence should include only the page number. For APA style, you need to also include the source's year of publication the first time the source is referenced.

MLA Style

According to Durrani, it's hard to find the right balance between appropriate taxation that allows government to function and excessive taxation that impedes economic growth (89).

APA Style

According to Durrani (2014), it's hard to find the right balance between appropriate taxation that allows government to function and excessive taxation that impedes economic growth (p. 89).

In MLA style, if you have listed more than one source by an author in the Works Cited, indicate which source you are citing by including a shortened title before the page number. In APA style, if you have listed more than one source from an author with the same publication year, indicate which source you're citing by adding a small letter (*a, b, c,* etc.) after the date:

MLA Style

According to Durrani, it's hard to find the right balance between appropriate taxation that allows government to function and excessive taxation that impedes economic growth ("Expectations" 89).

APA Style

According to Durrani (2014a), it's hard to find the right balance between appropriate taxation that allows government to function and excessive taxation that impedes economic growth (p. 89).

Again, you should turn to Chapter 28 (MLA Style) and Chapter 29 (APA Style) to learn how to cite other kinds of works.

Quoting

26.2 quote other authors and speakers.

When quoting an author or speaker, you are importing their exact words into your document. To signal that these words are not yours, always place quotation marks around them and include a parenthetical citation.

Quoting sounds pretty easy, but you can confuse your readers or even get yourself in trouble if you don't properly copy and cite the works of others. You might even be accused of plagiarism. Here are some helpful guidelines:

Brief Quotations

A brief quotation takes a word, phrase, or sentence directly from an original source. Always introduce and provide some background about the quotation: Do not expect a quotation to make your point by itself.

Words. If an author uses a word in a unique way, you can put quotes around it in your own text. After you tell your reader where the word comes from, you don't need to continue putting it inside quotation marks.

> **Acceptable quotation:** Using Gladwell's terms, some important differences exist between "explicit" learning and "collateral" learning (36).

> **Unacceptable quotation:** Using Gladwell's terms, some important differences exist between explicit learning and collateral learning (36).

Phrases. If you want to use a whole phrase from a source, you need to put quotation marks around it. Then weave the quote into a sentence, making sure it flows with the rest of your writing.

> **Acceptable quotation:** Tomorrow's educators need to understand the distinction between, as Gladwell puts it, "two very different kinds of learning" (36).

> **Unacceptable quotation:** Tomorrow's educators need to understand the distinction between, as Gladwell puts it, two very different kinds of learning (36).

Sentences. You can also bring entire sentences from another source into your document. Use a *signal phrase* (e.g., "As Gladwell argues,") or a colon to indicate that you are quoting a whole sentence.

> **Acceptable quotation:** As Gladwell argues, "Meta-analysis of hundreds of studies done on the effects of homework shows that the evidence supporting the practice is, at best, modest" (36).

> **Unacceptable quotation:** As Gladwell argues, meta-analysis of hundreds of studies done on the effects of homework shows that the evidence supporting the practice is, at best, modest.

Acceptable quotation using a colon: Gladwell summarizes the research simply: "Meta-analysis of hundreds of studies done on the effects of homework shows that the evidence supporting the practice is, at best, modest" (36).

Unacceptable quotation using a colon: Gladwell summarizes the research simply: Meta-analysis of hundreds of studies done on the effects of homework shows that the evidence supporting the practice is, at best, modest.

Long Quotations

Occasionally, you may need to quote a source at length. A quote longer than three lines should be formatted as a *block quote*. A block quote indents the entire quotation to separate it from your normal text. No quotation marks are used, and the citation appears at the end of the quote, outside the final punctuation.

A child is unlikely to acquire collateral learning through books or studying for the SAT exams, Gladwell explains. They do acquire it through play:

> The point is that books and video games represent two very different kinds of learning. When you read a biology textbook, the content of what you read is what matters. Reading is a form of explicit learning. When you play a video game, the value is in how it makes you think. Video games are an example of collateral learning, which is no less important. ("Brain" 2)

Block quote.

In asserting that collateral learning "is no less important" than explicit learning, Gladwell implies that American education may be producing students who are imbalanced—with too much content knowledge and too little facility in dealing with unstructured situations, the kinds of situations that a person is likely to face every day of his or her working life. (2)

Author explains what the quote means.

Use block quotes only when the original quotation cannot be paraphrased and must be preserved in its full length. Don't expect a long quotation to make your point for you. Instead, use the quote to support the point you are making.

Paraphrasing and Summarizing

When paraphrasing or summarizing, you are putting someone else's ideas into your own words. In some situations, using a paraphrase or summary is preferable to using a quote. Using too many quotations can make a text look choppy and might lead the reader to think that you are just stitching together passages from other people's works. Paraphrasing allows you to maintain the tone and flow of your writing.

26.3 use paraphrase and summary to explain the ideas of others.

There are four main differences between a paraphrase and a summary:

- A paraphrase handles only a portion of the original text, while a summary often covers its entire content.

- A paraphrase usually follows the organization of the original source, while a summary reorganizes the content to highlight the major points.

- A paraphrase is usually about the same length or a little shorter than the original text being paraphrased, while a summary is significantly shorter than the original text.

- A paraphrase *looks through* the text to convey what the author is saying, but summaries can also *look at* the text to explore an author's strategies, style, reasoning, and other choices (see Chapter 4, "Reading Critically, Thinking Analytically").

Figure 26.1 includes a source text that will be used to discuss paraphrasing and summarizing in this part of the chapter.

Paraphrasing

The goal of paraphrasing is to explain and describe a portion of the source's text in your own words. A paraphrase is usually about the same length or a little shorter than the material being paraphrased. For example, the following acceptable and unacceptable paraphrases explain Gladwell's distinction between "explicit" and "collateral" learning.

Acceptable Paraphrase

Gladwell explains that we can think of intelligence (or "smart," as he calls it) as having two related but distinct dimensions (36). On the one hand, there is the intelligence we associate with storing, accessing, and reproducing information and with the ability to solve certain kinds of problems. This is the kind of intelligence a person gets from reading books and, generally, from school—what Gladwell calls "explicit" learning. Then there's another kind of intelligence that we get through "collateral" learning. When people develop this kind of intelligence, they have the practical know-how needed to enter a confusing, complex, chaotic situation and quickly and perhaps intuitively develop a hierarchy of what needs to be done, how it should be done, and when it should be done. Both kinds of intelligence are important, Gladwell assures us, but we probably need to think long and hard about the "right balance" between them.

In this acceptable paraphrase, the writer used primarily her own words. When she used exact words from Gladwell's article, she placed them inside quotations. Now let's look at a paraphrase that is too close to the original source:

Unacceptable Paraphrase

Gladwell explains that being smart requires two kinds of thinking. When a person reads a textbook, he or she is engaging in explicit learning. Here the

The point is that books and video games represent two very different kinds of learning. When you read a biology textbook, the content of what you read is what matters. Reading is a form of explicit learning. When you play a video game, the value is in how it makes you think. Video games are an example of collateral learning, which is no less important.

Being "smart" involves facility in both kinds of thinking—the kind of fluid problem solving that matters in things like video games and I.Q. tests, but also the kind of crystallized knowledge that comes from explicit learning. If Johnson's book has a flaw, it is that he sometimes speaks of our culture being "smarter" when he's really referring just to that fluid problem-solving facility. When it comes to the other kind of intelligence, it is not clear at all what kind of progress we are making, as anyone who has read, say, the Gettysburg Address alongside any Presidential speech from the past twenty years can attest. The real question is what the right balance of these two forms of intelligence might look like. *Everything Bad Is Good for You* doesn't answer that question. But Johnson does something nearly as important, which is to remind us that we shouldn't fall into the trap of thinking that explicit learning is the only kind of learning that matters.

One of the ongoing debates in the educational community, similarly, is over the value of homework. Meta-analysis of hundreds of studies done on the effects of homework shows that the evidence supporting the practice is, at best, modest. Homework seems to be most useful in high school and for subjects like math. At the elementary-school level, homework seems to be of marginal or no academic value. Its effect on discipline and personal responsibility is unproved. And the causal relation between high-school homework and achievement is unclear: it hasn't been firmly established whether spending more time on homework in high school makes you a better student or whether better students, finding homework more pleasurable, spend more time doing it. So why, as a society, are we so enamored of homework? Perhaps because we have so little faith in the value of the things that children would otherwise be doing with their time. They could go out for a walk, and get some exercise; they could spend time with their peers, and reap the rewards of friendship. Or, Johnson suggests, they could be playing a video game, and giving their minds a rigorous workout.

FIGURE 26.1
Source Text

This excerpt from Malcolm Gladwell's Outliers *will be used in this chapter to demonstrate paraphrasing and summarizing.*

crystallized knowledge that comes from the content of what you read is what matters. Playing video games is an example of collateral learning. Here the value lies in how the game makes you think and results in adaptable problem-solving skills. Although many people think that explicit learning is the only kind that matters, both kinds are important. (36)

The highlights in this unacceptable paraphrase indicate where the writer has lifted words and phrases directly from Gladwell's article. Even though the writer cites the source, she should have placed these exact words and phrases inside quotation marks.

When paraphrasing, make sure it's your voice, and not the source's voice, that comes through. Notice how the voice in the unacceptable paraphrase is overwhelmed by the voice of the source. However, in the acceptable paraphrase the writer's voice comes through clearly.

Summarizing

When summarizing a source, you are capturing its principal idea or ideas in a condensed form. A summary often also explores and describes the author's choices, including the source's structure; its tone, angle, or thesis; its style; its underlying values; or its persuasive strategies. In the following summaries, the writers address the main idea in Gladwell's review: the right balance between "explicit" and "collateral" learning.

Acceptable Paragraph-Length Summary

In the final portion of "Brain Candy," Gladwell accepts Johnson's argument that video games can help develop valuable capacities and extends it further, suggesting that we overvalue "explicit" learning and undervalue "collateral" learning. But the real issue, Gladwell tells us, is not whether Americans are getting better at collateral learning or whether collateral learning is important. "The real question," asserts Gladwell, "is what the right balance of these two forms of intelligence might look like" (36). We need to discuss this question, Gladwell suggests, as a nation because many of the decision makers in education seem to think that explicit learning is all that matters without a healthy debate. We have failed to acknowledge, Gladwell reminds us, that play also results in an important kind of intelligence.

Notice how this summary focuses on Gladwell's main point and makes it prominent. An unacceptable summary usually relies too much on the wording of the original text, and it may not prioritize the most important points in the source text.

Unacceptable Summary

In the final portion of "Brain Candy," Gladwell accepts Johnson's argument that playing video games is valuable because of how it makes you think and extends it further, asking what the right balance between these two forms of intelligence would look like. Gladwell explains that books and video games deliver two very different kinds of learning (36). When you read, it's the content that matters. Reading is a form of explicit learning. Playing a video game is valuable because of the way it makes you think. Collateral learning is no less important than explicit learning. But the real question, Gladwell tells us, is figuring out the right balance of these two forms of intelligence. We need to discuss this question, Gladwell suggests, as a nation because many of the decision makers in education seem to be proceeding as if explicit learning is all that matters without a healthy debate. For example, a number of elementary schools have eliminated recess and replaced it with math or English (36). They have also increased the amount of homework, even though nobody knows whether spending more time on homework in high school makes you a better student or whether better students spend more time on their homework. Gladwell concludes that as a society, we are so enamored of homework because we do not understand the value of the things that children would otherwise be doing with their time. This is the triumph of the explicit over the collateral.

The highlighted phrases in this unacceptable summary show where the writer uses almost the same wording or structure as the original text. This is called "patchwriting," which writing scholar Rebecca Moore Howard defines as "copying from a source text and then deleting some words, altering grammatical structures, or plugging in one synonym for another" (xvii). Patchwriting is a form of plagiarism and is discussed later in this chapter .

Framing Quotes, Paraphrases, and Summaries

Your readers need to see the boundaries between your work and the material you are taking from your sources. To help your readers identify these boundaries, you should frame your quotations, paraphrases, and summaries by using signal phrases, by citing sources, and by making connections to your own ideas (Figure 26.2).

26.4 frame quotes, paraphrases, and summaries in your texts.

Signal Phrase. A signal phrase indicates where the source material comes from. The words "as" and "in" are often at the heart of a signal phrase (e.g., "As Gladwell argues," "In his article 'Brain Candy,' Gladwell states").

Direct Quotation. Material quoted directly from your source should be separated from your own words with commas, quotation marks, and other punctuation to indicate which words came directly from the source and which are your own.

Citation. A citation directs readers to the original source's location, identifying the exact pages or Web site. In MLA or APA documentation style, an in-text citation is used to cite the source. In other documentation styles, you might use a footnote or endnote.

Connection. When you connect the source's ideas to your ideas, you will make it clear how the source material fits in with your own statements and claims.

Figure 26.2 color codes these features. The following examples use these colors to highlight signal phrases, source material, citations, and connections.

As Malcolm Gladwell reminds us, many American schools have eliminated recess in favor of more math and language studies, favoring "explicit" learning over "collateral" learning ("Brain" 36). This approach is problematic, because it takes away children's opportunities to interact socially and problem-solve, which are critical skills in today's world.

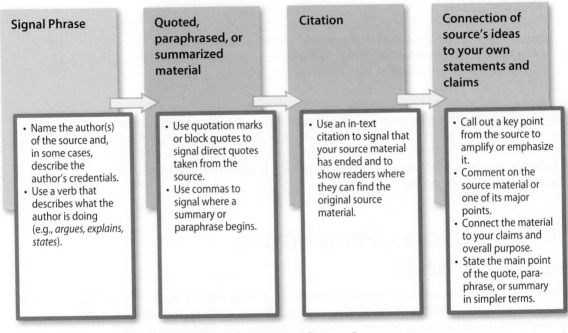

FIGURE 26.2 Framing Material from a Source

Material taken from a source should be clearly framed with a signal phrase, a citation, and a connection to your own statements and claims.

Speculating about why we so firmly believe that homework is critical to academic success, Gladwell suggests, "Perhaps because we have so little faith in the value of the things that children would otherwise be doing with their time" (36). In other words, Gladwell is arguing that we are so fearful of letting children play that we fill up their time with activities like homework that show little benefit.

Similarly, Pink describes several studies that show that the careers of the future will rely heavily on creativity and spatial recognition, which means people who can think with the right side of their brain will have the advantage (65). If so, then we also need to change our educational system so that we can strengthen our abilities to think with both sides of the brain, not just the left side.

As shown in this example, the frame begins with a signal phrase. Signal phrases typically rely on an action verb that indicates what the author of the source is trying to achieve in the material that is being quoted, paraphrased, or summarized. Figure 26.3 provides a helpful list of verbs you can use to signal quotes, paraphrases, and summaries.

The frame typically ends with a connection showing how the source material fits into your overall discussion or argument. Your connection should do one of the following things for your readers:

accepts	accuses	acknowledges
adds	admits	advises
agrees	alleges	allows
analyzes	announces	answers
argues	asks	asserts
believes	charges	claims
comments	compares	complains
concedes	concludes	confirms
considers	contends	countercharges
criticizes	declares	demonstrates
denies	describes	disagrees
discusses	disputes	emphasizes
explains	expresses	finds
grants	holds	illustrates
implies	insists	interprets
maintains	notes	objects
observes	offers	points out
proclaims	proposes	provides
quarrels	reacts	reasons
refutes	rejects	remarks
replies	reports	responds
reveals	shows	states
suggests	supports	thinks
urges	writes	

FIGURE 26.3 Verbs for Signal Phrases

Use verbs like these in your signal phrases to introduce quotations, paraphrases, and summaries.

- Call out a key point from the source to amplify or emphasize it.

- Expand on the source material or one of its major points.

- Connect the source material to your claims and overall purpose.

- Rephrase the main point of the source material in simpler terms.

When handled properly, framing allows you to clearly signal the boundaries between your source's ideas and your ideas.

Avoiding Plagiarism

The Council of Writing Program Administrators defines plagiarism this way:

26.5 avoid plagiarizing the words and ideas of others.

> **In an instructional setting, plagiarism occurs when a writer deliberately uses someone else's language, ideas, or other original (not common-knowledge) material without acknowledging its source.**

In college, plagiarism is a form of academic dishonesty, and it can lead to a failing grade on an assignment or even for the class. In the workplace, plagiarism is a form of copyright infringement in which one person illegally takes the ideas or words of someone else without that person's permission. Copyright infringement can lead to costly lawsuits and the firing of any employee who commits it.

Plagiarism is not always intentional. Sometimes writers forget to copy down their sources in their notes. Nevertheless, even accidental plagiarism may result in serious trouble with your professors, your university, or your employer. So it is crucial that you understand the kinds of plagiarism and learn to avoid them.

Academic Dishonesty

The most obvious form of plagiarism occurs when someone hands in work that is not his or her own. Everyone, including your professors, knows about "cheater Web sites" that sell or give away college papers. Everyone also knows about "borrowing" someone else's paper. And everyone knows it's easy to cut and paste a sample paper from the Internet. (If you found it, chances are good your professor will find it, too.)

And yet, some students foolishly try to get away with these kinds of plagiarism. Your professors aren't naive. If you hand in a paper that's not your own, you're being dishonest. When students get caught, they receive a failing grade for the class, which looks bad on their transcripts and is difficult to explain to future employers or graduate school admissions committees. They might even be expelled. This kind of plagiarism is clearly intentional, and few people have sympathy for someone who is so obviously cheating.

Ironically, people who buy, download, or copy papers often spend more time and energy finding the paper and worrying about the consequences of getting caught than they would if they just wrote the paper in the first place.

Patchwriting

Patchwriting was mentioned earlier in this chapter. Usually, patchwriting happens when someone cuts and pastes one or more paragraphs from a Web page or other source and then alters words and sentences to make them look like his or her own.

When done intentionally, patchwriting is clearly a form of academic dishonesty because the writer is presenting someone else's ideas as his or her own without attribution. Some students have even tried to patchwrite an entire paper. They cut and paste several paragraphs from one source or a variety of sources. Then they add some transitions and a few of their own sentences, while altering the words and sentences from the original. As a result, little of the paper is based on their own ideas. This kind of dishonesty usually leads to a failing grade for the assignment and for the class.

Patchwriting can happen unintentionally, especially when a writer copies sentences or paragraphs from a source and then forgets the material was taken from somewhere else. The writer might even cite the source, not realizing that the text that was included is too close to the original. Unfortunately, your professor cannot tell whether you were intentionally being dishonest or just made an honest mistake.

To avoid patchwriting, carefully identify your sources in your notes. Clearly mark any quotes taken from your sources with quotation marks, brackets, or some other kind of distinguishing mark. Then, when you use these materials in your document, make sure you quote, paraphrase, summarize, and cite them properly.

Ideas and Words Taken without Attribution

In college and in the workplace, you will often need to use ideas, words, phrases, or sentences from a source. When you do this, *you must correctly quote and cite that source.* That is, you must place those words inside quotation marks (or block quote them) and provide a citation that tells your reader precisely where you got those words. If you use ideas, words, phrases, or sentences without attribution, you could be charged with academic dishonesty or copyright infringement.

You do not need to cite a source when stating "common knowledge," which is information that is available in multiple sources and that your readers would consider accurate and indisputable. However, sometimes it is difficult to determine whether the information you are providing is common knowledge. If you aren't sure, cite the source. Citing a source will add support to your work, and it will help you avoid being accused of plagiarism.

The Real Problem with Plagiarism

No doubt, plagiarism is easier than ever with the Internet. It's also easier than ever to catch someone who is plagiarizing. Your professors can use *Google,* and they have access to plagiarism-checking Web sites. They often have access to collections of prior papers that were handed in before.

If you plagiarize, there is a good chance you will get caught. But the real problem with plagiarism is that you are cheating yourself. You're probably paying thousands of dollars for your education. Cheating robs you of the chance to strengthen your communication skills and prepare for advanced courses and your career.

Of course, there is pressure to do well in your classes, and you don't always have enough time to do everything you want. In the end, though, doing your own work will help you improve and strengthen your mind and abilities. Don't miss that opportunity.

Here are some helpful guidelines for citing, quoting, paraphrasing, and summarizing sources and avoiding plagiarism.

DECIDE What to Cite, Quote, Paraphrase, or Summarize

Ask yourself what kinds of materials should be cited, quoted, summarized, or paraphrased in your document. To guide your decision, keep your readers' needs and the genre in mind.

CITE Ideas or Information from Sources

Any ideas or information that you take from another source should be cited with a parenthetical citation.

QUOTE Words, Phrases, and Sentences and Cite Them

Any words, phrases, or sentences from another source should be placed in quotation marks and cited with MLA or APA documentation style.

PARAPHRASE Important Sources and Cite Them

When you paraphrase, you are using your own words and sentence structures to explain an author's or speaker's ideas. Paraphrases are usually about the same length as the original or a little shorter. When you use words from the original text, be sure to quote them. Paraphrases need to be cited.

SUMMARIZE Sources with Important Ideas and Cite Them

A summary captures the principal ideas of a source by summarizing the entire work or a major portion of it. Summaries are shorter than the original source material and present the main ideas. They often also explain an author's choices, such as organization, genre, persuasive strategies, and style.

USE Signal Phrases to Mark Quotes, Paraphrases, and Summaries

A *signal phrase* uses words like "as" or "in" to highlight for the readers where a source is being referenced. A variety of *signal verbs* can also highlight the beginning of a quote, paraphrase, or summary.

DON'T Plagiarize Intentionally or Unintentionally

Plagiarism, whether intentional or unintentional, is a form of academic dishonesty. It involves using someone else's words or ideas without giving that person proper credit. Intentional plagiarism usually leads to a failing grade for the paper and the course. Don't do it.

1. With your group, discuss the kinds of research you have done in the past, and how you have incorporated sources into your work. How do you think research in college will be handled differently?

2. Look at the example of "patchwriting" on pages 462–463. Discuss two or three strategies that can help you avoid patchwriting in your own work.

3. With your group, discuss what causes students to plagiarize. Then come up with two or three strategies professors could use to discourage and prevent it. Finally, discuss what professors and colleges should do when someone does plagiarize.

Talk About This

1. Choose a television or online commercial and then paraphrase and summarize it. What is the most challenging aspect of summarizing the commercial accurately?

2. Choose three quotations from a source and practice incorporating them into something you are writing for this class. Be sure to use a signal phrase or signal verb.

3. Choose three paragraphs from a source and purposely create an inappropriate "patchwritten" text. Then transform your patchwritten text into an appropriate paraphrase. As you rewrite the text, pay attention to the kinds of alterations you need to make.

Try This Out

1. **Summarize a source.** Choose a source text and write down a single sentence that summarizes the source's main point in your own words. Now write a one-paragraph summary of the source, highlighting its major ideas. Finally, turn your one-paragraph summary into a multiple-paragraph summary that includes quotes and citations.

2. **Explain how to handle plagiarism.** Write a brief position paper in which you discuss how your professors and university should handle plagiarism in the age of the Internet. Offer some ideas about how professors can steer students away from the temptation to plagiarize.

Write This

> Go to My **Writing**Lab to complete this chapter's exercises and test your understanding of its objectives.

27

Using MLA
Style

In this chapter you will learn how to—

27.1 use MLA parenthetical citations.

27.2 create bibliographic entries for a works-cited list.

27.3 prepare a works-cited list in MLA style.

Modern Language Association (MLA) documentation style helps you to keep track of your sources, while showing your readers where you found the supporting information in your document. MLA style is most commonly used in the humanities (i.e., English, history, philosophy, languages, art history). This style is also used in other scholarly fields because of its flexibility and familiarity.

In this chapter, you will learn how to use MLA style to reference your sources and create a list of "works-cited" at the end of your document. The models of MLA citations shown here are the ones most commonly used in college and in the workplace. If you cannot find a model that fits the source you are trying to cite, you should turn to the *MLA Handbook*, 8th ed. (2016). You can also look up examples on the *Purdue OWL* (owl.english.purdue.edu).

On the Internet, an increasing number of online citation generators are available such as *EasyBib, Citation Machine,* and *BibMe.* Your word processing software (*Word, WordPerfect*) will often have a built-in citation generator, or you can use reference manager software (*EndNote, Zotero*) to generate in-text citations and your works-cited list. We recommend using these citation generators because they can help you manage your sources and cite them accurately. However, you should always make sure the generator is following the most up-to-date MLA documentation style. Then, double-check all citations to make sure they were created correctly. Always remember that these citation generators are only as accurate as the information you feed into them.

Parenthetical Citations

When citing a source, you first need to include a *parenthetical reference*. A parenthetical reference usually appears at the end of the sentence that includes information from your source. For example:

27.1 use MLA parenthetical citations.

> Archeologists have shown that wild dogs diverged from wolves about ten thousand years ago (Jones 27).

> For example, in *The Robber Bride*, Atwood depicts the response of second wave feminism to postfeminism (Tolan 46), through the interactions of three friends with an aggressive vampire who has returned from the dead.

Note: For a key to the color highlighting used here and throughout this chapter, see the bottom of this page.

As shown here, a parenthetical reference includes two important pieces of information: the source's name (usually an author's name), followed by a single space with no comma, and the page number from the source where the information appeared. The first parenthetical reference above signals that the information was taken from page 27 in a work from someone named Jones. The second parenthetical reference signals that its information can be found on page 46 in a source written by someone named Tolan.

If readers want to, they can then turn to the "works-cited" at the end of the document to see the full citation, which will look like this:

> Jones, Steve. *Darwin's Ghost*. Ballantine, 2000.

> Tolan, Fiona. "Sucking the Blood Out of Second Wave Feminism: Postfeminist Vampirism in Margaret Atwood's *The Robber Bride*." *Gothic Studies*, vol. 9, no. 2, 2007, pp. 45-57.

The parenthetical reference and the full citation work together. The reference points to the works-cited list, which provides the information needed for locating the source.

When the Author's Name Appears in the Sentence

If you name the author in the sentence, then your parenthetical citation should include only the page number but not the author's name. For example:

> According to Steve Jones, a genetic scientist, archeologists have shown that wild dogs diverged from wolves about ten thousand years ago (27).

> In her recent article, Tolan (46) argues that Atwood's *The Robber Bride* is really an allegory of postfeminism, in which three second-wave feminists are confronted with the anxieties brought about by the postfeminist backlash.

Author Title Publication Online Source

Typically, a parenthetical reference appears at the end of the sentence, but as shown above, it can also appear immediately after the name of the source.

If the first part of your sentence draws information from a source but the remainder of the sentence represents your own thoughts, you should put the reference immediately after the source's material is used. For example:

> Glassner argues that naive Americans are victimized by a news media that is engaged in "fear-mongering" and other scare tactics (205), but I believe the American people are able to distinguish between real news and sensationalism.

Citing More Than One Source in the Same Sentence

If you want to cite multiple sources that are basically saying the same thing, you can use one parenthetical reference, separating the sources with semicolons:

> George Washington was the only logical choice for President of the United States, because he had the respect of the competing political factions that emerged after the signing of the Treaty of Paris in 1783 (Ellis 375; Irving 649).

If you are citing more than one source in the same sentence but they are making different points, you should put the parenthetical reference as close as possible to the information taken from each source. For example:

> Some historians view Cicero as a principled defender of the dying Roman Republic (Grant 29), while others see him as an idealistic statesman who stood helplessly aside as the Republic crumbled (Everett 321).

Citing a Source Multiple Times

In some situations, you will need to cite a source multiple times. If your document continues to use a single source, you should include only the page number in subsequent references as long as no other source comes between them.

> New owners often misread the natural signals from their puppy (Monks 139). One common problem is submissive urination in which a puppy shows submission by peeing. Owners often believe the puppy is acting defiantly, but it is really trying to signal submission. So punishing the dog is exactly the wrong thing to do, because it only encourages the puppy to be even more submissive, resulting in even more puddles on the floor (140).

In the example above, the full parenthetical reference is included early in the paragraph. The second reference, which is only a page number, is clearly referring back to the source in the first reference.

However, if another source is cited between two parenthetical references to the same source, the author's name from the first source would need to be repeated in a subsequent reference. For example:

New owners often misread the natural signals from their puppy (Monks 139). One common problem is submissive urination in which a puppy shows submission by peeing. Owners often believe the puppy is acting defiantly, but it is really trying to signal submission (Kerns 12). So punishing the dog is exactly the wrong thing to do, because it only encourages the puppy to be even more submissive, resulting in even more puddles on the floor (Monks 140).

In the example above, the author includes Monks in the last sentence's reference because the reference (Kerns 12) appears between the two references to the source written by Monks.

Citing a Source with No Page Numbers

If the source has no page numbers (or line numbers or paragraph numbers) you should not put any number in the in-text citation. Just put the author's last name in parentheses. Unnumbered paragraphs, like those on a Web page, do not need to be counted for the in-text citation.

Other Parenthetical References

A wide variety of parenthetical references are possible. Figure 27.1 shows models of the most commonly used parenthetical references. Choose the model that best fits your source. If none of these models fits the source you are trying to cite, you can combine these models to come up with something that will work. If you still cannot figure it out, consult the *MLA Handbook* or a reliable online resource, such as the *Purdue OWL*.

FIGURE 27.1
Types of MLA Parenthetical References

Type of Source	Example Parenthetical Reference
Single author	(Gerns 12)
Single author, multiple pages	(Barnes 5-9) or (Barnes 34, 121) *The hyphen signals a range of pages. The comma signals similar information can be found on two different pages.*
Two authors	(Hammonds and Gupta 203)
Three or more authors	(Hanson et al. 845) *A source with three or more authors should include the first author's last name, first name, followed by et al.*
Multiple sources in same reference	(Yu 34 ; Thames and Cain 98 ; Young et al. 23) *The semicolon divides the sources.*
Two or more works by the same author	(Tufte , *Visual* 25) and (Tufte , "Powerpoint" 9) *The first prominent word in the source's title is used. Italics signals a book, while quotation marks signal an article.*
Different authors with the same last name	(M. Smith 54) and (A. Smith 34) *The first letter abbreviates each author's first name.*
Corporate author	(NASA 12) or (Amer. Beef Assn. 232) *Abbreviate as much of the corporate name as possible. Periods are needed when abbreviating acronyms that are not commonly used.*
No author for book	(*Handling* 45) *Use the first prominent word in the title and put it in italics.*
No author for journal article or newspaper article	("Genomics" 23) *Use the first prominent word in the title and put it in quotation marks.*
No author for newspaper article	("Recession" A4) *The letter "A" is the section of the newspaper and the number is the page.*
Quoted in another source	(qtd. in Franks 94) *"qtd." stands for "quoted."*

continued

FIGURE 27.1
(continued)

Type of Source	Example Parenthetical Reference
Web page or other document with numbered paragraphs and no pagination	(Reynolds, par. 3) *If the source's paragraphs are numbered, use "par." (for paragraph) with the paragraph number, separated from the author's name by a comma. If the source has chapters or sections, use the labels "ch" or "sec." When citing consecutive parts, separate the numbers by a dash (e.g., chs. 2–4 means Chapters 2 through 4).*
Web page or other document with numbered paragraphs or other parts but no author and no pagination	("Friendly," par. 7) *Put the first prominent word in the title in quotes, with "par." standing for the word paragraph, separated from the author's name by a comma. If the source has chapters or sections, use the labels "ch" or "sec." When citing consecutive parts, separate the numbers by a dash (e.g., chs. 2–4 means Chapters 2 through 4).*

If you have a source that doesn't fit the models shown here, you can usually figure out how to cite it by combining the above reference models. If you still cannot figure out how to cite your source, consult the MLA Handbook *or an online guide.*

Preparing the List of Works-Cited

Your list of the works-cited appears at the end of your document. In this list, you should include full citations for all the sources you cite. Your works-cited list should be in alphabetical order by the author's last names and only include sources you cited in the document. When the author's name is not known, alphabetize the source by the first prominent word in its title (ignore words like *The, A,* or *An*).

27.2 create bibliographic entries for a works-cited list.

A typical works-cited entry will include specific information in the following color-coded order.

> Name of Author(s). Title of Source. Title of Container, Other Contributors, Version, Number, Publisher, Publication Date, Location, Container's Online Address.

Some items, such as an article or a song, will be included in a larger source, which MLA calls a "container." For example, an article is typically *contained* in a magazine, newspaper, or a website. Similarly, a song might be *contained* in an album or appear on a website like *YouTube*. Here are entries from three types of sources:

> Chew, Robin. "Charles Darwin, Naturalist, 1809-1882." *Lucidcafe*, 27 June 2012, www.lucidcafe.com/library/96feb/darwin.html.

Author Title Publication Online Source

Poresky, Louise. "Cather and Woolf in Dialogue: The Professor's House to the Light House." *Papers on Language and Literature,* vol. 44, no. 1, 2008, pp. 67-86.

Shreve, Porter. *When the White House Was Ours.* Houghton, 2008.

Including More Than One Source from an Author

If your works-cited list includes two or more sources from the same author, only the first entry should include the author's name. Afterward, entries should use three hyphens instead of the name. Multiple entries from one author should be alphabetized by the first prominent words in the titles.

Murphy, James. *Rhetoric in the Middle Ages: A History of Rhetorical Theory from Saint Augustine to the Renaissance.* U of California P, 1974.

---. *A Short History of Writing Instruction: From Ancient Greece to Modern America.* 2nd ed., Erlbaum, 2001.

Murphy, James, et al. *A Synoptic History of Classical Rhetoric.* 3rd ed., Erlbaum, 2003.

As shown above, if a single author is also listed as a coauthor for another entry, you should include the full name again without the three hyphens.

Citing a Source that Appears in Another Source (Containers)

Here's where things become a little more complicated. Sometimes, a source will appear in a first container that is then included in a second container. For example, let's say you want to cite an essay that originally appeared in a book (first container) but which you accessed from an online database (a second container). This source has two containers. The information would be cited the following way:

Author(s). Title of Source. Title of First Container, Other Contributors, Version, Number, Publisher, Publication Date, Location. Title of Second Container, Location.

To help you see how this second container works, here is an example of the same essay that was found in print and through an online source.

Ellison, Ralph. "The World and the Jug." *The Collected Essays of Ralph Ellison,* edited by John Callahan. Modern Library, 2003, pp. 155-188.

Torres 12

Works Cited

Barber, Paul. *Vampires, Burial, and Death*. Yale UP, 1989.

Bluestein, Gene. *Poplore: Folk and Pop in American Culture*. U of Massachusetts P, 1994.

Keyworth, Donald. "Was the Vampire of the Eighteenth Century a Unique Type of Undead Corpse?" *Folklore*, vol. 117, no. 3, 2006, pp. 1-16.

Todorova, Maria. *Imagining the Balkans*. Oxford UP, 1996.

FIGURE 27.2 Formatting a List of Works-Cited

MLA style requires that the heading "works-cited" be centered on the page. The margins should be one inch on all sides. The entries should be double-spaced.

Ellison, Ralph. "The World and the Jug." *The Collected Essays of Ralph Ellison,* edited by John Callahan. Modern Library, 2003, pp. 155-188. *Google Books,* books.google.com/books?id=GT3oSgZKvQoC&printsec=frontcover&dq=collected+essays&hl=en&sa=X&ved=0ahUKEwiBmJjQz6LMAhWis4MKHcMzCNEQ6AEIMTAD#v=onepage&q=collected%20essays&f=false.

Formatting a List of Works-Cited

Start the works-cited list on a new page with the centered heading "works-cited" at the top (Figure 27.2). Entries are double-spaced, in hanging indent format, which means the first line of each entry is not indented, but the rest are indented a half inch.

Citing Sources in the List of Works-Cited

27.3 prepare a works-cited list in MLA style.

The following examples of MLA citations are based on the guidelines in the *MLA Handbook for Writers of Research Papers* (8th edition, 2016). We have included models of the most common kinds of entries in a works-cited list. If you do not find a model for a source, you should turn to the *MLA Handbook*, style.mla.com, or a more comprehensive online source like the *Purdue OWL*.

Author | Title | Publication | Online Source

MLA List of Works-Cited

Books and Other Nonperiodical Publications

1. Book, One Author
2. Book, Two Authors
3. Book, Three or More Authors
4. Book, With Editor
5. Book, Corporate or Organization Author
6. Book, Edited Collection
7. Book, Translated
8. Book, Author Unknown
9. Book, Second Edition or Beyond
10. Book, in Electronic Form
11. Document, Government Publication
12. Document, Pamphlet
13. Foreword, Introduction, Preface, or Afterword
14. Sacred Text
15. Dissertation, Unpublished

Journals, Magazines, and Other Periodicals

16. Article, Journal with Volume and Issue Numbers
17. Article, Journal with Issue Number Only
18. Article, Edited Book
19. Article, Magazine
20. Article, Newspaper
21. Article, Author Unknown
22. Article, CD-ROM
23. Editorial
24. Comment from a Web Site
25. Review

Web Publications

26. Web Site, Author Known
27. Web Site, Corporate Author
28. Web Site, Author Unknown
29. Article from an Online Periodical
30. Article from an Online Scholarly Journal
31. Periodical Article Accessed through a Database (Web)
32. Blog Posting
33. *Twitter* Post
34. Podcast

Other Kinds of Sources

35. Film or Video Recording
36. Television or Radio Program
37. Song or Audio Recording
38. Online Video (e.g., *YouTube*)
39. Personal Correspondence, E-Mail, or Interview
40. Work of Art
41. Print Advertisement
42. Commercial
43. Speech, Lecture, or Reading
44. Image or Cartoon
45. Comic Book or Graphic Novel

Citing Books and Other Nonperiodical Publications

Books and other nonperiodical publications are perhaps the easiest to list in the works-cited list. A book citation will have some of the following features:

    ①   ②   ③   ④   ⑤

Author. *Title*. Other contributors, Publisher, year of publication.

The "other contributors" are people like editors, translators, illustrators, or producers who need to be identified in addition to the author. These names are preceded by a phrase identifying their contribution: *edited by, translated by, directed by, performance by,* and so on.

1. Book, One Author

Ambrose, Stephen. *Band of Brothers*. 3rd ed., Simon, 2001.

2. Book, Two Authors

Brett, Michael, and Elizabeth Fentress. *The Berbers: The Peoples of Africa*.
    Wiley-Blackwell, 1996.

3. Book, Three or More Authors

Fellman, Michael, et al. *This Terrible War: The Civil War and Its Aftermath*.
    Longman, 2007.

Note: When a source has three or more authors, use the first author's name followed by et al.

4. Book, With Editor

Albery, Ian, et al. *Complete Psychology*, 2nd ed. Edited by Graham Davey, Routledge, 2014.

5. Book, Corporate or Organization Author

American Psychiatric Association. *Diagnostic and Statistical Manual of Mental*
    Disorders. 4th ed., APA, 1994.

6. Book, Edited Collection

Mueller-Vollmer, Kurt, editor. *The Hermeneutics Reader*. Continuum, 1990.

7. Book, Translated

Dostoevsky, Feodor. *Notes from Underground*. 2nd ed. Translated by Michael Katz,
    Norton, 2001.

8. Book, Author Unknown

Physical Science. McGraw Hill, 2007.

9. Book, Second Edition or Beyond

Kottak, Conrad. *Anthropology: The Exploration of Human Diversity*. 12th ed., McGraw Hill, 2008.

10. Book, in Electronic Form

Darwin, Charles. *On the Various Contrivances by Which British and Foreign Orchids Are Fertilised by Insects*. 2nd ed., D. Appleton and Company, 1895. *Google Books*, books.google.com/books?id=Cv8zAQAAMAAJ&source=gbs_navlinks_s.

11. Document, Government Publication

Arguin, Paul, et al., editors. *Health Information for International Travel 2007-2008: The Yellow Book*. Centers for Disease Control and Prevention, 2007.

12. Document, Pamphlet

Torture, American Style. Historians Against the War, 2006.

13. Foreword, Introduction, Preface, or Afterword

Parker, Hershel. Foreword. *Moby-Dick*, by Herman Melville, Northwestern UP, 2001, pp. xiii-xvi.

14. Sacred Text

The Bible. The New Oxford Annotated Version, 3rd ed., Oxford UP, 2001.

15. Dissertation, Unpublished

Charlap, Marie-Helene. "Once with Women, Now with Women: A Qualitative Study of Identity." New York U, 2008. Dissertation.

Citing Journals, Magazines, and Other Periodicals

Citations for articles that appear in "containers," such as journals, magazines, and other regularly published periodicals, need to include additional information that identifies where the article was published.

A citation for an article contained in a journal, magazine, or other periodical publication includes the following features:

①   ②   ③   ④   ⑤

Author. "Article Title." *Journal Title,* Other contributers, volume number, issue number,

⑥   ⑦

date of publication, page numbers.

16. Article, Journal with Volume and Issue Numbers

Jovanovic, Franck. "The Construction of the Canonical History of Financial Economics." *History of Political Economy,* vol. 40, no. 2, 2008, pp. 213-42.

17. Article, Journal with Digital Objective Identifier (DOI) Numbers

Koi, Kent and Hamid Rabb. "Impact of Acute Kidney Injury on Distant Organ Function: Recent Findings and Potential Therapeutic Targets." *Kidney International,* vol. 89, no. 3, Mar. 2016, pp. 555-564. doi:10.1016/j.kint.2015.11.019.

18. Article, Edited Book

Goodheart, George. "Innate Intelligence Is the Healer." *Healers on Healing,* edited by Richard Carlson and Benjamin Shield, Putnam, 1989, pp. 53-57.

19. Article, Magazine

Zakaria, Fareed. "Obama's Vietnam: How to Salvage Afghanistan." *Newsweek,* 9 Feb. 2009, pp. 36-37.

20. Article, Newspaper

Herszenhorn, David. "Bipartisan Push to Trim Size of Stimulus Plan." *The New York Times,* 5 Feb. 2009, late ed., p. A1.

21. Article, Author Unknown

"The Big Chill Leaves Bruises." *The Albuquerque Tribune,* 17 Jan. 2004, p. A4.

22. Article, CD

Hanford, Peter. "Locating the Right Job for You." *Electronic Job Finder.* Career Masters, 2001.

23. Editorial

The Times Editorial Board. "Kobe Bryant (Finally) Heads to the Lockers." *The Los Angeles Times,* 1 Dec. 2015, www.latimes.com/opinion/editorials/la-ed-1201-kobe-retires-20151130-story.html.

24. Comment from a Web Site

LogicandReason. Comment on "How Reading a Novel Can Improve the Brain." ABC News, 12 Jan. 2014, 9:45 p.m., abcnews.go.com/Technology/reading-improve-brain/story?id=21501657.

25. Review

Toibin, Colm. Review of *The North Water* by Ian McGuire. *The New York Times Book Review*, 11 Apr. 2016, www.nytimes.com/2016/04/17/books/review/the-north-water-by-ian-mcguire.html?_r=0.

Citing Web Publications

When citing sources from the Web, the largest challenge involves the dates of the material. If a Web source does not include a date or the date is not specific, you should include the word "Accessed" and the date on which you last accessed the information. This accessed date is added because the site can be altered.

26. Web Site, Author Known

Nervi, Mauro. "Kafka's Life (1883-1924)." *The Kafka Project*, 1 Aug. 2011, www.kafka.org/index.php?biography.

27. Web Site, Corporate Author

"What is Usability?" The Usability of Knowledge. *User Experience Professionals' Association*, 2010, www.usabilitybok.org/what-is-usability. Accessed 12 Mar. 16.

28. Web Site, Author Unknown

"Animal Sentience." *OneKind*, 2010, www.onekind.org/education/animal_sentience/. Accessed 23 August 2016.

29. Article from an Online Periodical

Scutti, Susan. "Where Does Personality Reside in the Brain? The Frontoparietal Network Makes You Who You Are." *Medical Daily*, 18 Apr. 2016, www.medicaldaily.com/brain-personality-frontoparietal-network-who-you-are-382142.

30. Article from an Online Scholarly Journal

Dougherty, Timothy R. "Knowing (Y)Our Story: Practicing Decolonial Rhetorical History." *Enculturation*, no. 21, 20 Apr. 2016, enculturation.net/knowing-your-story.

31. Periodical Article Accessed Through a Database (Web)

Lu, Xiaofei, and Haiyang Ai. "Syntactic Complexity in College-Level English Writing: Differences among Writers with Diverse L1 Backgrounds." *Journal of Second Language Writing*, vol. 29, Sept. 2015, pp. 16-27. ScienceDirect, doi:10.1016/j.jslw.2015.06.003.

FIGURE 27.3 CITATION MAP: **Citing a Scholarly Journal on the Web**

A citation for an article from a scholarly journal on the Web includes the following features:

① Name of the author, last name first

② Title of the work in quotation marks

③ Name of the journal in italics

④ Volume number and issue number

⑤ Date of publication (year for scholarly journal)

⑥ Range of page numbers for whole article

⑦ Location (URL or DOI)

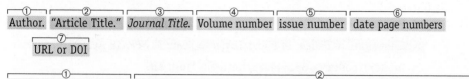

Author. "Article Title." *Journal Title.* Volume number issue number date page numbers
URL or DOI

Marmolego, Gloria, et al. "False Memory in Bilinguals: Does Switching Languages Increase False Memories?" *American Journal of Psychology* vol. 122, no. 1, 2009, pp. 1-16, www.jstor.org/stable/i27784368

FIGURE 27.4 CITATION MAP: **Citing an Article or Other Source from a Database or Other Electronic Collection**

If you need to cite a source that has two containers (an article in a journal in a database; a song in an album accessed on *YouTube*; or a poem from a book included in *GoogleBooks*, for example), the citation will have the following features:

① Name of the author, last name first

② Title of the work in quotation marks

③ Name of the container in italics

④ Volume number and issue number

⑤ Date of publication (year for scholarly journal)

⑥ Range of page numbers for whole article

⑦ Name of database

⑧ DOI or stable URL of article on database

⑨ Your date of access, if the site has no date, or changes frequently

Author. "Article Title." *Journal Title,* volume number, issue number, year, page range. *Database,* doi or stable URL.

McGee, Elizabeth, and Mark Shevlin. "Effect of Humor on Interpersonal Attraction and Mate Selection." *Journal of Psychology,* vol. 143, no. 1, 2009, pp. 67-77. *Academic Search Premier,* doi: 10.3200/JRLP. 143.1.67-77.

32. Blog Posting

Clancy, Jules. "An Embarrassing Peek at My Neglected Edible Garden." *Stonesoup*,
13 Apr. 2016, thestonesoup.com/blog/2016/04/edible-garden/.

33. Twitter Post

@WIRED. "Root is a little robot on a mission to teach kids how to http://bit.
ly/1NxyHDE." *Twitter*, 18 Apr. 2016, 12:05 p.m., twitter.com/WIRED/status/
722138895748636672?lang=en.

34. Podcast

"Is Yellowstone in Danger of Being 'Loved to Death'?" *NPR*, 18 Apr. 2016, www.
npr.org/podcasts/381444908/fresh-air. Fresh Air.

Citing Other Kinds of Sources

There are many other kinds of sources. Especially for performances, you may choose
to begin a citation with an artist's name, a director or producer's name, or the title of
the work. Consult the *MLA Handbook* for specific examples.

① Name of Author, Writer, or Performer (Last Name, First Name)

② Title of the work (italics for complete work, quotation marks for episode, song, or
part of a whole)

③ Title of container, in italics, if applicable

④ Other contributors

⑤ Publisher or broadcaster

⑥ Publication or broadcast date

⑦ Location (a city with state or country)

⑧ Title of second container (if applicable), in italics

⑨ Online source for second container (usually a web address)

35. Film or Video Recording

Cameron, James, director. *Avatar*. Twentieth Century Fox, 2009.

36. Television or Radio Program

"From Pole to Pole." Planet Earth, season 1, episode 1, *BBC*, 25 Mar. 2007. *Netflix*,
www.netflix.com/watch/70207859?trackId=13752289&tctx=0%2C0%2C6e182250
571593e11b44eab18ac6facd1a5efdae%3A024114377c329a254c89e1780a422f0143
0343dc. Accessed 28 Jan. 2014.

37. Song or Audio Recording

Pallot, Nerina. "Rousseau." *The Sound and the Fury*. Idaho Records, 11 Sept. 2015. *Spotify*, open.spotify.com/track/6YfrKVzJ5nfay7bQUeCb8V.

38. Online Video (e.g., *YouTube*)

"It's not you. Bad doors are everywhere." *YouTube*, uploaded by Vox, 26 Feb. 2016, www.youtube.com/watch?v=yY96hTb8WgI. Accessed 1 Mar. 2016.

39. Personal Correspondence, E-Mail, or Interview

Stradler, Josephine E. "Fwd: Business Proposal." Received by Pete Tommel, 4 Sept. 2014.

40. Work of Art

Degas, Edgar. *The Star*. 1879/81, The Art Institute of Chicago.

41. Print Advertisement

"We Stand for Saving Money." Geico. *Newsweek*, 26 Mar. 2012. Advertisement.

42. Commercial

"Share a Coke." Coca-Cola. ABC, 27 June 2014. Commercial.

43. Speech, Lecture, or Reading

Wallace, David Foster. "This is Water." Kenyon College Commencement Speech, 21 May 2005.

44. Image or Cartoon

United States Census Bureau. "World War II: 70 Years On." Infographic. U.S. *Department of Commerce*, 17 June 2015, www.census.gov/library/infographics/world-war-ii.html.

45. Comic Book or Graphic Novel

Lee, Stan, and Ditko, Steve. *Doctor Strange*. No. 53, Marvel Comics, 1993.

A Student's MLA-Style Research Paper

The document shown here uses MLA citation style. You can use this document to observe how an author uses MLA citation style under real conditions, including parenthetical references and a list of works-cited.

Author Title Publication Online Source

Naidus 1

Brian Naidus

PCD 3442

Dr. Will Crampton

12 May 2011

A Whole New World: A Background on the

Life of the Freshwater Shark

The shark has easily become one of the most popular and
recognizable marine species in our culture today. This animal is a
cartilaginous fish of the subclass Selachimorpha, which belongs to the
more notorious class, Chondrichthyes (Waggoner). This diverse group
has a plethora of variation and diversity; over 2,000 recorded, fossilized
species. The first sharks were thought to be introduced between 450
and 420 million years ago, with the earliest known fossil to be a
400 million year old shark known as Leonodus (Martin, "Origin").
Although the shark had evolved to inhabit almost strictly marine
environments, this species had specialized teeth, indicating that it may
have lived in freshwater habitats. This ancient species belonged to a
family, known as xenacanths, a group of early freshwater sharks that
existed at this time.

Currently, there are a few freshwater species of shark, which
remain mostly under the radar, due to their more popular oceanic family
members (Compagno et al., 54). The bull shark, *Carcharhinus leucas*, is a
species that is not only common in warm, coastal waters, but is also able
to tolerate freshwater (Curtis). It is often showcased for its extremely
aggressive behavior, and is undoubtedly the most recognized of the
43 members of the Selachimorpha that are said to have been reported in
freshwater habitats. Among these are the six members of the "River
Sharks," which reside in the East-Indian and West-Central Pacific
Oceans. There is very little known of these rare and possibly
endangered species, although they resemble, cohabit and are sometimes
mistaken for bull sharks themselves. Some sharks may tolerate brackish

Dates and figures
from credible
sources strengthen
the report.

Naidus 2

Fig. 1 Shark Teeth. Ancient multi-cusped teeth for grasping and swallowing prey whole.

water; however some have seemed to prefer water with low or no salinity. All these species share an interesting evolutionary past and their behavior and biology continues to mystify and question those who study them.

The history of sharks is far-branching and can lead to heavy debate. Some species may grow and shed tens of thousands of teeth within a matter of years. It is this reason that their species remains a personal favorite with paleontologists and have been extensively identified. The first fossilized sharks were recognized by their double-cusped teeth, which heavily favors the possibility that these individuals were a freshwater species (Martin, "Origins"). The teeth of these ancient fish were different than those of modern sharks (see fig. 1). Multi-cusped teeth primarily serve the shark to grasp its prey and swallow it whole, while modern teeth have evolved as serrated, single-cusped teeth,

When referencing an entire work, page number is not included.

which allow the shark to tear and gouge its prey and to refrain from swallowing its food whole.

Freshwater sharks can be found in two separate habitats. First they will arrive in coastal rivers via the sea. Secondly, sharks can be found in lakes, which have little or no direct contact with the sea (Budker 137). In the first scenario, freshwater sharks can choose in which habitat to live; temporal or seasonal factors allow the shark to either remain in the freshwater or return to brackish or marine coastal waters. However, if rivers dry up or change course, sharks may be quarantined in lakes, where they are subject to allopatric speciation. If they happen to survive, they will eventually give rise to the formation of new specialized species.

> The topic sentence should state the subject or point of the paragraph.

One of these sharks is the bull shark, or *Carcharhinus leucas*, the most infamous of all sharks to have freshwater ties. It could be the fish's broad habitat or resounding aggressiveness which has labeled it as the world's most dangerous shark. Not only can attacks occur in warm coastal waters, but bull shark incidents have been reported hundreds of miles up inland river systems! This species, which can get up to 500 pounds and 11 feet in length, can be known as other names such as the Zambezi Shark in Africa, or the Lake Nicaragua shark in Central America (Curtis). Their habitat stretches the globe; however these sharks prefer to stay in warm, shallow, murky waters either on the coast or in inland brackish or freshwaters.

Bull sharks presently have a vast habitat in the lakes of Central America. Sharks and sawfish can be seen in Lake Izabel, the largest lake in Guatemala; however they are most known to reside in the waters of Lake Nicaragua. These sharks were first believed to be Brown Sharks, and it wasn't until the 1960s however, that scientists determined that the sharks in Lake Nicaragua were in fact species of *Carcharhinus Leucas*. Much of what we know about these animals is because of the

Naidus 4

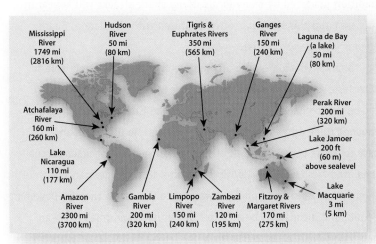

Fig. 2 Sightings of Bull Sharks in Fresh Water (Martin, "Freshwater").

Maps and other graphics should be placed where they can support specific points.

research put together by "The Status of the Freshwater Shark of Lake Nicaragua" assembled by Thomas Thorson, Donald Watson, and Michael Cowan in 1966.

Lake Nicaragua is connected to the sea by the San Juan River which distributes sharks from lake to sea. These 1966 studies reported that sharks use this path, and during times when the river level was low, they discovered that the sharks actually navigate upriver through rapids from the Caribbean, much as spawning salmon do (McCollam).

As shown in figure 2, the Bull Shark can be found in the Mississippi River in the United States and has been recorded in the Amazon River as far as 4000 km from sea! *Leucas* is also extremely prevalent in the Ganges River in India. These sharks have an indiscriminate palate; they will eat almost everything. In the Ganges, they often feed on deceased bodies fed to the river during funerals, a tradition practiced by many locals. Many shark attacks will appear in this area and this species is often confused with the Ganges Shark, *Glyphis gangeticus* (Curtis).

Sharks, which are primarily marine organisms, are only able to withstand and tolerate fresh water, depending on the animal's capability to change. History shows that the first recorded shark was thought to be a freshwater species. Many marine biologists and psychologists believe that all of the earliest marine specimens actually inhabited freshwater or slightly brackish water. Elasmobranches were thought to transition from freshwater into the sea in the mid-Devonian Period, and ultimately, be able to transfer back and forth between habitats (Gilbert et al. 265).

This point of view would be a definite milestone; if sharks evolved from their freshwater ancestors, then the ability for Elasmobranches to survive in saline water would likely be viewed as an impressive applied adaptation. The argument that freshwater precedents saltwater species is based on the fact that an organism's kidneys are more developed in freshwater fish species. This subject is extremely controversial, yet there is not enough evidence to deduce where the first sharks lived.

Most organisms would more than likely have trouble adjusting their eyesight from the different densities of water salinity. However, sharks as a whole rarely rely on their eyes; their other senses are much more important to them. River sharks inhabit murky waters with little or no visibility so it can be suggested that their small beady eyes are not much of a factor for deciding whether or not to venture into new salinities.

On the other hand, osmoregulation in sharks seems to ask the main question: how can a shark's circulatory and urinary systems deal with the change in the salinities? As we know, teleost fishes constantly drink sea water to keep a higher concentration of salt in their bodies.

Naidus 6

Unlike these fish, a shark's salt concentrations are hypertonic to the surrounding water, meaning they must keep a constant supply of water running through their gills. A few experiments have been done comparing the freshwater Bull Shark to its marine counterpart.

Looking at the Lake Nicaragua species, Thorson, Watson, and Cowan concluded that when juxtaposed with its marine equivalent, the freshwater species showcased a loss of osmotic pressure; it measured about two-thirds of that of the marine species. They concluded that the loss of pressure was due to a 20 percent reduction in bodily sodium and chloride (excreted by the rectal gland) and a reduction of half of the animal's urea production. These freshwater animals adapt by critically diluting their urine and increasing their urine rate to around 20 times of those in the ocean. In sum, the internal salt concentration of freshwater Elasmobranches is lower than their marine counterparts, but it is still extremely higher than the internal concentrations of saltwater game fishes (Martin, "Freshwater").

Freshwater sharks have lived a life in the shadows, while the abundant groups of marine sharks have shone in the spotlight. Nonetheless, many species do spend plenty of time in waters with lower salinities, and history reveals that our first sharks may have been freshwater-dwelling. Bull Sharks continue to have the most freshwater influence, and their broad habitat sometimes allows people to mistake them for other species, such as the river sharks of the Ganges River. These sharks have adapted to new waters mostly through techniques of osmoregulation and reduced osmotic pressure. Freshwater sharks can tell us a lot about the past, present, and future of any shark species, and they truly invoke a feeling of appreciation for one of the oldest and magnificent animals on the planet.

When describing the findings of an entire work and the reference is included in the sentence, no parenthetical citation is needed.

The conclusion summarizes the argument and ends with a final statement about the significance of the findings.

Works-Cited

Budker, Paul. *The Life of Sharks.* Columbia UP, 1971.

Compagno, Leonard, et al. *Sharks of the World.* Princeton UP, 2005.

Curtis, Tobey. "Bull Shark." *Ichthyology.* Florida Museum of Natural
History, www.flmnh.ufl.edu/fish/discover/species-profiles/
carcharhinus-leucas. Accessed 18 Mar. 2008.

Gilbert, Perry, et al. *Sharks, Skates, and Rays.* Johns Hopkins P,
1967.

Martin, R. Aidan. "Freshwater Sharks and Rays." *Physiology.*
ReefQuest Centre for Shark Research, www.elasmo-research.
org/education/topics/p_fw_rays.htm. Accessed 20 Mar. 2008.

---. "Origin of Modern Sharks." *Shark Evolution.* ReefQuest Centre
for Shark Research, www.elasmo-research.org/education/
evolution/origin_modern.htm. Accessed 20 Mar. 2008.

McCollam, Douglass. "The Bull Shark." *Slate,* 18 July 2001, www.
slate.com/articles/news_and_politics/the_gist/2001/07/the_
bull_shark.html.

"Shark Evolution." *Shark Evolution.* BioExpedition Publishing,
www.sharks-world.com/shark_evolution/. Accessed 27 Mar.
2008.

Thorson, Thomas, et al. "The Status of the Freshwater Shark of
Lake Nicaragua." *American Society of Ichthyologists and
Herpetologists,* vol. 1966, no. 3, 7 Sept. 1966, pp. 385-402.
JSTOR, doi:10.2307/1441058.

Waggoner, Ben. "Introduction to the Chondrichthyes." *UCMP,* www.
ucmp.berkeley.edu/vertebrates/basalfish/chondrintro.html.
Accessed 30 Mar. 2008.

Using APA Style

In this chapter you will learn how to—

28.1 use APA parenthetical citations.

28.2 create bibliographic entries for a References list.

28.3 prepare a References list in APA style.

A merican Psychological Association (APA) documentation style, like MLA style (Chapter 27), is a method for keeping track of the sources you are using to support your claims, while letting readers know where you found these sources. APA style is commonly used in the social sciences, physical sciences, and technical fields.

In this chapter, you will learn how to use APA style to reference your sources and create a list of "References" at the end of your document. The models of APA citations shown here are the ones most commonly used in college and in the workplace. For more information on APA style, consult the *Publication Manual of the American Psychological Association,* 6th ed. (2010).

Parenthetical Citations

When citing a source with APA style, you first need to include a parenthetical citation. This appears in the text of your document, usually at the end of the sentence that includes the information from your source. For example:

> Children and adults see the world differently, which can make their parents'
> divorce especially unsettling (Neuman, 1998, p. 43).

28.1 use APA parenthetical citations.

Among Africa's other problems, the one that is most significant may be its lack of reliable electrical energy (Friedman, 2008, p. 155).

Note: For a key to the color highlighting used here and throughout this chapter, see the bottom of the next page.

As shown here, a full parenthetical citation includes three important pieces of information: the source's name (usually an author's name), the year the source was published, and the exact location of information in the source (usually a page number).

If readers want to, they can then turn to the list of "References" at the end of the document to see the full citation, which will look like this:

Neuman, G. (1998). *Helping your kids cope with divorce the sandcastles way.* New York, NY: Random House.

In other words, the parenthetical citation and the full reference work together. The parenthetical citation points readers to the References list, which includes all the information needed to locate the source.

APA style also allows you to refer to a whole work by simply listing the author's name and the year of the source. For example:

Genetics are a new frontier for understanding schizophrenia (Swaminathan, 2008).

Autism and psychosis have been shown to be diametrical disorders of the brain (Crespi & Badcock, 2008).

In situations where you are specifically highlighting a study or author, you should move the full parenthetical reference up in the sentence:

According to one study (Adreason & Pierson, 2008), the cerebellum plays a key role in the onset of schizophrenia.

Three books (Abraham & Llewellyn-Jones, 1992; Boskind-White & White, 2000; Burby, 1998) have tried to explain bulimia to nonscientists.

When the Author's Name Appears in the Sentence

If you include the author's name in the sentence, your parenthetical citation should include only the year of the source and page number. The year should follow the name of the source, and the page number is usually placed at the end of the sentence. For example:

Neuman (1998) points out that children and adults see the world differently, which can make their parents' divorce especially unsettling (p. 43).

Friedman (2008) argues that Africa's most significant problem may be its lack of electrical energy (p. 155).

If one part of your sentence draws information from a source but the remainder of the sentence states your own thoughts, you should put the reference immediately after you describe the information from the source. For example:

As Dennet (1995) points out, scientists are uncomfortable with the idea that nature uses a form of reason (p. 213), but I think we must see nature as a life form that is looking out for its best interests.

Citing More Than One Source in the Same Sentence

In APA style, it is common to cite multiple sources that provide the same or similar information, separated with semicolons:

Several researchers (Crespi & Badcock, 2008; Shaner, Miller, & Mintz, 2004, p. 102; Swaminatha, 2008) have shown the toll that schizophrenia takes on a family.

In the sentence above, the writer is referring to entire works by Crespi and Badcock and by Swaminatha, but she is referring only to page 102 in the article by Shaner, Miller, and Mintz.

If you are citing more than one source in the same sentence, but they are making different points, you should put the parenthetical reference as close as possible to the information taken from each source. For example:

Depression is perhaps one of the most common effects of bulimia (McCabe, McFarlane, & Olmstead, 2004, p. 19), and this depression "almost always impairs concentration" (Sherman & Thompson, 1996, p. 57).

Citing a Source Multiple Times

In some situations, you will need to cite a source multiple times. If your document continues to use a single source, then subsequent citations should include only the page number, unless another source comes between them. For example:

> The side effects of brain tumor treatment can include fatigue, brain swelling, hair loss, and depression (Black, 2006, p. 170). Hair loss and other outward signs of treatment can be the most disturbing. Depression, however, perhaps needs more attention because it often requires patients to take antidepressants and stimulants (p. 249).

In the example above, the full parenthetical citation is included early in the paragraph. The second reference, which includes only a page number, is clearly referring back to the source in the first reference.

However, if another source is cited between two parenthetical citations to the same source, the author's name from the first source would need to be repeated in a subsequent reference. For example:

> The side effects of brain tumor treatment can include fatigue, brain swelling, hair loss, and depression (Black, 2006, p. 170). Hair loss and other outward signs of treatment can be the most disturbing. For instance, Becker (2003) discusses her obsession with hiding the incision where the tumor was removed (p. 231). Depression, however, perhaps needs more attention because it often requires patients to take antidepressants and stimulants (Black, 2006, p. 249).

In the example above, the author includes a full parenthetical reference to Black in the final sentence of the paragraph, because the reference to Becker (2003) appears between the first and second references to Black.

Other Parenthetical References

Figure 28.1 shows models of some common parenthetical citations. Choose the one that best fits your source. If none of these models fits the source you are trying to cite, you can use combinations of these models. If you still cannot figure it out, turn to the APA's *Publication Manual*.

Preparing the List of References

28.2 create bibliographic entries for a References list.

Your list of references appears at the end of your document. In this list, you should include full citations for every source you cite. A typical entry includes features like the name of the author, the date of publication, the title of the text, and the place of publication. Here are entries from three types of sources.

FIGURE 28.1
Types of APA Parenthetical References

Not all possible parenthetical references are shown here. If you have a unique source that doesn't fit these examples, you can usually figure out how to cite it by combining these reference models.

Type of Source	Example Parenthetical Reference
Single author	(Gerns, 2009, p. 12)
Single author, multiple pages	(Barnes, 2007, pp. 5–9) or (Barnes, 2007, pp. 34, 121) *The dash signals a range of pages. The comma suggests similar information can be found on two nonconsecutive pages. The "pp." signals multiple pages.*
Two authors	(Hammonds & Gupta, 2004, pp. 203) *The ampersand (&) is used instead of "and."*
Three authors	(Gym, Hanson, & Williams, 2005, p. 845) *The ampersand (&) is used instead of "and."*
More than three authors	*First reference:* (Wu, Gyno, Young, & Reims, 2003, p. 924) *Subsequent references:* (Wu et al., 2003, p. 924)
Six or more authors	*First and subsequent references:* (Williamson et al., 2004, p. 23)
Multiple sources in same parenthetical citation	(Thames & Cain, 2008; Young, Morales, & Cato, 2009; Yu, 2004) *The semicolon separates the sources.*
Two or more works by the same author	(Tufte, 2001, p. 23) and (Tufte, 2003) *The author's name is used with the date.*
Two or more works by the same author in the same year	(Tufte, 2001a, p. 23) and (Tufte, 2001b, p. 11) *The "a" and "b" signal two different works and will appear in the list of references also.*
Different authors with the same last name	(M. Smith, 2005, p. 54) and (A. Smith, 2007, p. 34) *The first letters abbreviate each author's first name.*
Corporate author	(National Aeronautics and Space Administration [NASA], 2009, p. 12) or (American Beef Association, 2006, p. 232) *Well-known acronyms, such as NASA, can be put in brackets the first time and then used in any following parenthetical references.* (NASA, 2009, p. 14)

continued

FIGURE 28.1
(continued)

Type of Source	Example Parenthetical Reference
No author for book	(*Handling Bulimia,* 2004, p. 45) *Use the full title of the source in italics.*
No author for journal article or newspaper article	("Genomics as the New Frontier," 2008, p. 23) *Put the full title in quotation marks.*
No author for newspaper article	("Recession," 2009, p. A4) *The letter "A" is the section of the newspaper and the number 4 is the page.*
Cited in another source	(as cited in Franks, 2007, p. 94)
Web page or other document with no pagination	(Reynolds, 2006, para. 3) *"para." stands for "paragraph," as counted down from the top of the page.*
Web page or other document with no author and no pagination	("Friendly," 2008, para. 7) *Put the first prominent word of the title in quotes, with "para." standing for "paragraph," as counted down from the top of the page.*

Servan-Schreiber, D. (2008). *Anti-cancer: A new way of life.* New York, NY: Viking.

Crespi, B., & Badcock, C. (2008). *Psychosis and autism as diametrical disorders in the social brain. Behavior Brain Science, 31*(3), 241–261.

Chew, R. (2008, February 1). Charles Darwin, naturalist, 1809–1882. *Lucidcafe.* Retrieved from http://www.lucidcafe.com/library/96feb/darwin.html

The References list should include *only* those sources you cite in your document. Do not include sources you consulted but did not cite in your paper.

Your References should list all the sources you cite in alphabetical order by the authors' last names. When an author's name is not known, the work is alphabetized by the first prominent word in its title. When alphabetizing, ignore words like *The, A,* or *An* if they are the first word in the title.

If you are listing two works by the same author in the same year, they should be alphabetized by the first prominent words in their titles and then distinguished by "a," "b," "c," and so on (e.g., 2007a, 2007b, 2007c).

> VAMPIRES IN HOLLYWOOD   12
>
> References
>
> Arthen, I. (2005, December 9). Real vampires. *FireHeart, 2*. Retrieved
>   from http://www.earthspirit.com/fireheart/fhvampire.html
>
> Barber, P. (1989). *Vampires, burial, and death*. New Haven, CT: Yale
>   University Press.
>
> Bluestein, G. (1994). *Poplore: Folk and pop in American culture*.
>   Amherst, MA: University of Massachusetts Press.
>
> Keyworth, D. (2006). Was the vampire of the eighteenth century a
>   unique type of undead corpse? *Folklore, 117*(3), 1–16.

FIGURE 28.2 Formatting a List of References

The "References" heading should be centered, and entries should be double spaced with hanging indentation (each line after the first is indented one-half inch).

Formatting a List of References in APA Style

Start the reference list on a new page with the centered heading "References" at the top (Figure 28.2). Entries are then listed double-spaced. Be sure to use hanging indent format, which means the first line of each entry is not indented, but the rest are indented a half inch.

In professional texts, however, your reference list should match the design of your document. The "References" heading should be consistent with other headings. If you are single-spacing the rest of your document, the reference list should be single-spaced, too, perhaps with spaces between entries.

Citing Sources in the List of References

The following list is not comprehensive. However, we have included models of the most common kinds of entries in a reference list. You can use these examples as models for your own citations. If you do not find a model for a source, you should turn to the APA's *Publication Manual*, sixth edition (2010).

28.3 prepare a References list in APA style.

APA List of References

Books and Other Non-Periodical Publications

1. Book, One Author
2. Book, Two Authors
3. Book, Three or More Authors
4. Book, Corporate or Organization Author
5. Book, Edited Collection
6. Book, Translated
7. Book, Author Unknown
8. Book, Second Edition or Beyond
9. Book, Dissertation or Thesis
10. Book, in Electronic Form
11. Document, Government Publication
12. Document, Pamphlet

Journals, Magazines, and Other Periodicals

13. Article, Journal with Continuous Pagination
14. Article, Journal without Continuous Pagination
15. Article, Edited Book
16. Article, Magazine
17. Article, Newspaper
18. Article, Author Unknown
19. Article, CD-ROM
20. Review

Web Publications

21. Web Site, Corporate Author
22. Web Page, Author Unknown
23. Article from an Online Periodical
24. Scholarly Journal Article with a Digital Object Identifier (DOI)
25. Scholarly Journal Article
26. Podcast

Other Kinds of Sources

27. Film or Video Recording
28. Television or Radio Program
29. Song or Audio Recording
30. Online Video (e.g., YouTube)
31. Personal Correspondence, E-Mail, or Interview

Citing Books and Other Nonperiodical Publications

A book citation will have some of the following features:

1. Name of the author, corporation, or editor with last name first (include "(Ed.)" or "(Eds.)" if the work is listed by editor)

2. Year the work was published, in parentheses (if unknown, use "n.d." for "no date")

3. Title of the work, in italics (capitalize only first word, proper nouns, and any word that follows a colon)

4. City and state or country where the work was published (use standard U.S. Postal Service abbreviations for states; spell out the full names of countries outside of the United States)

5. Publisher

    ①   ②   ③   ④

Author. (Year of publication). *Title of work*. City and state (or country) of

          ⑤

publication: Publisher.

1. Book, One Author

Jones, S. (2001). *Darwin's ghost: The origin of species updated*. New York, NY: Ballantine Books.

2. Book, Two Authors

Pauling, L., & Wilson, E. B. (1935). *Introduction to quantum mechanics*. New York, NY: Dover.

3. Book, Three or More Authors

Newnan, D. G., Eschenbach, T. G., & Lavelle, J. P. (2008). *Engineering economic analysis* (10th ed.). Oxford, England: Oxford University Press.

4. Book, Corporate or Organization Author

American Psychiatric Association. (1994). *Diagnostic and statistical manual of mental disorders* (4th ed.). Washington, DC: Author.

5. Book, Edited Collection

Mueller-Vollmer, K. (Ed.). (1990). *The hermeneutics reader*. New York, NY: Continuum.

6. Book, Translated

Habermas, J. (1979). *Communication and the evolution of society* (T. McCarthy, Trans.). Boston, MA: Beacon Press.

7. Book, Author Unknown

Handbook for the WorkPad c3 PC Companion. (2000). Thornwood, NY: IBM.

8. Book, Second Edition or Beyond

Williams, R., & Tollet, J. (2008). *The non-designer's web book* (3rd ed.). Berkeley, CA: Peachpit.

9. Book, Dissertation or Thesis

Simms, L. (2002). *The Hampton effect in fringe desert environments: An ecosystem under stress* (Unpublished doctoral dissertation). University of New Mexico, Albuquerque, NM.

10. Book, in Electronic Form

Darwin, C. (1862). *On the various contrivances by which British and foreign orchids are fertilised by insects.* London, England: John Murray. Retrieved from http://pages.britishlibrary.net/charles.darwin3/orchids/orchids_fm.htm

11. Document, Government Publication

Greene, L. W. (1985). *Exile in paradise: The isolation of Hawaii's leprosy victims and development of Kalaupapa settlement, 1865 to present.* Washington, DC: U.S. Department of the Interior, National Park Service.

12. Document, Pamphlet

The Colorado Health Network. (2002). *Exploring high altitude areas.* Denver, CO: Author.

Citing Journals, Magazines, and Other Periodicals

A citation for a journal, magazine, or other periodical publication includes the following features:

1. Name of the author, corporation, or editor; last name first, followed by initial of first name and any middle initials

2. Date of publication (year for scholarly journal; year, month, day for other periodicals)

3. Title of the work, not enclosed in quotation marks (capitalize only first word, proper nouns, and any word that follows a colon)

4. Title of the periodical in italics (capitalize all significant words)

5. Volume number (italicized) and issue number (not italicized, but enclosed in parentheses). If each issue begins with page 1, include the issue number.

6. Range of page numbers for whole article

       ①   ②   ③   ④   ⑤
Author. (Date of publication). Title of article. *Title of Journal, volume number*

     ⑥   ⑦
(issue number), page numbers.

13. Article, Journal with Continuous Pagination

Boren, M. T., & Ramey, J. (1996). Thinking aloud: Reconciling theory and practice. *IEEE Transactions on Professional Communication, 39,* 49–57.

14. Article, Journal without Continuous Pagination

Kadlecek, M. (1991). Global climate change could threaten U.S. wildlife. *Conservationist, 46*(1), 54–55.

15. Article, Edited Book

Katz, S. B., & Miller, C. R. (1996). The low-level radioactive waste siting controversy in North Carolina: Toward a rhetorical model of risk communication. In G. Herndl & S. C. Brown (Eds.), *Green culture: Environmental rhetoric in contemporary America* (pp. 111–140). Madison: University of Wisconsin Press.

16. Article, Magazine

Appenzeller, T. (2008, February). The case of the missing carbon. *National Geographic,* 88–118.

17. Article, Newspaper

Hall, C. (2002, November 18). Shortage of human capital envisioned, Monster's Taylor sees worker need. *Chicago Tribune,* p. E7.

18. Article, Author Unknown

The big chill leaves bruises. (2004, January 17). *Albuquerque Tribune,* p. A4.

19. Article, CD-ROM

Hanford, P. (2001). Locating the right job for you. *The electronic job finder* [CD-ROM]. San Francisco, CA: Career Masters.

20. Review

Leonhardt, D. (2008, November 30). Chance and circumstance. [Review of the book *Outliers* by M. Gladwell]. *New York Times Book Review,* p. 9.

Citing Web Publications

Citations for Web documents do not need to include your date of access if you can provide a publication date. However, you do need to provide either the URL from which a source was retrieved or a Digital Object Identifier (DOI). When including a URL or DOI, always insert a break *before* a slash, period, or other punctuation mark.

FIGURE 28.3 CITATION MAP: Citing Part or All of a Web Site

A citation for a Web publication will have some or all of the following features:

① Name of the author, corporation, organization, editor, or webmaster. For authors and editors, last name first followed by initials.

② Date of publication, in parentheses (year, month, day). If no date is given, write (n.d.) to indicate "no date."

③ Title of the individual page, document, or article.

④ Title of the Web site, in italics.

⑤ Retrieval information: the site's URL; do not add a period at the end of the URL.

①
Author of Web site. ② (Date published). ③ Title of document or *Title of Page*. ④ *Title of Overall Web Site*.

⑤
Retrieved

①
Arches National Park ② (n.d.). ③ *Nature & science*. ④ *National Park Service*.

⑤
Retrieved from http://www.nps.gov/arch/naturescience/index.htm

⑤ URL

④ Title of Web site

③ Title of page

FIGURE 28.4 **CITATION MAP: Citing a Journal Article with a DOI**

① Name of the author (last name, initials)

② Publication date

③ Title of article

④ Title of the journal in italics

⑤ Volume number in italics, and issue number (in parentheses, not italicized)

⑥ Page numbers

⑦ Digital Object Identifier. (It is easiest to cut and paste the DOI directly from the original document into your text.)

Author of article. (Publication date). Title of article. *Title of Journal, volume number*(issue number), page numbers. DOI

Pyles, L., & Cross, T. (2008). Community revitalization in post-Katrina New Orleans: A critical analysis of social capital in an African American neighborhood. *Journal of Community Practice, 16*(4), 383–401. doi:10.1080/10705420802475050

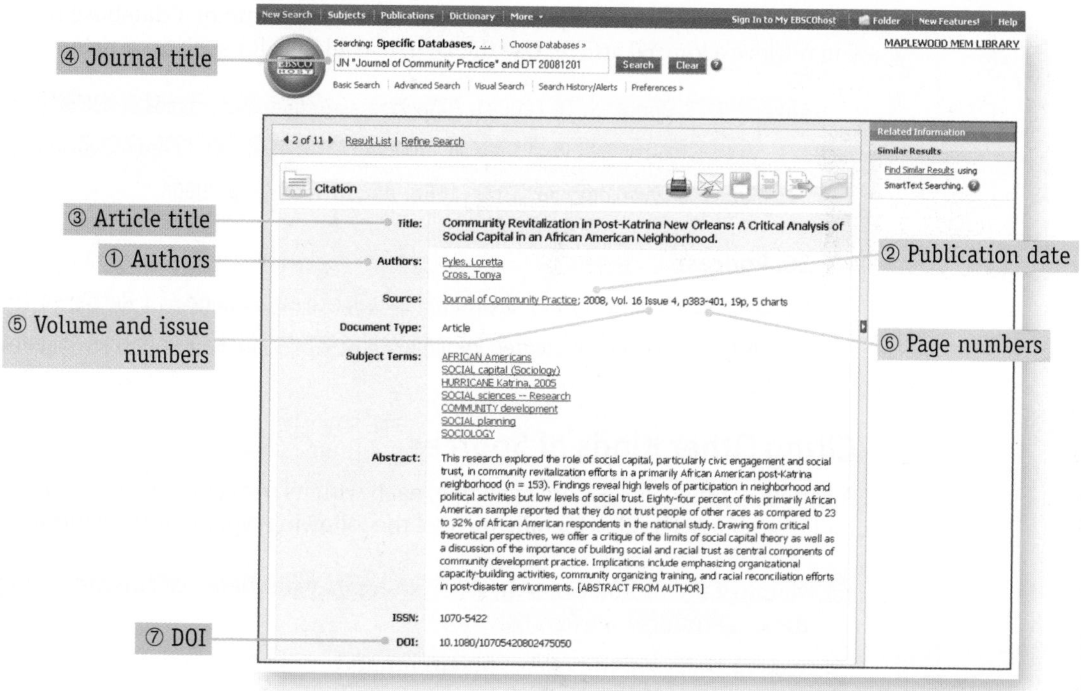

21. Web Site, Corporate Author

U.S. Fish and Wildlife Service. (2008). *Estuary restoration act of 2000*. Retrieved from
http://www.fws.gov/coastal/estuaryRestorationAct.html

22. Web Page, Author Unknown

Clara Barton: Founder of the American Red Cross. (n.d.). *American Red Cross Museum.*
Retrieved from http://www.redcross.org/museum/history/claraBarton.asp

23. Article from an Online Periodical

Vaitheeswaran, V. (2009, April 16). Medicine goes digital. *The Economist.* Retrieved
from http://www.economist.com/specialreports

24. Scholarly Journal Article with a Digital Object Identifier (DOI)

Blake, H., & Ooten, M. (2008). Bridging the divide: Connecting feminist histories and
activism in the classroom. *Radical History Review, 102,* 63–72.
doi:10.1215/01636545-2008-013

25. Scholarly Journal Article

The APA no longer requires you to include the name of a database from which
you retrieve a journal article. Use the DOI, if available, for such an article.

Ankers, D., & Jones, S. H. (2009). Objective assessment of circadian activity and
sleep patterns in individuals at behavioural risk of hypomania. *Journal of
Clinical Psychology, 65,* 1071–1086. doi:10.1002/jclp.20608

26. Podcast

Root, B. (2009, January 27). *Just one more book* [Audio podcast]. Retrieved from
http://www.justonemorebook.com/2009/01/27/interview-with-neil-gaiman

Citing Other Kinds of Sources

A variety of other sources are available, each with its own citation style. The citations
for these sources tend to include most of the following types of information:

1. Name of the producers, writers, or directors with their roles identified in parentheses (Producer, Writer, Director)

2. Year of release or broadcast, in parentheses

3. Title of the work (italics for a complete work; no italics for a work that is a segment, episode, or part of a whole)

4. Name of episode (first letter of first word capitalized)

5. Title of the program (italicized)

6. Type of program (in brackets), e.g., [Film], [Television series], [Song]

7. City and state or country where work was produced

8. Distributor of the work (e.g., HBO, Miramax, New Line)

9. Retrieval information, for works accessed online

27. Film or Video Recording

Jackson, P. (Director), Osborne, B., Walsh, F., & Sanders, T. (Producers). (2002). *The lord of the rings: The fellowship of the ring* [Motion picture]. Hollywood, CA: New Line.

28. Television or Radio Program

Paley, V. (Writer). (2009). Human nature, the view from kindergarten [Radio series episode]. In I. Glass (Producer), *This American Life*. Chicago, IL: WBEZ/Chicago Public Radio.

29. Song or Recording

Myer, L. (1993). Sometimes alone. On *Flatlands* [CD-ROM]. Ames, IA: People's Productions.

30. Online Video (e.g., YouTube)

Jones, M. (2013, April 7). *Anorexia story* [Video file]. Retrieved from https://www.youtube.com/watch?v=tefOtACvz88

31. Personal Correspondence, E-Mail, or Interview

Personal correspondence is not listed in the references list. Instead, the information from the correspondence should be given in the parenthetical citation:

This result was confirmed by J. Baca (personal communication, March 4, 2013).

A Student's APA-Style Research Paper

The document shown here uses APA style for parenthetical citations and the References list. The student writer followed his professor's requirements for formatting his paper; formatting guidelines in the APA *Publication Manual* are intended for submissions to professional journals.

Author   Title   Publication   Online Source

A header with an abbreviated title and page number is included on all pages.

Assortative Mating and Income Inequality

Austin Duus

University of New Mexico

Professor Krause

Economics 445: Topics in Public Finance

Assortative Mating and Income Inequality

Paul Ryscavage begins *Income Inequality in America* (1999) on the premise that the growth in income inequality in the United States in the last thirty years is driven by changes in technology, globalization, and "family structure." The first two factors seem intuitive. Returns-to-education in an economy where exchange is facilitated by personal computers and BlackBerries is both well-documented (Daugherty, 2008; Lynn, 2002) and offers explanatory logic on how an educated segment of the population's income gains could outpace those of the less-educated. However, family structure, the final element in Ryscavage's inequality trifecta, seems suspiciously far removed from the typical industrial activities of the economy. At first, this demographic nuance seems more polemical than empirical. The single-mom menace, the erosion of "family values," and the disappearance of the Ozzie-and-Harriet nuclear family seem more like ideological talking points than matters of economic fact.

What is stunning, however, is how small changes in the aggregate makeup of American households can drastically affect the distribution of income in that population. The proportion of single, female-headed households has increased due to the "independence effect" on the dissolution or preemption of marriages, among other things. Moreover, this type of household is the most likely to be poor (Cancian & Reed, 1999). Judith Treas (1987) refers to these changes in the context of the "feminization of poverty" (p. 283). This sociology catchphrase makes more sense when considered in the context of trends in female labor force participation and the marriage market.

Even more elemental to the question of family structure and its effects on income inequality are the underlying forces by which

> Multiple sources cited in the same sentence are separated by a semicolon. Sources should also be listed in alphabetical order

> When the author's name appears in the sentence, only the year is parenthetically cited, and the page number is cited at the end of the sentence.

ASSORTATIVE MATING 3

individuals choose to partner, and partners choose to sort, in all segments of the population. Beyond income inequality (or equality as the case may be), marriage [or nonmarital partnering] has "implications for . . . the number of births and population growth, labor-force participation of women, inequality in income, ability, and other characteristics among families, genetical [sic] natural selection of different characteristics over time, and the allocation of leisure and other household resources" (Becker, 1973, p. 814). In short, household formation is a largely economic decision, which, like other such decisions, is a choice determined by weighing the costs (including opportunity costs) against expected utility.

Three ellipsis points (...) indicate that some words have been omitted from within a quoted sentence.

Theoretical Framework

Individuals do not pair with other individuals to form households randomly. Instead, one can observe traits by which individuals tend to sort themselves and their mates. Garfinkel and McLanahan (2002) define this process of assortative mating as "the tendency of people to choose partners of similar age, race, educational attainment, and other social, psychological, and biological characteristics" (p. 417). More specifically, they are referring to *positive* assortative mating in which individuals choose similar partners. In the literature, this is sometimes referred to as homogamy. Individuals, for various reasons, sometimes find it advantageous to choose partners who are different from them. This is *negative* assortative mating.

Main headings are centered and boldfaced, using both uppercase and lowercase letters.

The Becker Theory

Gary Becker (1973) was the first to outline a theory of a marriage market. His claims were straightforward. Marriage, like all economic decisions, is an optimized utility function. "Persons marrying . . . can be assumed to expect to raise their utility level above what it would be were they to remain single." Moreover, like all utility functions, a

Secondary headings are flush left and boldfaced, using both uppercase and lowercase letters.

ASSORTATIVE MATING   4

marriage is optimized against a constraint. Potential mates are limited;
therefore, scarcity drives a market in which "many men and women
compete as they seek mates. . . . Each person tries to find the best mate,
subject to the restrictions imposed by market conditions" (p. 814).

> Use four ellipsis points to indicate material omitted between sentences in a quote.

      Becker (1973) found that people might choose to marry simply
because it is easier to have "sexual gratification, cleaning, and feeding"
(p. 818) in-house than to purchase those services. Also, conveniently,
"love" can "reduce the cost of frequent contact and of resource
transfers" (p. 819). Observations about who marries whom suggest
individuals sort by "IQ, education, height, attractiveness, skin color,
ethnic origin, and other characteristics" (p. 815). Sorting by some
heritable traits may be related to creating "desired" offspring.
Additionally, the choice to separate or divorce is determined by
opportunity cost. If there is more to lose, people will think twice about
going to divorce court.

> The findings of credible sources help the author make his point with greater authority.

Negative Assortative Mating

      Becker (1973) speculates there may be negative sorting in regard
to specific "psychological traits, such as a propensity to dominate,
nurture, or be hostile" (p. 824). However, central to Becker's theory of
the marriage market is an assumption of negative sorting in regard to
wages. Jepsen and Jepsen (2002) explain:

> Theories of the sexual division of labor predict that high-
> wage men will pair with low-wage women and that, once the
> couple forms a household, men will specialize in market
> production while women will specialize in home production.
> (p. 442)

> For a quotation of 40 or more words, use a block quote without quotation marks.

However, all empirical studies suggest the opposite is true. While
correlations between spousal wages tend to be very small, usually the
smallest of traits studied, they are positive. It is assumed, generally

without warrant, that male wages and female household production are substitutes, and gains in marriage result from this specialization. Becker (1991) finds the sexual division of labor so compelling as to claim in regard to same-sex couples, "households with only men or only women are less efficient because they are unable to profit from the sexual difference in comparative advantage" (p. 38). Becker, however, fails to specify how having a uterus gives one a "comparative advantage" in dishwashing and food preparation or the relationship between a Y chromosome and market work. It is also unclear why partners of the same sex cannot specialize.

When appropriate, author challenges limitations of sources.

Regardless of the problems with assuming gender essentialism in theory, empirically, Lam (1988) found even high-wage women exhibit a tendency to specialize in household production as they prefer even higher wage men. (Thus their opportunity cost to not participating in the labor market is lower in comparison to their spouses.) This means women do not necessarily specialize in household production because they are female. This finding is further validated when female labor force participation data are disaggregated into cohorts. Black women, for example, tend to participate in the labor force regardless of the income of their spouses (Jepsen & Jepsen, 2002; Treas, 1987).

Evidence for Assortative Mating

Traits Studied

Age. While men seek younger women and women seek slightly older men (Jepsen & Jepsen, 2002), on balance, people seek partners of an age similar to their own (Jaffe & Chacon-Puignau, 1995). Age, in most studies, generally has the "strongest positive assortative mating" (Lam, 1988, p. 478).

Use of multiple heading levels provides access points and makes the text easier to read.

IQ. Jepsen and Jepsen (2002) estimate the correlation as similar to the IQ correlation between siblings.

ASSORTATIVE MATING   6

Education. Lam (1988) calculates schooling being second only to age in positive assortative mating. Strikingly, the particular trait has experienced the largest boost in homogamy. Costa and Kahn (2000) note education as a primary driving force in how couples sort and then where they live. In fact, educational homogamy has increased while homogamy with respect to race, ethnicity, and age has decreased. This could be explained by educational sorting happening later. As individuals marry or partner later in life, they are more likely to partner with someone less like them. While people may choose to partner with someone of a different culture, age, or even weight, level of education seems to be increasingly important as a positive sorting mechanism—at least, among married couples.

Wage. Wage has the weakest correlation coefficient, ranging from .02 to .24 (Jepsen & Jepsen, 2002; Treas, 1987).

Differences by Type of Couple

Married Couples. Married couples tend to be the most homogamous in all factors but wage.

Cohabitating Couples. In general, market variables are more positive with unmarried couples than married couples, but less positive with nonmarket traits (Jepsen & Jepsen, 2002). With respect to race, age, and education, unmarried couples tended to be less homogamous than married couples, but more homogamous with earnings and hours worked. This is consistent with the idea of marriage self-selection, whereby financial independence is a disincentive to marry.

While median measures of unmarried couples in regard to age are identical to married couples, there is a much wider distribution of age differences. Unmarried parents tended to have a more substantial education gap than their married counterparts. However, this is primarily due to the education gap of parents who have never lived together (Garfinkel & McLanahan, 2002).

> Taken as a whole, these results suggest that mothers and fathers who do not marry each other may be less homogamous in terms of age and education than parents who marry . . . . Nonetheless, it appears that a high level of assortative mating still occurs. (p. 429)

Same-Sex Couples. Out of all the types of couples studied, female same-sex couples had the strongest positive assortative mating by wage. Unlike most studies, their wage correlation was statistically significant (Jepsen & Jepsen, 2002). Both male and female same-sex couples had a larger wage correlation than both unmarried and married opposite-sex couples. In contrast, the "estimated coefficient for race and age are noticeably larger for opposite-sex couples than for same-sex couples" (Jepsen & Jepsen, 2002, p. 444).

Black Couples. In many ways, African American family formation is a useful natural experiment on the effects of increased female labor force participation on income inequality. Unlike their White and Latino counterparts, Black women are likely to work regardless of the income of their spouses. Also, "relative to whites, African Americans report less willingness to marry a person of a lower socioeconomic status, and they express less desire to marry" (Jepsen & Jepsen, 2002, p. 437). So while two working spouses would be an equalizing force if upper-income women did not work, this is not the case with Black women.

While female labor force participation may increase inequality within the African American community, it may actually narrow the race-income gap. According to Danziger (1980), in "1974, nonwhite family income was 78 percent of white's; this ratio would have been only 71 percent if nonwhite wives had not worked more than did white wives" (p. 448).

When it would be unclear what source is cited, the authors' names are included in the parenthetical citation.

ASSORTATIVE MATING   8

Analysis

Impact on Income Inequality

Historically we find that female labor force participation was an equalizing force in the United States income distribution. Women's wages were compressed in the phenomenon of the occupational set of nurse/teacher/secretary. However, since World War II (when women first entered the workforce in large numbers), the diversity of market opportunities available to women has substantially increased and as marriage and other assortative mating is delayed well beyond high school, it is increasingly likely pairs will sort by wage as well as by the usual homogamous characteristics.

Conclusion

Currently, empirical data suggest the effects of more high-wage women entering the workforce are mixed (Danziger, 1980). Even for experiments in which all women participated in the labor force, the wage correlation might only increase to around .25 (Treas, 1987), which would have limited effects on the aggregate household income distribution.

Final analyses and conclusions are stated succinctly and prominently.

References

Becker, G. S. (1973). A theory of marriage: Part I. *Journal of Political Economy, 81,* 813–846. doi: 10.1086/260084

Becker, G. S. (1991). *A treatise on the family.* Cambridge, MA: Harvard University Press.

Cancian, M., & Reed, D. (1999). The impact of wives' earnings on income inequality: Issues and estimates. *Demography, 36,* 173–184. doi: 10.2307/2648106

Costa, D. L., & Kahn, M. E. (2000). Power couples: Changes in the locational choice of the college educated, 1940–1990. *Quarterly Journal of Economics, 115,* 1287–1315. doi:10.1162/003355300555079

Danziger, S. (1980). Do working wives increase family income inequality? *Journal of Human Resources, 15,* 445–451. doi:10.2307/145294

Garfinkel, I., & McLanahan, S. S. (2002). Assortative mating among unmarried parents: Implications for ability to pay child support. *Journal of Population Economics, 15,* 417–432. doi:10.1007/s001480100100

Jepsen, L. K., & Jepsen, C. A. (2002). An empirical analysis of the matching patterns of same-sex and opposite sex couples. *Demography, 39,* 435–453. doi:10.1353/dem.2002.0027

Lam, D. (1988). Marriage markets and assortative mating with household public goods: Theoretical results and empirical implications. *Journal of Human Resources, 23,* 462–487. doi:10.2307/145809

References begin on new page. All cited works are included and listed in alphabetical order by author.

The DOI is provided whenever available, even for print articles.

Ryscavage, P. (1999). *Income inequality in America.* Armonk, NY:
    Sharpe.

Treas, J. (1987). The effect of women's labor force participation on the
    distribution of income in the United States. *Annual Review of
    Sociology, 13,* 259–288. doi:10.1146/annurev.so.13.080187.001355

Go to **My**WritingLab to complete this chapter's
exercises and test your understanding of its objectives.

29

Writing with Social Networking

In this chapter, you will learn how to—

29.1 create a social networking site.

29.2 start your own blog.

29.3 contribute an article to a wiki.

29.4 upload videos and podcasts to the Internet.

Despite the mainstream media's needless fretting about whether people write anymore, in reality people are reading and writing more today than ever before. They write comments on *Instagram*, text each other, send e-mails, surf the Web, post on *Facebook*, share opinions on blogs, create *YouTube* videos and podcasts, and use *Twitter* to follow and comment on people and events. If we added up all the time spent on reading and writing through social media, we would almost certainly find that writing is more central to our lives today than for people at any other time in history.

Is This Writing?

Maybe you are wondering whether the new media tools we will discuss in this chapter should still be considered "writing." Blogging looks like writing, but what about social networking sites like *Twitter, Tumblr,* or *Instagram*, or video sharing sites like *YouTube*? Can we still call that writing?

Yes. We live in a time of great technological change, so our understanding of what it means to "write" and be "literate" needs to expand and evolve. This kind of revolution has happened before. When the printing press was introduced in Europe in the fifteenth century, it sparked the Renaissance by dramatically changing what writing looked like and how people used text. Before the printing press, "writing" meant handwritten texts, such as letters and illuminated manuscripts. Monks painstakingly copied books by hand in scriptoriums and circulated them among only a privileged few.

Much like the advent of the Internet today, the invention of the printing press suddenly offered wide access to new ideas and texts, significantly increasing literacy and the sharing of information. More than likely, the monks working in the scriptoriums of Medieval Europe would have been mystified by the kinds of writing that we take for granted today. The ability to mass produce books, newspapers, magazines, junk mail, brochures, and posters would have seemed odd and even threatening to them.

So it's not surprising that we are anxious about how the new communication technologies available today will change what we think of as "writing." Almost surely, writing will continue to evolve, becoming something new and different. The new technologies described in this chapter are only the beginning of that change.

Creating a Social Networking Site

Let's start with the easiest way to go public with your writing—creating a site on a social networking service like *Instagram, Facebook, Tumblr, LinkedIn,* or *Spoke*. The first three, *Instagram, Facebook,* and *Tumblr,* can help you connect and stay in touch with friends and family. Similarly, *LinkedIn* and *Spoke* facilitate networking in the workplace.

29.1 create a social networking site.

Social networking sites are also used by companies, nonprofit organizations, special interest groups, and political parties to stay in touch with and influence customers, supporters, and voters. For example, your college or university probably has *Instagram, Facebook, and Tumblr* sites that let you keep in touch with campus events (Figure 29.1).

FIGURE 29.1 Facebook Page for a University

Many companies and organizations use social networking to reach students, parents, donors, and other interested people.

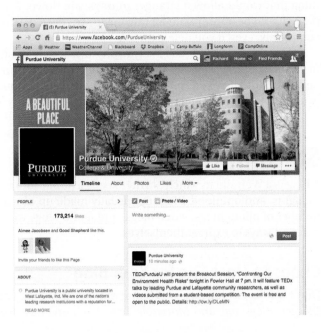

LinkedIn and *Spoke* are career-related social networking services that will help you connect with colleagues, business associates, and potential employers.

Choose the Best Site for You

Each social networking service is a little different. As you choose which one is best for you, think about your purpose. Right now, you probably just want to keep in touch with your friends. But as you move through college and into the workplace, your site may become a way to network with other people in your field.

Also, if you are using your site as a way to showcase your writing, keep in mind that some social networking sites are better than others at supporting longer forms of writing, such as memoirs, commentaries, reviews, position papers, and other kinds of extended texts.

Be Selective About Your "Friends"

It's tempting to add everyone you know or might want to know to your "Friends" list, but that isn't the best approach. You don't want so-called "friends" writing comments on your sites that would put you in a bad light. Employers, for example, routinely check the social networking sites of potential employees. So, only connect with people who are really your friends.

Update Your Profile Regularly

Keep your site up to date with your opinions, ideas, passions, and views on current events. However, don't post private information such as contact information or anything that would allow a stranger to track you down. Any pictures you put on your page should be appropriate for anyone to see (because these photos never disappear completely, even if you delete them).

Over time, your site will likely evolve into a tool for staying in touch with people in your field, professionals and clients, and people in your community. Your site will be less about what you did last weekend and more about your long-term interests, your life, your career, and how you're making a difference in the world.

Starting Your Own Blog

29.2 start your own blog.

A blog is a Web site in which a writer keeps a public journal of his or her experiences, thoughts, and opinions. Blogs are usually made up of words and sentences, but the number of photo blogs, video blogs, and audio blogs will increase as people explore different ways to express themselves.

Choose a Host Site for Your Blog

Don't pay for a blogging site. Some popular free blogging sites include *Wordpress*, *Blogger*, *Blogsome*, and *Moveable Type*. Each one has strengths and weaknesses, so

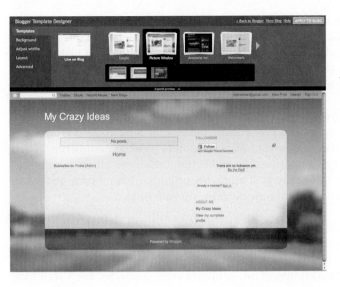

FIGURE 29.2 Choosing a Blog Template

The template you choose for your blog should fit your personality, purposes, and the kinds of topics you want to discuss on your blog.

you might look at each one to determine which will fit your needs and reach the people you want to speak to. Another kind of blog is a "microblog," like *Twitter*, which allows only a small number of words per post. *Twitter* was the groundbreaking microblogging site, but other microblogging services are now available.

When you sign up, your host site will ask you for some basic information—your name, your blog's name, and an e-mail address. You will then choose the template that fits your personality and the kinds of topics you want to discuss (Figure 29.2).

Writing and Updating Your Blog

When you have finished setting up your blog, you can start posting. You can, of course, write about anything that interests you, but here are some strategies for getting the most out of your blog.

Compose, Edit, and Publish Your Ideas. On your blogging site, you will see tabs or buttons on the screen that allow you to "compose," "edit," and "publish" your comments. Type some of your thoughts into the Compose screen and hit the Post or Publish button. Keep adding comments when you have something to share.

Personalize Your Blog. You can add photographs, profiles, polls, newsreels, icons, and other gadgets to your blog's layout. Pick features that are appropriate for the kind of blog you want to create, but don't go overboard with extra material that distracts readers from your ideas and arguments.

Develop Your Blogging Strategy. Your *blogging strategy* should concentrate your posts on a few topics that you really care about and want to comment about regularly. To develop your blogging strategy, make a list of five to ten issues (politics, fashion, sports, unicorns) that you would enjoy writing about even if no one read your posts. Then, boil that list down to a few that you want to post about at least once every week. Concentrate on making substantive comments about those topics, not just quips or snarky gibes. If you want people to visit your site regularly, you need to write about topics that they will find meaningful and interesting.

Let Others Join the Conversation. The initial settings for your blogging site will strictly control who can access and post comments to your blog. As you grow comfortable with your blog, you might want to allow others to write comments. When starting out, only allow "registered users" to add comments. If you allow "anyone" to comment, *spammers* and *trolls* may post annoying or embarrassing comments and images. Then you will need to spend time cleaning up your blog.

While blogging, be mindful about posting negative, slanderous, or callous comments about people, organizations, or companies. Your blog should not be a private journal in which you lash out at others. In some cases, bloggers have been sued for writing slanderous or libelous things about people or companies. So, keep your blog appropriate and based on facts you can verify.

Writing Articles for Wikis

29.3 contribute an article to a wiki.

Wikis are collaboratively written Internet sites that users can add to and edit. One of the most popular, of course, is *Wikipedia*, an online encyclopedia that allows users to add and edit information about almost any topic. Other popular wikis include *eHow, WikiHow, CookbookWiki, ProductWiki, Uncyclopedia,* and *Wikicars.* Figure 29.3 shows a user-written entry from *Wikitravel.* Your professors may ask you to add material to one of these wikis or contribute to a wiki dedicated to your class.

Write the Article

Like any kind of writing, you should begin by thinking about your topic, angle, purpose, readers, and the contexts in which your article will be used. Research your topic thoroughly, draft the article, and edit it carefully. Draft and edit your wiki article with a word processor. This approach will allow you to do all the drafting and revising before you upload it to the wiki. Include any appropriate graphics. You should also have your sources available, so they can be listed in "References," "External Links," and "Further Reading."

Make your article interesting and factually accurate. If your article is about something trivial or mundane, the wiki administrator will simply delete it. If your article is factually inaccurate, other wiki users will rewrite or even delete your work.

Add Your Article to the Wiki

Look for the button that says, "Create an article" or "Start the X article." Most wikis require you to have an account if you want to add an article. Once you log in, the wiki will provide a box where you can cut and paste your article from your word processor.

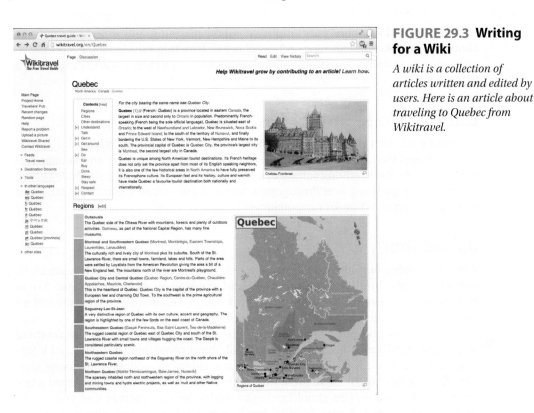

FIGURE 29.3 Writing for a Wiki

A wiki is a collection of articles written and edited by users. Here is an article about traveling to Quebec from Wikitravel.

Edit and proofread your article. Then click the Save Page button. At this point, your article will be added to the wiki.

You should return to your article periodically to make sure someone hasn't altered it to say something inaccurate. You might be pleasantly surprised to find that someone has expanded your article, providing information you didn't know about.

Putting Videos and Podcasts on the Internet

You can upload videos to Web sites like *YouTube, Vimeo, Yahoo! Screen,* and *Hulu.* Some popular podcasting sites include *Podcast Alley, iTunes,* Podcast.com, and *Podcast Feed.*

29.4 upload videos and podcasts to the Internet.

Create Your Video or Record Your Podcast

As with any kind of writing, if you want to create something worth watching or listening to, you should first consider your topic, angle, purpose, readers, and the contexts in which your work will be experienced. Then invent the content and draft a script.

Above all, don't bore your audience. Good planning and tight scripting will allow you to make something worth watching or listening to. After all, it's boring to watch or listen to a person ramble about a topic without a clear sense of purpose or a main point.

Edit Your Work

Edit your work with video- or sound-editing software. Some good video-editing software packages include *MS Movie Maker, Adobe Premiere, Final Cut,* and *iMovie.* The most common sound editing software packages for podcasts include *Adobe Audition, Audacity, Garage Band,* and *Propaganda.* Some of this software comes prepackaged with computers or is free for download.

Upload Your Video or Podcast

When your video or podcast is ready, find the "upload" link or button (Figure 29.4). You will be asked for a title, description, and some keywords called "tags." Try to include as many keywords as you can so that people searching the Web site will be more likely to come across your video or podcast.

These video and podcast sites are public, so don't show, do, or say anything illegal, unethical, or embarrassing. Be careful about providing your personal information. Even if you limit who can access your videos or podcasts, someone else, including friends, might share them with others. Again, as we have mentioned a few times in this chapter, you should only put things on the Internet that you would want viewed or shared with friends, family members, and your current or future employers.

FIGURE 29.4
Uploading a Video

Putting a video on YouTube is easier than ever. This page shows how to load a video by dragging it to the YouTube screen on your computer.

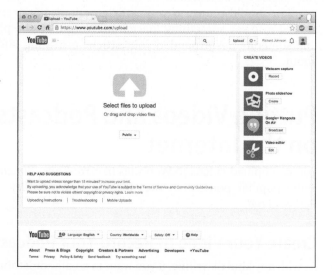

Google and the Google logo are registered trademarks of Google Inc., used with permission.

The social media tools you use to manage your personal life can be powerful platforms for sharing your ideas and arguments with a much larger community. Here's what you can do with these tools.

CREATE Your Profile on a Social Networking Site

Choose the social networking service that is most appropriate for your lifestyle and thoughts. Pick one that has the audience you most want to reach.

BLOG about What Matters to You

You're more likely to update your blog often—and write with a passion that engages and involves readers—if you choose a topic of ongoing personal interest.

SHARE Your Online Compositions

Post your work for others to see. But be strategic about who can see or follow you and how (or if) others can comment on or participate in your site.

PARTICIPATE in Knowledge Sharing on a Wiki Site

Share what you're learning in college by writing entries for wikis—or by correcting erroneous information on others' wikis. Be sure your information is accurate, well researched, and useful to others.

BROADCAST Your Ideas to the World

Use video and audio recording technologies to capture places, events, and people of interest to you and the community. Upload your work to a site where it can be widely shared and discussed.

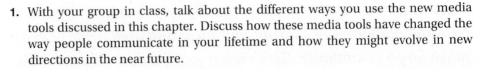

1. With your group in class, talk about the different ways you use the new media tools discussed in this chapter. Discuss how these media tools have changed the way people communicate in your lifetime and how they might evolve in new directions in the near future.

2. How are social networking sites, blogging, and audio and video sharing changing the workplace? How do members of your group expect new media to shape their careers?

3. Do you think people learn social skills online that they can use elsewhere? Or, are social media actually harmful to people's abilities to interact in the real world?

1. If you already have a social media site, revise it in ways that would make it appealing (or at least acceptable) to a future employer. You can change your settings to limit the kinds of materials that would be available to specific readers, like a future employer.

2. With a group of people from your class, shoot a small video or record a podcast. Upload the video or podcast to a video sharing Web site and send a link to your professor.

3. With a group in your class, think of a topic that interests all of you. Then, using three different wikis, read the articles written about that topic. What facts do these wiki articles have in common? What facts are different or missing from one or more of the articles? How do the articles approach the topic from different angles, and what do they choose to highlight?

1. **Learn about a new media tool.** Write a review of one of the new media tools discussed in this chapter. Discuss its future and how you think it will affect your life and your career.

2. **Write your ideas in a blog.** For two weeks, keep a blog in which you write about anything that interests you. Then write an e-mail to your professor in which you explain why you did or didn't enjoy blogging, and whether you think you will continue blogging in the future.

Creating a
Portfolio

In this chapter, you will learn how to—

30.1 create learning portfolios and showcase portfolios.

30.2 get started putting together a portfolio.

30.3 gather materials for your portfolio.

30.4 select the best artifacts to show your skills.

30.5 write a reflection on your work and growth.

30.6 present your materials for academic and career-related purposes.

30.7 create a résumé of your experience and skills.

Your portfolio is a collection of your best work, allowing you to exhibit your experiences, skills, knowledge, and potential. Creating a portfolio also gives you an opportunity to reflect on your writing, leading to deeper, more permanent learning. In college, you will probably need to assemble portfolios for specific courses or create a portfolio as a "capstone" to your studies in your major.

When applying for jobs, you can use your portfolio to show potential employers what you can do. As an employee, you may also be asked to include a portfolio as part of your annual performance evaluations, which are used to determine whether you will receive a promotion or a raise in salary.

Two Basic Kinds of Portfolios

There are two basic types of portfolios: *learning portfolios* and *showcase portfolios*.

Learning Portfolios. Learning portfolios focus on your progress toward mastering specific knowledge and skills. Your learning portfolio walks readers through the

30.1 create learning portfolios and showcase portfolios.

527

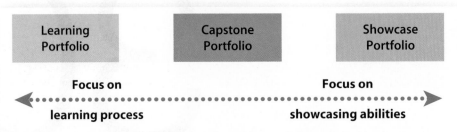

FIGURE 30.1 Kinds of Portfolios and Their Purposes

The focus of your portfolio depends on its purpose. The portfolios you create in school will focus more on the progress of your learning than the portfolios you create to find internships and jobs.

projects you completed for a course or it reviews your college career to show how you have progressed. Your learning portfolio demonstrates what you have accomplished by displaying finished products and occasionally drafts and notes.

Showcase Portfolios. Showcase portfolios display only finished products that demonstrate your work at its best. They are designed to highlight the knowledge and skills that you have mastered. They are like a snapshot that provides a rich and detailed depiction of your skills and know-how at the present moment.

A third kind of portfolio, usually called a "capstone portfolio" is a hybrid of these two (Figure 30.1). Like learning portfolios, capstone portfolios show your progress toward mastery of disciplinary knowledge. However, capstone portfolios usually do not include drafts or notes because they are designed to show your work at its best.

Getting Started on Your Portfolio

30.2 get started putting together a portfolio.

Creating a portfolio is not difficult. Just follow these four simple steps:

1. **Collect** your work in an ongoing "archive" in a binder, on your hard drive, or "in the cloud" on a Web-based server. Each item in your portfolio is called an *artifact*.

2. **Select** the artifacts that best exemplify your knowledge and skills. Your selections depend on who will be viewing your portfolio and why.

3. **Reflect** on what is in the portfolio. This brief reflection reviews your portfolio's materials and sometimes describes the skills and processes you've used to create them.

4. **Present** the portfolio as a complete package. Depending on how it will be used, your portfolio might be print, online, or multimedia.

Your portfolio should include documents, as well as any noteworthy photographs, presentations, and projects. It could also include electronic media, such as images, video, and audio stored on a flash drive or DVD.

Step One: Collect Your Work

Your archive is like a storehouse of raw material. This is where you keep copies of your work until you select them for your portfolio. Find a safe place for storing your archive. You could use your computer's hard drive, but a more reliable choice is a Web-based "cloud storage service." Your college might offer cloud storage or even an e-portfolio system. Alternatively, companies such as Dropbox, Google Drive, or Apple iCloud offer storage space free of charge.

30.3 gather materials for your portfolio.

For print documents, you should also designate a drawer in your desk or file cabinet for archive materials. Keep any projects, awards, letters, or other career-related documents in this drawer. Or, you can scan them and store them electronically on your computer or in cloud storage.

Right now, early in your college career, is a good time to create an archive. That way, you can get into the habit of saving your best work. As an added benefit, you will always know where your work is stored. The worst time to start an archive is when you are getting ready to graduate from college. At that point, much of your best work will have been forgotten or lost.

Archiving for a Specific Course

In some courses, your professor will require you to complete a portfolio that exhibits your work from the class. Make sure you understand what kinds of materials you will need to save for your portfolio. Some professors will ask that you save everything—notes, drafts, and polished copies. Other professors may want just final versions of your work in the portfolio. Here are some things you might be asked to save:

- All notes, including class notes, brainstorming, freewrites, journaling, and so on
- Rough drafts, informal writing, responses, and perhaps your professors' written comments on your drafts
- Peer reviews that you've done for others and that others have done for you
- Final drafts
- Electronic material, such as images, multimedia, blogs, Web-based discussions

Archiving for Your College Career

Your department or college may ask you to create a portfolio at various stages of your college career. For instance, at the end of your sophomore or junior year, your academic program may require you to submit a portfolio that illustrates your ability to write well and think critically. And at the end of your college career, you may be asked to create a capstone portfolio that illustrates what you have accomplished in your major field of study.

Items that you should save for this portfolio include the following:

- Awards or recognition of any kind
- Letters of reference from professors
- Scholarship letters and letters of acceptance
- Materials and evaluations from internships, co-ops, or jobs
- Copies of exams (preferably ones you did well on)
- Evidence of participation in clubs or special events and volunteer work

You never know what you will need, so keep anything that might be useful. If you regularly save these materials, you will be amazed at how much you accomplished during your college years.

Archiving for Your Professional Career

Employers often ask job applicants to bring a professional portfolio to interviews. It is also common for professionals to maintain a portfolio for promotions, performance reviews, and job searches. A professional portfolio could include these materials:

- Reflective cover letter that introduces the portfolio by describing your career goals, education, work experiences, skills, and special expertise
- Résumé
- Examples of written work, presentations, and other materials such as images, links to Web sites, and so on
- Diplomas, certificates, and awards
- Letters of reference

For job interviews, you should create two versions of your professional portfolio. The first version, which you should never give away, will hold all your original materials. The second version, called a "giveaway portfolio," should have copies of your materials that you can leave with interviewers.

Step Two: Select the Best Artifacts

30.4 select the best artifacts to show your skills.

You've been adding to your archive over a semester. Now it's time to begin the process of creating a portfolio. Keep in mind that a single archive can supply the material for several portfolios, each with a different purpose and audience.

Start by considering which of your archived artifacts will allow you to achieve your portfolio's purpose and meet the needs of your readers. Choose items carefully because the best examples of your work need to stand out. Select the key documents that help you achieve your purpose and catch your reader's interest.

Step Three: Reflect on Your Work

You may be asked to write two kinds of reflections for your portfolio, depending on how it will be used:

30.5 write a reflection on your work and growth.

Learning-Focused Reflections. These reflections tell the story of your progress in a class or an academic program. They show that you have made progress toward certain knowledge and skills. They also give you a chance to understand the course objectives more thoroughly and to master the course content even more completely.

Mastery-Focused Reflections. These reflections describe your mastery of certain bodies of knowledge and skills. In this kind of reflection, explain what you can do and how expertly you can do it.

Your Reflection as an Argument

Whether you are creating a learning portfolio or a showcase portfolio, your reflection needs to state an overall claim (i.e., a main point or thesis). Then the reflection should point to specific features of the portfolio as evidence that supports your claim.

Demonstrating these features, Figure 30.2 shows a learning-focused reflection written for a first-year writing course, and Figure 30.3 offers a mastery-focused reflection written by a job candidate. Notice how each reflection makes a claim about the writer's experience and abilities and then points to specific places in the portfolio where readers can find evidence supporting those claims. The first reflection, for a writing course, focuses on process and progress. The second, for a showcase portfolio, focuses almost exclusively on the job candidate's mastery.

Step Four: Present Your Materials

How you present your work is important. So don't just throw your materials into a manila envelope or fasten them together. That looks sloppy and unprofessional. You need to present your materials in an organized and attractive way, so your readers can find the documents they want to see. Use three-ring binder or a nice folder, or create an e-portfolio that you can post on the Internet or copy to a flash drive or DVD.

30.6 present your materials for academic and career-related purposes.

For a Specific Course. Most portfolios for a single course are organized chronologically from the earliest documents to the most recent documents. Your reflection should appear first as an introduction to the portfolio. And if you are asked to include drafts of papers, you should put them *behind* the final versions, not in front of them.

For a Capstone Course. A portfolio for a capstone course can be organized by courses, giving each course its own part and arranged in sequential order. You could also organize the portfolio by genres (e.g., reviews, analyses, reports, proposals) or by topic. Drafts are not typically included in capstone portfolios.

MEMORANDUM

Date: December 12, 2013

To: James Delkins

From: Luke Fine

Subject: Reflection Memo for Portfolio

___

Describes past experiences and early expectations

When I signed up for English 103, I wasn't sure what to expect. My teachers in high school always said I was a good writer, but they also warned me writing in college would be harder. They liked my creativity, but they also often criticized how I organized and expressed my creative ideas. So, one of my goals this semester was to strengthen my writing by learning how to better organize my words and improve my ability to write clearly. In this reflection memo, I will describe how I have tried to improve my writing while meeting the goals of this course.

States the purpose and main claim

Addresses course learning outcomes one by one

Mastering My Writing Process

Before coming to college, I honestly didn't know what a "writing process" was. For me, writing was a matter of sitting down and writing whatever came to mind. Then, I would move a few things around, figure out where paragraphs should be made, and clean up the grammar errors and typos. I guess I always knew this kind of writing wouldn't work in college, but I was getting high grades. Don't fix what isn't broken, as they say.

In English 103, I learned how to work back and forth through stages of writing, including inventing, drafting and organizing, improving the style, and designing the text. Editing and revising is now something

FIGURE 30.2 A Student's Learning-Focused Reflection

This reflection, created for a course in first-year composition, exemplifies one approach to the cover letter. The professor had asked for cover letters that described students' learning progress in terms of the four main course goals.

FIGURE 30.2
A Student's Learning-Focused Reflection

I use to improve my work. Comparing the first and final drafts of my proposal shows how I used my classmates' peer reviews. Every aspect of the final draft is more focused, clear, and compelling. For example, my title and introduction state my purpose clearly; my paragraphs all have good topic sentences; and my plan includes details that were missing in the first draft. I spent far more time revising than I did writing the first draft, but it all paid off.

Points to specific features of the portfolio as evidence that supports his claims

Using Genres

At first, the concept of genres didn't seem revolutionary. I had already learned how to write five-paragraph papers and was pretty good at it. Using genres just seemed like a new way of doing something I was already good at.

As we learned different genres, though, I began to see that each genre allows me to achieve a different purpose. My review, "When in Rome," of the classic movie, *Gladiator*, for instance, allowed me to explain why this movie is still widely watched today. I pointed out that its use of the revenge narrative was the plot line that held it together. I also explained how the historically accurate sets, more than the fighting scenes, are the real magic of the film. Before writing this review, I took movie reviews for granted. Now, I understand what makes a review effective or ineffective, and I can use a lively style to make my reviews interesting.

[Delkins goes on to discuss other ways in which he has met the goals of the course.]

In conclusion, I feel like I have come a long way in four months. Admittedly, I was a bit overconfident about my writing skills when I came to college. I knew I wasn't a great writer, but I always did well in my English classes. Now, as I look over the works in my portfolio, I see quite a bit of growth in my writing. I'm writing more clearly, my work is better organized, and I have developed a stronger voice. I'm including visuals and designing documents. These skills should be helpful in college, and they will help me succeed in my future.

Looks to the future, explaining how these skills will be important in college and beyond

Welcome to My Portfolio

Let me begin by thanking you for reviewing the materials in my portfolio. Here, I have collected examples of my best work to demonstrate my knowledge, experience, and abilities as a civil engineer. These materials will show you that I am well trained and innovative, and I have a solid background in the design, construction, and maintenance of interstate highways and bridges.

> States purpose and main point while acknowledging the readers.

The first section includes examples from my internships and cooperative experiences. I have included two reports that I wrote during my internship with the Michigan Department of Transportation. They show my ability to write detailed, accurate observations of road and bridge conditions, while making clear recommendations. The third document is a proposal for a research project on quick-setting concrete that I helped write during my co-op experience with New Horizons Construction.

> Explains the content and organization of the portfolio.

The second section shows materials created for my courses at Michigan State. Our professors used projects to teach us how to problem solve and come up with innovative solutions to challenging problems. The reports, proposals, specifications, and technical descriptions included here were selected to demonstrate the range of my abilities and my communication skills.

> Highlights key features of each section.

The third section includes letters of reference, awards, scholarships, and other recognition of my work at Michigan State and my internship and co-op experiences.

My goal in this portfolio is to show you that I am ready to begin contributing to your firm right away. If you would like to see other examples of my work, please call me at 517-555-1855 or e-mail me at rgfranklin@msu.edu.

> Concludes with a main point and contact information.

FIGURE 30.3 A Job Candidate's Mastery-Focused Reflection

In this reflection, a job candidate highlights a few of her strengths and experiences. The reflection serves mostly as an introduction to the portfolio.

For a Job Application Packet. Portfolios used for job searches typically follow the organization of a résumé. After your reflection, you should include parts like Education, Related Coursework, Work Experience, Skills, Awards, and Activities. Each part should have its own divider with a tab.

If you will be presenting your portfolio in person (e.g., in an interview or to a group), you should organize your material in a way that helps you orally explain your background and experiences. It should also look professional and focused.

Creating an E-Portfolio

Making an e-portfolio is not difficult, especially if you know how to create a basic blog or Web site. The blogging site *Wordpress* is a popular place to house e-portfolios. Many universities also have created their own hosting sites for e-portfolios.

Electronic portfolios have several advantages:

- They can be accessed from any networked computer.

- They can include multimedia texts such as movies, presentations, and links to Web sites you have created.

- They can include scanned-in documents that show comments that others have handwritten on your work.

- They provide interactivity for the reader. For example, the reflective letter can link directly to the documents in the portfolio or to items on the Internet.

- They include materials and links to information. For example, you might put links to your university and academic department to help interviewers learn about your educational background.

- They can be updated easily, and older versions can be archived.

- They provide customized access features for different readers.

- They eliminate copying costs.

Some e-portfolio services even allow you to maintain an electronic archive from which you can create a virtually limitless number of e-portfolios, each targeted for a specific purpose and audience.

Keeping Your Portfolio Up to Date

This semester, your professor may be asking you to create a portfolio only for your writing class. Right now, though, would be a good opportunity to also create your portfolio archive that you can use throughout your college career and beyond.

Each semester, spend a little time updating your portfolio. Look for chances to create documents that fill out any gaps in your portfolio. You can also find opportunities to add to your portfolio by joining clubs, doing volunteer work, and completing internships or co-ops.

It takes an hour or so each semester to update your portfolio. When you are nearing graduation and starting to look for a job, you will be thankful you did.

Creating a Starter Résumé

30.7 create a résumé of your experience and skills.

You professor may ask you to include a résumé in your portfolio. At this point in your college career, it probably doesn't seem like you need a résumé—at least not for a few more years. Increasingly, though, résumés are being used for college-related purposes, like scholarships, applications, and internships. Plus, if you create a "starter résumé" now, you can keep it up to date with new experiences.

A résumé is a profile of yourself that usually fits on one page (Figure 30.4). Like a profile, your résumé offers basic facts about your life. It should tell a story about your education, work experience, awards, and activities. Your résumé needs to make a good impression, because it is the first item your readers, including employers, will see.

For a college student or recent college graduate, the *archival résumé* is usually the most familiar and appropriate. It includes the following features:

Career objective. A career objective is a sentence or phrase that describes the career you are seeking.

Educational background. Your educational background should list your current college degree and any other degrees in reverse chronological order—most recent to least recent. List your major and minors. Sometimes career-related coursework is listed here.

Work experience. Any jobs, internships, or co-ops that you have held should be listed, starting with the most recent and working to the least recent.

Skills. Résumés often include a section listing career-related skills, such as leadership training, computer skills, languages, bookkeeping, and so on.

Awards and activities. List any awards you have earned and any organized activities in which you have participated. Scholarships can appear here.

References. Your references are the people who will vouch for you—professors, supervisors, and other professionals. In most résumés, the line "References available upon request" appears at the bottom of the page.

Again, you may not think you need a résumé right now, but starting one early in your college career will help you figure out what you need to accomplish before graduating. That way, when you are ready to graduate, you will have a competitive résumé for the career you want.

Anne Simmons Franklin

834 County Line Rd.   Home: 618-555-2993
Hollings Point, Illinois 62905   Mobile: 618-555-9167
                                       E-mail: afranklin@unsb5.net

Name and contact information placed up front.

CAREER OBJECTIVE

A position as a naturalist, specializing in agronomy, working for a distribution company that specializes in organic foods.

Career objective describes position sought.

EDUCATIONAL BACKGROUND

Bachelor of Science, Southern Illinois University, expected May 2015.
Major: Plant and Soil Science
Minor: Entomology
GPA: 3.2/4.0

WORK EXPERIENCE

Intern Agronomist, December 2013–May 2014
Brighter Days Organic Cooperative, Simmerton, Illinois

Work experience is supported with details.

- Consulted with growers on organic pest control methods. Primary duty was sale of organic crop protection products, crop nutrients, seed, and consulting services.
- Prepared organic agronomic farm plans for growers.
- Provided crop-scouting services to identify weed and insect problems.

Field Technician, August 2013–December 2013
Entomology Department, Southern Illinois University

- Collected and identified insects.
- Developed insect management plans.
- Tested organic and nonorganic pesticides for effectiveness and residuals.

SKILLS

Computer Experience: Access, Excel, Outlook, PowerPoint, and Word.
Global Positioning Systems (GPS). Database Management.
Machinery: Field Tractors, Combines, Straight Trucks, and Bobcats.
Communication Skills: Proposal Writing and Review, Public Presentations,
Negotiating, Training, Writing Agronomic and Financial Farm Plans.

Skills are listed separately for emphasis.

AWARDS AND ACTIVITIES

Awarded "Best Young Innovator" by the Organic Food Society of America
Member of Entomological Society of America
Vice-President, Entomology Club, Southern Illinois University,
2012–present

Awards and activities are listed later in the résumé.

REFERENCES AVAILABLE UPON REQUEST

FIGURE 30.4 A Résumé

This résumé was created by graduating senior.

Use this guide to help you begin and complete your portfolios.

COLLECT Your Work in an Archive

Get into the habit of saving your documents and projects in an archive. For a specific course, you may want to save *everything,* from notes to rough drafts to final drafts, from print documents to audio files to images to movies. For a capstone portfolio in the middle or at the end of your academic career, you will want to save a variety of examples of your best work. The safest and most convenient storage place is an electronic archive, provided by your school or other cloud-storage service.

SELECT the Works for a Specific Type of Portfolio

When you have a specific type of portfolio in mind, start selecting the works from your archive that will help you to achieve your purpose and that will be most useful for your readers.

REFLECT on What the Portfolio Shows: Your Learning Process, Your Abilities, and Your Experience

Every portfolio needs some kind of reflection or cover letter that introduces readers to the portfolio. In your reflection, make your argument about what the portfolio shows by pointing out to readers what they should notice.

PRESENT Your Portfolio

If you're using a binder or folder for your portfolio, include a table of contents and tabbed section dividers. If you're creating an e-portfolio, use an attractive Web page design, links, and an easy-to-use navigation system.

KEEP Your Portfolio Up to Date

Revisit your portfolio at the end of each semester. It will be useful when you begin your job search. Many professionals maintain an ongoing portfolio for career development, promotions, and new opportunities.

CREATE Your Starter Résumé

Even if your professor doesn't require a résumé for your portfolio, right now would be a good time to start one. That way, you can fill it in and update it throughout your college career.

1. Brainstorm the development of a portfolio for this course or another course. Describe to your group how you would collect, select, reflect on, and present your work.

2. Imagine your dream job and the portfolio and interview for this position. Analyze the rhetorical situation for this interview and portfolio. Briefly, write down notes that define the topic, angle, purpose, readers, and contexts for this kind of portfolio. Also, discuss how the rhetorical situation might change to suit different kinds of job interviews.

3. Imagine that your major requires that you create a capstone portfolio, including what you learned and how you learned it. Make a list of the kinds of artifacts that you will want to have saved for this portfolio, with a brief explanation of what each artifact would show about you.

Try
This
Out

1. Go online and find an e-portfolio created by a college student. What kinds of artifacts are included? Is there anything surprising about the documents or projects the student has included? How is the portfolio organized and designed? Does the organization make things easy to find? Does it make a good impression?

2. Go online and find at least two professional e-portfolios from people who are pursuing a career like the one you want to pursue. What is included in their portfolios? How well does the cover letter introduce and explain the contents of the portfolio? What specifically works well or could be improved?

3. Write the résumé you would like to have when you graduate from college. Put down your degree, major, and the year you will graduate. List jobs, internships, and co-ops you would like to have before graduating. Identify the skills you want to develop while you are at college. List the activities you want to participate in while at college. Your résumé should fit on one page.

Write
This

1. **Create a mini-portfolio.** With your most recent assignment in this course, create a mini-portfolio that charts your progress from prewriting through drafts and feedback to final drafts. Write a cover letter in which you reflect on your writing process for this assignment. In your reflection, make a claim about your learning and support it by pointing to specific places where you have improved each draft, and by explaining the choices you made and why.

2. **Critique an e-portfolio on the Internet.** Find an interesting e-portfolio on the Internet. Write a three-page rhetorical analysis in which you analyze its effectiveness. How does the author use reasoning (*logos*) to demonstrate his or her knowledge and abilities? How does he or she establish a sense of authority (*ethos*)? Where, if anyplace, does the author use emotion (*pathos*) to add personality to the portfolio?

> Go to My**Writing**Lab to complete this chapter's exercises and test your understanding of its objectives.

31

Succeeding on
Written Exams and Assessments

In this chapter, you will learn how to—

31.1 prepare yourself to succeed on a written examination.

31.2 begin the exam with confidence, while budgeting your time.

31.3 organize your ideas so you can answer questions quickly and effectively.

I n many classes, you will be asked to take written exams, which are also called "essay exams" or "essay tests." Written exams are used to evaluate how well you understand the course materials and whether you can apply what you learned. These exams allow you to demonstrate higher-order thinking skills such as interpreting ideas, applying new knowledge, analyzing solutions, synthesizing concepts, and evaluating assumptions.

In some situations, written exams are also used for *assessment*, which means they partially measure how well your academic program or your university is achieving its goals. Assessment exams are similar to the ones you took in high school or for college admissions (e.g., the SAT or ACT), but college assessment tests will ask you to demonstrate a more sophisticated understanding of critical reading, analytical reasoning, problem solving, audience analysis, and genre awareness.

Written exams can be stressful. Succeeding on these exams becomes much easier when you learn a few helpful test-taking strategies, while using the time-tested rhetorical strategies you have already learned in this book. In this chapter, you will learn a four-stage process for doing well on written exams: (1) preparing for the exam, (2) starting the exam, (3) answering the questions, (4) finishing the exam (Figure 31.1).

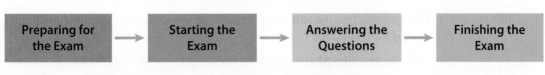

FIGURE 31.1 A Four-Stage Process for Successful Written Exams

To be successful on written exams, you should think of the writing process in four stages.

Step One: Prepare for the Exam

Studying course materials closely and taking good notes during lectures are important first steps for succeeding on exams. You can also internalize the material by *being active* with it. Here are some strategies for doing that.

31.1 prepare yourself to succeed on a written examination.

Meet with Study Groups

In your class or where you live, find two to five other dedicated students who are willing to meet regularly to study together and collaborate on projects. It helps to find group members who understand the material both better than you and also not as well as you. People who have already mastered the material can answer your questions and help you enrich your comprehension. Meanwhile, working with people who have not mastered the material can help you strengthen your own understanding. Teaching others is often the best way to master material yourself.

Set up a regular time and place to meet with your study group, perhaps one or two times a week. Your university's student union, a library, or a local café can be good places for regular meetings.

Ask Your Professor about the Exam

You can often improve your chances of succeeding by asking your professor about the exam during class or office hours. Your professor may be willing to provide you with sample questions or examples from previous semesters' tests. However, professors don't like it when students ask, "Will this be on the test?" Instead, ask more open-ended questions like these:

- What kinds of questions are likely to appear on the exam?

- What do you expect us to be able to do on the exam?

- How many questions will be on the exam, and how long should each one take to answer?

- What is the best way for us to prepare for this exam?

- Can you give us a list of five to ten major concepts or key ideas that we should master for this exam?

- Can you describe what a typical answer to the exam question would look like?

Pay Attention to Themes and Key Concepts

As you review your lecture notes and textbook, look for thematic patterns to help you organize and remember the course material. Ask yourself: Which are the fundamental ideas and topics that the professor and textbook have focused on? Which key concepts seem to be coming up over and over again? When the professor summarizes, what are the major points she or he keeps coming back to? What are some larger trends or concepts that seem to underlie all the ideas and theories learned in this class?

Study the Assessment Rubric or Scoring Guidelines

It's hard to study for an assessment exam, but you can often find the outcomes that are being measured. On the Internet, you can usually look up the rubrics or "scoring guidelines" for major assessment exams, including the CLA+, CAAP, ETS Proficiency Profile, and the GRE Analytic Writing section.[1] A rubric is a scoring grid that defines and describes the criteria being used to evaluate the completed written exams. You can use these criteria to shape your answers. For example, if the rubric states, "Establishes a clear thesis statement that makes an argumentative claim," then you know the evaluators will be specifically looking for this kind of argumentative thesis statement. Knowing what the evaluators are looking for will help you score higher on the test.

Create Your Own Questions and Rehearse Possible Answers

You and your study group could also come up with your own questions that might appear on the exam. Then, practice generating responses to them. To get ready for the exam, you can rehearse your responses a few different ways:

- **Talk to yourself:** Mentally run through your responses and, if possible, explain your answers out loud.

- **Talk to others:** Talk through possible answers with members of your study group. Your roommates and friends might also be willing to listen and offer suggestions.

---

[1] These exams are generally known by their acronyms. The full names are Collegiate Learning Assessment (CLA+), Collegiate Assessment of Academic Proficiency Test (CAAP), the Educational Testing Service (ETS) Proficiency Profile, and the Graduate Records Examination (GRE).

- **Outline or plan out responses:** By yourself or with others, use outlines to map out possible responses. Then express your answers orally or in writing.

- **Simulate the actual exam:** Write sample responses within the allotted amount of time. If you have test anxiety and tend to go blank before an exam, try to practice in the actual classroom where you will be taking the test.

Step Two: Start Your Written Exam

So the professor has just handed you the exam. Now what? Take a deep breath and relax. Avoid the impulse to just dive right in.

31.2 begin the exam with confidence, while budgeting your time.

Review the Exam Quickly to Gain an Overall Picture

Take a moment to review the whole exam. Pay attention to the kinds of questions and how much time is recommended for answering each one. Identify questions that are worth the most points so you can devote extra time to them.

As you read each question, jot down a few quick notes or a brief outline of an answer. Then, move on to the next question. These notes and outlines have two benefits: First, they help you warm up by putting your ideas down before you start writing, and, second, they will show your professor where you were going with each answer even if you run out of time. Your professor won't give you full credit for an outline or an incomplete response, but you might receive partial credit if it looked like you were going to answer the question correctly.

Also, questions on later parts of the exam will often help you form answers to questions that appear earlier in the exam. By giving the whole exam a review, you should begin to see the larger themes that make up the foundation of the exam.

Budget Your Time

Allocate your time properly, so you can answer all the questions. As shown in Figure 31.2, you might find it helpful to divide the time available into quarters. Spend the first quarter considering each question, jotting down some notes, and outlining a possible answer for each question. Devote the second and third quarters to actually drafting your answers one by one. Save most of the fourth quarter for revising, editing, and proofreading.

Step Three: Answer The Questions

When answering a written exam question, your goal is to demonstrate how much you *know* about the course material and what you can *do* with it. So for most questions, you will want to keep the organization and style of your response fairly simple and straightforward.

31.3 organize your ideas so you can answer questions quickly and effectively.

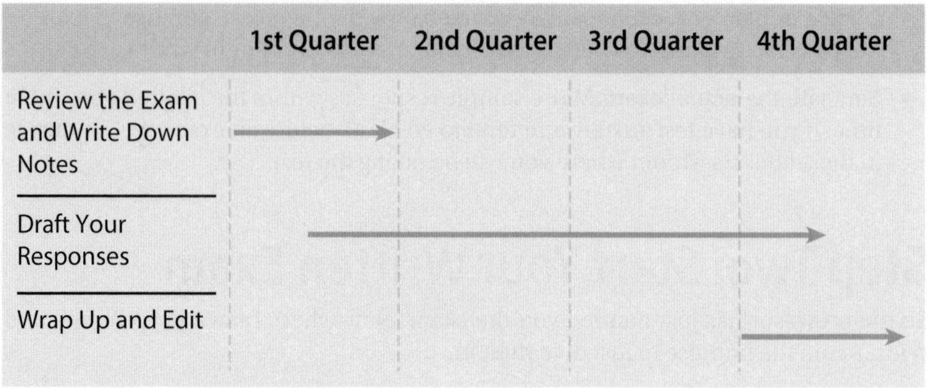

	1st Quarter	2nd Quarter	3rd Quarter	4th Quarter
Review the Exam and Write Down Notes	→			
Draft Your Responses		→		
Wrap Up and Edit				→

FIGURE 31.2 Budgeting Your Time

Don't just dive in and start writing. Take some of your total time to plan your answers, and be sure to leave time at the end to write conclusions and do some final insertions, editing, and proofreading.

Organize Your Answer

Remember that a written exam answer should always have an introduction, body, and conclusion. That advice might sound obvious, but under pressure, people often forget these three parts. Instead, they just start writing everything they know about the topic. This "shotgun" approach often leads to an unfocused burst of facts, names, and concepts that make little sense when looked at together.

As you think about the organization of your answer, keep the following three-part structure of a written answer in mind:

Introduction. Your introduction should state your main claim, which the rest of your answer will support. In your introduction, you might also restate the question, forecast the organization of your response, and provide some background information (e.g., historical facts, important people, or key terms). Your introduction should comprise just a few sentences.

Body. The body should be divided into two to five major points, with each point receiving a paragraph or two of coverage. Put your major points in the topic sentences at the beginning of your paragraphs. Then support each major point with facts, data, reasoning, and examples. Usually, you will find that the professor is asking you to do one of the following things:

- *Narrate* a historical event, story plot, or process (narrative or summary).

- *Explain* the importance of an event, person, or place (analysis).

- *Describe* something or explain how it works (description).
- *Define* something (definition).
- *Divide* something into groups or types (classification).
- *Compare* two or more things (comparison and contrast).
- *Argue* for or against a point (summary of both sides, argument for one).
- *Solve* a problem (description of problem and argument for a solution).

Once you know what your professor is asking you to do, the structure of your answer will become much more obvious.

Conclusion. Briefly indicate that you are wrapping up (e.g., "In conclusion,") and restate your main point. If time allows, you may also want to raise a new question or problem, describe the implications of your response, state the significance of the problem, or make a prediction about the future.

Step Four: Complete the Written Exam

Save some time at the end of the exam for revising and editing. You won't have many minutes left, so focus on improving completeness and clarity.

Checklist for Revising and Editing Written Exams

❐ Reread each prompt to make sure you answered the question.

❐ Look for any missing key points and determine if you have time to add them.

❐ Check whether your ideas are clear and easy to follow.

❐ Emphasize key terms and concepts by repeating them or highlighting them.

❐ Proofread for grammatical errors, spelling mistakes, and garbled handwriting.

Remember, you will gain nothing by racing through the exam and being the first person out the door. You won't look any smarter, and your professor really won't be impressed. So you may as well use every minute available to do the best job you can.

One Student's Written Exam

To demonstrate some of the ideas from this chapter, here is a typical written exam response. This student's answer is clear and straightforward. The organization is basic, and the style is plain. It's not perfect, but it achieves the student's goals of showing that he understands the course materials and can do something with that information.

Written Prompt: In your opinion, which world region or subregion has the greatest potential to improve its development status over the course of your lifetime? Why? What environmental, human, and/or economic resources could it depend on in this process?

Shane Oreck

Question 3B

Prominently identifies which question he is answering.

The region that has the greatest potential to improve is Latin America. The reasons for this are: its natural resources, technological potential, tourism potential, and human resources.

Introduction restates the question, makes a clear main claim, forecasts the answer, and uses keywords from lectures and readings.

First, countries within Latin America have a bounty of natural and biological resources. If these countries eventually become able to excavate these minerals in a more efficient manner, then their economies will boom. In the Amazon, many countries are looking toward this uncharted area in hopes of finding biological sources that will help in the areas of science and health. So with time and ingenuity, hopefully this will help Latin America's overall economy as well.

Second, because Latin America is so close to more technologically advanced countries, they have a great potential for technological advancement. This would be better accomplished through a new trade pact with countries in North America, China, and even Russia. If Latin America can make trade a more viable source of income, then the continent's economy will probably grow quickly, bringing with it technological advance and outside sources that could be of importance for these countries.

Each body paragraph begins with a strong topic sentence that announces a key point.

Third, tourism has great potential because of Latin America's beautiful oceans, views, landscapes, historical attractions, and architecture. They do face difficulties in terms of modern facilities and safety for Western guests, but if they can create the infrastructure, then, like Mexico, they could enjoy substantial economic relief from the money generated. Some Latin American countries, like Brazil, are already enticing travelers into their areas.

The writing style is simple and straightforward.

Lastly, Latin America has a vast array of human resources. Although current educational resources are lacking, these countries are heavily populated. With improved educational opportunity and greater availability of birth control (so that women can plan families and enjoy educational opportunities as well), the people of Latin America would be an enormous untapped resource in which to revitalize the region, economically and culturally.

It's true also that many other regions of the world, including China and India, would be candidates for greatest potential for improving their development status. But because of its location, abundance of mineral and biological resources, trade and technological potential, tourism, and human resources, Latin America certainly has the potential for creating a bright future. Besides, Latin America has been so poorly developed for so long, it seems due for a resurgence. Where else can it go but up?

> The conclusion wraps up with its main point and a look to the future.

Notice how this writer has responded to the prompt in a straightforward way. He uses a simple organizational pattern, with a clear introduction, body, and conclusion. The main points are easy to locate in each paragraph's topic sentence. Specific and meaningful facts, details, and reasoning are used to support claims.

Written exams can be challenging, but you will be more successful if you prepare properly. To do your best, follow these steps.

PREPARE for the Exam

Take good notes on lectures and readings, but also consider the key themes and issues that your professor keeps returning to. Form and regularly meet with a study group. Go to your professor and ask what the exam will look like, and what he or she wants to see in an exam response.

START the Exam

First read through the entire test to get the big picture, making note of how much time you have and the point value for each question. Budget your time so you can outline some answers, write out the exam, and revise and edit.

ANSWER the Questions

Make sure you understand what each question is asking you to do (explain, describe, define, classify, compare, argue for or against, or solve a problem). As you write, stay focused and try to maintain a simple, straightforward organization and style.

FINISH Up with Revising and Editing

Reread the questions and make sure your responses answer them. Make any adjustments needed and highlight places where you address the question directly. Save some time for proofreading.

1. Individually, freewrite an answer to this question: What is hard about taking written exams? After you've responded, discuss your answer with your group and come up with three strategies for making written exams more manageable.

2. In your group or in an informal written response, examine the student example in this chapter. Explain why its structure is appropriate for a written exam.

3. In your group, talk about the student example in this chapter in terms of a genre. What genre, rhetorical patterns, and argumentative strategies are used in this response? What other genres, rhetorical patterns, or argumentative strategies could the student use to organize this response, perhaps in a better way?

1. As an informal writing assignment, create at least two written exam prompts for another course you are taking. Share them with your group.

2. Find a textbook that has questions at the ends of the chapters and choose one question that you think could be on a written exam. Make an outline of how you would respond to that question. Discuss your outline with your group.

3. Type "sample written exam" into an Internet search engine and locate three examples of written exam questions. Analyze these questions and explain what kinds of content, organization, and style would be appropriate in an answer.

1. **Write a practice written exam response.** As practice, write a written exam response to a prompt created by your professor. When you are finished, compare your responses with those of your classmates.

2. **Argue for or against written exams in college.** Write a letter to the editor of your campus newspaper. In your letter, argue for or against the use of written exams as a way of testing and assessing students. If you are arguing against using written exams, what would be a suitable replacement for them?

Go to **My WritingLab** to complete this chapter's exercises and test your understanding of its objectives.

32

Presenting
Your Work

In this chapter, you will learn how to—

32.1 get started on developing your presentation.

32.2 organize your presentation with a good introduction, body, and conclusion.

32.3 design your visual aids.

32.4 deliver your presentation with confidence and style.

32.5 practice and rehearse your presentation.

Presenting your work in college courses and in the workplace is a common experience. More and more, professors are asking students to present their projects to an audience, usually their class. And almost any professional career will require you to present information, ideas, and opinions to others. Your ability to speak effectively in front of an audience will be an important cornerstone of your success.

Public speaking is even more important today as video streaming, video conferencing, and webinars have become common tools of the workplace. These media technologies make it possible to write and then present your material in real time and answer your audience's questions.

Most genres go hand in hand with public presentations. In your advanced college courses, you will be asked to present reviews, commentaries, and arguments as well as research papers. In the workplace, you will need to present profiles, reviews, proposals, and reports to your clients and supervisors.

In this chapter, you will learn some easy strategies for turning your documents into public presentations. As you learn and practice these simple techniques, your presentations will become more polished and persuasive.

Step One: Plan Your Presentation

Because this book is about writing, not public speaking, we are going to assume that you already have written a document that you need to turn into a presentation. Now it is time to repurpose your paper into a presentation for an audience.

32.1 get started on developing your presentation.

Ask a Few Key Questions to Get Started

Solid preparation is the key to successful public speaking. You can start by asking the Five-W and How questions:

- *Who* will be in my audience and what do they need?

- *What* do I want to accomplish with my presentation?

- *When* will I be asked to speak?

- *Where* will I be giving my presentation?

- *Why* am I presenting this information to this audience?

- *How* should I give the presentation?

Answer each of these questions separately. Your answers will help you figure out what you need to do to prepare for your presentation.

Keep in mind that your audience wants more from you than just the information in your document. After all, if they wanted to, they could just read it. So why do they want you to present it to them instead? A presentation gives the audience a chance to interact with you and ask questions. Your audience wants to see you in action. They want you to *perform* the material for them.

Choose the Appropriate Presentation Technology

Think about what technology will be available and which type would fit your presentation. The technology you choose depends on the audience's expectations and the place where you will be giving your talk. Each kind of presentation technology offers advantages and disadvantages. Figure 32.1 describes some of the advantages and disadvantages of each.

Allot Your Time

If you are new to speaking in public, a five- to ten-minute presentation might sound like a lifetime. The time, though, will go fast. A ten-minute presentation, for example, is only the equivalent of a four- or five-page double-spaced paper. So you will need to budget your time carefully to avoid going over the time allowed.

Figure 32.2 shows how to budget the time for a presentation with three major topics. Of course, if your presentation's body has fewer or more than three topics, you should make adjustments in the times allowed for each one. These time limits are flexible guidelines, not rigid rules.

FIGURE 32.1

Pros and Cons of Presentation Technologies

	Advantages	Disadvantages	Genres
 **Digital Projector**	• Can be dynamic and colorful • Allows for animation and sound • Creates a more formal atmosphere	• Requires a darkened room, which might inconvenience your audience • Diverts attention from the speaker to the screen • Computers are not completely reliable	Memoirs, Profiles, Reviews, Evaluations, Literary Analyses, Rhetorical Analyses, Arguments, Proposals, and Reports
 **Overhead Projector**	• Projectors are available in most workplaces and classrooms • Easy to print transparencies from most home printers	• May seem static and lifeless • Need to manually change transparencies during your presentation	Evaluations, Literary Analyses, Rhetorical Analyses, Arguments, Proposals, and Reports
 **Whiteboard, Chalkboard, Notepad**	• Allows speaker to create visuals on the spot • Audience pays more attention because speaker is moving	• Cannot be used with a large audience • Writing on board requires extra time • Ideas need to be transferred clearly to the board	Evaluations, Commentaries, Arguments, Proposals, and Reports
 **Poster Presentation**	• Allows audience to see whole presentation • Presents highly technical information clearly • Allows audience to ask specific questions	• Cannot be presented to more than a few people • Can be hard to transport	Memoirs, Profiles, Reviews, Evaluations, Literary Analyses, Rhetorical Analyses, Arguments, Proposals, and Reports
 **Handouts**	• Helps reinforce major points • Can offer more detail, data, and statistics • Audience has something to take home	• Handing them out can be distracting in large presentations • Audience members may read the handouts instead of listen to the talk	Profiles, Reviews, Literary Analyses, Rhetorical Analyses, Arguments, Proposals, Research Papers, and Reports

	5-Minute Presentation	10-Minute Presentation	20-Minute Presentation
Introduction	Half a minute	1 minute	1–2 minutes
Topic 1	1 minute	2 minutes	5 minutes
Topic 2	1 minute	2 minutes	5 minutes
Topic 3	1 minute	2 minutes	5 minutes
Conclusion	Half a minute	1 minute	1 minute
Questions and Answers	1 minute	2 minutes	3 minutes

FIGURE 32.2
Allotting Your Presentation Time

When planning your presentation, budget your time carefully to scale your talk to the time allowed.

Step Two: Organize Your Ideas

The organization of your presentation will typically follow the genre you are using to organize your document. Your talk should have a distinct beginning, middle, and end. That advice might seem obvious, but public speakers often forget to properly introduce their talk to the audience, or they abruptly end without summing up their main points.

32.2 organize your presentation with a good introduction, body, and conclusion.

There is an old speechmaking saying you should commit to memory: *Tell them what you're going to tell them. Tell them. Tell them what you told them.*

Introduction: Tell Them What You're Going to Tell Them

The introduction of your talk is almost always the most critical part of your presentation. At the beginning of your speech, you have a small window—perhaps a minute or two— to capture the audience's attention while stating your topic, purpose, and main point.

Speakers make some or all of the following moves in their presentation's introduction:

Identify your topic. Tell your audience what your presentation is about.

State the purpose of your presentation. Explain the objective of your talk.

State your main point. Tell them what you want to prove or support.

Stress the importance of your topic to the audience. Explain why this issue is important to them and why they should pay attention.

Offer background information on the subject. Provide enough information to familiarize the audience with your topic.

Forecast the structure of your talk. Tell them how your talk will be organized.

These moves can be made in any order.

You might also come up with a good *grabber* to start out your speech. A grabber captures the audience's attention by stating something interesting or challenging. Some effective grabbers include:

A rhetorical question: "Do you ever wonder why child actors tend to have personal problems when they become adults?"

A startling statistic: "A recent survey shows that 74 percent of women students report that they have been sexually harassed at this university. Meanwhile, 43 percent of male students report they have been harassed."

A compelling statement: "If nothing is done about global climate change, it is likely that polar bears will become extinct in the wild during our lifetime."

An anecdote: "Last year, I finally climbed my first mountain over 14,000 feet. In many ways, climbing that mountain affirmed to me that I had triumphed over the injuries I sustained in Afghanistan two years before."

An interesting observation: "Have you ever noticed that the word *ogre* appears in the middle of the word *progress*? I keep that ogre in mind whenever I'm trying to do something new, because I know something or someone is going to try to hold me back."

A show of hands: "Let's see a show of hands. How many of you think the pizza here in town leaves something to be desired?"

A good grabber identifies your topic while giving your audience something to think about.

The Body of Your Talk: Tell Them

In the body, state your major points and support them with facts, reasoning, examples, data, quotations, and other forms of proof you can offer.

In most situations, the body of your presentation should follow the same pattern as the body of your document. Divide your text into two to five major issues that you want to discuss with the audience. If you try to cover more than five topics, you risk overwhelming the audience with more new information than they can handle. So organize the body of your talk to feature the most important things you want them to remember.

Here's a good strategy that might help you strip down your talk to something you can handle in a small amount of time. Look through your document and ask yourself, "What does my audience *need* to know about this topic to make a decision?" Then cross out any material that goes beyond need-to-know information.

Conclusion: Tell Them What You Told Them

Once you signal that you are about to conclude, you will have the audience's heightened attention for the next two minutes. Take advantage of their attention by repeating your main point in a clear and memorable way. A typical conclusion will include some or all of the following moves:

Signal clearly that you are concluding. Make an obvious transition that signals the end of your talk, such as "Let me wrap up now" or "Finally."

Restate your main point. Tell your audience exactly what you have been trying to explain or prove in your talk.

Reemphasize the importance of your topic to the audience. Be clear about why the audience should care about your topic. Answer their "Why should I care?" questions.

Call the audience to action. If you want the people in your audience to do something, tell them what you think they should do. Be specific about the actions you want them to take.

Thank the audience. When you are finished, don't forget to say, "thank you." This phrase signals to the audience that your presentation is done, and it usually prompts them to applaud.

Remember to keep your conclusion brief. Once you say something like, "In conclusion," you have just one or two minutes to finish up. If you ramble beyond a couple of minutes, your audience will become restless and annoyed.

Question and Answer

At the end of your talk, you should be prepared to answer a few questions from the audience. The question and answer period offers you a good opportunity to interact with the audience and clarify your ideas. You should be ready to answer three types of questions:

A Request for Clarification or Elaboration. Questions that ask you to clarify or elaborate are opportunities to reinforce some of your key points. When you receive this kind of question, start out by rephrasing the question for the audience. Rephrasing will allow you to put the issue in your own words and state it loudly enough for the audience to hear. Then answer the question, expanding on the information in your talk. Try to use each question to restate one of your major points.

A Hostile Question. Occasionally, an audience member will ask a question that challenges the information you provided in your talk. Here is a good three-step strategy for answering these kinds of questions:

1. **Rephrase the question.** State the question in terms that will allow you to answer it in ways that reflect your own understanding or beliefs.

2. **Validate the question.** Tell the audience that you understand the questioner's concerns and even share them.

3. **Elaborate and move forward.** Explain that the course of action you are supporting handles the issue better or seems more reasonable.

The Heckling Question. In rare cases, an audience member will want to challenge you with a heckling question. In this situation, you need to recognize that the questioner is *trying* to sabotage your presentation. He or she wants you to become flustered. Don't let the heckler do that to you. After trying your best to answer a question or two from a heckler, simply say, "I'm sorry you feel that way. We have other people with questions. Perhaps we can meet after my talk to discuss your concerns." Then look away from that person. Usually, someone else in the audience will ask a question and you can move on.

When the question and answer period is over, you should briefly thank the audience again. This will usually prompt another round of applause.

Step Three: Design Your Visual Aids

32.3 design your
visual aids.

Visual aids will help you clarify your ideas and illustrate your main points for the audience. Perhaps the best way to create visual aids is to make slides with the presentation software (*PowerPoint*, *Keynote*, or *Presentations*) that was packaged with your word-processing software.

Format Your Slides

Whether you are presenting in a large lecture hall with a projector or to a few people with a poster presentation, slides are some of the best visual aids available (Figure 32.3). Here are some strategies for formatting your slides:

FIGURE 32.3
Creating Slides

Shown here are a title slide and a body slide from a profile paper repurposed as a presentation. The photographs add a strong visual identity to the slides.

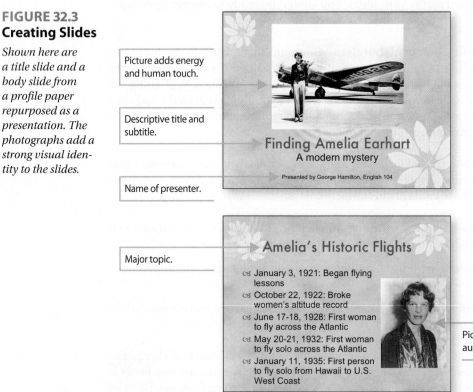

- Title each slide with an action-oriented heading.

- Put five or fewer major points on each slide. If you have more than five major points, divide that topic into two slides.

- Use left-justified text for most items on your slides. Centered text should only be used for slide titles.

- Use dark text on a white or light background whenever possible. Light text on a dark background can be difficult to read.

- Use bulleted lists of phrases instead of paragraphs or sentences.

- Use photos, icons, and graphics to keep your slides fresh and active for the audience. Make sure your graphics look good on the screen. Increasing the size of a Web-based graphic, for example, can make the image look blurry or grainy.

You will be tempted to pack too much material onto each slide. Don't do that. Effective slides, like the ones shown in Figure 32.3, need to be simple and easy to interpret. You don't want your audience trying to puzzle out the meaning of your complicated slides instead of listening to your talk.

Step Four: Prepare Your Delivery

The usual advice is to "be yourself" when you are speaking in public. Of course, that's good advice for people who are comfortable speaking in front of an audience. Better advice is to be an actor and play the role that fits your topic and your audience.

32.4 deliver your presentation with confidence and style.

Body Language

Ideally, the movements of your body should help you reinforce your message and maintain the audience's attention.

Dress Appropriately. Choose clothing that reflects your audience's expectations and the topic of your talk. Even when you are presenting to your classmates, you should view it as an opportunity to practice your professional persona. Dress as though you are presenting in a professional workplace.

Stand Up Straight. When speakers are nervous, they tend to slouch, lean, or rock back and forth. These movements look unprofessional and make it difficult for you to breathe regularly. Instead, keep your feet squarely under your shoulders with knees slightly bent. Keep your shoulders back and down and your head up to allow good airflow. If your shoulders are forward and up, you won't get enough air and the pitch of your voice will seem unnaturally high.

Use Open Hand and Arm Gestures. For most audiences, open hand and arm gestures will convey trust and confidence. Avoid folding your arms, keeping your arms at your sides, or putting both hands in your pockets, as these poses will convey a defensive posture that audiences do not trust.

Make Eye Contact. Each person in the audience should believe you made eye contact with him or her at least once during your presentation. If you are nervous about making eye contact, look at the audience members' foreheads instead. They will think you are looking them directly in the eye.

Move to Reinforce Major Points or Transitions. If possible, when you make important points, step forward toward the audience. When you make transitions in your presentation from one topic to the next, move to the left or right. Your movement across the floor will highlight the transitions in your speech.

Voice and Tone

As you improve your presentation skills, you should start paying more attention to your voice and tone.

Speak Lower and Slower. When speaking to an audience, you will need to speak louder than you normally would. As your volume goes up, so will the pitch of your voice, making it sound unnaturally high to the audience. By consciously lowering your voice, you should sound just about right. Also, nerves may cause you to speak too quickly. Silently remind yourself to speak slowly.

Use Pauses to Reinforce Your Major Points. Each time you make a major point, pause for a moment to let the audience commit it to memory.

Use Pauses to Eliminate Verbal Tics. Verbal tics like "um," "ah," "like," "you know," "OK?" and "See what I mean?" are nervous words and phrases that fill gaps between thoughts. If you have a verbal tic, train yourself to pause when you feel like using one of these sounds or phrases.

Minimize How Often You Look Down at Your Notes. Look at your notes as little as possible. Looking down at your notes causes your neck to bend, which restricts your airflow and makes your voice harder to hear. Plus, notes can become a distracting "safe place" that keeps you from engaging visually with your audience.

Step Five: Practice and Rehearse

32.5 practice and rehearse your presentation.

You should leave plenty of time to practice your presentation out loud. Even better advice, though, is to "rehearse" what you are going to say and how you are going to say it. Rehearsal allows you to practice your presentation in a more realistic setting.

Practice, Practice, Practice

Practice involves speaking your presentation out loud to yourself. As you are working through your presentation verbally, you should memorize its major points and gain a sense of its organization and flow. While practicing, you should:

- Listen for any problems with content, organization, and style.

- Edit and proofread your visuals and handouts.

- Decide how you are going to move around as you deliver the speech.

- Pay attention to your body language and voice.

If you notice any problems as you are practicing your presentation, you can stop and fix them right away.

Rehearse, Rehearse, Rehearse

The secret to polishing your presentation is to rehearse it several times. Unlike practice, rehearsal means speaking from beginning to end *without stopping*.

As much as possible, you want to replicate the experience of giving your real talk. After each rehearsal session, you should make any revisions or corrections. Recruit friends to listen as you rehearse your presentation. They will provide you with a live audience, so you can gauge their reactions to your ideas. Another possibility is recording your presentation, with either audiovisual or just audio equipment.

Practicing will help you find any major problems with your talk, but rehearsal will help you turn the whole package into an effective presentation.

Here are some helpful guidelines for developing and giving presentations.

ANSWER the Five-W and How Questions about Your Presentation

Think about the who, what, where, when, why, and how issues that will shape the content, organization, style, and design of your presentation.

CHOOSE the Appropriate Presentation Technology

Depending on the size of your audience and the room in which you will be speaking, consider what kind of presentation technology would best allow you to present your ideas.

ORGANIZE Your Ideas

More than likely, the genre of your document offers a good organization for your talk. Remember to "Tell them what you're going to tell them. Tell them. Tell them what you told them."

DESIGN Your Visual Aids

Slides work well for most presentations. Use presentation software, such as *PowerPoint, Keynote,* or *Presentations,* to convert your paper into a colorful and interesting set of slides. If slides aren't appropriate, you should look into the possibility of using a whiteboard or handouts.

THINK about Your Body Language

Consider issues like how you will dress and how you will stand and move when you are presenting. Practice making eye contact with people.

IMPROVE Your Voice and Tone

Work on speaking lower and slower, while using pauses to reinforce your major points. Also, use pauses to eliminate any verbal tics, such as "um," "ah," "like," and "you know."

PRACTICE and Rehearse

Ultimately, practice and rehearsal are the best ways to improve and polish your presentation. Use practice to help you revise your talk and correct errors. Use rehearsal to polish your presentation and make it as persuasive as possible.

1. In a small group, share your opinions about what works well in a presentation. Discuss effective and ineffective presenters (coaches, teachers, public speakers) that you have experienced in the past. What traits made these people effective or ineffective as public speakers?

2. Find a video clip online of a particularly problematic speech. Imagine that you and your group are this person's speaking coach. Being as helpful as possible, what advice would you give this person to improve his or her future presentations?

3. With your group, choose three things from this chapter that you would like to use to improve your presentation skills. Then take turns presenting these three things to your "audience."

1. Find a speech on a video Web site. In a brief rhetorical analysis, discuss the strengths and weaknesses of the presentation. Specifically, pay attention to the content, organization, style, and use of visuals in the presentation.

2. Outline a two-minute speech on a subject that you know well. Then, without much further thought, give a presentation to a small group of people from your class. Practice making the six introductory moves mentioned in this chapter and the five concluding moves.

3. Using presentation software, turn one of the papers you wrote for this class into slides. Break your paper down into major and minor points and add pictures and illustrations that will help your audience visualize your ideas. Print out your slides and look for any inconsistencies in wording or places where you could reorganize.

1. **Evaluate a public presentation.** Attend a public presentation on your campus. Instead of listening to the content of the presentation, pay attention to how it was organized and presented. Then write a review, a rave, or a slam of the presentation. Use the presentation strategies described in this chapter to discuss the strengths and weaknesses of the speaker and his or her talk.

2. **Repurpose a written text into a presentation.** Choose a major project for this course or another one and turn it into a presentation. Choose the appropriate presentation technology. Make sure you develop an introduction that captures your audience's attention. Divide the body of your paper into two to five major topics for your presentation. Then develop a conclusion that stresses your main points and looks to the future. When you have finished creating your talk, spend some time practicing and rehearsing it. Your professor may ask you to present your talk in class.

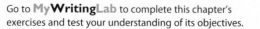

Go to **My WritingLab** to complete this chapter's exercises and test your understanding of its objectives.

Memoirs

The First Morning

EDWARD ABBEY

In this narrative, Edward Abbey tells the story of his first morning as a ranger in Arches National Monument. Abbey is considered one of America's best nature writers, and his works have inspired many outdoor enthusiasts. In this narrative, which is the first chapter of Abbey's book Desert Solitaire, *watch how he uses metaphors and detail to bring the desert to life and draw you into his story.*

This is the most beautiful place on earth.

There are many such places. Every man, every woman, carries in heart and mind the image of the ideal place, the right place, the one true home, known or unknown, actual or visionary. A houseboat in Kashmir, a view down Atlantic Avenue in Brooklyn, a gray gothic farmhouse two stories high at the end of a red dog road in the Allegheny Mountains, a cabin on the shore of a blue lake in spruce and fir country, a greasy alley near the Hoboken waterfront, or even, possibly, for those of a less demanding sensibility, the world to be seen from a comfortable apartment high in the tender, velvety smog of Manhattan, Chicago, Paris, Tokyo, Rio or Rome—there's no limit to the human capacity for the homing sentiment. Theologians, sky pilots, astronauts have even felt the appeal of home calling to them from up above, in the cold black outback of interstellar space.

For myself, I'll take Moab, Utah. I don't mean the town itself, of course, but the country which surrounds it—the canyonlands. The slickrock desert. The red dust and the burnt cliffs and the lonely sky—all that which lies beyond the end of the roads.

The choice became apparent to me this morning when I stepped out of a Park Service housetrailer—my caravan—to watch for the first time in my life the sun come up over the hoodoo stone of Arches National Monument.

I wasn't able to see much of it last night. 5 After driving all day from Albuquerque—450 miles—I reached Moab after dark in cold, windy, clouded weather. At park headquarters north of town I met the superintendent and the chief ranger, the only permanent employees, except for one maintenance man, in this particular unit of America's national park system. After coffee they gave me a key to the housetrailer and directions on how to reach it; I am required to live and work not at headquarters but at this one-man station some twenty miles back in the interior, on my own. The way I wanted it, naturally, or I'd never have asked for the job.

Leaving the headquarters area and the lights of Moab, I drove twelve miles farther north on the highway until I came to a dirt road in on the right, where a small wooden sign pointed the way: Arches National Monument Eight Miles. I left the pavement, turned east into the howling wilderness. Wind roaring out of the northwest, black clouds across the stars—all I could see were clumps of brush and scattered junipers along the roadside. Then another modest signboard:

WARNING: QUICKSAND
DO NOT CROSS WASH
WHEN WATER IS RUNNING

The wash looked perfectly dry in my headlights. I drove down, across, up the other side and on into the night. Glimpses of weird humps of pale rock on either side, like petrified elephants, dinosaurs, stoneage hobgoblins. Now and then something alive scurried across the road: kangaroo mice, a jackrabbit, an animal that looked like a cross between a raccoon and a squirrel—the ringtail cat. Farther on a pair of mule deer started from the brush and bounded obliquely through the beams of my lights, raising puffs of dust which the wind, moving faster than my pickup truck, caught and carried ahead of me out of sight into the dark. The road, narrow and rocky, twisted sharply left and right, dipped in and out of tight ravines, climbing by degrees toward a summit which I would see only in the light of the coming day.

Snow was swirling through the air when I crossed the unfenced line and passed the boundary marker of the park. A quarter-mile beyond I found the ranger station—a wide place in the road, an informational display under a lean-to shelter, and fifty yards away the little tin government housetrailer where I would be living for the next six months.

A cold night, a cold wind, the snow falling like confetti. In the lights of the truck I unlocked the housetrailer, got out bedroll and baggage and moved in. By flashlight I found the bed, unrolled my sleeping bag, pulled off my boots and crawled in and went to sleep at once. The last I knew was the shaking of the trailer in the wind and the sound, from inside, of hungry mice scampering around with the good news that the long lean lonesome winter was over—their friend and provider had finally arrived.

This morning I awake before sunrise, stick 10
my head out of the sack, peer through a frosty window at a scene dim and vague with flowing mists, dark fantastic shapes looming beyond. An unlikely landscape.

I get up, moving about in long underwear and socks, stooping carefully under the low ceiling and lower doorways of the housetrailer, a machine for living built so efficiently and compactly there's hardly room for a man to breathe. An iron lung it is, with windows and venetian blinds.

The mice are silent, watching me from their hiding places, but the wind is still blowing and outside the ground is covered with snow. Cold as a tomb, a jail, a cave; I lie down on the dusty floor, on the cold linoleum sprinkled with mouse droppings, and light the pilot on the butane heater. Once this thing gets going the place warms up fast, in a dense unhealthy way, with a layer of heat under the ceiling where my head is and nothing but frigid air from the knees down.

But we've got all the indispensable conveniences: gas cookstove, gas refrigerator, hot water heater, sink with running water (if the pipes aren't frozen), storage cabinets and shelves, everything within arm's reach of everything else. The gas comes from two steel bottles in a shed outside; the water comes by gravity flow from a tank buried in a hill close by. Quite luxurious for the wilds. There's even a shower stall and a flush toilet with a dead rat in the bowl. Pretty soft. My poor mother raised five children without any of these luxuries and might be doing without them yet if it hadn't been for Hitler, war and general prosperity.

Time to get dressed, get out and have a look at the lay of the land, fix a breakfast. I try to pull on my boots but they're stiff as iron from the cold. I light a burner on the stove and hold the boots upside down above the flame until they are malleable enough to force my feet into. I put on a coat and step outside. Into the center of the world, God's navel, Abbey's country, the red wasteland.

The sun is not yet in sight but signs of the advent are plain to see. Lavender clouds sail like a fleet of ships across the pale green dawn; each cloud, planed flat on the wind, has a base of fiery gold. Southeast, twenty miles by line of sight, stand the peaks of the Sierra La Sal, twelve to thirteen thousand feet above sea level, all covered with snow and rosy in the morning sunlight. The air is dry and clear as well as cold; the last fogbanks left over from last night's storm are scudding away like ghosts, fading into nothing before the wind and the sunrise.

The view is open and perfect in all direc- 15
tions except to the west where the ground rises and the skyline is only a few hundred yards away. Looking toward the mountains I can see the dark gorge of the Colorado River five or six miles away, carved through the sandstone mesa, though nothing of the river itself down inside the gorge. Southward, on the far side of the river, lies the Moab valley between thousand-foot walls of rock, with the town of Moab somewhere on the valley floor, too small to be seen from here. Beyond the Moab valley is more canyon and tableland stretching away to the Blue Mountains

fifty miles south. On the north and northwest I see the Roan Cliffs and the Book Cliffs, the two level face of the Uinta Plateau. Along the foot of those cliffs, maybe thirty miles off, invisible from where I stand, runs U.S. 6-50, a major east-west artery of commerce, traffic and rubbish, and the main line of the Denver-Rio Grande Railroad. To the east, under the spreading sunrise, are more mesas, more canyons, league on league of red cliff and tablelands, extending through purple haze over the bulging curve of the planet to the ranges of Colorado—a sea of desert.

Within this vast perimeter; in the middle ground and foreground of the picture, a rather personal demesne, are the 33,000 acres of Arches National Monument of which I am now sole in habitant, usufructuary, observer and custodian.

What are the Arches? From my place in front of the housetrailer I can see several of the hundred or more of them which have been discovered in the park. These are natural arches, holes in the rock, windows in stone, no two alike, as varied in form as in dimension. They range in size from holes just big enough to walk through to openings large enough to contain the dome of the Capitol building in Washington, D.C. Some resemble jug handles or flying buttresses, others natural bridges but with this technical distinction: a natural bridge spans a watercourse—a natural arch does not. The arches were formed through hundreds of thousands of years by the weathering of the huge sandstone walls, or fins, in which they are found. Not the work of a cosmic hand, nor sculptured by sand-bearing winds, as many people prefer to believe, the arches came into being and continue to come into being through the modest wedging action of rainwater, melting snow, frost, and ice, aided by gravity. In color they shade from off-white through buff, pink, brown and red, tones which also change with the time of day and the moods of the light, the weather, the sky.

Standing there, gaping at this monstrous and inhuman spectacle of rock and cloud and sky and space, I feel a ridiculous greed and possessiveness come over me. I want to know it all, possess it all, embrace the entire scene intimately, deeply, totally, as a man desires a beautiful woman. An insane wish? Perhaps not—at least there's nothing else, no one human, to dispute possession with me.

The snow-covered ground glimmers with a dull blue light, reflecting the sky and the approaching sunrise. Leading away from me the narrow dirt road, an alluring and primitive track into nowhere, meanders down the slope and toward the heart of the labyrinth of naked stone. Near the first group of arches, looming over a bend in the road, is a balanced rock about fifty feet high, mounted on a pedestal of equal height; it looks like a head from Easter island, a stone god or a petrified ogre.

Like a god, like an ogre? The personification [20] of the natural is exactly the tendency I wish to suppress in myself, to eliminate for good. I am here not only to evade for a while the clamor and filth and confusion of the cultural apparatus but also to confront, immediately and directly if it's possible, the bare bones of existence, the elemental and fundamental, the bedrock which sustains us. I want to be able to look at and into a juniper tree, a piece of quartz, a vulture, a spider, and see it as it is in itself, devoid of all humanly ascribed qualities, even the categories of scientific description. To meet God or Medusa face to face, even if it means risking everything human in myself. I dream of a hard and brutal mysticism in which the naked self merges with a nonhuman world and yet somehow survives still intact, individual, separate. Paradox and bedrock.

Well—the sun will be up in a few minutes and I haven't even begun to make coffee. I take more baggage from my pickup, the grub box and cooking gear, re-enter the trailer and start breakfast. Simply breathing, in a place like this, arouses the appetite. The orange juice is frozen, the milk, slushy with ice. Still chilly enough inside the trailer to tum my breath to vapor. When the first rays of the sun strike the cliffs I fill a mug with steaming coffee and sit in the doorway facing the sunrise, hungry for the warmth.

Suddenly it comes, the flaming globe, blazing on the pinnacles and minarets and balanced rocks, on the canyon walls and through the windows in the sandstone fins. We greet each other, sun and I, across the black void of ninety-three million miles. The snow glitters between us, acres of diamonds almost painful to look at. Within an hour all the snow exposed to the sunlight will be gone and the rock will be damp and steaming. Within minutes, even as I watch, melting snow begins to drip from the branches of a juniper nearby; drops of water streak slowly down the side of the trailerhouse.

I am not alone after all. Three ravens are wheeling near the balanced rock, squawking at each other and at the dawn. I'm sure they're as delighted by the return of the sun as I am and I wish I knew the language. I'd sooner exchange ideas with the birds on earth than learn to carry on intergalactic communications with some obscure race of humanoids on a satellite planet from the world of Betelgeuse. First things first. The ravens cry out in husky voices, blue-black wings flapping against the golden sky. Over my shoulder comes the sizzle and smell of frying bacon.

That's the way it was this morning.

A CLOSER LOOK AT
The First Morning

1. This memoir is filled with visual imagery and metaphors. Find five places where Abbey uses sensory detail (especially sight, sound, and touch) to heighten the readers' experience. How does he use this rich detail to make readers feel they are present in this place with him?

2. As Abbey explains, he is utterly alone in this new place. Then again, there are other creatures present and a landscape that he describes as coming alive. Nature itself might also be considered a character in this memoir. Where in this memoir does nature seem to be taking on a living role? In what ways does Abbey use nature as a character in his story?

3. Memoirs need more than just details. They should also include a plot that has a complication, a series of scenes or stages that move the memoir forward. A memoir should lead to some kind of new understanding or revelation that presents a moment of transformation or clarity in the writer. Describe the complication and revelation that occur here, pointing to and even quoting specific places in the text as evidence.

IDEAS FOR
Writing

1. Write a profile of a place that has special meaning for you. Like Abbey, you could also include a memoir-like "story" about your first encounter with this place. As you write your profile, pay special attention to the way that *place* helped you shape your understanding about yourself, some larger issue, or someone else. In other words, how did this place help define who you are and who you have become?

2. Using Abbey's memoir as a model, write a description of your college campus or a place on your campus or in your community. Use and even over-use metaphors, similes, personal narrative, and rich description to evoke a sensory experience for your readers.

The College Hazing That Changed My Life

THOMAS ROGERS

Thomas Rogers contributed this memoir to a series titled "Freshman Orientation" for the online magazine Salon.com, where he is an arts editor. As you read, notice how Rogers uses many of the key features of a memoir to tell a powerful story about his inner conflict that begins with his family, carries on through to his college days, and ends with a surprising resolution and new understanding.

I had no idea college was going to be so much like a gay porn movie. That's what I kept thinking as I stood in the middle of a sun-dappled backyard, dressed in nothing but a spandex unitard and running shoes, preparing to have oil poured over my body. For the last two hours, 10 other young rowers and I had been undergoing "initiation" to my university's varsity crew team. After two weeks of tryouts, we had finally made the grade, and this was our reward: An afternoon of embarrassing hazing activities, followed by a homoerotic climax that seemed to have come straight out of my 17-year-old gay subconscious.

Our team captain, a 200-pound hulk of a man, was walking from freshman to freshman with a large vat of vegetable oil, and letting it cascade all over them one by one. "Be prepared to have the worst acne of your lives over the next week," he warned us. A tarp nearby had also been covered in oil, and other members of the team were streaming into the backyard with bottles of beer to watch what was about to happen. When my turn came, I closed my eyes. As I felt the liquid drip into my shoes, he leaned over and said, "Get ready to wrestle."

College is a strange time. As soon as our parents drive away from our dorms, and leave us alone with our boxes of books and Ikea corkboard, we're free to make an extraordinary number of mistakes and end up in situations that may not teach us much about organic chemistry or Emily Dickinson, but let us figure out who we are and who we want to be. In my case, that situation involved man-on-man oil wrestling.

I had always been my family's black sheep when it came to sports. For as long as I could remember, my mom had been an obsessive long-distance runner. She logged about 50 miles per week, and when her friends ran half-marathons on weekends, she would run along, just to give them "emotional support." My dad, a tall, thin doctor, had competed in triathlons around Western Canada for a large portion of his adult life. And my older sister was a star. Ever since I was a young kid, she had always been an exceptionally talented athlete—a runner, swimmer, biker and rower. By the time I was graduating high school, she had worked her way to the top echelons of Canada's rowing community and was even considering trying out for the Olympic team.

I, on the other hand, was what some of my 5 disappointed sports coaches had consistently described as "physically awkward." Whereas my sister had inherited all of my parents' athletic genes, I had inherited all of their gangliest. I was tall and shaped like a stretched piece of Play-Doh with twigs stuck into it. My limbs had a tendency to do things that I didn't want them to do, like make me fall over boxes and down stairs. And, to make things worse, I was pathetically, pathologically shy. For most of my childhood, I was the wallflower who stood in the corner while the other kids threw balls at each other's faces (apparently I hung out with some pretty violent kids).

On top of that, I'd known I was gay since I was 8. While that discovery didn't send me into paroxysms of panic, it also made me want to keep to myself pretty much all of the time. I spent most of my early teens reading books and listening to a lot of Nine Inch Nails and ABBA. It wasn't that I didn't want to be a jock like the rest of my family—in fact, I was envious of my sister's talents—it's just that I was usually pretty mediocre at the sports I was enrolled in, and practice cut into time spent alone with my Walkman. And then, I discovered rowing.

As far as sports go, rowing is a remarkably bizarre and all-consuming one. You have to get up at 4:30 in the morning to sit in a very skinny boat facing backward and row around in a loop until you get very tired. You have to wear some very revealing spandex outfits. Given that our rowing club was located on a river near farmland, you also have to dodge rocks and tree stumps and the occasional bloated dead cow. And yet there was something magical about it. Every morning, I would get to see the sunrise before I went to school, and I loved the feeling of exhaustion I felt after every practice. In high school, I took the sport more and more seriously until something weird happened: I became sort of good.

Not only did becoming a jock boost my self-confidence, it was an antidote to my anxieties about my burgeoning homosexuality, about the girlish lilt that could emerge in my voice or my occasional extravagant hand motions. I had always been pretty comfortable with the idea that I was gay, but I was still struggling with the implication that it meant being less manly than the other boys. But jocks were manly. They were self-confident, and cool, and, somehow, better than people who weren't jocks. And if I became one, especially at college, I would be like that too.

When I arrived at tryouts, I discovered these people were much larger, more serious and gregarious than me. Everybody seemed to have gone to a private school with a fancy rowing team. One of the older guys, always surrounded by groups of women, kept referring to something called "The Raft," which turned out to be a large bed he used for group sex. Another, an enormous man who went by the nickname "Ice" (apparently he had just discovered "Top Gun"), claimed to be a former Abercrombie and Fitch model and the son of a Dutch ambassador. He would put rubbing alcohol on his blisters to show people how manly he was, and about one week into the tryouts, he told me to get him a sandwich because "there was a hierarchy on the team," and he was at the top and I was at the bottom. (This comment raised my eyebrows for multiple reasons.)

As different from me as they were, these were precisely the cool jocks I had always dreamed of being. These guys were self-confident, manly and attractive—and nobody seemed to question their abrasiveness. As Ice was fond of saying, while eating large amounts of tuna in the dorm cafeteria, the men on the rowing team could "bring it—athletically, academically and socially." Maybe their chutzpah would rub off on me. One week later, when I finally made the team—as a "bow seat" in the lightweight eight—I felt so much better about myself. Even if it did mean being surrounded by guys I was starting to feel iffy about.

A few days after they announced the lineup, we had to show up at one of our teammates' houses dressed in our unisuits and running shoes. I figured we were in for hazing, but I had hoped it would be more demure, like those trust games where people wear blindfolds and stand on crates and catch each other. Instead, we had to run around campus holding a boat on our shoulders singing "Row, row, row your boat" (unfortunately, this coincided with my university's annual medieval fair). We had to flex in front of the cafeteria during lunch time, and jump in the lake, and perform embarrassing skits in front of the dorms.

Then came the oil wrestling.

When I stepped onto that oil-covered tarp to face off against my opponent, I wasn't preoccupied by the insane homoeroticism of the moment. Instead, I was thinking about how this entire display was predicated on the fact that gay sexuality was laughable and gross. They had clearly chosen it as a hazing activity because the idea of man-on-man contact would make us as uncomfortable as possible. And the more I thought about it, the more I did feel dirty—and resentful.

It was with a tremendous amount of apprehension that I began to grapple with the opponent, a similarly skinny freshman named Kieran. As the crowd began to yell, "wrestle, wrestle, wrestle," we pushed each other over onto our backs, and tried to edge each other to the end of the tarp. Oil wrestling (who knew!) really is quite slippery. So we rolled around and spent a lot of time accidentally elbowing each other in the stomach. By this point, a bunch of twigs had already fallen into the oil, and kept jabbing me in the ribs, and the liquid got into my eyes. Clearly I wasn't putting up much of a show. I heard somebody nearby yell out, "Well, this is lame!"

But by the time Kieran pushed me off the 15 tarp and onto the grass, I had the first great revelation of my freshman year: Being a jock was bullshit. If this was the kind of macho, homophobic stuff I had to tolerate to be on a sports team, there was no point in even trying. If that meant admitting I was a mediocre athlete, that was fine with me. I had to come to terms with the fact that my gayness made me less butch than Ice, and that was better than being a douchebag. When the rowing season ended, I left the sport and turned instead toward outcasts like me—bookish kids, drama nerds and other queer kids. I never turned back.

Now, with some perspective, I can see I discovered something else in that moment, much bigger than my failure to be an all-star jock. I saw that I was never going to be normal. And it was time to stop being embarrassed by that—and start being excited about it.

A decade later, I still am.

A CLOSER LOOK AT
The College Hazing That Changed My Life

1. An effective memoir usually starts fast with a "lead" that draws the reader in and hints at the memoir's overall meaning or "theme." Sometimes, as in this case, it takes the reader right into heart of the main action before backing up and providing background. How effectively does this strategy work in this memoir?

2. Rogers sets the scene with rich and vivid details. He moves from various scenes, painting brief but compelling portraits of key people, from family members to his athletic team members. He also fills scenes with sensory details (sight, touch, sound, and smell). Find specific places where this variety and richness in detail make the memoir more powerful.

3. At the heart of any memoir (or story) is a complication that the author grapples with and needs to resolve. In this memoir, what is the conflict that draws readers in and makes this more than just a personal story? How does he resolve that conflict, and how would you describe his new understanding?

4. Memoirs usually conclude with a point or "implied thesis." How would you describe the author's new understanding? What general point (or points) does the author make?

IDEAS FOR
Writing

1. As we move from the world of family to new situations and friends, all of us face life's complications that we need to resolve for ourselves. Write a memoir that tells the story of your journey from family and youthful friends to new surroundings, how you faced that change and how you arrived at new understandings. Be sure to provide rich details about the scenes and the people in your memoir.

2. In the third paragraph, the author shifts the scene from the climactic wrestling scene (his scene-setting lead) to a brief comment about college life:

"College is a strange time." In college, he suggests, we learn about more than just the subjects studied in the classroom; we also learn about life and who we are. Drawing on your own personal college experience, write a commentary on this idea about broader learning. How has the college experience changed you? Do you think college *should* teach students about more than just subject matter? Should college do more than prepare you for a career?

Lines in the Sand

DEMETRIA MARTINEZ

In her autobiographical essays (like this one), novels, poetry, children's books, and journalism, Demetria Martinez writes about her life as an activist who has never shied away from controversy. Her writing addresses immigrant rights, religion, spirituality, Latina identity, and other issues. Notice how Martinez uses the memoir genre to poke fun at herself while making an argument urging her readers to examine their beliefs about what makes a person physically beautiful.

Ever since the Spanish and the Indians mixed over five hundred years ago, makeup has gone orange on Chicana complexions. Throughout my teens, twenties, and much of my thirties, I would emerge from drugstores, my wrists slashed with lipstick samples, my cheeks primed with blush, my jawline finished with foundation. Cover Girl, Maybelline, Revlon: I have graced cosmetic companies with more of my consumer dollars than I dare admit.

But those mirrors at the counters that glare like headlights? Take my word for it. They are part of a vast capitalist conspiracy against women with olive skin.

As any Chicana will tell you, the one mirror that never lies is your rearview mirror at high noon. The traffic light turns red. You peer through dangling rosary beads, hope springing eternal. You just bought enough makeup to touch up a Diego Rivera mural; you asked not for high art, merely good coverage.

But it is not to be. In the time it took to drive ten blocks from Walgreens, your blush, lipstick, and foundation have taken on a sorrowful orange flush. The guy behind you honks; God only knows when the light turned green. The only reason to hold your head up for the rest of the drive is your eye shadow, its colors fixed as beautifully as those in a Navajo sand painting.

So what exactly is olive skin?   5

My father is café con very little leche. Mom is peaches and cream. Why my coloring evokes the small ovoid fruit of a Mediterranean evergreen tree confounds me. For years curiosity has lured me into gourmet delis and international markets, where I have scrutinized jars of olives and bottles of virgin pressed oils looking for similarities to my own skin color. Nada.

I turn to the *American Heritage Dictionary*. The color olive, it says, is "A yellow green of low to medium lightness and low to moderate saturation." Huh?

"I can't keep on throwing away money on makeup at Walgreens," I confess to Charlotte, an African American who works in cosmetics at JCPenney.

Charlotte is examining my face like a surgeon about to lower the scalpel. "You've got a ton of yellow," she says. "A lot of my Hispanic ladies buy the wrong makeup because they don't think of themselves as on the yellow side. They think it's more of an Asian thing." She swirls a cotton pad in a powder compact labeled "Sand."

"Try this. Take the mirror outdoors and stand in the sun." she instructs. "Remember, you want to match your skin, not lighten it or darken it." 10

I forge ahead with the experiment in the blazing sun. Sand it is. Now this is a *real* discovery. Five hundred years after the conquest, this Chicana stumbles upon the perfect face powder, part of a line of makeup made for women of color by a supermodel who hails from Africa.

Call it cosmetic justice. The Spaniards were enamored of the concept of sangre limpia, yet their veins were saturated with the blood of Moors and Jews, African slaves and the indigenous peoples of the New World. Is it any wonder that daughters and sons of la raza Cósmica—indeed, all Latinos—subvert the color schemes imposed upon us by census and society alike?

One afternoon at a Chicago hotel I was putting on my face in preparation for a poetry reading I was to give that night with Nikki Giovanni.

Listening to National Public Radio, I was surprised to learn that the great physicist Stephen Hawking was speaking at a conference on cosmetology. I turned the volume up.

Cosmology, you idiot, I said to myself.

But I should have probed more deeply. The word "cosmetics" comes from the Greek word "kosmos," meaning order. Such etymologies can seem esoteric—until you turn forty. When my day came, I thought about the many cultures whose philosophies hold that physical beauty is a reflection of harmony, an order arising from good relations with others, nature, and the deities. 15

My makeup expenditures took a prodigious plunge.

Olive skin? Sisters, time to move on. Let's straighten our rearview mirrors and press on the gas pedal. Another five hundred years is just around the corner. Our little planet has an appointment for a makeover. We had better show up on time.

A CLOSER LOOK AT
Lines in the Sand

1. Describe the conflict (or complication) that Martinez struggles with and how she resolves this issue for herself. Is this an issue that non-Latinas must deal with? Do only women face these complications, or do men face them also? Drawing on your own personal experience, why do you think this remains a difficult conflict for so many?

2. In this memoir, Martinez describes several scenes in which she grapples with her efforts to conform to society's beliefs about beauty. How does she use humor and self-deprecation to bring about a feeling of intimacy with her readers and make them feel comfortable considering these issues?

3. Some memoirs include a question for readers to reflect on or an argumentative thesis that urges readers to believe or act in certain ways. Is the main point (or thesis) stated explicitly? If so, where? How would you re-state Martinez's main point even more explicitly?

IDEAS FOR
Writing

1. Write a rhetorical analysis of Martinez's memoir in which you explain how closely it follows the memoir genre. Look back at the description of the memoir genre's features in Chapter 5. Does this memoir follow the usual pattern? How well did she use style to hold your attention and draw you in to the drama?

Overall, explain why you felt this memoir offered a good example of the genre.

2. Write a memoir that describes how you changed your beliefs from accepting society's standards without question to embracing a revelation that led to a radical change in what you believed, how you behaved, or how you viewed an issue or other people. Use a memoir that tells the story of this change and encourages your readers to consider this change for themselves.

The Noble Experiment

JACKIE ROBINSON

As Told to Alfred Duckett

Before Jackie Robinson broke the "color barrier" in 1947, African Americans were not permitted to play on Major League Baseball teams but were segregated into the Negro leagues. Robinson was not only an outstanding athlete but also an outstanding human being who would face incredible challenges. Notice how this memoir focuses on two great men, Robinson himself and Branch Rickey.

In 1910 Branch Rickey was a coach for Ohio Wesleyan. The team went to South Bend, Indiana, for a game. The hotel management registered the coach and team but refused to assign a room to a black player named Charley Thomas. In those days college ball had a few black players. Mr. Rickey took the manager aside and said he would move the entire team to another hotel unless the black athlete was accepted. The threat was a bluff because he knew the other hotels also would have refused accommodations to a black man. While the hotel manager was thinking about the threat, Mr. Rickey came up with a compromise. He suggested a cot be put in his own room, which he would share with the unwanted guest. The hotel manager wasn't happy about the idea, but he gave in.

Years later Branch Rickey told the story of the misery of that black player to whom he had given a place to sleep. He remembered that Thomas couldn't sleep.

"He sat on that cot," Mr. Rickey said, "and was silent for a long time. Then he began to cry, tears he couldn't hold back. His whole body shook with emotion. I sat and watched him, not knowing what to do until he began tearing at one hand with the other—just as if he were trying to scratch the skin off his hands with his fingernails. I was alarmed. I asked him what he was trying to do to himself.

"'It's my hands,' he sobbed. 'They're black. If only they were white, I'd be as good as anybody then, wouldn't I, Mr. Rickey? If only they were white.'"

"Charley," Mr. Rickey said, "the day will 5 come when they won't have to be white."

Thirty-five years later, while I was lying awake nights, frustrated, unable to see a future, Mr. Rickey, by now the president of the Dodgers, was also lying awake at night, trying to make up his mind about a new experiment.

He had never forgotten the agony of that black athlete. When he became a front-office executive in St. Louis, he had fought, behind the scenes, against the custom that consigned black spectators to the Jim Crow section of the Sportsman's Park, later to become Busch Memorial Stadium. His pleas to change the rules were in vain. Those in power argued that if blacks were allowed a free choice of seating, white business would suffer.

Branch Rickey lost that fight, but when he became the boss of the Brooklyn Dodgers in 1943, he felt the time for equality in baseball had come. He knew that achieving it would be terribly difficult. There would be deep resentment, determined opposition, and perhaps even racial violence. He was convinced he was morally right, and he shrewdly sensed that making the game a truly national one would have healthy financial results. He took his case before the startled directors of the club, and using persuasive eloquence, he won the first battle in what would be a long and bitter campaign. He was voted permission to make the Brooklyn club the pioneer in bringing blacks into baseball.

Winning his directors' approval was almost insignificant in contrast to the task which now lay ahead of the Dodger president. He made certain that word of his plans did not leak out, particularly to the press. Next, he had to find the ideal player for his project, which came to be called "Rickey's noble experiment." This player had to be one who could take abuse, name-calling, rejection by fans and sportswriters and by fellow players not only on opposing teams but on his own. He had to be able to stand up in the face of merciless persecution and not retaliate. On the other hand, he had to be a contradiction in human terms; he still had to have spirit. He could not be an Uncle Tom. His ability to turn the other cheek had to be predicated on his determination to gain acceptance. Once having proven his ability as player, teammate, and man, he had to be able to cast off humbleness and stand up as a full-fledged participant whose triumph did not carry the poison of bitterness.

Unknown to most people and certainly to me, after launching a major scouting program, Branch Rickey had picked me as that player. The Rickey talent hunt went beyond national borders. Cuba, Mexico, Puerto Rico, Venezuela, and other countries where dark-skinned people lived had been checked out. Mr. Rickey had learned that there were a number of black

10

players, war veterans mainly, who had gone to these countries, despairing of finding an opportunity in their own country. The manhunt had to be camouflaged. If it became known he was looking for a black recruit for the Dodgers, there would have been all kinds of trouble. The gimmick he used as a coverup was to make the world believe that he was about to establish a new Negro league. In the spring of 1945 he called a press conference and announced that the Dodgers were organizing the United States League, composed of all black teams. This, of course, made blacks and pro-integration whites indignant. He was accused of trying to uphold the existing segregation and, at the same time, capitalize on black players. Cleverly, Mr. Rickey replied that his league would be better organized than the current ones. He said its main purpose, eventually, was to be absorbed into the majors. It is ironic that by coming very close to telling the truth, he was able to conceal that truth from the enemies of integrated baseball. Most people assumed that when he spoke of some distant goal of integration, Mr. Rickey was being a hypocrite on this issue as so many of baseball's leaders had been.

Black players were familiar with this kind of hypocrisy. When I was with the Monarchs, shortly before I met Mr. Rickey, Wendell Smith, then sports editor of the black, weekly Pittsburgh *Courier,* had arranged for me and two other players from the Negro league to go to a tryout with the Boston Red Sox. The tryout had been brought about because a Boston city councilman had frightened the Red Sox management. Councilman Isadore Muchned threatened to push a bill through banning Sunday baseball unless the Red Sox hired black players. Sam Jethroe of the Cleveland Buckeyes Marvin Williams of the Philadelphia Stars, and I had been grateful to Wendell for getting us a chance in the Red Sox tryout, and we put our best efforts into it. However, not for one minute did we believe the tryout was sincere. The Boston club officials praised our performance, let us fill out application cards, and said "So long." We were fairly certain they wouldn't call us, and we had no intention of calling them.

Incidents like this made Wendell Smith as cynical as we were. He didn't accept Branch Rickey's new league as a genuine project, and he frankly told him so. During this conversation, the Dodger boss asked Wendell whether any of the three of us who had gone to Boston was really good major league material. Wendell said I was. I will be forever indebted to Wendell because, without his even knowing it, his recommendation was in the end partly responsible for my career. At the time, it started a thorough investigation of my background.

In August 1945, at Comiskey Park in Chicago, I was approached by Clyde Sukeforth, the Dodger scout. Blacks have had to learn to protect themselves by being cynical but not cynical enough to slam the door on potential opportunities. We go through life walking a tightrope to prevent too much disillusionment. I was out on the field when Sukeforth called my name and beckoned. He told me the Brown Dodgers were looking for top ballplayers, that Branch Rickey had heard about me and sent him to watch me throw from the hole. He had come at an unfortunate time. I had hurt my shoulder a couple of days before that, and I wouldn't be doing any throwing for at least a week.

Sukeforth said he'd like to talk with me anyhow. He asked me to come to see him after the game at the Stevens Hotel.

Here we go again, I thought. Another time-wasting experience. But Sukeforth looked like a sincere person, and I thought I might as well listen. I agreed to meet him that night. When we met, Sukeforth got right to the point. Mr. Rickey wanted to talk to me about the possibility of becoming a Brown Dodger. If I could get a few days off and go to Brooklyn, my fare and expenses would be paid. At first I said that I couldn't leave my team and go to Brooklyn just like that. Sukeforth wouldn't take no for an answer. He pointed out that I couldn't play for a few days anyhow because of my bum arm. Why should my team object?

I continued to hold out and demanded to 15 know what would happen if the Monarchs fired me. The Dodger scout replied quietly that he didn't believe that would happen.

I shrugged and said I'd make the trip. I figured I had nothing to lose.

Branch Rickey was an impressive-looking man. He had a classic face, an air of command, a deep, booming voice, and a way of cutting through red tape and getting down to basics. He shook my hand vigorously and, after a brief conversation, sprang the first question.

"You got a girl?" he demanded.

It was a heck of a question. I had two reactions: why should he be concerned about my relationship with a girl; and, second, while I thought, hoped, and prayed I had a girl, the way things had been going, I was afraid she might have begun to consider me a hopeless case. I explained this to Mr. Rickey and Clyde.

Mr. Rickey wanted to know all about Rachel. 20 I told him of our hopes and plans.

"You know, you *have* a girl," he said heartily. "When we get through today, you may want to call her up because there are times when a man needs a woman by his side."

My heart began racing a little faster again as I sat there speculating. First he asked me if I really understood why he had sent for me. I told him what Clyde Sukeforth had told me.

"That's what he was supposed to tell you, " Mr. Rickey said. "The truth is you are not a candidate for the Brooklyn Brown Dodgers. I've sent for you because I'm interested in you as a candidate for the Brooklyn National League Club. I think you can play in the major leagues. How do you feel about it?"

My reactions seemed like some kind of weird mixture churning in a blender. I was thrilled, scared, and excited. I was incredulous. Most of all, I was speechless.

"You think you can play for Montreal?" he de- 25 manded. I got my tongue back. "Yes," I answered.

Montreal was the Brooklyn Dodgers' top farm club. The players who went there and made it had an excellent chance at the big time.

I was busy reorganizing my thoughts while Mr. Rickey and Clyde Sukeforth discussed me briefly, almost as if I weren't there. Mr. Rickey was questioning Clyde. Could I make the grade?

Abruptly, Mr. Rickey swung his swivel chair in my direction. He was a man who conducted himself with great drama. He pointed a finger at me "I know you're a good ballplayer," he barked. "What I don't know is whether you have the guts."

I knew it was all too good to be true. Here was a guy questioning *my* courage. That virtually amounted to him asking me if I was a coward. Mr. Rickey or no Mr. Rickey, that was an insinuation hard to take. I felt the heat coming up into my cheeks.

Before I could react to what he had said, he 30 leaned forward in his chair and explained.

I wasn't just another athlete being hired by a ball club. We were playing for big stakes. This was the reason Branch Rickey's search had been so exhaustive. The search had spanned the globe and narrowed down to a few candidates, then finally to me. When it looked as though I might be the number-one choice, the investigation of my life, my habits, *my* reputation, and my character had become an intensified study.

"I've investigated you thoroughly, Robinson," Mr. Rickey said.

One of the results of this thorough screening were reports from California athletic circles that I had been a "racial agitator" at UCLA. Mr. Rickey had not accepted these criticisms on face value. He had demanded and received more information and came to the conclusion that if I had been white, people would have said, "Here's a guy who's a contender, a competitor."

After that he had some grim words of warning. "We can't fight our way through this, Robinson. We've got no army. There's virtually nobody on our side. No owners, no umpires, very few newspapermen. And I'm afraid that many fans will be hostile. We'll be in a tough position. We can win only if we can convince the world that I'm doing this because you're a great ballplayer and a fine gentleman."

He had me transfixed as he spoke. I could 35 feel his sincerity, and I began to get a sense of how much this major step meant to him. Because of his nature and his passion for justice, he had to do what he was doing. He continued. The rumbling voice, the theatrical gestures, were gone. He was speaking from a deep, quiet strength.

"So there's more than just playing," he said. "I wish it meant only hits, runs, and errors—only the things they put in the box score. Because you know—yes, you would know, Robinson, that a baseball box score is a democratic thing. It doesn't tell how big you are, what church you attend, what color you are, or how your father voted in the last election. It just tells what kind of baseball player you were on that particular day."

I interrupted. "But it's the box score that really counts—that and that alone, isn't it?"

"It's all that *ought* to count," he replied. "But it isn't. Maybe one of these days it will be all that counts. That is one of the reasons I've got you here, Robinson. If you're a good enough man, we can make this a start in the right direction. But let me tell you, it's going to take an awful lot of courage."

He was back to the crossroads question that made me start to get angry minutes earlier. He asked it slowly and with great care.

"Have you got the guts to play the game no matter what happens?"

"I think I can play the game, Mr. Rickey," I 40 said.

The next few minutes were tough. Branch Rickey had to make absolutely sure that I knew what I would face. Beanballs would be thrown at me. I would be called the kind of names which would hurt and infuriate any man. I would be physically attacked. Could I take all of this and control my temper, remain steadfastly loyal to our ultimate aim?

He knew I would have terrible problems and wanted me to know the extent of them before I agreed to the plan. I was twenty-six years old, and all my life—back to the age of eight when a little neighbor girl called me a nigger—I had believed in payback, retaliation. The most luxurious possession, the richest treasure anybody has, is his personal dignity. I looked at Mr. Rickey guardedly, and in that second I was looking at him not as a partner in a great experiment, but as the enemy—a white man. I had a question, and it was the age-old one about whether or not you sell your birthright.

"Mr. Rickey," I asked, "are you looking for a Negro who is afraid to fight back?"

I never will forget the way he exploded.

"Robinson," he said, "I'm looking for a ball- 45
player with guts enough not to fight back."

After that, Mr. Rickey continued his lecture on the kind of thing I'd be facing.

He not only told me about it, but he acted out the part of a white player charging into me, blaming me for the "accident" and calling me all kinds of foul racial names. He talked about my race, my parents, in language that was almost unendurable.

"They'll taunt and goad you," Mr. Rickey said. "They'll do anything to make you react. They'll try to provoke a race riot in the ballpark. This is the way to prove to the public that a Negro should not be allowed in the major league. This is the way to frighten the fans and make them afraid to attend the games."

If hundreds of black people wanted to come to the ballpark to watch me play and Mr. Rickey tried to discourage them, would I understand that he was doing it because the emotional enthusiasm of my people could harm the experiment? That kind of enthusiasm would be as bad as the emotional opposition of prejudiced white fans.

Suppose I was at shortstop. Another player 50 comes down from first, stealing, flying in with spikes high, and cuts me on the leg. As I feel the blood running down my leg, the white player laughs in my face.

"How do you like that, nigger boy?" he sneers.

Could I turn the other cheek? I didn't know how I would do it. Yet I knew that I must. I had to do it for so many reasons. For black youth, for my mother, for Rae, for myself. I had already begun to feel I had to do it for Branch Rickey.

I was offered, and agreed to sign later, a contract with a $3,500 bonus and a $600-a-month salary. I was officially a Montreal Royal. I must not tell anyone except Rae and my mother.

A CLOSER LOOK AT
The Noble Experiment

1. Social justice is an important theme in this memoir. What are some of the social-justice issues that the two main characters—Branch Rickey and Jackie Robinson—must face? How does each character respond in a unique way and why?

2. Like any genre, the memoir genre is stretchy and allows authors to incorporate a variety of subjects and features. This memoir, for instance, focuses as much on the experiences, words, and actions of Branch Rickey as it does the author, Jackie Robinson. In what ways could you argue that this is still Robinson's memoir? For instance, who experiences the conflict, and who is moved to a transformation in understanding?

3. Jackie Robinson is regarded by most Americans as an important hero in the history of sports and civil rights, but few people even know who Branch Rickey was. What does Robinson's choice to share the spotlight with Rickey tell us about Robinson? What does it say more generally about how heroes rise to greatness?

IDEAS FOR
Writing

1. Write a memoir in which you describe a time in your life when someone inspired you to take on a challenge you thought you weren't ready for. Like Robinson, you should explain how this person helped you take an important step in your own life.

2. Write a review of *42*, which is a biographical sports movie about Jackie Robinson. Focus on the scene in the film that is based on the incidents described in "The Noble Experiment" and compare how the movie depicts the interactions between Rickey and Robinson with the description offered by Robinson. What is different? Which details are left out of the movie or added? Decide which version you found more powerful and explain why this is the case.

A FEW IDEAS FOR
Composing a Memoir

1. **Write a transition-to-college memoir.** The decision to attend college usually comes with some tension and even conflict. For you, what social, economic, familial, and personal issues led up to this change in your life? How did you feel about this transition into being a college student? How did it affect the people who are important to you? Describe the emotions you felt (optimism, pride, anxiety, etc.) and what caused those emotions. As you write, think of the larger theme or themes that give meaning to your story.

2. **Write a memoir about a positive turning point.** Describe this turning point by focusing on the "conflict" that you needed to overcome. Then write about how you and others evaluated the conflict and resolved it. How did this event or moment change you? Why was it so important? How did it help define who you are now? What is the broader lesson you learned about life from this experience?

3. **Create a multimodal memoir.** Repurpose a memoir you or someone else has written into a new multimodal memoir. You could change the medium to a presentation (Chapter 32, "Presenting Your Work"), to a poster, to electronic words and images (on a blog, Web site, etc.), or to audio. Consider supplementing your memoir with images, sounds, and interactivity. Don't simply add images or sounds, and don't simply dump the contents into your new medium. Rather, explore how these changes allow you to transform your original memoir into something new and different. How do these changes allow you to explore new ideas or go more deeply into others?

Go to **MyWritingLab** to complete this chapter's exercises and test your understanding of its objectives.

34

Profiles

Dave Grohl and the Foo Fighters

CARL WILKINSON

In this profile, Carl Wilkinson provides a rich verbal portrait of rock musician Dave Grohl, who was the drummer in the "seminal grunge band Nirvana" and continues to lead the successful band the Foo Fighters. He also shows how contemporary popular music is changing in response to Internet file sharing. Notice how Wilkinson combines research with rich details about Grohl, his studio, and Grohl's own words to help readers understand what makes Grohl "the perfect rock star."

A group of record company executives, sitting down to sketch the perfect rock star, may well come up with someone a little like Dave Grohl. He has the look—long, thick black hair; he has the talent—he plays the drums, guitar and piano, he sings and he writes his own songs; and, above all, he has both pedigree and credibility.

In the early 1990s, as drummer with seminal grunge band Nirvana, Grohl helped change the face of popular music. Today, as lead singer with stadium-filling rock giants Foo Fighters, he is a multi-millionaire who has sold more than 15 million albums worldwide, won six Grammy awards and is president of his own record label. Alongside Foo Fighters he has a number of side projects (including supergroup Them Crooked Vultures, with Led Zeppelin's John Paul Jones); a documentary about his band shot by Oscar-winning director James Moll was released last month and his seventh album, *Wasting Light*, is out on Monday. Now 42, Grohl—and his brand of rock "n" roll—has grown up, had kids and settled down.

How did a man who was just a drummer and who never intended to make money from music end up as one of the biggest and wealthiest rock stars of the decade, succeeding in the face of a record industry in crisis?

We meet at Studio 606, the 8,000 sq ft recording space he built in 2005 in the Northridge area of Los Angeles. Outside, the Californian spring sunshine throws stark shadows across a neighbourhood that estate agents would describe euphemistically as "mixed"; from inside this large utilitarian building, with its tinted windows, the blue sky looks almost overcast.

Grohl, who is tall, lean and has grown into [5] his slightly goofy looks, sets down the keys to his decidedly un-rock 'n' roll grey BMW estate, tucks his shoulder-length hair behind his ear and flips the lid on his laptop. "Sorry," he beams. "I've just got to check my e-mail. I want to see if my daughter got into private school." Grohl married Jordyn Blum in 2003, and they have two daughters, Violet Maye, aged four, and Harper Willow, one.

The upstairs lounge looks like a bachelor pad: there's a fridge, jukebox and widescreen TV with an eclectic selection of boxsets: The Office, ACDC and Bon Jovi gigs, and a tape of the Make-up and Effects trade show 1997. Scattered across the purple sofa are cushions covered with old band T-shirts (Slayer, The Police, Black Sabbath, Motorhead, Led Zeppelin) made by Grohl's mother. "She called up and said 'David, what do you want me to do with those T-shirts in the attic?'," says Grohl in a falsetto.

Downstairs, a vast recording studio complete with Persian rugs and a grand piano in the corner leads on to a warehouse filled with carefully labelled guitar cases, drums and assorted equipment. Among the platinum records, framed posters and photographs hanging in the corridor outside the soundproofed control room where we adjourn to talk is the iconic cover of Nirvana's 1991 album *Nevermind*, which celebrates its 20th anniversary in September.

Nevermind (and Nirvana) is both a gift and a curse to Grohl now. "For 16 years I've had to balance these two things: my love and respect of Nirvana and my love and respect of the Foo Fighters." He lifts first his right hand then his left and balances the two, the large feathers tattooed on both forearms gently rising and falling. "I wouldn't be here if it wasn't for Nirvana, there's no question. But I don't know if I'd be alive if it wasn't for the Foo Fighters. I try to keep them at a balance that is very respectful of each other."

Despite Grohl's desire to move on, the legacy of Nirvana's groundbreaking album still haunts him, and for good reason. *Nevermind* changed popular culture. Until the release of that album in 1991, music was dominated by pop giants such as Madonna, Michael Jackson and Whitney Houston. The alternative music scene was just that: lo-fi, raw-sounding and based on a punk DIY ethos that came to be known as grunge.

"Grunge emerged from the Pacific north- 10 west," explains the writer Mark Yarm, whose book *Everybody Loves Our Town: A History of Grunge* will be published in September to coincide with *Nevermind*'s anniversary. "It's unclear who coined the term, but it came to mean guitar bands who had a certain unkempt style and usually came from Seattle. It was a movement that was always supposed to transcend the cash. Success was viewed very warily. People like Nirvana's lead singer Kurt Cobain were resistant to success, yet very much sought it at the same time."

Grohl, who never imagined himself becoming a doctor, lawyer or writer, recorded his first album at 15 in a studio near his parents' house in Springfield, Virginia—a suburb of Washington, DC. "The intention wasn't to become U2, it was to satisfy that need to accomplish something outside of the mainstream system," he says.

That early anti-commercial intent symbolised the ethos of the alternative music scene. In 1990, Grohl became the drummer for Seattle-based band Nirvana, which had been formed by singer Kurt Cobain and bass player Krist Novoselic in 1987. Nirvana had already released a debut album, *Bleach* (1989), and the three-piece—Cobain, Novoselic and Grohl—toured small venues in a tiny van. It was a love of music that fuelled them, not the desire to become rich, famous rock stars.

All that changed when they teamed up with producer Butch Vig on their second album *Nevermind*. Where *Bleach* was a bona fide indie album released on the tiny Seattle-based Sub Pop label to which the band signed for an initial $600 advance, *Nevermind* was released by Geffen, a label owned by the Universal Music Group that was also home to the band's idols Sonic Youth.

"Sonic Youth's major label debut came out in 1990 and sold about 200,000 copies, which was considered a huge number in indie-rock circles back then," explains Yarm. "It was just inconceivable that another 'weird', underground band like Nirvana, who really looked up to Sonic Youth, could sell millions and millions of albums." Yet *Nevermind*, which was expected to sell around 200,000 copies, exploded.

"Many people point to the week in January 15 1992 when Nirvana knocked Michael Jackson—the King of Pop—off the top of the American charts as the moment alternative music truly went mainstream," says Yarm. To date, *Nevermind* has sold more than 26 million copies worldwide.

The album marked a sea-change in popular culture: it was the birth of a sound, a fashion and a lifestyle that was as big as punk or the swinging 60s before it. In the same year as *Nevermind* was released, Douglas Coupland published his famous novel *Generation X* and the theme tune for this new generation was Nirvana's breakthrough single "Smells Like Teen Spirit"—a raw, angry rallying cry that touched a nerve around the world.

Yet, for Grohl—at least initially—little changed. "It was just as much a shock to us as it was to everybody else. I think we were the last ones to believe it. Our world wasn't changing within all of that. We had a gold record and we were still touring in a van. And then it went platinum—we sold a million records— and we were still touring in a van; I was still sharing a room with Kurt when we had a platinum record. Even after we sold 10 million albums I was still living in a back room at my friend's house with a futon and a lamp." He does remember being sent his first credit card though. Never a big spender, he immediately rushed to his local Benihana, the chain of Japanese restaurants.

Thanks to Nirvana's success, record companies descended on Seattle, snapping up any band they could find. "It was a feeding frenzy," says Yarm. "One executive told me that all the flights from LA to Seattle were constantly booked. If one of those planes had gone down, it would have destroyed the music industry."

After the stratospheric success of *Nevermind*, Nirvana released just one further studio album, 1993's *In Utero*, and toured to breaking point. In 1994, lead singer Kurt Cobain, struggling with the pressure, was flown home to the US from Rome after taking an overdose during the European leg of the band's tour. On April 8 1994, Cobain was found dead at the house in Seattle he shared with his wife Courtney Love and their daughter Frances Bean. He had taken a heroin overdose and shot himself. His suicide shook the music world to its core, made global headlines and, in the eyes of many devastated fans, established Cobain as a tragic-romantic figure in the mould of Janis Joplin, Jim Morrison or Jimi Hendrix. He was 27 years old.

In the months after Cobain's death, Grohl [20] couldn't bring himself to play music. "After Nirvana ended in April 1994, I didn't really do much that year," explains Grohl. It wasn't until October 1994 that he felt ready to go back into the studio. "I didn't have a plan or any major career aspiration," he says. "I just felt like I needed to do something."

Over the course of five days, he recorded 13–14 of his songs in a small studio near his house, playing all the instruments and singing every song. Grohl distributed 100 copies of the recording to friends and music industry insiders and, reticent to step into the limelight so soon after Nirvana, he called the project Foo Fighters, the second world war term for an unidentified flying object, as it "sounded more like a band". Those recordings, which cost Grohl around $5,000, became Foo Fighters' self-titled debut album. Released in 1995, it established Grohl as one of the biggest rock musicians in the world.

It's practically unheard of for a drummer to make it as a lead singer—perhaps the only other famous example is Phil Collins, who forged a solo career after his time in Genesis. Yet Collins is not playing stadium gigs 20 years on. When almost every other band of his generation has fallen by the wayside, what is it about Grohl and Foo Fighters that still resonates?

"Their music is no nonsense, blue-collar everyman music," explains Butch Vig, who has produced the band's new album *Wasting Light*. "I think that people feel like they know the band. They can relate to their songs, but they can also relate to them as individuals." Today, after some personnel changes over the years, Foo Fighters consist of drummer Taylor Hawkins, guitarists Chris Shiflett and Pat Smear, bass player Nate Mendel and Grohl. They are a friendly, close-knit five-piece, who share jokes nonstop and banter about moments on tour. Over the course of 16 years and seven studio albums, the band has honed a particular brand of emotionally charged rock that has transcended their early grunge influences. Grohl writes melodies with the energy of punk rock that form an enviable greatest hits package guaranteed to fill any stadium in the world (in June 2008 the band played two consecutive shows at the 90,000-capacity Wembley Stadium).

The band's new album is in some ways a return to the sound and approach of their early records. "There's no question that history is a big part of this record," admits Grohl. Despite his shiny, well-equipped studio, he decided to record *Wasting Light* in his garage at home, and in a nod to his lo-fi, DIY roots, recorded to tape rather than digitally on a computer. Like *Nevermind*, *Wasting Light* is something of an antidote to the overproduced mainstream pop that currently fills the charts. It's not the only thing that sets the band apart.

The music industry has changed since Foo [25] Fighters released their first album in 1995. "Historically record sales accounted for the majority of band revenues," explains Chris Carey, senior economist at PRS for Music, a not-for-profit organisation which collects and distributes public performance royalties for composers, songwriters and music publishers. "As record sales have suffered in recent years the industry has looked to other areas for revenue. Synchronisations [music used in computer games and TV programmes] and merchandise sales have become increasingly important, and the boom in live music is well reported. It used to be that bands would tour at a loss to sell CDs. Nowadays music is often given away in order to generate buzz and promote live events."

How does this seismic shift in the record industry affect a band such as the Foo Fighters? "They've got an established fan base and a good track record, they're an act coming to the top of the market," says Carey. "Their revenues won't be representative of what a band coming into the market now would experience. That existing fan base, I'd imagine, will still buy physical albums and, I would expect, have a good amount of money to spend on concert tickets so what you can charge for a Foo Fighters gig is more than you could for a newer band. As a result their earning profile will be quite healthy: a good mix of live and recorded."

Today, thanks to industry pressures, many popstars often have to take the money wherever they can get it, whether it's corporate gigs, sponsorship deals or product placement in music videos. In the week I met Foo Fighters, the Libyan revolution was erupting and Beyoncé, Nelly Furtado and Usher had donated to charity their million-dollar fees earned playing for the Gaddafi family. "We've done corporate gigs to pay for touring," says Foo Fighters drummer Taylor Hawkins, "but we've never played for the Gaddafis! There's nothing wrong with getting paid to play music as long as it's in the realms of whatever moral standards you have . . . "

Despite the shift in the music industry, Foo Fighters, with a secure fan base and stable income have been able to pick and choose what they do. "I think at this point we've exceeded any of the expectations we had for this band— musically or financially," explains Grohl. "The most important thing is that we do what we do with the same integrity we had when we started 16 years ago. We're not a financially ambitious band—we're doing just fine. It comes down to how much do you really need?"

Nate Mendel, the band's bassist and longest-serving member after Grohl himself, agrees: "All these ways you can exploit your band commercially, we've done a lot of it, but compared to a band similar to us, we've held back. We wanted to be in a band that didn't have to do that. It's only our generation that's ever had a problem with it. Prior to and after 80s punk rock and the alternative music of the 90s nobody cared. It's only our generation that was cautious about exploiting their music."

"Punk-rock guilt," laughs Hawkins. "I'm flying in this private jet and eating lobster thermidor— but I'm not giving a song to Honda!"

As internet piracy has taken its toll on the record industry, revenue from live gigs and merchandise has become ever more important. "If you're not making money from records you have to make it somewhere else," says Carey. "Merchandise was up more than 20 per cent in 2009 growing at a good rate and in 2008 live music was up about 13-14 per cent which is boom growth."

Piracy and the decline in record sales won't have hit the Foo Fighters as hard as many other newer bands—which may explain why Grohl, who is president of his own label, Roswell Records, is unconcerned about file sharing. When he was growing up Grohl and his friends would swap tapes of their favourite bands despite campaigns warning that "home taping is killing the record industry". Today, the internet has really put a dent in the music business, Grohl acknowledges, but for him file sharing is simply an extension of those home-made mix-tapes. "To me, the most important thing is that people come and sing along when we pull into town on tour," he says. "Sharing music is not a crime. It shouldn't be. There should be a deeper meaning to making music than just selling downloads."

Grohl's experience with Nirvana has coloured the way he now runs Foo Fighters. "I learnt a lot of lessons from being in Nirvana. A lot of beautiful things and a lot of . . . " he pauses, "lessons of what not to do. I'm not a businessman, but when it comes to making music I've kind of figured out a way of doing it without anyone getting hurt." He drums his fingers, performing a short paradiddle against the arm of the leather sofa.

After his death, Cobain's estate passed to his wife, the singer Courtney Love, who in 1997, with Cobain's bandmates, formed Nirvana LLC, a limited liability company to oversee their interests. The three have at times fought over Nirvana's legacy, almost going to court in 2002 (a settlement was reached the day before proceedings were due to begin) and in 2009 scrapping over the use of Cobain's likeness in computer game *Guitar Hero 5*. In April 2006, Love sold

25 per cent of her share in Nirvana's catalogue to Primary Wave Music for a reported $50m.

When he formed Foo Fighters, Grohl set up 35 Roswell Records as a holding company for the band's entire music catalogue, which is then licensed to a record company for a six- to seven-year period at a time. "Unfortunately, a lot of musicians sign away their freedoms when they enter into these big business contracts. It's an age-old story. It's still happening. I don't think there's a place for that kind of outside control when it comes to being creative."

Are you a control freak? I ask. "Absolutely. No question. I am a controlling freak. I'm not a control freak, I'm a controlling freak. This is our baby. When it comes to making music, we have our own process, we have our own crooked democracy . . . "

Democracy? Or is it a benign dictatorship? "Well, yeah. Show me a band of five people where there's no leader . . . I just don't think it could happen. At the end of the day, it's my name at the bottom of the cheque."

Foo Fighters are now embarking on another stadium-filling world tour. As Grohl, the perfect rock star, headed off, I couldn't help thinking of the two fortune cookies I'd spotted earlier pinned to his fridge. "An interesting musical opportunity is in your near future," read one. The other said simply: "Study and prepare yourself and one day, your day will come."

A CLOSER LOOK AT
Dave Grohl and the Foo Fighters

1. Like most profiles, this one has a central theme. It examines not only the actual person (Grohl) but also what the person stands for or typifies. Sometimes a theme involves some sort of tension or an important question. What is the tension for Grohl, and what are the larger questions the profile raises and asks readers to ponder?

2. Rather than coming out and stating a thesis, Wilkinson poses three key questions (in paragraphs 3, 21, and 25), and in the final paragraph muses about fortune-cookie messages on Grohl's refrigerator. How do these questions and his final paragraph help direct readers toward certain take-away conclusions? How would you summarize the thesis of this profile?

3. By citing research from two sources, Wilkinson provides background information that describes the larger social context in which Grohl lives and works. The first source is a history of grunge music by Mark Yarm (paragraphs 10–15), the other an interview with music-industry economist Chris Carey (paragraphs 24 and 25). How does this research add to the profile's authority and move the main storyline forward?

IDEAS FOR
Writing

1. Write a profile that, like Wilkinson's, not only paints a rich portrait of someone who is a leader in his or her field but also examines a central question about the broader social, cultural, or professional context in which the subject lives and works. Your subject could be an artist or an ordinary person who would interest your readers. Include a memo written to your professor that states your purpose, your main point, and the readers you are targeting.

2. Choose an artist or performer that you admire and write a rave review about that person and his or her work (see Chapter 7). Provide some context about the contemporary scene that helps explain what makes this person and work so extraordinarily exemplary and wonderful.

Prudencia

JODY L. IPSEN

Jody Ipsen is a humanitarian worker for immigrant rights and a freelance writer. A version of this piece appeared in a newspaper, the Tucson Citizen, *titled "Immigration: Why Prudencia Died." Ipsen is collecting her profiles and other work into a book,* When the Women Wept: Cries from the Migrant Trail. *She has adapted one of her book's chapters into this brief profile.*

The tropical jungle, dense with massive tree canopies, palm fronds, mango trees, red coffee berries, tangled vines and creeping ferns against the morning sun explodes like a massive jade from the land. The early morning fog casts the gem in a gauzy film, like an ephemeral phantom that flees when the Maya sun rises. Through the winding roads of the tropics to the highlands of Guatemala, shepherds, dressed in their red and blue trajes (clothing specific to their region) tend their sheep. Small fires coil in vertical rings and roosters rouse the sleep. It is hard to imagine that in 1982, plus or minus a few years, Todos Santos, a village in the clouds, was torched to the ground by U.S.-trained paramilitary, who also massacred thousands of indigenous men, women and children. The civil war that spilt the blood and cut the heads off of thousands continues to haunt the living.

At night the hills of Guatemala heave with grief. Slain victims of the dirty little war weep for their dead children; they cry of starvation and disease; they howl for the pregnant mothers whose babies were cut out of their bellies; they wail when the bullets were shot out of U.S. helicopters; they bawl as they bleed to death from their severed limbs by the cold blooded killers. In the morning the trees drip with tears where their families were hanged.

Unfortunately many men and women flee Guatemala despite the peace accord that was signed in 1996. Under the Freedom of Information Act, the CIA released documents of its covert operations during the Cold War. According to the CIA report titled *Sterilizing a "Red Infection,"* David M. Barret readily admits the United States' clandestine complicity in the civil war resulting in hundreds of thousands of deaths. During the Cold War, the CIA and the U.S. government gained tremendous currency by selling fear that Guatemala was a rising communist country.

Both John Dulles, former Secretary of State, and Allen Dulles, former Director of the CIA, played pivotal roles in the overthrow of the Guatemalan government. Allen Dulles was a shareholder in The United Fruit Company. His investments were threatened by the possible expropriation of land that President Jacobo Árbenz Guzmán wanted returned to peasant farmers.

In December of 1958, John Foster Dulles said, "The United States of America does not have friends; it has interests." The interests of the United Fruit Company were of foremost importance despite an unforeseen turn of heinous events.

CIA documents reported that "Washington used the CIA and U.S. Ambassador John Peurifoy to support and direct certain Guatemalan military leaders in overthrowing Árbenz's government. It was also psychological warfare—cleverly deceptive efforts to persuade Guatemala's citizens and political/military leaders that a major invasion force was steadily moving toward the nation's capital. . . ."

Some eleven years later and thousands of miles away in the Sonoran desert, thirty-three concerned humanitarians caravanned along a dusty road to a remote region approximately twenty miles west of Tucson, Arizona. Discarded backpacks, filthy jeans, brittle water bottles and worn shoes spread across miles of greasewood, mesquite trees, and devil's claws. In the bed of a truck, Father Bob Carney covered his mouth and nose with a bandana to avoid choking on the fine dust that creates the stunning sunsets in Arizona. It was over 100 degrees at 5:30 PM and the heat burned our skin.

Prudencia Martin Gomez was from Todos Santos, Guatemala, a small Maya village in the Cuchumatanes Mountains. At nineteen, Prudencia was migrating to California to join her boyfriend, Ismael. She was abandoned by her group when she fell ill from dehydration and heat exposure. She died on June 15, 2007, in the Tucson Sector of the Sonoran desert. The recorded temperature that day was 115 degrees.

Her boyfriend, Ismael, a young man, had already migrated to the United States when he couldn't find work as a teacher in Todos Santos. Although he was raised by his grandparents near the western coast of Guatemala and was formally educated, he was shunned by his community when he returned, due in large part to his father's grisly involvement in the civil war.

Prudencia wasn't a casualty of the war, but 10 instead a victim of the devastating consequences that sprouted from the bloody aftermath. Families remain divided, communities are in chaos, and lack of trust for one another creates divisive animosity among the Mayas, especially those families who had ties to the war.

During the 1980's, Todos Santos was scorched to the ground. Crops were burned, homes were seared, Mayas were chopped to pieces. Other families fled to remote regions of the mountains, hiding from the military while subsisting on tree roots and vegetation. Many died from starvation, disease and blight.

Under the auspice of the United States' secret directives during the 1980's, Ismael's father was forced to join the ranks of the military or be murdered, and fought against his own ilk, which had deleterious effects on Ismael's professional opportunities.

Prudencia had heard the gruesome stories juxtaposed to the stories of wealth and of what dreams may come while weighing them against the few jobs available to Maya women, due to the lack of civil rights for women and because of racial tensions that exist between indigenous and non-indigenous peoples of Guatemala.

Prudencia was convinced that her future existed inside the United States of America.

Prudencia and Ismael were going to marry once he saved enough money to build them a home in Guatemala. Prudencia, with a petite frame and long black hair that flowed past her hips, had simple pleasures, like gazing at the stars and thinking of the promise of joining Ismael someday. In May of 2007, at the age of 19, she left Todos Santos to surprise her boyfriend, who was living somewhere in California. Like most migrants, she traveled with a coyote (guide), through the veins of Mexico's underground, avoiding immigration police and bandits who rob Central Americans. She then walked approximately fifty miles from the border of Sasabe, Mexico to the outskirts of Tucson, Arizona. With only a gallon of water and the clothes in her backpack, Prudencia trudged through the desert under the scorching summer sun for approximately four to five days. Coyotes often abandon the sick or injured migrants in order to get the remainder of their group across. She was later found dead by humanitarians who were notified by her boyfriend that she was left behind by the group.

By the end of the civil war in 1996, it is esti- 15 mated that over 200,000 people were murdered. In 2007, three thousand women were murdered in Guatemala. Many believe the murderers are the formerly U.S.-trained Guatemalan military and police. In an attempt to bring back the conservative mano dura party (iron fist), the military instills fear through mutilations in order to persuade the country only the fist can stop the violence. So many of the disappeared women are later found mutilated and remain forever unidentified.

Ostensibly, many of the migrants leaving Guatemala find themselves without work or in Ismael's situation, without a community. The fallout of the civil war continues despite the ongoing efforts of Amnesty International. The legacy of death and destruction due in large part to U.S. covert operations thwarts any mechanisms to restore Guatemalan life to prewar conditions.

According to Intelligence scholar, Christopher Andrew, "The Guatemala affair [was] a disreputable moment—Eisenhower was 'directly responsible' for 'death and destruction, yet showed no signs of embarrassment then or later over his 'bullying of a banana republic.'"

In July of 2008, a shrine was erected at the site where Prudencia died.

A CLOSER LOOK AT
Prudencia

1. Ipsen chooses not to begin with a description of her subject, Prudencia, and does not even mention her until the second paragraph of the second section. How does this delay affect your understanding of Prudencia?

2. Examine the overall structure. Ipsen moves back and forth from the Guatemalan civil war and the United States' role in that war to the story of Prudencia Martin Gomez. In what ways does this complex organization enhance your understanding of her subject?

3. Ipsen chooses not to come out and tell the reader what she believes is the message or theme of this profile. That is, she uses an "implied thesis" that leaves such conclusions to the reader. How would the impact of this piece have changed had she chosen to directly state her thesis?

4. Ipsen has chosen to give this profile a one-word title, not "Prudencia Martin Gomez" or "The Tragedy of Prudencia Martin Gomez," but just "Prudencia." While "Prudencia" refers literally to the person profiled, *prudencia* is Spanish for "prudence," which can mean "discretion, carefulness, and the foresight to avoid danger and mishap"; it can also mean "the habit of mind of discerning what is good and moral." How does this ironic double sense of *Prudencia* enhance the meaning of the profile? What larger questions does it raise? Who has acted prudently and who has not?

IDEAS FOR
Writing

1. Write a brief commentary responding to this profile. Do some research on the Guatemalan civil war and the United States' role in it. Do you believe the United States was justified in taking part in this civil war? When should the United States be involved in these kinds of situations, and when should it stand aside?

2. Ipsen has spent years as a humanitarian helping immigrants who risk their lives migrating to the United States. Obviously, she feels passionately about this social and political cause, and the individuals who are caught up in these conflicts. Write a letter to the editor in which you express your own views about immigration and the plight of people like Prudencia. When should the United States allow people like Prudencia to enter the country legally? What lines would you draw to keep illegal immigrants out?

Lorde: The Music Phenomenon of the Year

NATHAN HELLER

Nathan Heller is a film and TV critic for Vogue *magazine, where this profile of singer-songwriter Lorde appeared. As you read, notice that the author has spent a great deal of time with Lorde and combines that firsthand experience with other background information to paint a rich portrait that captures his subject in an interesting and fresh way.*

The music phenomenon of the year, seventeen-year-old Lorde has gone from the suburbs of Auckland to the top of the global charts.

Pop songs traditionally rest on pronouns: *you* and *me,* the two of *us* together. One of the most startling things about Ella Yelich-O'Connor, the seventeen-year-old singer-songwriter who records as Lorde, is that although those words make the expected showings, their meaning, like a lot about her work, comes refreshed and entirely turned around. Since Lorde's single "Royals" went to number one in the United States this past fall, making her the youngest artist to top the charts in more than 25 years, her unadorned, descriptively precise songs have defined a novel point of view in mainstream vocals. Lorde's *I* is disembodied; her *you* is coyly attentive. ("You haven't stopped smoking all night," she sings in "A World Alone," on her debut album, *Pure Heroine.*) The crucial pronoun in her lyrics, though, is *we.* Writing from the vantage of kids joined by their experience—"We'll never be royals"—Lorde traces a path of transforming identity and burgeoning ambition. It's the voice of youth, but also of striking sophistication, and in recent months it's made her one of the most promising talents in global pop.

For Lorde, a New Zealander who grew up in the Auckland suburbs, the rush of international attention has been welcome for its ever-changing challenges more than its wash of glamour. "It's nice to be using lots of my brain all the time," she confesses one autumn afternoon over lunch in Manhattan, at a Chelsea photographer's loft. Dressed casually, in knitted gray pants and a striped T-shirt, she pauses pensively between bites. "I feel like I'm not yet sitting comfortably in what I'm doing, and I definitely feel a hunger for branching out," she says in her lilting accent. Since being discovered at a school talent show and signed to a recording- and-development deal at twelve, she's followed a quick and precipitous path to fame. But unlike many fresh-faced singers racing up the charts, Lorde retains an active hand in her musical craft.

It's a couple of days before her birthday ("I'll probably just listen to 'Anthems for a Seventeen-Year-Old Girl,' " she deadpans; "I'll have, like, a self-reflection moment"), which she will celebrate outside New Zealand for the first time. Meanwhile, there's work to be done: a special concert for the Museum of Modern Art Film Benefit that evening, during which she'll meet David Bowie, one of several illustrious fans; some filming for her next music video in a couple of days; the demands of a rapid urban schedule. "It feels like coming home, in a sense, because every film is set here, and every TV show," she says of New York. "But also like another planet."

Industrious, imaginative, and intellectually 5 precocious, Lorde holds an equally exotic appeal for her audience. Offstage, she is arresting, with cutting blue eyes and a mane of curly brown hair. In her videos and photos, she often wears a mask of catlike makeup, giving her features a defamiliarized, almost otherworldly eccentricity. She says her style icons are "people like Grace Jones and David Bowie, who have such a sense of themselves." With a look that moves easily from sleek austerity to fantastical whimsy, she counts Comme des Garçons, Miu Miu, Moschino, and Simone Rocha among her favorite labels. (She wore Chanel to the MoMA event.) "The kind of clothes that I've found I like to wear over the past year and six months have all been things that make me feel powerful and strong," she says. "I wear a lot of pants. I wear a lot of long, structured dresses."

Over the past year, Lorde has developed an adoring fan base among young listeners, something that she is still adjusting to. "It's a fine line between being a role model and preaching to people. I never want to tell anyone how they should be, especially not someone my age," she says. "But, that being said, I'm conscious of the fact that people my age are reading what I say and listening to what I say, and that's cool—particularly for the girls who are into what I do."

What people of all ages love most, of course, is the music. As a songwriter, Lorde is exacting and understated, leaning away from the usual sweet nothings of international pop and toward lyrics that are experientially evocative and quietly anthemic. Her music is cool, rhythmic, and pared-down, combining the beats of the European dance floor with haunting synth overlays and pure-voice melody. Despite her youth, her style emerged almost fully formed, borne by her smoky vocal tones—a timbre that recalls Adele or Amy Winehouse without resembling either. "It wasn't until I had vocal lessons, when I was thirteen or fourteen, that singing really became kind of a tool, and something I could use to get across what I was feeling," she says. "Before then, the things that I had taught myself to do with my throat were instinctive, and stuff that I was mimicking from things that I had heard. I had quite a nasal, twangy voice." Early on, Lorde would bring her producer and writing partner, Joel Little, a set of finished lyrics, and they'd invent music to match: She quickly wrote "Royals"—"that old chestnut," she calls it—after stumbling on a vintage *National Geographic*

photo of Kansas City Royals player George Brett. She originally conceived of the song as "a big, blown-out soul jam." ("I still have videos on my Photo Booth of me just vocal-freestyling the lyrics. Which is crazy to watch—no one's ever going to see that.") She released the song on SoundCloud, a music-posting Web service, which helped propel its rise.

Little realized Lorde had gotten to a new level when they were working on "Tennis Court": "I was making the beat and she sat in the back of the studio silently for a few hours, putting together the chorus melody in her head. She wouldn't sing it to me or show me the lyrics or anything. Eventually she was like, 'OK, I think I've got it,' and sang me pretty much the chorus you hear now, and I was just like, 'Holy shit, I love you, but I kind of hate you.'"

Lorde's mother is Sonja Yelich, a distin- 10 guished New Zealand poet. (Her father is an engineer.) But the singer says she feels most at home in the creative register of prose. "I've never written poetry, but I've written short fiction for a long time, and that's the thing that I read, pretty much exclusively," she says. "It's much more similar to songwriting for me—having to make something big and get it into a small space." She's been a close reader of newer American writers (such as Wells Tower and Claire Vaye Watkins) as well as the old masters (Raymond Carver, Alice Munro, Kurt Vonnegut, Tobias Wolff). These days, her composition takes another approach: "Now when I have an idea and I write it, it comes out in the form of a song." Yet she still writes prolifically and elegantly on her blog ("last night, i played to a room of people whose names i worship, breathe like fine gold smoke, reverent," she mused after a recent performance) and has an active Twitter presence. "A lot of the writers that I like aren't really about narrative; they're just about perfectly formed sentences," she says. "That's always been something I've been drawn to—one word or five words that sit perfectly."

Lorde's life in Auckland, where she grew up the second of four children, stands in contrast to her fast-paced international career. She has two dogs, Jimmy Choo and Boss—one's big, the other small—and thinks of them a lot. "Dogs have this weird thing where you leave and they just think you're dead," she says. "When we go out of the room now, they get super stressed out, because they're like, 'Are they going to go away again?'" (She tends to be the dogs' favorite.) The fraught pull toward home has shown up in her work. "I had a strange kind of tussle writing the record, in that I had been in this place my whole life that I had ached to get out of," she explains. "I had wanted to live in a city. And then I had this experience of traveling and being in the biggest cities in the world. Coming back home, I realized that (a) where I live is beautiful and (b) did I want to grow up? Did I want to leave the suburbs? It was sort of a weird coming-of-age thing or something."

In "400 Lux," she describes an aimless cruise around the suburbs through a stream-of-consciousness reverie ("Dreams of clean teeth/I can tell that you're tired"). Little describes most of Lorde's lyrics as "references to specific moments and experiences she's had, so the listener is let in on something really personal . . . but only up to a point, because she doesn't spell everything out, so they retain a sense of mystery, too." The "400 Lux" chorus shifts in meaning across a line break—"I'm glad that we stopped kissing/the tar on the highway"—a pivot that changes the song from a teen ballad based on a limited store of experience into a rangy, restless dream.

Lorde's sensibility is full of such swerves and trapdoors, each pulling away from mainstream-pop conventions. So is her stage presence. In an industry that rewards glamour, sex, and high jinks, Lorde performs shows with quirky restraint, dancing "like Gollum," as she's put it, with a small repertoire of twitchy movements. Creating a provocative stage persona is a gesture she can appreciate in others but doesn't feel compelled to emulate. In making music videos, she combines scenes from suburban New Zealand and lush, surreal fantasies; at times, as in the video for "Tennis Court," which appeared last summer, she seems to be drawing less from pop conventions than from performance art.

"I definitely love writing pop music, but in terms of structure and formula—you know it,

and then you know it," she explains. "I'm probably always going to return to that kind of structure, but it's nice to branch out a bit." Recently, in beginning to think about material for a second album, she's been focusing more intensely on her instrumental lines. "I've been writing traditional pop songs, and recording them, and then making the instrumental equivalent—I'm just mucking around with stuff," she says, melting into teenage insouciance.

Something will have to change by the time 15 Lorde's second album arrives, if only because her life, these days, is not the same. Much of *Pure Heroine* chronicles the experience of being young and obscure on the edges of the First World. ("We live in cities/You'll never see on-screen," Lorde sings in "Team." "Not very pretty, but we sure know how to run things.") Now she is one of the most in-demand performers on the globe, with four Grammy nominations and a nearly sold-out North American tour this spring.

"Obviously, if I were to come out with a record about living in my town and doing the things that we always did, that wouldn't be accurate," she says. "I've always wanted someone in my position to write about what it's like to be in my position"—but how to do it without becoming tiresome? Songs like "Royals" lampoon the bling culture of rock and hip-hop from the point of view of an outsider, an approach that provoked its own controversy. (Some thought it was caricaturing African-American rap culture.) If Lorde, now very much inside, tries to report from fame's front lines, she'll have to do it with finesse. "Hopefully I don't write the record which is like, 'I'm sitting in my spa, and I'm very sad,'" she jokes.

Yet for a young artist who aspires not just to success but to a full career (her heroes are musicians, such as Bowie and Radiohead, who have reinvented themselves repeatedly), it seems a worthy challenge. Gimlet-eyed but far from cynical, her songs look toward a future when today's urbane, interconnected kids will run the world. And her precocious confidence makes that outcome irresistible. "I'm kind of over getting told to throw my hands up in the air," she sings elsewhere in "Team." "So there."

A CLOSER LOOK AT
Lorde: The Music Phenomenon of the Year

1. The author has interviewed and shadowed his subject. Where does it first become clear that the author has spent time with Lorde? What does the author discover about her from this firsthand experience that he couldn't have otherwise known about her?

2. In the second paragraph, the author observes that Lorde's lyrics use the word *we* in a way that "traces a path of transforming identity and burgeoning ambition." How does this observation set the tone and theme for the rest of the profile? In what ways does the theme of transformation and ambition mirror the conflicts of Lorde herself, as well as the generation she represents?

3. Find a general-reference entry about Lorde on an Internet encyclopedia (such as Wikipedia) or a popular-culture database (such as IMDb.com), and compare this entry with Heller's profile. What does Heller's profile tell you about Lorde that a reference-entry genre does not? What information is offered by reference entries that a profile writer would choose to leave out?

IDEAS FOR
Writing

1. Write a profile that, like Heller's, not only offers an interesting and personal portrait of someone but also suggests how this person represents his or her generation or some other group. A person doesn't need to be famous to be representative. If possible, choose someone you can interview and shadow so that you understand this individual's world and environment. Show how your subject's life, work, aspirations, and conflicts mirror those of some larger group of people.

2. Write a proposal that offers a plan for repurposing this profile to take it multimodal. You can propose incorporating multimodal elements such as pictures with captions, links to online videos, and others. You could also propose a radical repurpose that, for instance, redesigns this print profile into a 5-minute video profile. Explain why this multimodal transformation is needed, and then offer a detailed plan (such as a storyboard) for making these changes. Be sure to explain *why* you have made each choice.

Two Profiles of Griffith Park

These two profiles of Griffith Park, the largest municipal park in the United States, located in the city of Los Angeles, take very different approaches. The first profile appears on the website of Los Angeles Department of Recreation and Parks. The second is written by novelist and nonfiction writer Benjamin Percy for Outside, *a monthly magazine that focuses on outdoor recreation. As you read, notice how they differ in terms of style and content.*

City of Los Angeles Department of Recreation and Parks, General Information for Griffith Park

Times And Regulations:

Griffith Park is open to the public from 5:00 a.m. to 10:30 p.m. Bridle trails, hiking paths, and mountain roads are closed at sunset. The speed limit on all park roads is 25 mph and is strictly enforced. Brush fires present a definite safety hazard, especially from Spring to early Fall, when the natural chaparral and underbrush is very dry. Open fires are prohibited; barbecue pits are provided free of charge at picnic areas. In case of emergency in the park, notify the Ranger Station at (323) 913-4688 or dial 911. The Griffith Park Fire Recovery Blog offers updated park information.

Location:

Griffith Park lies just west of the Golden State Freeway (I-5), roughly between Los Feliz Boulevard on the south and the Ventura Freeway (SR 134) on the north. Freeway off-ramps leading to the park from I-5 are Los Feliz Boulevard, Griffith Park (direct entry) and Zoo Drive. Approaching the park on SR 134 eastbound, take either the Forest Lawn Drive or Victory Boulevard offramps. From SR 134 westbound, take Zoo Drive or Forest Lawn Drive. After leaving freeways, follow the signs into the park.

Narrative:

With over 4,210 acres of both natural chapparal-covered terrain and landscaped parkland and picnic areas, Griffith Park is the largest municipal park with urban wilderness area in the United States. Situated in the eastern Santa Monica Mountain range, the Park's elevations range from 384 to 1,625 feet above sea level. With an arid climate, the Park's plant communities vary from coastal sage scrub, oak and walnut woodlands to riparian vegetation with trees in the Park's deep canyons. The California native plants represented in Griffith Park include the California species of oak, walnut, lilac, mountain mahogany, sages, toyon, and sumac. Present, in small quantities, are the threatened species of manzanita and berberis.

Over the years recreational attractions have been developed throughout the Park, however an amazingly large portion of the Park remains virtually unchanged from the days Native American villages occupied the area's lower slopes. Today's Griffith Park offers numerous family attractions, an assortment of educational and cultural institutions, and miles of hiking and horseback riding trails, and provides visitors an ideal environment for enjoyable recreation activities.

Originally a part of the Spanish land grant, Rancho Los Feliz, the park was named for its former owner, Colonel Griffith J. Griffith. Born in Glamorganshire, South Wales, Griffith emigrated to the United States in 1865, eventually, making a personal fortune in California gold mine speculation. In 1882, Griffith settled in Los Angeles, and purchased a 4,071 acre portion of the Rancho Los Feliz, which stretched northward from the northern boundaries of the Pueblo de Los Angeles. On December 16, 1896, the civic-minded Griffith bequeathed 3,015 acres of his Rancho Los Feliz estate as a Christmas gift to the people of Los Angeles to be used as parkland. The enormous gift, equal to five square miles, was to be given to the city unconditionally—or almost so.

"It must be made a place of recreation and rest for the masses, a resort for the rank and file, for the plain people," Griffith said on that occasion.

"I consider it my obligation to make Los Angeles a happier, cleaner, and finer city. I wish to pay my debt of duty in this way to the community in which I have prospered."

Since Griffith's original gift, further donations of land, along with City purchases and the reversion of private land to public domain have expanded the Park to its present size. Col. Griffith died July 7, 1919, however, he had left a sizeable trust fund to complete the dreams he had for the park; specifically designating funds for the construction of a Greek amphitheater (the Greek Theatre, built 1930) and an observatory and hall of science (Griffith Observatory, built 1935.)

Griffith Park stands today a monument to the dedicated vision of one man—Griffith Jenkins Griffith, Park Commission, civic philanthropist, advocate of parklands, and fervent speaker of recreation for the health of Los Angeles.

Welcome to the Jungle

BENJAMIN PERCY

I'm not here for the silicone or Bentleys. I don't want to get my picture taken with a Marilyn Monroe impersonator. I've come to grind my teeth on a little of L.A.'s sweet grit.

My buddy James—a fast-talker with wild eyes and a grizzly bear of a beard—picks me up at LAX. He's lived here for three years but still keeps a GPS on the dash. "This city," he says, "makes no sense." He's talking about more than the tangle of roadways. He's talking about a city that is not so much a city as it is a mess of neighborhoods, each with its own personality, making L.A. a kind of smog-belching, schizophrenic beast.

We park along the L.A. River at Atwater Village and step into the concrete channel. I have alternating views of the freeway and the mist-haloed San Gabriel Mountains. This is not the barren watercourse from *Terminator 2*. Bass populate the river. Horseback riders splash along its banks. There are islands thick with trees that are decorated with garbage. I quickly spot a dozen species of waterfowl.

Ducks honk. Semis blast their horns. A group of spandex-clad bicyclists races by on the riverside path. James and I find a tunnel, full of graffiti and shadows and broken glass, that takes us under the freeway. When we emerge, we are at the doorstep of 4,000-acre Griffith Park, one of the largest urban wildernesses in the country.

We enter the 53-mile network of trails, and soon trees crowd around us, hushing the grumble of the city. At the end of our seven-mile hike, the sun begins to set, and the neon glow of the city makes the sky a bruised purple. We drive to Koreatown and Masan, a restaurant known for its monkfish stew, which we order, along with live octopus. The legs twist on our plates like dying snakes, and I chew them to a paste—if you don't, the suckers can latch on to your tongue.

"You want dessert?" James asks, and I say, "I want to shoot some guns."

Just past Skid Row we find the Los Angeles Gun Club, the kind of nondescript building that could pass for a paper-clip warehouse. Then you approach the door and hear the *snap-snap-snap* of muffled gunfire. Inside, the air is heavy with gun oil, and the walls are busy with racks of every firearm you can imagine. James and I opt for an AR-15, an assault rifle that jerks in my arms like something alive as I fire rounds down lane four. I am surrounded by men with forearm tats who fire pistols while their girlfriends clap and squeal. After blasting my way through three bricks of ammo, my hands are trembling and I can't shake the grin from my face.

"What do you think?" James asks.

"Unreal," I say.

A CLOSER LOOK AT
General Information for Griffith Park and Welcome to the Jungle

1. Profiles belong to a very "stretchy" and versatile genre. These profiles of Griffith Park differ greatly, but they both describe the same place.

   a. How do they differ in terms of the details they describe?

   b. How do they differ in purpose, angle, audience, and style?

   c. How do their titles forecast the content, angle, and style of each?

   d. How do their organizations differ? How do they begin and end?

   e. Finally, compare the two in a single sentence that follows a pattern like this one: "The Recreation and Parks piece makes me feel_____, while Percy's piece makes me feel_____." Then point out or quote specific places in each text that elicit that feeling.

2. The first profile is written for readers who visit the Los Angeles Recreation and Parks website, the second for people who enjoy reading *Outside* magazine. Use Google to find each website and speculate about the values and expectations of each set of readers. How would *Outside* readers react if they found "General Information" in the magazine? How would visitors to the Parks and Recreation website react if they encountered Percy's profile?

3. Which kind of profile would you most enjoy writing? Or would you rather write something that falls between the two? Explain your choice.

4. "Welcome to the Jungle" has more energy and snap partly because it tells a story. What narrative elements does Percy use to make this very short profile interesting?

IDEAS FOR
Writing

1. Choose a place you find interesting and write two short profiles of the place. For the first, imagine you work for a business or government agency that needs a serious and restrained profile for their website. The profile should present information clearly and in a way that would be appropriate for a wide range of readers. It should be neutral and objective in tone and style. For the second, imagine you have been asked to contribute a profile to a website or magazine you enjoy reading. Target those readers, using a tone that is energetic and entertaining. Amplify with metaphors and similes. Paint a rich picture with details about what the place smelled, sounded, and looked like. When you've finished, write a memo that explains the strategies you used to match the values and expectations of each reader type.

2. "Welcome to the Jungle" profiles both a place and experience. Write a place profile that also tells an interesting story about one of your personal experiences that happened in a special place. Set the scene in rich detail and use dialogue to provide texture. Your profile should help readers understand what is special about this place.

A FEW IDEAS FOR
Composing a Profile

1. **Write a profile of a place or an object.** While writing your profile, think of this place or object as a *person* rather than as an inanimate thing. Discuss its history, its unique characteristics, its relationships with people, and so on. Relate any stories you know about it. Make sure you keep your readers in mind as you write this profile. Write for readers who are interested in experiencing this place or object. How can you make your profile interesting and engaging for them?

2. **Repurpose a profile for children.** Find a profile of a famous person (e.g., Martin Luther King, Jr., Clara Barton, Abraham Lincoln, Maya Angelou, Cesar Chavez, Princess Diana) and rewrite it in a way that would be accessible and interesting to children who are five to ten years old. Include the original profile when you hand in your rewritten profile to your professor.

3. **Create a profile of someone in your family.** Use a style that would make your profile especially engaging to readers who don't know you, your family, or your community. Pay special attention to your use of detail, and show your subject in motion or doing things, if possible.

Go to **My**WritingLab to complete this chapter's exercises and test your understanding of its objectives.

Reviews

Frozen Tries and Fails to Be Both Traditional and Modern

DAN SCHINDEL

In this movie review, Dan Schindel writes a negative critique of Frozen, *one of the most popular and profitable movies of 2013. He focuses on the inconsistencies and even some of the hypocrisies of a Disney princess film that tries to break out of the genre. Watch how he highlights the weaknesses of the movie, according to him, while praising its strengths.*

Disney is in a strange place with its animated features, especially when it comes to fairy tales. In some ways, the studio is still struggling in a post-*Shrek* world, trying to figure out how to sell unironic sentimentality like dreams and true love to a more cynical audience. At the same time, the studio has become more corporately controlled, and everything is constantly focus-tested and second-guessed. As a result of this schizoid approach to filmmaking, many aspects of *Frozen* feel uncertain.

The story takes place in the kingdom of Arendelle, where the royal castle is sealed off from outsiders. Princess Elsa (Idina Menzel) possesses magic ice powers that are triggered by emotion. As a child, she almost killed her younger sister Anna (Kristen Bell) with these abilities, so she forgoes all human contact in order to keep her family safe.

When the time comes for Elsa's coronation as Queen, the castle is opened for foreign dignitaries. This thrills Anna, who has felt stifled during the years of seclusion. She immediately falls head over heels for the visiting Prince Hans (Santino Fontana), and the two become engaged after a few hours (and one musical number) of courtship. When they break this news to Elsa, she loses control and exposes her magic. Ashamed, Elsa runs away to the mountains, unknowingly casting all of Arendelle into a thick, unseasonable winter. Anna goes after her, picking up a few friends along the way: eccentric ice vendor Kristoff (Jonathan Groff), his reindeer companion Sven, and animate snowman Olaf (Josh Gad).

Disney has been trying to adapt Hans Christian Andersen's *The Snow Queen* since the 1940s, never quite able to make it work. Writer/director Jennifer Lee and co-director Chris Buck solved the problem by not actually adapting the book at all. The film has nothing in common with the original tale beyond a queen who controls snow. It's appropriate that the title was changed to the supremely generic-sounding *Frozen*, since the film doesn't have anything on its mind beyond the well-worn tropes of True Love, Friendship, and Believing In Yourself.

There are a few positive elements. The voice 5 actors all do nice jobs in both the emoting and singing departments, and there are a few terrific emotional beats along with a generous amount of good humor. Anna is a great protagonist—capable, smart, and awkward in a way that's (mostly) endearing and not too cutesy. And then there's Elsa, who is dealing with things Disney characters normally don't face, even if her situation feels like an X-Men riff (in keeping with recent trends, her ice tricks play a lot more like superpowers than any kind of magic). A better version of this film would focus more on her; the movie falters whenever Elsa isn't present, and we only get one-and-a-half Idina Menzel musical performances, which I'm pretty sure is criminal.

Frozen is stuck between playing its cliched themes straight and trying to subvert them. Like *Enchanted*, it tries to have its cake and eat it too. Making fun of "love at first sight" doesn't change the fact that a whole song was sung about it. Pointing out that an obvious bad guy's name sounds like "weasel" does not redeem the use of a blatantly obvious bad guy. The movie goes for both "traditional" and "hip," most evident in the jarringly modern, Whedonesque patter of the dialogue.

On occasion, though, the film pulls it off. Kristoff holds "conversations" with Sven in which he performs a silly voice for the reindeer. It's a clever twist on the talking animal sidekick. Olaf, despite being entirely toyetic, is a non-annoying presence, his comic relief wackiness buoyed by Gad's enthusiasm.

Frozen does its best to overcome traditional archetypes, but doesn't go far enough. It centers on a sibling relationship rather than a romantic one, but the interaction between Anna and Elsa is too limited. Even more frustrating is how nothing that happens to the characters on their journey impacts their development at all. When Elsa first runs off, she seems to embrace her powers, and while this loss of inhibition thankfully doesn't signal her transformation into a villain, it also doesn't change her in any other meaningful way.

Much of *Frozen* is reminiscent of *Tangled*, a similarly pleasant but ephemeral experience. The bicker-banter relationship between Anna and Kristoff is beat-for-beat a retread of the one between Rapunzel and Flynn, and Sven might as well be the horse Maximus. Worse, though, is that the animation looks nearly the same as it did in the former film. A lot of computer-animated films featuring humans are nigh indistinguishable, and this is no exception. It looks pretty, but technical prowess is not a substitute for true artistic ingenuity.

As a musical, *Frozen* is much more success- 10 ful than Disney's other recent attempts to revive the format, capturing the same feeling and Broadway-lite style as the films from Disney's "renaissance" in the early '90s. There are a few memorable songs, and most of them are well-integrated into the story, propelling the narrative forward or illustrating the characters' emotional states in a dynamic way. For example, the lyrics and melody of "Do You Want to Build a Snowman" are simple and unflashy, but the piece is effective because it organically conveys the passage of time and the growing gulf between Anna and Elsa as they age. It also helps that the movie has a decent amount of songs (*Tangled* had *four*. You call *that* a musical?), which are spaced evenly throughout the run-time. The only thing it lacks is a proper finale number.

The best song in the film is "Let It Go," in which Elsa expresses her exhilaration at being able to freely use her abilities for the first time in her life. It's an Idina Menzel power ballad, so of course it's great. Another standout is "For the First Time in Forever," which is sung ably by Bell and gets a nifty reprise later on as a duet with Menzel. Other critics have professed love for Gad's "In Summer," but I can't recall a single line of it. The soundtrack was written and composed by Robert Lopez and Kristen Anderson-Lopez, who are collectively responsible for the music of *Avenue Q, The Book of Mormon,* and 2011's *Winnie the Pooh.* The fact that such talented people produced such a mixed offering of songs is a tad disappointing.

Frozen is nice, and that's all. It's born out of warring needs to both play things safe and be truly bold, so while it's never outright bland, it lacks staying power. There's nothing new here, but it accomplishes the old inoffensively enough.

A CLOSER LOOK AT

Frozen Tries and Fails to Be Both Traditional and Modern

1. With your group, find five inconsistencies or weaknesses named by Schindel in the movie *Frozen*. Do the members of your group agree with Schindel's assessment of *Frozen* that "while it's never outright bland, it lacks staying power"?

2. Make a list of three movies that you personally like but others find flawed. Compare your list with those of other group members. Then, choose one of the movies from your list and defend it. Why, despite its flaws, do you consider it an entertaining and worthwhile movie?

3. Of course, Disney produces princess movies because they rake in huge profits. Discuss the princess-movie genre with your group. What are the major features of this genre, and how do various Disney movies stretch the genre to offer new and original takes on the prototypical princess story?

IDEAS FOR

Writing

1. A "movie trailer" mashup uses songs or images from one movie to create something funny with scenes from another movie. For example, search for "Brokeback to the Future" or "Avatar/Pocahontas" on YouTube. Write a review in which you choose one of these mashups and discuss why it is funny or insightful.

2. Write a rebuttal or counterargument to Schindel's review of the movie *Frozen*. Keep in mind that *Frozen* was a smash hit when it was released and it's still popular today. Do you think Schindel was wrong about the movie, or do you think the movie is popular despite the flaws he points out?

Why We Crave Horror Movies

STEPHEN KING

This curious article was first published in Playboy *in January 1981 when Stephen King was emerging as one of the great horror writers. It's not a standard review, but it has many of this genre's elements. Watch how King stretches the genre to achieve an interesting purpose.*

I think that we're all mentally ill: those of us outside the asylums only hide it a little better—and maybe not all that much better, after all. We've all known people who talk to themselves, people who sometimes squinch their faces into horrible grimaces when they believe no one is watching, people who have some hysterical fear—of snakes, the dark, the tight place, the long drop . . . and, of course, those final worms and grubs that are waiting so patiently underground.

When we pay our four or five bucks and seat ourselves at tenth-row center in a theater showing a horror movie, we are daring the nightmare.

Why? Some of the reasons are simple and obvious. To show that we can, that we are not afraid, that we can ride this roller coaster. Which is not to say that a really good horror movie may not surprise a scream out of us at some point, the way we may scream when the roller coaster twists through a complete 360 or plows through a lake at the bottom of the drop. And horror movies, like roller coasters, have always been the special province of the young; by the time one turns 40 or 50, one's appetite for double twists or 360-degree loops may be considerably depleted.

We also go to re-establish our feelings of essential normality; the horror movie is innately conservative, even reactionary. Freda Jackson as the horrible melting woman in *Die, Monster, Die!* confirms for us that no matter how far we may be removed from the beauty of a Robert Redford or a Diana Ross, we are still light-years from true ugliness.

And we go to have fun. 5

Ah, but this is where the ground starts to slope away, isn't it? Because this is a very peculiar sort of fun indeed. The fun comes from seeing others menaced—sometimes killed. One critic has suggested that if pro football has become the voyeur's version of combat, then the horror film has become the modern version of the public lynching.

It is true that the mythic, "fairytale" horror film intends to take away the shades of gray . . . . It urges us to put away our more civilized and adult penchant for analysis and to become children again, seeing things in pure blacks and whites. It may be that horror movies provide psychic relief on this level because this invitation to lapse into simplicity, irrationality and even outright madness is extended so rarely. We are told we may allow our emotions a free rein . . . or no rein at all.

If we are all insane, then sanity becomes a matter of degree. If your insanity leads you to carve up women like Jack the Ripper or the Cleveland Torso Murderer, we clap you away in the funny farm (but neither of those two amateur-night surgeons was ever caught, heh-heh-heh); if, on the other hand your insanity leads you only to talk to yourself when you're under stress or to pick your nose on the morning bus, then you are left alone to go about your business . . . though it is doubtful that you will ever be invited to the best parties.

The potential lyncher is in almost all of us (excluding saints, past and present; but then, most saints have been crazy in their own ways), and every now and then, he has to be let loose to scream and roll around in the grass. Our emotions and our fears form their own body, and we recognize that it demands its own exercise to maintain proper muscle tone. Certain of these emotional muscles are accepted—even exalted—in civilized society; they are, of course, the emotions that tend to maintain the status quo of civilization itself. Love, friendship, loyalty, kindness—these are all the emotions that we applaud, emotions that have been immortalized in the couplets of Hallmark cards. . . .

When we exhibit these emotions, society 10 showers us with positive reinforcement; we learn this even before we get out of diapers. When, as children, we hug our rotten little puke of a sister and give her a kiss, all the aunts and uncles smile and twit and cry, "Isn't he the sweetest little thing?" Such coveted treats as chocolate-covered graham crackers often follow. But if we deliberately slam the rotten little puke of a sister's fingers in the door, sanctions follow—angry remonstrance from parents, aunts and uncles; instead of a chocolate-covered graham cracker, a spanking.

But anticivilization emotions don't go away, and they demand periodic exercise. We have such "sick" jokes as, "What's the difference between a truckload of bowling balls and a truckload of dead babies?" (You can't unload a truckload of bowling balls with a pitchfork . . . a joke, by the way, that I heard originally from a ten-year-old.) Such a joke may surprise a laugh or a grin out of us even as we recoil, a possibility that confirms the thesis: If we share a brotherhood of man, then we also share an insanity of man. None of which is intended as a defense of either the sick joke or insanity but merely as an explanation of why the best horror films, like the best fairy tales, manage to be reactionary, anarchistic, and revolutionary all at the same time.

The mythic horror movie, like the sick joke, has a dirty job to do. It deliberately appeals to all that is worst in us. It is morbidity unchained, our most base instincts let free, our nastiest fantasies realized . . . and it all happens, fittingly enough, in the dark. For those reasons, good liberals often shy away from horror films. For myself, I like to see the most aggressive of them—*Dawn of the Dead*, for instance—as lifting a trap door in the civilized forebrain and throwing a basket of raw meat to the hungry alligators swimming around in that subterranean river beneath.

Why bother? Because it keeps them from getting out, man. It keeps them down there and me up here. It was Lennon and McCartney who said that all you need is love, and I would agree with that.

As long as you keep the gators fed.

A CLOSER LOOK AT
Why We Crave Horror Movies

1. List the three qualities (criteria) that Stephen King argues are the characteristics of an excellent horror film. Do you agree with these criteria? Would you add or subtract some of them? How does King use these criteria to sort the good horror movies from the bad?

2. King's style is especially interesting in this article. He seems to be making a straightforward argument about the difference between good horror movies and bad horror movies. But occasionally, he throws a strange sentence at the readers, creating a pained laugh or a dark thought. Find a handful of these moments in the article. How does he use style to bring about this dark humor?

3. This review is about horror movies, but King's real motive is to explore the psychology behind people's fascination with such movies. He identifies several reasons why people crave horror films. Highlight these reasons and discuss them with a group in your class. Do you agree with King, or do you think people have other reasons for enjoying horror movies?

IDEAS FOR
Writing

1. Write a rebuttal to King's article in which you dispute his reasoning or offer different reasons why people like to see horror movies. In your rebuttal, you could challenge King's criteria, or you could question whether he is right about why people enjoy blood and gore. You might even challenge the worth of these kinds of movies altogether. You don't need to completely disagree with King, but you should distinguish your argument from his in a significant way.

2. Rent or go see a horror film, perhaps one based on a Stephen King novel. Write a review of the movie using King's evaluation criteria in this article as the basis of your review. Unlike King's argument, your review does not need to define the criteria. Instead, assume King's criteria reflect "common expectations" that most moviegoers will accept. Unlike King, you do not need to make a broader argument about the psychology of these movies. Instead, review the movie as though you were writing for a newspaper or a movie review blog.

Why Watching Christian Blockbuster *Noah* Is Like Sitting in a Giant Bathtub

DOROTHY WOODEND

In this review of the movie, Noah, *Dorothy Woodend discusses the challenges of making a religiously themed movie, even with a major star like Russell Crowe in the lead. She uses humor to offset some of her sharper criticisms. Notice how she compares the familiar story of Noah from the Bible with this Hollywood version—and emerges impressed by the simple grace of the original source while disappointed with the Hollywood adaptation.*

"Are you there, God? It's me, Noah!"

It would have been nice if Darren Aronofsky had found a way to work this line into his new Biblical epic, "Noah." The film has just about everything else, including animals marching two by two, beards bushy enough to blot out the sun, giant transformers made out of boulders, divine smiting, and so much glowering Russell Crowe one might be forgiven for dampening one's movie seat.

The decision to make a movie about Noah and his big boat might seem a highly questionable enterprise, but bad ideas never seem to stop anyone lately. The bigger, the badder, the better, and with a running time of approximately 120,000 minutes, Aronofsky's latest joins the ranks of films that never seem to end.

The tale that you remember from your childhood wouldn't make for much a movie, so there is a lot of extrapolation that must be added on with bits of wire and binder twine. But in all this vast expanse and longwinded exposition, there is very little that feels real. Not real in the sense of "Gee, those computer generated animals look awfully lifelike," but more importantly, real as in "Hmm, I feel some genuine emotion happening down there." Or simply, "I have wet my pants."

In the center of all this stands Russell Crowe, 5 thick of body, and sporting various hairstyles that wouldn't look out of place on Vancouver's Main Street: long and mane-like, shaved and serious, or sticking out like a drunk porcupine. Meaty in every sense of the word, you could chew on him for a while before you even made much of a dent. Russell gives his portrayal of the Biblical patriarch the old college try. Old is the operative word here, since in the original story Noah was over 500 years old before things even got going.

Jennifer Connelly, who plays Noah's wife Naameh, has come a very long way from her first outing with Aronofsky, one "Requiem for a Dream," which, if you recall, involved a deeply unfortunate sex scene. No more up the bum for this lady! In "Noah," she is the matriarch of the holiest family, stripped of eyeliner and forced to wear artfully woven clothes that look like they came from Eileen Fisher's new collection. She may have a name that sounds like it came from the front end of a sheep, but she is holier-than-thou all the way through the movie. The rest of the cast do their thespian best, but they often seem confused by the proceedings.

The only person who seems to be having fun is crazy old Ray Winstone, channeling antediluvian reality by way of Essex.

'What the hell?'

Unlike religious epics of old, "Noah" does not take place in some Hollywood back-lot version of ancient Egypt, but is rather a bowdlerized version of the Old Testament mixed with science fiction. God is somewhere lurking behind the clouds, but so are some strange fantasy beasts and a magical Methuselah (played by Anthony Hopkins). The entire thing seems odd and out of joint, like it was put together in the dark. It is hard even to encapsulate the plot without sounding vaguely insane, but we will press on.

The story kicks off with a lesson in geneal- 10 ogy. Adam and Eve begat Cain, Abel and some other schlub named Seth. Cain bonked Abel with a rock, and then went on to begat Ray Winstone. "What the hell?" is the only reasonable thing to say to that. Meanwhile, Seth popped out a few kids of his own, one of whom eventually gives rise to our Noah, the last good guy on earth.

When little Noah is just a sliver of a boy— who doesn't look a day over 259—his father Lemech gives little Noah a history lesson.

Their interlude is cut short by the arrival of ruffians of Cainish descent. Noah's father gets mightily dead, and our little hero scampers off to find a safer place to grow up.

Cut forward a few hundred years and Noah and his fashionably déshabillé family are out gathering nuts and berries. With three sons (Shem, Ham and wee Japheth), Noah has his work cut out for him merely to survive. Under the auspices of the descendants of Cain, things haven't worked out too well. Vast cities, fuelled by some explosive golden stuff in the ground that is never fully explained, have sprung up and died. The place is a mess, a blighted landscape that looks a lot like northern Alberta.

More ruffians show up and are summarily slaughtered by our peace-loving patriarch. Seems God has a plan for Noah and he wastes no time in being utterly obscure about it. After a series of dreams featuring drowned worlds and animated snakes, Noah and his family set off on a quest to find the oldest Meth-man in the world. Along the way they pick up a wounded girl, Ila, whose entire family has been slaughtered, and they take her along for the ride. Here is where the director's cross-eyed vision really gets going.

On the run from yet more Cainites, the fam- 15 ily head into the badlands where they encounter The Watchers. The Watchers are fallen angels, cursed by God for being uppity. They look a lot like prehistoric Transformers and rumble about like Nick Nolte, so naturally one of them is also voiced by said Nolte.

Instead of bashing Noah's head in, they help him reach his grandfather Methuselah's mountain. I don't quite know what Sir Anthony Hopkins was aiming for with his portrayal of the oldest man in the world, but he ends up somewhere between Yoda and Riff Raff from the Rocky Horror Picture Show. Before you know it, Granddad drugs Noah, gives him a magic seed, and—presto!—God makes trees.

Time for a pee break

After this whiz bang trip, things quiet down for a moment. The entire middle chapter of the film is given over to the creation of the ark itself: lots of boiling of tar and hewing of wood. If you have to go pee, do it now. For one thing, not much happens, plus when all that water shows up you may feel certain sympathy in your bladder.

As Noah and family toil and strain, the intricacies of old-timey marriage come to the fore. Ila (played by Emma Watson) has grown up into a beautiful young woman, but she is barren. Even as she and Shem romp like horny puppies in the woods, brother Ham, who also desires himself a girlfriend, lurks and watches.

Just like the Bible said, horniness will be the end of us. Ham has a sausage and he wants to use it. He demands that his parents find him a woman. But storm clouds are gathering, as well as a passel of raggedy rapey-types led by a guy named Tubal-cain (Winstone), a direct descendant of the original murderous Cain and self-declared king of the world. In Genesis 4:22, Tubal-cain is referred to as "forger of all instruments of bronze and iron." The film takes this literally and supplies him with weapons aplenty—the better to murder folks with. Tubal and his mob set up camp around Noah's boat, and await the coming storm. To pass the time, they amuse themselves with lots of raping and animal eviscerations.

It's little wonder that God has had enough 20 and finally the rain descends. It looks a lot like Vancouver last Wednesday.

All wet

It's easy to poke a stick at "Noah." The film is so bloated it's like something that's been drifting in the water for days. Certainly it's hysterical and ridiculous. That's just the beginning though. The sheer bombast of the thing speaks more to the ambition of the director, which seems to be in keeping for so many filmmakers these days. Given time and money and big stars, what can they do but assemble vast, tottering layer-cake films—movies so clotted with cream, fruit, nuts, and assorted fripperies that they seem to forget the point is to tell a story and tell it well. (I am looking directly at you, Wes Anderson.) All the whipped ganache in the universe makes no difference when the damn thing is hollow at its core.

"Noah" suffers from something of the same fate; it is stuffed to the brim, but missing the one key thing that matters, namely that we care what happens to these folks. Most of the film just feels silly, except for one scene, in which something older, and decidedly more brutal comes to the fore. For only a moment you catch a glimpse, more correctly a whiff, of something. Call it sulfur and brimstone, some primitive reek of the days when the Old Testament was something to be genuinely feared. The hard, cold mineral odor of it is there in the scene, in which Noah must decide whether to murder two new born babies, because it is God's Will.

But where is God exactly? He doesn't get any speaking parts, and the most visible evidence we get of the ongoing confab between Noah and him is some rainbow sprinkles, and of the course the deluge that wipes away all humanity. Unlike the constant celestial chatter that marks the actual biblical text, in this film all is silent. God speaks only in bad CGI (Computer God Imagery) that consists of animated snakes, people hitting other people with rocks and a lot of trees. I wish he would say

something—anything really—but no such luck. With no word from on high, we're stuck with humans on big old boat, and the only thing they have to do is sit around listening to animals snort and fart in their sleep.

The film, for all its insanity, is no fun. It feels more like an endurance contest than anything else. The high beauty of biblical language is also distinctly absent. Instead we get drivelly lines like "Men broke the world." Not once, but twice. The fact this is apparently true (at least according to the latest comprehensive UN climate change report) is something else entirely.

But the inconvenient truth can't be dis- 25 counted either: "Noah," like all end-of-world fantasias that have preceded it, speaks to some deep and lingering sense that we need punishment. Humanity is like a gaggle of naughty teens who threw a massive house party while our parents were away and now there's a toilet on the lawn and vomit in the vestibule. We have some explaining to do, with our oceans full of acid and plastic.

Punishment is cited over and over again as a necessary and good thing. A dad that spanks your bottom is better than the dad that simply isn't there. In the film, much ado is made about the fact that no one has heard from God in a while. In his absence, men have grown plucky and defiant.

All this changes when the water comes. Suddenly we're in a Brueghel painting, the screams of the damned drowning out the sound of the storm. But a patriarchal deity who kills everything just to start again—what kind of a God is that? Entire books have been written about what a meanie God is in the Old Testament. That's not news, nor is the allegory that resource extraction is to blame for global calamity. So what is new exactly?

Maybe it's the same old thing, writ again. Aronofsky's version has become even longer, more elaborate and much more expensive, but with worse dialogue.

The sin of pride brings about a fall. Aronofsky set about making an epic, and threw in everything he could think of: homicidal megalomania, rock monsters, horny teens, berry picking and magical in vitro. He's mixed it up and poured it out, but aside from a few scattered moments (Crowe is suitably impressive), nothing endures. It all drains away, leaving one damp and unsatisfied.

There are bits and fragments of the epic [30] drama that has kept the story going since the Epic of Gilgamesh (written in 650 B.C.). But these are only tiny whispers lost in the giant bathtub of a movie.

It is curious that not many critics have stepped up and said this is a terrible film—nonsensical, overblown and grandiose. I have spared you the worst of it, including the requisite end-of-act fight scene, where Noah and Tubal-ligation-cain wrestle and grunt atop of the sleeping animals. Or, the later bits that involve Noah inventing wine and getting naked-ass drunk in the sand. If you weren't familiar with the original biblical text, you would have no idea what was

happening in this scene. The general reception of the film seems to be one of apologia, along of the lines of, "Yes, it's not great, but at least it's trying hard."

The real problem is that "Noah" is a story badly told. A good story endures because it is beautiful and clear. You can't really do any better than: "In the beginning God created the heaven and the earth. And the earth was without form, and void; and darkness was upon the face of the deep. And the Spirit of God moved upon the face of the waters.

"And God said, Let there be light: and there was light."

How do you possibly top the clarity of these words? You can't. The only place the film has any real power is here, in the original text. It doesn't really matter whether you believe that God wrote it or not—it's one hell of a story.

A CLOSER LOOK AT
Why Watching Christian Blockbuster *Noah* Is Like Sitting in a Giant Bathtub

1. Find three places where Woodend uses humor to offset some of her criticisms of the movie. With your group, discuss the purpose of this kind of humor in a negative review. Did you find these funny moments helpful or problematic?

2. With your group, list some other big-budget movies that received negative reviews and did not do well at the theaters. What are some of the common qualities of a big-budget film flop? Use Woodend's review to identify some of these qualities.

3. Recently, religious films have made a comeback in popularity, so it's not surprising that the producers of a film like *Noah* might want to pursue that market. However, this movie was panned by both secular and religious reviewers. With your group, come up with a list of three qualities that make a film based on a religious story popular. Then, discuss what might make a religious film unpopular.

IDEAS FOR
Writing

1. Write your own negative review of a movie. Choose a movie that was considered a flop in its day. Write a review in which you use humor to lightly mock the movie and explain why it was not worth seeing.

2. In Woodard's review, the presence of Russell Crowe in *Noah* seems to be its only bright spot.

Write a profile of an actor or actress who can carry even a bad movie. In your profile, explain why this person's acting, appearance, or past successes can still attract audiences to movies that are otherwise not very good.

Tomb Raider: Definitive Edition

RYAN TALJONICK

In this review of a video game, Ryan Taljonick offers a positive review of the video game Tomb Raider: Definitive Edition. *The* Tomb Raider *series has been around for a long time (by video game standards), so selling a next generation version of an old game can be a challenge. Pay attention to Taljonick's use of the action adventure genre to explain why this video game is a success.*

Lara Croft is dead. This time, she was ripped apart by wolves. Death has also come in a variety of other forms: boulders, bear traps, spikes to the throat—each over-the-top execution a display of vulnerability. These shocking moments are heavy-handed with their message, but it comes across loud and clear: Lara Croft, the *new* Lara Croft, isn't a pistol-wielding superhero. She's an inexperienced adventurer caught in the middle of a harrowing sequence of events. The only thing more surprising than the brutality Lara endures during Crystal Dynamic's *Tomb Raider* reboot is just how polished the whole experience is—now even more shiny in the Definitive Edition. *Tomb Raider* is still a fantastic game and an excellent origin story for one of gaming's original treasure seekers.

After getting shipwrecked on a mysterious island during her first-ever archaeology expedition, Lara finds herself in one life-or-death situation after another. Her crew is missing, and the island's cult-like inhabitants are eager to kill her. The narrative's dark, distressing tone is established right from the start, and never once does it stray during *Tomb Raider*'s 15-hour campaign. This consistency builds a great deal of tension and intrigue, and you'll be eager to keep playing to see what happens next.

Throughout the game, you're tasked with solving elaborate puzzles and taking on sporadic groups of enemies; in addition to plenty of platforming and exploration. After you finish *Tomb Raider*'s long-winded tutorial, it easily rivals the best *Uncharted* has to offer—and that's not a claim made lightly. Where *Uncharted* props itself up on Nathan Drake's charm, platforming prowess, and ability to shoot dudes in the head

without getting bummed out, *Tomb Raider*'s foundation is one of excellent pacing, and an ominous story of survival.

The development of Lara's character is an integral part of that experience. She's a far cry from the stylish adventurer you used to know. In the stead of a dolled up gunslinger is a do-what-it-takes female lead who's intelligent and capable. It's unsettling to watch her brave some truly disturbing situations—at times, *Tomb Raider* is more survival horror than action adventure—but she *deals with it* because death is the only alternative, culminating in her gratifying evolution from a green explorer to a seasoned survivor. It's a shame that caliber of character development doesn't extend to the supporting cast. Her shipwrecked friends are pretty generic characters who, while rarely annoying, just aren't memorable.

But what those characters lack in magnetism is more than made up for by the incredible personality and mystery of the island setting. It's a bizarre place filled with ancient shrines, World War II-era bunkers, and all sorts of relics and trinkets spanning multiple centuries. It's always clear that something *strange* is going on, and the island's secrets tease you right up until the very end. You explore a huge variety of environments, sectioned off into hub-like zones, all of which give clues that help you uncover the island's overall enigma. From underground ruins and snow-laden mountain tops to lush forests and grim oceanside cliffs, no one area ever feels like a rehash of another, and the sheer amount of detail in each is impressive.

During Lara's journey, you encounter plenty of dangers. Traps, hostile cultists, and vicious animals alike will stand in your way. Nearly every battle feels like an intense fight to the death instead of just another shootout, despite the fact you rarely encounter more than five or six enemies at a time. The bad-guy AI is great for the most part, as foes will kick over tables to form barricades or shoot off flares to call for help. Best of all, they often react realistically to your shots. Cap an enemy in the leg, for example, and he'll go down to the ground where you can finish him off with a melee execution. Usually a climbing-axe to the skull. Nasty!

Lara's inexperience shows through early on, as her shots are inaccurate and weak. By defeating enemies, solving puzzles, and finding the many collectibles hidden on the island, you gain experience points and resources for upgrading Lara's skills and weapons. Other games that try to emulate the growth of an unseasoned character don't pull it off with quite the same aplomb as *Tomb Raider* does—by the end of the adventure, Lara's transformation into a powerful heroine is noticeable, and feels natural.

But *Tomb Raider* isn't all about fighting. It's totally common to spend five minutes exchanging fire with a group of enemies, then go 45 without seeing a soul. These breaks in battle are filled with great platforming segments, clever puzzles, and adrenaline-pumping set piece moments, and the pacing throughout is unrivaled by any other game in the genre. Even the rate at which Lara obtains new weapons and equipment—like rope arrows that open up new sections of some zones on the island—is admirable, as you snag new gear right up until the final chapters.

Tomb Raider's single-player campaign alone is worth the price of admission for newcomers, but its multiplayer component will be a welcome addition for those looking for a bit more longevity. Multiplayer maps are filled with climbable ledges, zip lines, and level-specific traps that are perfect for scoring easy kills. There are some pretty decent modes to keep things interesting for awhile, too, such as Cry for Help in which one team must capture a series of control points before the other kills and loots 20 players. That said, the multiplayer doesn't feel as genre-defining as the campaign, as it doesn't really introduce anything new to keep you interested after a dozen matches or so.

Even if you've never been a huge fan of Lara Croft's fortune-hunting adventures, *Tomb Raider* is sure to impress. Its expert sense of pacing, captivating setting, and dark tone create a truly memorable experience that's further enhanced by an immense level of detail. Lara Croft, the *old* Lara Croft, is dead. In place of a dolled-up gunslinger is a do-what-it-takes survivor—and I hope she hasn't had her fill of adventuring just yet.

Is the Definitive Edition worth buying? The improvements are too subtle and gimmicky for me to recommend that experienced Tomb Raiders—people who have already finished the game on PS3 or Xbox 360—drop $50 / £40 on the next-gen version. However, if you own a PS4 or Xbox One, and you *haven't* yet experienced the new *Tomb Raider*, then you should leap any chasm and murder any hired merc who stands in your way until you've got this playing on your console . . . It's still brilliant, and the Definitive Edition is the superior version.

10

A CLOSER LOOK AT
Tomb Raider: Definitive Edition

1. This review isn't all positive. With your group, list five problems that Taljonick identifies in *Tomb Raider: Definitive Edition*. Despite these flaws, why does he still recommend buying this video game?

2. Video games and movies often share genres. For example, the action adventure genre is popular in both video games and movies. Choose a movie genre that is not commonly shared with video games (e.g., romantic comedy). With your group, discuss what kind of video game might be made from this unused genre. Do you think it would be successful? Why or why not?

3. Video games are played by both genders, and yet the main characters of action adventure video games tend to be male. The *Tomb Raider* franchise is one of the exceptions, because it stars a female lead, Lara Croft. Do you think the female lead in *Tomb Raider* makes it unique? If so, why? If not, why is *Tomb Raider* just like other action adventure games?

IDEAS FOR
Writing

1. An often-unnoticed feature of video games is that they frequently have interesting and intriguing soundtracks. Write a music review of the soundtrack from a video game. What makes the music interesting or dull? How does the music relate well (or not) to the video content of the game?

2. Think of a movie that would make a good video game. Write a pitch in which you attempt to sell your idea to a video game company. What would make the video game popular? What would be the plot of the video game and how closely would it follow the plot of the movie?

A FEW IDEAS FOR
Composing a Review

1. **Write a review of something you absolutely did not enjoy.** Your topic could be a movie, play, restaurant, book—just about anything. Be creative. Keep in mind, though, that your review will be for public viewing, so you want to be fair while explaining what you did not like about the subject. Then add a brief cover letter written to your professor and your classmates in which you discuss some of the challenges of writing a negative review.

2. **Write a review of three of your favorite movies in a specific genre.** Your review should discuss them together and argue that they are some of the best examples of this genre. What are some of your and your readers' common expectations about this genre? How do these particular movies succeed within the genre, and where do they stray from it? Compare and contrast these three movies to show how they are similar and how they are different.

3. **Find a review on the Internet that you disagree with.** Then write a rebuttal review in which you argue against the other reviewer and show why your subject is actually better or worse than the reviewer said. Your review should be written for the same Web site in which you found the original review.

Go to **MyWritingLab** to complete this chapter's exercises and test your understanding of its objectives.

Literary Analyses

Stopping by Woods on a Snowy Evening

ROBERT FROST

Robert Frost (1874–1963) was a popular poet during his lifetime. Many of his poems, like "Stopping by Woods on a Snowy Evening," appear to be simple observations of nature or country life but on other levels address larger philosophical and social themes. Frost considered this among his greatest poems, calling it "my best bid for remembrance." Read this poem several times, paying attention to the scene, the language, what happens, and the feeling that is evoked by the "music" of the poem.

Whose woods these are I think I know.
His house is in the village though;
He will not see me stopping here
To watch his woods fill up with snow.

My little horse must think it queer   5
To stop without a farmhouse near
Between the woods and frozen lake
The darkest evening of the year.

He gives his harness bells a shake
To ask if there is some mistake.   10
The only other sound's the sweep
Of easy wind and downy flake.

The woods are lovely, dark and deep,
But I have promises to keep,
And miles to go before I sleep,   15
And miles to go before I sleep.

A CLOSER LOOK AT
Stopping by Woods on a Snowy Evening

1. Poetry combines the sense of written words with the sound of the spoken words. Read this poem aloud and listen carefully to determine what feeling or mood is created by the sound of the poem. How does the sound match or reinforce the sense of the words?

2. Describe the poem's plot—not just the events that happen but also how character and events create some kind of conflict between characters or within a character. What *conflict* do you think the speaker is experiencing? Point specifically to the poem itself to explain what leads you to that understanding.

3. How do poems like this one, which has no clear resolution, cause you to think more deeply? Does the lack of resolution make the poem frustrating for you or more interesting?

IDEAS FOR
Writing

1. Write a parody of "Stopping by Woods on a Snowy Evening." Imitate the structure, style, and if possible the sound of the poem, focusing on some activity and place in which the speaker finds herself or himself. For instance, you might begin a poem titled "Looking into the Refrigerator on a Sunday Morning" with these lines: "Whose milk this is I think I know./I need it for my cornflakes though. . . ." The point is to play with the poetic form and have fun by using it to describe an incongruous situation.

2. Write a brief review of "Stopping by Woods on a Snowy Evening," another poem, or some other cultural work, such as a song. (See Chapter 7 for more on reviews.) Early in your review, present a specific set of common expectations that you believe any good poem should be able to meet.

An Overview of "Stopping by Woods on a Snowy Evening"

STEVEN MONTE

Steven Monte is an associate professor of English at College of Staten Island–City University of New York who has published widely on American poets and poetry. In this interpretation of Frost's great poem, Monte urges readers to look beyond the poem's simplicity to the strangeness and power of the poem to evoke multiple and ambiguous meanings. As you read, pay attention to the way that Monte never strays far from the poem's words (quoting them throughout) to arrive at an interesting and insightful understanding of the poem.

With the exception of "The Road Not Taken," "Stopping by Woods on a Snowy Evening" is probably Frost's best-known poem. As with many well-known poems, we may feel that familiarity equals understanding or that a poem we have read or heard enough times can't surprise us anymore. This is especially the case with "Stopping by Woods," which is not only one of the most popular American poems, but is also one written in a clear and seemingly direct style. We might even say that we like the poem precisely because of its simplicity and effortless feel. But as with a person we've been acquainted with for a long time but don't really know, a familiar poem may change when we encounter it in unfamiliar circumstances. Where once we saw only surface and clearly defined qualities, suddenly we see depths and ambiguity. For this to happen with a poem, we often only need to stop and reflect on our experience, like the speaker in Frost's poem. One of the messages of "Stopping by Woods" seems to be just that pausing and reflecting on experience help us re-enter life with a new understanding and sense of direction.

The plot of "Stopping by Woods" is straightforward: a man (we assume) narrates his experience of driving some sort of horse-drawn vehicle by privately owned woods on a snowy evening.

He stops, and then contemplates how strange his halt must seem to the horse, given that it is cold and dark and there is no farmhouse in sight. The horse shakes his harness bell, an action that the man interprets as the animal asking "if there is some mistake." The man then listens to the wind and the snow and ends his account with some remarks on his experience, his responsibilities to the world, and the distance he needs to travel before he sleeps. The story could easily be true—it certainly aims to be "true to life"—but it is hard not to interpret it symbolically. Many readers over the years have felt that the man's journey toward sleep represents life's "journey" toward death, though Frost himself insisted that the last two lines were not an invocation of death. Another popular way of reading the poem is to understand the man's rejection of the woods as an acceptance of social duty and personal responsibility.

But "Stopping by Woods" is a much stranger poem than may appear at first. From the opening lines, we know that the story is being told from the speaker's point of view ("Whose woods these are I think I know"), but we may never bother to consider whom the man is addressing. The addressee of the poem can only be the man himself, who seems to be narrating the events as they occur to him, or thinking "aloud" to himself. This odd, subjective perspective is worth puzzling over, if only because it allows us to see just how self-conscious the man is. Why is he so concerned about being seen stopping by the woods? Is it simply because he fears he will be accused of trespassing on someone else's property? Perhaps he feels guilty that he has temporarily suspended his business and does not wish to be seen or see himself as someone who shirks responsibility. Or it could be that he feels guilty for indulging in a fantasy, for he is attracted to something he feels he should resist. It is hard to say what the woods represent for the man—rest, death, nature, beauty, solitude, oblivion—but it is clear that he feels he should not allow himself to give in to his desire to stay there. There is moreover a sexual dimension to his fantasy: the feminine woods ("lovely, dark and deep") are set against a

world of men where promises must be kept—the world of property and business.

Whatever depths "Stopping by Woods" possesses, it gives us the impression of simplicity. How does the poem manage this? Most obviously, its language remains conversational throughout and it generally avoids twisting around the word order of spoken speech. "Stopping by Woods" also contains only one word with more than two syllables. When the poem does alter the expected word order, as in "Whose woods these are I think I know," the sound and the sense of the line help us forget that there is anything odd going on. We don't feel the line should read "I think I know whose woods these are" because we get the sense that the speaker is expressing the thought as it occurs to him: he is especially concerned with remembering who owns the woods, and he expresses his uncertainty by following his first thought with the phrase "I think I know." The insistent rhythms of the poem—every line except one is exceptionally regular in beating out "ta-dum, ta-dum, ta-dum, ta-dum"—and the frequent rhymes add to the illusion of simplicity. Caught in the flow of the poem, we tend not to notice that the lines "Between the woods and frozen lake/The darkest evening of the year" neither follow logically from the lines that come before them nor form a complete sentence on their own. Once again, we might feel that we are listening to the thoughts of the speaker. He is situating himself in place ("Between the woods and frozen lake") and time ("The darkest evening of the year"), where "darkest" may imply the "longest" evening of the year, December 22, the winter solstice. By calling the evening "darkest," the man suggests that he has reached a low point or a moment of crisis.

Another reason why "Stopping by Woods" 5 seems simple is that it is structured around many familiar oppositions. A complete list of these oppositions would be unusually long for such a short poem: man and nature, masculine and feminine, emptiness and fullness, business and pleasure, movement and stopping, society and solitude, life and death, activity and sleep, and so on. Such familiar distinctions may make us feel at home in the poem, but they may also be disturbing. The categories either seem too fixed (should we only associate men with activity and business?) or too fluid (which is empty, life or death?). Oppositions also help determine the poem's organization: "Stopping by Woods" constantly alternates between inner thoughts and descriptions of the world outside. Even within its descriptive mode, the poem shifts from the visual details of the first stanza ("He will not see . . . To watch his woods") to the sounds of the third stanza ("harness bells . . . The only other sound's the sweep"). Meanwhile the second and the fourth stanzas are more reflective. In the second stanza, the man imagines what the horse is thinking. The details of "the woods and frozen lake" may be in the man's line of vision, but they may also be his way of placing the scene on a mental map, just as "darkest evening" may place the day on a mental calendar. The fourth stanza is even more subjective in its description of the woods as "lovely, dark and deep." All of this inward and outward movement and the poem's oppositions make us feel that the man is being pulled in different directions and needs to make a decision.

But before looking at the decision the man makes in the last stanza, it is worthwhile to stop and examine some of the odd features of his descriptions. Why is his horse "little"? Why is the wind "easy" and the flake "downy"? It is not enough to say "because they *are* little, easy, and downy," or even "because they appear that way to the man," for we would still be left wondering why he chose to describe these things and not others. A somewhat more inventive if unkind explanation is that Frost needed to fill up his lines with these adjectives in order to keep the poem's rhythm insistent. But perhaps we can do better. By calling the horse "little," Frost gives us a sense of the smallness of the figures in the landscape. We furthermore sense that the man is not rich and is probably fond of his animal. "Easy" and "downy" may in their own way hint at what the man is feeling. Part of the attraction of the scene seems to lie in its promise of ease and softness, its contrast to the hard world of men.

The description of the woods in the final stanza leads into the strangest and most memorable section of the poem. Why does this last stanza haunt us? It begins innocently enough and even sounds like a cliche: "The woods are lovely." But the vagueness of the description, the pulse of the line, and the repetition of sounds ("dark and deep") suggest that we are entering a kind of dreamworld. The drowsy repetition of "And miles to go before I sleep" completes this effect, and we sense that the poem is enacting what the man is feeling. The poem's close feels satisfying because it deviates from, and then reinforces, patterns that the poem has established earlier. The first three stanzas have rhymes in the first, second, and fourth lines. The third line then rhymes with the first line of the following stanza, helping us feel that all four stanzas connect like links in a chain. But the established rhythms and rhymes are disrupted in the final stanza. The line "But I have promises to keep" is not as rhythmically insistent as the other lines of the poem. It also contains the poem's only three-syllable word, "promises." Just as the man attempts to shake off his dreamy attraction to the woods, we are brought up short with this jarring line. The last two lines then feel like a fade out, not simply because of the repetition, but due to the return of the rhythm and the absence of a new linking word: all four lines of this stanza rhyme.

The speaker in "Stopping by Woods" "wakes up" to a knowledge of what he must do. He apparently decides to return to the real world and cease his dreaming. He is leaving nature and returning to society, and in so doing makes us feel that there is some irony in the poem's title: he was only "stopping by" nature, as if on a social call. At the beginning of the poem he was unsure ("I think I know"); at the end he has gained some kind of knowledge. We can think of the experience he has by the woods as either a temporary diversion or a recurring moment in his life that helps him go on. In this straight reading of the poem, the man's experience, though forcing him to confront the fact of death and the difficulties of life, consoles him (and the reader) in the end. But if this moment is, or has the potential to be, a recurrent moment in life, the poem may not be as consoling as we first thought. In this dark reading of the poem, we can't be sure whether the man has come to a decision or merely postponed it. He never actually says he has moved on and, if anything, he seems on his way to sleep. Even supposing he does continue on his journey, it is not clear that the road ahead represents a more appealing alternative to the woods. Real life may seem emptier now, and all those familiar oppositions that help us make sense of our lives are open to question. If we equate stopping by woods with reading a poem, we will confront a similar dilemma. As the man's experience should suggest, however, it is not a question of choosing between alternatives so much as it is becoming aware of new possibilities. In looking closely at poem, we don't cancel our first experience of reading so much as we enrich it and make it more strange.

A CLOSER LOOK AT
An Overview of "Stopping by Woods"

1. Read through this literary analysis again, this time noting the places where Monte asks a specific interpretive question about Frost's poem. For instance, in paragraph 3 he asks, "Why is he so concerned about being seen stopping by the woods? Is it simply because he fears he will be accused of trespassing on someone else's property?" He asks similar questions in paragraphs 4, 5, 6, and 7. How does he use these interpretive questions to move his literary analysis forward?

2. Consult Chapter 17, "Choosing a Style." Choose one of these features of style and one two- to five-sentence passage from Monte's literary analysis and explain how Monte's passage illustrates effective style.

For instance, you might wish to explain how Monte weaves the poem's words with his own, or how he tells readers what they should notice about those quotations.

3. Carefully reread Monte's first paragraph, and note especially the final sentence, which states a possible interpretation for—or claim about—Frost's poem. Now reread the final paragraph, which begins by reiterating a similar interpretation but also suggests just as strongly a different interpretation, a "dark reading of the poem." Does he believe one reading is superior to the other? If not, then what exactly does he want us to understand about the poem?

IDEAS FOR
Writing

1. Choose any work from popular culture (a TV show, a song, a movie, a graphic work, etc.) and write a review that interprets that work in parallel fashion to Monte's interpretation of Frost's poem. Specifically, Monte argues that Frost's poem *appears* simple and straightforward, but a more careful reading shows that it is actually complex, meaningful, and interesting. Make a similar argument in your review of your chosen work from popular culture.

2. Monte assumes that a poem that does not lead to a specific reading but allows for multiple ambiguous readings is superior to a poem that has a straightforward meaning or point. Write an argument that supports or rebuts Monte's suggestion that complex poems are superior.

Touched by a Vampire

LAURA MILLER

Laura Miller is the senior books writer for and cofounder of the Web site Salon. *She also contributes to the* New York Times *and the* New Yorker. *"Touched by a Vampire" was written for* Salon *and reviews the popular* Twilight *series of vampire novels written by Stephenie Meyer. As you read this piece, pay attention to the questions that Miller raises and addresses.*

A minute past midnight on August 2, bookstores across the country will for the first time repeat a ritual once reserved for a single author: J. K. Rowling. They'll stay open late and begin selling copies of *Breaking Dawn* by Stephenie Meyer, the fourth novel of the *Twilight* series, at the first moment they're officially permitted to do so. Tens of thousands of fans plan to congregate for these release parties, message boards have shut down to guard against leaked spoilers, and as many as a million readers will be blocking out an entire weekend to bury themselves in the book.

The preceding three installments in the series—*Twilight, New Moon* and *Eclipse*—occupy the top slots in *Publishers Weekly's* bestseller list for children's fiction (they are categorized as Young Adult, or YA, titles), and are among the top five overall bestsellers on *USA Today's* list. In May, *Publishers Weekly* reported that 5.3 million copies of the *Twilight* books had sold in the U.S. alone. When a movie based on the first novel comes out in December, expect to see book sales jump to numbers that approach Rowling's eight-figure numbers.

No wonder the media has heralded *Twilight* as the next Harry Potter and Meyer as the second coming of J. K. The similarities, however, are largely commercial. It's hard to see how *Twilight* could ever approach Harry Potter as a cultural phenomenon for one simple reason: the series' fan base is almost exclusively female. The gender imbalance is so pronounced that Kaleb Nation, an enterprising 19-year-old radio show host-cum-author, has launched a blog called Twilight Guy, chronicling his experiences reading the books. The project is marked by a spirit that's equal parts self-promotion and scientific

inquiry—"I am trying to find why nearly every girl in the world is obsessed with the *Twilight* books by Stephenie Meyer"—and its premise relies on the fact that, in even attempting this experiment, Nation has made himself an exceptional guy indeed. Bookstores have been known to shelve the *Twilight* books in both the children's and the science fiction/fantasy sections, but they are—in essence and most particulars—romance novels, and despite their gothic trappings represent a resurrection of the most old-fashioned incarnation of the genre. They summon a world in which love is passionate, yet (relatively) chaste, girls need be nothing more than fetchingly vulnerable, and masterful men can be depended upon to protect and worship them for it.

The series' heroine, Bella Swan, a 16-year-old with divorced parents, goes to live with her father in the small town of Forks, Wash. (a real place, and now a destination for fans). At school, she observes four members of a fabulously good-looking and wealthy but standoffish family, the Cullens; later she finds herself seated next to Edward Cullen in biology lab and is rendered nearly speechless by his spectacular beauty. At first, he appears to loathe her, but after a protracted period of bewilderment and dithering she discovers the truth. Edward and his clan are vampires who have committed themselves to sparing human life; they call themselves "vegetarians." The scent of Bella's blood is excruciatingly appetizing to Edward, testing his ethical limits and eventually his emotional ones, too. The pair fall in love, and the three books detail the ups and downs of this interspecies romance, which is complicated by Bella's friendship with

Jacob Black, a member of a pack of Native American werewolves who are the sworn enemies of all vampires.

Comparisons to another famous human girl 5 with a vampire boyfriend are inevitable, but Bella Swan is no Buffy Summers. *Buffy the Vampire Slayer* was at heart one of those mythic hero's journeys so beloved by Joseph Campbell-quoting screenwriters, albeit transfigured into something sharp and funny by making the hero a contemporary teenage girl. Buffy wrestled with a series of romantic dilemmas—in particular a penchant for hunky vampires—but her story always belonged to *her.* Fulfilling her responsibilities as a slayer, loyalty to her friends and family, doing the right thing and cobbling together some semblance of a healthy life were all ultimately as important, if not more important, to her than getting the guy. If Harry Potter has a vampire-loving, adolescent female counterpart, it's Buffy Summers.

By contrast, Bella, once smitten by Edward, lives only for him. When he leaves her (for her own good) at the beginning of *New Moon,* she becomes so disconsolate that she resorts to risking her own life, seeking extreme situations that cause her to hallucinate his voice. This practice culminates in a quasi-suicidal high dive into the ocean, after which, on the brink of drowning, she savors visions of her undead boyfriend: "I thought briefly of the clichés, about how you're supposed to see your life flash before your eyes. I was so much luckier. Who wanted to see a re-run, anyway? I saw *him,* and I had no will to fight . . . Why would I fight when I was so happy where I was?" After Edward returns, the only obstacle she can see to her eternal happiness as a member of the glamorous Cullen family is his stubborn refusal to turn her into a vampire: He's worried that she'll lose her soul.

Otherwise directionless and unsure of herself, Bella's only distinguishing trait is her clumsiness, about which she makes frequent self-deprecating jokes. But Bella is not really the point of the *Twilight* series; she's more of a place holder than a character. She is purposely made as featureless and ordinary as possible in order to render her a vacant, flexible skin into which

the reader can insert herself and thereby vicariously enjoy Edward's chilly charms. (His body is as hard and cold as stone, an ick-inducing detail that this reader, for one, found impossible to get past.) Edward, not Bella, is the key to the *Twilight* franchise, the thing that fans talk about when explaining their fascination with the books. "Perfect" is the word most often used to describe him; besides looking like a male model, Edward plays and composes classical music, has two degrees from Harvard and drives several hot cars very, very fast. And he can read minds (except, mysteriously, for Bella's). "You're good at everything," Bella sighs dreamily.

Even the most timorous teenage girl couldn't conceive of Bella as intimidating; it's hard to imagine a person more insecure, or a situation better set up to magnify her insecurities. Bella's vampire and werewolf friends are all fantastically strong and fierce as well as nearly indestructible, and she spends the better part of every novel alternately cowering in their protective arms or groveling before their magnificence. "How well I knew that I wasn't good enough for him" is a typical musing on her part. Despite Edward's many protestations and demonstrations of his utter devotion, she persists in believing that he doesn't mean it, and will soon tire of her. In a way, the two are ideally suited to each other: Her insipidity is the counterpart to his flawlessness. Neither of them has much personality to speak of.

But to say this is to criticize fantasy according to the standards of literature, and Meyer—a Mormon housewife and mother of three—has always been frank about the origins of her novels in her own dreams. Even to a reader not especially susceptible to its particular scenario, *Twilight* succeeds at communicating the obsessive, narcotic interiority of all intense fantasy lives. Some imaginary worlds multiply, spinning themselves out into ever more elaborate constructs. *Twilight* retracts; it finds its voluptuousness in the hypnotic reduction of its attention to a single point: the experience of being loved by Edward Cullen.

Bella and her world are barely sketched— 10 even Edward himself lacks dimension. His inner life and thoughts are known to us only through what Bella sees him say or do. The characters, such as they are, are stripped down to a minimum, lacking the texture and idiosyncrasies of actual people. What this sloughing off permits is the return, again and again, to the delight of marveling at Edward's beauty, being cherished in his impermeable arms, thrilling to his caresses and, above all, hearing him profess, over and over, his absolute, unfailing, exclusive, eternal and worshipful adoration. A tiny sample:

"Bella, I couldn't live with myself if I ever hurt you. You don't know how it's tortured me . . . you are the most important thing to me now. The most important thing to me ever."

"I could see it in your eyes, that you honestly believed that I didn't want you anymore. The most absurd, ridiculous concept—as if there were any way that I could exist without needing you!"

"For this one night, could we try to forget everything besides just you and me?" He pleaded, unleashing the full force of his eyes on me. "It seems like I can never get enough time like that. I need to be with you. Just you."

Need I add that such statements rarely issue from the lips of mortal men, except perhaps when they're looking for sex? Edward, however, doesn't even insist on *that*—in fact, he refuses to consummate his love for Bella because he's afraid he might accidentally harm her. "If I was too hasty," he says, "if for one second I wasn't paying enough attention, I could reach out, meaning to touch your face, and crush your skull by mistake. You don't realize how incredibly *breakable* you are. I can never, never afford to lose any kind of control when I'm with you." As a result, their time together is spent in protracted courtship: make-out sessions and sweet nothings galore, every shy girl's dream.

Yet it's not only shy girls who crush mightily 15 on Edward Cullen. One of the series' most avid fan sites is *Twilight Moms*, created by and for grown women, many with families of their own. There, as in other forums, readers describe the effects of Meyer's books using words like "obsession" and "addiction." Chores, husbands and children go neglected, and the hours that aren't spent reading and rereading the three novels are squandered on forums and fan fiction. "I have no desires to be part of the real world right now," posted one woman. "Nothing I was doing before holds any interest to me. I do what I have to do, what I need to do to get by and that's it. Someone please tell me it will ease up, even if just a little? My entire world is consumed and in a tailspin."

The likeness to drug addiction is striking, especially when you consider that literary vampirism has often served as a metaphor for that form of enthrallment. The vampire has been a remarkably fluid symbol for over a hundred years, standing for homosexuality, bohemianism and other hip manifestations of outsider status. Although the connection between the blood-sucking undead and romance fiction might seem obscure to the casual observer, they do share an ancestor. Blame it all on George Gordon, aka Lord Byron, the original dangerous, seductive bad boy with an artist's wounded soul and in his own time the object of as much feminine yearning as Edward Cullen has been in the early 21st. Not only did Byron inspire such prototypical romantic heroes as Heathcliff and Mr. Rochester (a character Meyer has listed as among her favorites), he was the original pattern for the vampire as handsome, predatory nobleman. His physician, John William Polidori, wrote "The Vampyre," a seminal short story that featured just such a figure, Lord Ruthven, patently based on the poet. Before that, the vampires of folklore had been depicted as hideous, bestial monsters.

Bram Stoker's Count Dracula was the English bourgeoisie's nightmare vision of Old World aristocracy: decadent, parasitic, yet possessed of a primitive charisma. Though we members of the respectable middle class know they intend to eat us alive, we can't help being dazzled by dukes and princes. Aristocrats imperiously exercise the desires we repress and are the objects of our own secret infatuation with hereditary hierarchies. Anne Rice, in the hugely popular *Vampire Chronicles*, made her vampire Lestat a bisexual rock star—Byron has also been called the first of those—cementing the connection between vampire noblemen and modern celebrities. In recent years, in the flourishing subgenre known as paranormal romance, vampires play the role of leading man more often than any other creature of the night, whether the mode is noir, as in Laurell K. Hamilton's Anita Blake series of detective novels or chick-lit-ish, as in MaryJanice Davidson's Queen Betsy series.

The YA angle on vampires, evident in the *Twilight* books and in many other popular series as well, is that they're high school's aristocracy, the coolest kids on campus, the clique that everyone wants to get into. Many women apparently never get over the allure of such groups; as one reader posted on *Twilight Moms*, "*Twilight* makes me feel like there may be a world where a perfect man does exist, where love can overcome anything, where men will fight for the women they love no matter what, where the underdog strange girl in high school with an amazing heart can snag the best guy in the school, and where we can live forever with the person we love," a mix of adolescent social aspirations with what are ostensibly adult longings.

The "underdog strange girl" who gets plucked from obscurity by "the best guy in school" is the 21st century's version of the humble governess who captures the heart of the lord of the manor. The chief point of this story is that the couple *aren't* equals, that his love rescues her from herself by elevating her to a class she could not otherwise join. Unlike Buffy, Bella is no hero. "There are so many girls out there who do not know kung fu, and if a guy jumps in the alley they're not going to turn around with a roundhouse kick," Meyer once told a journalist. "There's a lot of people who are just quieter and aren't having the Prada lifestyle and going to a special school in New York where everyone's rich and fabulous. There's normal people out there and I think that's one of the reasons Bella has become so popular."

Yet the Cullens, although they don't live in New York, *are* rich and fabulous. *Twilight* would be a lot more persuasive as an argument that an "amazing heart" counts for more than appearances if it didn't harp so incessantly on Edward's superficial splendors. If the series is supposed to be championing the worth of "normal" people, then why make Edward so exceptional? If his wealth, status, strength, beauty and accomplishments make him the "best" among all the boys at school, why shouldn't the same standard be applied to the girls, leaving Bella by the wayside? Sometimes Edward seems to subscribe to that standard, complaining about having to read the thoughts of one of Bella's classmates because "her mind isn't very original." But then, neither is Bella's. In a sense, Bella is absolutely right: She's not "good enough" for Edward—at least, not according to the same measurements that make Edward "perfect." Yet by some miracle she—unremarkable in every way—is exempt from his customary contempt for the ordinary. Then again, by choosing her he proves that she's *better* than all the average people at school.

Such are the tortured internal contradictions of romance, as nonsensical as its masculine counterpart, pornography, and every bit as habit forming. Search a little deeper on the Internet and you can find women readers both objecting to the antifeminist aspects of *Twilight* and admitting that they found the books irresistible. "Sappy romance, amateurish writing, etc.," complained one. Still, "when I read it, I just couldn't put it down. It was like an unhealthy addiction for me. . . . I'm not sure how I could read through it, seeing how I dislike romances immensely. But I did, and when I couldn't get *New Moon* I almost had a heart attack. That book was hypnotizing."

Some things, it seems, are even harder to kill than vampires. The traditional feminine fantasy of being delivered from obscurity by a dazzling, powerful man, of needing to do no more to prove or find yourself than win his devotion, of being guarded from all life's vicissitudes by his boundless strength and wealth—all this turns out to be a difficult dream to leave behind. Vampires have long served to remind us of the parts of our own psyches that seduce us, sapping our will and autonomy, dragging us back into the past. And they walk among us to this day.

20

A CLOSER LOOK AT
Touched by a Vampire

1. What are the features and moves that would identify this piece as a literary analysis? What are the features and moves that would identify it as a review? What other genres and genre features are mixed into this literary analysis?

2. In several places, Miller compares the *Twilight* series to the TV show *Buffy the Vampire Slayer* and *Twilight*'s characters (Bella and Edward) to the characters in *Buffy*. Which series does Miller find superior? What criteria does she use to evaluate one as superior to the other? In other words, what is it that makes one better or more interesting?

3. "Touched by a Vampire" can be seen as a "genre-based analysis" of the *Twilight* books, since Miller evaluates the books in relation to how they adhere to the romance genre. Miller writes that the *Twilight* books "are—in essence and most particulars—novels, and . . . represent a resurrection of the most old-fashioned incarnation of the genre." Does Miller, overall, approve or disapprove of the romance genre and of these books? Find specific places in "Touched by a Vampire" that support your conclusions.

IDEAS FOR
Writing

1. Miller takes features from many of the genres described in this book and fuses them into "Touched by a Vampire," which can be seen as a fusion of review, rant, evaluation, literary analysis, and commentary, just to name a few. Using Miller's "genre fusion" strategy, write a similar piece about a book, movie, song, band, television show, or other cultural work that you have found effective or ineffective, or that had a profound influence on you or left you cold.

2. Write a position paper that either challenges or supports Miller's position about the value of and healthfulness of reading romance novels.

Reader's Guide to Langston Hughes

This profile, which appeared on the leading poetry website, Poets.org, is an introduction to Langston Hughes, through his poetry. Many of the details of Hughes's life are left out of the profile, while the poetry itself takes center stage. Watch how this profile uses Hughes's poetry to tell a deeper story about his life and times.

I. Introduction

In Langston Hughes's landmark essay, "The Negro Artist and the Racial Mountain," first published in *The Nation* in 1926, he writes, "An artist must be free to choose what he does, certainly, but he must also never be afraid to do what he must choose." Freedom of creative expression, whether personal or collective, is one of the many legacies of Hughes, who has been called "the architect" of the black poetic tradition. He is certainly one of the world's most universally beloved poets, read by children and teachers, scholars and poets, musicians and historians.

Langston Hughes became the voice of black America in the 1920s, when his first published poems brought him more than moderate success.

Throughout his lifetime, his work encompassed both popular lyrical poems, and more controversial political work, especially during the thirties. He expressed a direct and sometimes even pessimistic approach to race relations, and he focused his poems primarily on the lives of the working class. When he writes that an artist must be unafraid, in "The Negro Artist and the Racial Mountain," he is not only defending the need for his own work, but calling forth the next generation of poets, not only giving them permission to write about race, but charging them with the responsibility of writing about race.

He writes, in the same essay, "I am ashamed for the black poet who says, 'I want to be a poet, not a Negro poet,' as though his own racial world were not as interesting as any other world." For Hughes, who wrote honestly about the world into which he was born, it was impossible to turn away from the subject of race, which permeated every aspect of his life, writing, public reception and reputation. That said, his subject matter was extraordinarily varied and rich: his poems are about music, politics, America, love, the blues, and dreams. No list could be inclusive enough. Hughes wrote poems about ordinary people leading ordinary lives, and about a world that few could rightly call beautiful, but that was worth loving and changing. Unfortunately, as with many of our great American poets (Emily Dickinson, Robert Frost), the variety and challenging nature of his work has been reduced in the public mind through the repeated anthologizing of his least political, most accessible work. His most famous poem, "Dreams," is to be found in thousands of English textbooks across America. Memorized by countless children and adults, "Dreams" is among the least racially and politically charged poems that he wrote:

> Hold fast to dreams
> For if dreams die
> Life is a broken-winged bird
> That cannot fly.

> Hold fast to dreams
> For when dreams go

> Life is a barren field
> Frozen with snow.

Though this is a poem of hope, it seems significant that he writes, in the second stanza, "when" instead of "if," a testimony to the difficulty of his own life, and the lives he so closely observed in his work. A later poem, "Dream Variations," articulates that very dream and is only slightly less well-known, or known primarily because of the last line, which became the title of John Howard Griffin's seminal work on race relations in the sixties.

> To fling my arms wide
> In some place of the sun,
> To whirl and to dance
> Till the white day is done.
> Then rest at cool evening
> Beneath a tall tree
> While night comes on gently,
>   Dark like me—
> That is my dream!

> To fling my arms wide
> In the face of the sun,
> Dance! Whirl! Whirl!
> Till the quick day is done.
> Rest at pale evening . . .
> A tall, slim tree . . .
> Night coming tenderly
>   Black like me.

This poem is much more characteristic of how Hughes was able to use image, repetition, and his almost hypnotic cadence and rhyme to marry political and social content to the structures and form of poetry.

Some of Hughes's major poetic influences 5 were Walt Whitman, Carl Sandburg, Paul Laurence Dunbar, and Claude McKay. He also recognized W.E.B. Dubois as a master of prose, and the long ignored stories and novels of Charles Chesnutt, which have recently gained more critical attention for both their structural complexity and political content. It was the marriage of these widely varying aesthetics, modernism mixed with an almost religious devotion to the power of repetition and musicality in the blues, that gave rise to Hughes's voice, which sounded like no other voice that came before it.

Hughes once wrote, "Our folk music, having achieved world-wide fame, offers itself to the genius of the great individual American composer who is to come." The idea of using the familiarity of music with the structural complications of other traditions is illustrated by a number of Hughes poems. Some of his poems, such as "Po' Boy Blues," are so much in the Blues tradition that it's impossible to read them without hearing the 12-bar blues behind the words.

> When I was home de
> Sunshine seemed like gold.
> When I was home de
> Sunshine seemed like gold.
> Since I come up North de
> Whole damn world's turned cold.

The genius here is not that the poem is so markedly different than the blues, but that presenting this form *as* poetry allowed the blues tradition the intellectual respect it deserved; putting the blues on the page demanded that they be taken seriously, and opened the door to future study and scholarship. However, just as Hughes believed that folk music would inspire a virtuoso composer to transform it, he himself transformed the language of poetry by integrating blues structures into poems such as "The Weary Blues."

> Droning a drowsy syncopated tune,
> Rocking back and forth to a mellow croon,
>   I heard a Negro play.
> Down on Lenox Avenue the other night
> By the pale dull pallor of an old gas light
>   He did a lazy sway . . .
>   He did a lazy sway . . .
> To the tune o' those Weary Blues.
> With his ebony hands on each ivory key
> He made that poor piano moan with melody.
>   O Blues!
> Swaying to and fro on his rickety stool
> He played that sad raggy tune like a musical
>   fool.
>   Sweet Blues!

> Coming from a black man's soul.
>   O Blues!
> In a deep song voice with a melancholy tone
> I heard that Negro sing, that old piano moan—
>   "Ain't got nobody in all this world,
>   Ain't got nobody but ma self.
>   I's gwine to quit ma frownin'
>   And put ma troubles on the shelf."

> Thump, thump, thump, went his foot on the floor.
> He played a few chords then he sang some more—
>   "I got the Weary Blues
>   And I can't be satisfied.
>   Got the Weary Blues
>   And can't be satisfied—
>   I ain't happy no mo'
>   And I wish that I had died."
> And far into the night he crooned that tune.
> The stars went out and so did the moon.
> The singer stopped playing and went to bed
> While the Weary Blues echoed through his head.
> He slept like a rock or a man that's dead.

This poem is much more structurally complex than "Po' Boy Blues." The blues that appear in quotation marks are traditional in form: a line is repeated and then altered. But the poetry surrounding those "traditional" blues/lines is much more difficult to classify; each line seems to be influenced by the blues, but also makes its own form, relying on the repetition of a single rhyme for its power at the end, yet departing radically from the "expected" shape of music. At the beginning, the small, indented explanations almost seem like a longing to burst into song, which doesn't actually happen until later in the poem. There is a modernist quality to this structure in that it borrows the technique of collage, but it isn't implemented in quite the same way. The quotations that one finds in Ezra Pound or T. S. Eliot have the effect of dividing traditions, as if poems were being cast off the Tower of Babel. In Hughes's work, the traditions are united.

Formally, however, the poem "Let America be America Again" is far more ambitious. Like

Whitman, Hughes uses the technique of *anaphora*, or repetition, as a rhetorical device that unifies the disparate elements of the poem:

I am the poor white, fooled and pushed apart,
I am the Negro bearing slavery's scars.
I am the red man driven from the land,
I am the immigrant clutching the hope I
    seek—
And finding only the same old stupid plan
Of dog eat dog, of mighty crush the weak.

I am the young man, full of strength and hope,
Tangled in that ancient endless chain
Of profit, power, gain, of grab the land!
Of grab the gold! Of grab the ways of satisfying
    need!
Of work the men! Of take the pay!
Of owning everything for one's own greed!

I am the farmer, bondsman to the soil.
I am the worker sold to the machine.
I am the Negro, servant to you all.
I am the people, humble, hungry, mean—
Hungry yet today despite the dream.
Beaten yet today—O, Pioneers!
I am the man who never got ahead,
The poorest worker bartered through the
    years.

These lines seem as if they could have been pulled straight from Whitman's poem "The Sleepers" except that Hughes is rhyming at the same time, which doubly unifies the stanzas. And where Whitman's poetry was open and inclusive, Hughes's poem is more pessimistic about the nature of America, even angry. The opening lines, which long for the past:

Let America be America again.
Let it be the dream it used to be.

are transformed by the end of the poem into:

O, let America be America again—
The land that never has been yet—

And yet must be—the land where *every* man
    is free.

As an American poet, Hughes offers a call to change to his readers as an alternative to Whitman's optimism. With both his politics and his formal innovations, he has influenced countless poets of different styles and schools in the twentieth and twenty-first century including Yusef Komunyakaa, Afaa Michael Weaver, Kevin Young, Robert Creeley, Frank O'Hara, Gwendolyn Brooks, Rita Dove, Martín Espada, and others. The question for the 21st-century reader of Hughes's work is how to read his poems without reducing his work to politics or denying the political complexity. He himself saw the politics and poetry as inseparable writing:

Most of my own poems are racial in theme and treatment, derived from the life I know. In many of them I try to grasp and hold some of the meanings and rhythms of jazz. I am as sincere as I know how to be in these poems and yet after every reading I answer questions like these from my own people: "Do you think Negroes should always write about Negroes?" "I wish you wouldn't read some of your poems to white folks." "How do you find anything interesting in a place like a cabaret?" "Why do you write about black people? You aren't black." "What makes you do so many jazz poems?"

The formal devices, rhetoric, anaphora, and rhyme as well as his original and compelling integration of the Blues, all of which make his poems so memorable and beloved, come from a cultural tradition that had never had a voice in poetry. In that sense, Hughes's use of forms was *itself* political, not just the content of his poems.

A CLOSER LOOK AT
Reader's Guide to Langston Hughes

1. This profile spends little time on the biographical facts of Hughes's life. What are some of the facts that you would have expected in a review like this one but weren't included?

2. With your group, choose one of the poems that was reproduced in this profile. Read it closely and inter-

pret its meaning. How does a poem reveal something about the poet who wrote it?

3. Music and poetry share a long parallel history. In this profile, what are five parallels that the author draws between music and the poetry of Hughes?

IDEAS FOR
Writing

1. Write a brief bio of Langston Hughes that provides a fuller picture, including the biographical facts of his life that are mostly left out of this profile.

2. Choose another poet. Write a profile like this one in which you use her or his works to explain the poet's life and times.

A FEW IDEAS FOR
Composing a Literary Analysis

1. **Write a literary analysis of a favorite work.** Choose a book, poem, movie, play, or other work that you find absolutely wonderful. Invite your readers to consider the work through a new and interesting angle and show them how that angle can lead to new and interesting insights that go beyond the obvious.

2. **Write a literary analysis about a persuasive work.** Choose a literary work that you feel tries to persuade readers about a certain belief or attitude. Write a literary analysis that focuses on how the literary work persuades its readers (see Chapter 22, "Using Argumentative Strategies"). Very few literary works make explicit claims, but they can often be more influential than straightforward arguments. For instance,

it is possible to see Paul Laurence Dunbar's "We Wear the Mask" (page 125) as making an argument against racial discrimination. Your analysis should explain what claim the literary work makes and how effectively it makes its case.

3. **Write a literary analysis of a nonprint work.** Experience a literary work both on the traditional printed page and in a digital mode and analyze how these different modes of presentation affect your experience as a reader. In your analysis, focus on how the changes in modes and media change your experience. What is emphasized and what new understandings are made possible by a change in media? What is de-emphasized or left out when the medium changes?

Go to **My**Writing**Lab** to complete this chapter's exercises and test your understanding of its objectives.

Rhetorical Analysis

The "Spectacularly Unhelpful" Second Amendment

GARRETT EPPS

In this rhetorical analysis, Garrett Epps examines one of the most controversial amendments to the U.S. Constitution in the Bill of Rights—the Second Amendment, which relates to the "right of the people to keep and bear arms." As you read, notice how Epps closely examines the word usage and grammar of the Second Amendment to reveal how difficult it can be to settle on a single interpretation. Epps is a professor of law at the University of Baltimore who often writes about legal issues for Slate.com.

The most controversial amendment to the Bill of Rights is also the most confusingly worded.

While some parts of the Constitution are as dry as the English law's ancient Statute of Frauds, others are as delicate and suggestive as a poem by Emily Dickinson, offering empty spaces we are invited to fill. Dickinson's poetry is deliberately terse and operates by image and suggestion far more than by narration or exposition. It forces us to read carefully, with an openness to the multiple meanings suggested by every word or phrase, and no certainty that how we read them is correct: generations of school children have learned to read using poems like "I'm nobody. Who are you?" As Walt Whitman is the father of American poetry, Dickinson is the mother. Dickinsonian reading is as much a part of the American mind as is Fundamentalism.

What would reading the Constitution with a Dickinsonian eye entail? Certainly we must become involved as much in what is not said as in what is. The language of the Constitution is compressed—in 7,000 words it evokes an entire nation—and practical unpacking of that text necessarily involves some of the tricks we learn encountering poems as apparently simple, yet baffling, as these words, written by Dickinson in 1865, as the United States suffered through civil war and social revolution:

> Revolution is the Pod
> Systems rattle from
> When the Winds of Will are stirred
>   Excellent is Bloom

The poem proceeds by juxtaposing an idea—revolution—with an image—the seed-pod of a plant. It does not contain a lesson about revolution; instead it forces the reader to expand his or her idea of it, to see it in a new way.

Let's apply a Dickinsonian eye to an important provision of the Bill of Rights:

> A well regulated Militia,
> being necessary to the security of a free
>   State, the right of the people to keep
>   and bear Arms,
> shall not be infringed.

"Revolution is the pod" does not describe; the Second Amendment does not, truly, prescribe. Instead, it evokes the image of a militia, then weds it to two important concepts—on the one hand a "free State," on the other "the people" and their rights. Generations of scholars and judges have puzzled over this verbal collage. Who are "the people"? Are they an organized group of villagers assembled for "training day" on the village green, or solitary wilderness settlers toting home-forged rifles for protection against bears and cougars?

Many readers find in the Second Amendment 5 a larger unstated vision of America as a polity in which an armed people "regulate" the state rather than the reverse, in which the individual is empowered to resist with deadly force unwelcome interference by either the government or the neighbors. (Just to make matters more confusing, a common usage in eighteenth-century America defined a "regulator" as a member of an extra-legal band of violent vigilantes.) Others, equally plausibly, deny this image, finding instead the important meaning of the amendment in the words "well regulated," and drawing from that the image of a republic in which the states are collectively armed for defense against rebels within and enemies without.

The duel of meanings is closely akin to the studied ambiguity of poetry. All discussions of what constitutional scholar Sanford Levinson recently called "the embarrassing Second Amendment" are shaped by complex images, by notions of what it is to be American, to be a citizen, or indeed to be a man. That it attracts the mythic imagination isn't surprising; its text offers one of the most puzzling conundrums in the entire Constitution.

"A well regulated militia being necessary to the security of a free state," it begins. This is the only provision of the Bill of Rights to have a preamble, and one of only two provisions in the entire Constitution. (The other is the so-called Patent and Trademark Clause, which introduces the congressional power to create limited monopolies as designed "To promote the Progress of Science and useful Arts.") It is also the only place in the Bill of Rights, indeed one of only three places in the Constitution, in which the present tense is used—"a well-regulated militia being necessary." (In the Tenth Amendment, the powers not delegated to the federal government "are reserved to the states respectively or to the people"; in the Citizenship Clause of the Fourteenth Amendment, "all persons born or naturalized in the United States, and subject to the jurisdiction thereof, are citizens of the United States and of the states wherein they reside.") This is in sharp contradistinction to what might be called the prophetic future tense of the rest of the document: "Congress shall have the power," or "the executive power shall be vested in a President." The first clause of the Second Amendment is matter-of-fact, almost offhand. As we all know, it seems to say, a militia is important to "a free state."

What is a "free state"? Does it mean a state of the Union, or any organized sovereign government? Is a well-regulated militia essential to the United States as a free nation independent of other nations, or to its constituent states, sovereign and to some degree independent of their federal father? If it were possible to determine what this means, it might answer the key question about the Second Amendment, which is: does the amendment protect (1) the power of the states to maintain militias as part of the "common," that is, national, defense; (2) the power of the states to arm themselves against possible federal oppression; (3) the right of individuals to "keep and bear arms" for militia service; or (4) the individual right to do so for personal protection?

If the amendment is a structural protection for states, then state governments would have had and would continue to have plenary authority to regulate weapons inside their borders. Nothing in the Constitution says that states have to maintain militias. If they chose not to, then possession of weapons by individuals would be of little use to the amendment's purpose, and they could ban them altogether. If they choose to maintain militias, they could limit any individual right to the kinds of arms it would be useful for citizens to possess in the event of emergency. They could perhaps even limit possession to people of military age, whose ownership of weapons would be useful. Or they might even have the power—as some communities in the American West have tried to do over the years— to require citizens to maintain a workable weapon in their homes so as to be ready for service at a moment's notice. The amendment would simply prevent the federal government from overriding these state choices.

On the other hand, if the right to "keep and bear arms" is a protection of the individual against tyranny from any source, then states, like the federal government, would be at least limited in (though not necessarily totally disabled from) the restrictions they wish to impose on individuals. The amendment's text speaks of a beneficiary of the right—"a free state," which implies an organized government; and a holder of the right, "the people," which implies possession and use in some collective form. What it never says is, "a person." The Fifth Amendment provides rights to individual "person[s]." The Second does not do so explicitly; this however cannot be conclusive, as the Fourth protects the right of "the people" against unreasonable search and seizure, and that right can only be meaningful if it is extended to individual.

Here the Framers' overall rhetorical approach is spectacularly unhelpful. As we have noted before, both the 1787 Convention and the First Congress adopted a grudging, tight-lipped tone toward the states. In only one place in either the Bill of Rights or the original Constitution is a right explicitly given to the states at the expense of the federal government. Suggestively enough, that solitary "state right" (more properly a "reserved power") relates to the organization and leadership of the state militia. That suggests an unusual degree of solicitude toward state power in this area, an interpretation that makes even more sense when we consider the radical military structure set up by the original Constitution.

Under the Articles of Confederation, all military forces were to be raised, provisioned, and organized by the states. The Confederation had the sole prerogative of "determining on peace or war," unless a state found itself either (1) actually invaded by another country (preemptive war against sovereign nations by the states without congressional consent being apparently barred by omission); (2) forewarned of a plan by "some nation of Indians" to invade the state (preemption in this case being allowed without congressional consultation); or (3) "infested by pirates" (the language suggesting that raids by pirates from outside the state's territory would not permit state reprisal without congressional approval, but that an actual pirate base on state territory could be attacked without consultation).

But despite Congress's predominance in the area of deciding on war, the entire military force of the Confederation was to be maintained by the states. The Confederation was to defray "charges of war" by raising funds through a direct requisition against the states based strictly on the value of land within their borders. But the military units were to be raised by the states, and the state legislatures would also designate the "regimental officers" ("all officers of or under the rank of colonel") even in wartime, when the forces would presumably be under joint Confederation command.

In the event of war, the Congress would set a number of troops needed and send each state a requisition "in proportion to the number of white inhabitants of such State." The states were to raise the troops required and "cloath, arm and equip them in a solid-like manner, at the expense of the United States" and then march them to the "place appointed" to be taken into the national service.

A cumbersome system indeed, and it would [15] be unworkable if individual states had no ready supply of trained men and materiel in case of emergency. Accordingly, the Articles required that "every State shall always keep up a well-regulated and disciplined militia, sufficiently armed and accoutered, and shall provide and constantly have ready for use, in public stores, a due number of field-pieces and tents, and a proper quantity of arms, ammunition and camp equipage."

Thus, under the Articles, the states not only could but must maintain fully combat-ready militias, while the Confederation would have no forces not directly supplied and staffed by the states. The prospect of the Confederation sending such troops against state governments, instead of foreign enemies, was virtually nil.

By contrast, consider the military setup under the 1787 Constitution. Congress could directly "raise and support armies," in time of peace or war. Congress could fund those armies by taxing the people of the states, without state consent. States could maintain militias and could appoint their officers. However, the organization and discipline of the militias was under congressional control at all times. In addition, the federal government could call the militias into the "actual service of the United States" at any time. When it did, the president would be their commander-in-chief. Once called into federal service, the militia could be used not only to "repel invasions" but to "execute the laws of the union [and] suppress insurrections"—in other words, to bend recalcitrant state governments to the federal will. Perhaps in no other area did the change from the Articles to the Constitution make a more drastic shift of authority from the states to the Union.

States were no longer required to maintain militias. The language seemed to take their existence for granted; but what would a state's "reserved power" to appoint officers avail if Congress, using its power to prescribe the discipline under which they would be maintained, were to overreach and order them disbanded? It's easy to imagine the horror of the veterans of '76 at the idea of a standing army kept by a Congress specifically empowered to take over, and perhaps disarm and disband, the state militias. The "shot heard 'round the world" had been fired when British regular troops, sent by a distant central government, marched to Lexington and Concord to seize the militia's weapons. Nothing in the Constitution would prevent that from happening again.

It would be quite logical, then, to read the Second Amendment as a direct response to this concern. The phrase "well-regulated militia" was directly lifted out of the Articles to refer to the state militaries ("every State shall always keep up a well-regulated and disciplined militia"). The Second Amendment could be read as reaffirming that state militias were essential, either to the state's freedom or to the well-being of the Union. Thus the federal power to discipline and call out the militia could not be expanded by construction to permit their dissolution. That reading is made even more logical when we consider that the Second Amendment, like all the provisions of the Bill of Rights, was initially read to apply only to the federal government. Nothing in it would apply to a state's power to regulate weapons ownership by its own people, if the state government so chose.

But this argument is far from conclusive. If the drafters of the Second Amendment were thinking purely of empowering the states and clarifying the status of the militia, then they have only themselves to blame for subsequent misunderstandings that have arisen. They could easily have said, "the power of the states to maintain a well-regulated militia, and to allow their people to keep and bear arms therefor, shall not be abridged." But they had trouble uttering the word "state" in the context of "power," as we have seen. Ensuring federal power, and limiting state authority, was a far more pressing concern of the Framers. And they chose the word "right," rather than "power"; if the word in this context refers to a state government, it would mark the only place in the entire Constitution—as written and amended from 1787 until now—where a state power is referred to as a "right." In every other context, the word "right" refers to an individual prerogative rather than a governmental power.

Constitutional historian Leonard W. Levy, a man of great learning and unambiguous opinion, deduced from the amendment's language that the Second Amendment must guarantee an entirely individual right:

> The very language of the Amendment is evidence that the right is a personal one, for it is not subordinated to the militia clause. Rather the right is an independent one, altogether separate from the maintenance of a militia. Militias were possible only because the people were armed and possessed the right to be armed. The right does not depend on whether militias exist.

Levy is a historian, not a linguist, and a real grammarian (ever-popular as a party guest) might say that the Militia Clause actually is grammatically subordinate to the Keep and Bear Clause, with the participle "being" to imply a cause-and-effect relationship: "Because (or since) a well regulated militia is essential to the security of a free state, the right of the people to keep and bear arms shall not be infringed." That reading arguably makes more sense than reading them as co-ordinate phrases: "A well-regulated militia is essential to the security of a free state and (or while we're on the subject) the right of the people to keep and bear arms shall not be infringed." If there is no subordinate relationship between the two clauses, then why would not the drafters have used the same aspect for both? The Militia Clause is in the present tense; the Keep and Bear Clause is in the future.

20

Consider the difference between saying, "The financial situation is quite critical, and I will have macaroni and cheese for lunch," and "The financial situation being quite critical, I shall have macaroni and cheese for lunch." Levy would apparently accept subordination, either grammatically or conceptually, only if the drafters had said, "Because and only because the right to keep and bear arms . . ." The co-ordinate reading of the two phrases seems to arise from a disposition to find a personal right in the language, rather than from the language itself.

That disposition might legitimately arise from the history of the phrase. "The right to keep and bear arms" went back to ancient disputes between king and Parliament, and to attempts by Catholic kings to disarm Protestant subjects. After the Glorious Revolution of 1688, William III granted his subjects the Bill of Rights, which specified that "subjects which are Protestants may have arms for their defence suitable to their conditions and as allowed by law." That language provides fodder for both sides of the argument. It says that the arms are to be kept, not for defense of the Realm but for "their (i.e., personal) defence," which supports the idea of a personal right. On the other hand, it grants a highly qualified right, one which is limited by (1) a subject's religion; (2) a subject's "standing," or rank in the English social structure; and, most important, (3) laws set by Parliament, which, since it can "allow" the bearing of arms, must very likely also be able to "disallow" it. The English right to bear arms thus is a qualified one, enforceable against the Crown alone, and perhaps designed to safeguard the authority of Parliament as much as the liberty of the subject.

The argument is complicated by the important constitutional fact that the Fourteenth Amendment, enacted much later, has the effect of providing that many if not all the guarantees of the Bill of Rights now apply against both the states and the federal government. If the Second Amendment protected only a state's right to maintain a militia, it would make little sense to regard it as applying against the state—"a well-regulated state militia is essential, and so the state shall not have the power to regulate

weapons" is a classic non sequitur. On the other hand, if it created a personal right against the federal government that could be abridged by the state (as the English right was provided against the king but subject to Parliament), the very nature of the right is changed—from qualified and purposive to categorical and absolute—by saying that the state also cannot limit it.

In all, the textual and structural evidence is 25 in equipoise, though, as the earlier Levy quote illustrates, very few commentators are willing to admit the depth of its ambiguity. The argument seems currently to be tipped one way or another by extratextual ideas of American history, the nature of freedom and even the essence of manliness. Many Americans profoundly believe that the American Revolution was won by a completely unorganized popular movement, in which self-sufficient yeomen in fur and homespun dusted off ancient flintlocks and deployed individually against the Redcoats from behind trees and walls. The actual struggles of Congress and the leadership of the Army to construct a professionally trained and supplied force display the Patriot movement less than gloriously. They have tended to be eclipsed by the myth of the self-sufficient country rifleman. If America won its independence with grandpappy's squirrel gun, then any threat to current personal armories is a dagger pointed at the national heart.

Other historical images are equally persuasive, perhaps at an unconscious level. If we regard the Militia Clause as having some relation to the "keep and bear arms" language, of course, it's not necessary to designate the state militia power as the sole purpose of the clause. A more refined question might be, what personal right to bear arms would further the end of providing a citizenry trained and equipped to serve the militia in time of emergency? And how would that right be balanced against the kinds of restrictions on personal possession of weapons that might actually be counterproductive by restricting the power of the militia to "execute the Laws of the Union, suppress Insurrections and repel Invasions." Personal possession of hand grenades, field artillery, armor-piercing bullets, or tactical nuclear weapons might reasonably be thought to undercut the militia function. Semi-automatic weapons and powerful handguns might or might not, in individual hands, further the purposes of the militia. These questions, like other important constitutional questions, are surely amenable to arguments more finely reasoned than most of those employed in popular discourse about the Second Amendment.

In 2008, the Supreme Court decided that the Second Amendment guarantees a personal, individual right to possess a handgun in the home for self-protection. Two years later the Court decided that this right applies, by force of the Fourteenth Amendment, against the states as well as against the federal government. The Court is now, for the first time in our history, committed to spelling out the extent of the personal right, and we can expect questions of this sort to come up. It is thus in the interests of everyone concerned with the role of firearms in society to contribute more than images and myths to a reasoned resolution of this question—and during such discussions, perhaps we should all keep our hands where others can see them.

A CLOSER LOOK AT
The "Spectacularly Unhelpful" Second Amendment

1. In this rhetorical analysis, author Garrett Epps compares the Second Amendment to an Emily Dickinson poem and asks us to "apply a Dickinsonian eye" to our reading of it. According to Epps, in what ways is the Second Amendment like a Dickinson poem?

2. Epps doesn't present us with a single interpretation of the Second Amendment. That is, he does not tell us "what it really means." Instead, he makes an argument *about* interpreting the Second Amendment. What main point does Epps make about how we should interpret it?

3. Epps doesn't state his own interpretation of the Second Amendment, whether he feels it supports or does not support an individual's right to bear arms. Find places in the text where you think Epps reveals his actual beliefs about the issue, and explain why you think he is pro-gun control or pro-right to bear arms.

IDEAS FOR
Writing

1. Write a response to this rhetorical analysis of the Second Amendment. Discuss whether you think it's important for ordinary Americans to understand not only *what* the U.S. Constitution says but also *how* it says it. Do you feel that American citizens should understand, as Epps argues, that the "rhetorical choices" made by the authors of the Bill of Rights make it difficult to interpret? Or should we leave these decisions to legal scholars and judges? Why would it be important for the average citizen to understand the complexities of interpreting the Second Amendment?

2. If Epps's rhetorical analysis is not read very carefully and thoughtfully, it would be difficult to follow his logic. Repurpose his analysis for an audience that might not have the patience to read through it carefully by making it multimodal. Create a video or audio presentation that presents (or refutes) Epps's main point in a way that less attentive readers could follow.

Sleuthing Patriotic Slogans

GARY SLOAN

In the United States, slogans are hard to escape. They are ever-present on radio and television, and, when walking or driving, we see them just about anywhere. In this rhetorical analysis, Gary Sloan, a retired English professor, digs a little deeper into the meaning of these slogans. Notice how he questions whether the slogans have any deeper meaning by paying close attention to the words themselves.

In this best of times and worst of times, the American landscape is dotted with signs, billboards, posters, and stickers emblazoned with patriotic slogans. In my hometown, merchants have scrawled on their display windows a smorgasbord of venerable shibboleths: "United We Stand," "Support the Troops," "Pray for the Troops," "Let Freedom Ring," "Home of the Brave," "God Bless America." Taped on many windows is a flyer that reads: "Pro-America Rally in Railroad Park. Bring lawn chairs, flags, and snacks. Dress patriotic."

When I read the flyer, I thought: Shouldn't that be "Dress *patriotically*?"

Because I have spent much of my life studying and teaching language, I respond inappropriately to patriotic slogans: I parse them grammatically and try to explicate them the way I would an obscure fragment in an essay. Like Hamlet, I sometimes become sicklied over with the pale cast of thought when I shouldn't be thinking at all. The slogans are designed to evoke warm feelings of camaraderie and unity, not grimaces and cocked brows.

Yet I persist in my folly. To wit: Many patriotic slogans are in the imperative mood. They issue a command ("Support the Troops," "Pray for the Troops"). Commands are risky. They create resistance in natural-born rebels and in patriophobes (those with an excessive fear of patriotism).

Are "Let Freedom Ring" and "United We 5 Stand" logically compatible? If everyone exercises freedom of speech and conscience, will we all stand united? Instead of assenting to the war against Iraq, some may opt to ring their dissent.

How does one "Support the Troops"? Letters? Pep rallies? Boxes of homemade cookies? Can one support the troops by urging them to obey their consciences even if their consciences conflict with their orders?

"Home of the Brave." Hmm. Brave in what sense? Obviously, many Americans aren't physically brave. Millions are afraid to walk the streets at night or open their doors to strangers. If "brave" refers to moral courage, might the bravest Americans be those who resist the will of the majority? Might it require more bravery to protest Operation Iraqi Freedom than to support it?

"God Bless America" is almost as inscrutable as the utterances of a Delphi oracle. Grammatically, the words are in the subjunctive mood. They express a wish or a prayer: "Please, God, bless America," or "May God bless America."

The real conundrum: What do the words mean? In what sense is God to bless America? With good health, bouncing babies, supportive spouses? Good schools? High IQs? Philosophical wisdom? Fat paychecks, sirloin steaks, sport-utility vehicles, faster computers, more cable channels, bigger boom boxes? Competitive Superbowls? Better face-lifts and liposuction? Speedier cruise missiles, smarter smart bombs, stealthier stealth bombers? Continued monopoly of the planet's natural resources?

And does "America" mean Americans? If so, does it comprise all Americans, including murderers, rapists, thieves, swindlers, embezzlers, muggers, liars, cheats, bullies, pederasts, pornographers, conceited airheads, slobs, slum lords, domestic tyrants, bigots, and racists?

Or does "America" refer to land, spacious 10 skies and amber waves of grain? Or to some platonic ideal of government embodied in the Declaration of Independence and the Con-stitution, worthy of being blessed even if some Americans aren't?

Now, if I can just figure out how to dress patriotic.

A CLOSER LOOK AT
Sleuthing Patriotic Slogans

1. Sloan suggests that some political slogans have an impact that runs opposite to their intended effect. Sometimes, they command us to do things or think in a particular way. Why do these commands actually undermine their message, according to Sloan?

2. Grammatical issues seem to be at the heart of much of Sloan's irritation with patriotic slogans. What kinds of grammar problems does he suggest cause these slogans to be questionable and less than solid?

3. Toward the end of the article, Sloan questions whether patriotic slogans are really meant for all Americans. When we think of Americans more broadly, including all citizens, what are the problems with these simple slogans?

IDEAS FOR
Writing

1. Look through a magazine or watch television to collect some slogans of your own. How do the slogans that you collected work? When held up to close scrutiny, as in Sloan's article, do they have weaknesses or make questionable assumptions? Write a commentary in which you defend or challenge the use of slogans to persuade people.

2. Find an advertisement on television or *YouTube* that uses a slogan prominently and write a review in which you explain why you think the advertisement is or is not effective. What makes it persuasive? Where are its shortcomings? How might the advertisement be made more effective?

Shooting from the Hip, with a Smile to Boot

LIBBY COPELAND

In the 2008 election, the emergence of Alaska Governor Sarah Palin as a national politician was meteoric. Her acceptance speech for vice-presidential candidate at the Republican National Convention electrified the conservative base, and she became an instant celebrity. In this rhetorical analysis, Libby Copeland, a writer for the Washington Post, *explains Palin's use of style to win people over. Copeland does not use the word* ethos, *but pay attention to how issues involving reputation and image underlie this analysis.*

The heart of Sarah Palin's appeal is—Wait, did you see that? There! She did it again: wrinkled up her nose in a way that either looks like a sneer or is adorably reminiscent of Samantha from "Bewitched." Depending on whom you talk to.

Next time you see a clip of the Republican vice presidential nominee, try this exercise. Mute your TV and just watch that face. How often do you see someone in political life so extravagantly expressive? The eyebrows go up, the shoulder leans in, the thumb jauntily gestures backward, the tongue actually fixes in the cheek. To mock Barack Obama, she licks her finger and holds it to the imaginary wind! And that smile, that nearly ever-present smile, which either indicates—oh, dear, here we go again—that she's sarcastic and dismissive or that she's letting you in on a very clever joke.

People love her so. People hate her so. At the heart of it is the delivery, a style of speaking we'll see again in tomorrow night's debate, a style that reaches past folksy and veers into the territory of—to hell with it, cue the charges of sexism—cute.

"She's perky, she's spunky," says Republican speechwriter Landon Parvin, who has written for both Presidents Bush. "She has this quality—in a 1950s comedy, her father would call her 'Button.'"

And?   5

"This allows her to get away with murder," he says.

All you wannabe hockey moms who imagine yourselves having coffee with Sarah Palin and swapping five-minute dinner recipes? Who find it endearing when Palin refers to her husband as "my guy"? Who like the smiling certainty in her tone, the determination in her squint? This is for you.

And all you Pal-lergics who dislike not only her hard-edged politics but that spoonful of sugar she serves it with? Who say her manner reminds you of—we'll quote here from a Pal-lergic named Judi Dickerson who coaches actors on dialogue—"the snotty head cheerleader in high school who was untouchable because she was always gonna win"? This is for you, too.

Sarah Palin is many things—somber is not one of them. There's something about her delivery that suggests she's almost always having fun. You know how they call Joe Biden the happy warrior? Palin has a similar quality—the ability to attack without seeming angry. Some of that is the smile on her face and the evident humor in her voice, as Sheila Tate, Nancy Reagan's former press secretary, points out.

But there's a lot more at work. It starts with   10
the way Palin's delivery allows her to leap through the camera into your living room. Perhaps in part because of her background as a television reporter and beauty pageant competitor, she seems to understand how the camera works.

"What she knows is that the camera is a thief," says Republican strategist Ron Bonjean, who has worked for former House speaker Dennis Hastert and former Senate majority leader Trent Lott, among others. "The camera will steal your emotions and make you flat, and what she's doing is over-emphasizing her emotions, over-emphasizing her delivery, in order to get that realness across to the camera."

The realness is what her fans talk about—that she's like them, that she doesn't seem contrived. "We feel like she talks like we do," says Susan Geary, a Richmond retiree who attended a McCain-Palin rally in Fairfax last month. "Like she's sitting in your kitchen."

There's a consistency to Palin's appeal—if you go back and look at old clips of her, you see many of the same stylistic elements—the warmth and the eager delivery, the voice that drops and rises emphatically, the dropped g's.

"That's been her bread and butter for 20 years, from the day she sat down in front of the TV cameras to do her sportscasting," says Anchorage-based pollster Ivan Moore. "Her success in her political career has been based on being able to project this enormously friendly, enormously appealing physical presence—and, some people would argue, use it to conceal this very much more ruthless and nakedly political character."

Palin's fans are drawn to her story, that folk- 15 hero combination of caribou-hunting toughness and traditional femininity that John McCain's campaign has played up. For many Palin supporters, her attractiveness does not weaken her appeal—rather, it balances those tales of valor on the tundra. Supporters have charged her critics with sexism but at the same time, at the GOP convention, delegates wore buttons that said "Hottest VP From the Coolest State." For a while, Cindy McCain was introducing Palin as a "true Western woman," evoking images of pretty prairie wives with rifles who could out-hunt their husbands and still get dinner on the table. (Hot chicks with guns being a beloved American archetype.)

They are also drawn to the notion of Palin's PTA-mom-just-like-you-ness, which is enhanced by the hair, which has not been cut short in the style of many political women, and the voice, which has not been brought down to a deeper register, or stripped of its Alaska-by-way-of-middle-America nasality. Palin does more than mention her five children as biographical fact in appearances—she also speaks in mom language. What other major political figure would attempt what she said at her welcome-home rally in Fairbanks last month?

"I see some of our staff members here and cabinet members," she told the audience at a rally. "I can't wait to give you guys a hug."

Palin's huggability is evidence of her accessibility—or of her lack of gravitas, depending on where you sit. When she met Pakistani President Asif Ali Zardari in New York recently, he called her "gorgeous" and joked he might hug her. In response, she laughed.

Much of Palin's appeal—as well as what some find grating—is about the language she chooses, which is folksy in the extreme. She says "heck" and "darn" and "gosh" and "shoot" and "oh, gee." She says, "Guys and gals, our regulatory system is outdated." And: The nation's financial system "needs some shakin' up and some fixin'." She pronounces things "awesome" and "cool," as in: "He's an awesome bundle of joy" (baby Trig) and "It was so cool growin' up in this church and gettin' saved here" (the Wasilla Assembly of God). The critics—she calls 'em "haters."

Could central casting produce a more ideal 20 messenger for the new Republican populism?

"I'm sure she's not from Alaska—she's been sitting on a Hollywood sound stage for years waiting for this," says Paul Costello, the former press aide to Rosalynn Carter and Kitty Dukakis. "She's so unbelievably perfect. . . . Even the red ruby shoes that she's been wearing."

In speeches, Palin's comedic timing is spot-on and her intonation is exaggerated, sweeping her audience along on the current of her message. "Very story-timely," says John Neffinger, a communications consultant who coaches corporate speakers and Democratic congressional candidates. "She varies her intonation all over the place so you know exactly what feelings she's trying to convey. Lots of warmth, very sing-songy."

In the few interviews she has given, or when taking question from voters, Palin speaks with speed and a rat-a-tat delivery, as if a pause were a sign of weakness. Sometimes she drops her voice to a rock-and-roll growl. Her hands move in concert, pointing to her lips, jabbing over her shoulder. Her delivery is "decisive, task-focused," says Ken Brousseau, who consults with executive search firm Korn/Ferry International on corporate leadership styles. "Very black and white." Contrast that with Barack Obama's more deliberative style, his long "uuuhs," his concessions to the opposition. ("John, you're absolutely right," in the presidential debate, over and over.)

When she's forced outside her comfort zone, as has happened a few times of late, Palin tends to "slip back to her talking points," as CBS's Katie Couric recently put it. John McCain is a maverick. Lots of things need some shakin' up. Palin may try to turn a question around ("In what respect, Charlie?") or stall when asked for examples to bolster her argument ("I'll try to find you some and I'll bring 'em to ya!").

"Forgive me, Mrs. Palin," faux Katie Couric 25 said to faux Sarah Palin on last week's "Saturday Night Live," "but it seems to me that when cornered you become increasingly adorable."

There's a youthfulness and an enthusiasm there—Palin is all emoticons; Rachel Ray as candidate for higher office. (When she ran for mayor of Wasilla in 1996, her campaign ad boasted upbeat, jazzy music and a slogan reminiscent of daytime TV: "Positively Sarah.") She speaks with supreme confidence (Ya can't blink, Charlie). On Monday, she said she looked forward to meeting Senate veteran Joe Biden at their debate.

"I've been hearing about his Senate speeches since I was in, like, the second grade," she told an audience in Columbus, Ohio—emphasizing her youth, as well as suggesting an unusual attentiveness to the earliest speeches of Biden, who was sworn in when she was 8.

Perhaps, suggests former Miss America Kate Shindle, an undecided Republican, there's a touch of the pageant world to Palin's voice, to her careful adherence to sound bytes, and that "cheerful aggressiveness" that Shindle calls "part cheerleader, part news anchor, and part drill sergeant."

The confidence is underscored by something Palin does frequently at the ends of her sentences. She sets her lips in forceful line (perfectly captured by Tina Fey in her first "Saturday Night Live" impersonation) as if to communicate that the matter is settled.

Now mute the television again. Watch 30 Palin's body. She expresses excitement through encouraging nods as well as what Karen Bradley—a University of Maryland dance professor who studies body movement—calls this "little shoulder wiggle." And watch that nose wiggle—which Parvin, the Republican speechwriter, says sometimes conveys "a cute determination" and sometimes "a cute distastefulness." And sometimes, it operates as a sort of "exclamation point," conveying agreement, he says. He calls her "Gidget goes to Washington."

"She is playing into a cultural stereotype," says Drew Westen, a psychiatry professor at Emory University who also works as a Democratic consultant and wrote *The Political Brain: The Role of Emotion in Deciding the Fate of the Nation*. And the stereotype? Westen cites Marlo Thomas in *That Girl*, Mary Tyler Moore in *The Dick Van Dyke Show*, Sally Field in *The Flying Nun*—a model of perky femininity that "was really salient in the early '60s before the sexual revolution and the cultural revolution took hold."

These physical and rhetorical habits set Palin in relief to Hillary Clinton, who projected great strength but much less of what one Democratic political consultant calls "traditional feminine warmth." Which was why it caused such a splash when Clinton once told a crowd, "I'm your girl"—there is little that's girly about Hillary Clinton's public persona. Palin calls herself a "gal" and it's utterly believable.

"She's not a woman trying to deliver a speech like a man, and there is an integrity to that," says Parvin.

And all of which means Sarah Palin is either great or awful, depending on whom you talk to, because her style and her conservative beliefs are either post-feminist or the antithesis of feminism. If Palin's cuteness is disarming to her supporters, it is troubling to those who worry that she lacks intellectual heft, and infuriating to those who feel she's being coddled. Not too long ago, CNN anchor Campbell Brown suggested the McCain campaign was being sexist by shielding Palin from interviews. Acting coach Dickerson suggests that Palin gets to be as nakedly political as any other candidate while being shielded from retaliation because of the perception that she is, after all, just a gal.

"You have a very glamorous, pretty woman35 with, actually, a very girly delivery—but what comes out of her are the words of a very savvy, very tough politician," says Dickerson. "It creates a mixed message of allowing her to really say anything that she wants."

Then again, who decides what's fair? Sarah Palin is hugging us all into confusion.

A CLOSER LOOK AT
Shooting from the Hip, with a Smile to Boot

1. In the article, find five rhetorical qualities that Copeland suggests Palin uses to persuade her audiences. Do you agree that Palin uses these qualities in a strategic way? What impact does Palin's style have on you as a viewer?

2. Copeland also suggests that Palin's style has a reverse effect on some people. In other words, some people "hate her so." Why does Palin's style have this effect, according to Copeland?

3. This article relies on some interesting stylistic devices itself. Find five different times when Copeland's own writing style seems to stand out. How does she use detail, metaphors, similes, and other stylistic devices to enhance her message?

IDEAS FOR
Writing

1. Looking back on the 2008 election, what were your reactions to the rhetorical styles of Palin and Obama? Clearly, both of them are formidable public speakers. How are their styles similar? How are they different? Write a response to this article in which you compare and contrast the speaking styles of Palin and Obama.

2. Find a video of Sarah Palin speaking on *YouTube* or another video Web site. Using the qualities highlighted in this article, write a review of her speech in which you critique her style and her use of *ethos* to make her speech more persuasive. Do you find her style effective or not?

"Eating Fresh" in America: Subway Restaurant's Nutritional Rhetoric

JESSICA LUNDGREN

In this rhetorical analysis, Jessica Lundgren takes a careful look at the rhetorical strategies used in Subway Restaurant's television ads. As you read, notice how the author explains how Subway uses a variety of rhetorical strategies to mislead viewers into thinking that its fast food is more healthful than it really is. Lundgren wrote this when she was an undergraduate studying at Pennsylvania State University.

Increasingly, many American fast food restaurants are marketing their food as being healthier, often by introducing new menu items that have less fat, fewer calories, and that fit into a broader range of nondiscretionary categories of the food pyramid. However, no fast food restaurant has focused on the "healthiness" of its products to the extent that Subway Restaurant has over the past near decade. In 2000, the restaurant's famous "Jared" campaign first shared the story of Jared Fogle, who lost 245 pounds in one year by following a diet that consisted primarily of Subway sandwiches ("The Subway Diet"). This campaign's influence on consumers was clear, as it was followed by a one-year sales increase of 47.5% for the restaurant (McGrath and MacMillan 159). The campaign advertised seven types of subs that contain six grams of fat or less—although the restaurant's menu includes not-so-healthy items as well. While Subway's sales continue to grow rapidly (and with Jared still appearing in many of its commercials), America's obesity rates also are increasing at a shocking pace. The role that popular restaurants such as Subway play in the American diet is important to consider in contemplating the obesity crisis, as Americans currently consume about one-third of their daily calories while dining out (Jacobson). To understand how restaurants like Subway influence the American diet, it is critical to examine their advertising strategies in order to ascertain specifically how their advertisements work to persuade potential customers. In particular, the increasingly common "healthy" fast food ads must be analyzed in terms of their potential to misguide viewers about the nutritional benefits of consuming fast food.

A recent study performed by Chandon and Wansink indicates that the average Subway diner has been misled by the restaurant's commercials, even if this is unintentional on Subway's part. As a result of an effect Chandon and Wansink have designated the "health halo," customers extend the "healthiness" of a selection of Subway's sandwiches to apply to all subs that the restaurant serves, even if a sub has additional, less-healthy toppings such as mayonnaise and other sauces that add to the fat and caloric content. The study shows that a person eating a Subway meal will estimate that it has, on average, 151 fewer calories than a McDonald's meal—when, in actuality, it has approximately the same number. The investigation also finds that people ordering a foot-long Italian BMT sandwich at Subway are much more likely to add higher-calorie drinks and cookies to their meal than people who order a McDonald's Big Mac, even though the Subway sandwich actually has twice the caloric value of the burger. In other words, the average person who eats at Subway believes that the "healthiness" of the sandwiches there compensates for the relative "unhealthiness" of side dishes such as cookies: by choosing to eat what they perceive to be a healthy meal, Subway diners feel that they have earned the right to consume additional items that they believe to be less healthy.

This type of research has made clear that the advertising methods used by Subway somehow have played an important role in distorting customers' perceptions of the nutritional content of the restaurant's products. The connection between exposure to fast food advertising and gaining weight is difficult to conclusively examine, but a 2006 study performed by Chou, Rashad, and Grossman suggests that a relationship does exist between viewing more fast food commercials and being overweight. The study examines the body mass index (BMI) values of children living within distinct television marketing areas in the U.S., and the amount of time that the children living in those specific areas spent viewing fast food ads on television.[1] Through this analysis, a strong positive relationship was found between time spent watching fast food ads and the probability that children were overweight. The study considers that children who watch more television (and thus see more fast food advertising) have higher BMI values because they probably engage in less physical activity and therefore burn fewer calories. Beyond this cause, however, the researchers stress that viewing fast food ads is likely to independently contribute to weight gain, because such advertising encourages children to develop an early habit of consuming unhealthy foods.

With the influential nature of fast food advertising and its effects on caloric intake and being overweight already having been explored by studies such as these, it is my intention to provide a close look at the rhetorical nature of fast food advertising through a specific focus on Subway Restaurant's television advertisements. Despite the importance of studying the rhetoric used in advertisements of "healthy" fast food, I have not identified any previously performed studies of the subject. Therefore, in my investigation, I intend to define and to provide examples of some of the primary rhetorical methods that Subway repeatedly uses in its advertisements, and to offer an explanation of how the restaurant's use of rhetoric may cause consumers to misunderstand the nutritional value of Subway's menu items.

For the purposes of my study, I define rheto- 5 ric as the persuasive methods applied by Subway

Restaurant to entice television viewers to purchase its products. I specifically concentrate on ads that make a deliberate appeal to the nutritional and health concerns of the average television viewer; I designate this rhetorical focus as "nutritional rhetoric." In a cultural environment that is increasingly permeated by news stories about health and especially about the obesity epidemic, it seems reasonable to assume that much of the American television audience has been primed to be acutely receptive to this form of rhetoric. I will analyze eight recent Subway television advertisements that I located online.[2] After viewing these ads several times, I identified five rhetorical strategies that repeatedly were used in making appeals to consumers. In my analysis, I will examine the advertisements in terms of their use of these strategies. I have classified the following approaches as being critical aspects of Subway's nutritional rhetoric: (1) the making of nutritional claims, (2) a visual rhetoric that makes the restaurant's "healthy" food options appear to be numerous and exciting (in addition to being nutritious), (3) the comparison of the Subway product with the products of other, less "healthy" fast food restaurants, (4) the clear indication that the physical manifestations of eating poorly, and hence being overweight, are unattractive or undesirable, and (5) the association of the Subway product with a person who is physically fit.

Analysis

To provide a background for my analysis of Subway's specific rhetorical practices, I will describe the general premises of eight "healthy" Subway commercials. I chose these commercials because they have all been aired fairly recently and because they all include references to eating well and/or being physically fit. Four of the commercials are part of Subway's Fresh Fit campaign, which began to air in March 2007. These advertisements all present characters who, it is implied, are not maintaining healthy lifestyles. The ads all mention that Subway's Fresh Fit menu "fits into the American Heart Association's approach to a healthy lifestyle." The other four commercials feature a nationally or internationally successful athlete who indicates that Subway sandwiches are a part of his or her diet.

Nutritional Claims

Subway's Fresh Fit campaign emphasizes that the restaurant currently offers "new, better-for- you sides and drinks." The advertisements show that these new sides and drinks include apple slices, Baked Lays potato chips, raisins, low-fat milk, and bottled water. It is important to note that the restaurant does not refer to these sides and drinks as being "healthy," but simply as "better-for-you." This distinction implies that the restaurant intends to be cautious about how it directly characterizes its products; it does not make explicit verbal claims that might be disputed by people who see a discrepancy between the phrases "healthy" and "better-for-you." For example, it is easy to say that a bag of Baked Lays is "better-for-you" than a greasier variety of chips, but to claim that Baked Lays are therefore "healthy" would be perceived as questionable by many nutrition-conscious viewers.

The restaurant's concern (perhaps from a legal standpoint) about being misread is highlighted further in the fine print that appears at the bottom of the screen in each of the Fresh Fit ads. The fine print in two of the commercials states that the "Subway Fresh Fit Meals are not a diet program," while in the two other commercials it is noted, "Subway Fresh Fit Meals are not a diet program, they are a better way to eat." Both examples of these fine-print statements remain on-screen for approximately four seconds. It seems safe to assume that these clarifications, being on-screen for such a short time and in a very small font, would easily escape the attention of the average television viewer. While most viewers may not notice these details, it still is important to be aware that Subway recognizes, if only in the fine print, that its meals are not in themselves "a diet program." Ironically, however, the statement that "they are a better way to eat" seems to be flawed: Subway cannot safely assume that its meals are naturally "a better way to eat" for every person.

The Fresh Fit campaign also focuses on the concept that the Fresh Fit meal "fits into the American Heart Association's approach to a healthy lifestyle." In this way, the commercials attempt to build up the restaurant's ethos by associating the brand with the American Heart Association (AHA) and the concept of leading a "healthy lifestyle." For American consumers who are concerned with their cardiovascular health—which likely includes a large portion of the population, being that cardiovascular disease is the top killer of Americans—this could serve as a particularly strong appeal.

Visual Rhetoric

Like any company that advertises food items, 10 Subway attempts to make its products visually appealing to consumers. The sandwiches shown in Subway's commercials are extra thick, packed with many toppings, and stand out clearly against plain white backgrounds—which may influence viewers to subconsciously associate Subway with the pure whiteness of medical facilities, lending greater power to the restaurant's healthy image. For its healthier products, Subway uses specific visual strategies. The restaurant seems to want its "better-for-you" products to come off as exciting and numerous. The Fresh Fit commercials include dynamic shots of apple slices flying through the air while water pours over them, as well as images of sliced strawberries falling into a bowl of low-fat yogurt. Each commercial includes images of a sandwich surrounded by a selection of sides and drinks that constantly alternates, as if to emphasize the multitude of "better-for-you" options that exists at Subway. In addition, the camera pans across a large spread of items, including a glass of milk, bowls of raisins and apples, and ripe tomatoes. Some viewers potentially could be misled by the images of sandwiches that are shown in the commercials. While it may not be noticeable to most viewers, the sandwiches in these advertisements appear to lack cheese. The sandwiches also appear to contain more lean choices of meats, such as turkey and ham (rather than meatballs, roast beef, or bacon), and the majority of their substantial width is comprised of lettuce, tomatoes, and other vegetables. Yet because the sandwiches are extremely thick, some viewers might wrongly assume that they contain cheese, heavy dressings, and other sources of additional calories, grams of fat, and sodium. As a related note, a visit to Subway reveals that its sandwiches often are much thinner than they appear to be in the restaurant's ads (an observation that rival sandwich company Quizno's has taken advantage of in its own commercials). Furthermore, while the sandwiches in these advertisements are thick with vegetables, an image that enhances their apparent health value, a typical sandwich made at the restaurant probably would not contain so many veggies, unless a Subway diner were to specifically order the peppers, cucumbers, onions, lettuce, spinach, tomatoes, and olives that often are packed onto the advertised sandwiches. A decrease in vegetable content might significantly reduce the nutritional value of the sandwich. Due to this ambiguous visual presentation of advertised sandwiches, an uninformed consumer might order a sandwich that, while similar to those shown in Subway's ads, actually is not equally healthy.

Rhetoric of Comparison

MacArthur and Cuneo take note of the current trend of "comparative ads," which are used in attempts to demonstrate why one company's product is superior to a related company's product. In one of their examples, the authors describe Papa John's claim that Pizza Hut's dough, unlike its own, is not fresh but instead comes out of the freezer. Subway Restaurant recently has used this approach to compare its sandwiches to the "greasy fast food" offered by other restaurants like McDonald's and Burger King. The Fresh Fit campaign in particular uses comparison to present the argument that Subway's food is healthier than other restaurants' fast food options.

These advertisements portray people who, instead of placing orders for food, literally are ordering fat. One man asks for a "jelly belly" while his female companion orders "cottage cheese thighs." A voiceover then intervenes:

"Instead of greasy fast food, try the new Subway Fresh Fit meal." The commercial then provides examples of the "better-for-you" options that Subway offers, as I have described previously. While the Fresh Fit commercials do not directly state which restaurants Subway is being compared to, the super-size options and bright red décor of the spoofed establishments make it fairly clear who the targets are. Other advertisements, however, are absolutely direct in their comparisons. In an advertisement featuring Subway's Jared and the champion figure skater Kimmie Meissner, the announcer states that "the delicious Subway Foot-Long Club" has "less than half the fat of a Big Mac."

These comparisons establish the logos of the advertisements. They present the television viewer with negative images or facts related to rival companies, and then contrast this information with the "better-for-you" nature of a specific type of Subway meal. This approach may influence a consumer to feel that he or she has received strong evidence that Subway Restaurant sells healthier food than other fast food restaurants. Equipped with this understanding, a person may feel that he or she is prepared to make informed and health-conscious decisions concerning future fast food meals.

The flaw of this rhetorical approach is clear: comparative advertisements do not show a complete picture of Subway or its competitors. While Subway's Fresh Fit menu contains items that likely are far healthier than many or even the majority of items on other restaurants' menus, Subway's menu as a whole contains sandwiches that rival the "unhealthiness" of the Big Mac and other fast food products: Subway's six-inch Chicken and Bacon Ranch sub has 30 grams of fat, and many other of its six-inch sandwiches exceed 20 grams of fat. At the same time, Subway's commercials ignore that many of its competitors offer healthier options in addition to their not-so-healthy items—just as Subway does. Burger King's menu includes garden salads with fat-free dressing, apples that are sliced to look like French fries, and the Tendergrill Chicken Sandwich which, with 7 grams of fat and 1,090 mg of sodium, is comparable to many of the "healthy"

Subway sandwiches. McDonald's Grilled Snack Wraps have 10 or fewer grams of fat, fewer than 300 calories, and approximately 800 mg of sodium. McDonald's hamburgers (250 calories) and two of the grilled chicken sandwiches (420 and 470 calories) on its menu also contain about 10 grams of fat. Clearly, Subway's "6 grams of fat or less" sandwiches, ranging from 230 to 370 calories and 500 to 1,290 mg of sodium, are not strikingly different from the healthier options at these other fast food establishments.

Subway's comparative ads carefully choose the nutritional aspects on which they base their comparisons. When the Big Mac claim is made in the Meissner commercial, for example, the fine print on the screen says about the Foot-Long Subway Club: "Contains 2620mg sodium. No claim is made regarding comparative calories." This makes clear that Subway's commercials may not be entirely upfront about their sandwiches' nutritional content: A sodium content of 2,620 mg exceeds the maximum of 2,300 mg/day that the American Heart Association recommends for healthy adults, and the Big Mac actually contains less than half the sodium that the Foot-Long Club contains. Likewise, the lack of a "claim . . . regarding comparative calories" seems to imply that the Subway Club has a higher caloric value than the Big Mac does: nutritional information publicly provided by the two restaurants exposes that the Foot-Long Club (640 calories) indeed does have a greater caloric content than the Big Mac (540 calories). While comparative advertising might, on the surface, appear to allow consumers to make more informed decisions about their fast food choices, in truth this type of ad is more likely to provide people with misleading or incomplete information that might result in deluded decision making.

Implied Undesirability of Weight Gain

The premise of several of the Fresh Fit commercials is that greasy fast food items will result in weight gain, and that this increased amount of body fat is undesirable primarily because of its physical appearance. The rhetorical nature of the perception of body fat in American culture is explored by Sonya Christine Brown, who asserts,

"Body shape and size are aspects of physical ethos that Americans focus on" (10). She states: "Fat is . . . perceived as the visible, physical evidence that a body is likely to be unhealthy, unwell, unfit" (39), and adds that "to be fat is to be scorned." The relationship between fat and ethos clearly is a rhetorical basis of Subway's advertisements. In one ad, a man pulls up to a drive-through window and asks, "Can I get the love handles, double chin, and some blubber?" The female in his car requests the same, but substitutes for the blubber "thunder thighs and a badonkadonk butt." Another, similar advertisement is located in an office setting, where one character announces his intention to go to "Burger Town." He takes the orders of his coworkers, which include "the can-my-butt-look-any-bigger meal," "the extra-tight-pants combo," the "feel-so-bloated-I-just-want-to-sleep-for-three-days meal," and "a-bucket-of-please-keep-your-shirt-on."

In addition to its appeals to ethos, this aspect of Subway's advertisements employs pathos to get the consumer's attention by insinuating that (1) if people consume certain types of fast food, they likely will become overweight or obese and that (2) the consumer himself should fear becoming overweight or obese and (3) as a way to protect himself from this fate, he should choose instead to eat the healthier fast food options that are offered at Subway. This approach attempts to plant in the consumer's mind suspicion regarding other fast food establishments, and then asks the consumer to consider that Subway actually can prevent him or her from acquiring "blubber."

One of the Fresh Fit commercials specifically targets the parents of young children. This commercial shows a young boy sitting on a couch with a plate of brownies on his lap while he plays a video game called "Snakka." The game's character chows down on French fries, a hot dog, and a burger, while the boy takes a big bite out of his brownie. The video game character, who initially had been able to run quickly, now slowly proceeds to the center of the screen, where a large ice cream sundae awaits him. When he jumps to reach the sundae, his large belly becomes stuck in a passageway and "GAME OVER" flashes onto the screen. At this point, a voiceover asks, "What kind of eating habits are your kids learning?" The Fresh Fit menu then is introduced. Like the other Fresh Fit ads, this commercial focuses on the point that unwelcome weight gain will result from the making of poor nutritional choices. This advertisement is unique, though, in that it asks parents to question how they are raising their children in terms of the eating habits that they are being taught. The answer to the underlying question—Are you a good parent?—hinges on whether the viewer is enabling his or her children to eat well. After asking this tough question, Subway provides a simple answer: Subway can aid parents in teaching their children to eat right. This rhetorical approach attempts to create a sense of insecurity in parents who want to do what is best for their children, and then it attempts to take advantage of the resulting vulnerability by offering its product as an easy solution.

Athletes and Jared as Subway Diners

Like many American companies, Subway uses athletes or other physically fit individuals to promote its products. McDonald's recent use of the Ronald McDonald character exemplifies this type of approach. In 2005, the restaurant unveiled the clown's new image as an in-shape supporter of children's health; at the annual Ronald McDonald convention, a leader in the corporation's marketing department even "threatened to fire clowns who didn't get fit" (MacArthur). To investigate Subway's own attempts to associate the restaurant with physically fit people, I examined four Subway advertisements that use athletes. Kikkan Randall, an Olympic cross-country skier training for the 2010 Winter Games, is featured in two of them. The other two ads include Subway's spokesman Jared Fogle paired up with U.S. champion figure skater Kimmie Meissner in one ad and NFL player Reggie Bush in the other.

The Reggie Bush ad actually shows the NFL [20] player eating a Subway sandwich. While Kikkan Randall and Kimmie Meissner are not shown eating food at Subway, both athletes imply that Subway is an important part of their diets. Randall says, "Something keeps me going, pushing myself to new heights . . . Is it the fame? The records? The future gold? Right now, it's just dinner tonight!" as she walks toward a Subway. Meissner, in her advertisement, tells Jared that the Subway Club "Fills me up so I can skate for hours." In Meissner's case, Subway is linked directly to her successful athletic performance. For Subway, the upholding of a healthful image is essential, so it seems particularly advantageous for the restaurant to portray winning athletes as consumers of its product. By associating an athlete with Subway food, the restaurant appeals to the television viewer through logos: if a person who is in peak physical health eats Subway, then it *must* be good for me, too.

When Jared is featured in the commercial alongside an athlete, it adds another dimension in support of the restaurant's logos. In the Reggie Bush ad, Jared briskly walks while Reggie sprints across a football field; Jared lifts his laundry basket while Reggie curls weights; and Jared skims a net over the surface of his above-ground pool while Reggie relaxes next to a large pool with a mansion in the background. The voiceover then says, "No matter how different you are, you've gotta love the Subway Foot-Long Club." The argument is apparent: Subway can be an important and healthful part of the diets of athletes as well as the diets of average people.

Conclusion

Fast food makes up a large portion of many millions of Americans' diets: every day, one in four Americans visits a fast food restaurant (Schlosser 3). While a diet chiefly consisting of fast food aided Subway's Jared in his extreme weight loss, it is highly unlikely that a diet based on fast food is the healthiest choice for most people. Nonetheless, consumers will continue to frequent fast food restaurants, and a close examination of the role that fast food plays in America's upward obesity trend remains necessary. My preceding analysis looked at some of the approaches used by Subway Restaurant that potentially could influence the average consumer to choose a meal that might not be as healthy as he or she perceives it to be. It is clear that there is a great need for further and more technical investigations of how "healthy" fast food advertisements lead customers to consume meals that would not fit a nutritionist's standards for a healthy dietary choice. In America, merely one-third of the adult population currently maintains body mass indexes that are considered to be medically healthy. America's increasing rates of obesity and overweight are undeniably significant in that they have the potential to negatively affect both the physical and the psychological well-being of Americans. They also are significant in terms of the massive healthcare costs that are associated with obesity, along with the strain that is being placed on the American healthcare system as a result of increasing incidences of obesity-related illnesses (Manson et al.). I view my study as a contribution to the discourse surrounding fast food advertising and as a stimulus for increased analysis of the ways in which fast food commercials may lead consumers to make misinformed nutritional decisions.

With so much at stake, it is critical that future research be done to determine how consumers might be enabled to make more accurate evaluations of the nutritional content of their fast food options. While it is unlikely that many restaurants voluntarily will alter their advertising strategies to make it absolutely clear to the customer what is "healthy" and what is not, other types of helpful changes to restaurants' approaches might be introduced. According to a press release from Subway, beginning in March 2007 every Subway in America introduced new menus that include an "appleshaped icon [to allow] customers to easily identify and order the 'better-for-you' options" ("Subway Restaurants"). Although Subway could take another step and provide more specific nutritional information on its menu, it is significant that the restaurant has made an attempt to make its menu more accessible to customers who are interested in making healthier choices. If every fast food restaurant were to provide its customers with direct and easy-to-comprehend nutritional facts on its menus, perhaps misconceptions about restaurants' products would

not be as sizeable as they are today. It is important to investigate how these types of changes might permit the average American to make more informed and healthier decisions while dining at a fast food restaurant.

Notes

1. The amount of time spent viewing fast food advertisements was calculated by the researchers using reported hours of children's television viewing as obtained by the National Longitudinal Survey of Youth in 1996, 1998, and 2000, and using fast food television advertisement data collected by Competitive Media Reporting from 1996 to 1999.

2. I viewed additional advertisements that I excluded from my analysis, because they lacked references to the health value of Subway's products. Subway's "Fresh Moment" series of ads and the "Subway Dinner Theatre" series (starring Jon Lovitz) both were excluded.

I would like to thank Dr. Xiaoye You for sharing his expertise and encouragement throughout the drafting and revision of this article.

Works Cited

American Heart Association. "Sodium Recommendations." 27 July 2007. Dec. 2007 <http://www.americanheart.org/presenter.jhtml?identifier=538>.

Brown, Sonya Christine. "Body/Image/Narrative: Contemporary Rhetoric of Body Shape and Size." Diss. U of Maryland, College Park, 2005.

Chandon, Pierre, and Brian Wansink. "The Biasing Health Halos of Fast-Food Restaurant Health Claims: Lower Calorie Estimates and Higher Side-Dish Consumption Intentions." *Journal of Consumer Research* 34.3 (2007): 301–14.

Chou, Shin-Yi, Inas Rashad, and Michael Grossman. "Fast-Food Restaurant Advertising on Television and Its Influence on Childhood Obesity." *National Bureau of Economic Research Working Paper*

Series (2006): 1-43. Dec. 2007 <http://www.aeaweb.org/annual_mtg_papers/2007/0106_1015_2004.pdf>.

Jacobson, Michael F. "The Hidden Cost of Eating Out." *Nutrition Action Healthletter* (April 2004): 2.

MacArthur, Kate. "Health-Minded Ronald Buffs Image." *Advertising Age* 76.30 (2005): S12.

MacArthur, Kate, and Alice Z. Cuneo. "Why Big Brands Are Getting into the Ring." *Advertising Age* 78.21 (2007): 6. Manson, JoAnn E., Patrick J. Skerrett, Philip Greenland, and Theodore B. VanItallie. "The Escalating Pandemics of Obesity and Sedentary Lifestyle." *Archives of Internal Medicine* 164.3 (2004): 249–58.

McGrath, Rita Gunther, and Ian C. MacMillan. *Marketbusters: 40 Strategic Moves That Drive Exceptional Business Growth.* Cambridge: Harvard Business School Press, 2005.

Schlosser, Eric. *Fast Food Nation.* New York: Harper Perennial, 2005.

"The Subway Diet: Jared Fogle Becomes a Celebrity by Losing Weight." *CBS News* 3 Sept. 2004. Dec. 2007 <http://www.cbsnews.com/stories/2004/03/02/48hours/main603484.shtml>.

"Subway Restaurants Introduce New 'Subway Fresh Fit' Menu Nationwide." *PR Newswire* 8 Mar. 2007.

A CLOSER LOOK AT

"Eating Fresh" in America: Subway Restaurant's Nutritional Rhetoric

1. According to Lundgren, what are the main strategies used by Subway, what does Subway want viewers to believe about its products, and how effectively do the marketers make their case? Find specific places in the text to back up your responses.

2. Rhetorical analyses can alert readers to serious issues and help them understand that they are being misled and how it is being done. How does Lundgren make her case that Subway's use of misleading advertisements is an important issue? Point to specific places where she gives reasons and evidence that back up her position that we should care about the company's deceptive rhetoric.

3. This rhetorical analysis includes a great amount of research that supports Lundgren's overall claim that Subway's ads are misleading. How effectively does she use these sources? Are her sources credible?

IDEAS FOR
Writing

1. Write a rhetorical analysis of this rhetorical analysis. Identify Lundgren's main claim and the rhetorical strategies she uses to persuade her readers that they should care about Subway's misleading rhetoric and that she is correct that they are in fact misleading. Use the ideas and terms offered in Chapter 9, "Rhetorical Analyses," both to analyze her analysis and to organize your own analysis of it.

2. Write a rhetorical analysis that, like this one, examines the rhetorical strategies used by a major company to persuade consumers that its product or service is healthier or better for the environment than that of its competitors. Like Jessica Lundgren, you should describe the ad (or ad campaign) and state your main point about what the company wants consumers to believe, the strategies it is using to persuade them, and overall how effective the ad (or campaign) is. You should then analyze the product or service by considering two to five rhetorical concepts and how the ad (or campaign) uses them.

A FEW IDEAS FOR
Composing a Rhetorical Analysis

1. **Write a rhetorical analysis focused on metaphors.** Chapter 9, "Rhetorical Analyses," talks briefly about how metaphors are used in writing. Find a common metaphor that is used in our society (e.g., "Time is money," "Thought is light," "War on cancer," "Argument is war") and then find examples of that metaphor in public use. In your rhetorical analysis, discuss how the metaphor shapes how people see particular issues. Discuss some of the perhaps unintended meanings or consequences of the metaphor you chose.

2. **Write a rhetorical analysis of three texts.** Compare and contrast the persuasive strategies used in these three texts. Show how different rhetorical strategies are intended to have different persuasive effects.

3. **Critique an ad found on a Web site.** Your ad critique should study the advertisement's uses of rhetorical strategies to persuade people to buy a particular product or use a specific service. How does the advertisement use *logos, ethos, pathos,* and visual appeals to try to be persuasive? Do you find the advertisement effective or not? Turn your ad critique into an electronic document (blog, Web site, *PowerPoint*) and link to the site with the ad.

Go to My**Writing**Lab to complete this chapter's exercises and test your understanding of its objectives.

Commentaries

Being Against Gay Marriage Doesn't Make You a Homophobe

BRANDON AMBROSINO

Rather than simply arguing for or against gay marriage, Brandon Ambrosino offers a new perspective on this controversial issue by examining and commenting on how we argue with each other—what's fair, what's appropriate, what moves people's understanding forward, and what stalls it. As you read, notice how the author summarizes and quotes from arguments on both sides of the issue to make his point.

Does being against gay marriage make someone anti-gay?

The question resurfaced last week when Cardinal Timothy Dolan, Archbishop of New York, claimed on *Meet the Press* that the Catholic Church is unfairly "caricatured" as anti-gay. *The Huffington Post's* Paul Raushenbush quickly wrote up a response, saying that "The hard reality that Cardinal Dolan and all Christians need to face up to is that the Catholic Church along with every other church whether Orthodox, Protestant or Catholic has been horrifically, persistently and vehemently anti-gay for almost all of its history."

Then Raushenbush hauled out a familiar argument: "Let's just be very clear here—if you are against marriage equality you are anti-gay. Done."

As a gay man, I found myself disappointed with this definition—that anyone with any sort of moral reservations about gay marriage is *by definition* anti-gay. If Raushenbush is right, then that means my parents are anti-gay, many of my religious friends (of all faiths) are anti-gay, the Pope is anti-gay, and—yes, we'll go here—first-century, Jewish theologian Jesus is anti-gay. That's despite the fact that while some religious people don't support gay marriage in a sacramental sense, many of them are in favor of same-sex civil unions and full rights for the parties involved. To be sure, most gay people, myself included, won't be satisfied until our loving, monogamous relationships are graced with the word "marriage." But it's important to recall that many religious individuals do support strong civil rights for the gay members of their communities.

What exactly do we mean when we say 5 "anti-gay," or "homophobic"? Often when I try to understand where my conservative opponents are coming from, my gay friends accuse *me* of being homophobic. It isn't homophobic of me to try to understand why someone might be opposed to marriage equality. Giving someone the benefit of the doubt takes courage; dismissing him before considering his argument—well, that seems a bit phobic. Beside—me? Homophobic? I write essays about being gay, and then I publish them, and everyone goes, "Oh yeah, he's gay." I have no reservations about my sexuality, so as far as the accusation of homophobia goes: that gay ship has already sailed to Disneyland, with a speedo-clad Tom Daley carved into the bow.

If it's "anti-gay" to question the arguments of marriage-equality advocates, and if the word "homophobic" is exhausted on me or on polite dissenters, then what should we call someone who beats up gay people, or prefers not to hire them? Disagreement is not the same thing as discrimination. Our language ought to reflect that distinction.

I would argue that an essential feature of the term "homophobia" *must* include personal animus or malice toward the gay community. Simply having reservations about gay marriage might be anti-gay *marriage*, but if the reservations are articulated in a respectful way, I see no reason to dismiss the person holding those reservations as anti-gay people. In other words, I think it's quite possible for marriage-equality opponents to have flawed reasoning without necessarily having flawed character. When we hastily label our opposition with terms like "anti-gay," we make an unwarranted leap from the first description to the second.

To me, recognizing the distinction between opposing gay marriage and opposing gay *people* is a natural outgrowth of an internal distinction: When it comes to my identity, I take care not to reduce myself to my sexual orientation. Sure, it's a huge part of who I am, but I see myself to be larger than my sexual expression: I contain my gayness; it doesn't contain me. If it's true that my gayness is not the most fundamental aspect of my identity as Brandon, then it seems to me that someone could ideologically disapprove of my sexual expression while simultaneously loving and affirming my larger identity. This is what Pope Francis was getting at when he asked, "When God looks at a gay person, does he endorse the existence of this person with love, or reject and condemn this person?" The Pope probably won't be officiating gay marriages any time soon. But because he differentiates between a person's sexual identity and her larger identity as a human being, he is able to affirm the latter without offering definitive commentary on the former. Maybe his distinction between Brandon and Gay Brandon is misguided, but it isn't *necessarily* malicious, and that's the point.

Rob Schenck, current chairman of the Evangelical Church Alliance, told me that while he believes that marriage is between one man and one woman, this belief is a "source of internal conflict" and "consternation" for him. How, he candidly asks, is denying marriage to gay people "consistent with loving your neighbor?" Schenck has no plans to change his social stance on this issue, but he serves as a good reminder that not all gay-marriage opponents are unthinking and bigoted. Sure, there are plenty of religious people who are actually homophobic, and find in their Bible convenient justification for these biases. But let's not forget about people like Rob who, though he opposes marriage equality, appreciates the reminder from gay advocates "that love is as important as anything else."

Though I'd like to see Rob change his mind, I don't imagine he will. For him, the procreative potential of the male-female sexual union is what marriage was designed for. But even if Rob's opinions don't change, I still don't believe he's a bigot. Just as I distinguish between my sexual expression and the larger identity that contains it, I think it's quite possible to distinguish between his political or theological expression (Conservative Rob) and his human identity (Rob). If he were disgusted by gay people, or thought they should be imprisoned, or wanted to see the gayness beat out of them, then that might implicate his human identity, in part because it would suggest a troubling lack of compassion. But the way he respectfully articulates his position on this issue doesn't give me grounds to impugn his *character*. I can think his logic flawed, his conclusions unwarranted, and his activism silly, and yet still think him to be a good person. In fact, these are the feelings I have for many of my religious friends, and I'm sure those same feelings are returned!

The secular cases being made against gay 10 marriage, as well, often have little to do with any kind of animus towards gay people themselves. Rather than appeal to an archaic notion of God's "intentions," these arguments instead focus on the vested interest the state has in legislating sexual relationships. Those who argue in this way don't see marriage as a sacrament, but as a child-rearing institution whose regulation is in society's best interest. Not a very good argument? Totally. Not a very good person who makes that argument? I need more information.

As a gay man thinking through the issue of marriage equality, I've come to the conclusion that, although it's a no-brainer for me, this issue is complicated to a great number of people. To demonize as anti-gay the millions of Americans currently doing the difficult work of thinking through their convictions is, in my opinion, very troubling.

It's true that as an LGBT person, I am Otherized against the sexual norm. But at the same time, I have an ethical obligation to my Other—the people unlike me—as well. On this issue, my Others include conservatives, fundamentalists, and more than a few folks from the square states. If my primary ethical obligation to my neighbor is to allow and affirm his moral agency, so long as it does not lead him to commit acts of violence, then what happens when I take away his right to peacefully disagree with me?

We shouldn't have to resort to trumped up charges of bigotry to explain why opponents of gay marriage are wrong. Calling someone "anti-gay" when his behavior is undeserving of that label doesn't only end civil discussion—it degrades the foundation that undergirds a democratic, pluralistic society. Though gay rights' opponents have at times vilified us, I hope that we're able to rise above those tactics.

A CLOSER LOOK AT
Being Against Gay Marriage Doesn't Make You a Homophobe

1. Good commentaries usually engage readers right away by clearly announcing the issues they are examining and their main points (or theses). Identify three to five strategies Ambrosino uses to draw readers in and help them quickly see the issue he's examining and his main point.

2. Describe an experience in which someone (perhaps you) was discussing a controversial issue and then labeled another individual a "bad person" (or "stupid," "insensitive," "cowardly," etc.) because of the position he or she held on that issue. What does such "name calling" do to the quality of the conversation? Why do you think some people resort to name calling when debates get heated?

3. Ambrosino makes it clear that he's an openly gay man. What does his identity have to do with the point he's trying to make? How does this information strengthen or perhaps weaken his argument?

IDEAS FOR
Writing

1. Write a commentary about an issue you care about that, like this one, offers a fresh angle by criticizing *how* some people are arguing about it and urges readers to argue differently. Be sure to make clear the argumentative moves that you feel shouldn't be used by summarizing and quoting the arguments of others. Also, explain why these moves harm the quality of the argument. Finally, offer suggestions about how people can more constructively argue about this issue so that both sides understand each other and perhaps can even come to some kind of mutual understanding.

2. Respond to Ambrosino's commentary with your own commentary that extends its argument in a new direction. Ambrosino asks whether it's appropriate to label as bigots people who oppose gay marriage. A more general question would be, is it *ever* appropriate to use name calling and labeling in an argument? Are there times when such strategies are called for?

Female Chauvinist Pigs

ARIEL LEVY

In this commentary, which is from the introduction of her book, Female Chauvinist Pigs, *Ariel Levy argues that women are actually taking steps back by embracing an over-sexualized popular culture. Pay attention to how Levy uses her own experiences and examples from popular culture to press home her main points.*

I first noticed it several years ago. I would turn on the television and find strippers in pasties explaining how best to lap dance a man to orgasm. I would flip the channel and see babes in tight, tiny uniforms bouncing up and down on trampolines. Britney Spears was becoming increasingly popular and increasingly unclothed, and her undulating body ultimately became so familiar to me I felt like we used to go out.

Charlie's Angels, the film remake of the quintessential jiggle show, opened at number one in 2000 and made $125 million in theaters nationally, reinvigorating the interest of men and women alike in leggy crime fighting. Its stars, who kept talking about "strong women" and "empowerment," were dressed in alternating soft-porn styles—as massage parlor geishas, dominatrixes, yodeling Heidis in alpine bustiers. (The summer sequel in 2003—in which the Angels' perilous mission required them to perform stripteases—pulled in another $100 million domestically.) In my own industry, magazines, a porny new genre called the *Lad Mag*, which included titles like *Maxim, FHM,* and *Stuff,* was hitting the stands and becoming a huge success by delivering what *Playboy* had only occasionally managed to capture: greased celebrities in little scraps of fabric humping the floor.

This didn't end when I switched off the radio or the television or closed the magazines. I'd walk down the street and see teens and young women—and the occasional wild fifty-year-old—wearing jeans cut so low they exposed what came to be known as butt cleavage paired with miniature tops that showed off breast implants and pierced navels alike. Sometimes, in case the overall message of the outfit was too subtle, the shirts would be emblazoned with the *Playboy* bunny or say Porn Star across the chest.

Some odd things were happening in my social life, too. People I knew (female people) liked going to strip clubs (female strippers). It was sexy and fun, they explained; it was liberating and rebellious. My best friend from college, who used to go to Take Back the Night marches on campus, had become captivated by porn stars. She would point them out to me in music videos and watch their (topless) interviews on *Howard Stern*. As for me, I wasn't going to strip clubs or buying Hustler T-shirts, but I was starting to show signs of impact all the same. It had only been a few years since I'd graduated from Wesleyan University, a place where you could pretty much get expelled for saying "girl" instead of "woman," but somewhere along the line I'd started saying "chick." And, like most chicks I knew, I'd taken to wearing thongs.

What was going on? My mother, a shiatsu 5 masseuse who attended weekly women's consciousness-raising groups for twenty-four years, didn't own makeup. My father, whom she met as a student radical at the University of Wisconsin, Madison, in the sixties was a consultant for Planned Parenthood, NARAL, and NOW. Only thirty years (my lifetime) ago, our mothers were "burning their bras" and picketing *Playboy*, and suddenly we were getting implants and wearing the bunny logo as supposed symbols of our liberation. How had the culture shifted so drastically in such a short period of time?

What was almost more surprising than the change itself were the responses I got when I started interviewing the men and—often—women who edit magazines like *Maxim* and make programs like *The Man Show* and *Girls Gone Wild*. This new raunch culture didn't mark the death of feminism, they told me; it was evidence that the feminist project had already been achieved. We'd earned the right to look at *Playboy*; we were empowered enough to get Brazilian bikini waxes. Women had come so far, I learned, we no longer needed to worry about objectification or misogyny. Instead, it was time for us to join the frat party of pop culture, where men had been enjoying themselves all along. If Male Chauvinist Pigs were men who regarded women as pieces of meat, we would outdo them and be Female Chauvinist Pigs: women who make sex objects of other women and of ourselves.

When I asked female viewers and readers what they got out of raunch culture, I heard similar things about empowering miniskirts and feminist strippers, and so on, but I also heard something else. They wanted to be "one of the guys"; they hoped to be experienced "like a man." Going to strip clubs or talking about porn stars was a way of showing themselves and the men around them that they weren't "prissy little women" or "girlygirls." Besides, they told me, it was all in fun, all tongue-in-cheek, and for me to regard this bacchanal as problematic would be old-school and uncool. I tried to get with the program, but I could never make the argument add up in my head. How is resurrecting every stereotype of female sexuality that feminism endeavored to banish good for women? Why is laboring to look like Pamela Anderson empowering? And how is imitating a stripper or a porn star—a woman whose job is to imitate arousal in the first place—going to render us sexually liberated?

Despite the rising power of Evangelical Christianity and the political right in the United States, this trend has only grown more extreme and more pervasive in the years that have passed since I first became aware of it. A tawdry, tarty, cartoonlike version of female sexuality has become so ubiquitous, it no longer seems particular. What we once regarded as a kind of sexual expression we now view as sexuality. As former adult film star Traci Lords put it to a reporter a few days before her memoir hit the best-seller list in 2003, "When I was in porn, it was like a back-alley thing. Now it's everywhere." Spectacles of naked ladies have moved from seedy side streets to center stage, where everyone—men and women—can watch them in broad daylight. *Playboy* and its ilk are being "embraced by young women in a curious way in a postfeminist world," to borrow the words of Hugh Hefner.

But just because we are post doesn't automatically mean we are feminists. There is a widespread assumption that simply because my generation of women has the good fortune to live in a world touched by the feminist movement, that means everything we do is magically imbued with its agenda. It doesn't work that way. "Raunchy" and "liberated" are not synonyms. It is worth asking ourselves if this bawdy world of boobs and gams we have resurrected reflects how far we've come, or how far we have left to go.

A CLOSER LOOK AT
Female Chauvinist Pigs

1. In this article, Levy discusses how being a "feminist" has changed. What are some of the reasons she believes many women who consider themselves liberated have reverted back to objectifying other women and themselves?

2. Levy points out that many women believe the feminist battles have already been won. And now, because women have achieved equality, they believe expressions of their sexuality are part of their earned freedom. Do you agree that women now have equal opportunities with men in all ways? If not, what are some ways in which men and women aren't equal?

3. This article relies heavily on examples to support its arguments. Find three examples in the article. What effect do these examples have on the readers? Why are examples sometimes more persuasive than facts or reasoning?

IDEAS FOR
Writing

1. Many people would say that Americans are more conservative now than ever. Often, pundits talk about the United States as being a "center-right" nation. Write an argument in which you explore how and why an overall conservative culture also tolerates a thriving raunch industry. Or, discuss why you think the United States is not really conservative after all.

2. Write a profile of a public figure who was once known for using his or her looks or sexuality to gain attention. Choose someone who has been out of the spotlight for several years. How did this person rise to fame? When was the turning point in his or her career? What is he or she doing now?

Recovering America's Exceptionalism

BEN S. CARSON

In this commentary, conservative columnist Ben S. Carson calls on Americans to "reclaim the values upon which our nation was built." As you read, pay close attention to the way Carson argues that we should remember the values of the past as a way to guide our future decisions about current issues.

In 1831, Alexis de Tocqueville, the famous French historian, came to America to study our nation. Europeans and others were fascinated with the success of the fledgling nation, then barely 50 years old and already competing on the world stage.

Such a thing had never before occurred, and Tocqueville was determined to discover the secret. He was duly impressed by our governmental structure, including the separation of powers, but he was in awe of the public educational system, which rendered its recipients completely literate by the completion of second grade. This depth of education was generally only found among the aristocracy in Europe.

Let's put aside the diversionary arguments about lack of educational access for all, which was a huge mistake, and concentrate on the tremendous advantage afforded our predecessors

by education. Early settlers not only mastered reading, writing and arithmetic, but also shared practical skills, all of which enabled them to traverse and tame a rugged and frequently hostile terrain from sea to shining sea.

As isolated communities sprang up throughout the nation, they were able to thrive through innovation, industry and compassion. The "can-do" attitude involved hard labor, but it also included a sense of responsibility for those who through injury or other hardships could no longer care for themselves. The spirit of caring, although diminished, remains an important part of who we are today.

Tocqueville was impressed by the fiery sermons that emphasized the word of God and not the social mores of the day. He concluded his American analysis by saying, "America is great because she is good. If America ever ceases to be 5 good, she will cease to be great." America was different because we openly acknowledged the role of God in our lives.

Some will say, "Carson is a religious fanatic because he believes in God and the Bible." Interestingly, the very same people are quick to invoke the name of God and recommend prayer at times of national and personal tragedy. Hypocrisy is their frequent companion.

Some will say America can never make claims of "goodness" owing to her history of slavery. Although it was by far the worst atrocity in our history, we paid a horrendous price in lives lost or destroyed in a Civil War that all but incapacitated a young nation. The guilt, shame and humility that resulted from this dark American episode will teach us and stigmatize us well into the future. Learning from mistakes is a sign of wisdom and goodness.

What is disturbing in the pursuit of goodness is the turning of a blind eye toward corruption, much like the Romans did before the fall of their empire. Episodes such as the Internal Revenue Service scandal should alarm all Americans, regardless of political affiliation. The fact that one party has characterized it as a "phony scandal" tells you a great deal about the loss of honesty in our society.

The fact that one party is willing to use its majority status to cram a health care bill down the throats of the minority party and the American people and then refuses to acknowledge the obvious illegitimacy of a bill passed largely on the basis of false information provides a barometer on the lack of importance placed on virtue in our society today. How can such a society in any way claim to be good?

How can a society that kills millions of 10 innocent unborn babies and then labels anyone opposing the practice "anti-woman" claim even a modicum of goodness? How can a nation that uses its news media to subtly trash traditional families, promote a drug-filled lifestyle and ridicule faith in God claim the mantle of righteousness?

I could go on pointing out how far we have strayed from our Judeo-Christian roots. For some, such a departure cannot come soon or dramatically enough. However, I believe the majority of Americans understand that we are different from everyone else, and that difference had a great deal to do with our rapid rise to the pinnacle of world power and wealth.

As we depart from our former values of decency, honesty, compassion and fairness, our status as a blessed nation will also be diminished.

Our decline is not necessary if we can learn from the mistakes of others and reclaim the values upon which our nation was built. I am not advocating for a national religion, but I do think we should seriously consider the words of John Adams, who said, "Our Constitution was made only for a moral and religious people. It is wholly inadequate for the government of any other."

America can be great, but it requires real courage and conviction to resist the urge to be "cool." None of this means we should impose Judeo-Christian values on those who wish to adopt a different kind of lifestyle, but it does mean we should not allow an alternative lifestyle to be imposed upon us.

Fairness is a two-way street, and so is toler- 15 ance. If the majority refuses to fight for its rights, while a vocal minority uses a compliant media to try to fundamentally change America, we will have only ourselves to blame.

A CLOSER LOOK AT
Recovering America's Exceptionalism

1. Commentaries usually announce the topic, angle, and main point (or thesis) early on. Where does Carson announce his main point? In your own words, how would you state his main point more clearly and completely?

2. Commentaries often describe the beliefs of people who have opinions that oppose those of the author. When an author states those opposing viewpoints fairly and completely, he or she can more successfully counter them. Where does Carson consider opposing viewpoints? How fairly does he represent those opposing positions?

3. Play the Believing and Doubting Game with Carson's commentary. When you're believing, what aspects are strongest and most compelling? When doubting, what weaknesses would you point out? Finally, synthesize these two positions and state where you stand on this issue.

IDEAS FOR
Writing

1. Write a rhetorical analysis of "Recovering America's Exceptionalism." Choose Carson's use of rhetorical strategies (such as *ethos*, *pathos*, and *logos*) and describe how and where he uses those strategies. Be sure to summarize, quote, and cite the text. Finally, evaluate the effectiveness of Carson's commentary. How strong a case does he make for his position?

2. Write a brief proposal that offers a solution to the problem of corruption (one of Carson's targets for criticism) and, as Carson puts it, "America's decline." What is the real problem that America faces as it tries to achieve fair and transparent government leadership? What approach to this issue would be considered fair to most Americans and would be practical? Discuss the costs and benefits of your plan, showing why your solution would be the best way to address these issues.

Will America Forget Its Veterans?

KAYLA WILLIAMS

Kayla Williams is a veteran of the Iraq War who is married to another veteran, Brian, whom she first met in a mountain outpost during the war and who later was wounded by a roadside bomb that resulted in significant brain injury. In this brief commentary, Williams uses personal narrative to make her case that Americans should support all veterans after their return home.

When the camera first panned to Michelle Obama sitting next to Sgt. 1st Class Cory Remsburg, a wounded warrior, during President Obama's State of the Union message last month, my breath caught in my throat. This proud noncommissioned officer was a guest of the first lady, and his presence alone was forcing all who saw him to remember that America remains a nation at war.

Later, the president told the story of meeting Remsburg shortly before he was injured on his 10th combat deployment, and of the long and grueling path to recovery he still travels. My family knows that road all too well. My husband,

Brian, sustained a penetrating traumatic brain injury from a roadside bomb in Iraq in October 2003, long before many of today's systems and services available to support wounded troops and military families existed. He "slipped through the cracks," and we both spent time on unemployment while waiting for his benefits to start after he was medically retired from the Army. He received no rehabilitation for his brain injury and got only sporadic mental-health care for his debilitating post-traumatic stress disorder.

And yet, we persevered, forming a supportive network of fellow veterans and gradually finding a new place in our community, with new ways to serve. It took six years before Brian could read a book again, but last month, he began using the GI Bill to attend college. Like Remsburg, we never quit.

My biggest fear is that the American people will forget us--their veterans. I worry that as the visible reminders of the wars in Iraq and Afghanistan fade from popular consciousness, so will the attention paid to troops, military families, and veterans. Yet the needs of US veterans will not end when the war does; they will just be beginning. Though over a lifetime veterans are more highly educated, employed, and paid than their civilian counterparts, the period of reintegration can be challenging.

Coming home to a nation distracted by celebrity gossip and seemingly oblivious to the 5 experiences of deployed troops was jarring and disconcerting. As a woman veteran, I felt particularly invisible. Many people had no idea that women were serving in combat alongside men, despite what the regulations said about keeping us out of direct ground combat jobs and units. Reentering the workforce was challenging. It was tough to translate military skills and experiences into civilian terms, and to adjust to a less hierarchical, more collaborative environment. Attending college classes with people fresh out of high school can feel like being in a war-tested version of the Adam Sandler movie "Billy Madison."

Brian and I are very fortunate: Over the years, he has enjoyed tremendous cognitive and psychological improvement, we have been able to access mental-health care when needed, and we have both used benefits we earned from the Department of Veterans Affairs. Today, we are contributing community members, solid employees, proud parents, and a strong married couple.

As today's troops come home, become veterans, and reenter civilian society, communities across the country should come together to ensure they have a smoother transition than we did. The military gave them superb practical and leadership skills they can put to good use here at home; give them the chance to use them. We never forgot about you while we were deployed. Don't forget about us when we come home.

A CLOSER LOOK AT
Will America Forget Its Veterans?

1. All commentaries try to persuade readers to believe or do something. What does Williams want her readers to understand, believe, and do? Where does she state this main point?

2. This is a very brief commentary that reveals only some of the details Williams includes in her 272-page memoir titled *Plenty of Time When We Get Home*. Why do you think Williams has chosen to write so brief a commentary? What would be lost if she had written a commentary that was, say, two or three times longer? Finally, what strategies does she use to keep her argument brief?

3. This commentary is similar to a memoir in the way that it narrates personal experience to achieve its effect. Why is Williams's use of personal narration compelling?

IDEAS FOR
Writing

1. Choose an issue you feel strongly about and about which you have personal experience. Write a memoir that, like this one, uses your personal experience to persuade readers to believe something or do something. You may choose to make your memoir multimodal, using graphics, audio, or other features to make your argument more compelling.

2. Write a profile of someone who, like Williams and her husband, has made a great sacrifice for others or for some larger cause. You can choose someone you know, or you could choose someone you can research thoroughly. How does this person feel about the sacrifices he or she made? Does your subject believe that these sacrifices were worth it and appreciated by others?

A FEW IDEAS FOR
Composing a Commentary

1. **Write a commentary for a news Web site.** Choose a controversial issue that interests you and find a relevant story on a news Web site like *CNN, MSNBC,* or *FoxNews.* Do some research on the subject and write a commentary in which you respond to and offer your opinion on this issue.

2. **Write a commentary comparing two views.** Find two commentaries on the same topic in magazines or on a news Web site. Where do these commentaries differ? Where are their views similar? Which commentator do you tend to agree with and why? Then, write your own commentary in which you discuss both sides of this issue and reveal your own opinion.

3. **Write a letter to the editor for a news Web site.** Choose one of the four commentaries printed in this chapter and challenge or support its argument. What are this person's weakest arguments? Where do you agree with the commentary? What might you add, based on your own experience?

Go to My**Writing**Lab to complete this chapter's exercises and test your understanding of its objectives.

CHAPTER 39

Arguments

A More Perfect Union

BARACK OBAMA

Barack Obama delivered this speech on March 18, 2008, before he was nominated as the 2008 Democratic Party presidential candidate. The speech is, in part, a reaction to television and Internet news stories that displayed the speeches of Obama's pastor, Jeremiah Wright. In those speeches, Wright denounced the American government for committing crimes against African Americans and other people of color. Critics of Obama charged that his position must reflect that of his pastor and that his political views, therefore, must be far more extreme than he had indicated. Obama delivered this speech to clarify his views about race in America's past, present, and future. Pay attention to the way he carefully criticizes Wright's statements (calling them both "wrong" and "divisive") but also explains why it is understandable that some people would come to hold such positions.

"We the people, in order to form a more perfect union."

Two hundred and twenty-one years ago, in a hall that still stands across the street, a group of men gathered and, with these simple words, launched America's improbable experiment in democracy. Farmers and scholars, statesmen and patriots who had traveled across an ocean to escape tyranny and persecution finally made real their declaration of independence at a Philadelphia convention that lasted through the spring of 1787.

The document they produced was eventually signed but ultimately unfinished. It was stained by this nation's original sin of slavery, a question that divided the colonies and brought the convention to a stalemate until the founders chose to allow the slave trade to continue for at least twenty more years, and to leave any final resolution to future generations.

Of course, the answer to the slavery question was already embedded within our Constitution—a Constitution that had at its very core the ideal of equal citizenship under the law; a Constitution that promised its people liberty, and justice, and a union that could be and should be perfected over time.

And yet words on a parchment would not be 5 enough to deliver slaves from bondage, or provide men and women of every color and creed their full rights and obligations as citizens of the United States. What would be needed were Americans in successive generations who were willing to do their part—through protests and struggle, on the streets and in the courts, through a civil war and civil disobedience and always at great risk—to narrow that gap between the promise of our ideals and the reality of their time.

This was one of the tasks we set forth at the beginning of this campaign—to continue the long march of those who came before us, a march for a more just, more equal, more free, more caring and more prosperous America. I chose to run for the presidency at this moment in history because I believe deeply that we cannot solve the challenges of our time unless we solve them together—unless we perfect our union by understanding that we may have different stories, but we hold common hopes; that we may not look the same and we may not have come from the same place, but we all want to move in the same direction—towards a better future for our children and our grandchildren.

This belief comes from my unyielding faith in the decency and generosity of the American people. But it also comes from my own American story.

I am the son of a black man from Kenya and a white woman from Kansas. I was raised with the help of a white grandfather who survived a Depression to serve in Patton's army during

World War II and a white grandmother who worked on a bomber assembly line at Fort Leavenworth while he was overseas. I've gone to some of the best schools in America and lived in one of the world's poorest nations. I am married to a black American who carries within her the blood of slaves and slaveowners—an inheritance we pass on to our two precious daughters. I have brothers, sisters, nieces, nephews, uncles and cousins, of every race and every hue, scattered across three continents, and for as long as I live, I will never forget that in no other country on Earth is my story even possible.

It's a story that hasn't made me the most conventional candidate. But it is a story that has seared into my genetic makeup the idea that this nation is more than the sum of its parts—that out of many, we are truly one.

Throughout the first year of this campaign, 10 against all predictions to the contrary, we saw how hungry the American people were for this message of unity. Despite the temptation to view my candidacy through a purely racial lens, we won commanding victories in states with some of the whitest populations in the country. In South Carolina, where the Confederate Flag still flies, we built a powerful coalition of African Americans and white Americans.

This is not to say that race has not been an issue in the campaign. At various stages in the campaign, some commentators have deemed me either "too black" or "not black enough." We saw racial tensions bubble to the surface during the week before the South Carolina primary. The press has scoured every exit poll for the latest evidence of racial polarization, not just in terms of white and black, but black and brown as well.

And yet, it has only been in the last couple of weeks that the discussion of race in this campaign has taken a particularly divisive turn.

On one end of the spectrum, we've heard the implication that my candidacy is somehow an exercise in affirmative action; that it's based solely on the desire of wide-eyed liberals to purchase racial reconciliation on the cheap. On the other end, we've heard my former pastor, Reverend Jeremiah Wright, use incendiary language to express views that have the potential

not only to widen the racial divide, but views that denigrate both the greatness and the goodness of our nation; that rightly offend white and black alike.

I have already condemned, in unequivocal terms, the statements of Reverend Wright that have caused such controversy. For some, nagging questions remain. Did I know him to be an occasionally fierce critic of American domestic and foreign policy? Of course. Did I ever hear him make remarks that could be considered controversial while I sat in church? Yes. Did I strongly disagree with many of his political views? Absolutely—just as I'm sure many of you have heard remarks from your pastors, priests, or rabbis with which you strongly disagreed.

But the remarks that have caused this recent 15 firestorm weren't simply controversial. They weren't simply a religious leader's effort to speak out against perceived injustice. Instead, they expressed a profoundly distorted view of this country—a view that sees white racism as endemic, and that elevates what is wrong with America above all that we know is right with America; a view that sees the conflicts in the Middle East as rooted primarily in the actions of stalwart allies like Israel, instead of emanating from the perverse and hateful ideologies of radical Islam.

As such, Reverend Wright's comments were not only wrong but divisive, divisive at a time when we need unity; racially charged at a time when we need to come together to solve a set of monumental problems—two wars, a terrorist threat, a falling economy, a chronic health care crisis, and potentially devastating climate change; problems that are neither black or white or Latino or Asian, but rather problems that confront us all.

Given my background, my politics, and my professed values and ideals, there will no doubt be those for whom my statements of condemnation are not enough. Why associate myself with Reverend Wright in the first place, they may ask? Why not join another church? And I confess that if all that I knew of Reverend Wright were the snippets of those sermons that have run in an endless loop on the television and *YouTube*, or if Trinity United Church of Christ conformed to the caricatures being peddled by some commentators, there is no doubt that I would react in much the same way.

But the truth is, that isn't all that I know of the man. The man I met more than twenty years ago is a man who helped introduce me to my Christian faith, a man who spoke to me about our obligations to love one another; to care for the sick and lift up the poor. He is a man who served his country as a U.S. Marine; who has studied and lectured at some of the finest universities and seminaries in the country, and who for over thirty years led a church that serves the community by doing God's work here on Earth—by housing the homeless, ministering to the needy, providing day care services and scholarships and prison ministries, and reaching out to those suffering from HIV/AIDS.

In my first book, *Dreams from My Father,* I described the experience of my first service at Trinity:

> People began to shout, to rise from their seats and clap and cry out, a forceful wind carrying the reverend's voice up into the rafters. . . . And in that single note—hope!—I heard something else; at the foot of that cross, inside the thousands of churches across the city, I imagined the stories of ordinary black people merging with the stories of David and Goliath, Moses and Pharaoh, the Christians in the lion's den, Ezekiel's field of dry bones. Those stories—of survival, and freedom, and hope—became our story, my story; the blood that had spilled was our blood, the tears our tears; until this black church, on this bright day, seemed once more a vessel carrying the story of a people into future generations and into a larger world. Our trials and triumphs became at once unique and universal, black and more than black; in chronicling our journey, the stories and songs gave us a means to reclaim memories that we didn't need to feel shame about. . . memories that all people might study and cherish—and with which we could start to rebuild.

That has been my experience at Trinity. Like 20 other predominantly black churches across the country, Trinity embodies the black community in its entirety—the doctor and the welfare mom, the model student and the former gang-banger. Like other black churches, Trinity's services are full of raucous laughter and sometimes bawdy humor. They are full of dancing, clapping, screaming, and shouting that may seem jarring to the untrained ear. The church contains in full the kindness and cruelty, the fierce intelligence and the shocking ignorance, the struggles and successes, the love and yes, the bitterness and bias that make up the black experience in America.

And this helps explain, perhaps, my relationship with Reverend Wright. As imperfect as he may be, he has been like family to me. He strengthened my faith, officiated my wedding, and baptized my children. Not once in my conversations with him have I heard him talk about any ethnic group in derogatory terms, or treat whites with whom he interacted with anything but courtesy and respect. He contains within him the contradictions—the good and the bad—of the community that he has served diligently for so many years.

I can no more disown him than I can disown the black community. I can no more disown him than I can my white grandmother—a woman who helped raise me, a woman who sacrificed again and again for me, a woman who loves me as much as she loves anything in this world, but a woman who once confessed her fear of black men who passed by her on the street, and who on more than one occasion has uttered racial or ethnic stereotypes that made me cringe.

These people are a part of me. And they are a part of America, this country that I love.

Some will see this as an attempt to justify or excuse comments that are simply inexcusable. I can assure you it is not. I suppose the politically safe thing would be to move on from this episode and just hope that it fades into the woodwork. We can dismiss Reverend Wright as a crank or a demagogue, just as some have dismissed Geraldine Ferraro, in the aftermath of her recent statements, as harboring some deep-seated racial bias.

But race is an issue that I believe this nation cannot afford to ignore right now. We would be making the same mistake that Reverend Wright made in his offending sermons about America—to simplify and stereotype and amplify the negative to the point that it distorts reality.

The fact is that the comments that have been made and the issues that have surfaced over the last few weeks reflect the complexities of race in this country that we've never really worked through—a part of our union that we have yet to perfect. And if we walk away now, if we simply retreat into our respective corners, we will never be able to come together and solve challenges like health care, or education, or the need to find good jobs for every American.

Understanding this reality requires a reminder of how we arrived at this point. As William Faulkner once wrote, "The past isn't dead and buried. In fact, it isn't even past." We do not need to recite here the history of racial injustice in this country. But we do need to remind ourselves that so many of the disparities that exist in the African-American community today can be directly traced to inequalities passed on from an earlier generation that suffered under the brutal legacy of slavery and Jim Crow. Segregated schools were, and are, inferior schools; we still haven't fixed them, fifty years after *Brown v. Board of Education,* and the inferior education they provided, then and now, helps explain the pervasive achievement gap between today's black and white students.

Legalized discrimination—where blacks were prevented, often through violence, from owning property, or loans were not granted to African-American business owners, or black homeowners could not access FHA mortgages, or blacks were excluded from unions, or the police force, or fire departments—meant that black families could not amass any meaningful wealth to bequeath to future generations. That history helps explain the wealth and income gap between black and white, and the concentrated pockets of poverty that persists in so many of today's urban and rural communities.

A lack of economic opportunity among black men, and the shame and frustration that came from not being able to provide for one's family, contributed to the erosion of black families—a problem that welfare policies for many years may have worsened. And the lack of basic services in so many urban black neighborhoods—parks for kids to play in, police walking the beat, regular garbage pick-up and building code enforcement—all helped create a cycle of violence, blight, and neglect that continue to haunt us.

This is the reality in which Reverend Wright and other African Americans of his generation grew up. They came of age in the late fifties and early sixties, a time when segregation was still the law of the land and opportunity was systematically constricted. What's remarkable is not how many failed in the face of discrimination, but rather how many men and women overcame the odds; how many were able to make a way out of no way for those like me who would come after them.

But for all those who scratched and clawed their way to get a piece of the American Dream, there were many who didn't make it—those who were ultimately defeated, in one way or another, by discrimination. That legacy of defeat was passed on to future generations—those young men and increasingly young women who we see standing on street corners or languishing in our prisons, without hope or prospects for the future. Even for those blacks who did make it, questions of race, and racism, continue to define their worldview in fundamental ways. For the men and women of Reverend Wright's generation, the memories of humiliation and doubt and fear have not gone away; nor has the anger and the bitterness of those years. That anger may not get expressed in public, in front of white co-workers or white friends. But it does find voice in the barbershop or around the kitchen table. At times, that anger is exploited by politicians, to gin up votes along racial lines, or to make up for a politician's own failings.

And occasionally it finds voice in the church on Sunday morning, in the pulpit and in the pews. The fact that so many people are surprised to hear that anger in some of Reverend Wright's sermons simply reminds us of the old truism that the most segregated hour in American life occurs on Sunday morning. That anger is not always productive; indeed, all too often it distracts attention from solving real problems; it keeps us from squarely facing our own complicity in our condition, and prevents the African-American community from forging the alliances it needs to bring about real change. But the anger is real; it is powerful; and to simply wish it away, to condemn it without understanding its roots, only serves to widen the chasm of misunderstanding that exists between the races.

In fact, a similar anger exists within segments of the white community. Most working- and middle-class white Americans don't feel that they have been particularly privileged by their race. Their experience is the immigrant experience—as far as they're concerned, no one's handed them anything, they've built it from scratch. They've worked hard all their lives, many times only to see their jobs shipped overseas or their pension dumped after a lifetime of labor. They are anxious about their futures, and feel their dreams slipping away; in an era of stagnant wages and global competition, opportunity comes to be seen as a zero sum game, in which your dreams come at my expense. So when they are told to bus their children to a school across town; when they hear that an African American is getting an advantage in landing a good job or a spot in a good college because of an injustice that they themselves never committed; when they're told that their fears about crime in urban neighborhoods are somehow prejudiced, resentment builds over time.

Like the anger within the black community, these resentments aren't always expressed in polite company. But they have helped shape the political landscape for at least a generation. Anger over welfare and affirmative action helped forge the Reagan Coalition. Politicians routinely exploited fears of crime for their own electoral ends. Talk show hosts and conservative commentators built entire careers unmasking bogus claims of racism while dismissing legitimate discussions of racial injustice and inequality as mere political correctness or reverse racism.

Just as black anger often proved counterproductive, so have these white resentments distracted attention from the real culprits of the middle class squeeze—a corporate culture rife with inside dealing, questionable accounting practices, and short-term greed; a Washington dominated by lobbyists and special interests; economic policies that favor the few over the many. And yet, to wish away the resentments of white Americans, to label them as misguided or even racist, without recognizing they are grounded in legitimate concerns—this too widens the racial divide, and blocks the path to understanding. [35]

This is where we are right now. It's a racial stalemate we've been stuck in for years. Contrary to the claims of some of my critics, black and white, I have never been so naive as to believe that we can get beyond our racial divisions in a single election cycle, or with a single candidacy—particularly a candidacy as imperfect as my own.

But I have asserted a firm conviction—a conviction rooted in my faith in God and my faith in the American people—that working together we can move beyond some of our old racial wounds, and that in fact we have no choice if we are to continue on the path of a more perfect union.

For the African-American community, that path means embracing the burdens of our past without becoming victims of our past. It means continuing to insist on a full measure of justice in every aspect of American life. But it also means binding our particular grievances—for better health care, and better schools, and better jobs—to the larger aspirations of all Americans—the white woman struggling to break the glass ceiling, the white man who has been laid off, the immigrant trying to feed his family. And it means taking full responsibility for our own lives—by demanding more from our fathers, and spending more time with our children, and reading to them, and teaching them that while they may face challenges and discrimination in their own lives, they must never succumb to despair or cynicism; they must always believe that they can write their own destiny.

Ironically, this quintessentially American—and yes, conservative—notion of self-help found frequent expression in Reverend Wright's sermons. But what my former pastor too often failed to understand is that embarking on a program of self-help also requires a belief that society can change.

The profound mistake of Reverend Wright's 40 sermons is not that he spoke about racism in our society. It's that he spoke as if our society was static; as if no progress has been made; as if this country—a country that has made it possible for one of his own members to run for the highest office in the land and build a coalition of white and black; Latino and Asian, rich and poor, young and old—is still irrevocably bound to a tragic past. But what we know—what we have seen—is that America can change. That is the true genius of this nation. What we have already achieved gives us hope—the audacity to hope—for what we can and must achieve tomorrow.

In the white community, the path to a more perfect union means acknowledging that what ails the African-American community does not just exist in the minds of black people; that the legacy of discrimination—and current incidents of discrimination, while less overt than in the past—are real and must be addressed. Not just with words, but with deeds—by investing in our schools and our communities; by enforcing our civil rights laws and ensuring fairness in our criminal justice system; by providing this generation with ladders of opportunity that were unavailable for previous generations. It requires all Americans to realize that your dreams do not have to come at the expense of my dreams; that investing in the health, welfare, and education of black and brown and white children will ultimately help all of America prosper.

In the end, then, what is called for is nothing more, and nothing less, than what all the world's great religions demand—that we do unto others as we would have them do unto us. Let us be our brother's keeper, Scripture tells us. Let us be our sister's keeper. Let us find that common stake we all have in one another, and let our politics reflect that spirit as well.

For we have a choice in this country. We can accept a politics that breeds division, and conflict, and cynicism. We can tackle race only as spectacle—as we did in the OJ trial—or in the wake of tragedy, as we did in the aftermath of Katrina—or as fodder for the nightly news. We can play Reverend Wright's sermons on every channel, every day and talk about them from now until the election, and make the only question in this campaign whether or not the American people think that I somehow believe or sympathize with his most offensive words. We can pounce on some gaffe by a Hillary supporter as evidence that she's playing the race card, or we can speculate on whether white men will all flock to John McCain in the general election regardless of his policies.

We can do that.

But if we do, I can tell you that in the next 45 election, we'll be talking about some other distraction. And then another one. And then another one. And nothing will change.

That is one option. Or, at this moment, in this election, we can come together and say, "Not this time." This time we want to talk about the crumbling schools that are stealing the future of black children and white children and Asian children and Hispanic children and Native American children. This time we want to reject the cynicism that tells us that these kids can't learn; that those kids who don't look like us are somebody else's problem. The children of America are not those kids, they are our kids, and we will not let them fall behind in a 21st-century economy. Not this time.

This time we want to talk about how the lines in the emergency room are filled with whites and blacks and Hispanics who do not have health care; who don't have the power on their own to overcome the special interests in Washington, but who can take them on if we do it together.

This time we want to talk about the shuttered mills that once provided a decent life for men and women of every race, and the homes for sale that once belonged to Americans from every religion, every region, every walk of life. This time we want to talk about the fact that the real problem is not that someone who doesn't look like you might take your job; it's that the corporation you work for will ship it overseas for nothing more than a profit.

This time we want to talk about the men and women of every color and creed who serve together, and fight together, and bleed together under the same proud flag. We want to talk about how to bring them home from a war that never should've been authorized and never should've been waged, and we want to talk about how we'll show our patriotism by caring for them, and their families, and giving them the benefits they have earned.

I would not be running for president if I 50 didn't believe with all my heart that this is what the vast majority of Americans want for this country. This union may never be perfect, but generation after generation has shown that it can always be perfected. And today, whenever I find myself feeling doubtful or cynical about this possibility, what gives me the most hope is the next generation—the young people whose attitudes and beliefs and openness to change have already made history in this election.

There is one story in particular that I'd like to leave you with today—a story I told when I had the great honor of speaking on Dr. King's birthday at his home church, Ebenezer Baptist, in Atlanta.

There is a young, twenty-three-year-old white woman named Ashley Baia who organized for our campaign in Florence, South Carolina. She had been working to organize a mostly African-American community since the beginning of this campaign, and one day she was at a roundtable discussion where everyone went around telling their story and why they were there.

And Ashley said that when she was nine years old, her mother got cancer. And because she had to miss days of work, she was let go and lost her health care. They had to file for bankruptcy, and that's when Ashley decided that she had to do something to help her mom.

She knew that food was one of their most expensive costs, and so Ashley convinced her mother that what she really liked and really wanted to eat more than anything else was mustard and relish sandwiches. Because that was the cheapest way to eat. 55

She did this for a year until her mom got better, and she told everyone at the roundtable that the reason she joined our campaign was so that she could help the millions of other children in the country who want and need to help their parents too.

Now Ashley might have made a different choice. Perhaps somebody told her along the way that the source of her mother's problems were blacks who were on welfare and too lazy to work, or Hispanics who were coming into the country illegally. But she didn't. She sought out allies in her fight against injustice.

Anyway, Ashley finishes her story and then goes around the room and asks everyone else why they're supporting the campaign. They all have different stories and reasons. Many bring up a specific issue. And finally they come to this elderly black man who's been sitting there quietly the entire time. And Ashley asks him why he's there. And he does not bring up a specific issue. He does not say health care or the economy. He does not say education or the war. He does not say that he was there because of Barack Obama. He simply says to everyone in the room, "I am here because of Ashley."

"I'm here because of Ashley." By itself, that single moment of recognition between that young white girl and that old black man is not enough. It is not enough to give health care to the sick, or jobs to the jobless, or education to our children.

But it is where we start. It is where our union grows stronger. And as so many generations have come to realize over the course of the two hundred and twenty-one years since a band of patriots signed that document in Philadelphia, that is where the perfection begins.

A CLOSER LOOK AT
A More Perfect Union

1. Read "A More Perfect Union" a second time or watch it on the Internet, noting those portions of the speech that most stand out for you. In some places, Obama begins several sentences in a row with the same word or phrase (a technique that is called *anaphora*). What effect do those passages have on the audience?

2. Find this speech on *YouTube* and watch it. Describe how seeing and hearing the speech was different than reading it. What ideas and key points came through stronger? What did you notice about the speech that you didn't notice while reading it?

3. If you were going to state the main point of this speech in a sentence or two, what would it be? Read the speech again or listen to it with the transcript in front of you. This time, though, highlight or underline the words, phrases, and sentences that seem to state important, larger points. Then look back on what you have highlighted and try to capture in your own words what Obama is trying to convey.

IDEAS FOR
Writing

1. Obama delivered this speech in part to answer public demands that he explain in precise and direct terms his beliefs and guiding principles about race in America. In this sense, the speech could be said to belong to the "manifesto" genre, which is a blend of the commentary, memoir, and other genres such as profiles and proposals. Write a manifesto that makes a public declaration of the principles that you believe in and the values that guide your life. Your response may be political, religious, philosophical, or personal.

2. Write a rhetorical analysis of "A More Perfect Union" that focuses on any aspect of the speech: its use of *ethos, pathos, logos,* or style and arrangement. Use this focus on one or two aspects to arrive at a new insight about the speech that goes beyond the obvious.

Princeton Mom vs. the Facts

LISA ENDLICH HEFFERNAN

The so-called "Princeton Mom," Susan Patton, has created a cottage industry around offering conservative advice to college women. Her popularity has also spurred resistance from people, like Heffernan, who challenge this kind of advice to college women. In this commentary, notice how Heffernan uses the "facts" to question the traditional advice offered to young women.

Susan Patton is attracting a great deal of attention with her polemic on the virtues of attracting a husband in college. Her underlying theme, that the university setting is the ideal feeding ground for husbands, leaves many women up in arms over the suggestion that the goal of getting a guy should be right up there with getting a degree. In what can only be described as scare tactics, she offers her version of motherly advice, which is that women need to find the smartest guys in college and pursue them as marriage prospects. It may be in her upcoming book she will fill in the facts that back up her many assertions, but her argument does not hold up, not because the message is offensive, although it is. Rather, because the argument does not square with the facts.

Patton begins her argument on sure footing. Marriage, or some other form of relationship, is a big factor in women's happiness. But the fact that she neglects to mention is that marriage is even more important for men. It is men who should be far more desperate to find a partner, as their health, happiness, and longevity depend on it. Multiple studies show that married men have a lower risk of disease, less loneliness and depression and that men with more educated wives enjoy a lower death rate. One cannot help but wonder if it is not men who should be seeking out college educated women as life partners, rather than the reverse.

Patton argues that spending the decade of one's 20's focused on career will leave women with few marriage prospects as they approach 30 because men reaching this milestone will look for younger women as partners. She exhorts future thirtysomethings not to put themselves in the precarious position of having to compete with girls much younger. But again, the problem with this argument lies in the facts. On average, men marry women two years younger. Two years, not ten years.

Next, Patton resorts to the lowest of all arguments, the one that kept girls from higher education for generations and to this day keeps women from asserting themselves in the classroom and the workplace in the same way that men do: Men don't like women who are too smart, or too educated. Without resorting to facts, Patton asserts, "Those men who are as well-educated as you are often interested in younger, less challenging women." Can we just pause for a moment and recognize this as the monumental insult to men that it is? And then we can move on to the facts. Among college-educated married women, Pew found that only 36 percent were married to less-educated men.

Times have changed, and college-educated 5 women are just as likely to marry as women without degrees. As Pew found, "Young women with college degrees are now just as likely as less-educated women to marry, and the timing of their marriages are increasingly similar. This was not the case in 1990. Back then, less-educated women were more likely to marry than were better-educated women, and they tended to do so at a younger age."

College, Patton argues, is the best place to find a husband because of the plentiful supply of well-educated like-minded men. The well-educated part is obvious, but like-minded might be harder to prove. College is a diverse place with people, luckily, of widely divergent views. But, nonetheless, the average age of marriage for college educated men is 28. The notion that they would be thinking about marriage, looking for a mate, or even a girlfriend for the very long haul, seems unlikely when, on average, their wedding date is still six to eight years away.

Finally, in perhaps the most offensive passage, Patton exhorts women to keep in touch with the smart men, particularly the super smart ones as they will be in demand. She presumes that marriage is an economic arrangement where women need to seek out the highest earner. First, college-educated women earn on their own, as Patton pointed out about herself, and do not necessarily need men in this role. Second, income prospects are not the criteria used in selecting a spouse. Research shows that among the reasons to get married, financial stability ranked fifth after more important reasons like love, lifelong commitment, companionship, and having children. Men and women are equally likely to rank love as their most important reason.

Patton stakes out a controversial viewpoint, and it is receiving widespread attention. While there are those who agree with her and others who disagree, her arguments should be held up to the light of fact. Young women should not be scared into action based on a world view from another era, that does not square with today's facts. The *New York Times* pointed out that college-educated women have the lowest divorce rate and therefore, "by age 30, and especially at ages 35 and 40, college-educated women are significantly *more* likely to be married than any other group." In reality it is the college-educated woman who is the prize. Her husband can expect a higher level of income, a healthier life, and longer marriage.

A CLOSER LOOK AT
Princeton Mom vs. the Facts

1. In this argument, Heffernan claims that the facts demonstrate that Patton's conservative advice to college women is misguided. With your group, identify three of these facts in Heffernan's argument. Do you agree that the facts undermine Patton's advice to college women?

2. One of Heffernan's major complaints about Patton's advice is that it seems to suggest that marriage is primarily an economic arrangement. With your group, discuss the reasons why people get married. How important is economics to a marriage in your opinion?

3. Young people are given a great amount of advice, especially when they are in college. With your group, make a list of five common pieces of advice that college-aged people are given. Discuss this advice with your group. Do you think this kind of advice is helpful or not?

IDEAS FOR
Writing

1. Imagine you are ten years older than you are right now. Write a commentary in which you offer your younger self advice about how to make the best of your college experience. Think about the person you want to be ten years from now. Then, tell yourself how your college experience fits into that plan.

2. The "Princeton Mom" phenomenon began with a letter to the editor in the Princeton student newspaper. Write your own letter to the editor in which you offer advice to people of your own gender about how they should view relationships while at college.

The Dangers of the Drinking Age

JEFFREY A. MIRON AND ELINA TETELBAUM

In this article, Miron and Tetelbaum argue against the belief that a drinking age of 21 years old saves lives or keeps students from drinking. Their argument is that raising the drinking age nationally to 21 has had many unintended consequences, such as a rise in binge drinking and disrespect for the law. In this article, pay attention to how the authors use statistics to support their major points and counteract opposing views.

For the past 20 years, the U.S. has maintained a Minimum Legal Drinking Age of 21 (MLDA21), with little public debate about the wisdom of this policy. Recently, however, more than 100 college and university presidents signed the Amethyst Initiative, a public statement calling for "an informed and dispassionate public debate over the effects of the 21-year-old drinking age."

The response to the Amethyst Initiative was predictable: Advocates of restricted access and zero tolerance decried the statement for not recognizing that the MLDA21 saves lives by preventing traffic deaths among 18- to 20-year-olds. The president of Mothers Against Drunk Driving, for example, accused the university heads of "not doing their homework" on the relationship between the drinking age and traffic fatalities.

In fact, the advocates of the MLDA21 are the ones who need a refresher course. In our recently completed research, we show that the MLDA21 has little or no life-saving effect.

To understand why, a bit of history is useful. 5

When the U.S. repealed the prohibition of alcohol in 1933, states were free to legalize, regulate or prohibit access to it as they saw fit. Most legalized but regulated it. In particular, 32 states adopted an MLDA of 21, while 16 chose an MLDA between 18 and 20. With few exceptions, these disparities persisted through the late 1960s.

Between 1970 and 1976, 30 states lowered their MLDA from 21 to 18. These changes coincided with other national efforts to enfranchise youth, exemplified by the 26th Amendment, which granted those 18+ the right to vote.

In 1984, however, Congress passed the Federal Underage Drinking Act (FUDAA), which withholds transportation funding from states that do not have an MLDA21. The justification given for the act was that higher MLDAs would result in fewer traffic fatalities.

By the end of 1988, after passage of the FUDAA, all states adopted an MLDA21. Several states had adopted an MLDA21 before the FUDAA, but the other states were less eager to change. Several passed MLDA21 legislation but set it up for repeal if the FUDAA were held unconstitutional. Others enacted "sunset provisions" in case federal sanctions expired. But when the Supreme Court upheld the FUDAA, states faced a strong incentive to maintain an MLDA21.

Our research compares traffic fatality rates in states before and after they changed their MLDA from 18 to 21. In contrast to all earlier work, however, we examined separately the impact in states that adopted an MLDA21 on their own and those that were coerced by the FUDAA.

The results are striking. Virtually all the life- 10 saving impact of the MLDA21 comes from the few early-adopting states, not from the larger number that resulted from federal pressure. Further, any life-saving effect in those states that first raised the drinking age was only temporary, occurring largely in the first year or two after switching to the MLDA21.

Our results thus challenge both the value of the MLDA21 and the value of coercive federalism. While we find limited evidence that the MLDA21 saves lives when states adopted it of their own volition, we find no evidence it saves lives when the federal government compels this policy.

This makes sense if a higher MLDA works only when state governments can set a drinking age that responds to local attitudes and concerns—and when states are energized to enforce such laws. A policy imposed from on high, especially one that is readily evaded and opposed by a large fraction of the citizenry, is virtually guaranteed to fail.

The major implication of these results is that the drinking age does not produce its main claimed benefit. Moreover, it plausibly generates side effects, like binge drinking and disrespect for the law—the very behavior that events planned for this month's alcohol awareness theme are designed to deter.

If we are to truly tackle the dangers of youth drinking, we must admit that the National-21 experiment has failed. We welcome the surgeon general's recent call to action to reduce underage drinking, to the extent that it provides tips for families and educators to curb the dangers of alcohol abuse.

The federal government has taken alcohol 15 policy out of these parties' hands, however, by imposing an ineffective policy on everyone. An awareness campaign can only do so much when the most significant impediment to change is not on college campuses but in Washington.

A CLOSER LOOK AT
The Dangers of the Drinking Age

1. The authors explain how the current drinking age of 21 came about. Review these historical details. How does this historical information help build a context so readers can better understand this issue?

2. According to the authors, why exactly is the minimum drinking age of 21 years not working in most states? Find the places where they make these points.

3. Study this article with a group of others from your class. If you were trying to poke holes in the authors' argument, where are some weak points that you would consider challenging?

IDEAS FOR
Writing

1. Write a proposal in which you argue that states should again have the power to set their own drinking ages. Explain the problem with the national standard of 21 years old and explore its effects. Then, argue that your state should have the power to set its own drinking age. Explain what age you believe is appropriate. Then, argue out the costs and benefits of adopting the age you recommend.

2. Write an argument in which you summarize this article and then argue against or for it. Explain both sides of the drinking issue by reviewing research on this subject. Then, argue against their point of view or use their argument as the basis for a broader argument that supports their major points.

Women in the World: An Age of Participation

HILLARY CLINTON

Hillary Clinton gave this speech at the Women in the World Summit in 2012. As you read her speech, pay attention to the ways she uses real stories to make the case that social progress depends on people who actively support the rights and freedoms of women.

It has not been as strenuous as it has been inspiring, to have had the chance throughout my life, but certainly in these last 20 years, to have the privilege of meeting women and girls in our own country and then throughout the world who are taking a stand, whose voices are being heard, who are assuming the risks that come with sticking your neck out, whether you are a democracy activist in Burma or a Georgetown law student in the United States.

My life has been enriched, and I want yours to be as well. I am thrilled that so many of you have taken the time out of your own lives to celebrate these stories of these girls and women. And of course, now I hope that through your own efforts, through your own activism, through the foundations, through your political involvement, through your businesses, through every channel you have, you will leave here today thinking about what you too can do. Because when I flag in energy, when I do recognize that what my friends are telling me—that I need more sleep—is probably true, I think about the women whom I have had the honor to work with. Women like Dr. Gao, who is about—well, she's shorter than the podium. She is in her 80s now. She did have bound feet. She became a doctor and she was the physician who sounded the alarm about HIV/AIDS despite the Chinese Government's efforts for years to silence her.

Or I think about Vera, the activist from Belarus whom I met. She's worked so hard to shine a spotlight on the abuses happening right inside Europe one more time—another regime that believes silencing voices, locking up dissidents, rigging elections, is the only way to stay in power. So she and her allies brave the abuse every single day to say no, there is another way.

Or Inex, who I got to know during our efforts on behalf of the peace process in Northern Ireland. And she was reaching across all of these deep divides between the communities there, trying to forge understanding and build bridges. And like Muhtaren, the Pakistani young woman who had been so brutally assaulted for some absurd remnant out of an ancient belief in settling scores between families which should have no place in any country in the 21st century. She was expected to kill herself. Well, of course; you've been shamed, you've been dishonored; through no fault of your own, you are now dead to us, so just finish the job. Well, she not only didn't, but she is a living rebuke to not only those who assaulted her but to the government that did not recognize it needs to protect all of its girls and women, because without their full involvement in their society, there can never be the progress that is so necessary.

We know about their stories. Somehow, we 5 have seen their struggles break through the indifference and the resistance to telling the stories of girls and women who are struggling against such odds across the world.

But they also represent so much more. Because this hall is filled with women and men who are on the front lines fighting for change, for justice, for freedom, for equal rights. And there are tens of millions more who need our support. So what does it mean to be a Woman in the World? Well, I too believe it means facing up to the obstacles you confront, and each of us confront different kinds. It means never giving up—giving up on yourself, giving upon your potential, giving up on your future. It means waking early, working hard, putting a family, a community, a country literally on your back, and building a better life.

You heard from Zin Mar Aung, the Burmese democracy activist who spoke earlier. When I met her late last year when I, on your behalf, on behalf of our country, went to Burma, I discussed with her and other activists what civil society would now be able to do to further the political and the economic reforms that the people so desperately need. And we did honor her along with nine extraordinary other women as International Women of Courage at the State Department.

She, as you could see, came out of prison not embittered, although she had every right to be so, but determined, determined to make her contribution. She didn't have time to feel sorry for herself, to worry whether her hair was the right shade or the right length. She got to work. And because of her, she's founded four organizations, she's working with young people and women to build civil society and citizenship. She raises funds for orphanages, she helps the families of political prisoners trying tore-enter into society, and she is one of those watering the seeds of democracy.

Or consider the young Nepali woman Suma, who sang so beautifully for us. You know what her story was. Six years old, sold into indentured servitude, working under desperate conditions, not allowed to go to school, not even allowed to speak her own native language. But then finally rescued by an NGO, an organization supported by the United States State Department, your tax dollars, called Room to Read, helped her enroll in a local school. We've helped 1,200 girls across India, Nepal, Bangladesh, and Sri Lanka complete their secondary education.

So there is much we can do together. And I have to tell you, I thought it was exquisitely appropriate as I woke up and was getting ready this morning to open *The New York Times* front page and see Christine Lagarde and Angela Merkel there. I know both of them and I think they are worthy of our appreciation and admiration, because they have hard jobs. Christine, who was

10

here, is demonstrating not only her leadership at the IMF but also sending a message that there is no longer any reason that women cannot achieve in business, finance, the economy. And Chancellor Merkel is carrying Europe on her shoulders, trying to navigate through this very difficult economic crisis.

Now, I also heard a report of the call to action and the passion that Leymah Gbowee, our Nobel Peace Prize winner, along with President Ellen Johnson Sirleaf from Liberia summoned you to. Now, for those of you who have seen the movie *Pray the Devil Back to Hell*, you know what happened in Liberia in the spring of 2003. But for others of you who may not yet have seen it, I urge you to do so, because thousands of women from all walks of life—Christians and Muslims together—flooded the streets, marching, singing, praying. Dressed all in white, they sat in a fish market under the hot sun under a banner that said: "The women of Liberia want peace now."

And they built a network and they delivered for their children and for future generations. It was an extraordinary accomplishment. And when the peace talks finally happened in Ghana—not in Liberia—they went to Ghana. They staged a sit-in at the negotiations, linked arms, blocked the doors until the men inside reached an agreement. So the peace was signed, the dictator fled, but still they did not rest. They turned their energies to building an enduring peace. They worked to elect Ellen Johnson Sirleaf, who became the first woman ever elected president of an African country. And in January, I had the honor of attending her second inauguration.

I just saw my good friend, President Jahjaga of Kosovo. She's a very young president, but already her life is a testament for what women can do to promote peace and security. She was still a student when the war started. She saw so much suffering. She wanted to help. So after finishing her studies, she became a police officer. She worked closely with international troops to forge a fragile peace. She rose through the ranks and eventually became the leader of the new Kosovo police force. And then just last year, she became the first woman elected president anywhere in the Balkans. (Applause.) And she has worked to bring her country together to promote the rule of law, ethnic reconciliation, regional stability—all the while standing up for the rights and opportunities of women and girls.

You can look around the world today and you can see the difference that individual women leaders are making. Dilma Rousseff in Brazil, former Chilean President Michelle Bachelet, who's now leading UN women. They carry an enormous load for the rest of us, because it is hard for any leader—male or female. But I don't fear contradiction when I say it is harder for women leaders. There are so many built-in expectations, stereotypes, caricatures that are still deeply embedded in psyches and cultures.

When I sat down alone for dinner with Aung 15 San Suu Kyi back in November, it really did feel like meeting an old friend, even though it was the first time we've had a chance to see each other in person. Of course, from afar I had admired her and appreciated her courage. I went to the house where she had been unjustly imprisoned. Over dinner, we talked about the national struggle, but we also talked about the personal struggle. How does one who has been treated so unjustly overcome that personal sense of anger, of the years that were lost, families that were no longer seen, in order to be a leader that unites and brings people together? Nelson Mandela set such a high standard, and he often told me how going to prison forced him to overcome the anger he felt as a young man, because he knew when he walked out that prison door, if he were still angry, if he still was filled with hatred, he would still be in prison.

Now, Aung San Suu Kyi, like Nelson Mandela, would have been remembered in history forever if she had not made the decision to enter politics, as he did as well. So there she is at, I think, 67, out traveling in an open car through the heat of the countryside, meeting crowds of tens of thousands, even hundreds of thousands, absorbing their hopes that they are putting on to her. She knows that when she crosses into politics, even though it is ultimately the way change is made that can last, she moves from being an icon

to a politician. I know that route. And I know how hard it is to be able to balance one's ideals, one's aspirations, with the give and take of any political process anywhere in the world.

Now, we can tell stories all night and we can talk about the women who have inspired us. But what inspires me is not just who they are, but what they do. They roll their sleeves up and they get to work. And this has such important implications for our own country and for our national security, because our most important goals—from making peace and countering extremism to broadening prosperity and advancing democracy—depend to a very large degree on the participation and partnership of women.

Nations that invest in women's employment, health, and education are just more likely to have better outcomes. Their children will be healthier and better educated. And all over the world, we've seen what women do when they get involved in helping to bring peace. So this is not just the right thing to do for us to hold up these women, to support them, to encourage their involvement; this is a strategic imperative.

And that's why at the State Department, I've made women a cornerstone of American foreign policy. I've instructed our diplomats and development experts to partner with women, to find ways to engage and build on their unique strengths, help women start businesses, help girls attend school, push that women activists will be involved in peace talks and elections. It also means taking on discrimination, marginalization, rape as a tactic of war. I have seen the terrible abuses and what that does to the lives of women, and I know that we cannot rest until it is ended.

In December, we launched a U.S. National 20 Action Plan on Women, Peace, and Security, which is our roadmap for how we accelerate and institutionalize efforts across the United States Government to advance women's participation. And we're taking on some really tough problems. We're trying to build local capacity. We're giving grants to train women activists and journalists in Kenya in early-warning systems for violence. We're supporting a new trauma center for rape victims in Sudan. We're helping women in the Central African Republic access legal and economic services. We're improving the collection of medical evidence for the prosecution of gender-based violence in the Democratic Republic of the Congo.

And that's just the beginning, because from around the world, from Iraq and Afghanistan to Sudan to the new transitional democracies in the Middle East and North Africa, we're expecting our embassies to develop local strategies to empower women politically, economically, and socially.

But we are watching carefully what is happening. We are concerned about the revolutions in the Middle East and North Africa. They held so much promise, but they also carried real risks, especially for women. We saw women on the front lines of the revolutions, most memorably in Cairo's Tahrir Square. They marched, they blogged, they tweeted, they risked their lives alongside their sons and brothers—all in the name of dignity and opportunity. But after the revolution, too often they have found their attempts to participate in their new democracies blocked. We were delighted that our great Supreme Court Justice Ruth Bader Ginsburg went on a State Department-sponsored trip to Egypt and Tunisia. And while there, she rightly said the daughters of the Middle East "should be able to aspire and achieve based on the talent God gave them and not be held back by any laws made by men."

Just a few weeks ago in a town hall meeting in Tunis, a young woman wearing a headscarf stood up and talked about her experience working in partnership with the U.S. Embassy in a program that we call Bridge to Democracy. She said that often people she met were surprised that a young women wearing a hijab would work with Americans, and that we would work with her. Gradually, she said, these preconceptions broke down and increasingly people are just eager to find new partners to help build their new democracy. I told her that in America, in Tunisia, anywhere in the world, women should have the right to make their own choices about what they wear, how they worship, the jobs they

do, the causes they support. These are choices women have to make for themselves, and they are a fundamental test of democracy.

Now, we know that young woman in Tunisia and her peers across the region already are facing extremists who will try to strip their rights, curb their participation, limit their ability to make choices for themselves. Why extremists always focus on women remains a mystery to me. But they all seem to. It doesn't matter what country they're in or what religion they claim. They want to control women. They want to control how we dress, they want to control how we act, they even want to control the decisions we make about our own health and bodies. Yes, it is hard to believe that even here at home, we have to stand up for women's rights and reject efforts to marginalize any one of us, because America needs to set an example for the entire world. And it seems clear to me that to do that, we have to live our own values and we have to defend our own values. We need to respect each other, empower all our citizens, and find common ground.

We are living in what I call the Age of 25 Participation. Economic, political, and technological changes have empowered people everywhere to shape their own destinies in ways previous generations could never have imagined. All these women—these Women in the World— have proven that committed individuals, often with help, help from their friends, can make a difference in their own lives and far beyond.

So let me have the great privilege of ending this conference by challenging each of you. Every one of us needs to be part of the solution. Each of us must truly be a Woman in the World. We need to be as fearless as the women whose stories you have applauded, as committed as the dissidents and the activists you have heard from, as audacious as those who start movements for peace when all seems lost. Together, I do believe that it is part of the American mission to ensure that people everywhere, women and men alike, finally have the opportunity to live up to their own God-given potential. So let's go forth and make it happen.

A CLOSER LOOK AT
Women in the World: An Age of Participation

1. Clinton argues that we are living in an "Age of Participation" and that people are empowered through "economic, political, and technical changes" that are happening all around them. With your group, discuss what you believe she means by an Age of Participation.

2. As Clinton points out, developing countries are often viewed as places where women's rights are most at risk. Yet, only a little over a century ago, women in the United States were not far ahead of where women in developing countries are today. According to Clinton, the progress of a society depends greatly on the progress of women's rights. With your group, use the history of the United States to discuss whether this premise is true.

3. Clinton's main point in this speech can be hard to find. Locate a few sentences that seem to express her main point. Then, with your group, discuss what she is really trying to argue in this speech.

IDEAS FOR
Writing

1. Using an Internet search engine, find a transcript or video of Clinton's 2013 speech titled "Helping Women Isn't Just a 'Nice' Thing to Do," which was given a year after the speech printed here. Compare the two speeches. Write a commentary in which you react to Clinton's arguments in these speeches.

2. Write a profile of a woman in politics whom you admire. In your profile, discuss what qualities have made this woman successful and admirable. You can also discuss her flaws if appropriate.

A FEW IDEAS FOR
Composing an Argument

1. **Write an argument on an important issue.** Try to give the topic a local slant by choosing an issue that concerns your campus or your community. It might be the community you physically work or live in, or a virtual community of people who share the same interests. Even if you want to talk about a national or global issue, try to find the local angle. For instance, rather than just writing about global warming generally, approach that issue by discussing what is happening on your campus or within your community.

2. **Write an argument responding to an article.** Find an article that states a position you strongly disagree with. Try to summarize the opposing article's argument so objectively that even a person who holds that position would agree that you have treated it fairly. Then express your own opinion in a way that shows your views are more reasonable than your opponent's views.

3. **Create a multimedia argument.** Your argument should argue for a specific belief or course of action. Choose an incident from your own life that sets the stage or leads to a lesson about the issue you are arguing. Try to highlight details that allow you to explore both sides of the issue. Consider blending in features of other genres, such as memoirs, profiles, and proposals. Try experimenting with organizations that creatively use the flexibility of the medium you chose for this project.

Go to My**WritingLab** to complete this chapter's exercises and test your understanding of its objectives.

40

Proposals

Ethical Chic: How Women Can Change The Fashion Industry

ELIZABETH SCHAEFFER BROWN

In this brief proposal, Elizabeth Brown explores the ongoing problems with the manufacturing of clothing around the world. She explains how women consumers can make a difference with a few thoughtful choices.

Globalization has made it easier than ever to ignore where our clothes come from. Are the workers paid equitably? Are their working conditions safe? Are their communities healthy? Many consumers may find it difficult to answer these questions, in part because most retail clothing makers don't disclose adequate information about production.

Here's the truth: When a garment is made in the developing world, the average percentage of the final retail cost that goes to the garment worker ranges from 0.5 - 4 percent. Most of us accept this status quo as the norm. Even the U.S. government, one of the largest consumers on the planet, orders clothing from the kind of factories that have killed so many people in Bangladesh.

For a long time, men have opened doors for each other in business. I believe that if we are to solve this issue, then we need more women to rise to leadership positions in the fashion industry. Women like Joey Adler from Industrial Revolution II (a client of mine at Uncommon Union)—and even celebrities like Olivia Wilde—are already opening doors and putting more ethical plans into action. As more women take on more authority as leaders in the fashion industry, they are poised to challenge the long-standing assumption that our ethics are limited by market forces.

The world is ready for women to remake the fashion of fashion—to bring into vogue putting people first. Here are a few ways we can get started:

Brand Ethical Fashion as Cool

Begin to educate consumers about the impor- 5 tance of ethical fashion. Social entrepreneurs on the sourcing side of the equation know that, in order to change how we think about commerce and how we conduct business as entrepreneurs, leaders and consumers, the industry needs to work hard to develop customers who will make ethical choices.

Start by identifying public figures and entertainment stars—e.g., trendsetters like Donna Karan (Urban Zen) and Hugh Jackman (Laughing Man)—who care about developing an ethical framework for capitalism. Leverage their authority and influence to bring ethical fashion into the forefront of public attention. Rather than trying to appeal to people's conscience, begin to make the ethical choice the fashionable one.

Consider the Product

Develop a product with a clearly defined ethical pedigree. To do so, you need to be able to document the life cycle of the product from inception to the store shelf. Who designed the product? Who made it? What is it made from? To what extent was the welfare of the people involved in the process taken into account?

The answers to all these questions need to serve the purpose of marketing the product. Some stages of a product's lifecycle (especially in the developing world) can be difficult to verify and control, so be careful. You need to offer proof.

Market Smart

Lastly, use both the quality and appeal of the product and its pedigree as a marketing tool. Many if not most people want to make the ethical choice—they just need help getting there. Educate consumers about the long chain of events starting with textile production and ending with the store purchase. Whenever possible, show public figures wearing the product or discussing the product.

Make it personal: Use photographs and 10 story to creative a narrative about the product so that consumers feel that they are not just buying an object but becoming part of a story.

If consumers then begin to ask questions and demand accountability—if humanitarian, health, and environmental concerns start to drive the fashion industry—ethically sourced fashion will become the norm. The status quo will change. In the end, change depends on the willingness of workers, consumers, and entrepreneurs to step into the unknown. Let us be some of the first to insist on a better world.

A CLOSER LOOK AT
Ethical Chic: How Women Can Change the Fashion Industry

1. In this proposal, Brown does not spend a great amount of time describing the problem or exploring its causes and effects. Instead, she moves quickly to her solution for the problem. With your group, discuss why she uses this strategy. What are the advantages to putting the solution up front? What are some of the risks?

2. Brown suggests that one part of the solution is getting women into leadership roles in the manufacturing of clothing. Yet, women make the majority of clothing buying decisions in the United States.

With your group, discuss whether you think women would be more influential as corporate leaders in the fashion industry or as savvy consumers of clothing products.

3. Do some preliminary Internet research into the origins of the clothing and shoes you are wearing right now. Find the labels in your clothing and run searches on the companies that made them. With your group, discuss what you found out about where your clothes were made as well as the companies that made them.

IDEAS FOR
Writing

1. The ethical production of all items is important. Think of something you use every day, such as a car, electronics, shoes, electricity, or food, and investigate its origin. Write a proposal similar to Brown's in which you develop a plan for making sure this product is made in a way that respects the rights of workers. You can also come up with a plan for protecting the environment during the manufacturing of this product.

2. Write a counterstatement in which you are skeptical of Brown's solution to this problem. The truth is, many women are already influential leaders in the fashion industry, and women already have the power to make informed choices. Yet, these manufacturing-related ethical problems continue. Think of another solution that might solve this problem and offer it in your counterstatement.

Reforming College Sports

JOHN U. BACON

John Bacon is a prominent sportswriter who is widely published on sports websites. In this proposal, he discusses options for creating minor leagues in professional football and basketball. Pay attention to the way he explains the reasons why the current college athletic system exists and how he uses this explanation to develop a plan for solving the problem.

Big Ten Commissioner Jim Delany—who might be the smartest man in college sports—stood outside the Big Ten's brand new offices recently, telling a group of reporters, "Maybe in football and basketball, it would work better if more kids had a chance to go directly into the professional ranks. If they're not comfortable and want to monetize, let the minor leagues flourish."

It isn't clear if Delany's comments reflected his deeply held beliefs, an offhand comment, or just a daring bluff—but if it's the latter, it isn't as daring as it seems.

By challenging the NFL and NBA to start their own minor leagues, Delany doesn't have much to lose. He knows they won't, because they have every reason not to. They've used the college leagues to develop their players from the day the pro leagues started. Why would they derail the gravy train now?

And even if they did, it wouldn't cost the Big Ten much, if anything.

But if we call Delany's bluff and play it out, 5 we'll see it leads to one idea that could actually save what we love most about college football: the passion no other sport can match.

The Unexamined Root Of The Problem

I came to the same conclusion Delany did several years ago, though for different reasons.

Working on a book proposal a decade ago, I was struck by the essential difference between American football and basketball on the one hand, and just about every sport in the world on the other: football and basketball developed primarily as college games. When the NFL and NBA opened decades later, they simply hired the best college players available, but it still took the pro leagues decades to challenge the popularity of college football and basketball. The NFL didn't get a permanent foothold until the classic 1958 title between the New York Giants and the Baltimore Colts, and the NBA Finals were still on tape-delay until Magic and Bird joined the league in 1979.

Why does this matter? Because by starting after college football and basketball were already established, the NFL and NBA were freed from having to develop viable minor leagues of their own, making them virtually the only sports in the world that don't have them. Roughly a century ago, Major League Baseball and the NHL could not rely on the nascent college programs to fill their rosters, so they had to create their own minor leagues.

And that's why today, almost every high school football and basketball star has just one path to the big leagues: the NCAA. This makes no sense. Athletes and universities *can* benefit each other, but they shouldn't *need* to. Pele never had to worry about passing 12 credits before playing in his first World Cup, and the University of Chicago figured out it didn't need a football team to be a world-class university. As former University of Chicago president Robert

Maynard Hutchins liked to say, "Football is to education as bullfighting is to agriculture." He backed it up in 1939, when he pulled the Maroons out of the Big Ten. Today, Chicago's admissions department is the fourth most selective in the country, behind only those of Harvard, Yale and Princeton.

When a committed student-athlete enrolls 10 in a four-year college, everyone involved receives at least some benefit. The athlete gets a free education, an enduring asset no matter what he does on the field, and the college enjoys reflected glory from his performance. But when we require a gifted athlete with little or no interest in higher education to enroll in a four-year college to get to the NFL or NBA, he is more likely to fail in the classroom, which may actually prevent him from pursuing a promising athletic career—something that happens only in America—and the school's academic reputation will take a very public hit. Nobody wins.

So, how do we fix this?

The Pro And Cons Of Paying Players

Everyone agrees it's increasingly difficult to support the farce that the NCAA is foisting upon us, but we can't agree on how to fix it. In recent years we've seen proposals ranging from school-sponsored minor league teams to ending big-time college sports altogether.

The most popular idea sits between those two extremes: give up the ruse, and pay the players. After all, everyone seems to be making millions off the athletes, except the athletes.

Consider the skyrocketing salaries of Division I football coaches, which now average more than $2 million a year, an increase of 750 percent (adjusted for inflation) since 1984, about twenty times more than professors' salaries increased over the same period. In 2012, the highest-paid state employee in twenty-seven states was a football coach, and in thirteen it was a basketball coach. The number of states whose highest-paid public employee was a university president? Four. The explosion in CEO pay, and the rationales that go with it, would be a fair comparison.

This chasm between the value of the play- 15 ers' scholarships and their coaches' salaries will only become more obscene with the arrival of the four-team playoff this season, whose TV rights alone will be worth $5.64 billion over twelve years, or about $470 million a year—all for three games. In the NCAA basketball tournament this past spring, March Madness generated $1 billion—in ad revenue alone.

As I wrote in *Fourth and Long*:

They will tell you it's the cost of doing business—but what's the business, exactly? When 60 Minutes *interviewed [former Domino's Pizza CEO-turned-Michigan athletic director] Dave Brandon that fall, he said the "business model is broken." What he failed to grasp was that it is not supposed to be a business in the first place. After all, what business doesn't have to pay shareholders, partners, owners, taxes, or the star attractions, the players and the band?*

This mindset seems particularly true of the contemporary CEOs as-athletic directors, for whom no amount is enough.

"As one digs deeper into the national character of the Americans," Alexis de Tocqueville wrote, almost two hundred years ago, "one sees that they have sought the value of everything in this world only in the answer to this single question: how much money will it bring in?"

More recently, Homer Simpson told his boss, Monty Burns, "You're the richest man I know." "Yes," Burns replied. "But you know, I'd trade it all for just a little more."

And that's the problem. Like Asian carp invading your freshwater paradise, once the money-grubbers take over, their appetites are insatiable, and they are impossible to remove.

The most serious threat to big-time college athletics is not the endless scandals, which affect only those who get caught, but the rampant greed, which affects everybody. As Michael Kinsley has famously said, "The scandal isn't what's *illegal*. The scandal is what's *legal*."

With so many millions sloshing around the athletes, it's no surprise they're reaching their limits. And it's not just "Johnny Football" Manziel, a uniquely unsympathetic figure, either, but Kain Colter, Northwestern's pre-med quarterback, who has taken to wearing an armband with "A.P.U." on it, for All Players United, in support of those fighting to protect their rights, and their safety.

Certainly, the idea of giving the players a stipend of a thousand or two a year—which the NCAA almost passed four decades ago—so they can pay for a dinner date, a winter coat or a trip home, is long overdue. But even that modest proposal will cost more than its proponents imagine, since Title IX will dictate all scholarship athletes receive the same stipend, be they the All-American quarterback or the second-string coxswain on the women's crew team.

Thus, when people talk about $20,000 "salaries" for college athletes, the cost at the biggest programs, which have some 700 student-athletes, will quickly exceed $10 million. And before you know it, you're talking real money.

If you think for a second these payments will 20 be deducted from the coaches' bloated salaries, I have a "Johnny Football" autograph to sell you. No, these salaries will be piled on to the mountain of money that college athletic departments already spend every year. And they will pay for that pile, of course, by extracting still more millions from alternate jersey sales, rising seat license "donations," corporate partnerships, and the ads that come with them—the very things that are alienating lifelong fans.

If I'm right that the biggest threat to college football is not scandal but greed, paying the players will only exacerbate the sport's central problem, setting up the kind of tug-of-wars we see in pro sports that turn everybody off. Pouring more gasoline on a fire will not make it smaller. Paying players will not solve the problem it is intended to solve—the players will soon want more, just like the coaches, and not without reason—but it will create many new problems that will threaten the future of the sport.

Universities already have a difficult time controlling their athletic departments, and the pay-to-play plans will not make it any easier. They will turn the student-athletes into bona fide employees, which will open a Pandora's box of legal issues, and questions from the IRS.

The pay-to-play proposals also assume the current record TV ratings, sweetheart corporate deals and sold-out stadiums will continue far into the future. But we've already seen plenty of signs that the fans are also nearing their breaking point.

Penn State fans travel an average of four hours to see their Nittany Lions play—as hardcore as any fans in college football. But Penn State snapped its six-year streak of 100,000-plus crowds more than a year before Jerry Sandusky was arrested, thanks to an aggressive seat-license program.

Three thousand fans dropped their season tickets in 2010, when the seat-license program was introduced, three thousand more did the next year, and the departures have only accelerated since. When I attended the University of Central Florida-Penn State game this fall, my friends estimated there were no more than 85,000 fans in the stands that night—no matter what they announced as the "official paid attendance."

Penn State fans are not the canaries in the coalmine. They are the coalminers. And if they're starting to climb out of their favorite mine, no program is safe.

The cost for a family of four to attend a 25 Michigan football game, with average seats and no hotel rooms or restaurant meals, runs about $500—more than a day at Disneyworld. And Mickey never loses. While the Michigan athletic department claims the streak of 100,000-plus crowds, dating back to 1975, has never been broken, the game against Akron revealed wide swaths of empty seats, particularly in the student section—your future season ticket holders.

If you crank up the seat licenses, the TV timeouts and the endless ads another notch or two to pay players' salaries, you will risk losing a generation of fans, and the whole enterprise will erode.

The question of paying the players will become truly academic if there's no money to pay them.

When did you last attend a boxing match or a horse race? If the bottom can fall out of those once robust sports, it can happen to college football, too. And if you like Off-Track Betting Parlors, and the empty stands they create, you're going to love the future of big-time college sports.

Creating Two Tracks To The Big Leagues

Despite the many good reasons to pay the players, I think there are better reasons not to—and a better way to fix the problem that paying the players is intended to fix.

Delany might not be serious about his dare, 30 but I am.

In my previous book, **Three and Out**, I wrote, "For those rare stars, I've always believed, the NFL and NBA should set up viable minor leagues to give such players a real choice—the same one high school hockey and baseball players have."

That came out two years ago. The need for this change is much more urgent today.

What football and basketball players need is what baseball and hockey players have enjoyed for almost a century: a viable minor league, so players who don't want to be college students, and prefer to be paid in cash instead of scholarships, can do just that.

This would cut down on the majority of problems that beset both sports, almost overnight. Johnny Football? Sign all you want. "One and done" becomes "None and done." Go!

Delany's bold statement aside, you have to 35 believe that if the NFL and NBA actually called his bluff, he might fear losing some of the NCAA's

most exciting players to the new minor leagues – and with them, some of the appeal of college football and basketball.

Fret not. As I write in *Fourth and Long:*

College athletes are more passionate playing for a scholarship than pro athletes are playing for millions. And we admire them more for this very reason. It's the difference between citizen soldiers volunteering for the army and hired Hessians. Give us the doughboys, the G.I. Joes, and the grunts fighting for a cause.

And this is why we watch: not for perfection, but passion—the same reason over a million fans watch the Little League World Series every summer. This point is easily proven: the worst team in the NFL would crush the best team in college football, every year. Yet college football is the only sport in the world that draws more fans to its games than the big league teams it feeds. The attendance at Michigan, Ohio State, and Penn State typically averages 50 percent more than that of the NFL teams in those states—and often doubles it. No minor league baseball or hockey team comes close to matching the attendance of their parent clubs.

This basic truth escapes both the proponents of paying players and the NCAA executives who try to squelch minor leagues from starting: college football is selling romance, not prowess. If ability were the only appeal, we'd move NFL games to Saturday and watch those games instead. But if you lose the romance of college football, you will lose the fans of college football.

In 2005, former Michigan athletic director Bill Martin commissioned a professionally conducted survey, which revealed that Michigan football season-ticket holders were doggedly loyal, with slightly more than half of them holding their seats for more than two decades. They were about 50 percent more likely to buy Michigan basketball season tickets than season tickets for any professional team. Only 9 percent of Michigan season-ticket holders also bought season tickets to any professional team, and this survey was taken when Michigan basketball was down and the Detroit Red Wings and Pistons were just a few years away from their latest titles.

This tells us a basic truth: College football fans don't just love football. They love college football—the history, the traditions, the rituals, and the rivalries that surpass those of the pro game. They are attracted to the belief that it's based on ideals that go beyond the field, do not fade with time, and are passed down to the next generation.

We don't have to wonder if creating a separate minor league system will work. We already know: Just check out college hockey. The players who would rather have a paycheck than a scholarship can jump straight to the minor leagues—and they do. Because the players who opt for college are not forced to do so by the NHL, the graduation rates tend to be much higher in college hockey, and the scandals much fewer. College hockey fans love them all the more, because they know the guys they're cheering for have chosen to be college hockey players. They're the real deal.

In hockey, at least, both the minor leagues and the colleges deliver the players and the fans exactly what they promise. The only games they play are on the ice.

How To Make It Honest

OK, but why would the NFL and NBA ever go for this, and voluntarily invest millions of their own money to create something they've been getting for free since they started? They wouldn't, of course, so you'd have to force them.

But forcing them can be accomplished in 40 one step: bring back freshmen ineligibility. If you want to make it honest, that's how you do it.

In fact, freshmen ineligibility was the rule from 1905, the year the NCAA was founded, until 1972, and for a simple reason: colleges actually believed their athletes should be students first, and this is how they proved it. It gave all athletes a year to get their feet on the ground, and catch up where needed. Dean Smith and Terry Holland argued before the Knight Commission about the merits of freshmen ineligibility—but that was nine years ago, and nothing has changed. Until the NCAA, the leagues, the presidents and the athletic directors bring back freshmen ineligibility, you should not take them seriously when they speak of "student-athletes." They do not mean it.

By requiring *all* student-athletes to be actual student-athletes, many elite athletes will opt out—but there's no way the NFL or the NBA will let talented 18-year olds wander off if they might be able to help their teams win games. So, the NFL and NBA would almost certainly do what they should have done decades ago: Prepare players for their leagues, with their own money, by starting their own minor league teams.

Creating two paths to the pros will throw a bucket of cold water on the overheated facilities arms race, the soaring coaches' salaries and the insane TV contracts. Yes, those things exist in college hockey and baseball, but nowhere near on the same scale. Restoring a sense of proportion is what we're seeking here.

Yes, we need other reforms, too. We need to put an end to the NCAA's absurd charade of posing as the sheriff when it's really the saloon-keeper. Universities should hire athletic directors who've spent their working lives nurturing student-athletes, not "maximizing the revenue streams" of their "brand." And we should require all universities to reinstate true faculty oversight of their athletic programs.

"Without faculty control," Michigan's leg- 45 endary athletic director, Don Canham, wrote in an essay that came out after his death in 2005, "the presidents are running up to $70 million budget programs (Michigan, Ohio State, Stanford, Texas, etc.) with no oversight. What $70-million business could conduct business without a board of control?" In the eight years since Canham warned of "unbridled expansion," Michigan's budget has more than doubled. Guess he knew something.

All these changes are needed, but creating a second path to the pros is the key. And—as Smith, Holland and Canham himself urged—restoring freshmen ineligibility is the way to do it.

No, this solution will not create a perfect world. There will still be athletes who aren't bona fide college students. There will still be coaches and boosters happy to break the rules. And there will still be an outsized mania for the sport. The goal is not perfection, but sanity—to protect the integrity of the universities the players are representing, to protect the players from being trapped, and to preserve the passion the players and fans still feel for their favorite game.

The time to save this century-old game is now. And creating minor leagues to preserve college athletics, while giving all athletes a real choice, is the way to do it.

It's time to call Mr. Delany's bluff.

A CLOSER LOOK AT
Reforming College Sports

1. This argument is a proposal, even though it isn't called one. With your group, use the genre to discuss how this argument includes many of the features of a typical proposal. Then, discuss how it doesn't follow the proposal genre.

2. Bacon offers several reasons why the current system of college athletics exists. What causes does he mention? What are some of the effects of this problem? With your group, come up with three other effects of this problem.

3. If Bacon's plans were implemented, what do you think would happen to college athletics? What are some of the potential downsides of this reform? What are some of the potential upsides? With your group, discuss whether the benefits outweigh the costs.

IDEAS FOR
Writing

1. Identify a problem on your college campus that should be corrected. Write a proposal to the university administration (or another named source) in which you explain its causes and effects. Then, offer a plan for solving the problem. Conclude by explaining the costs and benefits of your solution.

2. Write a profile of a contemporary or historical sports figure. The person could be a role model or a scoundrel. She or he could be great or obscure. Try to capture this person's story and personality in your profile. What makes or made this person unique and noteworthy?

A Modest Proposal

JONATHAN SWIFT

*Jonathan Swift (1667–1745) was an Irish clergyman who was among the most skilled satirists
ever to write in any language. Like most satires,* A Modest Proposal *appears on the surface
to approve of something ludicrous in order to attack a real social problem. As you read this
selection, keep in mind that it was published anonymously in 1729 and that readers would have
been expecting to read a serious and straightforward proposal for addressing the intolerable
conditions and treatment of the Irish poor, not a satire.*

*For preventing the children of poor peo-
ple in Ireland, from being a burden on
their parents or country, and for making them beneficial to the publick.*

It is a melancholy object to those, who walk
through this great town, or travel in the country,
when they see the streets, the roads and cabbin-
doors crowded with beggars of the female sex,
followed by three, four, or six children, all in rags,
and importuning every passenger for an alms.
These mothers instead of being able to work for
their honest livelihood, are forced to employ all
their time in stroling to beg sustenance for their
helpless infants who, as they grow up, either turn
thieves for want of work, or leave their dear native country, to fight for the Pretender in Spain,
or sell themselves to the Barbadoes.

I think it is agreed by all parties, that this
prodigious number of children in the arms, or on
the backs, or at the heels of their mothers, and
frequently of their fathers, is in the present de-
plorable state of the kingdom, a very great additional grievance; and therefore whoever could
find out a fair, cheap and easy method of making
these children sound and useful members of the
common-wealth, would deserve so well of the
publick, as to have his statue set up for a pre-
server of the nation.

But my intention is very far from being con-
fined to provide only for the children of professed beggars: it is of a much greater extent, and
shall take in the whole number of infants at a
certain age, who are born of parents in effect as
little able to support them, as those who demand
our charity in the streets.

As to my own part, having turned my 5
thoughts for many years, upon this important
subject, and maturely weighed the several
schemes of our projectors, I have always found
them grossly mistaken in their computation. It is
true, a child just dropt from its dam, may be supported by her milk, for a solar year, with little
other nourishment: at most not above the value
of two shillings, which the mother may certainly
get, or the value in scraps, by her lawful occupation of begging; and it is exactly at one year old
that I propose to provide for them in such a manner, as, instead of being a charge upon their parents, or the parish, or wanting food and raiment
for the rest of their lives, they shall, on the contrary, contribute to the feeding, and partly to the
cloathing of many thousands.

There is likewise another great advantage in
my scheme, that it will prevent those voluntary
abortions, and that horrid practice of women
murdering their bastard children, alas! too frequent among us, sacrificing the poor innocent
babes, I doubt, more to avoid the expence than
the shame, which would move tears and pity in
the most savage and inhuman breast.

The number of souls in this kingdom being
usually reckoned one million and a half, of these
I calculate there may be about two hundred
thousand couple whose wives are breeders; from
which number I subtract thirty thousand couple,
who are able to maintain their own children, (although I apprehend there cannot be so many,
under the present distresses of the kingdom) but
this being granted, there will remain an hundred
and seventy thousand breeders. I again subtract

fifty thousand, for those women who miscarry, or whose children die by accident or disease within the year. There only remain an hundred and twenty thousand children of poor parents annually born. The question therefore is, How this number shall be reared, and provided for? which, as I have already said, under the present situation of affairs, is utterly impossible by all the methods hitherto proposed. For we can neither employ them in handicraft or agriculture; we neither build houses, (I mean in the country) nor cultivate land: they can very seldom pick up a livelihood by stealing till they arrive at six years old; except where they are of towardly parts, although I confess they learn the rudiments much earlier; during which time they can however be properly looked upon only as probationers: As I have been informed by a principal gentleman in the county of Cavan, who protested to me, that he never knew above one or two instances under the age of six, even in a part of the kingdom so renowned for the quickest proficiency in that art.

I am assured by our merchants, that a boy or a girl before twelve years old, is no saleable commodity, and even when they come to this age, they will not yield above three pounds, or three pounds and half a crown at most, on the exchange; which cannot turn to account either to the parents or kingdom, the charge of nutriments and rags having been at least four times that value.

I shall now therefore humbly propose my own thoughts, which I hope will not be liable to the least objection.

I have been assured by a very knowing 10 American of my acquaintance in London, that a young healthy child well nursed, is, at a year old, a most delicious nourishing and wholesome food, whether stewed, roasted, baked, or boiled; and I make no doubt that it will equally serve in a fricasie, or a ragoust.

I do therefore humbly offer it to publick consideration, that of the hundred and twenty thousand children, already computed, twenty thousand may be reserved for breed, whereof only one fourth part to be males; which is more than we allow to sheep, black cattle, or swine, and my reason is, that these children are seldom the fruits of marriage, a circumstance not much regarded by our savages, therefore, one male will be sufficient to serve four females. That the remaining hundred thousand may, at a year old, be offered in sale to the persons of quality and fortune, through the kingdom, always advising the mother to let them suck plentifully in the last month, so as to render them plump, and fat for a good table. A child will make two dishes at an entertainment for friends, and when the family dines alone, the fore or hind quarter will make a reasonable dish, and seasoned with a little pepper or salt, will be very good boiled on the fourth day, especially in winter.

I have reckoned upon a medium, that a child just born will weigh 12 pounds, and in a solar year, if tolerably nursed, encreaseth to 28 pounds.

I grant this food will be somewhat dear, and therefore very proper for landlords, who, as they have already devoured most of the parents, seem to have the best title to the children.

Infant's flesh will be in season throughout the year, but more plentiful in March, and a little before and after; for we are told by a grave author, an eminent French physician, that fish being a prolifick dyet, there are more children born in Roman Catholick countries about nine months after Lent, the markets will be more glutted than usual, because the number of Popish infants, is at least three to one in this kingdom, and therefore it will have one other collateral advantage, by lessening the number of Papists among us.

I have already computed the charge of 15 nursing a beggar's child (in which list I reckon all cottagers, labourers, and four-fifths of the farmers) to be about two shillings per annum, rags included; and I believe no gentleman would repine to give ten shillings for the carcass of a good fat child, which, as I have said, will make four dishes of excellent nutritive meat, when he hath only some particular friend, or his own family to dine with him. Thus the squire will learn to be a good landlord, and grow popular among his tenants, the mother will have eight shillings neat profit, and be fit for work till she produces another child.

Those who are more thrifty (as I must confess the times require) may flea the carcass; the skin of which, artificially dressed, will make admirable gloves for ladies, and summer boots for fine gentlemen.

As to our City of Dublin, shambles may be appointed for this purpose, in the most convenient parts of it, and butchers we may be assured will not be wanting; although I rather recommend buying the children alive, and dressing them hot from the knife, as we do roasting pigs.

A very worthy person, a true lover of his country, and whose virtues I highly esteem, was lately pleased, in discoursing on this matter, to offer a refinement upon my scheme. He said that many gentlemen of this kingdom, having of late destroyed their deer, he conceived that the want of venison might be well supply'd by the bodies of young lads and maidens, not exceeding fourteen years of age, nor under twelve; so great a number of both sexes in every country being now ready to starve for want of work and service: And these to be disposed of by their parents if alive, or otherwise by their nearest relations. But with due deference to so excellent a friend, and so deserving a patriot, I cannot be altogether in his sentiments; for as to the males, my American acquaintance assured me from frequent experience, that their flesh was generally tough and lean, like that of our school-boys, by continual exercise, and their taste disagreeable, and to fatten them would not answer the charge. Then as to the females, it would, I think, with humble submission, be a loss to the publick, because they soon would become breeders themselves: And besides, it is not improbable that some scrupulous people might be apt to censure such a practice, (although indeed very unjustly) as a little bordering upon cruelty, which, I confess, hath always been with me the strongest objection against any project, how well soever intended.

But in order to justify my friend, he confessed that this expedient was put into his head by the famous Salmanaazor, a native of the island Formosa, who came from thence to London, above twenty years ago, and in conversation told my friend, that in his country, when any young person happened to be put to death, the executioner sold the carcass to persons of quality, as a prime dainty; and that, in his time, the body of a plump girl of fifteen, who was crucified for an attempt to poison the Emperor, was sold to his imperial majesty's prime minister of state, and other great mandarins of the court in joints from the gibbet, at four hundred crowns. Neither indeed can I deny, that if the same use were made of several plump young girls in this town, who without one single groat to their fortunes, cannot stir abroad without a chair, and appear at a play-house and assemblies in foreign fineries which they never will pay for; the kingdom would not be the worse.

Some persons of a desponding spirit are in 20 great concern about that vast number of poor people, who are aged, diseased, or maimed; and I have been desired to employ my thoughts what course may be taken, to ease the nation of so grievous an incumbrance. But I am not in the least pain upon that matter, because it is very well known, that they are every day dying, and rotting, by cold and famine, and filth, and vermin, as fast as can be reasonably expected. And as to the young labourers, they are now in almost as hopeful a condition. They cannot get work, and consequently pine away from want of nourishment, to a degree, that if at any time they are accidentally hired to common labour, they have not strength to perform it, and thus the country and themselves are happily delivered from the evils to come.

I have too long digressed, and therefore shall return to my subject. I think the advantages by the proposal which I have made are obvious and many, as well as of the highest importance.

For first, as I have already observed, it would greatly lessen the number of Papists, with whom we are yearly over-run, being the principal breeders of the nation, as well as our most dangerous enemies, and who stay at home on purpose with a design to deliver the kingdom to the Pretender, hoping to take their advantage by the absence of so many good Protestants, who have chosen rather to leave their country, than stay at home and pay tithes against their conscience to an episcopal curate.

Secondly, The poorer tenants will have something valuable of their own, which by law may be made liable to a distress, and help to pay their landlord's rent, their corn and cattle being already seized, and money a thing unknown.

Thirdly, Whereas the maintainance of an hundred thousand children, from two years old, and upwards, cannot be computed at less than ten shillings a piece per annum, the nation's stock will be thereby encreased fifty thousand pounds per annum, besides the profit of a new dish, introduced to the tables of all gentlemen of fortune in the kingdom, who have any refinement in taste. And the money will circulate among ourselves, the goods being entirely of our own growth and manufacture.

Fourthly, The constant breeders, besides 25 the gain of eight shillings sterling per annum by the sale of their children, will be rid of the charge of maintaining them after the first year.

Fifthly, This food would likewise bring great custom to taverns, where the vintners will certainly be so prudent as to procure the best receipts for dressing it to perfection; and consequently have their houses frequented by all the fine gentlemen, who justly value themselves upon their knowledge in good eating; and a skilful cook, who understands how to oblige his guests, will contrive to make it as expensive as they please.

Sixthly, This would be a great inducement to marriage, which all wise nations have either encouraged by rewards, or enforced by laws and penalties. It would encrease the care and tenderness of mothers towards their children, when they were sure of a settlement for life to the poor babes, provided in some sort by the publick, to their annual profit instead of expence. We should soon see an honest emulation among the married women, which of them could bring the fattest child to the market. Men would become as fond of their wives, during the time of their pregnancy, as they are now of their mares in foal, their cows in calf, or sow when they are ready to farrow; nor offer to beat or kick them (as is too frequent a practice) for fear of a miscarriage.

Many other advantages might be enumerated. For instance, the addition of some thousand carcasses in our exportation of barrel'd beef: the propagation of swine's flesh, and improvement in the art of making good bacon, so much wanted among us by the great destruction of pigs, too frequent at our tables; which are no way comparable in taste or magnificence to a well grown, fat yearly child, which roasted whole will make a considerable figure at a Lord Mayor's feast, or any other publick entertainment. But this, and many others, I omit, being studious of brevity.

Supposing that one thousand families in this city, would be constant customers for infants' flesh, besides others who might have it at merry meetings, particularly at weddings and christenings, I compute that Dublin would take off annually about twenty thousand carcasses; and the rest of the kingdom (where probably they will be sold somewhat cheaper) the remaining eighty thousand.

I can think of no one objection that will pos- 30 sibly be raised against this proposal, unless it should be urged that the number of people will be thereby much lessened in the kingdom. This I freely own, and 'twas indeed one principal design in offering it to the world. I desire the reader will observe, that I calculate my remedy for this one individual Kingdom of Ireland, and for no other that ever was, is, or, I think, ever can be upon Earth. Therefore let no man talk to me of other expedients: Of taxing our absentees at five shillings a pound; Of using neither cloaths, nor houshold furniture, except what is of our own growth and manufacture; Of utterly rejecting the materials and instruments that promote foreign luxury; Of curing the expensiveness of pride, vanity, idleness, and gaming in our women; Of introducing a vein of parsimony, prudence, and temperance; Of learning to love our country, wherein we differ even from Laplanders, and the inhabitants of Topinamboo; Of quitting our animosities and factions, nor acting any longer like the Jews, who were murdering one another at the very moment their city was taken; Of being a little cautious not to sell our country and consciences for nothing; Of teaching landlords to have at least one degree of mercy towards their tenants. Lastly, of putting a spirit of honesty, industry, and skill into our shop-keepers, who, if a resolution could now be taken to buy only our native goods, would immediately unite to cheat and exact upon us in the price, the measure, and the goodness, nor could ever yet be brought to make one fair proposal of just dealing, though often and earnestly invited to it.

Therefore I repeat, let no man talk to me of these and the like expedients, 'till he hath at least some glympse of hope, that there will ever be some hearty and sincere attempt to put them into practice.

But, as to my self, having been wearied out for many years with offering vain, idle, visionary thoughts, and at length utterly despairing of success, I fortunately fell upon this proposal, which, as it is wholly new, so it hath something solid and real, of no expence and little trouble, full in our own power, and whereby we can incur no danger in disobliging England. For this kind of commodity will not bear exportation, and flesh being of too tender a consistence, to admit a long continuance in salt, although perhaps I could name a country, which would be glad to eat up our whole nation without it.

After all, I am not so violently bent upon my own opinion, as to reject any offer, proposed by wise men, which shall be found equally innocent, cheap, easy, and effectual. But before something of that kind shall be advanced in contradiction to my scheme, and offering a better, I desire the author or authors will be pleased maturely to consider two points. First, As things now stand, how they will be able to find food and raiment for a hundred thousand useless mouths and backs. And secondly, There being a round million of creatures in humane figure throughout this kingdom, whose whole subsistence put into a common stock would leave them in debt two million of pounds sterling; adding those who are beggars by profession to the bulk of farmers, cottagers and labourers, with their wives and children, who are beggars in effect; I desire those politicians who dislike my overture, and may perhaps be so bold to attempt an answer, that they will first ask the parents of these mortals, whether they would not at this day think it a great happiness to have been sold for food at a year old, in the manner I prescribe, and thereby have avoided such a perpetual scene of misfortunes, as they have since gone through, by the oppression of landlords, the impossibility of paying rent without money or trade, the want of common sustenance, with neither house nor cloaths to cover them from the inclemencies of the weather, and the most inevitable prospect of intailing the like, or greater miseries, upon their breed for ever.

I profess, in the sincerity of my heart, that I have not the least personal interest in endeavouring to promote this necessary work, having no other motive than the publick good of my country, by advancing our trade, providing for infants, relieving the poor, and giving some pleasure to the rich. I have no children, by which I can propose to get a single penny; the youngest being nine years old, and my wife past child-bearing.

A CLOSER LOOK AT
A Modest Proposal

1. How closely does Swift adhere to the main features and structure of a proposal? Point to specific passages where the author describes and analyzes the problem, explains the specific plan for solving the problem, and lists the benefits and costs of the plan. What other features of a modern proposal does this satire use?

2. *A Modest Proposal* uses irony to make its argument. In other words, Swift says one thing but means something entirely different. First, summarize what the narrator literally proposes. Then state what you believe Swift really meant for his readers to understand. Finally, describe some of the subtle strategies (such as style, evidence, structure, *ethos, pathos, logos*) Swift uses to make this supposed proposal feel real.

3. As discussed in Chapter 12, writers use proposals to convince readers that a specific plan will solve an important problem. If this is the case, then is *A Modest Proposal* really a proposal? Or is it a piece of writing that uses readers' expectations about proposals to achieve some other

purpose? In terms of its purpose, what genre does it most align with: a commentary, argument paper, rant, or some other genre? How does Swift's playing with the genre of the proposal help him (or hurt him) in terms of achieving his intended purpose?

IDEAS FOR
Writing

1. Imitating Swift's *A Modest Proposal*, write a mock proposal that on the surface makes a ludicrous proposition but actually criticizes or attacks some injustice or some policy you feel strongly about. Like Swift, you should fashion your mock proposal so that it closely resembles the proposal genre. Include a reflective memo to your professor that describes your true intentions and purpose. This memo should also describe the proposal strategies that you used to play with this genre.

2. Write a rhetorical analysis of Jonathan Swift's *A Modest Proposal*. Be sure to define Swift's rhetorical purpose. Is he trying to persuade, and if so, to what beliefs or position? Or is he merely trying to entertain? Or is it some combination? Also, describe the rhetorical strategies that are used. Focus on just one or two rhetorical strategies, such as *ethos, pathos, logos,* or style. Finally, evaluate the work: How effectively does it engage its readers and achieve its rhetorical purpose?

With 7 Billion on Earth, a Huge Task Before Us

JEFFREY D. SACHS

Jeffery D. Sachs, professor of health policy and management and director of the Earth Institute at Columbia University, is a world leader on international economics, sustainability, and poverty alleviation. As you read this brief proposal, written for CNN.com, pay attention to the way he analyzes the global problem we are facing, the methods he uses to convince his readers of its importance, and his proposed solutions.

Just 12 years after the arrival of the 6 billionth individual on the planet in 1999, humanity will greet the 7 billionth arrival this month. The world population continues its rapid ascent, with roughly 75 million more births than deaths each year. The consequences of a world crowded with 7 billion people are enormous. And unless the world population stabilizes during the 21st century, the consequences for humanity could be grim.

A rising population puts enormous pressures on a planet already plunging into environmental catastrophe. Providing food, clothing, shelter, and energy for 7 billion people is a task of startling complexity.

The world's agricultural systems are already dangerously overstretched. Rainforests are being cut down to make way for new farms; groundwater used for irrigation is being depleted; greenhouse gases emitted from agricultural activities are a major factor in global climate change; fertilizers are poisoning estuaries; and countless species are threatened with extinction as we grab their land and water and destroy their habitats.

The economic challenges are equally huge. Population is growing most rapidly in the world's poorest countries—often the places with the most fragile ecological conditions. Poor people tend to have many more children, for several reasons. Many live on farms, where children can be engaged in farm chores.

Poor societies generally suffer from high 5 rates of child mortality, leading parents to have more children as "insurance" against the possible deaths of children. Girls rarely make it to high school, and are often married at a very young age, leading to early childbearing. And modern methods of contraception may be unavailable or unaffordable.

When poor families have six or eight children, many or most of them are virtually condemned to a lifetime of poverty. Too often, parents lack the wherewithal to provide decent nutrition, health care and education to most of them. Illiteracy and ill health end up being passed from generation to generation. Governments in poor countries are unable to keep up, their budgets overmatched by the need for new schools, roads and other infrastructure.

So the arrival of the 7 billionth person is cause for profound global concern. It carries a challenge: What will it take to maintain a planet in which each person has a chance for a full, productive and prosperous life, and in which the planet's resources are sustained for future generations? How, in short, can we enjoy "sustainable development" on a very crowded planet?

The answer has two parts, and each portends a difficult journey over several decades.

The first part requires a change of technologies—in farming, energy, industry, transport and building—so that each of us on average is putting less environmental stress on the planet. We will have to make a worldwide transition, for example, from today's fossil-fuel era, dependent on coal, oil and gas, to an era powered by low-carbon energies such as the sun and wind. That will require an unprecedented degree of global cooperation.

The second key to sustainable development is the stabilization of the global population. This is already occurring in high-income and even some middle-income countries, as families choose to have one or two children on average. The reduction of fertility rates should be encouraged in the poorer countries as well. Rapid and wholly voluntary reductions of fertility have been and can be achieved in poor countries. Success at reducing high fertility rates depends on keeping girls in school, ensuring that children survive, and providing access to modern family planning and contraceptives.

Two centuries ago, the British thinker 10 Thomas Robert Malthus famously warned that excessive population growth would cut short economic progress. That is a threat still with us today, but it is a warning, not an inevitable outcome.

We face an urgent task: to adopt more sustainable technologies and lifestyles, and work harder to achieve a stable population of some 8 billion or so by mid-century, rather than the current path, which could easily carry the world to more than 10 billion people by 2100.

A CLOSER LOOK AT
With 7 Billion on Earth, a Huge Task Before Us

1. This proposal, though very brief, follows the classic proposal structure closely. Turn to the At-A-Glance section at the beginning of Chapter 12 and mark the places where Sachs introduces the topic and problem, describes and analyzes the problem, proposes a plan, and concludes by looking to the future. Which features get the most attention? Which features could use more explanation?

2. Proposals need to show readers that the problems they address are serious and deserve attention. How does Sachs argue for such importance? Describe his argumentative strategies in terms of *ethos, pathos,* and *logos* (consult Chapter 22, "Using Argumentative Strategies"). How effective are his strategies? What other strategies could he have used to convince his readers of his topic's importance?

3. Sachs does not go into much detail about the costs and benefits of his proposed two-part plan. Do you think his plan is feasible? What are the costs and benefits associated with his plan?

IDEAS FOR
Writing

1. Write a rhetorical analysis that explains whether Sachs's proposal successfully meets the writing situation at hand. Be sure to consider the audience and their reading situation (reading this on a website) and how well the brevity meets that situation. How well does Sachs accomplish his overall purpose?

2. In his work as director of the Earth Institute, Jeffrey Sachs attempts to find solutions to enormous global problems. Write a profile of a person who is tackling a major social, political, or economic problem, such as poverty, justice, education, sustainability, and so forth. (You could also profile a group of people or an organization.) Describe the values that motivate your subject and explain what makes your subject interesting and inspiring.

A FEW IDEAS FOR
Composing a Proposal

1. **Write a proposal to solve a hometown problem.** List five things that irritated you about the place where you grew up. Choose one. Then define the problem or irritation and figure out its causes and effects. Develop a plan for solving that problem and offer a step-by-step solution. Conclude your proposal by explaining why the costs of your plan are worth the benefits of solving the problem. Your proposal should be written for publication in a local newspaper where you grew up.

2. **Write a "modest proposal" of your own.** If you run an Internet search, you will find many proposals titled "A Modest Proposal." Most of them are modeled in some way on Jonathan Swift's *A Modest Proposal*, a satire in which he suggests an absurd solution to a real problem. Write your own modest proposal in which you suggest an absurd solution to a serious problem in your community.

3. **Create a podcast proposal for improving your life.** What are the causes and effects of the problem? What would you need to do to fix this aspect of your life? What would be some of the benefits if you followed your plan, and what would be the costs? Although you are the primary reader of this proposal, write it so that others will understand what you are trying to accomplish. Then turn your proposal into a podcast, so you can listen to it in the future.

Go to **My WritingLab** to complete this chapter's exercises and test your understanding of its objectives.

CHAPTER 41

Reports

The NSDUH Report:
Major Depressive Episode among Full-Time College Students and Other Young Adults, Aged 18 to 22

The series of NSDUH reports offers the latest research on issues involving mental illness, especially involving illnesses related to substance abuse. While reading this report, pay attention to how the authors use their findings to support their conclusions about depression among college students.

In Brief

- Combined data for the years 2008 to 2010 show that 8.4 percent of full-time college students aged 18 to 22 and 8.2 percent of other young adults (part-time college students and those not currently enrolled in college) aged 18 to 22 experienced a major depressive episode (MDE) in the past year

- Although both groups had similar rates of past year MDE, other young adults with MDE were more likely than full-time college students with past year MDE to report that the mood related to their MDE very severely impaired their important activities and relationships and to report that they experienced more than 60 days in the past year when they were totally unable to carry out their normal activities

- Despite greater severity of symptoms among other young adults with MDE, both groups were equally likely to receive specialty mental health treatment (43.9 vs. 40.4 percent)

Tragic events on college campuses in recent years and a growing awareness of the significance of prevention and early intervention for mental disorders have focused new attention on the mental health needs of young adults. Research indicates that about half of Americans will meet the criteria for a disorder from the *Diagnostic and Statistical Manual of Mental Disorders*, fourth edition (DSM-IV),[1] sometime in their lifetime, with first onset usually in childhood or adolescence.[2] New information from the National Survey on Drug Use and Health (NSDUH) regarding the prevalence and severity of mental health disorders among young adults who are in college and among those who are not in college (and about whom less is generally known) can therefore be very useful to policy makers and behavioral health providers.

Using combined data from the NSDUH for 2008 to 2010, this issue of *The NSDUH Report* focuses on the prevalence of past year major depressive episode (MDE) among college students and other young adults (part-time college students and those not currently enrolled in college) aged 18 to 22.[3] The report compares the prevalence of MDE for these two groups by gender and race/ethnicity. The extent to which full-time college students and other young adults aged 18 to 22 with MDE report that their symptoms interfere with their important activities and their personal relationships (based on the Sheehan Disability Scale, or SDS) is also described.[4] The report also indicates the proportion of each group that reported that they received specialty mental health treatment.[5]

For this analysis, respondents were classified as college students if they reported that they were in their first through fourth year (or higher) at a college or university and that they were a full-time student. Respondents who were on break from college were considered enrolled if they intended to return to college or university when the break ended.

MDE by Demographic Characteristics

Combined data from the 2008 to 2010 NSDUH surveys show that 8.4 percent of full-time college students aged 18 to 22 experienced MDE in the past year; similarly, 8.2 percent of other young adults aged 18 to 22 experienced MDE in the past year. For both full-time college students and other young adults aged 18 to 22, females were more likely than males to have had a past year MDE (Table 1). Among full-time college students, 12.0 percent of females had a past year MDE compared with 4.5 percent of males;

TABLE 1 Major Depressive Episode (MDE) in the Past Year among Persons Aged 18 to 22, by Full-Time College Status and Demographic Characteristics: Percentages, 2008 to 2010

Demographic Characteristic	Full-Time College Students (%)	Other Young Adults (%)
Total	8.4	8.2
Aged 18 to 20	8.2	8.1
Aged 21 to 22	8.6	8.3
Male	4.5	5.5*
Female	12.0	11.3
Non-Hispanic White	8.4	9.4
Non-Hispanic Black	7.4	6.2
Non-Hispanic American Indian/Alaska Native	–	4.6
Non-Hispanic Native Hawaiian or Other Pacific Islander	–	–
Non-Hispanic Asian	6.3	4.2
Non-Hispanic Persons of Two or More Races	17.6	17.8
Hispanic	9.1	6.4*

*The difference between full-time college students and other young adults was statistically significant at the .05 level.
– Estimate not reported due to low precision.
Source: 2008 to 2010 SAMHSA National Surveys on Drug Use and Health (NSDUHs).

among other young adults aged 18 to 22, 11.3 percent of females had a past year MDE, compared with 5.5 percent of males. No differences were observed with regard to age (18 to 20 year olds vs. 21 to 22 year olds) for either full-time college students or other young adults.

The prevalence of MDE differed by racial/ethnic categories. Among full-time college students, the percentage with past year MDE ranged from 6.3 percent among Asians to 17.6 percent among persons of two or more races. Among other young adults aged 18 to 22, the rates of past year MDE ranged from 4.2 percent among Asians to 17.8 percent among persons of

two or more races. Hispanic full-time college students were more likely than other Hispanic young adults to have had past year MDE (9.1 vs. 6.4 percent).

Reported Severity of Symptoms

Although the overall proportion of individuals aged 18 to 22 with past year MDE was similar among full-time college students and other young adults, differences between the two groups were apparent in the severity of depressive symptoms and in the degree to which symptoms impaired important activities and relationships (Table 2). For example, 8.2 percent

TABLE 2 Severity of Impairment due to Symptoms of Depression among Persons Aged 18 to 22 with Past Year Major Depressive Episode (MDE), by Full-Time College Status: Percentages, 2008 to 2010

Severity of Impairment	Full-Time College Students (%)	Other Young Adults (%)
Home Management: No Interference	6.5	3.0*
Home Management: Mild	23.3	21.7
Home Management: Moderate	43.0	40.3
Home Management: Severe	23.0	28.1*
Home Management: Very Severe	4.1	6.9*
Ability to Work: No Interference	6.0	6.5
Ability to Work: Mild	31.4	28.5
Ability to Work: Moderate	39.9	38.1
Ability to Work: Severe	19.2	20.5
Ability to Work: Very Severe	3.5	6.4
Close Relationships: No Interference	2.7	2.4
Close Relationships: Mild	19.4	18.3
Close Relationships: Moderate	31.6	33.4
Close Relationships: Severe	38.0	32.9*
Close Relationships: Very Severe	8.2	13.0*
Social Life: No Interference	3.1	3.7
Social Life: Mild	16.9	15.0
Social Life: Moderate	32.2	35.8
Social Life: Severe	39.2	32.2*
Social Life: Very Severe	8.6	13.3*

* The difference between full-time college students and other young adults was statistically significant at the .05 level.
Source: 2008 to 2010 SAMHSA National Surveys on Drug Use and Health (NSDUHs).

FIGURE 1 Maximum Level of Severity of Impairment due to Symptoms of Depression among Persons Aged 18 to 22 with Past Year Major Depressive Episode (MDE), by Full-Time College Status: 2008 to 2010

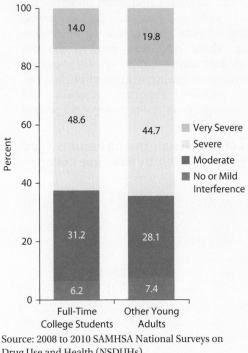

Source: 2008 to 2010 SAMHSA National Surveys on Drug Use and Health (NSDUHs).

FIGURE 2 Number of Days in the Past Year Unable to Carry Out Normal Activities due to Symptoms of Depression among Persons Aged 18 to 22 with Past Year Major Depressive Episode (MDE), by Full-Time College Status: 2008 to 2010

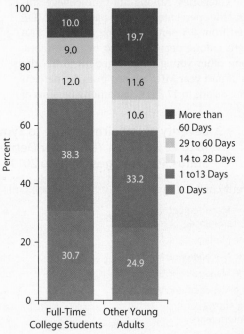

Source: 2008 to 2010 SAMHSA National Surveys on Drug Use and Health (NSDUHs).

of full-time college students reported that they experienced very severe impairment in their ability to maintain close relationships, whereas 13.0 percent of other young adults reported this level of impairment.

Among full-time college students aged 18 to 22 with past year MDE, 14.0 percent reported that the maximum severity level of their MDE was very severe (Figure 1).[6] Among other young adults aged 18 to 22, however, the percentage reporting that the maximum severity level of their MDE was very severe was 19.8 percent. Although only 10.0 percent of full-time college students aged 18 to 22 with past year MDE reported that there were more than 60 days in the past year when they were totally unable to carry out normal activities, for other young adults aged 18 to

22, this percentage was 19.7 percent (Figure 2). Similarly, 30.7 percent of full-time college students with past year MDE reported there were no days in the past year when they were totally unable to carry out their normal activities, but only 24.9 percent of other young adults reported that this was the case.

Receipt of Specialty Mental Health Treatment

Full-time college students aged 18 to 22 with past year MDE and other young adults with past year MDE were equally likely to receive specialty mental health treatment in the past year (43.9 and 40.4 percent, respectively) (Figure 3). The percentage of full-time college students aged 18

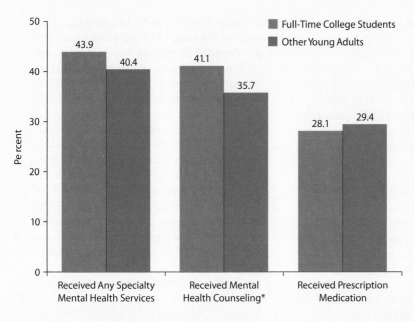

FIGURE 3 Receipt of Specialty Mental Health Treatment in the Past Year among Persons Aged 18 to 22 with Past Year Major Depressive Episode (MDE), by Full-Time College Status: 2008 to 2010

* The difference between full-time college students and other young adults is statistically significant at the .05 level.

Source: 2008 to 2010 SAMHSA National Surveys on Drug Use and Health (NSDUHs).

to 22 with past year MDE who received specialty mental health counseling was slightly higher than the percentage of other young adults with past year MDE who received mental health counseling (41.1 vs. 35.7 percent).

However, full-time college students and other young adults with past year MDE were almost equally likely to receive prescription medication for their MDE (28.1 and 29.4 percent, respectively).

Discussion

Overall, the prevalence of past year MDE was similar among full-time college students and other young adults aged 18 to 22 (8.4 and 8.2 percent, respectively). However, other young adults aged 18 to 22 with MDE were generally more likely to report that the mood related to their MDE very severely impaired their important activities and relationships and were also more likely than full-time college students to report a higher number of days in the past year during which they were unable to carry out their normal activities because of MDE. Despite the reported greater severity of their symptoms, full-time college students with MDE and other young adults aged 18 to 22 with MDE were equally likely to receive specialty mental health

treatment, although other young adults were more likely than full-time college students to have received mental health counseling.

Considerable controversy surrounds the question of whether rates of psychiatric disorders and mental health treatment differ between college students and their peers who do not attend college.[7] Although much attention has been focused on the mental health problems and service needs of full-time college students, the results presented here suggest that other young adults aged 18 to 22 experience similar, and possibly more serious, mental health issues. It is possible that the reason for this is that young adults aged 18 to 22 who are not full-time college students experience different kinds of stresses related to employment (and unemployment) or family responsibilities. These factors may contribute to the increased severity of MDE symptoms and greater functional impairment reported by these other young adults. Further, it is possible that full-time college students are more likely than other young adults aged 18 to 22 to have access to health insurance and/or to specialty mental health and other medical and support services provided by their colleges. The mental health problems and treatment needs of young adults aged 18 to 22 who are not full-time college students may thus warrant increased investigation and attention.

End Notes

1. American Psychiatric Association. (1994). *Diagnostic and statistical manual of mental disorders* (4th ed.). Washington, DC: Author.

2. Kessler, R. C., Berglund, P., Demler, O., Jin, R., Merikangas, K. R., & Walters, E. E. (2005). Lifetime prevalence and age-of-onset distributions of DSM-IV disorders in the National Comorbidity Survey Replication. *Archives of General Psychiatry, 62*(6), 593-602.

3. MDE is defined using diagnostic criteria in the DSM-IV, which specifies a period of 2 weeks or longer during which there is either depressed mood or loss of interest or pleasure and at least four other symptoms that reflect a change in functioning, such as problems with sleep, eating, energy, concentration, and self-image. In assessing MDE, no exclusions were made for MDE caused by medical illness, bereavement, or substance use disorders.

4. The Sheehan Disability Scale (SDS) measures the impact of MDE on a person's life. The SDS asks adults aged 18 or older to give a rating of 0 to 10 (with 10 being the highest) for the level of impairment caused by the disorder in each of four role domains: (1) home management, (2) work, (3) close relationships with others, and (4) social life. Respondents with unknown severity of SDS role impairment data or for whom particular activities were not applicable were excluded.

5. Treatment for depression is defined as seeing or talking to a doctor or other professional or using prescription medication in the past year for depression.

6. Maximum severity is defined as the highest level of impairment caused by the disorder in any one of the four role domains. For example, if an individual reported no impairment in three of the role domains and a 7 in the fourth role domain, the maximum severity value would be 7.

7. Blanco, C., Okuda, M., Wright, C., Hasin, D. S., Grant, B. F., Liu, S. M., & Olfson, M. (2008). Mental health of college students and their non-college attending peers: Results from the National Epidemiologic Study on Alcohol and Related Conditions. *Archives of General Psychiatry, 65*(12), 1429-1437.

A CLOSER LOOK AT
Major Depressive Episode among Full-Time College Students and Other Young Adults, Aged 18 to 22

1. This report is rather complex and includes many statistics. With your group, identify the three major findings in this report.

2. As the report suggests, depression is a problem for some college students. What are the some of the implications of depression in their lives?

3. On the Internet, find some treatment options to manage depression in college-aged students. Identify three resources at your college for helping students who are experiencing depression.

IDEAS FOR
Writing

1. Using the findings in this report, write a commentary in which you argue that more attention should be paid to depression-related issues involving college students.

2. On the Internet, research other mental illnesses that tend to affect college-aged students. Choose one of these conditions for further study. Write a report in which you discuss this mental illness and how it can be treated, paying special attention to treatment options for college-aged students.

7 Days on Craigslist's Casual Encounters

SAMUEL AXON

Samuel Axon, the Digital Entertainment Reporter at the online magazine Mashable, *takes an empirical approach to finding out who uses and what really happens at the "hookup" section of Craigslist, the best-known national online network of classified advertising. Although this report does not follow the classic organization and style of the report, notice how Axon stretches the genre to fit his readers' needs and values.* **Caution: As a student, you should not conduct an online experiment like this one, because posing as someone else online might be dangerous or violate your university's research ethics policies.**

Many people use Craigslist to find roommates, cheap furniture, used cars or part-time jobs. But there's another function: Sex.

I decided to dive into Craigslist's "Casual Encounters"—a section made for no-strings hookups—to see if any of what I assumed about that virtual place was true. Is it populated entirely by perverted sexual deviants, serial killers, prostitutes and scammers as rumors insist? Or can two regular people really make the connection that the section's name suggests?

I should admit that I had no intention to actually hook up with someone, should the opportunity arise, if for no other reason than it would be inappropriate and manipulative to an unwitting partner to do so and write about it. But it's not a stretch to say that even if you abstain from the goal, spending a week on Casual Encounters can teach you a lot about human beings and how the web has changed how we pursue one of our most essential and important desires.

It goes without saying that the content of this article is not intended for children or those made uncomfortable by such topics. But if you're interested, read on for the story of my seven days on Craigslist's Casual Encounters— my failures, near misses, discoveries, insights and successes. Following that, I interviewed two women to learn how they used the site successfully for their own fulfillment.

The Experiment

I began with a listing announcing myself to the 5 women of my city.

Each day I tried a different approach to see what would be most effective, though I never lied or posted fake photographs. One day my message was intended to be sweet and normal; I suggested starting with drinks and fun conversation to see if we had chemistry, then going back to my place to cuddle on the couch with a movie and see where that led. Another day, I described it as a rebound. In yet another, I explicitly detailed sexual activities and used very aggressive language.

Ultimately, only the "sweet and normal" was successful, even though very few posts by women had that same tone (more on that later). I received about a half-dozen responses each day. Most were scams, some were men, some were prostitutes, and just one was legit.

Barking Up the Wrong Tree

All the responses I got from real people on my first day weren't from women—they were from men. I made it very clear in my post that I was only interested in women, but a large number of men chose to ignore that.

They all offered oral sex. I responded to them politely, saying, "Just interested in women, but thanks for the offer! Have a good one." Most didn't write back after that. One responded: "Really man, can be cool and relaxing."

I began to suspect that no women actually 10 used the site. The stereotype is that women are interested in relationships, and that only men would be interested in totally casual sex, right? We know that's not true, though. In fact, I was inspired to write this article when a friend told me many of her female friends had owned up to using it.

But where were they? I was only getting messages from gay or bisexual men!

An Army of Scammers

Over the next couple of days, I actually received a lot of posts from women. Or at least, they said they were women. To be honest, I doubted the veracity of the claims.

It didn't take long to realize that almost all the replies I received were scams. The situation is so severe on Craigslist Casual Encounters that posts by real women who are actually seeking hook-ups are often flagged for removal at the slightest cause for suspicion.

The most common scams are "safe dating" websites. An alleged woman will write a man saying she's interested, but that because of the Craigslist-based serial killers and rapists in the news, she needs some extra assurance that it's safe. If you follow the link she provides, the website asks you for your credit card number—y'know, so it can do a background check to make sure you're not a criminal. Right.

My favorite scam: One individual tried to get 15 me to buy him or her virtual currency in online games like MapleStory before agreeing to hand over contact information. Yeah, right—moving on!

Taking Initiative

What little luck I'd had so far. The week was half over and I hadn't had a single bite. I decided I would have to take the initiative, so in addition to posting my own ads, I started responding to every ad from any woman who seemed at all interesting.

I cast a wide net in my searches, looking up posts by straight or bisexual women between the ages of 18 and 35 who lived anywhere in Chicagoland—a large metropolitan area that's home to close to five million females. Most of the women wanted something very specific they couldn't find in their normal lives: Someone to help play out a particular fantasy, someone vastly older than them or someone of another race.

Very few of the women who were advertising seemed to be looking for anything I would consider a "normal encounter." Nevertheless, I tailored each response to whatever they were looking for. I typically wrote two or three paragraph replies and matched the tone of their own messages, then attached a couple of tasteful photos of myself.

I didn't get a single reply from an actual prospect this way. It turned out that most of the ads were fakes from scammers, and quite a few fell into another category all together.

Love ~~Don't~~ Does Cost a Thing

Prostitution is what made Craigslist controver- 20 sial. There's technically another section for that—"Adult Services," formerly "Erotic Services"—but that's not the only place you'll find practitioners of the world's oldest profession.

The prostitutes of Craigslist speak in code, but it's not a difficult one to learn. They advertise "French lessons"—an odd thing to advertise under "Casual Encounters," don't you think? Well, it's obviously a euphemism for something else. Many of the ads that weren't from scammers were from prostitutes.

The ads are so obvious that it's surprising the euphemisms are effective in fending off law enforcement. Then again, maybe they *are* law enforcement. What a mess!

Success?

Amidst all those failures, I had one near-success. A woman wrote in response to my sweet "cuddling first" ad saying she was in town for only a couple of months, and that she was frustrated she couldn't find a relationship. When she sent her pictures, she looked plain but attractive.

We exchanged a couple of e-mails over the course of two hours, tossing back and forth lists of interests and the like. She made it clear that she wanted to meet up, and while she talked about starting slow, it was clear that it would indeed be a casual encounter. But when I suggested a time to meet—the last message from me before I would reveal myself and back out—there was no reply.

At least, not yet. The next day, she e-mailed 25 me saying she was deeply apologetic and that she'd fallen asleep. She said she'd like to meet up sometime. So yes, there are women on Craigslist. Well, at least one!

The Other Perspective, Part 1: My Fake Female Ad

You've probably guessed by now that the experiences for heterosexual men and women on Craigslist's casual encounters are quite different.

I observed that for every ad a woman posts, there are at least 20 from men. If nothing else, that imbalance ought to alter the experience.

To get the female perspective, I did two things: I posted a fake ad as a woman to see what kinds of responses I would get, and I interviewed two women who have had success hooking up on casual encounters in the past. First, the ad.

"I just broke up with my boyfriend and while it was the right thing to do, it's been rough because I still have all this physical passion and sexual energy and I don't know where to direct it," I wrote. "I feel this is the best way because I don't want to hurt him by hooking up with someone we both know."

As for potential suitors, I asked only that they supply a photo and "be attractive and not creepy." I clicked "post" and waited. There was a five minute delay before my ad appeared, then I started receiving about one response per minute.

Most of them were careful to say "I don't do 30 this often." Some were attractive, some weren't. Some sent pictures of themselves naked along with the word "Hi." Others wrote a single paragraph making it very clear just how normal and nice they thought they were, and included the sort of photo you would find on a Facebook profile. There were a lot of expressions of sympathy over my fake breakup. I was hearing from men of all types, and it seemed I had my pick of the litter.

After about thirty minutes, though, my post was flagged for removal. I thought I'd made it look legit, but as we learned earlier, folks have good reason to be hawkish about scammers.

The Other Perspective, Part 2: Interviews with Craigslist Women

After the end of my test run with Craigslist casual encounters, I decided to get more insight into the female experience with the site by interviewing two women who said they had successes meeting up with men on Casual Encounters.

Their problem was the opposite of mine. They had too many options to pick from, but they both dealt with the numerous choices in the same way.

Both women ultimately responded to men who they felt put effort into writing long, personal messages as opposed to quick notes. Multiple paragraphs of insightful and relatable prose won out—but only after the initial test of physical appearance. One said that only 5 to 10% of the men who responded to her ad made it past the initial, picture-based judgment. Both said they immediately eliminated men who opened with pictures of genitalia—a very common practice. However, looks were important.

My favorite anecdote: One of the women I 35 interviewed said she once had a crush on a client at her job, but couldn't make a move without compromising her professionalism. However, she was looking through Casual Encounters and saw an ad from a man, and she recognized his writing style—it was her old client! She sent him a message to see if it was him, asking a question only he would be able to answer. He proved his identity and they ended up hooking up.

One of the women said she would go to Casual Encounters when she was looking for a very specific sexual experience—something you can't always count on from a one night stand that starts at a club or bar. The other said her reasons could be summed up as "curiosity, boredom, and convenience." She also said "it's a safe way to reach out in ways you might be too shy to in person."

"There are a lot of shady people, or at least people doing shady things on Craigslist," one said. "But once you get over the embarrassment of actually posting or responding to something on Craigslist, it has the potential to be very rewarding. The trick is to keep an open mind and not have any real expectations. At the very least, it's mildly entertaining."

So What is Casual Encounters Really Like?

After all this exploration, I'll say that Craigslist casual encounters is a place where people go to find very specific things from each other that they might not be able to conveniently locate in the real world. Some of those things are very alternative.

It's a last, best hope for some people who are looking to make a personal connection, but it's full of spam, unwanted attention, crime, and, well . . . crazy people. You might not find what you're looking for, but you're sure to find something interesting regardless.

Put another way, Craigslist casual encoun- 40 ters is a sexual microcosm of the rest of the Internet.

A CLOSER LOOK AT
7 Days on Craigslist's Casual Encounters

1. Although this text may not look like some of the other reports in this section, it does conform to the genre's conventions in many ways. Make a list of the ways it does and does not conform.

2. Find the research question and the hypothesis. How clearly are these stated?

3. Axon takes an empirical approach to his research question by conducting a kind of "experiment." How does this approach make the report more or less interesting and persuasive?

IDEAS FOR
Writing

1. You should not do an experiment similar to the one Axon describes, because pretending you are someone else online could be dangerous. Also, you could violate other people's rights or your university's ethics codes for research. Write a commentary in which you discuss some of the ways in which posing as someone else online, especially on Web sites like Craigslist, could put a researcher in jeopardy or violate the rights of others.

2. Write a rhetorical analysis of "7 Days on Craigslist's Casual Encounters" that explains how well Axon achieves his purpose. First, go to Mashable.com and do a full audience analysis (as described in Chapter 3). Now write your rhetorical analysis, focusing on how Axon adapts and stretches the report genre to suit the attitudes, beliefs, and expectations of Mashable readers.

Freshman Fifteen: Fact or Fiction?

JENNIFER A. CARITHERS-THOMAS, SHELLEY H. BRADFORD, CHRISTOPHER M. KESHOCK, STEVEN F. PUGH

Published in the College Student Journal, *this research report examines the so-called "freshman fifteen," which refers to the average amount of weight students supposedly gain during their first year of college. The authors of this study used a survey to assess the accuracy of this widespread belief. As you read, pay attention to the way they frame their research question and the methods they use to answer it.*

Abstract

The present study examined the validity of the concept known as Freshman Fifteen. The sample included 52 freshman college students enrolled in a physical education class. Three issues were addressed: a) amount (if any) of weight gain during the first year in college, b) perceptions on the reasons for any weight gain, and c) strategies for losing unwanted weight gain. Results indicated that nearly two-thirds (62%) of the sample reported weight gain (M = 10.8 lbs.). These findings did not find strong support for the notion of Freshman Fifteen. Implications for college administrators were noted.

Introduction

The expression "Freshman Fifteen" is a term used to describe the weight gain by students during their first year of study in college (Thomas, 2006). This specific topic has been recently discussed by researchers, clinicians, and nutritionists. Brown (2008) reviewed the extant literature and found more than 140 newspaper articles about freshman weight gain, 20 peer reviewed articles, 141 university newspaper articles and 19 popular magazine articles on this issue, including eight books. A Google search of the term "Freshman Fifteen" yielded 7,630,000 links and articles specifically designed to provide advice, hints, and strategies to help college students avoid gaining the dreaded "Freshman Fifteen" (Google, 2009). With 1.5 million students entering United States colleges or universities each fall, the Freshman Fifteen could be considered an epidemic (Malinauskas, Auinger, & Klein 2006).

The purpose of this study was to validate or negate the premise that freshman college students are likely to gain 15 pounds during their first year of college. Moreover, this study asked respondents to identify the causes of weight gain peculiar to the freshman year and inquired about specific methods that can be implemented to control weight gain. This type of research is necessary to determine if weight gain occurs and, more importantly, what behaviors can be modified to diminish the probability of further weight gain. Furthermore, if the assertion is true that students gain weight, regardless of the specific amount of pounds, universities have an obligation to provide programs, resources, and services to educate their students about the concept of the Freshman Fifteen.

Review of the Literature

The seminal reference to the concept of the "Freshman Fifteen" was found in 1989 that chronicled a college freshman's fight against weight gain (see Brown, 2008). This 15 pounds of perceived weight gain that has been investigated, analyzed, evaluated, and debated for almost two decades and refers to the popular belief that students gain an average of 15 pounds during their first year of college (Hodge, Jackson, & Sullivan 1993). An extensive review of the literature validates that weight gain typically and predictably occurs; yet a weight gain of 15 pounds has not been substantiated by most research endeavors. Some research shows that the average weight gain to be only 8.8 pounds (Howell, Mewborn, Randle & Fowler-Johnson, 1985). A study by Hoffman, Policastro, Quick, and Lee (2006) found that a mean of 7 pounds is gained during the first year. In another study, 59% of the volunteers gained weight in their freshman year (Graham & Jones, 2000);

however, the amount of weight gained was calculated at 4.6 pounds (2000). A study conducted by researchers at Michigan State University revealed that of the 110 respondents, the average weight gain was 7 pounds, again substantially less than the predetermined 15 (Hodge et al., 1993). In fact, the authors concluded that the majority of the female students in the sample remained the same weight during their first six months of college. The Journal of American College Health reported that about 70% of students will gain a significant amount of weight between the start of college and the end of sophomore year (Jung, Bray, & Ginnis 2008). The researchers also found that the average weight gain is closer to 9 pounds as opposed to 15 pounds. Researchers studying men and women found that although both sexes gain weight, men appeared to gain more and experience a larger increase in body mass index (Mihalopoulous, Raedeke, Aeby, Smith, & Dallas 2008).

A recent study found that 90% of first year college students are aware of the freshman 15, yet many students chose to ignore the warning signs related to weight gain (Jung et al., 2008; Wyshak, 2007). The possible reasons of this superfluous weight gain are limitless in the college atmosphere. Many researchers suggest that this weight gain is attributed to the newfound freedom and accompanying stress associated with the shift to college life. Other researchers claim that the excess weight gain is due to an increase in caloric consumption through the intake of alcohol and unhealthy snacking (Jung et al., 2008).

Moreover, few personal characteristics have been found to distinguish women who gain, lose, or maintain their weight. In fact, contrary to predictions, self-esteem, body image, and locus of control were unconnected to weight change among women who gained weight (Hodge et al., 1993). Yet, those women who lost weight and evaluated their appearance, fitness, and health more positively lose less weight. This suggests that a favorable body image may mitigate against a pursuit of slimness (Hodge et al., 1993).

Method

Participants

The participants of this study were students who had completed their freshman year of college at the University of South Alabama. The sample comprised 52 female and male students who were enrolled in tennis and weight training physical education courses.

Instrumentation

Previous researchers who had studied the "Freshman Fifteen" concept had collected measurements such as height and weight, body mass, percentage of body fat, total fat mass, and waist and hip circumferences (Jung et al., 2006; Morrow et al., 2006). The current survey measure sought specific information about the amount of weight gain, loss, or maintenance during a student's freshman year. Another section asked students about factors that contributed to weight gain such as late night snacking, drinking, stress, and social eating. A final section asked students to identify the specific approaches they utilized to lose weight (if they acknowledged that weight had been gained); for example, dieting, increasing one's activity, making better food choices, and decreasing one's amount of stress. These data were collected during the Spring semester of 2009.

Results and Discussion

Nearly two-thirds of our sample admitted to weight gain during their freshman year. Of the 32 students (62%) who reported weight gain, the average weight gain of the respondents was 10.78 pounds (range 2 lbs.-28 lbs.). Only six students reported a weight gain exceeding 15 pounds. Of the 18 females sampled who reported weight gain, the average weight gain was 10.5 pounds. Of the 14 males sampled that gained weight, the average increase in weight was measured at 11.14 pounds. Nine students (17.3%) reported that they actually lost weight during their freshman year. The average amount of weight loss was 9.44 pounds (range 2-30 lbs.). Interestingly, eleven students (21.15%) reported maintaining their weight (7 males; 4 females). Participants identified the most plausible reason or reasons

TABLE 1 Major Factors Identified to Account for Weight Gain

Reasons	Percentage
Late-night snacking	20.8
Cafeteria food selection	12.9
Social eating	11.9
Irregular schedule	11.9
General stress	10.9
Decreased activity	10.9
Lack of "healthy foods"	8.9
Social drinking	6.9

for their weight gain. Table 1 presents the rank order of critical factors.

Participants noted several ways that they could lose their weight gain. Students identified increasing activity to be the best way to achieve weight loss (25.24%). Making better food choices (24.27%) and decreasing the amount of fast food consumed (19.42%) also ranked high on the list. In addition, students acknowledged the importance of decreasing snack ingestion (11.65%), dieting (10.68%), decreasing stress (3.88%), and decreasing the amount of drinking (2.91%); interestingly, less than one percent of our sample stated that they would use an over-the-counter diet pill.

The current findings indicated that a sizeable majority of college students gain weight as freshman; however, the amount of weight gain appears to be moderate (about 10 lbs.). Moreover, it seems that young college students are aware of the factors that contribute to their weight gain and various methods that can be implemented which should lead to weight loss.

Also, the current findings support prior research endeavors that reported that many freshman students do not gain weight. In fact, 24% of our sample was able to maintain their weight and 17% were able to lose weight. Further, our findings corroborate the conclusions of earlier research efforts on the "Freshman Fifteen" issue (e.g., Hoffman et al., 2005; Howell et al., 1985; Mihalopoulous et al., 2008).

Implications for College Administrators

College preventative programs that accentuated the importance of good nutrition, consistent exercise, and healthy behaviors could possibly reverse the propensity to gain weight. Dieticians or nutritionists could be more involved in planning meals in the cafeteria setting to provide healthier food selections, such as salads, wraps, and vegetables. Physical education courses could be required for all freshman students to promote the importance of exercise. Colleges could engage nurses or other health care providers to offer seminars on the health benefits of exercise and consistent physical activity in the prevention of chronic diseases associated with obesity. Additionally, colleges should provide exercise equipment and gym facilities that students could use daily in designated areas of student housing. Educational endeavors for all students should consider annual physicals and health fairs that stress proper nutrition, exercise, and the maintenance of healthy behaviors.

The current study has several limitations; for example, the sample size is small and was obtained from one educational setting. Future research should focus on longitudinal data regarding weight loss/gain and concomitant health behaviors that promote stable weight maintenance.

References

Brown, C. (2008). The information trail of "Freshman 15": A systematic review of health myth within the research and popular literature. *Health Information Library*, 25, 1–12.

Google. (2009). Freshman 15. Retrieved February 8, 2009 from www.google.com.

Graham, M., & Jones, A. (2000). Freshman 15; Valid theory or harmful myth? *Journal of American College Health*, 50, 171–173.

Hodge, C, Jackson, L., & Sullivan, L. (1993). The "Freshman 15" facts and fantasies about weight gain in college women. *Physiology of Women Quarterly*, 17, 119–126.

Hoffman, D. Policastro, P., Quick, V., & Lee, S. (2002). Changes in body weight and fat mass of men and women in the first year of college: A study of the "Freshman 15". *Journal of American College of Health*, 55, 52–55.

Howell, M. F., Mewbom, C. R., Randle, Y., & Fowler-Johnson, S. (1985). Risk of excess weight gain in university women: A 3 year community controlled analysis. *Addictive Behaviors*, 10, 15–28.

Jung, M., Bray, S., & Ginis, M. (2008). Behavior change and the Freshman 15: Tracking physical activity and dietary patterns in first-year university women. *Journal of American College Health*, 56, 523–530.

Malinauskas, B., Raedeke, T., Aeby, V., Smith, J., & Dallas, M. (2006). Dieting practices, weight perceptions and body composition: A comparison of normal weight, overweight, and obese college females. *Nutrition Journal*, 5, 11–15.

Mihalopoulos, N., Auinger, P., & Klein, J. (2008). The Freshman 15: Is it real? *Journal of American College Health*, 56, 531–533.

Morrow, M., Heesch, K., Dinger, M., Hull, H., Kneehans, A., & Fields, D. (2006). Freshman 15: Fact or fiction? *Obesity*, 74, 1438–43.

Thomas, J. (2006). Weight gain awareness. The Freshman 15: A nutrition student public speaking project. *Journal of Nutrition, Education and Behavior*, 38, 383–386.

Wyshak, G. (2007). Weight change, obesity, mental health, and health perception: Self-reports of college-educated women. *Primary Care Companion Journal of Clinical Psychiatry*. 9, 48–54.

A CLOSER LOOK AT
Freshman Fifteen: Fact or Fiction?

1. This study examines the accuracy of a belief that is commonly held among college students. List some other beliefs about college life that may or may not be true. How could you design a research study to assess the accuracy of those beliefs?

2. A report's research question should be addressed in its introduction. Reread the introduction, including "Review of the Literature." In a single complete sentence, state this report's research question as a question. Then, explain in your own words what is already known about the topic and why this research would be of interest to college students.

3. Consulting the methods section, describe the participants who were studied and how weight gain was assessed. Do you think this study's results accurately reflect how much weight change occurred and the causes for those changes? Why or why not?

IDEAS FOR
Writing

1. Write a rebuttal that argues that the findings of this research report cannot be entirely trusted. Pay special attention to limitations (weaknesses) of its methods. For instance, you might describe why the participants in this study may not be typical of all college students (hint: use the Internet to learn about "sampling bias"). You might also explain why using surveys may not reveal the truth about weight change or the causes of weight change. Finally, offer some ideas for improving the methods.

2. Write a brief memoir that describes how your dietary or exercise habits changed (or did not) when you first started college or some other new and stressful situation. Like all memoirs, yours should offer insight into the challenges that you faced as well as a main point (or lesson) that provides a new understanding for your readers.

More Than Just a Pretty Face: Men's Priority Shifts Toward Bodily Attractiveness in Short-term versus Long-term Mating Contexts

JAIME C. CONFER, CARIN PERILLOUX, DAVID M. BUSS

Biologists have long studied how various animal species choose their mates. For instance, why are peacocks with the longest tail (a disadvantage for escaping predators) chosen by mates more often than shorter-tailed peacocks? This scientific inquiry asks a similar question about humans: What physical characteristics influence men's and women's choices of partners, and does choice strategy vary across situations?

Abstract

Studies of physical attractiveness have long emphasized the constituent features that make faces and bodies attractive, such as symmetry, skin texture, and waist-to-hip ratio. Few studies, however, have examined the reproductively relevant cues conveyed by faces and bodies as whole units. Based on the premise that fertility cues are more readily assessed from a woman's body than her face, the present study tested the hypothesis that men evaluating a potential short-term mate would give higher priority to information gleaned from her body, relative to her face, than men evaluating a potential long-term mate. Male and female participants (N = 375) were instructed to consider dating an opposite sex individual, whose face was occluded by a "face box" and whose body was occluded by a "body box," as a short-term or long-term mate. With the instruction that only one box could be removed to make their decision about their willingness to engage in the designated relationship with the occluded individual, significantly more men assigned to the short-term, compared to the long-term, mating condition removed the body box. Women's face versus body information choice, in contrast, was unaffected by the temporal dimension of the mating condition. These results suggest that men, but not women, have a

condition-dependent adaptive proclivity to prioritize facial cues in long-term mating contexts, but shift their priorities toward bodily cues in short-term mating contexts.

1. Introduction

The importance of physical attractiveness and the biological correlates of various attributes has received much empirical attention since Darwin (1871) noted the precedence given to physical attractiveness, especially in women: "In civilized life man is largely, but by no means exclusively, influenced in the choice of his wife by external appearance" (p. 738). Despite much research having been devoted to attractiveness, most studies have focused on the specific features that contribute to overall attractiveness (for a review, see Sugiyama, 2005). Symmetry (Perrett et al., 1999), averageness (Langlois & Roggman, 1990; but see Grammer & Thornhill, 1994 for sex-specific effects), and sexual dimorphism (Johnston, Hagel, Franklin, Fink, & Grammer, 2001) have been shown to affect facial attractiveness. Contributors to bodily attractiveness include waist-to-hip-ratio (Singh, 1993) and body mass index (Tovée, Maisey, Emery, & Cornelissen, 1999). Other specific bodily traits, such as muscularity (Frederick & Haselton, 2007), breast size (Furnham & Swami, 2007), and leg length

(Sorokowski & Pawlowski, 2008) have been the focus of recent empirical research. Lacking, however, is research on the relative importance of faces and bodies as whole units, and whether the prioritization of facial or bodily attractiveness is dependent upon the intended duration of the mating context (short-term versus long-term mating)—a context of well-documented importance in mate preferences (Buss & Schmitt, 1993).

Aspects of physical attractiveness have been hypothesized to be "attractive" because they have been recurrently and closely associated with individuals' health, age, and hormonal status throughout human evolutionary history (Symons, 1979; Williams, 1975). Certain fitness-dependent cues relating to a woman's *current fertility* and her *reproductive value* (a measure of *future* reproductive potential that is strongly correlated with a woman's age) are conveyed through the face and body with substantial overlap. For example, a woman's current fertility can be assessed through increases in facial (Roberts et al., 2004) and bodily attractiveness (Kirchengast & Gartner, 2002) that occur at ovulation. Similarly, health-correlated cues of reproductive value can be conveyed through both the face and the body. Pocked-marked facial skin, for example, reveals a history of disease (Buss, 1994), while increased leg length is correlated with a multitude of health benefits: lower risks of cardiovascular disease (Gunnell, Whitley, et al., 2003), diabetes (Davey Smith et al., 2001) and cancer (Gunnell, May, Ben-Sholomo, Yarnell, & Smith, 2003). Finally, age-dependent cues also related to reproductive value, such as taut facial skin and firm breasts (Symons, 1979), can be diagnosed through a woman's face and body. Clearly, information regarding a woman's fertility and reproductive value can be gleaned from both her face and body.

Nevertheless, one component, the face or the body, may convey relatively richer information about a particular health or hormonal status variable than the other. Thus, our central hypothesis is that *although many cues regarding a woman's health and fertility can be gleaned from both her face and her body, each component conveys a subset of cues that are not conveyed by the other component.* The results of several studies have indicated that the face and body make independent contributions toward overall attractiveness (e.g., Currie & Little, 2009; Peters, Rhodes, & Simmons, 2007), supporting the tenability of this basic premise. We hypothesized that a woman's face provides relatively richer information regarding her reproductive value; and conversely, that a woman's body conveys stronger cues to her current fertility. These two dimensions peak at different ages, necessitating a tradeoff such that one could not secure a woman who is simultaneously at the pinnacle of reproductive value and fertility. In human populations, reproductive value peaks around age 17, whereas fertility peaks around age 24 (Buss, 1994; Symons, 1979; Williams, 1975). Accordingly, Jones (1996) notes that ". . . male preferences may have led to the evolution both of cues in the female figure that advertise sexual maturity and of cues in the face that advertise youth" (p. 103; see also Symons, 1979).

Empirical evidence supports the premise that female faces and bodies provide information that is not entirely redundant. Facial features appear to be particularly effective cues of youth and health. Aside from obvious facial indicators of youth, such as homogeneous skin and the absence of wrinkles and sagginess (Fink, Grammer, & Thornhill, 2001), preferences have also been demonstrated for neotenous facial traits (e.g., large eyes; Cunningham, 1986). Features such as these are considered "feminine" because they are sensitive to the rise in estrogen levels that accompanies puberty and persists throughout a woman's reproductive lifespan (Thornhill & Gangestad, 2008). As women age and approach menopause, however, androgens increase relative to estrogen levels, causing their facial features to take a more masculine form (e.g., thinner lips; Gangestad & Scheyd, 2005), rendering specific facial features effective proxies for assessing a woman's age and consequently, her reproductive value.

Women's bodies provide a window to several variables related to their *current fertility* (as contrasted with reproductive value) that cannot be ascertained through their facial characteristics alone. A woman's body shape is subjected to what Singh (1993) refers to as a "wide first pass filter," a quick heuristic that unconsciously evaluates whether a woman is currently capable of conceiving. For example, information obtained from a woman's waist-to-hip ratio (WHR) informs three concerns paramount to a woman's reproductive condition: (1) pregnancy status, (2) fertility, and possibly, (3) ovulatory status. First, as a woman progresses through pregnancy, her WHR exceeds 1.0, a clear indication that she is currently incapable of conceiving. For example, a young pregnant woman has high reproductive value, but a fertility of zero. This highlights the fact that fertility and reproductive value are partially dissociable, and that bodily cues are a powerful source of information regarding current fertility. Second, women with unusually high WHRs have greater difficulty conceiving than women with sex-typical WHRs (Singh, 1993, Zaadstra et al., 1993); therefore, the hormonal profile necessary for conception can be assessed through a woman's WHR. Finally, based on evidence that women's WHRs may slightly decrease at ovulation (Kirchengast & Gartner, 2002), a woman's figure could also reveal whether or not she is at peak cycle fertility. In addition to waist-to-hip ratio, a woman's body mass index signals her ability to sustain pregnancy and lactation (Lake, Power, & Cole, 1997) as well as her supply of the fatty acids that support fetus neurodevelopment (Lassek & Gaulin, 2008). Bodily traits such as these can be appraised at a glance to assess a woman's current fertility.

Historically, a man's reproductive success depended in part on selecting a mate high in fertility with appreciable reproductive value. However, because there are substantial costs involved in exclusively attempting to secure such a woman (e.g., missed sexual opportunities), men typically make tradeoffs that depend on whether a short-term or long-term mate is sought. Theoretically, for men pursuing a short-term mate, a woman's current fertility is more paramount than her reproductive value (Buss & Schmitt, 1993). Thus, unlike men pursuing a long-term mating strategy, men pursuing short-term mating opportunities should possess evolved psychological mechanisms that are activated less by

cues to a woman's reproductive value than by cues to her current fertility. This logic formed the basis of our prediction: *Men assigned to evaluate a woman as a short-term mate would give higher priority to information gleaned from her body than from her face, compared to men assigned to evaluate a woman as a long-term mate.*

Although there is compelling evidence that both sexes have evolved short-term and long-term mating strategies (Buss & Schmitt, 1993), individuals naturally differ in the extent to which they pursue one mating strategy over another, a construct labeled sociosexual orientation (SOI-R) (Gangestad & Simpson, 1990). We hypothesized that SOI-R would affect the relative priority given to facial and bodily cues, in addition to the effect of the mating condition to which participants were assigned. Based on the same rationale for the assigned short-term and long-term mating contexts, we anticipated that those who naturally pursue short-term relationships (as measured by the SOI-R, with higher scores indicating less restricted SOI-R; Penke & Asendorpf, 2008) would assign a higher priority to bodily attractiveness than those pursuing mainly long-term committed relationships. Our central hypothesis would receive additional support if both the individual differences in SOI-R and the contextual effects that result from assigning participants to mating conditions produce similar patterns of information prioritization.

We saw no *a priori* grounds for predicting that women would experience an analogous conditional shift in body versus face priority across the two mating contexts for two reasons. First, women were predicted not to differentially prioritize cues of current fertility because men's fertility does not show the same precipitous age-dependent drop-off as women's fertility. As a result, there has been relatively weaker selection pressure on women to attend to such cues. Second, to the degree that women seek physical indicators of good genes in a mate (Gangestad & Thornhill, 1997; Penton-Voak et al., 1999), hormonally dependent characteristics indicative of good genes appear to be equally reflected in men's faces and bodies (Folstad & Karter, 1992; Gangestad, Thornhill, & Yeo, 1994; Thornhill & Gangestad,

1993). Previous research has shown that testosterone-based cues of masculinity (e.g., wide jaw) are correlated with actual and perceived health (Rhodes, Chan, Zebrowitz, & Simmons, 2003). Because such cues have also been correlated with fluctuating asymmetry as assessed through the face and the body (Gangestad, & Thornhill, 2003), information about a man's health can be gleaned from both sources. Thus, in contrast to men, we expected no difference in the priority that women would give to a man's facial and bodily attractiveness as a function of mating context.

2. Methods

2.1. Participants

The sample consisted of 381 university students (194 male, 187 female) who agreed to participate in exchange for course credit. The data from six participants who did not identify themselves as heterosexual were excluded, resulting in a data set of 192 men (age M = 18.85, SD = 1.29) and 183 women (age M = 18.69, SD = 1.45). Approximately one quarter of the sample (51 men and 57 women) reported being in a committed romantic relationship.

2.2. Materials and procedure

Two clothed, full body photographs, one of a man and one of a woman, were purchased from a stock photography database for use in the present study. Individual difference measures, including sex, relationship status, and participants' SOI-R (Penke & Asendorpf, 2008), were obtained from participants prior to experimentation.

After accessing the experiment online, participants viewed an image of an opposite sex individual whose face was occluded by a "face box" and whose body was occluded by a "body box." A stick figure was superimposed over the face and body boxes to indicate which part of the photographed individual lay underneath (see Fig. 1). Having been randomly assigned to one of two mating conditions, participants were instructed to first imagine themselves as single and then to consider the possibility of dating the opposite sex individual behind the boxes as either a short-term mate (i.e., one night stand) or a long-term mate (i.e., a committed relationship

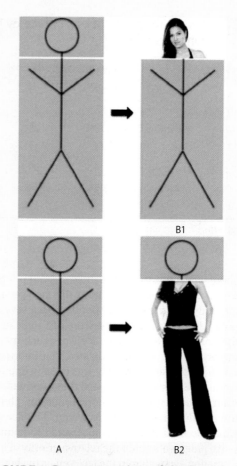

FIGURE 1 Demonstration of the box removal procedure (for male participants). Column (A) represents the opposite sex image that is first presented to participants occluded by a "face box" and a "body box." Column (B) represents the image that is presented to participants upon removal of the "face box" (B1) or "body box" (B2).

partner), depending on their assigned condition. To experimentally test the relative importance of facial and bodily attractiveness, participants were instructed that they could only remove one box (the "face box" or "body box") to inform their decision about whether or not they would engage in the designated relationship with the occluded person.

After participants selected a box to remove, they were asked, "When you made your decision

TABLE 1 Cross-tabulation of box choice by long-term or short-term mating context and sex

Males		Face box	Body box	Females		Face box	Body box
LT	Observed	68	23	LT	Observed	60	22
	Expected	55.5	35.5		Expected	56.9	25.1
	% within LT	75%	25%		% within LT	73%	27%
ST	Observed	49	52	ST	Observed	67	34
	Expected	61.5	39.5		Expected	70.1	30.9
	% within ST	49%	51%		% within ST	66%	34%
Total		61%	39%	Total		69%	31%

LT, long term; ST, short term.

about which box to remove, how did you prioritize information gathered from the face versus the body?" Participants responded on a seven-point Likert scale wherein a score of 1 indicated that information from the face was much more important, a score of 4 indicated that information from the face and body was equally important, and a score of 7 indicated that information from the body was much more important. Thus, the two dependent variables were (1) choice of which occluding box to remove, and (2) quantitative judgments about the relative priority of information gleaned from the face versus the body. Although unnecessary, the face or body of the opposite sex individual underneath was subsequently revealed, in accordance with each participant's selection. Participants were fully debriefed as to the purpose of the study.

3. Results

3.1. Face versus body box choice

To evaluate whether participants chose to remove the face or body box more often, we first conducted an exploratory analysis which revealed a general trend to choose the face box over the body box in male participants (face: 61%; $\chi^2_1 = 9.19$, $N = 192$, $p_{rep} = .99$, $\varphi = .22$) and in female participants (face: 69%; $\chi^2_1 = 27.55$, $N = 183$, $p_{rep} > .99$, $\varphi = .39$). We then conducted χ^2 cross-tabulation analyses within each sex to examine the effect of mating context on box choice, taking into account the inherently unequal expected

frequencies of box choice. Table 1 presents the observed and expected frequencies for each mating condition by sex. Men removed the face box when told to consider the target as a long-term mate with greater frequency than expected by chance (observed 68; expected 55.5). In contrast, men removed the body box when told to consider the target as a short-term mate with greater frequency than expected by chance (observed 52; expected 39.5), $\chi^2_1 = 13.81$, $N = 192$, $p_{rep} > .99$, $\varphi = .27$. Women did not differ from chance levels in their choice for box removal, $\chi^2_1 = 0.99$, $N = 183$, $p_{rep} = .75$, $\varphi = .07$. Fig. 2 illustrates

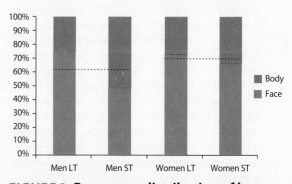

FIGURE 2 **Frequency distribution of box choice by mating context and sex. Expected frequencies of box choice, based on average frequencies by sex, are indicated with dashed lines.**

box choice within each mating condition by sex, compared to the frequencies expected by chance.

3.2. Rated priority assigned to facial and bodily information

Collecting Likert scale data on the priority that participants assigned to the information from the face and body boxes allowed us to also conduct t-tests within each sex. For this variable, higher scores indicated a greater priority placed on information from the body box. Two females who did not respond to this question were not included in the analyses for the priority variable. In line with the prediction, men who were told to evaluate the target as a short-term mate assigned the body box significantly higher priority (mean $\pm$ S.E. $= 3.75 \pm 0.15$) than did men told to evaluate the target as a long-term mate (mean $\pm$ S.E. $= 3.00 \pm 0.13$), $t_{190} = -3.72$, $p_{rep} > .99$, $d = .52$. Women assigned similar priority to the body box in both the short-term (mean $\pm$ S.E. $= 3.21 \pm 0.15$) and long-term mating conditions (mean $\pm$ S.E. $= 2.93 \pm 0.15$), $t(179) = -1.32$, $p_{rep} = .82$, $d = .19$.

3.3. Individual differences in SOI-R

To explore the hypothesis that the priority given to facial or bodily information is affected by an individual's SOI-R, we correlated participants' priority scores with their SOI-R scores, with higher SOI-R scores indicating less restricted sociosexual orientation. For women, only the SOI Desire subscale score was significantly correlated with their box priority ratings, $r = .18$, $N = 175$, $p_{rep} = .963$. For men, however, their overall SOI-R score, as well as all subscales, were significantly correlated with their box priority ratings (SOI Total: $r = .25$, $N = 183$, $p_{rep} = .994$; SOI Behavior: $r = .14$, $N = 188$, $p_{rep} = .923$; SOI Attitude: $r = .25$, $N = 189$, $p_{rep} = .994$; SOI Desire: $r = .19$, $N = 188$, $p_{rep} = .971$).

4. Discussion

Simply assigning men to a short-term mating condition, as opposed to a long-term mating condition, caused them to increase the priority given to information obtained from a woman's body. Women assigned to the short-term and long-term mating conditions all gave greater priority to information obtained from an opposite

sex individual's face. These results, as shown through both box choice and priority ratings, empirically support the hypothesis that men attend to bodily cues more in short-term than long-term mating contexts. In contrast, women's relative preferences were unaffected by mating condition, suggesting that women consistently prioritize facial cues over bodily cues. The adaptive shift in men's mating psychology was also reflected as a stable individual difference in men's SOI scores, with unrestricted men giving greater priority than restricted men to information obtained from a woman's body. Thus, men who most benefit from assessing current fertility, as opposed to reproductive value, showed greater interest in a woman's bodily cues.

Despite the conditional shift that focused men's interest toward a woman's body, both men and women chose to reveal the face of the opposite sex image at greater than chance levels when collapsed across conditions (despite the smaller absolute size of the face box, which one could argue contains less information than the larger body box). If the purpose of removing the face or body box was to assess overall attractiveness, these results are consistent with previous research indicating that the face is a better predictor of overall attractiveness than the body (Furnham & Reeves, 2006; Peters et al., 2007; Riggio, Widaman, Tucker, & Salinas, 1991). Because health is valued in both short-term and long-term mates, and because indicators of a robust immune system, such as symmetry, averageness, and sexual dimorphism, are abundantly accessible from an individual's face, facial attractiveness should be given greater weight, all else equal, than bodily attractiveness. Moreover, the face can convey social signals, such as reciprocal romantic interest, which are valued across sex and mating contexts.

The obtained pattern of results mirrors the findings of Currie and Little (2009) who showed that ratings of facial attractiveness better predicted overall attractiveness than did ratings of bodily attractiveness. Likewise, Currie and Little discovered a context-dependent shift in male raters, wherein ratings of bodily attractiveness better predicted ratings of overall attractiveness in a short-term relationship context than in a long-term relationship context. These findings provide convergent evidence that a woman's face and body convey at least somewhat non-redundant cues of female mate quality (but see Thornhill & Grammer, 1999).

Given that our results were obtained from a relatively young sample, future studies should replicate these results using a more diverse sample of participants. The forced choice procedure used in the present study allowed us to isolate the variables of interest in order to illuminate a context-dependent shift; however, this approach sacrificed ecological validity in regard to the mate assessment circumstances of everyday life. Methods that are more ecologically valid allow multiple cues to be assessed at once, for example, by allowing cues indicative of genetic quality and parental investment capacity to be evaluated simultaneously (Perilloux, Webster, & Gaulin, 2010). Within most cultures, men and women typically utilize cues from both a potential mate's face and body to assess his or her desirability as a mate. Thus, future studies should utilize a methodology that can elucidate how participants simultaneously assign relative priorities to both faces and bodies.

The current study provides evidence that for men, but not for women, priority shifting takes place based on the pursuit of short-term and long-term mating strategies. This methodology is conducive to many avenues of future research which aim to differentiate the relative importance placed on facial and bodily traits in a context-dependent manner, such as whether women's priorities of short-term and long-term mates' faces and bodies vary across the menstrual cycle along with documented fluctuations in sexual desire (Penton-Voak et al., 1999). Traits associated with SOI-R (Thornhill & Gangestad, 2008) and traits associated with parenting effort (Roney, Hanson, Durante, & Maestripieri, 2006) may be expressed in unequal concentrations across a man's face and body.

The present study utilized an evolutionarily informed perspective to hypothesize and document an increase in the relative importance of bodily information to men in a short-term mating context. Our hypothesis received further support when men who were dispositionally inclined to short-term mate showed a similar shift toward bodily cues as men in the assigned short-term mating condition. This study provides the empirical support for the hypothesized sex differences in the prioritization of facial and bodily attractiveness, while adding to a cumulative body of evidence highlighting the importance of temporal context in predicting mating decisions.

Acknowledgments

The authors thank Greg Hixon for his verification of our statistical procedures and members of the Buss Lab for their helpful feedback.

References

Buss, D. M. (1994). *The evolution of desire: Strategies of human mating.* New York: Basic Books.

Buss, D. M., & Schmitt, D. P. (1993). Sexual strategies theory: A contextual evolutionary analysis of human mating. *Psychological Review, 100,* 204–232.

Cunningham, M. (1986). Measuring the physical in physical attractiveness: Quasi-experiments on the sociobiology of female facial beauty. *Journal of Personality and Social Psychology, 50,* 925–935.

Currie, T. E., & Little, A. C. (2009). The relative importance of the face and body in judgments of human physical attractiveness. *Evolution and Human Behavior, 30,* 409–416.

Darwin, C. (1871). *The descent of man, and selection in relation to sex.* London: J. Murray.

Davey Smith, G., Greenwood, R., Gunnell, D., Sweetnam, P., Yarnell, J., & Elwood, P. (2001). Leg length, insulin resistance, and coronary heart disease risk: The Caerphilly Study. *Journal of Epidemiology and Community Health, 55,* 867–872.

Fink, B., Grammer, K., & Thornhill, R. (2001). Human (*Homo sapiens*) facial attractiveness in relation to skin texture and color. *Journal of Comparative Psychology, 115,* 92–99.

Folstad, I., & Karter, A. J. (1992). Parasites, bright males, and the immunocompetence handicap. *The American Naturalist, 139,* 603–622.

Frederick, D. A., & Haselton, M. G. (2007). Why is muscularity sexy? Tests of the fitness indicator hypothesis. *Personality and Social Psychology Bulletin*, 33, 1167–1183.

Furnham, A., & Reeves, E. (2006). The relative influence of facial neoteny and waist-to-hip ratio on judgments of female attractiveness and fecundity. *Psychology, Health, & Medicine*, 11, 129–141.

Furnham, A., & Swami, V. (2007). Perception of female buttocks and breast size in profile. *Social Behavior and Personality*, 35, 1–8.

Gangestad, S. W., & Scheyd, G. J. (2005). The evolution of human physical attractiveness. *Annual Review of Anthropology*, 34, 523–548.

Gangestad, S. W., & Simpson, J. A. (1990). Toward an evolutionary history of female sociosexual variation. *Journal of Personality*, 58, 69–96.

Gangestad, S. W., & Thornhill, R. (1997). The evolutionary psychology of extra-pair sex: The role of fluctuating asymmetry. *Evolution and Human Behavior*, 18, 69–88.

Gangestad, S. W., & Thornhill, R. (2003). Facial masculinity and fluctuating asymmetry. *Evolution and Human Behavior*, 24, 231–241.

Gangestad, S. W., Thornhill, R., & Yeo, R. A. (1994). Facial attractiveness, developmental stability, and fluctuating asymmetry. *Ethology and Sociobiology*, 15, 73–85.

Grammer, K., & Thornhill, R. (1994). Human (*Homo sapiens*) facial attractiveness and sexual selection: The role of symmetry and averageness. *Journal of Comparative Psychology*, 108, 233–242.

Gunnell, D., May, M., Ben-Sholomo, Y., Yarnell, J., & Smith, G. D. (2003). Height, leg length and cancer: The Caerphilly Study. *Nutrition and Cancer*, 47, 34–39.

Gunnell, D., Whitley, E., Upton, M. N., McConnachie, A., Davey Smith, G., & Watt, G. C. M. (2003). Associations of height, leg length and lung function with cardiovascular risk factors in the Midspan Family Study. *Journal of Epidemiology and Community Health*, 57, 141–146.

Johnston, V. S., Hagel, R., Franklin, M., Fink, B., & Grammer, K. (2001). Male facial attractiveness: Evidence for hormone-mediated adaptive design. *Evolution and Human Behavior*, 22, 251–267.

Jones, D. (1996). *Physical attractiveness and the theory of sexual selection*. Ann Arbor, MI: Museum of Anthropology, University of Michigan.

Kirchengast, S., & Gartner, M. (2002). Changes in fat distribution (WHR) and body weight across the menstrual cycle. *Collegium Antropologicum*, 26, 47–57.

Lake, J. K., Power, C., & Cole, T. J. (1997). Women's reproductive health: The role of body mass index in early and adult life. *International Journal of Obesity*, 21, 432–438.

Langlois, J. H., & Roggman, L. A. (1990). Attractive faces are only average. *Psychological Science*, 1, 115–121.

Lassek, W. D., & Gaulin, S. J. C. (2008). Waist-to-hip ratio and cognitive ability: Is gluteofemoral fat a privileged store of neurodevelopmental resources? *Evolution and Human Behavior*, 29, 26–34.

Penke, L., & Asendorpf, J. B. (2008). Beyond global sociosexual orientations: A more differentiated look at sociosexuality and its effects on courtship and romantic relationships. *Journal of Personality and Social Psychology*, 95, 1113–1135.

Penton-Voak, I. S., Perrett, D. I., Castles, D. L., Kobayashi, T., Burt, D. M., Murray, L. K., et al. (1999). Menstrual cycle alters face preference. *Nature*, 399, 741–742.

Perilloux, H. K., Webster, G. D., & Gaulin, S. J. C. (2010). Signals of genetic quality and maternal investment capacity: The dynamic effects of fluctuating asymmetry and waist-to-hip ratio on men's ratings of women's attractiveness. *Social Psychological and Personality Science*, 1, 32–42.

Perrett, D. I., Burt, D. M., Penton-Voak, I. S., Lee, K. J., Rowland, D. A., & Edwards, R. (1999). Symmetry and human facial attractiveness. *Evolution and Human Behavior*, 20, 295–307.

Peters, M., Rhodes, G., & Simmons, L. W. (2007). Contributions of the face and body to overall attractiveness. *Animal Behavior*, 73, 937–942.

Rhodes, G., Chan, J., Zebrowitz, L. A., & Simmons, L. W. (2003). Does sexual dimorphism in human faces signal health? *Proceedings of the Royal Society of London*, 270, S93–S95.

Riggio, R. E., Widaman, K. F., Tucker, J. S., & Salinas, C. (1991). Beauty is more than skin deep: Components of attractiveness. *Basic and Applied Social Psychology*, 12, 423–439.

Roberts, S. C., Havlicek, J., Flegr, J., Hruskova, M., Little, A. C., Jones, B. C., et al. (2004). Female facial attractiveness increases during the fertile phase of the menstrual cycle. *Proceedings of the Royal Society of London*, 271, S270–S272.

Roney, J. R., Hanson, K. N., Durante, K. M., & Maestripieri, D. (2006). Reading men's faces: Women's mate attractiveness judgments track men's testosterone and interest in infants. *Proceedings of the Royal Society of London B*, 273, 2169–2175.

Singh, D. (1993). Adaptive significance of female physical attractiveness: Role of waist-to-hip ratio. *Journal of Personality and Social Psychology*, 65, 293–307.

Sorokowski, P., & Pawlowski, B. (2008). Adaptive preferences for leg length in a potential partner. *Evolution and Human Behavior*, 29, 86–91.

Sugiyama, L. S. (2005). Physical attractiveness in adaptationist perspective. In D. M. Buss (Ed.), *The handbook of evolutionary psychology* (pp. 292–343). Hoboken, NJ: Wiley.

Symons, D. (1979). *The evolution of human sexuality*. New York: Oxford University Press.

Thornhill, R., & Gangestad, S. W. (1993). Human facial beauty: Averageness, symmetry, and parasite resistance. *Human Nature*, 4, 237–269.

Thornhill, R., & Gangestad, S. W. (2008). *The evolutionary biology of human female sexuality*. New York: Oxford University Press.

Thornhill, R., & Grammer, K. (1999). The body and face of woman: One ornament that signals quality? *Evolution and Human Behavior*, 20, 105–120.

Tovée, M. J., Maisey, D. S., Emery, J. L., & Cornelissen, P. L. (1999). Visual cues to female physical attractiveness. *Proceedings of the Royal Society of London*, 266, 211–218.

Williams, G. C. (1975). *Sex and evolution*. Princeton, NJ: Princeton University Press.

Zaadstra, B. M., Seidell, J. C., VanNoord, P. A. H., Te Velde, E. R., Habbema, J. D. F., Vrieswijk, B., et al. (1993). Fat and female fecundity: Prospective study of body fat distribution in conception rates. *British Medical Journal*, 306, 484–487.

A CLOSER LOOK AT
More Than Just a Pretty Face

1. The title of this article has two distinctive parts. The first part before the colon is a familiar and memorable saying. The part after the colon does something different. What does this second part do?

2. How closely do the organization and features of this scientific report follow the reports genre as described in Chapter 13? Highlight places that follow the genre and any places that don't.

3. This report appeared in *Evolution and Human Behavior*, a scientific journal in the field of "evolutionary psychology," which examines how human behavior may in part be influenced by the way evolution has driven human biology. Go to the Web and find one or two articles about this field that are easy to understand but authoritative. When you have a better grasp of the field, discuss whether Confer, Perilloux, and Buss succeed in convincing you that they have reached the correct conclusions. Do you think they have really figured out why people are attracted to others in various situations?

4. This article is addressed primarily to experts in the science of evolutionary psychology. There are parts that a non-specialist, like you and your classmates, might not understand (for instance, the complex statistics in the results section). Even so, if you read closely, you will probably be able to understand the basics. Which parts were most helpful to you as a nonspecialist? Which parts are probably not useful to nonspecialists?

5. The writers begin with the assumption that much of our mate-choosing preferences are based in the biology of reproduction: We choose our mates in part according to the likelihood that they will help us produce offspring that will survive. In other words, we are at least partly similar to birds, reptiles, and other animals. How would you respond to that assumption? For you, is that very idea plausible, ridiculous, or somewhere in between?

IDEAS FOR
Writing

1. Like experts in any field, scientists often need to explain the complexities of their field to wider audiences or ordinary people. A nurse might need to talk about nutrition guidelines to a patient, a restaurant chef about food preparation to a food critic, or a lawyer about complex legal issues to a jury. Now it's your turn to play expert. Imagine that you are one of the authors of this study and a journalist wants to do a feature story about how men choose mates, but the journalist is unclear about what the study did and found. Write an e-mail to this journalist explaining, in layperson's terms, what you did and what you discovered in this study.

2. Write a commentary based on this article that encourages your readers either to accept and use the findings or fundamentally question them. If you choose to accept and embrace the findings, explain why the findings are important to your readers. If you choose to question these findings, explain why readers should not make too much of them; for instance, you might be concerned young men will use them to rationalize considering women as sexual objects as "natural." Whichever you choose, be sure to back up your argument with reasoning and evidence.

A FEW IDEAS FOR
Composing a Report

1. **Develop a methods section for a report.** List five questions about life on your campus that you would like to answer. Pick one and develop a methodology for answering that question. Use your methodology to generate facts, data, and other support. Then write a report to the dean of students at your university in which you present and discuss your results and offer recommendations.

2. **Write a summary of a report.** Find a report on the Internet or elsewhere that studies a topic related to your major or a personal interest. Describe what it says in your own words, but do not offer your own opinion. The purpose of your summary is to give an overview of the report's major points, not to offer your own views about the topic.

3. **Create a multimedia report about your major.** For students who might be interested in your major field of study, create a multimedia research report that explains the requirements for graduation and the kinds of careers available for people who earn a degree in your major. Research this topic through the Internet, print sources, and interviews with counselors and professors.

Go to **My WritingLab** to complete this chapter's exercises and test your understanding of its objectives.

Research Papers

The Public Overwhelmingly Wants It: Why Is Taxing the Rich So Hard?

ALYSSA BATTISTONI

Alyssa Battistoni takes on a question that has occurred to many people: Why not ask more from people who already have more than enough money? After all, the gap between the wealthy and the middle class has grown dramatically in the past two decades. By doing research on this question, the author explores the power of the wealthy over politicians and how the rich, as a minority, have more influence on government than others. Look at the ways Battistoni supports her arguments with a balance of facts and emotional appeals.

When even the *New York Times,* the supposed bleeding heart of the liberal media, is asking whether it's more "perilous politically" to accept tax increases for 3 percent of households or benefit cuts for everyone, you'd assume that even Americans who aren't rich are opposed to raising taxes on those who are ("Will Voters," par. 4). But you'd be wrong: nearly three-quarters of Americans support raising taxes on the wealthy ("Washington Post-ABC News Poll," item 14). So why is raising taxes on the wealthy so hard—or why do we think it is?

The obvious answer is that rich people have political clout—but can it really be so simple? A growing mound of evidence suggests that while wealthy people's preferences may not be the only factor in political decision-making, it's a worrisomely important one. In a recent study, Princeton political scientist Larry Bartels found that senators outright ignored the views of their least advantaged constituents while catering to the preferences of the wealthy (4). Princeton's Martin Gilens has also found that policy changes reflect the preferences of the most affluent, while the preferences of poor and middle-income Americans have almost no bearing (794).

Political scientists Lawrence Jacobs and Benjamin Page have found that the preferences of foreign policymakers correspond more to the preferences of executives of multinational companies than to the general public (115). Page and Jeffrey Winters estimate that the top 10 percent of income earners hold about 90 percent of

materially based political power, and that "each member of the top 1 percent averaged more than 100 times the power of a member of the bottom 90 percent; about 200 times if the index is calculated in terms of the more politically relevant non-home wealth" (736). These numbers are staggering, and should be seriously troubling to anyone who thinks political equality worth defending. Indeed, by Page and Winter's definition of oligarchy as "the extreme political inequalities that necessarily accompany extreme material inequalities," it's pretty hard to argue that the United States isn't an oligarchic society (732).

The simple fact of the matter is that the people who can afford to fund and engage in Beltway politics, from idea-generating to legislation-drafting, are disproportionately wealthy, so it's difficult to suss out just how much of politicians' deference to the preferences of the wealthy is responsiveness to the wealthy themselves as opposed to the general alignment of rich people's interests with those of influential elites, organized special interest groups, business lobbies, and those of policymakers themselves.

Because of course, plenty of politicians are 5 themselves wealthy—the median net worth of members of Congress is just under a million dollars (Gilson and Perot, sec. 4). Being wealthy doesn't necessarily mean you're a shill for lower taxes—indeed, John Kerry and Jay Rockefeller, two of the richest senators, have advocated more progressive tax rates—but it certainly means that most representatives have a different perspective on economic matters than the average American. Indeed, the 10 richest members of Congress—supporters of progressive taxation or no—all voted to extend the Bush tax cuts. (Gilson and Perot, sec. 4)

Of course, it's no secret that as political campaigns have grown increasingly more expensive, campaign contributions have grown increasingly more important: the 2010 midterms cost $4 billion (Klein, par. 1), and President Obama is already planning to spend a billion dollars on his bid for reelection (Overby, par. 1). Meanwhile, citizens in the top income quarter provide nearly three-quarters of campaign contributions, while those in the lowest quintile account for just 2 percent. But as Bartels notes, campaign contributions don't explain the whole story.

If anything, we probably understate the political influence of the rich. In part, that's because we can't quite comprehend the magnitude of economic inequality and the extent to which political power is correlated with it. The real numbers—like that the wealthiest 300,000 Americans received as much income as the bottom 150 million—sound too crazy to be true (Johnston, par. 5). As a result, proposals to raise taxes on the wealthy are so often dismissed as wild-eyed populist rhetoric—"soaking the rich"—rather than legitimate, reasonable policy prescriptions.

Furthermore, while we take for granted that the wealthy have more political power than the average citizen, we figure that the sheer numbers of middle class and low-income voters can outweigh the preferences of the rich in swaying public officials. Robert Reich, for example, has argued that the rich have the political power to block higher tax rates "only if we let them," saying "here's the issue around which Progressives, populists on the right and left, unionized workers, and all other working people who are just plain fed up ought to be able to unite" (par. 14). And indeed, that kind of coalition-building is the basis for much progressive politics. But as the wealth and power of the most privileged Americans increases, it's becoming harder and harder for the rest of us to keep up even in the aggregate.

So instead we're getting caught in a negative feedback cycle: as the rich get richer and more powerful, policies are increasingly aligned with their interests, which increases inequality still further. Meanwhile, the middle and working classes are left with shrinking incomes and correspondingly less and less power to demand investment in a more equitable economy—and a broader tax base. Unions used to be able to counter the power of the wealthy, but their decline has left the average worker with little recourse. Instead of presenting an organized alternative to the views endorsed by the rich, average Americans are left to voice their political preferences through the vague format of an opinion poll. It's no wonder that, as political scientists Jacob Hacker and Paul Pierson write, "America's public officials have rewritten the rules of American politics and the American economy in ways that have benefitted the few at the expense of the many" (6).

So while it's absolutely true that the rich pay far more in income taxes than the rest of us (Robyn and Prante, par. 3)—the wealthiest 1 percent of Americans pay 38 percent of income tax—that tiny fraction of the population also receives about 24 percent of income, accounts for about 34 percent of net worth, and holds 42.7 percent of financial wealth (net worth minus the value of one's home) (Domhoff, par. 16). And those are statistics from before the crash—though there are only tentative estimates of current wealth distribution, many economists actually think it's gotten more unequal.

Since average people's wealth is largely tied up in their homes, the wealth of the median household has dropped an estimated 36 percent since the housing bubble popped, while the wealth of the top 1 percent has fallen a comparatively small 11 percent (Wolff, 33). As Bartels concludes, "the economic order of the contemporary United States poses a clear and profound obstacle to realizing the democratic value of political equality" (32). In other words, as long as economic inequality is as extreme as it is now, political equality will remain an ideal rather than a reality. We need to make this case over and over again—right now we're in danger of drawing exactly the wrong lessons from the economic nightmare of the past few years.

In a *Wall Street Journal* piece a couple of weeks ago, former California economic forecaster Brad Williams states "We created a revenue cliff. . . . We built a large part of our government on the state's most unstable income group" (Frank, par. 5). The people protesting with signs reading "We Love Jobs," he suggested, were "missing the real point." But it's Williams who's missing the point: what we really did was build a large part of our economy around an unstable income group and industry, and what we need to do is build an economy with a broader base and more evenly distributed resources.

Indeed, many arguments given against raising taxes are in fact reasons for decreasing the financial and political power of the wealthy. Worried that rich people will leave the state, or even the country, to avoid property or income tax? Don't build an economy that depends on a small number of people who have the resources to leave sticking around. Worried that rich people won't invest in their businesses or create new jobs if we tax them? Don't build an economy that depends on a few wealthy people hiring the rest of us. Worried that rich people's incomes are too volatile? Don't build an economy so heavily dependent on financial markets. And make no mistake: although the *Journal* would have you believe the distribution of wealth is a naturally occurring phenomenon, state investment and regulation plays an essential role in the structure of the economy. If we want a more equal playing field, we can have it—but we need to start now.

Works Cited

Bartels, Larry. "Economic Inequality and Political Representation." Aug 2005. Web. 25 Apr 2011.

Domhoff, G. William. "Who Rules America: Wealth, Income, and Power." *Who Rules America?* Jan 2011. Web. 25 Apr 2011.

Frank, Robert. "The Price of Taxing the Rich." *Wall Street Journal* 26 Mar 2011. Web. 25 Apr 2011.

Gilens, Martin. "Inequality and Democratic Responsiveness." *Public Opinion Quarterly* 69.5 (2005): 778–796. Print.

Gilson, Dave, and Carolyn Perot. "It's the Inequality, Stupid." *Mother Jones.* Web. 25 Apr 2011.

Haker, Jacob, and Paul Pierson. *Winner-Take-All-Politics.* New York, NY: Simon & Schuster, 2010. Print.

Jacobs, Lawrence, and Benjamin Page. "Who Influences U.S. Foreign Policy." *American Political Science Review* 99.1 (2005): 107–123. Print.

Johnston, David Cay. "Income Gap Is Widening, Data Shows." *New York Times* 29 Mar 2007. Web. 25 Apr 2011.

Klein, Ezra. "More Money, More Problems." *Newsweek* 31 Oct 2010. Web. 25 Apr 2011.

Overby, Peter. "2012: The Year Of The Billion-Dollar Campaigns?" *National Public Radio* 18 Feb 2011. Web. 25 Apr 2011.

Reich, Robert. "Why We Must Raise Taxes on the Rich, ASAP!" *RobertReich.org* 4 Apr 2011. Web. 25 Apr 2011.

Robyn, Mark, and Gerald Prante. "Summary of Latest Federal Individual Income Tax Data." *Tax Foundation.* Web. 25 Apr 2011.

"Washington Post-ABC News Poll." Web. 25 Apr 2011.

"Will Voters Accept Tax Increases?—Room for Debate." 13 Apr 2011. Web. 25 Apr 2011.

Winters, Jeffrey, and Benjamin Page. "Oligarchy in the United States." *Perspectives on Politics* 7.4 (2009): 731–751. Print.

Wolff, Edward. "Recent Trends in Household Wealth in the United States: Rising Debt and the Middle-Class Squeeze—an Update to 2007." Mar 2010. Print.

A CLOSER LOOK AT
The Public Overwhelmingly Wants It: Why Is Taxing the Rich So Hard?

1. One of Battistoni's main arguments is that politicians often overlook the needs of the public, because they share the same views as wealthy and powerful business executives. Why, according to Battistoni, do politicians think and behave this way? According to Battistoni's argument, what are some of the effects of this kind of thinking by politicians?

2. The author sounds angry and frustrated. Identify five places in this research paper where she creates this style or tone. In what ways does Battistoni express her anger and frustration at the power of the rich over politicians?

3. The author also argues that the United States is actually too dependent on the rich to pay taxes.

She writes, "What we really did was build a large part of our economy around an unstable income group and industry, and what we need to do is build an economy with a broader base and more evenly distributed resources." Do you think she is contradicting herself at this point? In the end, is she really arguing for more taxes on the rich?

IDEAS FOR
Writing

1. Write a commentary in which you express your own views on taxes. Do you think some people are overburdened with taxes? Do you think some people don't pay enough taxes? Use research to support and explain your views.

2. Write an elevator pitch in which you briefly explain how you would make politicians more responsive to the general public. (The pitch is a microgenre of the proposal, described in Chapter 12.) Right now, most people agree that politicians are overly influenced by special interest groups, wealthy donors, labor unions, and corporate lobbyists, while they are not listening to regular people. In your elevator pitch, explain how you would change the political system so politicians hear about the needs and concerns of all.

Rapture Ready: The Science of Self Delusion

CHRIS MOONEY

In this research paper, Chris Mooney explores why people often believe things that can be proven wrong. Reviewing psychology and political-science research on reasoning and denial, he discusses studies that show how the reasoning processes of conservatives and progressives often depend more on their prior beliefs and expectations than on factual evidence and solid reasoning. Pay attention to the way that Mooney does more than just report his sources' findings; he uses them to inform his own argument and back up his claims.

"A man with a conviction is a hard man to change. Tell him you disagree and he turns away. Show him facts or figures and he questions your sources. Appeal to logic and he fails to see your point" (Festinger, Riecken, & Schacter, 1956, p. 3). So wrote the celebrated Stanford University psychologist Leon Festinger and his coauthors, in a passage that might have been referring to climate change denial—the persistent rejection, on the part of so many Americans today, of what we know about global warming and its human causes. But it was too early for that—this was the 1950s—and Festinger and his coauthors were actually describing a famous case study in psychology.

Festinger and several of his colleagues had infiltrated the Seekers, a small Chicago-area cult whose members thought they were communicating with aliens—including one, "Sananda," who they believed was the astral incarnation of Jesus Christ. The group was led by Dorothy Martin, a Dianetics devotee who transcribed the interstellar messages through automatic writing.

Through her, the aliens had given the precise date of an Earth-rending cataclysm: December 21, 1954. Some of Martin's followers quit their jobs and sold their property, expecting to be rescued by a flying saucer when the continent split asunder and a new sea swallowed much of the United States. The disciples even went so far as to remove brassieres and rip zippers out of their trousers—the metal, they believed, would pose a danger on the spacecraft.

Festinger and his team were with the cult when the prophecy failed. First, the "boys upstairs" (as the aliens were sometimes called) did not show up and rescue the Seekers. Then December 21 arrived without incident. It was the moment they had been waiting for: How would people so emotionally invested in a belief system react, now that it had been soundly refuted?

At first, the group struggled for an explanation. But then rationalization set in. A new message arrived, announcing that they'd all been spared at the last minute. Festinger summarized the extraterrestrials' new pronouncement: "The little group, sitting all night long, had spread so much light that God had saved the world from destruction" (p. 171). Their willingness to believe in the prophecy had saved Earth from the prophecy!

From that day forward, the Seekers, previously shy of the press and indifferent toward evangelizing, began to proselytize. "Their sense of urgency was enormous" (p. 171), wrote the researchers. The devastation of all they had believed had made them even more certain of their beliefs.

In the annals of denial, it doesn't get much more extreme than the Seekers. They lost their jobs, the press mocked them, and there were efforts to keep them away from impressionable young minds. But while Martin's space cult might lie at on the far end of the spectrum of human self-delusion, there's plenty to go around. And since Festinger's day, an array of new discoveries in psychology and neuroscience has further demonstrated how our preexisting beliefs, far more than any new facts, can skew our thoughts and even color what we consider our most dispassionate and logical conclusions. This tendency toward so-called "motivated reasoning" helps explain why we find groups so polarized over matters where

the evidence is so unequivocal: climate change, vaccines, "death panels," the birthplace and religion of the president, and much else. (For an overview of the phenomenon of motivated reasoning, see Kunda, 1990.) It would seem that expecting people to be convinced by the facts flies in the face of, you know, the facts.

The theory of motivated reasoning builds on a key insight of modern neuroscience: As Damasio explains, reasoning is actually suffused with emotion (or what researchers often call "affect"). Not only are the two inseparable, but our positive or negative feelings about people, things, and ideas arise much more rapidly than our conscious thoughts, in a matter of milliseconds—fast enough to detect with an EEG device, but long before we're aware of it. That shouldn't be surprising: Evolution required us to react very quickly to stimuli in our environment (p. 144). It's a "basic human survival skill," explains political scientist Arthur Lupia of the University of Michigan (personal communication). We push threatening information away; we pull friendly information close. We apply fight-or-flight reflexes not only to predators, but to data itself.

We're not driven only by emotions, of course—we also reason, deliberate. But reasoning comes later, works slower—and even then, it doesn't take place in an emotional vacuum. Rather, our quick-fire emotions can set us on a course of thinking that's highly biased, especially on topics we care a great deal about.

Consider a person who has heard about a scientific discovery that deeply challenges her belief in divine creation—a new hominid, say, that confirms our evolutionary origins. What happens next, explains political scientist Charles Taber of Stony Brook University, is a subconscious negative response to the new information—and that response, in turn, guides the type of memories and associations formed in the conscious mind (personal communication). "They retrieve thoughts that are consistent with their previous beliefs," says Taber, "and that will lead them to build an argument and challenge what they're hearing."

In other words, when we think we're reasoning, we may instead be rationalizing. Or to use an analogy offered by University of Virginia psychologist Jonathan Haidt: We may think we're being scientists, but we're actually being lawyers (2000, p. 10). Our "reasoning" is a means to a predetermined end—winning our "case"—and is shot through with biases. They include "confirmation bias," in which we give greater heed to evidence and arguments that bolster our beliefs, and "disconfirmation bias," in which we expend disproportionate energy trying to debunk or refute views and arguments that we find uncongenial.

That's a lot of jargon, but we all understand these mechanisms when it comes to interpersonal relationships. If I don't want to believe that my spouse is being unfaithful, or that my child is a bully, I can go to great lengths to explain away behavior that seems obvious to everybody else—everybody who isn't too emotionally invested to accept it, anyway. That's not to suggest that we aren't also motivated to perceive the world accurately—we are. Or that we never change our minds—we do. It's just that we have other important goals besides accuracy—including identity affirmation and protecting one's sense of self—and often those make us highly resistant to changing our beliefs when the facts say we should.

Modern science originated from an attempt to weed out such subjective lapses—what that great 17th century theorist of the scientific method, Francis Bacon, dubbed the "idols of the mind." Even if individual researchers are prone to falling in love with their own theories, the broader processes of peer review and institutionalized skepticism are designed to ensure that, eventually, the best ideas prevail.

Our individual responses to the conclusions 15 that science reaches, however, are quite another matter. Ironically, in part because researchers employ so much nuance and strive to disclose all remaining sources of uncertainty, scientific evidence is highly susceptible to selective reading and misinterpretation. Giving ideologues or partisans scientific data that's relevant to their beliefs is like unleashing them in the motivated-reasoning equivalent of a candy store.

Sure enough, a large number of psychological studies have shown that people respond to scientific or technical evidence in ways that justify their preexisting beliefs. In a classic 1979 experiment (Lord, Ross, & Lepper), pro- and anti-death penalty advocates were exposed to descriptions of two fake scientific studies: one supporting and one undermining the notion that capital punishment deters violent crime and, in particular, murder. They were also shown detailed methodological critiques of the fake studies—and in a scientific sense, neither study was stronger than the other. Yet in each case, advocates more heavily criticized the study whose conclusions disagreed with their own, while describing the study that was more ideologically congenial as more "convincing."

Since then, similar results have been found for how people respond to "evidence" about affirmative action, gun control, the accuracy of gay stereotypes (Munro & Ditto, 2010), and much else. Even when study subjects are explicitly instructed to be unbiased and even-handed about the evidence, they often fail. And it's not just that people twist or selectively read scientific evidence to support their preexisting views. According to research by Yale Law School professor Dan Kahan and his colleagues, people's deep-seated views about morality, and about the way society should be ordered, strongly predict whom they consider to be a legitimate scientific expert in the first place—and thus where they consider "scientific consensus" to lie on contested issues.

In Kahan's research, individuals are classified, based on their cultural values, as either "individualists" or "communitarians," and as either "hierarchical" or "egalitarian" in outlook (Kahan, Jenkins-Smith, & Braman, 2011, p. 148). (Somewhat oversimplifying, you can think of hierarchical individualists as akin to conservative Republicans, and egalitarian communitarians as liberal Democrats.) In this study, subjects in the different groups were asked to help a close friend determine the risks associated with climate change, sequestering nuclear waste, or concealed carry laws: "The friend tells you that he or she is planning to read a book about the issue but would like to get your opinion on whether the author seems like a knowledgeable and trustworthy expert" (p. 153). A subject was then presented with the résumé of a fake expert "depicted as a member of the National Academy of Sciences who had earned a Ph.D. in a pertinent field from one elite university and who was now on the faculty of another" (p. 153). The subject was then shown a book excerpt by that "expert," in which the risk of the issue at hand was portrayed as high or low, well-founded or speculative. The results were stark: When the scientist's position stated that global warming is real and human-caused, for instance, only 23 percent of hierarchical individualists agreed the person was a "trustworthy and knowledgeable expert" (p. 163). Yet 88 percent of egalitarian communitarians accepted the same scientist's expertise. Similar divides were observed on whether nuclear waste can be safely stored underground and whether letting people carry guns deters crime. The alliances did not always hold. In another study (Kahan, Braman, Monahan, Callahan, & Peters, 2010), hierarchs and communitarians were in favor of laws that would compel the mentally ill to accept treatment, whereas individualists and egalitarians were opposed.

In other words, people rejected the validity of a scientific source because its conclusion contradicted their deeply held views—and thus the relative risks inherent in each scenario. A hierarchal individualist finds it difficult to believe that the things he prizes (commerce, industry, a man's freedom to possess a gun to defend his family) could lead to outcomes deleterious to society (Kahan et al., 2010). Whereas egalitarian communitarians tend to think that the free market causes harm, that patriarchal families mess up kids, and that people can't handle their guns. The study subjects weren't "antiscience"—not in their own minds, anyway. It's just that "science" was whatever they wanted it to be. "We've come to a misadventure, a bad situation where diverse citizens, who rely on diverse systems of cultural certification, are in conflict," says Kahan (Cone & Kahan, 2010).

And that undercuts the standard notion that the way to persuade people is via evidence and argument. In fact, head-on attempts to persuade can sometimes trigger a backfire effect, where people not only fail to change their minds when confronted with the facts—they may hold their wrong views more tenaciously than ever.

20

Take, for instance, the question of whether Saddam Hussein possessed hidden weapons of mass destruction just before the US invasion of Iraq in 2003. When political scientists Brendan Nyhan and Jason Reifler (2010) showed subjects fake newspaper articles in which this was first suggested (in a 2004 quote from President Bush) and then refuted (with the findings of the Bush-commissioned Iraq Survey Group report, which found no evidence of active WMD programs in pre-invasion Iraq), they found that conservatives were more likely than before to believe the claim. (The researchers also tested how liberals responded when shown that Bush did not actually "ban" embryonic stem-cell research. Liberals weren't particularly amenable to persuasion, either, but no backfire effect was observed.)

Another study gives some inkling of what may be going through people's minds when they resist persuasion. Northwestern University sociologist Monica Prasad and her colleagues wanted to test whether they could dislodge the notion that Saddam Hussein and Al Qaeda were secretly collaborating among those most likely to believe it—Republican partisans from highly GOP-friendly counties. So the researchers set up a study in which they discussed the topic with some of these Republicans in person (Prasad, Perrin, Bezila, Hoffman, Kindleberger, Manturuk, & Powers, 2009). They would cite the findings of the 9/11 Commission, as well as a statement in which George W. Bush himself denied his administration had "said the 9/11 attacks were orchestrated between Saddam and Al Qaeda."

As it turned out, not even Bush's own words could change the minds of these Bush voters—just 1 of the 49 partisans who originally believed the Iraq-Al Qaeda claim changed his or her mind. Far more common was resisting the correction in a variety of ways, either by coming up with counterarguments or by simply being unmovable:

Interviewer: [T]he September 11 Commission found no link between Saddam and 9/11, and this is what President Bush said. Do you have any comments on either of those?

Respondent: Well, I bet they say that the Commission didn't have any proof of it but I guess we still can have our opinions and feel that way even though they say that. (Prasad et al., 2009, p. 154)

The same types of responses are already being documented on divisive topics facing the current administration. Take the "Ground Zero mosque." Using information from the political myth-busting site FactCheck.org, a team at Ohio State (Nisbet & Garrett, 2010) presented subjects with a detailed rebuttal to the claim that "Feisal Abdul Rauf, the Imam backing the proposed Islamic cultural center and mosque, is a terrorist-sympathizer." Yet among those who were aware of the rumor and believed it, fewer than a third changed their minds.

A key question—and one that's difficult to answer—is how "irrational" all this is. On the one hand, it doesn't make sense to discard an entire belief system, built up over a lifetime, because of some new snippet of information. "It is quite possible to say, 'I reached this pro-capital-punishment decision based on real information that I arrived at over my life,'" explains Stanford social psychologist Jon Krosnick (personal communication). Indeed, there's a sense in which science denial could be considered keenly "rational." In certain conservative communities, explains Yale's Kahan, "People who say, 'I think there's something to climate change,' that's going to mark them out as a certain kind of person, and their life is going to go less well" (Cone & Kahan, 2010).

This may help explain a curious pattern Nyhan and Reifler found when they tried to test the fallacy that President Obama is a Muslim (2010). When a nonwhite researcher was administering their study, research subjects were amenable to changing their minds about the president's religion and updating incorrect views. But when only white researchers were present, GOP survey subjects in particular were more likely to believe the Obama Muslim myth than before. The subjects were using "social desirabililty" to tailor their beliefs (or stated beliefs, anyway) to whoever was listening.

Which leads us to the media. When people grow polarized over a body of evidence, or a resolvable matter of fact, the cause may be some form of biased reasoning, but they could also be receiving skewed information to begin with—or a complicated combination of both. In the Ground Zero mosque case, for instance, a separate study (Nisbet & Garrett, 2010) showed that survey respondents who watched Fox News were more likely to believe the Rauf rumor and three related ones—and they believed them more strongly than non-Fox watchers.

Okay, so people gravitate toward information that confirms what they believe, and they select sources that deliver it. Same as it ever was, right? Maybe, but the problem is arguably growing more acute, given the way we now consume information—through the Facebook links of friends, or tweets that lack nuance or context, or "narrowcast" and often highly ideological media that have relatively small, like-minded audiences. Those basic human survival skills of ours, says Michigan's Arthur Lupia, are "not well-adapted to our information age" (personal communication).

If you wanted to show how and why fact is ditched in favor of motivated reasoning, you could find no better test case than climate change. After all, it's an issue where you have highly technical information on one hand and very strong beliefs on the other. And sure enough, one key predictor of whether you accept the science of global warming is whether you're a Republican or a Democrat. The two groups have been growing more divided in their views about the topic, even as the science becomes more unequivocal.

So perhaps it should come as no surprise that more education doesn't budge Republican views. On the contrary: In a 2008 Pew survey, for instance, only 19 percent of college-educated Republicans agreed that the planet is warming due to human actions, versus 31 percent of non-college educated Republicans. In other words, a higher education correlated with an increased likelihood of denying the science on the issue. Meanwhile, among Democrats and independents, more education correlated with greater acceptance of the science.

Other studies have shown a similar effect: Republicans who think they understand the global warming issue best are least concerned about it; and among Republicans and those with higher levels of distrust of science in general, learning more about the issue doesn't increase one's concern about it. What's going on here? Well, according to Charles Taber and Milton Lodge of Stony Brook, one insidious aspect of motivated reasoning is that political sophisticates are prone to be more biased than those who know less about the issues. "People who have a dislike of some policy—for example, abortion—if they're unsophisticated they can just reject it out of hand," says Lodge. "But if they're sophisticated, they can go one step further and start coming up with counterarguments" (personal communication, April 12, 2011). These individuals are just as emotionally driven and biased as the rest of us, but they're able to generate more and better reasons to explain why they're right—and so their minds become harder to change.

That may be why the selectively quoted emails of Climategate were so quickly and easily seized upon by partisans as evidence of scandal. Cherry-picking is precisely the sort of behavior you would expect motivated reasoners to engage in to bolster their views—and whatever you may think about Climategate, the emails were a rich trove of new information upon which to impose one's ideology.

Climategate had a substantial impact on public opinion, according to Anthony Leiserowitz, director of the Yale Project on Climate Change Communication. It contributed to an overall drop in public concern about climate change and a significant loss of trust in scientists (personal communication, April 5, 2011). But—as we should expect by now—these declines were concentrated among particular groups of Americans: Republicans, conservatives, and those with "individualistic" values. Liberals and those with "egalitarian" values didn't lose much trust in climate science or scientists at all. "In some ways, Climategate was like a Rorschach test," Leiserowitz says, "with different groups interpreting ambiguous facts in very different ways."

So is there a case study of science denial that largely occupies the political left? Yes: the claim that childhood vaccines are causing an epidemic of autism. Its most famous proponents are an environmentalist (Robert F. Kennedy Jr., 2009) and numerous Hollywood celebrities (most notably Jenny McCarthy [2011] and Jim Carrey). The *Huffington Post* gives a very large megaphone to denialists. And Seth Mnookin, author of the new book *The Panic Virus* (2011), notes that if you want to find vaccine deniers, all you need to do is go hang out at Whole Foods.

Vaccine denial has all the hallmarks of a belief system that's not amenable to refutation. Over the past decade, the assertion that childhood vaccines are driving autism rates has been undermined by multiple epidemiological studies (see Mooney, 2009). It has been undermined as well by the simple fact that autism rates continue to rise, even though the alleged offending agent in vaccines (a mercury-based preservative called thimerosal) has long since been removed.

Yet the true believers persist—critiquing each new study that challenges their views, and even rallying to the defense of vaccine-autism researcher Andrew Wakefield, after his 1998 *Lancet* paper—which originated the current vaccine scare—was retracted and he subsequently lost his license (General Medical Council, 2010, p. 9) to practice medicine. But then, why should we be surprised? Vaccine deniers created their own partisan media, such as the website Age of Autism, that instantly blast out critiques and counterarguments whenever any new development casts further doubt on anti-vaccine views.

It all raises the question: Do left and right differ in any meaningful way when it comes to biases in processing information, or are we all equally susceptible?

There are some clear differences. Science denial today is considerably more prominent on the political right—once you survey climate and related environmental issues, anti-evolutionism, attacks on reproductive health science by the Christian right, and stem-cell and biomedical matters. More tellingly, anti-vaccine positions are virtually nonexistent among Democratic officeholders today—whereas anti-climate-science views are becoming monolithic among Republican elected officials.

Some researchers have suggested that there are psychological differences between the left and the right that might impact responses to new information—that conservatives are more rigid and authoritarian, and liberals more tolerant of ambiguity. Psychologist John Jost of New York University has further argued that conservatives are "system justifiers": They engage in motivated reasoning to defend the status quo.

This is a contested area, however, because as soon as one tries to psychoanalyze inherent political differences, a battery of counterarguments emerges: What about dogmatic and militant communists? What about how the parties have differed through history? After all, the most canonical case of ideologically driven science denial is probably the rejection of genetics in the Soviet Union, where researchers disagreeing with the anti-Mendelian scientist (and Stalin stooge) Trofim Lysenko were executed, and genetics itself was denounced as a "bourgeois" science and officially banned.

The upshot: All we can currently bank on is the fact that we all have blinders in some situations. The question then becomes: What can be done to counteract human nature itself?

Given the power of our prior beliefs to skew how we respond to new information, one thing is becoming clear: If you want someone to accept new evidence, make sure to present it to them in a context that doesn't trigger a defensive, emotional reaction.

This theory is gaining traction in part because of Kahan's work at Yale. In one study (Kahan, Braman, Slovic, Gastil, & Cohen, 2007), he and his colleagues packaged the basic science of climate change into fake newspaper articles bearing two very different headlines—"Scientific Panel Recommends Anti-Pollution Solution to Global Warming" and "Scientific Panel Recommends Nuclear Solution to Global Warming" (p. 5)—and then tested how citizens with different values responded. Sure enough, the latter framing made hierarchical individualists much more open to accepting the fact that humans are causing global warming. Kahan and his colleagues infer that the effect occurred because the science had been written into an alternative narrative that appealed to their pro-industry worldview.

You can follow the logic to its conclusion: Conservatives are more likely to embrace climate science if it comes to them via a business

or religious leader, who can set the issue in the context of different values than those from which environmentalists or scientists often argue. Doing so is, effectively, to signal a détente in what Kahan has called a "culture war of fact" (Kahan et al., 2007). In other words, paradoxically, you don't lead with the facts in order to convince. You lead with the values—so as to give the facts a fighting chance.

References

Cone, J. (Interviewer), & Kahan, D. (Interviewee). (2010, June 10). Cultural Cognition Project, Part 2. [Interview transcript]. Retrieved from http://seagrant.oregonstate.edu/blogs/communicatingclimate/transcripts/Episode_10b_Dan_Kahan.html

Damasio, A. R. (1994, October). Descartes' error and the future of human life. *Scientific American, 271*(4), 144.

Festinger, L., Riecken, H. W., & Schacter, S., (1956). *When prophecy fails: A social and psychological study of a modern group that predicted the destruction of the world.* Minneapolis: University of Minnesota Press.

General Medical Council. (2010, May 24). Determination on serious professional misconduct (SPM) and sanction [Letter to Jeremy Wakefield]. Retrieved from http://www.gmc-uk.org/Wakefield_SPM_and_SANCTION.pdf_32595267.pdf

Haidt, J. (2001). The emotional dog and its rational tail: A social intuitionist approach to moral judgment. *Psychological Review. 108*, 814-834. doi: 10.1037/0033-295X.108.4.814

Kahan, D. M., Braman, D., Monahan, J. Callahan, L., & Peters, E. (2010). Cultural cognition and public policy: The case of outpatient commitment laws. *Law and Human Behavior 34*, 118-140. doi: 10.1007/s10979-008-9174-4

Kahan, D. M., Braman, D., Slovic, P., Gastil, J., & Cohen, G. (2007, October 3). The second national risk and culture study: Making sense of—and making progress in—the American culture war of fact. *The Cultural Cognition Project at Yale Law School.* Retrieved from http://www.scribd.com/doc/3446682/

The-Second-National-Risk-and-Culture-Study-Making-Sense-of-and-Making-Progress-In-The-American-Culture-War-of-Fact

Kahan, D. M., Jenkins-Smith, H., & Braman, D. (2011). Cultural cognition of scientific consensus. *Journal of Risk Research 14*, 147–174. doi: 10.1080/13669877.2010.511246

Kennedy, Robert F. Jr. (2009, February 24). Vaccine Court: Autism debate continues. *The Huffington Post.* Retrieved from http://www.huffingtonpost.com/robert-f-kennedy-jr-and-david-kirby/vaccine-court-autism-deba_b_169673.html

Kunda, Z. (1990). The case for motivated reasoning. *The Psychological Bulletin, 108,* 480–498. doi: 10.1037/0033-2909.108.3.480

Lord, C. G., Ross, L., & Lepper, M. R. (1979). Biased assimilation and attitude polarization: The effects of prior theories on subsequently considered evidence. *Journal of Personality and Social Psychology 37,* 2098–2109. doi: 10.1037/0022-3514.37.11.2098

McCarthy, Jenny. (2011, January 10). In the vaccine-autism debate, what can parents believe? *The Huffington Post.* Retrieved from http://www.huffingtonpost.com/jenny-mccarthy/vaccine-autism-debate_b_806857.html

Mnookin, Seth. (2011). *The panic virus: A true story of medicine, science, and fear.* New York: Simon & Schuster.

Mooney, Chris. (2009, May 6). Why does the vaccine/autism controversy live on? *Discover.* Retrieved from http://discovermagazine.com/2009/jun/06-why-does-vaccine-autism-controversy-live-on

Munro, G. D., & Ditto, P. H. (1997). Biased assimilation, attitude polarization, and affect in reactions to stereotype-relevant scientific information. *Personality and Social Psychology Bulletin 23,* 636–653. doi: 10.1177/0146167297236007.

Nisbet, E. & Garrett, K. (2010, October 14). Fox News contributes to spread of rumors about proposed NYC mosque: CNN and NPR promote more accurate beliefs. Retrieved from http://http://www.comm.ohio-state.edu/kgarrett/MediaMosqueRumors.pdf

Nisbet, E. & Garrett, K. (2010, October 27). Belief in rumors hard to dispel: Fact checking easily undermined by images, unrelated facts. PDF. Retrieved from http://www.comm.ohio-state.edu/kgarrett/FactcheckMosqueRumors.pdf

Nyhan, B., & Reifler, J. (2010). When corrections fail: The persistence of political misperceptions. *Political Behavior, 32,* 303–330. doi: 10.1007/s11109-010-9112-2

Pew Research Center for the People & the Press. (2008, May 8). A deeper partisan divide over global warming. Retrieved from http://people-press.org/files/legacy-pdf/417.pdf

Prasad, M., Perrin, A. J., Bezila, K., Hoffman, S. G., Kindleberger, K., Manturuk, K., & Powers, A. S. (2009). "There must be a reason": Osama, Saddam, and inferred justification. *Sociological Inquiry 79,* 142–162. doi: 10.1111/j.1475-682X.2009.00280.x

Wakefield, A. J., Murch, S. H. Anthony, A., Linnell, J., Casson, D. M., Malik, M., ... Walker-Smith, J. A. (1998). Ileal-lymphoid-nodular hyperplasia, non-specific colitis, and pervasive developmental disorder in children. *The Lancet 351,* 637–641. doi: 10.1016/S0140-6736(97)11096-0

A CLOSER LOOK AT
Rapture Ready: The Science of Self Delusion

1. Mooney is basically arguing that reasoning is not the way people usually figure out what they believe. According to Mooney, how do people form and defend their beliefs—even when their beliefs are provably wrong?

2. According to Mooney's research, what are the basic differences between conservatives and progressives about how they see the world and what they choose to believe? How do these differences sometimes lead them to engage in self-delusion?

3. Late in the article, Mooney offers a few strategies for persuading people to consider ideas that they may disagree with. What are two ways that Mooney mentions to persuade people?

IDEAS FOR
Writing

1. Choose one of the examples of self-delusion that Mooney mentions in this research paper. Write a commentary in which you explain and explore this case of self-delusion. Discuss its history and the evidence offered by its believers. At the end of your commentary, explain whether you think this self-delusion is harmful and what you think should be done about it.

2. Write a memoir in which you describe a time when you couldn't persuade someone to do something or believe something. What happened as you made your arguments? Use your memoir to explain why you think this person didn't believe what you were saying.

3. Write an argument in which you try to argue for or against a controversial point. Instead of just expressing your opinion, though, try to "frame" the debate in terms that someone who is politically opposite to you will understand. For example, if you are arguing for "clean energy" with someone who doesn't believe in climate change, how can you reframe the debate in a way that he or she will find more persuasive?

Taking on Creationism: Which Arguments and Evidence Counter Pseudoscience?

MARK GREENER

In this research paper, Mark Greener addresses an audience of scientists to address the question, "Should scientists engage in the creationism/evolution debate, and if so what evidence and argumentative strategies are most compelling to nonscientists?" As you read, notice how Greener cites a variety of sources to summarize the debate and summarize recommendations from authoritative scientists.

As the noted geneticist and evolutionary biologist Theodosius Dobzhansky (1900–1975) famously commented, "nothing in biology makes sense except in the light of evolution." However, creationism in its many forms insists that everything in nature was created by a deity: from the movement of chloride ions through a channel in response to the binding of a ligand, to the bizarre life-forms that were deposited in the Burgess Shale more than 500 million years ago. To any mainstream biologist, creationism sounds ludicrous and scientists have repeatedly fought attempts to introduce the teaching of creationism generally, and intelligent design particularly, into school curricula. However, like many scientists and commentators, Jerry Coyne, Professor of Ecology and Evolution at the University of Chicago, IL, USA, fears that the social impact of these movements could extend far beyond the purely scientific debate. Therefore, scientists need to counter the claims of the proponents of creationism and determine which arguments best support the case for evolutionary theory and, more generally, support science itself in the public arena.

From its heartland in America's 'Bible belt', creationism is slowly extending its reach. "It's difficult to quantify, but my strong sense is that creationism is spreading across Europe," said Simon Conway Morris, Professor of Evolutionary Palaeobiology at the University of Cambridge, UK. "Ten years ago the movement was negligible. Today, it is clearly more substantial." Last year, the Guardian reported that 59 schools in the UK were using information about intelligent design as "a useful classroom resource" (Randerson, 2006).

Biologists have long-debated whether and how to respond to claims that the theory of evolution must be taught together with more or less biblical interpretations of the origins of life on Earth. However, the fervour of the anti-evolutionary lobby means that it is now a question of how, not whether, biologists must educate the public about evolution and natural selection. Yet, scientists face a dilemma. The danger is that if scientists engage the proponents of creationism and intelligent design in direct debate, they risk giving further credence to anti-evolutionary arguments by inferring that the ideas are worthy of discussion. Conversely, a failure to engage in debate could allow creationists to argue that biologists cannot, rather than will not, counter their arguments.

Creationism itself is not a unified movement; its various incarnations encompass a gamut of philosophical positions (Scott, 2000), including intelligent design. As Michael Coates, in the Department of Organismal Biology and Anatomy at the University of Chicago, IL, USA, noted: "[intelligent design] covers a wide spectrum of beliefs—just as creationists include anything from believers in a god that did no more than light the blue touch-paper of life, the universe and everything, through to a strongly interventionist deity who counts dead sparrows, answers prayers and directs the occasional thunderbolt."

The Catholic Church—one of the most his- 5 torically ardent opponents of Darwin's grand theory of evolution—has made its peace with the subject. Before he became Pope Benedict XVI, Cardinal Joseph Ratzinger wrote that, "[w]e

cannot say: creation or evolution, inasmuch as these two things respond to two different realities. The story of the dust of the earth and the breath of God, which we just heard, does not in fact explain how human persons come to be but rather what they are. It explains their inmost origin and casts light on the project that they are. And, vice versa, the theory of evolution seeks to understand and describe biological developments. But in so doing it cannot explain where the 'project' of human persons comes from, nor their inner origin, nor their particular nature. To that extent we are faced here with two complementary— rather than mutually exclusive—realities" (Ratzinger, 1995).

Proponents of intelligent design might accept some minor aspects of evolutionary theory. However, intelligent design by definition denies that mutation and natural selection can explain, for example, the evolution of chordates from echinoderms. It draws its intellectual roots from a Teleological argument that has been supported by some philosophers since Plato's Timaeus. The English theologist William Paley (1743-1805) formulated the most famous example: if one found a watch, the order, complexity and purpose would argue for a watchmaker. Similarly, because the universe shows order, complexity and purpose, there must be a creator.

According to Conway Morris, such teleological seeds often fall on fertile ground. "Many creationists are genuinely astonished by the diversity of living organisms," he said. "[A]s biologists, we tend to use mechanistic metaphors, which implicitly encourage the idea of a maker. So, one can see why the idea of an intelligent designer appeals to someone not versed in evolutionary theory. [Intelligent design] is not science and I think it's bad theology, but I can see why people hold the view."

This might explain why so many educated people take intelligent design seriously, as Coyne commented: "Intelligent design is attracting some serious attention, it's not just a few quacks who think that the earth is flat." During a debate held in May, three out of the ten Republican candidates for the US presidency said that they did not believe in evolution. "We should worry when the fundamentalists start to run public budgets and gain, or attempt to gain, political influence," Coates said.

Intelligent design and creationism do not just limit themselves to refuting the theory of evolution; the attack on science extends to other fields including geology, astronomy and even scientific materialism. The Center for Science and Culture (Seattle, WA, USA), which describes itself as "the nation's leading think-tank challenging various aspects of evolutionary theory" comments on its website: "We think the materialistic world view that has dominated Western Intellectual life since the late 19th century is false and we want to refute it [...] Materialism is a dehumanising philosophy" (Discovery Institute, 2003). Coyne commented, "[c]reationism is an attack on the materialistic basis of science [...] This carries forward into [the creationist] view of other evidence. Many creationists believe that global warming is a hoax, for example. They simply don't accept scientific evidence."

Coyne agrees with the British evolutionary biologist Richard Dawkins, one of the staunchest defenders of evolutionary theory, that engaging creationists in direct debate is a waste of time. "The whole history of the debate shows us that such debates of rhetorical fencing are futile," he said. Conway Morris, however, objects to the intellectual arrogance of some biologists. "Some of the more extreme secularists who effectively say that anyone who believes in [intelligent design] is stupid don't help to move the debate forward," he said. "It's insulting and it's not surprising that the debates become acrimonious."

A better strategy might therefore be to let the scientific evidence speak for itself. "It's hard for anyone to claim that evolution hasn't taken place when they're presented with the evidence," Coyne agreed. "And it's worth pointing out that many people who believe in God also regard evolution as fact. The two aren't incompatible." However, countering the rhetoric of the proponents of intelligent design and creationism with scientific evidence is not an easy task; evolutionary theory does not quite stir the belief and passion in most people that the grandeur of an Almighty does. Given the difficulties, what evidence can biologists use to counter creationist dogma?

For example, how can biologists counter the creationist argument that there are still many missing links in the fossil record that make evolutionary theory unworkable? Conway Morris noted that an understanding of what those missing links are is a good start. He pointed out that a marked phenotypic change, facilitating rapid evolution, might arise from a single-nucleotide polymorphism. "Life often seems as if it walks on a knife edge," he said. "But in cases such as this there won't be an intermediate in the fossil record." In any case, the fossil record contains numerous transitional forms that allow the reconstruction of, for example, the development of the modern whale (Balaena spp.) from the hippo-like Diacodexis spp., which existed some 50 million years ago. Missing links emerge regularly and it is quite likely that palaeontologists have simply not discovered them all yet.

Some biologists find that evolutionary convergence offers a powerful argument against intelligent design and highlights the effectiveness of natural selection. Creationists often cite the eye as a complex organ that could not have evolved without intervention. However, Conway Morris counters that, "[y]ou can track the evolution of the eye on several different occasions [...] Despite very different origins, the pathways converge." He cited the examples of the octopus and the trout; both have a similarly altered lens composition that corrects for spherical aberration. "They both produced the ideal parabola as described by physicists," he explained. "But then again, both had to adapt to overcome the same limitation, so is it that surprising that they solved it in the same way?" In other words, the ancestors of the octopus and trout were selected for because these changes to their eye conferred increased fitness to the organism—they were better able to see and escape predators, and find food—and hence the change was propagated. No design was required, only the natural selection of a series of advantageous mutations.

Other examples of convergent evolution include silk, copper proteins and carbonic anhydrase. "Through examples such as this we can see the footprints of history even without the fossil record," Conway Morris said. "There's almost a sense that these examples have to work in this way because of the environmental circumstance. Rather than being random, common phenotypes developed to adapt to common pressures."

"In instances of convergence, evolutionary evidence is found in the detail," Coates commented. "Molluscan and vertebrate lens composition might be remarkably similar, but vertebrate retinal structure remains 'back to front'. A designer would orient the tips of photoreceptors so that they point towards the light source, and the parts of the retina that carry signal towards the brain should be farther removed. This seems fair enough, and this is how the squid retina is built, but vertebrate examples are assembled the other way around—perversely, light has to plunge the full depth of the retina to reach the point of reception."

Similarly, the HOX gene family that controls limb formation in vertebrates offers another example of evolution in action. "The evolution of paired fins into limbs with digits is a classic example of morphological transformation," Coates said. "Evidence for homology between paired fins and limbs is compelling—from an evolutionary perspective, vertebrate limbs are best viewed as a specialized subset or kind of paired fins." Indeed, the pattern of morphological change—the evolutionary sequence of anatomical transformation—is pretty well established. "This sets an agenda for developmental biology, concerning questions about differences between fin buds and limb buds, cell populations, tissues, signals and patterns," Coates added. "As these questions are answered, the evolutionary transition from fins to limbs is likely to become an exemplar of changing pattern and process underpinning large-scale morphological change."

However, although biologists can present good arguments for evolution, they still need to reach out to the general public and explain those arguments and engage in a dialogue. "Part of the answer is to introduce more evolutionary biology into early school curricula," Coates commented. "Children need to grow up with the fact of evolution, and [the] awareness that it underpins biology. Teachers should be encouraged to be bold enough to talk about this early and often,

from infants onwards—whatever the parents' faiths or the school governors' and/or trustees' faiths. There seems to be a widespread fear of treading on toes." Coyne added that, "[t]oo often school science regards evolution as a given and focuses on the mechanisms, mimicry and so on [...]. It rarely presents the evidence from, for example, the fossil record."

In any case—like in any scientific field—there are still numerous areas of controversy in evolutionary theory. "Evolutionary theory remains a really fertile field," Coyne agreed. "For example, we don't understand how species form." His main area of research aims to ascertain whether speciation involves many or only a few genes, whether genetic drift plays a significant role, and whether the movement of transposable elements causes hybrid sterility or whether it undermines viability.

Similarly, Conway Morris has built his reputation on another controversy: the interpretation of the Burgess Shale that records an explosion of the numbers and types of life-form during the Cambrian period. His research group has recently submitted two papers that illustrate how body plans as amazingly diverse as those found in the shale might have emerged, and how nature ended up with organisms as different as starfish and fish. However, the basic question of what caused the Cambrian explosion—why life needed to adapt so quickly—remains open. "Before the Cambrian, life evolved fantastically slowly, then there was this sudden seachange," Conway Morris said. "An increase in oxygen levels is one possibility, but we don't really know."

The British geneticist and evolutionary biologist J.B.S. Haldane (1892–1964), one of the pioneers of classical population genetics, which reconciled Mendelian and Darwinian theory, once remarked that "fossil rabbits in the precambrian" would invalidate evolution. But his quip makes a serious point and highlights a key difference between evolutionary theory and creationism: as with any scientific theory, Darwinism is constantly challenged and reinforced by new evidence. Creationism, on the other hand, rejects scientific theory and new evidence and favours a more or less narrow world-view based on divine intervention. Therefore, until a Precambrian rabbit comes bounding out of the fossil record, the theories of natural selection and evolution remain the only valid explanations of how life on Earth developed.

References

Discovery Institute (2003) The "Wedge Document": "So What?". Seattle, WA, USA: Discovery Institute. www.discovery.org

Randerson J (2006) Revealed: rise of creationism in UK schools. London, UK: Guardian, Nov 27 (http://education.guardian.co.uk/schools/story/0,,1957858,00.html)

Ratzinger J (1995) In the Beginning: A Catholic Understanding of the Story of Creation and the Fall. Grand Rapids, MI, USA: Eerdmans

Scott EC (2000) The Creation/Evolution Continuum. Oakland, CA , USA: National Center for Science Education.www.ncseweb.org

A CLOSER LOOK AT
Taking on Creationism

1. For a research paper, an author should identify the topic, state the purpose, state the main point/thesis, offer background information, and stress the importance of the topic to readers. Examine the introductory paragraphs and point out the specific places where Greener makes each of these moves. As a group, write one or two sentences that summarize Greener's topic, purpose, main point/thesis, and reasons for believing the topic is important.

2. Would you characterize this research paper as "expository" (explaining the topic without arguing for one side) or "argumentative" (choosing a side and using research to support that side)? Develop an argument for each characterization: In what ways is this an expository research paper, and in what ways is it argumentative?

3. In this research paper, Greener uses online, print, and empirical sources to offer background information and explain why the topic is important. For his recommendations about whether and how to debate, however, he relies mostly on empirical sources (interviews). What strategies does Greener use to establish the authority of each of his interviewees?

IDEAS FOR
Writing

1. Write a rhetorical analysis of Greener's research paper. Explain its historical context, including who his target audience is, where it appeared, and why Greener wrote it (his purpose). Then analyze the text in terms of reasoning (*logos*), credibility (*ethos*), and emotion (*pathos*), making sure to define each of these concepts. In the end, explain whether it is effective or persuasive, and why it is or is not.

2. Write an explainer (see Chapter 13) in which you explore the arguments for and against the question, "Should scientists engage in the evolution/creationism debate?" You can use Greener's research paper as a source, and you can consult others as well. Why do some scientists say that creationists should be simply ignored, and why do others argue that scientists should join in?

Darwin's Paradigm Shift[1]

TIM M. BERRA, PH.D., University Professorial Fellow, Charles Darwin University & Professor Emeritus, Dept. Of Evolution, Ecology & Organismal Biology, The Ohio State University 1760 University Dr., Mansfield, Ohio 44906 USA

In this research paper, Tim Berra explains the history of Darwin's theory of evolution. Then, he goes on to discuss one of this theory's implications and impacts on science. The discussion is mostly factual with minimal opinion included. Look closely at the author's strategies for staying objective about a controversial issue.

Charles Darwin (1809–1882) was an extraordinary man by any standard. The theory of evolution by natural selection, as elaborated in his book *On the Origin of Species* (1859) (Figure 1.1), is considered by historians and philosophers of science to be one of the most important far-reaching ideas ever had by the human mind (Dennett 1995). Before exploring this grandiose statement, a brief review of Darwin's life and scientific accomplishments is in order. Then I will address the implications of his very useful insights that extend beyond science and profoundly impact the progress of humanity

An Outline of Darwin's Life

Charles Darwin was born into a wealthy English family on 12 February 1809. His father, Robert Waring Darwin (1766–1848), was a prominent physician, as was his grandfather Erasmus Darwin (1731–1802). His mother was Susannah Wedgwood (1765–1817), the daughter of Josiah Wedgwood (1730–1795), the pottery manufacturer and entrepreneur. Josiah was also a close friend of Erasmus Darwin.

Darwin's father sent Charles to medical school at Edinburgh University in 1825 and removed him in 1827, when it became obvious that Charles was not interested in a medical career. Robert Darwin then decided that Charles should study to be a clergyman in the Church of England, sending him to Cambridge University in 1828. In 1831 Charles graduated tenth in his class among those who did not take an honors degree. He then received an invitation orchestrated by his professor, John Stevens Henslow (1796–1861), to be an unpaid naturalist-companion to Captain Robert FitzRoy (1805–1865) on a surveying voyage around the world on the H.M.S. *Beagle* (1831–1836). Darwin later described this opportunity as "the first real training or education of my mind."

On his return from the nearly five-year *Beagle* voyage, Darwin found that he was accepted as a serious scientist, and he had no desire to become a clergyman. He began working on the specimens collected during the voyage. He married his first cousin, Emma Wedgwood (1808–1896), and they eventually moved from London to Down House in Kent. They had 10 children, seven of whom survived to adulthood. In the years after the voyage, Charles was often ill, but nevertheless highly productive. He entered his ideas about how species form in a series of notebooks. This included a branching, treelike diagram that reflected the common origin and relatedness of organisms. This early evolutionary tree showed that classification should be genealogical (Pietsch 2012; Mindell 2013).

This tree's implications, however, extended far 5 beyond taxonomy. Darwin kept his revolutionary

[1]Berra, Tim M. 2013. *Darwin & His Children: His Other Legacy*. Oxford University Press, New York.

ideas private for 20 years, except to broach them to his closet scientific colleagues: geologist Charles Lyell (1797–1875), botanist Joseph Dalton Hooker (1817–1911), and his American botanist correspondent at Harvard University, Asa Gray (1810–1888) (Porter 1993). In 1858 Darwin received a letter from naturalist Alfred Russel Wallace (1823–1913), who, like Darwin, was inspired by the writings of Thomas Malthus (1766–1834). Wallace outlined ideas on natural selection and speciation that were nearly identical to Darwin's. This letter, combined with urging from Lyell and Hooker, prompted him to complete and publish *On the Origin of Species* in 1859. Darwin continued to perform experiments and publish on a variety of topics right up to the time of his death, of heart disease, on 19 April 1882. He was laid to rest with pomp and ceremony in Westminster Abbey, a few feet from Isaac Newton. Further details can be pursued in two of the most comprehensive biographies of Darwin (Desmond and Moore 1991; Browne 1995, 2002), a concise biography (Berra 2009), and, of course, Darwin's autobiography (Barlow 1958).

Synopsis of Darwin's Scientific Achievements

Educated citizens are generally aware of *On the Origin of Species,* as well as Darwin's account of his voyage around the world in the H.M.S. *Beagle* through his *Journal of Researches* (1839) (Figure 1.1), a book now universally known as *The Voyage of the Beagle. The Voyage* and *The Origin* have never been out of print. Almost all of Darwin's books have been translated into multiple foreign languages, numbering 33 by last count (Freeman 1977). *The Origin* itself has been published in at least 29 languages, 11 in Darwin's lifetime. Only his work on barnacles appears solely in English.

Most people are surprised to learn that Darwin also made many other major contributions to geology, zoology, and botany through his observations, experiments, and writings. His books have been chronicled (Berra 2009), so I will just briefly outline the breadth of his influence. Darwin explained how coral reefs form (1842) and contributed to geological observations on movements within the earth (1844) and the deformation theory of metamorphic rock (1846). In a pioneering four-volume

work that took eight years to complete, he described all known fossil and living barnacle species (1851–1854). Darwin explained how orchids are pollinated by insects (1862) and how plants climb (1865), and he catalogued the bewildering amount of variation in domestic plants and animals (1868) (Figure 1.1). He delineated human origins and sexual selection (a special form of natural selection) in multiple species in ways never before articulated (1870–1871), and discussed human and animal emotions in the same terms (1872). The latter work was one of the first books to use photographs to illustrate a point (Prodger 2009).

Darwin showed how insectivorous plants on poor-quality soils utilize nitrogen-rich insects to provide that essential nutrient (1875), and demonstrated that the offspring of cross-pollinated plants were more numerous and vigorous than self-pollinated ones (1876, 1877). His observations of growth within plants laid the foundation for the field of plant growth hormones (1880). His work on earthworms (1881) is a classic study in ecology. Any one of these achievements, by itself, could constitute a life's work for most scientists.

Darwin's Legacy

Darwin was born and educated at a time when "special creation" was the prevailing scientific view. That is, God created the universe and all species a few thousand years ago, and they were unchangeable. "Revelation," not research, provided this view. Darwin began the H.M.S. *Beagle* voyage with this belief. During his lifetime the age of the earth was increasingly recognized as much more ancient, a concept suggested by James Hutton (1769–1797), Georges Cuvier (1769–1832), and Charles Lyell (1797–1875) (Bowler 1984; Larson 2004). Observations made during the voyage led Darwin to question the Genesis creation myth and the immutability of species. He found marine fossils thousands of feet above sea level and reasoned that the land had been elevated by movements within the earth, not inundated in great biblical flood. The fossil mammals he uncovered in South America resembled living mammals from the same area. He wondered why this should be if each species

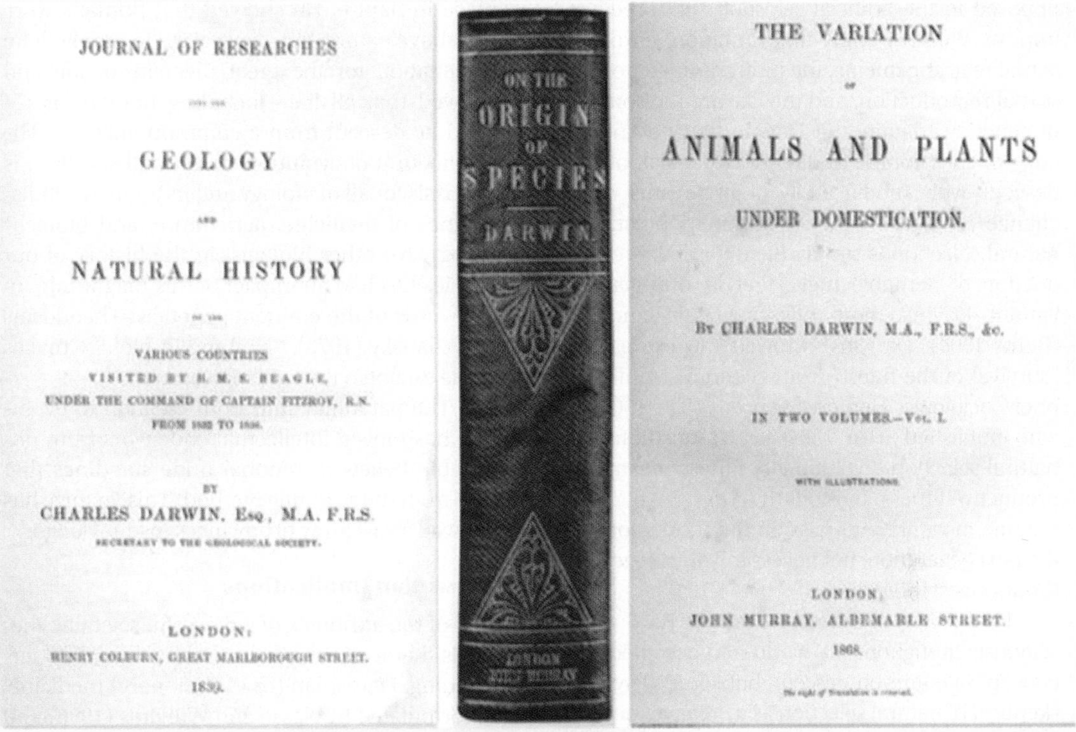

FIGURE 1.1

Left: The title page of Darwin's Journal of Researches, *published in its own right as a stand-alone book. It was originally published as volume 3 of Captain FitzRoy's narrative.* The Voyage of the Beagle *was first used as the title in 1905. Center: The spine of the first edition of* On the Origin of Species, *by Charles Darwin, published by John Murray of London on 24 November 1859. All 1,500 copies of the first printing were ordered before the official date of publication. Right: The title page of the first edition of* The Variation of Animals and Plants. *Herbert Spencer's phrase "survival of the fittest" is used by Darwin for the first time here. The material included in this book extends the first chapter of* The Origin.

was specially created. Extinction was barely recognized in those days. If each species was created in place, why did the animals on islands off continental areas resemble those on the nearest landmass? Why were there so many species in an island group that looked very similar but had slight differences from island to island? In *The Voyage of the Beagle*, Darwin concluded that it was as if "one species had been taken and modified for different ends." None of these things made sense from a creationist perspective. As he wrote to Hooker in 1844, "I am almost convinced (quite contrary to the opinion I started with) that species are not (it is like confessing a murder) immutable" (Burkhardt et al. 1985-, 3:2).

The elegant simplicity of Darwin's reasoning can be distilled as follows. There is variation in nature, and many more offspring are generated than can survive; therefore there is a struggle for life in which favorable variations are preserved and unfavorable variations are removed. This leads to evolution, which he defined as "descent with modification," and to the formation of new species. Nature is doing the selecting for the forms best adapted to a particular environment, so Darwin called the process natural selection—as opposed to the artificial selection that breeders impose. We now know that mutation, chromosomal rearrangements, the indiscriminateness of sexual reproduction, and the like are the sources of genetic variation, but Darwin had no knowledge of such topics. Today we can speak of the descent with modification of organisms as a change in gene frequency within populations; natural selection is simply the differential reproduction of heritable traits, that is, one genetic variant leaving more offspring than another (Berra 1990). Darwin borrowed the expression "survival of the fittest" from economist/philosopher/sociologist Herbert Spencer (1820–1903)—who published it in 1864—as a substitute for natural selection. Evolutionary fitness means reproductive fitness. In modern terms, the fittest is the one most likely to pass on the most genes to the next generation, not necessarily the biggest or the strongest individual.

By the time of Darwin's death in 1882, most scientists thoughout the world had accepted the concept of common descent, but some were still skeptical of natural selection as a creative mechanism (Bowler 1984). The public was less accepting.

When the first printing of *On the Origin of Species* appeared on 24 November 1859, it precipitated one of those rare events in the history of science: a paradigm shift. Philosopher Thomas Kuhn (1962) used this term to refer to the replacement of one world view by another. Examples of a paradigm shift in science include the replacement of the earth-centered Ptolemaic system by the sun-centered Copernican system, and of Newtonian physics by relativity and quantum physics.

Darwin's work neatly dovetailed into the wider pattern of scientific advances that were occurring during his lifetime. Lyell and others had provided the necessary geological time frame for evolution to operate. The writings of Georges Cuvier, Thomas Malthus, Robert Chambers (1802–1871), Herbert Spencer, Alfred Russel Wallace, and many others helped set the evolutionary stage. By 1859 evolution by natural selection was an idea ready to burst forth. Darwin and the publication of *The Origin* made it happen. Darwin, through *The Origin* and his books that followed, changed the way humans view their place in nature. He showed that humans were not above nature, but a part of it. He supplied the explanation for the great diversity of life and showed that all life—including human—is related by descent from a common ancestor. His explanation of evolution via natural selection is the basis for all of biology and its applied subdisciplines of medicine, agriculture, and biotechnology. No other biologist in the history of our species has had an impact of this magnitude. In the words of the eminent geneticist Theodosius Dobzhansky (1973), "Nothing in biology makes sense except in the light of evolution."

The paradigm shift from creation to evolution has moved intellectual endeavors from untestable beliefs to rational understandings that flow from the scientific method. This, in turn, has allowed a vast array of advances in knowledge.

Darwinian Implications

One of the attributes of a powerful scientific theory is that it enables future research and understanding. Darwinian (or evolutionary) medicine, as formulated by Nesse and Williams (1996) and expanded by Stearns and Koella (2008) and Gluckman et al. (2009), explains how some disease symptoms, such as fever, may be a response favored by natural selection as a defense against pathogens. Some conditions generally considered to be genetic diseases, such as sickle cell anemia, may allow differential survival of its victims in malarial zones, a phenomenon called balanced polymorphism (Berra 1990). Evolutionary thinking explains the arms race waged by pathogens and hosts that prevents either from being completely eliminated. The development of resistant bacteria through the flagrant overuse of antibiotics is easily explained by Darwinian reasoning. A drug will kill the susceptible bacteria, but bacteria with a preexisting resistant mutation are unaffected and can build up the next generation. Then, when that antibiotic is later needed for a bacterial infection, the drug is ineffective. This is evolution, pure and simple.

A similar process occurs in agriculture with the overapplication of pesticides and the formation of pesticide-resistant pathogens, insects, and noxious plants. Australians are very familiar with warfare between myxomatosis and rabbits:

the virus initially killed 99 percent of the rabbits (an invasive, or nonnative, species in Australia), but, given enough time, the surviving rabbits returned in force, since the virus evolved in the direction of less virulence and the process of natural selection among the rabbits resulted in more resistance to the virus (Berra 1998).

Evolutionary psychology and evolutionary ethics, as explored by Barkow et al. (1992) and popularized by Wright (1994), help explain the origin of morality. Peacemaking among nonhuman primates, through the calming effect of mutual grooming to diffuse aggression, may be seen as the precursor of what became morality in humans (de Waal 1989). Modern religions are recent human inventions--a mere few thousand years old. The antecedents of morality, on the other hand clearly evolved before humanity, as reflected in the empathy exhibited by bonobos (*Pan paniscus)* and the reciprocity of chimpanzees (*P. troglodytes*) (de Waal 2005). The awareness and sensitivity demonstrated by humans' closest relatives may be the underlying driver of prosocial behavior (de Waal 2012, 2013). Kin selection, where an individual voluntarily sacrifices for a close genetic relative, makes sense in an evolutionary context, because some of the same genes of the individual making the sacrifice will be passed on by the kin who survives. Hamilton (1972) refers to this as inclusive fitness. A realization that humans share kinship with all animal life has helped to raise consciousness about how we treat other animals (Singer 1977).

The ancestry of the AIDS virus, HIV-1 (human immunodeficiency virus-1), has been traced to SIVcpz (simian immunodeficiency virus) carried by our closest living relative, the chimpanzees, *P. troglodytes* (Bailes et al. 2003). This is not surprising from an evolutionary perspective. Somewhere in high school today there is a student whose future research may contribute to better control of the AIDS epidemic. What chance of that would there be if evolution weren't taught properly in high school?

Even religion is now being explained as having an evolutionary origin: a natural phenomenon that arose once the brain evolved a critical mass and complexity (Dennett 2006). Bloch (2008) suggested that the evolution of imagination was a requisite for the emergence of religion, which he considered a logical extension of human sociality. Previously, this emergence of modern human behavior was thought to have occurred about 35,000-40,000 years ago, the time of the Upper Paleolithic "revolution," as manifested by an explosion of image making and cultural transformations (White 2003). However, recent discoveries in South Africa of engraved ochres (Henshilwood et al. 2002) and of small bladelets made from heat-treated stone (K. Brown et al. 2012) demonstrate that humans had already evolved the capacity for complex thought at least 70,000 years ago. Acceptance of authority (necessary for group cohesion and survival), enforced by tool use and language, and combined with a confusion between coincidence and cause and effect, can result in the establishment of a religious belief that becomes dominant in a culture (Wolpert 2007). Religion encourages beliefs and rituals—which may appear absurd to outsiders—that unite in-group cohesiveness but also promote conflict with out-groups (Atran and Ginges 2012).

Those whose religion requires a literal interpretation of the Bible fear that a paradigm shift from supernaturalism to methodological naturalism (a naturalistic causation for nature's phenomena) threatens their beliefs. The 1925 Scopes trial—nicknamed the "monkey trial" and the "trial of the century"—in Dayton, Tennessee, has come to symbolize the struggle of religion against science in popular culture; the trial later inspired the play and film *Inherit the Wind* (Larson 1997). Such creationists are particularly vocal in America, which has a longstanding tradition of anti-intellectualism (Pigliucci 2002; Numbers 2006). This has resulted in a series of creationist legal challenges to evolution that have been decided in favor of evolution (Berra 1990). The most important legal cases are against creationists or government entities that have adopted creationist policies, thus violating part of the US Constitution. These legal decisions include *Epperson v. Arkansas, McLean v. Arkansas, Edwards v. Aguillard,* and *Kitzmiller v. Dover*. In the latter case, intelligent design (ID) creationists influenced the Dover, Pennsylvania, School Board to adopt their ideas, an action that was challenged in the courts by a group of parents. The ID creationist philosophy, which posits that life is too complex to have arisen by natural means and therefore had a supernatural origin, has been critiqued in Pennock (2001) and exposed as a threat to science education by Forrest and Gross (2004). In the concluding portion of his decision, Judge John E. Jones III (2005) determined that the school board's policy of teaching intelligent design violated the Establishment Clause (the separation of church and state) of the First Amendment to the US Constitution. He wrote: "In making this determination, we have addressed the seminal question whether ID is science. We have concluded that it is not and moreover that ID cannot uncouple itself from its creationist, and thus religious, antecedents. . . . The breathtaking inanity of the board's decision is evident when considered against the factual backdrop which has now been fully revealed though this trial." For those who want to dive deeper into the miracle-strewn world of the anti-science crowd and explore this interesting case further, Padian (2007) reviewed three books based on the Dover trial.

Modern Evolutionary Synthesis

Darwin, of course, had no knowledge of genes, chromosomes, or how inheritance worked. This required additional input, arising from an understanding of Gregor Mendel's (1822–1884) genetic work. Biotechnology, whether in the form of genetically modified crops, designer drugs, gene therapy, or the human genome project, derives from Darwin's and Mendel's profound insights into how nature operates.

The modern evolutionary synthesis grew from Darwin's explanation of natural selection and Mendel's demonstration that inheritance was particulate—that is, that it can be passed from generation to generation by "particles," now known as genes (Dobzhansky 1937)—augmented by the research of mathematically oriented population geneticists such as J. B. S. Haldane, Ronald A. Fisher, Sewall Wright, Thomas Hunt Morgan, Theodosius Dobzhansky; paleontologist George Gaylord Simpson; botanist G. Ledyard Stebbins Jr.; biologist Julian Huxley (Thomas Henry Huxley's grandson); and the most important

evolutionary biologist since Darwin, Ernst Mayr. This fusion of knowledge moved evolutionary science forward to the middle of the twentieth century (Larson 2004). James D. Watson and Francis Crick's 1953 demonstration that the molecular structure of DNA (deoxyribonucleic acid) allowed for genetic coding was a huge breakthrough, one that ultimately made it possible to sequence the three billion chemical base pairs that compose the human genome and identify the approximately 20,000–25,000 genes in human DNA (Lander et al. 2001; Venter et al. 2001).

TV viewers are familiar with DNA analysis, popularized on various CSI (crime scene investigation) programs. DNA-sequencing techniques—where the arrangements of the A-T-C-G nucleotides are compared—can convict or exonerate people accused of crimes. Similar techniques can confirm or deny paternity in disputed cases, or can ensure that the expensive grouper fillets you purchase are not flesh from a lesser species. Such evolutionary tests are accepted by the judicial system because they pass the Daubert standard for scientific evidence: the techniques were subject to empirical testing, published in peer-reviewed journals, and accepted by the scientific community (Mindell 2009).

Recent discoveries in evolutionary developmental biology, known as evo-devo, have shown that very similar genes are present in very dissimilar animals. These body-shaping genes are controlled by DNA switches (called enhancers) that turn them on or off at various times during development. Such enhancers are a major factor in the development of morphology, the branch of biology that deals with the form of living organisms and with relationships between their structure (Carroll 2005). The above examples are just a smattering of the benefits to society that flow directly from the creative power of Charles Darwin's theory of evolution by means of natural selection.

The Human Genome Project spawned ENCODE (Encyclopedia of DNA Elements), whose mission was to describe all of the functional elements encoded in our genome. The 6 September 2012 issue of *Nature* published six coordinated ENCODE papers, while 24 related papers were published elsewhere in the same week. (Further exploration of this complicated, state-of-the-art 25 topic is facilitated at www.nature.com/encode/.) In addition to well-known coding elements, ENCODE explained the hidden genetic switches that regulate development and turn other genes on and off. This new knowledge showed that the term "junk DNA" was just a manifestation of our incomplete understanding. Today's biologists are fortunate to have the very broad shoulders of Charles Darwin to support and make possible their elaboration of how biology works.

The paradigm shift (Berra 2008) instigated by Darwin has made more obvious the superiority of the scientific method as a means of understanding the world around us. It is ironic that the legacy of a man once destined for the church has been to replace supernaturalism with methodological naturalism.

References

Atran, Scott and Jeremy Ginges. 2012. Religious and Sacred Imperatives in Human Conflict. *Science* 336: 855–857.

Bailes, E., F. Gao, F. Bibollet-Ruche, V. Courgnaud, M. Peeters, P. Marx, B. H. Han, and P. M. Sharp. 2003. Hybrid Origin of SIV in Chimpanzees. *Science* 300: 1713.

Barkow, J. H., L. Cosmides, and J. Tooby (Eds.). 1992. *The Adapted Mind.* Oxford University Press, Oxford.

Barlow, Nora (Ed.) 1958. *The Autobiography of Charles Darwin, 1809–1882: With Original Omissions Restored.* W. W. Norton, New York.

Berra, Tim M. 1990. *Evolution and the Myth of Creationism.* Stanford University Press, Stanford, CA.

Berra, Tim M. 1998. *A Natural History of Australia.* University of New South Wales Press/Academic Press, Sydney/San Diego.

Berra, Tim M. 2008. Charles Darwin's paradigm shift. *The Beagle, Records of the Museum and Art Galleries of the Northern Territory* 24: 1–5.

Berra, Tim M. 2009. *Charles Darwin: The Concise Story of an Extraordinary Man.* Johns Hopkins University Press, Baltimore.

Bloch, Maurice. 2008. Why Religion Is Nothing Special but Is Central. *Philosophical Transactions of the Royal Society, B* 363: 2055–2061.

Bowler, Peter J. 1984. *Evolution: the History of an Idea.* University of California Press, Berkeley.

Brown, Kyle S., et al. 2012. An Early and Enduring Advanced Technology Originating 71,000 Years Ago in South Africa. *Nature* 491: 590–593.

Browne, Janet. 1995. *Charles Darwin: A Biography. Vol. 1, Voyaging.* Princeton University Press, Princeton, NJ.

Browne, Janet. 2002. *Charles Darwin: A Biography. Vol. 2, The Power of Place.* Knopf, New York.

Burkhardt, Frederick, et al. (Eds.). 1985 –. *The Correspondence of Charles Darwin.* 19+ vols. Cambridge University Press, Cambridge. [This project is expected to include 30 volumes and to be completed around 2025.]

Carroll, Sean B. 2005. *Endless Forms Most Beautiful: The New Science of Evo Devo and the Making of the Animal Kingdom.* W. W. Norton, New York.

Darwin, Charles. 1859. *On the Origin of Species by Means of Natural Selection; or, The Preservation of Favoured Races in the Struggle for Life.* John Murray, London.

de Waal, Frans. 1989. *Peacemaking among Primates.* Harvard University Press, Cambridge, MA.

de Waal, Frans. 2005. *Our Inner Ape.* Riverhead Books, New York.

de Waal, Frans. 2012. The Antiquity of Empathy. *Science* 336: 874–876.

de Waal, Frans. 2013. *The Bonobo and the Atheist: In Search of Humanism among the Primates.* W. W. Norton New York.

Dennett, Daniel C. 1995. *Darwin's Dangerous Idea.* Touchstone, New York.

Dennett, Daniel C. 2006. *Breaking the Spell: Religion as a Natural Phenomenon.* Viking, New York.

Desmond, Adrian and James Moore. 1991. *Darwin: The Life of a Tormented Evolutionist.* Warner Books, New York.

Dobzhansky, Theodosius. 1973. Nothing in Biology Makes Sense Except in the Light of Evolution. *American Biology Teacher* 35: 125–129.

Forrest, Barbara and Paul R. Gross. 2004. *Creationism's Trojan Horse: The Wedge of Intelligent Design.* Oxford University Press, Oxford.

Freeman, R. B. 1977. *The Works of Charles Darwin: An Annotated Bibliographical Handlist.*

2nd edition, revised and enlarged. Archon Books, Hamden, CT.

Gluckman, Peter, Alan Beedle, and Marl Hanson. 2009. *Principles of Evolutionary Medicine.* Oxford University Press, Oxford.

Hamilton, William D. 1972. Altruism and Related Phenomena, Mainly in the Social Insects. *Annual Review of Ecology and Systematics* 3: 193-232.

Henshilwood, Christopher S., et al. 2002. Emergence of Modern Human Behavior: Middle Stone Age Engravings from South Africa. *Science* 295: 1278-1280.

Jones John E., III. 2005. Memorandum Opinion. In the United States District Court for the Middle District of Pennsylvania. *Tammy Kitzmiller, et al. Plaintiff s v. Dover Area School Board Defendants.* 400 F. Supp. 2d 707, Docket No. 04cv2688.

Kuhn, Thomas S. 1962. *The Structure of Scientific Revolutions* University of Chicago Press, Chicago.

Lander, Eric S., et al. 2001. Initial Sequencing and Analysis of the Human Genome. *Nature* 409: 860-921.

Larson, Edward J. 1997. *Summer for the Gods: The Scopes Trial and America's Continuing Debate Over Science and Religion.* Basic Books, New York.

Larson, Edward J. 2004. *Evolution: The Remarkable History of a Scientific Theory.* Modern Library, New York.

Mindell, D. P. 2009. Evolution in the Everyday World. *Scientific American* 300: 82-88.

Mindell, D. P. 2013. The Tree of Life: Metaphor, Model, and Heuristic Device. *Systematic Biology* 62: 479-489.

Nesse, Randolph M. and George C. Williams. 1996. *Why We Get Sick.* Vantage Books, New York.

Numbers, Ronald L. 2006. *The Creationists: From Scientific Creationism to Intelligent Design.* Expanded Edition. Harvard University Press, Cambridge, MA.

Padian, Kevin. 2007. The Case of Creation. *Nature* 448: 253-254.

Pennock, Robert T. 2001. *Intelligent Design Creationism and Its Critics: Philosophical, Theological, and Scientific Perspectives.* MIT Press, Cambridge, MA.

Pietsch, Theodore W. 2012. *Trees of Life: A Visual History of Evolution.* Johns Hopkins University Press, Baltimore.

Pigliucci, Massimo. 2002. *Denying Evolution: Creationism, Scientism, and the Nature of Science.* Sinauer Associates, Sunderland, MA.

Porter, D[uncan] M. 1993. On the Road to the *Origin* with Darwin, Hooker, and Gray. *Journal of the History of Biology* 26: 1-38.

Prodger, Phillip. 2009. *Darwin's Camera: Art and Photography in the Theory of Evolution.* Oxford University Press, Oxford.

Singer, Peter. 1977. *Animal Liberation: Towards an End to Man's Inhumanity to Animals.* Granada, London.

Stearns, Stephen C. and Jacob C. Koella. 2008. *Evolution in Health and Disease.* 2nd edition. Oxford University Press, Oxford.

Venter, J. Craig, et al. 2001. The Sequence of the Human Genome. *Science* 291: 1304-1351.

White, Randall. 2003. *Prehistoric Art: The Symbolic Journey of Humankind.* H. N. Abrams, New York.

Wolpert, Lewis. 2007. *Six Impossible Things before Breakfast: The Evolutionary Origin of Belief.* W. W. Norton, New York.

Wright, Robert. 1994. *The Moral Animal.* Pantheon Books, New York.

A CLOSER LOOK AT
Darwin's Paradigm Shift

1. In this research paper, Berra writes, "By the time of Darwin's death in 1882, most scientists throughout the world had accepted the concept of common descent, but some were still skeptical of natural selection as a creative mechanism." According to the author, why were scientists and the public skeptical of Darwin's theories, and why are many people skeptical today?

2. The author includes a great amount of historical information. How is he using this historical information to lay the groundwork for discussing the importance and implications of Darwin's theories?

3. This research paper could be classified as an "expository" research paper, because it mostly explains and offers factual information, while not making an overt argument. Nevertheless, it is argumentative in places. Locate three of those "argumentative" moments in this research paper. How is the author using argument in this otherwise expository research paper?

IDEAS FOR
Writing

1. The cornerstone of Darwin's theory of evolution is the concept of "natural selection." According to the author, what is natural selection and why is it critical to Darwin's theory of evolution? Write a brief in which you explain the concept of natural selection and explain why it is necessary in Darwinian evolution.

2. Create a five-source annotated bibliography about the history of Darwin's theory of evolution. Include only sources that discuss the history of this theory. Do not include articles or books that argue for or against the theory. Combine your annotated bibliography with the bibliographies from your group in class. How many sources did all of you have in common? How many sources were unique to your list? Talk about why you came up with the same or different sources on this topic.

A FEW IDEAS FOR
Composing a Research Paper

1. **Write a research paper about a contemporary issue.** Choose an issue that is prominent in the national or local media right now. Your research paper's topic does not need to be new, but you should find a new angle that makes this issue fresh and interesting. Your research paper should be about an issue that you care about but also something you can write about in an informed way. You should ask your professor whether you need to write an "expository" or "argumentative" research paper for this assignment.

2. **Write a research paper that responds to someone else's argument.** Look for an article that makes an argument you consider wrongheaded or at least misinformed. Then, do research on this topic and explain why the facts support a different conclusion and undercut the article you are responding to. Your research paper should use the original article as a starting place, but you should go beyond simply writing a rebuttal. Instead, write a full research paper on the subject that explores the issue in depth.

3. **Develop a research Web site.** In many situations a research Web site is actually more useful than a research paper. These kinds of Web sites collect or make links to sources that readers can use to inform themselves and do their own research on the topic. The Web site you create should gather these sources of information into a usable form. It should also offer some discussion about which sources you found most useful (or not). Try to provide materials and links that address all sides of the issue, not just sources that agree with your opinion.

Go to My**WritingLab** to complete this chapter's exercises and test your understanding of its objectives.

This handbook will answer your questions about English grammar and usage. It will also help you write correctly and clearly.

1 Sentences

Every sentence has at least one subject and at least one verb, begins with a capital letter, and ends with end punctuation (a period, question mark, or exclamation point). In college writing and beyond, you will be asked to communicate complex ideas. Use this handbook to help you understand the wide variety of sentence types while avoiding grammatical errors.

1A Fragments

Sentence fragments are errors in which partial sentences are treated as complete sentences—begun with a capital letter and ended with a period. The fragment may be a subordinate clause, a phrase, or a combination of subordinate elements. Each of these is a fragment because it lacks a subject or a verb, or it begins with a subordinating word. Only independent clauses can make independent statements.

Subordinate Clause Fragment

Recognition. A subordinate clause has a subject and a verb but is not an independent clause because it includes a subordinate connector.

Some common subordinating connectors, grouped by function, include:

Time: *after, before, once, since, until, whenever*
Place: *where, wherever*
Cause: *as, because, since*
Contrast: *although, even though, though, while*
Condition: *even if, if*
Result: *in order that, so, so that*
Alternative: *than, whether*

Relative pronouns, such as *who, whom, whose, whatever, why,* and *unless,* can also be subordinate connectors.

Any clause beginning with one of these words is *subordinate* and should not be written as a sentence. Here are examples of clause fragments (italicized):

The Vikings revolutionized shipbuilding with the keel. *Which allowed their ships to go faster and farther without stopping for supplies.*

Norway's Lapps are believed to be a nomadic people of Asian heritage. *Who follow reindeer herds through Norway's cold, rugged land.*

Because the northern part of Norway is so far north. It has long periods during the summer when the sun shines 24 hours a day.

Correction.   There are two main ways of correcting clause fragments: (1) attaching them to the preceding or following sentence, and (2) removing or changing the subordinating connector. These sentences illustrate both types of correction:

The Vikings revolutionized shipbuilding with the keel. *This innovation* allowed their ships to go faster and farther without stopping for supplies. The subordinating word of the fragment is changed.

Norway's Lapps are believed to be of Asian heritage—nomadic people who follow reindeer herds through Norway's cold, rugged land. The fragment is connected to the preceding sentence with a dash.

Because the northern part of Norway is so far north, it has long periods during the summer when the sun shines 24 hours a day. The fragment is connected to the following sentence with a comma.

Phrase Fragment

Phrase fragments lack a subject, a verb, or both. The most common phrases written as fragments are *verbal phrases* and *prepositional phrases*.

Recognition.   A *verbal phrase* is a word group made up of a verb form and related modifiers and other words. As opposed to *verb phrases,* which are made up of verb parts (such as *has been gone*), a verbal phrase is constituted with a *verbal,* a word formed from a verb but not functioning as a verb. *Going,* for example, is a verbal, as is *gone.*

There are three kinds of verbals: gerunds, participles, and infinitives. Gerunds end in -*ing*; participles end in either -*ing* (present) or -*ed* (regular past); infinitives are usually introduced by *to*. Here are a few examples of how verbals are formed from verbs:

Verb	Present Participle and Gerund	Past Participle	Infinitive
snap	snapping	snapped	to snap
go	going	gone	to go
has	having	had	to have

Verbals function primarily as adjectives and nouns, most often in verbal phrases.

In the following examples, the italicized verbal phrases are fragments because they are written as sentences:

Eero Saarinen designed the 630-foot Gateway Arch for the St. Louis riverfront. *Imagining a giant stainless steel arch.* Participial phrase modifying *Eero Saarinen*

Critics said that cranes could not reach high enough. *To lift the steel sections into place.* Infinitive phrase modifying *high*

Saarinen knew that precision was of utmost importance. In *building the arch.* Gerund phrase as object of preposition *In*

Correction.   Verbal phrase fragments can be corrected in one of two ways: (1) by connecting them to a related sentence, or (2) by expanding them into a sentence. Both ways are illustrated below:

Eero Saarinen designed the 630-foot Gateway Arch for the St. Louis riverfront. *He imagined a giant stainless steel arch.* The verbal fragment is expanded to a sentence.

Critics said that cranes could not reach high enough *to lift the steel sections into place.* The verbal fragment is connected to a related sentence.

Saarinen knew that precision was of utmost importance in *building the arch.* The gerund phrase, object of the preposition *in*, is connected to a related sentence.

Recognition.   A *prepositional phrase* is a word group made up of a preposition and its object. Together they contribute meaning to a sentence, usually modifying a noun or a verb. Like subordinating conjunctions, prepositions show relationships, such as time, place, condition, and cause. Common prepositions include *about, above, among, below, but, by, from, in addition to, into, like, out of, past, regarding, toward,* and *until.*

In the following examples, prepositional phrases have been written as sentences and are therefore fragments:

The Vikings were descendents of Teutonic settlers. *Like most of today's Norwegians.*

Norway is a land of natural beauty. *From its fjord-lined coast to frigid Lapland.*

Correction.   Prepositional phrase fragments can also be corrected (1) by connecting them to a related sentence, or (2) by expanding them into a sentence.

> The Vikings were descendents of Teutonic settlers, *like most of today's Norwegians.* **or** *Like most of today's Norwegians,* the Vikings were descendents of Teutonic settlers. The prepositional phrase is connected to a related sentence.

> Norway is a land of natural beauty. *Its charm extends from its fjord-lined coast to frigid Lapland.* The prepositional phrase is expanded into a sentence.

Incomplete Thoughts

Sometimes fragments are simply errors in punctuation—the writer uses a period when a comma or no punctuation would be correct. A more difficult type of fragment to correct is the incomplete thought, such as this one:

> A large concrete dock 50 feet short of a wooden platform anchored in the middle of the bay.

With fragments of this sort, the writer needs to insert the missing information. The reader doesn't know what happens—what the dock does or what is done to it. The fragment might be revised like this:

> A large concrete dock *juts out, stopping* 50 feet short of a wooden platform anchored in the middle of the bay.

Acceptable Fragments

You probably encounter fragments every day. Titles are often fragments, as are answers to questions and expressions of strong emotion.

> **Titles:** *Gates of Fire: An Epic Novel of the Battle of Thermopylae*
> **Answer to question:** "How many more chairs do we need?" "Fifteen."
> **Expression of strong emotion:** "What a great concert!"

And much advertising uses fragments:

> Intricate, delicate, exquisite. Extravagant in every way.

> Another successful client meeting. Par for the course.

Finally, writers quoting spoken words might use fragments:

> Claire asked Erin, "Why would you do that?"

> Erin shrugged. "Because."

Common as they are in everyday life, fragments are usually unacceptable in academic or workplace writing. When you do choose to use a fragment, you should do it intentionally, and only after carefully considering your readers and the effect that you want to achieve.

1B Comma Splices

Comma splices consist of two independent clauses (clauses that can stand alone as sentences) improperly joined together by a comma as one sentence. Here are two examples:

> The economy of Algeria is in trouble, many citizens blame the government.

> The death of any soldier is tragic, however, death by friendly fire is particularly disturbing.

Recognition.   The first step in avoiding comma splices is to identify them. Because they happen only in sentences with at least two independent clauses, you can test your sentences by substituting periods for commas. If you end up with two complete sentences, you probably have a comma splice. In testing the first of the two preceding examples we come up with the following result:

> The economy of Algeria is in trouble.
> Many citizens blame the government.

Both of these clauses obviously qualify as complete sentences, so they must be independent clauses. They therefore cannot be connected with a comma. Remember this simple rule of punctuation: *Periods and commas are not interchangeable*. If a period is correct, a comma is not.

Correction.   You can revise comma splices using five different strategies.

1. Separate the independent clauses using a comma and a *coordinating conjunction*. There are seven—and *only* seven—coordinating conjunctions. As a memory aid, their first letters spell F-A-N-B-O-Y-S:

for	**b**ut
and	**o**r
nor	**y**et
	so

   To correct a comma splice, begin the second independent clause with one of these conjunctions preceded by a comma. For example:

   The economy of Algeria is in trouble, *and* many citizens blame the government.

2. Separate the independent clauses using a semicolon (with or without a transitional adverb). Semicolons are often interchangeable with periods and therefore can be used to separate independent clauses. For example:

   The economy of Algeria is in trouble; many citizens blame the government.

   The death of any soldier is tragic; *however,* death by friendly fire is particularly disturbing.

In the second example, *however* is a transitional adverb. Unlike coordinating conjunctions, *transitional adverbs* are not conjunctions and so do not join sentence elements. They do, however, connect ideas by showing how they relate to one another. Like conjunctions, they can show addition, contrast, result, and other relationships. Some of the most common transitional adverbs are *also, in addition, next, finally, for example, however, meanwhile, therefore,* and *then.*

A semicolon should always precede the transitional adverb that begins the second independent clause. A comma usually follows the transitional adverb, although in some instances, as in the following example, the comma is omitted:

Air bags deflate within one second after inflation; *therefore* they do not interfere with control of the car.

Some comma splices result when writers use transitional adverbs as if they were coordinating conjunctions. If you have trouble distinguishing transitional adverbs from coordinating conjunctions, remember that none of the coordinating conjunctions is longer than three letters, and all of the transitional adverbs are four letters or longer. Also, keep in mind that transitional adverbs are movable within the sentence while coordinating conjunctions are not; for example, the preceding example could be rewritten as:

Air bags deflate within one second after inflation; they do not *therefore* interfere with control of the car.

3. Make one of the independent clauses subordinate to the other by inserting a subordinating conjunction. When one of the clauses explains or elaborates on the other, use an appropriate subordinating conjunction to make the relationship between the two clauses more explicit (see 1A, Fragments). Consider the following comma splice and its revision:

Henry forgot to fill in his time card on Friday, he is going to have a hard time getting paid for the overtime he put in last week.

Because Henry forgot to fill in his time card on Friday, he is going to have a hard time getting paid for the overtime he put in last week.

4. Rewrite one of the independent clauses as a modifying phrase. A *modifying phrase* serves as an adjective or adverb within a sentence. By rewriting one of the independent clauses as a phrase, you can eliminate unneeded words. For example, consider the following comma splice and its revision:

The celebrity couple smiled for the camera, they were glowing of wealth and fame.

The celebrity couple smiled for the cameras, glowing of wealth and fame.
Here, *glowing of wealth and fame* acts as an adjective modifying the noun *couple.*

5. Punctuate each independent clause as a separate sentence. No law of grammar, punctuation, or style says you must present the two independent clauses together within one sentence. The example from before is perfectly acceptable written as follows:

The economy of Algeria is in trouble. Many citizens blame the government.

It may be to your advantage to divide long and/or complex independent clauses into separate sentences. Doing so may help convey your meaning to readers more clearly.

1C Fused Sentences

Fused sentences, sometimes called *run-on sentences,* are similar to comma splices. However, instead of a comma between the two independent clauses, there is no punctuation; the two independent clauses simply run together. For example:

The United States has 281 lawyers per 100,000 people Japan has only 11 attorneys per 100,000.

The World Cup is the most popular sporting event in the world you would never know it based on the indifferent response of the average American.

Recognition.   Unlike the comma splice, there is no punctuation in the fused sentence to guide you to the end of the first independent clause and the beginning of the second. As a result, it can be more challenging to identify independent clauses within fused sentences, particularly if the sentence also contains modifying phrases or dependent clauses set off by commas. The best way to do this is to read from the beginning of the sentence (reading aloud may help) until you have found the end of the first independent clause. Consider the following example:

Even though I was still sick with the flu, I attended the awards banquet as my family watched, the coach presented me with the trophy for most valuable player.

This fused sentence contains two subordinate clauses (*Even though I was still sick with the flu* and *as my family watched*), each one attached to one of the two independent clauses (*I attended the awards banquet* and *the coach presented me with the trophy*).

Correction.   Revise fused sentences using any one of the same five strategies for correcting comma splices (see 1B Comma Splices for more information on each strategy).

1. Separate the independent clauses using a comma and a coordinating conjunction. For example:

The United States has 281 lawyers per 100,000 people, *but* Japan has only 11 attorneys per 100,000.

2. Separate the independent clauses using a semicolon (with or without a transitional adverb). For example:

The United States has 281 lawyers per 100,000 people; Japan has only 11 attorneys per 100,000.

The World Cup is the most popular sporting event in the world; *however,* you would never know it based on the indifferent response of the average American.

3. Make one of the independent clauses subordinate to the other by inserting a subordinating conjunction. The newly formed dependent clause should explain the remaining independent clause. For example, consider the following fused sentence and its revision:

I run a marathon my feet get sore.

Whenever I run a marathon, my feet get sore.

4. Rewrite one of the independent clauses as a modifying phrase. Remember, modifying phrases act as adjectives or adverbs. Consider the following fused sentence and its revision:

Last night the tomcats fought outside my window they were crying and hissing for what seemed like hours.

Last night the tomcats fought outside my window, crying and hissing for what seemed like hours. Here, the phrase *crying and hissing* acts as an adjective modifying the noun *tomcats*.

5. Punctuate each independent clause as a separate sentence. As with comma splices, you can write the independent clauses (and their related phrases and dependent clauses) as separate sentences. Indeed, this is often the easiest way to handle fused sentences. For example:

I attended the awards banquet even though I was still sick with the flu. As my family watched, the coach presented me with the trophy for most valuable player. Here, the subordinate clause attached to the first independent clause *even though I was still sick with the flu* was also moved to the back of the first sentence for better readability.

1D Parallelism

Correctly used parallelism results when two or more grammatically equivalent sentence elements are joined. The sentence elements can be nouns, verbs, phrases, or clauses. (See 1E Coordination and Subordination.)

Parallelism becomes a problem when dissimilar elements are joined in pairs, in series, in comparisons using *than* or *as,* or in comparisons linked by correlative conjunctions. Consider the following examples of faulty parallelism:

She did not like rude customers or taking orders from her boss. The two elements in the pair are not parallel.

We were having a hard time deciding what to do in the afternoon: go snorkeling, go fishing, or swim out to the sand bar. The last of the three elements in the series is not parallel.

Michael decided to complete his degree next semester rather than studying abroad for another year. The two elements compared using *than* are not parallel.

My sister not only lost the race but also her leg got hurt. The two elements compared by the correlative conjunction *not only . . . but also* are not parallel. Other correlative conjunctions include *both . . . and, either . . . or, neither . . . nor, whether . . . or,* and *just as . . . so.*

Faulty parallelism can be corrected in various ways:

She did not like *dealing with* rude customers or taking orders from her boss. Words were added to the first element to make it parallel to the second.

We were having a hard time deciding what to do in the afternoon: go snorkeling, go fishing, or *go swimming*. The last element was rewritten to make it parallel with the others in the series.

Michael decided to complete his degree next semester rather than *to study* abroad for another year. The verb form of the second element is changed from a participle to an infinitive to make it parallel with the verb form in the first element.

My sister not only lost the race but also *hurt her leg*. The second element was rewritten to make it parallel with the first element.

1E Coordination and Subordination

When dealing with complex ideas, you will often need to explain relationships among things, ideas, places, people, events, and so forth. Most sentence relationships involve either coordination or subordination. That is, sentence elements are either grammatically equal to other elements (coordination) or grammatically dependent on other parts (subordination).

Coordination

When two or more equivalent sentence elements appear in one sentence, they are coordinate. These elements can be words, phrases, or clauses. Only parallel elements can be coordinated: verbs linked with verbs, nouns with nouns, phrases with phrases, and clauses with clauses (See 1D Parallelism). For example:

Broccoli and *related vegetables* contain beta-carotene, a substance that may reduce the risk of heart attack. Two nouns are joined by a coordinating conjunction.

We *ran, swam,* and *cycled* every day while we were at the fitness camp. Three parallel verbs are joined in a series with commas and a coordinating conjunction.

American medical devices are equally remarkable, *giving life to those with termi-nally diseased organs, giving mobility to those crippled with arthritic joints and deadened nerves,* and even, miraculously, *restoring the sense of hearing to those deprived of it.—Atlantic.* The participial (verbal) phrases are joined by commas and a final coordinating conjunction. Also, embedded in the second participial phrase, two coordinate noun phrases are joined by a coordinating conjunction: *arthritic joints and deadened nerves.*

The term "Big Bang" is common usage now with scientists, but it originated as a sarcastic rejection of the theory. Two independent clauses are joined by a comma and a coordinating conjunction.

Subordination

Subordinate elements show where the emphasis lies in sentences and modify ele-ments with independent clauses. A subordinate element—either a phrase or clause—is dependent on the element it modifies for its meaning. It often provides a fuller meaning than could be achieved exclusively through the use of independent elements.

For example:

For walking and jogging, the calorie expenditure is greater for people of greater body weight. The subordinate element is a prepositional phrase, modifying *is greater.*

Increasing both speed and effort in aerobic activities, the exerciser burns more calories. The subordinate element is a verbal phrase, modifying *exerciser.*

Because sedentary people are more likely to burn sugar than fat, they tend to be-come hungry sooner and to overeat. The subordinate clause modifies the verb *tend.*

People *who exercise on a regular basis* change certain enzyme systems *so that they are more likely to burn fat than sugar.* There are two subordinate clauses, one beginning with *who* and modifying *People,* and one beginning with *so that* and modifying the verb *change.*

Effective writing contains both coordination and subordination—coordination that sets equivalent elements side by side, and subordination that makes some elements dependent on others.

1F Mixed Sentences

A mixed sentence is a problem that occurs when two or more parts of a sentence do not make sense together. It is called faulty predication when a subject and predicate are mismatched. This kind of problem usually occurs when writers are striving to ex-press complex relationships. For example:

By driving to the movie was how we saw the accident happen. The prepositional phrase *By driving to the movie* is treated as the subject of the verb *was*. Prepositional phrases cannot serve as subjects.

Just because the candidate once had a drinking problem doesn't mean he won't be a good mayor now. The adverb clause *because the candidate once had a drinking problem* is treated as the subject of the verb *doesn't mean*. Adverbs modify verbs and adjectives and cannot function as subjects.

A CAT scan is when medical technicians take a cross-sectional X-ray of the body. The adverb clause *when medical technicians take a cross-sectional X-ray of the body* is treated as a complement of the subject *CAT scan*—another function adverbs cannot serve.

The reason I was late today is because my alarm clock broke. The subject, *reason*, is illogically linked with the predicate, *is because*. *Reason* suggests an explanation, so the predicate, *is because*, is redundant.

For cases of faulty predication, either revise the subject so it can perform the action expressed in the predicate or revise the predicate so it accurately depicts an action performed by the subject. When you are writing, avoid these patterns: *is when, is where*, and *The reason . . . is because*.

There are often many ways to revise mixed sentences:

While driving to the movie, we saw the accident happen.

Just because the candidate once had a drinking problem, we can't conclude that he won't be a good mayor.

A CAT scan is a cross-sectional X-ray of the body.

The reason I was late today is that my alarm clock broke.

1G Shifts

Shifts occur when writers lose track of their sentence elements. Shifts occur in a variety of ways:

In person

In music, where left-handed people seem to be talented, the right-handed world puts *you* at a disadvantage. Shift from *people*, third person, to *you*, second person

In tense

Even though many musicians *are* left handed, instruments *had been designed for right handers*. Shift from present tense to past perfect

In number

A left-handed *violinist* has to pay extra to buy *their* left-handed violin. Shift from singular to plural

In mood

Every time the *violinist played, she could always know* when her instrument was out of tune. Shift from the indicative mood, *violinist played,* to the subjunctive mood, *she could always know*

In voice

The sonata *was being practiced* by the violinists in one room while the cellists *played* the concerto in the other room. Shift from the passive voice, *was being practiced,* to the active voice, *played*

In discourse type

She said, "*Your violin is out of tune,*" and that *I was playing the wrong note.* Shift from the direct quotation, *"Your violin is out of tune,"* to the indirect quotation, *that I was playing the wrong note*

Once you recognize shifts, revise them by ensuring that the same grammatical structures are used consistently throughout the sentence:

In music, where left-handed *people* seem to be talented, the right-handed world puts *them* at a disadvantage.

Even though many musicians *are* left handed, instruments *have been designed* for right handers.

Left-handed *violinists* have to pay extra to buy *their* left-handed violins.

Every time the violinist *played,* she *knew* when her instrument was out of tune.

The violinists *practiced* the sonata in one room while the cellists *played* the concerto in the other room.

She said, "*Your violin is out of tune and you are playing the wrong note.*"

1H Dangling and Misplaced Modifiers

Dangling and misplaced modifiers are words and word groups that are phrased or positioned in ways that make the meaning of a sentence unclear and sometimes even ludicrous:

Reaching to pick up the saddle, the obnoxious horse may shake off the blanket. The dangling verbal phrase appears to relate to *horse.*

To extend lead out of the eversharp pencil, the eraser cap is depressed. The dangling verbal phrase implies that *the eraser cap* does something.

The eversharp pencil is designed to be used permanently, *only periodically replacing the lead.* The dangling verbal phrase implies that the pencil replaces the lead.

Dick *only* had to pay ten dollars for his parking ticket. The misplaced adverb should immediately precede *ten*.

Theodore caught a giant fish in the very same spot where he had lost the ring *two years later*. The misplaced adverb phrase confusingly appears to modify the last part of the sentence instead of, correctly, the first part.

Errors of this type are difficult for writers to recognize because these errors do not seem ambiguous to them.

Recognition. Verbal phrases always have implied but unstated subjects. In other words, somebody or something is performing the action of the verbal phrase, but the phrase itself does not say who or what. For clarity, that implied subject should be the same as the subject of the sentence or clause.

Correction. The way to correct dangling and misplaced modifiers depends on the type of error. Misplaced modifiers can often be moved to a more appropriate position:

Dick had to pay *only* ten dollars for his parking ticket.

Two years later, Theodore caught a giant fish in the very same spot where he had lost the ring.

Dangling modifiers usually require some rewording:

As you reach to pick up the saddle, the obnoxious horse may shake off the blanket. The dangling verbal phrase is converted to a clause.

To extend lead out of the eversharp pencil, *depress the eraser cap.* The main clause is revised so that *you* is the implied subject of *depress* (as it is for *To extend*).

The eversharp pencil is designed to be used permanently, *only periodically needing the lead replaced.* The dangling verbal phrase is revised so that the implied subject of *needing* is *pencil.*

1l Restrictive and Nonrestrictive Modifiers

Some modifiers are essential to a sentence because they *restrict,* or limit, the meaning of the words they modify; others, while adding important information, are not essential to the meaning of a sentence. The first type is called restrictive and the second nonrestrictive:

Restrictive

People *who plan to visit Europe* should take time to see Belgium. Relative clause modifying and identifying *People*

The industrialized country *between the Netherlands and France on the North Sea* is constitutionally a kingdom. Prepositional phrases modifying and identifying *country*

The Kempenland was thinly populated *before coal was discovered there.* Subordinate clause modifying *was populated* and giving meaning to the sentence

Language and cultural differences have created friction *that has existed for centuries.* Relative clause modifying and identifying *friction*

Nonrestrictive

Belgium has two major populations: the Flemings, *who live in the north and speak Flemish,* and the Walloons, *who live in the south and speak French.* Two relative clauses, the first modifying *Flemings* and the second modifying *Walloons*

With Brussels in the middle of the country, both groups inhabit the city. Prepositional phrases, together modifying *inhabit*

NATO's headquarters is in Brussels, *where it has been since its beginning in 1950.* Subordinate clause modifying *Brussels*

Covering southeastern Belgium, the sandstone Ardennes mountains follow the Sambre and Meuse rivers. Participial (verbal) phrase modifying *mountains*

If you think the distinction between restriction and nonrestriction is not worth making, consider the following sentences, the first restrictive and the second nonrestrictive:

People who wear braces on their teeth should not eat caramel apples.

People, who wear braces on their teeth, should not eat caramel apples.

Set off with commas, the nonrestrictive *who* clause implies that all people wear braces on their teeth and should not eat caramel apples, which is clearly not the case. It does not *restrict,* or limit, the meaning of *people.* In the first sentence, however, the *who* clause does restrict, or limit, the meaning of *people* to only those who wear braces on their teeth. Often only the writer knows the intended meaning and therefore needs to make the distinction by setting off, or not setting off, the modifier.

Here are a few guidelines that might help you in making this fine distinction:

1. A modifier that modifies a proper noun (one that names a person or thing) is usually nonrestrictive, because the name is sufficient identification. Notice *Flemings* and *Walloons* in the previous example.

2. A *that* clause is almost always restrictive.

3. Adverbial subordinate clauses (those beginning with subordinating conjunctions such as *because* and *when*) are almost always restrictive and are usually not set off with commas when they appear at the end of their sentences. If they appear at the beginning of sentences, they are almost always set off with commas.

4. A nonrestrictive modifier at the beginning of a sentence is followed by a comma, one at the end is preceded by a comma, and one in the middle is enclosed with two commas.

1J Adjectives and Adverbs

Adjectives and adverbs, often called *modifiers,* modify nouns and verbs. Adjectives modify nouns; that is, they describe, limit, explain, or alter them in some way. Adverbs modify verbs, adjectives, and other adverbs, telling more than the words by themselves would tell: drive *carefully* (adverb modifying a verb), *unexpectedly* early (adverb modifying an adjective), drive *very* carefully (adverb modifying an adverb). Adverbs usually tell how, where, when, and how much.

Adjectives and adverbs occasionally present some problems for writers. Be careful not to use adjectives when adverbs are needed, as in this incorrect sentence:

> The governor suspected that the legislators were not taking him *serious.* The sentence element receiving modification is the verb *were not taking,* yet the modifier *serious* is an adjective, which can only modify nouns. The correct modifier for this sentence is the adverb *seriously.* (If you are not sure whether a word is an adjective or an adverb, check your dictionary, which should identify parts of speech.)

Another problem in form concerns the *comparative* and *superlative* degrees. The comparative form of adjectives and adverbs shows a greater degree between two things, as in these correct sentences:

> Your luggage is *stronger* than mine. Adjective comparing *your luggage* and *mine*

> Your luggage survives airport baggage handling *better* than mine does. Adverb comparing how the two *survive* handling

The comparative degree is formed by adding -*er* to shorter adjectives and adverbs (*strong, stronger; hard, harder*). Longer words are preceded by *more* (*beautiful, more beautiful; seriously, more seriously*). Do not use -*er* with *more* (not *more harder*).

The superlative form shows a greater degree among three or more things, as in these correct sentences:

> This is the *strongest* luggage I have ever seen. Adjective comparing the present luggage to all other luggage the writer has seen

> Your luggage survives airport baggage handling *best* of all luggage I've seen. Adverb comparing how all luggage the writer has seen survives handling

The superlative degree is formed by adding -*est* to shorter adjectives and adverbs (*strong, strongest; hard, hardest*). Longer words are preceded by *most* (*beautiful, most beautiful; seriously, most seriously*). Do not use -*est* with *most* (not *most strongest*).

2 Verbs

Verbs often tell what the subject is doing:

> The company *agreed* to plead guilty to criminal charges.

> Nearly every miner *can name* a casualty of black lung disease.

Another common function of verbs is to link subjects to complements:

Logan *is* an isolated county in the corner of the state.

Sometimes the verb tells something about the subject, as the following passive verb does:

Casualties of mining *cannot be measured* only by injuries.

Through changes in form, verbs can tell the time of the action (past, present, future), the number of the subject (singular or plural), and the person of the subject (first person, *I, we;* second person, *you;* third person, *he, she, it, they*).

2A Tense

Writers can encounter problems with verbs because verbs, unlike most other words in English, have many forms, and a slight shift in form can alter meaning:

The fish *has jumped* into the boat.

The fish *have jumped* into the boat.

The meaning changes from one fish to more than one fish jumping into the boat. Observe how the verb *vanish* changes in the following sentences to indicate differences in time, or *tense:*

Present	Many agricultural jobs *vanish.*
Past	Many agricultural jobs *vanished.*
Future	Many agricultural jobs *will vanish.*
Perfect	Many agricultural jobs *have vanished.*
Past Perfect	Many agricultural jobs *had vanished.*
Future Perfect	Many agricultural jobs *will have vanished.*

Omitting an *-ed* ending or using the wrong helping verb can give readers a false message.

Helping (Auxiliary) Verbs.   It is also important to use a form that is a *finite,* or an actual, verb. In the following example, the word that appears to be a verb (italicized) is not a finite verb:

The fish *jumping* into the boat.

The word *jumping* does not have one of the primary functions of verbs—telling the time of the action, called *tense.* The time of the occurrence could have been the past (*the fish were jumping*), the present (*the fish are jumping*), or the future (*the fish will be jumping*). We also don't know whether the writer meant one fish or many. The *-ing* form is a *verbal* and requires a helping, or auxiliary, verb to make it finite, or able to tell time: words such as *am, is, are, was, were* (forms of *be*). Other helping verbs are *do* and *have.*

Irregular Verbs.   Most verbs change forms in a regular way: *want* in the present becomes *wanted* in the past, *wanting* with the auxiliary *be* (i.e., *is wanting*), and *wanted* with the auxiliary *have* (i.e., *have wanted*). Many verbs change irregularly, however—internally rather than at the ending. Here are a few of the most common irregular verbs:

Base Form	Past Tense	Present Participle	Past Participle
be (is, am, are)	was, were	being	been
come	came	coming	come
do	did	doing	done
drink	drank	drinking	drunk
give	gave	giving	given
go	went	going	gone
grow	grew	growing	grown
lie	laid	lying	lain

Check your dictionary for the forms of other verbs you suspect may be irregular.

The verb form that is perhaps the most troublesome is the *-s* form in the present tense. This form is used for all singular nouns and the pronouns *he, she,* and *it.* (See 2D Subject-Verb Agreement.)

2B Voice

English sentences are usually written in the active voice, in which the subject of the sentence is the doer of the action of the verb:

> Scott misplaced the file folder. *Scott,* the subject of the sentence, performed the action, *misplaced.*

With the passive voice, the doer of the action is the object of a preposition or is omitted entirely:

> The file folder was misplaced by Scott. *File folder* is now the subject of the sentence.

> The file folder was misplaced. The person doing the action is not named.

Choose the passive voice when it is appropriate to the genre and to your readers' needs. For genres such as memoirs, profiles, and literary analyses, you will probably choose active voice because readers of these genres usually want to know who is doing what to whom. In other situations, you may choose to use the passive voice, either because you do not know the doer's identity or because the doer's identity is unimportant or obvious to the reader. When writing a lab report in a chemistry course, for instance, your reader does not need to be told who specifically combined the chemicals. Finally, the passive voice can be useful if you want to keep the subjects consistent within a paragraph.

2C Mood

In most writing and speaking, the most commonly used mood by far is the *indicative mood*, which is used to make statements, to ask questions, and to declare opinions. For example:

> Not many people today *think* the world *is* flat. Makes a statement

Does anybody today *think* the world is flat? Asks a question

Members of the Flat Earth Society *should reevaluate* their thinking. Declares an opinion

Verbs in the *imperative mood* issue commands, requests, or directions. Imperative verbs never change form. When the subject of an imperative verb is not explicitly identified, it is understood to be *you.*

Julia, *stop* teasing your baby brother. Issues a command

Please *complete* this report by tomorrow morning. Issues a request

Turn right at the light and *drive* for another two blocks. Issues directions

Verbs in the *subjunctive mood* communicate wishes, make statements contrary to fact, list requirements and demands, and imply skepticism or doubt. They usually appear in clauses introduced by *if, that, as if,* and *as though.* Use the base form of the verb for the present tense subjunctive. For the past tense subjunctive of the verb *be,* use *were* for all subjects.

She wishes that her son's best friend *were* more responsible. Communicates a wish

If the world *were* to end tomorrow, we would not have to pay taxes anymore. Makes a statement contrary to fact

The jury summons requires that your cousin *arrive* punctually at 8:00 a.m. and *sign* in with the court clerk. Lists requirements

His girlfriend talks as if she *were* a pop music diva. Implies skepticism

Be sure to select the correct verb forms to express indicative, imperative, and subjunctive moods.

2D Subject-Verb Agreement

Errors in subject-verb agreement occur only with present tense verbs and the verb tenses that use present tense forms of helping verbs (such as *have* and *be*). And, except for the irregular verb *be* (with its forms *am, is, are, was, were*), the problem centers on third-person singular verbs with their *-s* ending. Here is the problem illustrated. Notice that only the verbs in the third-person singular are different. Unfortunately, all nouns are third person and, when singular, require this form in the present tense.

	Present		Present Perfect	
	Singular	**Plural**	**Singular**	**Plural**
First person	I work	we work	I have worked	we have worked
Second person	you work	you work	you have worked	you have worked
Third person	he (she, it) works	they work	he (she, it) has worked	they have worked

It is the -*s* form, then, that you need to watch for to avoid errors in subject-verb agreement. Here are some issues that may cause problems.

Intervening Subordinate Element

When a subject and a verb are side by side, they usually do not present a problem. Often, however, writers separate them with subordinate elements, such as clauses, prepositional or verbal phrases, and other elements. The result may be a subject-verb agreement error. The following sentence illustrates this problem:

> The realization that life is a series of compromises never occur to some people. The subject is *realization*, a singular noun, and should be followed by the singular verb *occurs*. The corrected sentence would read "The realization that life is a series of compromises never occurs to some people."

Subject Complement

Subject complements follow some verbs and rename the subject, although they are not always in the same number as the subject. Because a singular subject may have a plural complement, and vice versa, confused writers might make the verb agree with the complement instead of the subject. Here's an example:

> The result of this mistake are guilt, low self-esteem, and depression. The subject is *result*, not *guilt, low self-esteem,* and *depression*; the singular subject should be followed by the singular verb *is*. The corrected sentence would read "The result of this mistake is guilt, low self-esteem, and depression."

Compound Subject

Two or more words may be compounded to make a subject. Subjects connected by *and* and *but* are plural, but those connected by *or* and *nor* are singular or plural depending on whether the item closer to the verb is singular or plural:

> The young mother and the superior student *are* both candidates for compulsive perfectionism. Two subjects, *mother* and *student*, are joined by *and* and take a plural verb.

> Promotions or an employee award *tells* the perfectionist he or she is achieving personal goals. When two subjects, *promotions* and *award*, are joined by *or*, the verb agrees with the nearer one; in this sentence, a singular verb is required.

> An employee award or promotions *tell* the perfectionist he or she is achieving personal goals. Here the plural verb, *tell*, agrees with *promotions*, the closer of the two subjects.

Indefinite Pronoun as Subject

Although these words often seem plural in meaning, most of them are singular grammatically. When indefinite pronouns are the subjects of sentences or clauses, their verbs are usually singular:

> Everyone *has* at some time worried about achieving goals. The singular indefinite pronoun *everyone* takes a singular verb, *has*.

Each car and truck on the highway *was* creeping along on the icy pavement. The singular indefinite pronoun, *each*, requires a singular verb, *was*.

Neither of us *is* going to worry about being late. The singular indefinite pronoun, *neither*, takes a singular verb, *is*.

Nevertheless, some of us *are* going to be very late. The indefinite pronoun *some* (like *all, any,* and *none*) is singular or plural depending on context; compare "Some of the book *is* boring."

Inverted Sentence Order

Examples of inverted order are questions, plus sentences beginning with *there*. Sentences like these demand closer attention to agreement.

Have the results of the test come back yet? The plural subject, *results*, takes a plural verb, *have*.

There *are* many special services provided just for kids at hotels, ski lodges, and restaurants. The plural subject, *services*, takes a plural verb, *are*. *There* is never a subject; it only holds the place for the subject in an inverted sentence.

Intervening Relative Clause

Subordinate clauses that begin with the relative pronouns *who*, *which*, or *that* present special problems in subject-verb agreement. Their verbs must agree with their own subjects, not with a word in another clause. These subordinate clauses demand special attention because whether the pronouns are singular or plural depends on their antecedents. These sentences illustrate agreement within relative clauses:

Every person who *attends* the baseball game will receive a free cap. *Who*, the subject of *attends*, means "person," a singular noun.

John is one of the few people I know who *care* about frogs. *Who*, the subject of *care*, means "people," a plural noun.

John is the only one of all the people I know who *cares* about frogs. *Who* in this sentence means "one."

3 Pronouns

Pronouns can have all the same sentence functions as nouns; the difference is that pronouns do not have the meaning that nouns have. Pronouns refer only to nouns. Whenever that reference is ambiguous or inconsistent, there is a problem in clarity.

3A Pronoun Case

Case is a grammatical term for the way nouns and pronouns show their relationships to other parts of a sentence. In English, nouns have only two case forms: the regular form (the one listed in a dictionary, such as *year*) and the possessive form (used to show ownership or connection, such as *year's*; possessive nouns are discussed at 5J Apostrophe).

Pronouns, however, have retained their case forms. Here are the forms for personal and relative pronouns:

	Subjective	Objective	Possessive
Personal	I	me	my, mine
	you	you	your, yours
	he	him	his
	she	her	her, hers
	it	it	its
	we	us	our, ours
	they	them	their, theirs
Relative	who	whom	whose
	whoever	whomever	whosever

Notice, first, that possessive pronouns, unlike possessive nouns, do not take apostrophes—none of them. Sometimes writers confuse possessive pronouns with contractions, which do have apostrophes (such as *it's,* meaning *it is* or *it has;* and *who's,* meaning *who is;* for a further discussion, see 5J Apostrophe).

Another problem writers sometimes have with pronoun case is using a subjective form when they need the objective or using an objective form when they need the subjective.

Subjective Case.   Use the subjective forms for subjects and for words referring to subjects, as in these examples:

Among the patients a nutritionist sees are the grossly overweight people *who* have tried all kinds of diets. *Who* is subject of the verb *have tried* in its own clause.

They have a life history of obesity and diets. *They* is the subject of *have.*

He and the patient work out a plan for permanent weight control. *He* and *patient* are the compound subjects of *work.*

The patient understands that the ones who work out the diet plan are *he* and the nutritionist. *He* and *nutritionist* refer to *ones,* the subject of the clause.

Notice that pronoun case is determined by the function of the pronoun in its own clause and that compounding (*he and the patient*) has no effect on case.

Objective Case.   Use the objective forms for objects of all kinds:

"Between *you* and *me,*" said the patient to his nutritionist, "I'm ready for something that works." *You* and *me* are objects of the preposition *between.*

An exercise program is usually assigned the patient for *whom* dieting is prescribed. *Whom* is the object of the preposition *for.*

The nutritionist gives *her* a suitable alternative to couch sitting. *Her* is the indirect object of *gives.*

Modest exercise combined with modest dieting can affect *him or her* dramatically. *Him or her* is the direct object of *can affect.*

Having advised *them* about diet and exercise, the nutritionist instructs dieters about behavioral change. *Them* is the object of the participle *having advised.*

Notice again that the case of a pronoun is determined by its function in its own clause and is not affected by compounding (*you and me*).

Possessive Case.

Use the possessive forms to indicate ownership. Possessive pronouns have two forms: adjective forms (*my, your, his, her, its, our, their*) and possessive forms (*mine, yours, his, hers, its, ours, theirs*). The adjective forms appear before nouns or gerunds; the possessive forms replace possessive nouns.

The patient purchased *his* supplements from the drug store *his* nutritionist recommended. Adjective form before nouns

His swimming every day produced results faster than he anticipated. Adjective form before gerund

His was a difficult task to accomplish, but the rewards of weight loss were great. Possessive form replacing possessive noun

3B Pronoun Reference

Personal and relative pronouns (see list under 3A Pronoun Case) must refer unambiguously to their antecedents. Pronouns and antecedents must agree.

Here are sentences in which the pronouns do not clearly refer to their antecedents:

The immunologist refused to admit fraudulence of the data reported by a former colleague in a paper *he* had cosigned. More than one possible antecedent. *He* could refer to *immunologist* or to *colleague.*

In Carolyn Chute's book *The Beans of Egypt, Maine, she* treats poverty with concern and understanding. Adjective used as intended antecedent (possessive nouns function as adjectives). In this case, *Carolyn Chute's* modifies *book* and cannot serve as an antecedent of the pronoun *she.*

It says in the newspaper that the economy will not improve soon. Implied antecedent. There is no antecedent for *it.*

At Ajax *they* have tires on sale till the end of the month. Implied antecedent. There is no antecedent for *they.*

Faulty pronoun reference is corrected by clarifying the relationship between the pronoun and its intended antecedent:

The immunologist refused to admit fraudulence of the data reported by a former colleague in a paper *the immunologist* had cosigned. *The immunologist* replaces the unclear pronoun *he.*

In *her* book *The Beans of Egypt, Maine, Carolyn Chute* treats poverty with concern and understanding. The possessive pronoun *her* replaces the possessive noun and refers to the noun subject, *Carolyn Chute*.

The newspaper reports that the economy will not improve soon. The unclear pronoun *it* is replaced by its implied antecedent, *newspaper*.

Ajax has tires on sale till the end of the month. The unclear pronoun *they* is replaced by *Ajax*.

3C Pronoun Agreement

Pronouns must agree with their antecedents in number, person, and gender. (See the list of pronouns in 3A Pronoun Case.)

Compound Antecedents

If the antecedents are joined by *and,* the pronoun is plural; if they are joined by *or,* the pronoun agrees with the nearer antecedent. Here are examples of correct usage:

In the pediatric trauma center, the head doctor and head nurse direct *their* medical team. The pronoun *their* refers to both *doctor* and *nurse*.

The head doctor or the head nurse directs *his or her* team. The pronouns *his or her* refer to the closer antecedent, *nurse* (because the gender of the nurse is not known, the neutral alternatives are used).

The head doctor or the other doctors give *their* help when it is needed. The pronoun *their* agrees with the closer antecedent, *doctors*.

Indefinite Pronouns as Antecedents

As their name implies, indefinite pronouns do not refer to particular people or things; grammatically they are usually singular but they are often intended as plural. Some common indefinite pronouns are *all, any, anybody, each, either, everybody, neither, no one, nothing, one, some, somebody,* and *something*.

Like nouns, these pronouns can serve as antecedents of personal and relative pronouns. But because most of them are grammatically singular, they can be troublesome in sentences. Here are examples of correct usage:

Everyone in the trauma center has *his or her* specific job to do. **or** All the personnel in the trauma center have *their* specific jobs to do. The neutral, though wordy, alternative *his or her* agrees with the singular indefinite pronoun *everyone*. The second sentence illustrates the use of the plural when gender is unknown.

Each of them does *his or her* job efficiently and competently. **or** *All* of them do *their* jobs efficiently and competently. *Each* is singular, but *all* can be either singular or plural, depending on context (compare "*All* literature has *its* place").

Shifts in Person

Agreement errors in *person* are shifts between *I* or *we* (first person), *you* (second person), and *he, she, it,* and *they* (third person). These errors are probably more often a result of carelessness than of imperfect knowledge:

Last summer *I* went on a canoeing trip to northern Manitoba. It was *my* first trip that far north, and it was so peaceful *you* could forget all the problems back home. The person represented by *you* was not present. The writer means *I*.

See also 1G Shifts.

3D Relative Pronouns

Use relative pronouns to introduce clauses that modify nouns or pronouns. Personal relative pronouns refer to people. They include *who, whom, whoever, whomever,* and *whose.* Nonpersonal relative pronouns refer to things. They include *which, whichever, whatever,* and *whose.*

Use *which* to introduce nonrestrictive clauses and *that* to introduce restrictive clauses (see 1I Restrictive and Nonrestrictive Modifiers). Use *who* to refer to the subject of the sentence and *whom* to refer to an object of the verb or preposition. Following are examples of common errors:

The lawyer *that* lost the case today went to law school with my sister. Uses impersonal relative pronoun *that*

Conflict between the two parties led to the lawsuit *that* was finally settled today. The relative pronoun *that* introduces a nonrestrictive clause that modifies *lawsuit*. Nonrestrictive clauses supply extra information to the sentence, not defining information.

The case resulted in a ruling, *which* favored the plaintiff. The relative pronoun *which* introduces a restrictive clause that modifies *ruling*. Restrictive clauses supply defining information.

Later, the lawyer *whom* lost the case spoke with the jurors *who* we had interviewed. The first relative pronoun *whom* refers to the subject *lawyer* while the second relative pronoun *who* refers to the object of the verb *had interviewed.*

Once you recognize relative pronoun errors, it is usually easy to fix them:

The lawyer *who* lost the case today went to law school with my sister.

Conflict between the two parties led to the lawsuit, *which* was finally settled today.

The case resulted in a ruling *that* favored the plaintiff.

Later, the lawyer *who* lost the case spoke with the jurors *whom* we had interviewed.

4 Style

Style is a choice you make as a writer in response to the rhetorical situation. In Chapter 17, "Choosing a Style," you learned several strategies for using style in ways that are appropriate for your purpose, readers, and genre. Here, you will learn strategies for writing with clarity and conciseness. You will also learn strategies for recognizing when certain kinds of language are and are not appropriate.

4A Conciseness

Concise writing shows that you are considerate of your readers. You do not need to eliminate details and other content to achieve conciseness; rather, you cut empty words, repetition, and unnecessary details.

Follow these guidelines to achieve conciseness in your writing:

1. **Avoid redundancy.** Redundant words and expressions needlessly repeat what has already been said. Delete them when they appear in your writing.

2. **Avoid wordy expressions.** Phrases such as *In the final analysis* and *In the present day and age* add no important information to sentences and should be removed and/or replaced.

3. **Avoid unnecessary intensifiers.** Intensifiers such as *really, very, clearly, quite,* and *of course* usually fail to add meaning to the words they modify. Delete them when doing so does not change the meaning of the sentence, or when you could replace the words with a single word (for instance, replacing *very good* with *excellent*).

4. **Avoid excess use of prepositional phrases.** The use of too many prepositional phrases within a sentence makes for wordy writing. Always use constructions that require the fewest words.

5. **Avoid negating constructions.** Negating constructions using words such as *no* and *not* often add unneeded words to sentences. Use shorter alternatives when they are available.

6. **Use the passive voice only when necessary.** When there is no good reason to use the passive voice, choose the active voice.

Here are more examples of wordy sentences that violate these guidelines, with unnecessary words in italics:

If the two groups *cooperate together,* there will be *positive benefits* for both. Uses redundancy

There are some people *who* think the metric system is un-American. Uses wordy expression

The climb up the mountain was *very* hard on my legs and *really* taxed my lungs and heart. Uses unnecessary modifiers

On the day of his birth, we walked *to the park down the block from the house of his mother.* Uses too many prepositional phrases

She *did not like* hospitals. Uses negating construction when a shorter alternative is available

The door *was closed* by that man over there. Uses passive voice when active voice is preferable

Corrections to the wordy sentences above result in concise sentences:

If the two groups cooperate, both will benefit. This correction also replaces the wordy construction *there will be . . . for both* with a shorter, more forceful alternative.

Some people think the metric system is un-American.

The climb up the mountain was hard on my legs and taxed my lungs and heart.

On his birthday, we walked to the park near his mother's house.

She hated hospitals.

That man over there closed the door.

4B Appropriate Language
Effective writers communicate using appropriate language.

Suitability
Some situations require *formal language.* Formal language communicates clearly and directly with a minimum of stylistic flourish. Its tone is serious, objective, and often detached. Formal language avoids slang, pretentious words, and unnecessary technical jargon. *Informal language,* on the other hand, is particular to the writer's personality or social group and assumes a closer and more familiar relationship between the writer and the reader. Its tone is casual, subjective, and intimate. Informal language can also employ slang and other words that would be inappropriate in formal writing.

As informal language is rarely used within most academic, technical, or business settings, the following examples show errors in the use of formal language:

The director told the board members to *push off.* Uses informal language

Professor Oyo *dissed* Marta when she arrived late to his class for the third time in a row. Uses slang

The *aromatic essence* of the gardenia was intoxicating. Uses pretentious words

The doctor told him to take *salicylate* to ease the symptoms of *viral rhinorrhea.* Uses unnecessary jargon

Employing formal language correctly, these examples could be revised as follows:

The director told the board members to leave.

Professor Oyo spoke disrespectfully to Marta when she arrived late to his class for the third time in a row.

The scent of the gardenia was intoxicating.

The doctor told him to take aspirin to ease his cold symptoms.

Sexist Usage
Gender-exclusive terms such as *policeman* and *chairman* are offensive to many readers today. Writers who are sensitive to their audience, therefore, avoid such terms, replacing them with expressions such as *police officer* and *chairperson* or *chair.* Most sexist usage in language involves masculine nouns, masculine pronouns, and patronizing terms.

Masculine Nouns.   Do not use *man* and its compounds generically. For many people, these words are specific to men and do not account for women as separate and equal people. Here are some examples of masculine nouns and appropriate gender-neutral substitutions:

Masculine Noun	Gender-Neutral Substitution
mailman	mail carrier
businessman	businessperson, executive, manager
fireman	firefighter
man-hours	work hours
mankind	humanity, people
manmade	manufactured, synthetic
salesman	salesperson, sales representative, sales agent
congressman	member of Congress, representative

Making gender-neutral substitutions often entails using a more specific word for a generalized term, which adds more precision to writing.

Masculine Pronouns.   Avoid using the masculine pronouns *he, him,* and *his* in a generic sense, meaning both male and female. Consider the following options:

1. Eliminate the pronoun.

   Every writer has an individual style. Instead of Every writer has his own style.

2. Use plural forms.

   Writers have their own styles. Instead of A writer has his own style.

3. Use *he or she, one,* or *you* as alternates only sparingly.

   Each writer has his or her own style. Instead of Each writer has his own style.
   One has an individual writing style. Instead of He has his own individual writing style.
   You have your own writing style. Instead of A writer has his own style.

Patronizing Terms.   Avoid terms that cast men or women in gender-exclusive roles or imply that women are subordinate to men. Here are some examples of biased or stereotypical terms and their gender-neutral substitutions:

Biased/Stereotypical Term	Gender-Neutral Substitution
lady lawyer	lawyer
male nurse	nurse
career girl	professional, attorney, manager
coed	student
housewife	homemaker
stewardess	flight attendant
cleaning lady	housecleaner

Biases and Stereotypes

Most writers are sensitive to racial and ethnic biases or stereotypes, but they should also avoid language that shows insensitivity to age, class, religion, and sexual orientation.

5 Punctuation, Mechanics, and Spelling

Punctuation is a system of signals telling readers how the parts of written discourse relate to one another. Punctuation provides readers with cues for interpreting the writer's words as the writer intended them to be understood.

5A End Punctuation

A period is the normal mark for ending sentences. A question mark ends a sentence that asks a direct question, and an exclamation point ends forceful assertions.

Period .

Sentences normally end with a period.

> Studies suggest that eating fish two or three times a week may reduce the risk of heart attack. Statement

> Eat two or three servings of fish a week. Mild command

> The patient asked whether eating fish would reduce the risk of heart attack. Indirect question

Avoid inserting a period before the end of a sentence; the result will be a fragment (see 1A Fragments). Sentences can be long or short; their length does not determine their completion. Both of the following examples are complete sentences:

> Eat fish. Mild command; the subject, *you*, is understood

> In a two-year study of 1,000 survivors of heart attack, researchers found a 29 percent reduction in mortality among those who regularly ate fish or took a fish oil supplement. Statement; one sentence

Question Mark ?

A sentence that asks a direct question ends in a question mark.

> How does decaffeinated coffee differ from regular coffee?

Do not use a question mark to end an indirect question:

> The customer asked how decaffeinated coffee differs from regular coffee.

With quoted questions, place the question mark inside the final quotation marks:

> The customer asked, "How does decaffeinated coffee differ from regular coffee?"

Exclamation Point   !

The exclamation point tells readers that the sentence should be interpreted as forceful or dramatic.

> Fire!

> Shut that door immediately!

Because they give the impression of shouting, exclamation points are rarely needed in formal business and academic writing.

5B Semicolon   ;

Semicolons are mainly used for connecting two (or sometimes three) independent clauses.

> Dengue hemorrhagic fever is a viral infection common to Southeast Asia; it kills about 5,000 children a year.

Sometimes the second clause contains a transitional adverb (see 1B Comma Splices):

> Dengue has existed in Asia for centuries; *however,* it grew more virulent in the 1950s.

Do not use a comma where a semicolon or period is required; the result is a comma splice (see 1B Comma Splices). In contrast, a semicolon used in place of a comma may result in a type of fragment (see 1A Fragments):

> In populations where people have been stricken by an infectious virus, survivors have antibodies in their bloodstreams; *which prevent or reduce the severity of subsequent infections.* The semicolon makes a fragment of the *which* clause.

Do not confuse the semicolon with the colon (see 5D Colon). While the semicolon connects independent clauses, a colon ordinarily does not.

The semicolon is also used to separate items in a series when the items contain internal commas:

> Scientists are researching the effects of staphylococcus bacteria, which cause infections in deep wounds; influenza A virus, which causes respiratory flu; and conjunctivitis bacteria, which have at times caused fatal purpuric fever.

5C Comma   ,

The comma is probably the most troublesome mark of punctuation because it has so many uses. Its main uses are explained here.

Compound Sentences.   A comma joins two independent clauses connected with a coordinating conjunction (see 1B Comma Splices):

> Martinique is a tropical island in the West Indies, *and* it attracts flocks of tourists annually.

Do not use the comma between independent clauses without the conjunction, even if the second clause begins with a transitional adverb:

Faulty: Martinique is a tropical island in the West Indies, it attracts flocks of tourists annually. Two independent clauses with no conjunction creates a comma splice.

Faulty: Martinique is a tropical island in the West Indies, consequently it attracts flocks of tourists annually. Two independent clauses with transitional adverb creates a comma splice.

Introductory Sentence Elements.   Commas set off a variety of introductory sentence elements, as illustrated here:

When the French colonized Martinique in 1635, they eliminated the native Caribs. Introductory subordinate clause

Choosing death over subservience, the Caribs leaped into the sea. Introductory participial (verbal) phrase

Before their death, they warned of a "mountain of fire" on the island. Introductory prepositional phrase

Subsequently, the island's volcano erupted. Introductory transitional adverb

Short prepositional phrases sometimes are not set off with commas:

In 1658 the Caribs leaped to their death.

Sometimes, however, a comma must be used after a short prepositional phrase to prevent misreading:

Before, they had predicted retribution. Comma is required to prevent misreading

Nonrestrictive and Parenthetical Elements.   Words that interrupt the flow of a sentence are set off with commas before and after.

In this class are nonrestrictive modifiers (see 1B Restrictive and Nonrestrictive Modifiers), transitional adverbs (see 1B Comma Splices), and a few other types of interrupters. Here are examples:

This rugged island, *which Columbus discovered in 1502,* exports sugar and rum. Nonrestrictive *which* clause; commas before and after

A major part of the economy, *however,* is tourism. Interrupting transitional adverb; commas before and after

Tourists, *attracted to the island by its climate,* enjoy discovering its culture. Interrupting participial (verbal) phrase (see 1A Fragments); commas before and after

A popular tradition in Martinique is the Carnival, *which occurs just before Lent each year.* Nonrestrictive *which* clause; one comma

Martinique is an overseas department of France, *a status conferred in 1946.* An absolute, ending the sentence (participial phrase plus the noun it modifies)

Series
Commas separate items in a series:

Martiniquans dance to *steel drums, clarinets, empty bottles, and banjos.* Four nouns

Dressing in colorful costumes, dancing through the streets, and thoroughly enjoying the celebration, Martiniquans celebrate Carnival with enthusiasm. Three participial (verbal) phrases

Martinique has a population of over 300,000, its main religion is Roman Catholicism, and its languages are French and Creole dialect. Three independent clauses

Various sentence elements can make up a series, but the joined elements should be grammatically equivalent (see 1D Parallelism, which discusses faulty parallelism). Common practice calls for a comma before the conjunction joining the last item in the series.

Quotations
Commas set off quoted sentences from the words that introduce them:

"A wise man," says David Hume, "proportions his belief to the evidence."

According to Plato, "Writing will produce forgetfulness" in writers because "they will not need to exercise their memories." The second clause is not set off with a comma.

"*X* on beer casks indicates beer which paid ten shillings duty, and hence it came to mean beer of a given quality," reports *The Dictionary of Phrase and Fable.*

Quotations introduced with *that* and other connectors (such as *because* in the second sentence here) are not set off with commas. Commas at the end of quotations go inside the quotation marks.

Coordinate Adjectives
Commas separate adjectives that equally modify a noun:

The "food pyramid" was designed as a *meaningful, memorable* way to represent the ideal daily diet. Two adjectives modify the noun *way* equally.

When you're not sure about using a comma, try inserting the coordinating conjunction *and* between the two adjectives to see if they are truly coordinate (*meaningful and memorable*). Do not use a comma between adjectives that are not coordinate or between the last adjective and the noun being modified. (See also 1J Adjectives and Adverbs.)

Addresses and Dates
Use a comma to separate city and state in an address, but not to set off the zip code:

Glen Ridge, New Jersey 07028 *or* Glen Ridge, NJ 07028

In a sentence, a state name is enclosed in commas:

The letter from Glen Ridge, New Jersey, arrived by express mail.

Dates are treated similarly:

January 5, 1886 *but* 5 January 1886

The events of January 5, 1886, are no longer remembered. When other punctuation is not required, the year is followed by a comma.

Commas to Avoid

A comma does mean pause, but not all pauses are marked by commas. Use a comma only when you know you need one. Avoid the following comma uses:

1. To set off restrictive sentence elements:

   People, *who want a balanced diet,* can use the food pyramid as a guide. The restrictive *who* clause is necessary to identify *people* and should not be set off with commas.

2. To separate a subject from its verb and a preposition from its object:

   People who want a balanced diet, can use the food pyramid as a guide. The comma following the *who* clause separates the subject, *people,* from its verb, *can use.* Treat the noun phrase (*People who want a balanced diet*) as if it were a single word.

   The bottom level of the food pyramid contains food from grains, *such as,* bread, cereals, rice, and pasta. The preposition *such as* should not be followed by a comma.

3. To follow a coordinating conjunction (see 1B Comma Splices):

   The food pyramid describes a new approach to a balanced diet. But, the meat and dairy industries opposed it. The coordinating conjunction *but* should not be set off with a comma.

4. To separate two independent clauses (see 1B Comma Splices) not joined with a coordinating conjunction:

   The pyramid shows fewer servings of dairy and meat products, therefore consumers would buy less of these higher-priced foods. The comma should be replaced with a semicolon (5B).

5. To set off coordinate elements joined with a coordinating conjunction:

   Vegetables and fruits are near the bottom of the pyramid, *and should be eaten several times a day.* The coordinating conjunction *and* joins a second verb, *should be eaten,* not a second independent clause; therefore no comma is needed.

5D Colon :

Colons connect two sentence parts, as a hinge connects a door to its frame. Colons tell readers that a second part of the sentence is coming and that the second part will complement the first part by providing either: (1) a list that has been anticipated in the first part, or (2) an explanation, restatement, or elaboration of the first part:

> The space shuttle *Challenger* lifted off on January 28, 1986, with a seven-member crew: Francis R. Scobee, Michael J. Smith, Ronald E. McNair, Ellison S. Onizuka, Judith A. Resnik, Gregory B. Jarvis, and Christa McAuliffe. The list explains *crew.*

> A twelve-member investigating team discovered the cause of the disaster: a leak in one of the shuttle's two solid-fuel booster rockets. The phrase explains *the cause of the disaster.*

Do not use colons interchangeably with semicolons (see 5B Semicolon). Colons ordinarily are followed by a phrase or phrases, but they are often followed by an independent clause:

> A twelve-member investigating team discovered the cause of the disaster: a leak was found in one of the shuttle's two solid-fuel booster rockets. Both sides of the colon contain an independent clause.

Avoid using colons after verbs and prepositions (see 1A Fragments):

> The two causes of the O-ring failure were cold temperatures and design deficiencies. No colon after *were*

> The commission investigating the disaster noted a number of failures in communication, such as one within the National Aeronautics and Space Administration. No colon after *such as*

Colons have a few other set uses:

Time:	10:15 a.m.
Salutation in a business letter:	Dear Patricia Morton:
Biblical reference:	Genesis 2:3

5E Dash   —

The dash separates sentence elements like a comma, but suggests greater emphasis:

> In *The War of the Worlds* (1898), science fiction writer H. G. Wells described an intense beam of light that destroyed objects on contact—the laser.

It is also used to set off a nonrestrictive sentence element (see 1I Restrictive and Nonrestrictive Modifiers) that might be confusing if set off with commas:

> A number of medical uses—performing eye surgery, removing tumors, and unclogging coronary arteries—make the laser more than a destructive weapon. The three explanatory items separated by commas are set off from the rest of the sentence with dashes.

A dash is sometimes used in place of a colon when a colon might seem too formal:

> Besides its medical uses, the laser serves many other functions—reading price codes, playing compact audio discs, and sending telephone messages.

Use the dash with caution; overuse defeats the purpose of giving special emphasis to special parts of your writing. Overuse might also give readers the impression that you aren't familiar with alternative means of punctuation.

5F Quotation Marks   " "

The main use for quotation marks is to set off direct quotations:

> Professor Charlotte Johnson announced, "Interdisciplinary science is combining fields of scientific knowledge to make up new disciplines."

> "Biochemistry," she went on to say, "combines biology and chemistry."

Quotations within quotations are marked with single quotation marks:

> "The term 'interdisciplinary science' thus describes a change in how processes are investigated," she concluded.

Periods and commas (see 5C Comma) always go inside the end quotation marks; colons and semicolons almost always go outside the quotation. Dashes, question marks, and exclamation points go inside or outside depending on meaning:

> "Do you know the various branches of the physical sciences?" asked Professor Johnson. Question mark goes inside quotation marks because it applies to the quotation.

> Did the professor say, "Histology deals with tissues and cytology with the fine structures of individual cells"? Question mark goes outside quotation marks because it applies to the surrounding sentence, not the quotation.

Do not use quotation marks to set off indirect quotations:

> The professor said that histology and cytology are different branches of study.

Also, do not use quotation marks when you are using a long quotation. Instead, place the quoted material in its own block of text that is all indented and omit the quotation marks. (See Chapter 26, "Quoting, Paraphrasing, and Citing Sources," for more information on properly formatting long quotes.)

Another use for quotation marks is to enclose titles of works that are not published separately, including short stories, poems, songs, chapters, and essays:

> "You Are a Man," by Richard Rodriguez

> "The Incident," by Countee Cullen

Do not enclose titles of your own essays in quotation marks when they are in title position. (See 5K Italics for treatment of titles of works that are published separately.)

Quotation marks are sometimes used to indicate to readers that you are using a word or phrase in a special sense, but be careful not to overuse this function:

> The "right" way to do a thing is not always the best way.

5G Other Marks

Parentheses   ( )

Parentheses enclose interrupting elements. They usually add explanatory information that might seem digressive to the topic.

> The Particle Beam Fusion Accelerator *(PBFA II)* is a device designed to produce energy by fusion. Parentheses set off an abbreviation that will henceforth be used in place of the full term.

> The PBFA II stores up to 3.5 million joules of energy. *(One joule is the amount of energy expended by a one-watt device in one second.)* Parentheses set off an explanation framed as a complete sentence.

Parentheses are always used in pairs. They might have internal punctuation (as in the second example), but marks related to the sentence as a whole go outside the parentheses:

> During fusion *(joining of two atomic nuclei to form a larger nucleus),* mass is converted to energy. Parenthetical element is followed by a comma, showing that it relates to *fusion.* If it had been preceded by a comma, it would appear, illogically, to relate to *mass.*

Brackets   [ ]

Square brackets are used to indicate to the reader that the writer has inserted words into quoted material:

> Describing the Great Depression, Frederick Lewis Allen says, "The total amount of money paid out in wages *[in 1932]* was 60 percent less than in 1929." The words *in 1932* were not part of the original text.

Some writers use brackets to enclose brief parenthetical material within parentheses:

> Jules Verne *(Journey to the Center of the Earth* [1864]) described giant apes and a vast subterranean sea at the core of the earth. The date of publication is parenthetical to the title of the book.

Ellipsis Dots   . . .

Ellipsis dots (spaced periods) are used in quotations to indicate where words have been omitted. Three spaced periods mark omissions within a sentence. If the omission comes at the end of your sentence but not at the end of the original sentence, use four spaced periods.

> One of the legacies of the Great Depression, says Frederick Lewis Allen, is that "if individual Americans are in deep trouble, . . . their government [should] come to their aid." Words following a comma in the original sentence are omitted within the sentence. The brackets enclose an inserted word.

> This idea, adds Allen, "was fiercely contested for years. . . ." Allen's sentence did not end at *years,* where the quoted sentence ends.

Make sure that the omitted words do not distort the meaning of the original selection.

5H Capitalization

The rules for capitalization are relatively fixed. Following are examples of situations calling for capitalization.

1. Beginning of a sentence:

In 1929, the whole credit structure of the American economy was shaken.

2. Proper names or nouns:

With the onset of the *Great Depression, President Hoover* at first tried to organize national optimism. Historical period or event; person

Bankers on *Wall Street,* manufacturers in *Detroit,* and legislators in *Washington* all had an effect on the economy. Place

President Hoover set up the *Reconstruction Finance Corporation* to aid banks and businesses. Person; institution

Jell-O, Pepsi, Rice Krispies Trade names

Aunt Beatrice, Grandmother Dietz, Dad Relationships when they are part of the name; but not *my dad* and *my aunt and uncle*

3. Titles:

Death at an Early Age, by Jonathan Kozol; *The Dancing Wu Li Masters: An Overview of the New Physics,* by Gary Zukav. Capitalize first and last words, words following colons, and all other words except articles (*a, an,* and *the*) and conjunctions and prepositions of fewer than five letters (*and, but, in, by,* etc.).

Avoid capitalizing common nouns; for example:

For many people, the *winter* of 1902 was bleak. Seasons

Many people moved *south* to a warmer climate. Compass directions

Simon Waterson was a *professor of history* at the time. Titles that are not part of proper names

5I Abbreviation

While abbreviations are part of the language, not all are acceptable in all circumstances. A general guideline is that they are less common in formal prose than in less formal circumstances. The following examples are arranged from most acceptable to least acceptable in written prose.

Titles with proper names

Dr. Paul Gordon   Paul Gordon, Ph.D.
George Grossman, Jr.

Times and dates

11:15 A.M. *or* 11:15 a.m.   53 B.C.E   C.E. 371

Names of organizations and countries

NATO   CIA   NBC

Use *U.S.* as an adjective (*in a U.S. city*) and *United States* as a noun (*a city in the United States*).

Latin abbreviations (write out except in source citations and parenthetical comments)

etc.	and so forth (*et cetera*—applies to things)
i.e.	that is (*id est*)
e.g.	for example (*exempli gratia*)
cf.	compare (*confer*)
et al.	and others (*et alii*—applies to people)
N.B.	note well (*nota bene*)

Abbreviations to be avoided in most prose

The school board not bd. met on Tuesday not Tues. February not Feb. 3.

William not Wm. Townsend was a guest lecturer in the economics not econ. class.

Townsend arrived from Pittsburgh, Pennsylvania not *PA* or *Penn.,* late last night. Consult your dictionary when you have questions about specific abbreviations.

5J Apostrophe ʼ

The apostrophe has two main uses in English—to mark possessive nouns and to show contractions—plus a few specialized uses. Avoid all other uses.

Possessive Nouns

Ownership or connection is marked on nouns with apostrophes:

Norton's résumé is short and concise. The résumé belongs to Norton.

This week's newsletter will be a little late. The newsletter of this week

The article's title is confusing. The title of the article

To make nouns possessive, follow one of these steps:

1. For singular nouns, add *'s* (*nature* + *'s* = *nature's*; *Tess* + *'s* = *Tess's*).

2. For plural nouns ending in *s*, add *'* (*strangers* + *'* = *strangers'*).

3. For plural nouns not ending in *s*, add *'s* (*men* + *'s* = *men's*).

Do not use apostrophes to make nouns plural. (See 5N Spelling.) And do not use apostrophes with possessive and relative pronouns. (See 3A Pronoun Case.) For example:

The *Harris's* are in Florida. Incorrectly uses apostrophe to make the noun *Harris* plural

The family lost *it's* home in the fire. Incorrectly uses apostrophe with the pronoun *it* to make it possessive

Contractions

Apostrophes stand in place of omitted letters in contractions:

doesn't	does not	who's	who is *or* who has
isn't	is not	let's	let us
it's	it is *or* it has	we'll	we will

Because contractions reflect a casual style, they are usually not acceptable in formal writing. Do not confuse the contracted *it is* (*it's*) and *who is* (*who's*) with the possessive pronouns *its* and *whose*. (See 3A Pronoun Case.)

Special Uses

Plurals of letters, numbers, and words used as terms

I am hoping to get all *A*'s this year.

The memo had four misspelled *there*'s. See 5K Italics, which discusses italicizing words used as terms.

All the *7*'s are upside down in the 1990s catalog. The plural for years is usually formed without apostrophes.

Omitted letters or numbers

We'll never forget the summer of '*78*. Restrict to informal writing.

"Be *seein'* ya," Charlie said. Dialect in quoted speech.

5K Italics

Italic type, which slants to the right, has specialized uses.

Titles of works published independently

The Atlantic Monthly (magazine)

A Farewell to Arms (book)

Leaves of Grass (book-length poems)

The Wall Street Journal (newspaper)

American Idol (television program)

The Glass Menagerie (play)

Ships, aircraft, spacecraft, and trains

Challenger (spacecraft)

Leasat 3 (communications satellite)

San Francisco *Zephyr* (train)

Italics are also used for words, letters, and numbers used as themselves in a sentence:

The process of heat transfer is called *conduction.*

The letter *e* is the most commonly used vowel.

Many people consider *13* to be an unlucky number.

Italics can also be used for emphasis:

"I said, '*Did* you buy the tickets?' not '*Would* you buy the tickets?'"

Although underlining was used as a substitute for italics in the past, writers generally avoid it nowadays because underlining is used for other purposes (for example, to indicate a hyperlink in Web and other electronic writing).

5L Hyphens   -
Hyphens divide words at the ends of lines, form compound words, and connect spelled-out numbers.

Dividing Words
There are three general rules to remember when using hyphens to divide words at the ends of lines: (1) always divide between syllables, (2) don't divide one-syllable words, and (3) don't divide words so that only two letters carry over to the second line. Consider the following examples:

In the end, after months of waiting and mountains of legal fees, the court *rul-ed* against him. Incorrectly divides the one-syllable word *ruled.*

Needless to say, when the court ruled against him, he was not *particular-ly* pleased. Incorrectly divides the word *particularly* so that only the last two letters carry over to the second line.

Forming Compound Words
Knowing when to hyphenate compound words can be tricky because some compound words can be written as single words (for example, *graveyard* or *postmaster*) while others can be written as two separate words (for example, *place kick* or *executive secretary*). Complicating matters further, compound adjectives take hyphens when they precede nouns but not when they follow nouns. Here are some examples of the correct and incorrect use of hyphens:

My *ex-husband* is a *pro-Communist* crackpot. Use hyphens after the prefix *ex-* and any prefix placed before a proper name, in this case *pro-* before *Communist.*

In general, though, most words formed with prefixes are written as one word; for example, *antisocial* or *multicultural.*

The *post-mortem* revealed that her *brother in law* died of natural causes. This sentence contains two hyphenation errors. First, the compound word *post-mortem* should be written as a single word, *postmortem* (see comment on prefixes in the preceding example). Second, the compound noun *brother in law* should be hyphenated as *brother-in-law.*

The *secretary treasurer* discouraged the group from making *highly-risky* investments. This sentence contains two hyphenation errors. First, the compound noun *secretary treasurer* requires a hyphen. Second, *-ly* adverbs such as *highly* are written as separate words when they precede adjectives such as *risky.*

Connecting Spelled-Out Numbers
Use hyphens to link compounds of spelled out numbers and to link numbers to nouns. For example:

twenty-fifth time	six-year-old
nine-page letter	35-year-old
132-page report	

Whenever you have a question about dividing words and hyphenating compound words, use your dictionary. Dots usually mark syllables, and hyphens mark hyphenated compounds.

5M Numbers
Use the following guidelines to handle numbers in writing:

1. Spell out numbers requiring two words or less and write numerals for numbers requiring three or more words. In practice, this means you will write out numbers *one* to *ninety-nine* and write numerals for *100* and above.

2. Spell out numbers that begin sentences. For long numbers this can lead to awkward sentences. In such instances, you should consider revising the sentence to move the number away from the beginning of the sentence so it can be written in numerals.

3. Make exceptions for numbers used in special figures. In these instances, numbers are usually written as numerals. Special figures of this type include days and years; pages, chapters, and volumes; acts, scenes, and lines; decimals, fractions, ratios, and percentages; temperatures; addresses, statistics; and amounts of money.

Consider the following examples:

The company mailed *twenty-one* parcels yesterday.

She bought *2,200* acres of ranch land with her lottery winnings.

One hundred and fifty-two cows drowned in the flood.

The Japanese attacked Pearl Harbor on December *7, 1941.*

The famous "To be, or not to be" soliloquy appears in act *3*, scene *1* of *Hamlet.*

The suspect resided at *221* Dolores Street, apartment *3B.*

5N Spelling

Your spelling checker will flag most misspelled words and suggest alternatives, but it will often miss unintended homonyms (for instance, accepting *Brutish Literature* when you meant to type *British Literature*). Because you should not rely solely on a spell checker, here is a review of the most useful and dependable rules of spelling.

Doubling a Final Consonant

When adding a suffix such as *-ing* or *-ed* to a word that ends in a consonant, double the final consonant to keep the internal vowel short; for example, *permit, permitted; stop, stopped.* Double the final consonant when all three of the following are true:

1. The word ends in a consonant preceded by a vowel.

2. The word is one syllable or the accent is on the final syllable.

3. The suffix begins with a vowel.

Here are some other examples:

sit	sitting	prefer	preferred
put	putting	occur	occurrence

Words Containing *ie* or *ei*

The familiar rhyme about using *ie* or *ei* is true most of the time—enough times that it is worth remembering: *i* before *e* except after *c* when the sound is long *e.* Thus, words such as these follow the rule:

receive	believe	weight
ceiling	chief	beige

There are a few common exceptions: *caffeine, either, neither, seize,* and *weird.* Another common word that the rule does not address is *friend* (spelled *i* before *e,* but the sound is not long *e*).

Final *e*

To add an ending to a word that ends in a silent *e,* drop the *e* when the ending begins with a vowel:

believe + able = believable	believe + ed = believed
hope + ing = hoping	hope + ful = hopeful

When the consonant preceding the final *e* is a soft *c* or *g,* the *e* is dropped only when the ending begins with *e* or *i*:

change + ing = changing   change + able = changeable
nice + er = nicer   nice + ly = nicely

Final *y*

To add an ending to a word with a final *y* preceded by a consonant, change the *y* to *i* except when your ending is *-ing:*

happy + ly = happily   study + ing = studying
apply + es = applies   apply + ing = applying
try + ed = tried   try + ing = trying

When the final *y* is preceded by a vowel, keep the *y:*

play + ed = played   play + ful = playful

employ + ed = employed   employ + ment = employment

but

say + s = says   say + d = said
pay + ment = payment   pay + d = paid

Never change the *y* when adding an ending to a proper noun: *the Barrys.*

Plurals

Plural nouns ordinarily have an *s* ending:

boy + s = boys   car + s = cars

Words that end in *ch, s, sh, x,* or *z* require *-es:*

box + es = boxes   church + es = churches

Words ending in *o* are a little more troublesome. If the *o* is preceded by a vowel, add *s:*

radio + s = radios   video + s = videos

If the *o* is preceded by a consonant, ordinarily add *-es:*

hero + es = heroes   potato + es = potatoes

A few common words take either *s* or *-es:*

tornados, tornadoes   zeros, zeroes   volcanos, volcanoes

Some words form their plurals internally or do not have a plural form. Do not add an *s* to these words:

child, children   deer, deer

man, men   fish, fish

Compound words ordinarily have an *s* at the end of the compound:

textbook, textbooks   snowshoe, snowshoes
text edition, text editions

But when the first word of the compound is the main word, add the *s* to it:

sisters-in-law   attorneys-general

Whenever you are in doubt about the correct plural ending, check your dictionary.

Homonyms

Some of the most troublesome words to spell are homonyms, words that sound alike but are spelled differently. Here is a partial list of the most common ones:

accept, except	it's, its	than, then
affect, effect	know, no	their, there, they're
already, all ready	lead, led	to, too, two
cite, sight, site	maybe, may be	whose, who's
forth, fourth	passed, past	your, you're

A few other words, not exactly homonyms, are sometimes confused:

breath, breathe	loose, lose
choose, chose	precede, proceed
lightning, lightening	quiet, quite

Check the meanings of any sound-alike words you are unsure of in your dictionary.

Appendix
Readings Arranged by Theme

GENDER

FAMILY

ETHICS

LANGUAGE AND RHETORIC

SOCIAL JUSTICE

RELIGION AND SPIRITUALITY

WORK AND CAREER

Credits

National Institute of Arthritis and Musculoskeletal and Skin Diseases. *Healthy Muscles* page. National Institute of Arthritis and Musculoskeletal and Skin Diseases, http://www.niams.nih.gov/Health_Info/Kids/healthy_muscles.asp.

Natural Resources Defense Council. "Stop Electrocuting Patagonia." November 2007.

NSDUH. "Major Depressive Episode Among Full-Time College Students and Other Young Adults, Aged 18 to 22" The NSDUH Report, May 3, 2012.

National Park Service. "Arches National Park" screenshot.

Obama, Barack. "A More Perfect Union", March 18, 2008.

NSDUH Report. "Major Depressive Episode Among Full-Time College Students and Other Young Adults, Aged 18 to 22." *The NSDUH Report*, May 3, 2012.

Online Etymology Dictionary. "Escape comes from the Old French word "eschaper," which literally meant "to get out of one's cape, leave a pursuer with just one's cape."

Pearson Education, Inc. "Basic Organization for a Memoir."

Pearson Education, Inc. "Dynamics of Humans vs. Zombies with More Education." Graph from Lakeland (2010) and Messer (2010).

Pearson Education, Inc. Figure 1.4 "A Writing Process."

Pearson Education, Inc. Figure 2.1 "Five Elements of the Rhetorical Situation."

Pearson Education, Inc. Figure 2.2 "Creating a Concept Map About Your Topic."

Pearson Education, Inc. Figure 3.1 "Elements of a Brief Reader Profile."

Pearson Education, Inc. Figure 3.2 "Maslow's Hierarchy of Needs."

Pearson Education, Inc. Figure 3.3 "A Reader Analysis Worksheet."

Pearson Education, Inc. Figure 3.5 "The Importance of Context."

Pearson Education, Inc. Figure 4.2 "Toggling Between Looking Through and Looking At a Text."

Pearson Education, Inc. Figure 4.3a "Playing the Believing and Doubting Game."

Pearson Education, Inc. Figure 5.1 "Brainstorming to Find Topics."

Pearson Education, Inc. Figure 5.2 "Making a Map of the Scene."

Pearson Education, Inc. Figure 5.3 "Creating a Tone with a Concept Map."

Pearson Education, Inc. Figure 6.1 "Using Cubing to Inquire About Your Subject."

Pearson Education, Inc. Figure 7.1 "Brainstorming to List Common Expectations."

Pearson Education, Inc. Figure 11.1 "Brainstorming to Identify Major Points of Contention."

Pearson Education, Inc. Figure 11.3 "Designing an Argument."

Pearson Education, Inc. Figure 12.1 "Using a Concept Map to Develop a Plan."

Pearson Education, Inc. Figure 12.2 "Costs and Benefits of Your Plan."

Pearson Education, Inc. Figure 12.3 "Drafting the Problem Section."

Pearson Education, Inc. Figure 12.4 "Drafting the Plan Section."

Pearson Education, Inc. Figure 12.6 "Mapping an Authoritative Tone."

Pearson Education, Inc. Figure 13.1 "Brainstorming on Your Topic."

Pearson Education, Inc. Figure 13.2 "Inventing Your Methods with a Concept Map."

Pearson Education, Inc. Figure 13.3 "Outlining a Methodology."

Pearson Education, Inc. Figure 13.4 "The Cyclical Nature of Research."

Pearson Education, Inc. Figure 13.5 "First Half of a Report."

Pearson Education, Inc. Figure 13.6 "Second Half of a Report (Two Patterns)"

Pearson Education, Inc. Figure 14.1 "Organizing Sections in a Research Paper."

Pearson Education, Inc. Figure 14.2 "Designing a Research Paper."

Pearson Education, Inc. Figure 15.1 "Using a Concept Map."

Pearson Education, Inc. Figure 15.3 "A Storyboard that Illustrates the Major Parts of a Text."

Pearson Education, Inc. Figure 15.4 "A First Draft that Uses *Logos, Pathos,* and *Ethos* for Support."

Pearson Education, Inc. Figure 15.6 "Outlining with Presentation Software."

Pearson Education, Inc. Figure 16.1 "Three Ways to Outline a Paper."

Pearson Education, Inc. Figure 16.2 "A Starter Outline."

Pearson Education, Inc. Figure 18.2 "Using Vertical Alignment."

Pearson Education, Inc. Figure 18.4 "Serif vs. Sans Serif Typefaces."

Pearson Education, Inc. Figure 18.5 "Using Contrast."

Pearson Education, Inc. Figure 18.12 "A Diagram."

Pearson Education, Inc. Figure 19.1 "The Four Levels of Revising and Editing."

Pearson Education, Inc. Figure 19.2 "Rough Draft."

Pearson Education, Inc. Figure 19.3 "Global Revision."

Pearson Education, Inc. Figure 19.4 "Substantive Editing."

Pearson Education, Inc. Figure 20.1 "The Shape of a Paragraph."

Pearson Education, Inc. Figure 20.2 "Organizational Patterns for Sections."

Pearson Education, Inc. Figure 21.1 "The Narrative Pattern."

Pearson Education, Inc. Figure 21.2 "Three Kinds of Cause and Effect."

Pearson Education, Inc. Figure 21.3 "Three Patterns for Comparison and Contrast."

Pearson Education, Inc. Figure 22.1 "The Region of Arguable Claim.

Pearson Education, Inc. Figure 22.2 "Developing and Sharpening an Arguable Claim."

Pearson Education, Inc. Figure 22.3 "Three Types of Proofs for Supporting an Argument."

Pearson Education, Inc. Figure 22.8 "Common Logical Fallacies."

Pearson Education, Inc. Figure 23.2 "Tuckman's Four Stages of Teaming."

Pearson Education, Inc. Figure 23.3 "Sample Peer Response Worksheet."

Pearson Education, Inc. Figure 24.1 "Following a Research Process."

Pearson Education, Inc. Figure 25.2 "The Research Triangle."

Pearson Education, Inc. Figure 25.5 "Types of Survey Questions."

Pearson Education, Inc. Figure 26.2 "Framing Material from a Source."

Pearson Education, Inc. Figure 26.3 "Verbs for Signal Phrases."

Pearson Education, Inc. Figure 27.1 "Types of MLA Parenthetical References."

Pearson Education, Inc. Figure 27.2 "Formatting a List of Works Cited."

Pearson Education, Inc. Figure 28.1 "Types of APA Parenthetical References."

Pearson Education, Inc. Figure 28.2 "Formatting a List of References."

Pearson Education, Inc. Figure 30.1 "Kinds of Portfolios and Their Purposes."

Pearson Education, Inc. Figure 30.2 "Student's Learning-Focused Reflection."

Pearson Education, Inc. Figure 30.3 "A Job Candidate's Mastery-Focused Reflection."

Pearson Education, Inc. Figure 30.4 "A Résumé."

Pearson Education, Inc. Figure 31.1 "A Four-Stage Process for Successful Written Exams."

Pearson Education, Inc. Figure 31.2 "Budgeting Your Time."

Pearson Education, Inc. Figure 32.1 "Pros and Cons of Presentation Technologies."

Pearson Education, Inc. Figure 32.2 "Allotting Your Presentation Time."

Pearson Education, Inc. Figure 32.3 "Creating Slides."

Pearson Education, Inc. "Literary Analysis."

Pearson Education, Inc. "Making 'The Story of an Hour' Make Sense."

Pearson Education, Inc. "Profiles Structure."

Pearson Education, Inc. "Reviews Diagram."

Pearson Education, Inc. "Rhetorical Analysis."

Pearson Education, Inc. "Sample Written Exam Questions."

Pearson Education, Inc. "Student's Reading Response to "We wear the mask."

Pearson Education, Inc. "When you label alcohol as forbidden fruit, it only becomes more attractive."

Pearson Education, Inc. "Why My Generation Doesn't Care About Performance Enhancement."

Pennsylvania Commission on Crime and Delinquency. "Percentage of Youth Reporting Bullying at School or Sexual Harassment on the Internet in the Past Year." 2011 Pennsylvania Youth Survey Report.

People for the Ethical Treatment of Animals. "Chicks Love a Vegetarian." Used with permission.

Percy, Benjamin. "Welcome to the Jungle from Outside Magazine", May 02, 2011. Copyright © 2011 by Benjamin Percy. First appeared in Outside Magazine; June 2011, published by Outside Magazine. Reprinted by permission of Curtis Brown, Ltd.

Pew Research Center. "The Rising Cost of Not Going to College" Pew Research Center, Washington, D.C. (February 11, 2014). http://www.pewsocialtrends.org/2014/02/11/THE-RISING-COST-OF-NOT-GOING-TO-COLLEGE/. Reprinted with permission.

"Poets.org Guide to Langston Hughes," Poets.org. Reprinted by permission of the Academy of American Poets, 75 Maiden Lane, Suite 901, New York, NY 10038. www.poets.org. Reprinted with permission.

Purdue University Facebook page. Used with permission.

Riley, Grace. "Facts About Flip-Flops," eHow, www.ehow.com /info_8353316.

Robinson, Jackie and Alfred Duckett. Excerpt from *I Never Had it Made: An autobiography of Jackie Robinson* by Jackie Robinson and Alfred Duckett. Copyright © 1995 by Rachel Robinson. Reprinted by permission of HarperCollins Publishers.

Rogers, Thomas. "The College Hazing That Changed My Life," September 20, 2011. This article first appeared in Salon.com, at http://www.Salon.com An online version remains in the Salon archives. Reprinted with permission.

Rosenzweig, Paul, Steven P. Bucci, Charles D. Stimson, and James Jay Carafano. "Drones in U.S. Airspace: Principles for Governance" from *Backgrounder*, The Heritage Foundation, September 20, 2012.

Rough, Jim. "A Rebirth of 'We the People'" from *The Good Society*, Vol. 12(2), pages 44–48, Copyright © 2004 by The Pennsylvania State University Press. Reprinted by permission of The Pennsylvania State University Press.

Sachs, Jeffrey. "With 7 Billion on Earth, a Huge Task Before Us." From CNN.com, © 2011 Turner Broadcast Systems, Inc. All rights reserved. Used by permission and protected by the Copyright Laws of the United States. The printing, copying, redistribution, or retransmission of this content without express written permission is prohibited.

Sanderson, Helen. "Diving In." Used with permission.

Schindel, Dan. "*Frozen* Tries and Fails to be Both Traditional and Modern." *Movie Mezzanine*, November 28, 2013. Reprinted with permission.

Seattle Department of Transportation. "How Downtown Employees Get to Work." 2011.

Sloan, Gary. From "Sleuthing Patriotic Slogans." http://www.alternet.org/story/15617/sleuthing_patriotic_slogans, April 10, 2003.

Steele, Matthew. Executive Summary, SCC Café Proposal, Matthew Steele, Associated Students of the University of Washington. Reprinted with permission.

Stepp, Laura Sessions. Cover of *Unhooked: How Young Women Pursue Sex, Delay Love and Lose at Both* by Laura Sessions Stepp, Riverhead Books, an imprint of Penguin Group (USA). Used with permission.

Swift, Jonathan. From "A Modest Proposal: A Modest Proposal for Preventing the Children of Poor People From Being a Burthen to Their Parents or Country, and for Making Them Beneficial to the Publick" by Jonathan Swift, 1729.

Taljonick, Ryan. "Tomb Raider: Definitive Edition." January 28, 2014. © 2014 *Future US, Inc.* All rights reserved. Article reprinted with permission.

Turnbow, Katelyn. "Lives not worth the money?" May 28, 2009. Used with permission.

U.S. Department of Health and Human Services. "2012 National Survey on Drug Use and Health."

University of Illinois Press. website screen capture (http://ajp.press.illinois.edu/122/1/marmolejo.html) from the article, "False memory in bilinguals: Does switching languages increase false memories?" by Gloria Marmolejo, Kristen A. Diliberto-Macaluso, and Jeanette Altarriba from American Journal of Psychology 122:1 (Spring 2009). Reprinted with permission.

Whatley, Jean Ellen. Excerpt from "My Ex Went to Prison for Sex-Crimes," February 6, 2012. This article first appeared in Salon.com, at http://www.Salon.com. An online version remains in the Salon archives. Reprinted with permission.

Wilkinson, Carl. "Dave Grohl and the Foo Fighters." Used with permission.

Williams, Kayla. "Will America Forget Its Veterans?" *Christian Science Monitor*, February 18, 2014. Reprinted with permission.

Willis, Eric. "Hot for Creature." *Washington City Paper*, January 18, 2008.

Woodend, Dorothy. "Why Watching Christian Blockbuster *Noah* is Like Sitting in a Giant Bathtub," alternet.org, April 7, 2014. Reprinted with permission.

World Freerunning Parkour Federation. "What is Parkour?" Excerpt courtesy of the World Freerunning Parkour Federation, LLC (www.wfpf.com).

"Writing for a Wiki," Wikipedia. Published by Project 21, a program of the National Center for public Policy Research. Used with permission.

Index

Note: Figures are indicated by an *f* following a page number.

Rhetorical Knowledge

By the end of first-year composition, students should

- Learn and use key rhetorical concepts through analyzing and composing a variety of texts
- Gain experience reading and composing in several genres to understand how genre conventions shape and are shaped by readers' and writers' practices and purposes
- Develop facility in responding to a variety of situations and contexts calling for purposeful shifts in voice, tone, level of formality, design, medium, and/or structure
- Understand and use a variety of technologies to address a range of audiences
- Match the capacities of different environments (e.g., print and electronic) to varying rhetorical situations

PART 1 Getting Started provides strategies and a helpful selection of key rhetorical terms to help you analyze, compose for, and reflect on the writing situations you'll encounter in college and beyond.

PART 2 Using Genres to Express Ideas covers ten genres commonly taught in college and/or used in the workplace and ten connected "microgenres."

PART 3 Developing a Writing Process helps you become a versatile writer who adapts organization, style, and design strategies to audience, purpose, and genre.

PART 6 Getting Your Ideas Out There shows you how to use a variety of technologies to express your ideas powerfully and appropriately.

PART 7 Anthology of Readings provides accessible and engaging readings that exemplify how writers both adhere to and diverge from the conventions of ten major genres.

Critical Thinking, Reading, and Composing

By the end of first-year composition, students should

- Use composing and reading for inquiry, learning, critical thinking, and communicating in various rhetorical contexts
- Read a diverse range of texts, attending especially to relationships between assertion and evidence, to patterns of organization, to the interplay between verbal and nonverbal elements, and to how these features function for different audiences and situations
- Locate and evaluate (for credibility, sufficiency, accuracy, timeliness, bias and so on) primary and secondary research materials, including journal articles and essays, books, scholarly and professionally established and maintained databases or archives, and informal electronic networks and internet sources
- Use strategies—such as interpretation, synthesis, response, critique, and design/redesign—to compose texts that integrate the writer's ideas with those from appropriate sources

PART 1 Getting Started helps you use your understanding of the rhetorical situation and critical-reading strategies to evaluate and respond to what others have written.

PART 2 Using Genres to Express Ideas includes invention strategies for each genre and takes you through the writing process to communicate effectively and clearly in a variety of media.

PART 3 Developing a Writing Process integrates critical thinking with critical composing across all stages of the writing process.

PART 4 Strategies for Shaping Ideas explains how to recognize argumentative and other rhetorical strategies used by writers and put them to use in your own work.

PART 5 Doing Research offers practical and effective strategies for locating, evaluating, incorporating, and citing primary, secondary, and empirical sources.

PART 7 Anthology of Readings includes questions and writing assignments that will help you understand rhetorical strategies, inquiry, and critical thinking.